Neurocognitive Pathways of Emotion Processing and Quality of Life in Childhood Neurodevelopmental Disorders

Kalliopi Megari
https://orcid.org/0000-0002-5861-7199
University of York Europe Campus, Greece

IGI Global
Scientific Publishing
Publishing Tomorrow's Research Today

Vice President of Editorial	Melissa Wagner
Director of Acquisitions	Mikaela Felty
Director of Book Development	Jocelynn Hessler
Production Manager	Mike Brehm
Cover Design	Jose Rosado

Published in the United States of America by
IGI Global Scientific Publishing
701 East Chocolate Avenue
Hershey, PA, 17033, USA
Tel: 717-533-8845 | Fax: 717-533-7115
Website: https://www.igi-global.com E-mail: cust@igi-global.com

Library of Congress Cataloging-in-Publication Data

Names: Megari, Kalliopi, 1981- editor
Title: Neurocognitive pathways of emotion processing and quality of life in childhood neurodevelopmental disorders / edited by Kalliopi Megari.
Description: Hershey, PA : IGI Global Scientific Publishing, [2027] | Includes bibliographical references and index. | Summary: "This book will provide a comprehensive examination of the neurocognitive and emotional challenges faced by children with neurodevelopmental disorders (NDDs), such as autism spectrum disorder, ADHD, and learning disabilities. It will integrate insights from neuroscience, psychology, and education to highlight how these challenges affect learning, social interactions, and overall well-being. A central focus will be placed on the role of emerging technologies— including neuroimaging, artificial intelligence, wearable devices, and virtual reality—in advancing assessment, monitoring, and intervention strategies. By combining traditional approaches with innovative digital tools, the work aims to outline a framework for more personalized and scalable interventions"-- Provided by publisher.
Identifiers: LCCN 2026005970 (print) | LCCN 2026005971 (ebook) | ISBN 9798337370729 h/c | ISBN 9798337370736 s/c | ISBN 9798337370743 ebook
Subjects: LCSH: Developmental disabilities--Treatment--Technological innovations | Developmental disabilities--Prevention--Technological innovations | Developmental disabilities--Diagnosis--Technological innovations | Developmentally disabled children--Psychology | Neurodivergent children--Psychology | Emotional problems of children--Treatment
Classification: LCC RJ506.D47 N47 2026 (print) | LCC RJ506.D47 (ebook)
LC record available at https://lccn.loc.gov/2026005970
LC ebook record available at https://lccn.loc.gov/2026005971

British Cataloguing in Publication Data
A Cataloguing in Publication record for this book is available from the British Library.

Table of Contents

Detailed Table of Contents

Early childhood is a critical developmental period during which rapid changes occur in children's neuropsychological and socioemotional development, which lay the foundations for its later sentimental, social and cognitive function and behaviour. Disability is now defined from a biopsychological model which recognizes that limitations are a result of the interaction of biological malfunction and environmental factors.The majority of disabilities are associated with atypical brain development and differentiations in cognitive function such as memory, social information processing and attention. Additionally neurodevelopmental disabilities affect intensively socio-emotional growth and skills since they are often accompanied by difficulties in emotional regulation, social interaction, and communication. It is important to note that these difficulties are not a static situation. They are influenced by the context in which the child lives, which indicates the importance of early recognition of symptoms and planning appropriate intervention

Neurodevelopmental Disorders represents heterogeneous group of developmental disorders characterized by impairments in cognitive, communicative, behavioural, motor and adaptive development, emerging during the developmental period with lifelong persistence. Over successive decades, there has been marked significant progress in conceptualizations of these disorders, moving beyond narrowly defined views of childhood psychopathology to multidimensional developmental conditions influenced by neurobiological, genetic, environmental and sociocultural factors. Drawing primarily on the Diagnostic and Statistical Manual of Mental Disorders (DSM-I through DSM-5-TR) and complementary international frameworks, the chapter traces historical shifts in diagnostic thinking, addresses neurobiological and genetic bases of NDDs, highlights cultural and cross-cultural issues in diagnosis. The current chapter brings together developmental, clinical and policy perspectives that can help researchers, educators, clinicians and policymakers.

This chapter focuses on elucidating the causes/foundations of neurodevelopmental disorders like attention deficit hyperactivity disorder, autism spectrum disorder, Intellectual Disability, Learning disorders, Communication disorders and motor disabilities. This also focuses on delineating the biological and psychological impact of the disorders and quality of childhood and by bridging the gap of building more awareness for different interventions and therapies that bring improvements in behavioural aspects like aggression, hyperactivity; physiological aspects like stimming and providing a better and improved lifestyle for the children. Interventions like emotional and family support, and medications and therapies like occupational therapy, speech and language therapy, behavioural therapies and other developmental therapies that would help promote overall development. These therapies not only

Understanding typical development alongside neurodevelopmental disorders offers an integrative framework for appreciating the full spectrum of human developmental diversity. Typical developmental milestone provides essential reference points, while the study of neurodevelopmental disorders illuminates atypical trajectories shaped by dynamic gene-environment interactions, neural plasticity and contextual influences. Contemporary perspectives such as developmental psychopathology, neurodiversity and dimensional models challenge deficit- based views and emphasize continuity, individual variability and strengths-based understanding. The chapter highlights the importance of early identification, culturally responsive assessment and individualized, family-centered interventions, with education systems playing a central role in inclusion. Within the Indian context, alignment with the Rights of Persons with Disabilities Act (2016) and the National Education Policy (2020) supports a shift toward rights based, inclusive and sustainable practices across the lifespan.

Separation Anxiety Disorder (SAD) is highly prevalent in children with Autism Spectrum Disorder (ASD), with attentional control deficits increasing vulnerability to anxiety, particularly SAD and phobias. These difficulties often intensify emotional dysregulation, hyper-responsivity, avoidance, and social withdrawal. This chapter integrates current research on SAD in ASD and reviews neuropsychological frameworks underlying its development. It highlights the role of attentional control in anxiety, SAD, and impairments in emotional regulation and self-control. Findings underscore the involvement of the amygdala, hippocampus, and prefrontal cortex in regulating responses to separation-related cues, as well as the negative impact of oxytocin network dysregulation on SAD symptoms in ASD. Overall, attentional control emerges as a key factor in the development and maintenance of SAD. The review emphasizes the need for anxiety-specific assessment tools for ASD, attention-based interventions, and further research to improve functional outcomes for children with co-occurring ASD and SAD.

Preface

The expanding body of research in developmental neuroscience, neuropsychology, cognitive science, and child psychiatry has fundamentally transformed contemporary perspectives on childhood neurodevelopmental disorders. While early investigations focused predominantly on cognitive impairment, behavioral manifestations, and diagnostic classification, there is now broad recognition that emotional functioning constitutes a critical dimension of neurodevelopment, influencing social adaptation, academic achievement, mental health, and overall quality of life. Consequently, the systematic examination of the neurocognitive mechanisms underlying emotion processing has emerged as a major area of interdisciplinary inquiry, providing valuable insights into both typical and atypical developmental trajectories.

This volume, "Neurocognitive Pathways of Emotion Processing and Quality of Life in Childhood Neurodevelopmental Disorders", seeks to present a comprehensive synthesis of current theoretical frameworks, empirical evidence, and emerging research directions concerning the intricate relationships among brain development, emotional processing, neurocognitive functioning, and quality of life in children with neurodevelopmental disorders. By integrating contributions from diverse scientific disciplines, the book aims to advance understanding of the biological, psychological, and environmental mechanisms that shape emotional competence and adaptive functioning across childhood and adolescence.

Neurodevelopmental disorders encompass a heterogeneous group of conditions characterized by early-onset alterations in brain development that affect cognitive, communicative, motor, behavioral, and social functioning. Increasing evidence demonstrates that disturbances in emotional processing—including emotion perception, emotional awareness, affective regulation, empathy, social cognition, reward processing, and decision-making—are common across these disorders and frequently contribute to difficulties extending beyond the core diagnostic features. These alterations influence children's capacity to establish interpersonal relationships, engage successfully within educational environments, maintain psychological well-being, and participate meaningfully in family and community life. Elucidating the neurocognitive architecture underlying these processes is therefore essential for improving diagnostic precision, informing individualized intervention strategies, and promoting more favorable developmental outcomes.

Recent advances in structural and functional neuroimaging, computational neuroscience, molecular genetics, developmental psychopathology, and cognitive neuroscience have substantially enriched our understanding of the neural systems supporting emotional functioning. Investigations of distributed brain networks—including cortical and subcortical circuits involved in emotion perception, executive control, salience detection, social cognition, and affective regulation—have revealed increasingly sophisticated models of how atypical neurodevelopment influences emotional and behavioral adaptation. Simultaneously, longitudinal research has emphasized the dynamic interactions between biological maturation and environmental experiences, highlighting the importance of developmental timing, neuroplasticity, family relationships, educational contexts, and sociocultural influences in shaping emotional competence throughout childhood.

An equally significant development within the field has been the growing emphasis on quality of life as a multidimensional construct that extends well beyond symptom reduction or functional impairment. Contemporary conceptualizations recognize quality of life as encompassing physical health, emotional well-being, social participation, educational engagement, autonomy, family functioning, and subjective life satisfaction. This broader perspective reflects a paradigm shift toward person-centered and family-centered models of care, acknowledging that successful intervention should ultimately enhance meaningful participation in everyday life while supporting resilience, self-determination, and long-term psychosocial adjustment.

The chapters comprising this volume reflect these evolving perspectives by examining the neurobiological substrates of emotion processing, developmental models of emotional competence, disorder-specific patterns of affective functioning, advances in neuropsychological assessment, biomarkers of emotional regulation, and evidence-based therapeutic interventions. Particular emphasis is placed on the reciprocal interactions among neurocognitive mechanisms, environmental influences, and developmental experiences, recognizing that emotional functioning emerges from the continuous interplay between neural maturation and contextual factors operating across multiple ecological systems. The chapters have to do with:

OVERVIEW OF CHAPTERS

Chapter 1: Neuropsychological And Social-Emotional Development In Early Childhood: Typical And Atypical Pathways

Early childhood is a critical developmental period during which rapid changes occur in children's neuropsychological and socioemotional development, which lay the foundations for its later sentimental, social and cognitive function and behaviour. Disability is now defined from a biopsychological model which recognizes that limitations are a result of the interaction of biological malfunction and environmental factors.The majority of disabilities are associated with atypical brain development and differentiations in cognitive function such as memory, social information processing and attention. Additionally neurodevelopmental disabilities affect intensively socio-emotional growth and skills since they are often accompanied by difficulties in emotional regulation, social interaction, and communication. It is important to note that these difficulties are not a static situation. They are influenced by the context in which the child lives, which indicates the importance of early recognition of symptoms and planning appropriate intervention

Chapter 2: Definitions and classification of NDDs: Conceptual, Diagnostic and Developmental Perspectives

Neurodevelopmental Disorders represents heterogeneous group of developmental disorders characterized by impairments in cognitive, communicative, behavioural, motor and adaptive development, emerging during the developmental period with lifelong persistence. Over successive decades, there has been marked significant progress in conceptualizations of these disorders, moving beyond narrowly defined views of childhood psychopathology to multidimensional developmental conditions influenced by neurobiological, genetic, environmental and sociocultural factors. Drawing primarily on the Diagnostic and Statistical Manual of Mental Disorders (DSM-I through DSM-5-TR) and complementary international frameworks, the chapter traces historical shifts in diagnostic thinking, addresses neurobiological and genetic bases of NDDs, highlights cultural and cross-cultural issues in diagnosis. The current chapter brings together developmental, clinical and policy perspectives that can help researchers, educators, clinicians and policymakers.

Chapter 3: Neurodevelopmental Disorders in Childhood: Aetiology, Psychological Impact, and Therapeutic Approaches

This chapter focuses on elucidating the causes/foundations of neurodevelopmental disorders like attention deficit hyperactivity disorder, autism spectrum disorder, Intellectual Disability, Learning disorders, Communication disorders and motor disabilities. This also focuses on delineating the biological and psychological impact of the disorders and quality of childhood and by bridging the gap of building more awareness for different interventions and therapies that bring improvements in behavioural aspects like aggression, hyperactivity; physiological aspects like stimming and providing a better and improved lifestyle for the children. Interventions like emotional and family support, and medications and therapies like occupational therapy, speech and language therapy, behavioural therapies and other developmental therapies that would help promote overall development. These therapies not only help the children but also the parents in having a better environment at home, have better communication with the children, and help solve any strenuous situations or circumstance.

Chapter 4: Parallel Circles. Living with the Neurodiversity within the Family

This study is a literature review that attempts to understand the parenting experiences of neurodivergent people. It focuses on quantitative and qualitative studies describing thoughts and feelings of neurodivergent parents, the difficulties and challenges of parenting and managing these in everyday life. Reference is also made to research examining anxiety, acceptance or rejection, parental self-regulation and self-efficacy, family functioning, the impact of parenting on the above and the provision of support to parents. Finally, findings from research related to the impact of parents' characteristics on supportive programs for parents and children are presented. The findings of this study highlight the importance of understanding and the need for support for neurodivergent parents in order to improve their lives and daily routines in both crisis and normal times.

Chapter 5: Interconnected Minds: Executive Function, Memory, and Learning in Neurodiverse Childhoods

This chapter examines inclusive education through the lens of cognitive architecture, focusing on how neurodiverse learners interact with learning environments that implicitly assume tightly integrated executive, attentional, linguistic, and memory systems. Drawing on contemporary models of executive function, memory and retrieval, attention regulation, and mutualistic coupling, it argues that many educational barriers arise not from deficits in ability, but from persistent mismatches between instructional design and the internal coordination demands placed on learners. The chapter critically evaluates prominent inclusive and neuro-affirming frameworks, including Universal Design for Learning (UDL), FEDIS+R, and dignity-oriented approaches, acknowledging their ethical and structural contributions while highlighting limitations in cognitive specificity. In so doing, the chapter positions inclusive education as an evidence-informed reconfiguration of learning environments – one that supports durable, transferable, and meaningful engagement for cognitively diverse learners.

Chapter 6: The role of Neuropsychological assessment and Biomarkers towards Accurate Diagnosis and quality of life in Attention-Deficit/Hyperactivity Disorder

Attention-deficit/hyperactivity disorder (ADHD) is a common neurodevelopmental condition characterized by persistent inattention, hyperactivity, and impulsivity, which can lead to considerable functional difficulties. ADHD exhibits a high degree of variability, presenting in various forms across individuals and age groups, thereby complicating the diagnostic process significantly. However, the increasing recognition of the neurobiological foundations of ADHD has driven researchers to identify biomarkers that enhance the diagnostic precision. This review aims to provide a comprehensive overview of the latest advancements in biomarkers and neuropsychological assessment for ADHD diagnosis. More specifically, it will place an emphasis on the importance of early diagnosis, the necessity for enhanced diagnostic criteria, and the use of biomarkers and cognitive assessments in directing tailored interventions and optimizing patient outcomes.

Chapter 7: Understanding the Inside: The biological and genetic underpinnings of ASD and ADHD and their effects on children

This chapter investigates the biological and genetic foundations of Autism Spectrum Disorder (ASD) and Attention-Deficit Hyperactivity Disorder (ADHD) in children, framing them as neurodevelopmental conditions with evolving trajectories affecting learning, socialisation, and quality of life (QoL). It details polygenic architectures, shared risks in synaptic signalling and rare variants (e.g., SHANK3, CHD8 in ASD; DRD4, SLC6A3 in ADHD), alongside unique profiles impacting cortical development and striatal function. Neurobiological models reveal overlapping fronto-striatal disruptions, neurotransmitter imbalances (dopamine, serotonin,

GABA), and connectivity variances: ASD's social under-connectivity versus ADHD's executive deficits. Intersections in emotion regulation, sensory processing, and executive functions contrast with divergences in social cognition and reward systems. Developmental outcomes include comorbid maladaptive behaviours, peer challenges, and adaptive gaps, underscoring needs for epigenetic research, biomarkers, and neurodiversity-aligned interventions.

Chapter 8: Foundations of Typical Development and Neurodevelopment Disorders: Definitions, Classification, Conceptual Frameworks and Indian Context

Understanding typical development alongside neurodevelopmental disorders offers an integrative framework for appreciating the full spectrum of human developmental diversity. Typical developmental milestone provides essential reference points, while the study of neurodevelopmental disorders illuminates atypical trajectories shaped by dynamic gene-environment interactions, neural plasticity and contextual influences. Contemporary perspectives such as developmental psychopathology, neurodiversity and dimensional models challenge deficit- based views and emphasize continuity, individual variability and strengths-based understanding. The chapter highlights the importance of early identification, culturally responsive assessment and individualized, family-centered interventions, with education systems playing a central role in inclusion. Within the Indian context, alignment with the Rights of Persons with Disabilities Act (2016) and the National Education Policy (2020) supports a shift toward rights based, inclusive and sustainable practices across the lifespan.

Chapter 9: Attentional Control in Co-occurring Separation Anxiety among Children with Autism Spectrum Disorder: A Narrative Review

Separation Anxiety Disorder (SAD) is highly prevalent in children with Autism Spectrum Disorder (ASD), with attentional control deficits increasing vulnerability to anxiety, particularly SAD and phobias. These difficulties often intensify emotional dysregulation, hyper-responsivity, avoidance, and social withdrawal. This chapter integrates current research on SAD in ASD and reviews neuropsychological frameworks underlying its development. It highlights the role of attentional control in anxiety, SAD, and impairments in emotional regulation and self-control. Findings underscore the involvement of the amygdala, hippocampus, and prefrontal cortex in regulating responses to separation-related cues, as well as the negative impact of oxytocin network dysregulation on SAD symptoms in ASD. Overall, attentional control emerges as a key factor in the development and maintenance of SAD.

The review emphasizes the need for anxiety-specific assessment tools for ASD, attention-based interventions, and further research to improve functional outcomes for children with co-occurring ASD and SAD.

Chapter 10: Social Cognition and Core Cognitive Processes in Neurodevelopmental Disorders: Exploring Theory of Mind, Attention, Memory, Executive Functions, and Language

This chapter provides an in-depth examination of the core impairments of children with Neurodevelopmental Disorders with a particular focus on Social Cognition (Theory of Mind), Attention, Memory, Executive Functions and Language. Specifically, it presents the conceptual definitions, typical developmental trajectories and underlying neuroscientific mechanisms of these domains. Synchronously, it clarifies the deviations evident in children with NDDs and emphasizes on Social Cognition as a central transdiagnostic construct to scrutinize its bidirectional relationships with Attention, Memory, Executive Functions and Language, uncovering overall and disorder-specific trends. Furtherly, this paper delineates the consequences of these impairments on children's daily, social and academic functioning, mental and physical health, as well as quality of life

A defining objective of this volume is to facilitate the translation of scientific knowledge into clinical, educational, and public health practice. As precision medicine, artificial intelligence, digital health technologies, and computational approaches become increasingly integrated into developmental research, opportunities continue to expand for more individualized assessment, early identification of risk, and targeted intervention. Nevertheless, these scientific advances must be accompanied by careful consideration of ethical principles, equitable access to services, cultural diversity, interdisciplinary collaboration, and the perspectives of children and families whose lived experiences remain indispensable to meaningful progress within the field.

This book has been prepared for researchers, clinicians, psychologists, psychiatrists, neurologists, pediatricians, speech and language therapists, occupational therapists, educators, and graduate students engaged in the study and management of childhood neurodevelopmental disorders. It is intended to provide both a rigorous scientific foundation and an integrative conceptual framework through which readers may better understand the complex relationships linking neurodevelopment, emotional functioning, and quality of life.

It is our hope that this volume will contribute to the advancement of interdisciplinary scholarship by fostering dialogue among the neurosciences, behavioral sciences, clinical medicine, education, and rehabilitation. Equally, we aspire for it to encourage the development of innovative research methodologies, refined theoretical models, and evidence-based interventions that improve not only diagnostic and therapeutic outcomes but also the broader lived experiences of children with neurodevelopmental disorders.

Ultimately, the scientific significance of this field resides not solely in advancing knowledge of the developing brain, but in translating that knowledge into practices that promote human flourishing. By deepening our understanding of the neurocognitive pathways through which emotions influence development, adaptation, and well-being, we move closer to realizing a future in which every child with a neurodevelopmental disorder is afforded the opportunity to achieve optimal health, meaningful participation, and the highest attainable quality of life.

Kalliopi Megari
University of York, Europe Campus, Greece

Acknowledgments

The completion of this edited volume represents the culmination of a collaborative endeavor involving the dedication, expertise, and commitment of numerous individuals and institutions. As editor, I'm deeply grateful to all those whose contributions have made this work possible.

First and foremost, I extend our sincere appreciation to the distinguished authors who contributed chapters to this volume. Their scholarly excellence, intellectual insight, and willingness to share their expertise have resulted in a comprehensive and interdisciplinary examination of the neurocognitive mechanisms underlying emotion processing and their implications for quality of life in childhood neurodevelopmental disorders. Their commitment to scientific rigor and academic collaboration has been instrumental in achieving the objectives of this book.

I'm equally indebted to the reviewers whose thoughtful evaluations and constructive recommendations significantly enhanced the quality, clarity, and scientific integrity of the individual chapters. Their careful assessment and generous investment of time have strengthened this volume and ensured that it reflects current developments within this rapidly evolving field. My sincere gratitude is also extended to the editorial and publishing team for their professional guidance, encouragement, and meticulous attention throughout every stage of the publication process. Their expertise and commitment have been invaluable in transforming this project into its final form.

This volume has greatly benefited from the collective efforts of an international community of researchers, clinicians, neuroscientists, psychologists, psychiatrists, pediatricians, educators, speech and language therapists, occupational therapists, and rehabilitation specialists whose work continues to expand our understanding of childhood neurodevelopmental disorders. Their scientific contributions have established the foundation upon which much of the knowledge presented in this book has been built.

I wish to acknowledge the universities, research institutes, hospitals, and professional organizations that foster interdisciplinary collaboration and support scientific investigation in developmental neuroscience, neuropsychology, child mental health, and related disciplines. Continued institutional support remains essential for advancing research that ultimately improves clinical practice and educational outcomes.

Above all, I express our profound respect and gratitude to the children, adolescents, and families living with neurodevelopmental disorders. Their experiences, resilience, and participation in clinical care and research continue to deepen our understanding of neurodevelopment and emotional functioning. Their voices remind us that the ultimate purpose of scientific inquiry is to improve lives, promote inclusion, and support the full participation of every child within family, school, and society.

On a personal note, I'm grateful to our colleagues, mentors, students, collaborators, friends, and families for their encouragement, patience, and unwavering support throughout the preparation of this volume. Their confidence and understanding have sustained us during the many stages of this editorial undertaking.

As editor, it is my hope that this volume will serve as a valuable resource for researchers, clinicians, educators, and students while fostering interdisciplinary dialogue and inspiring future investigations into the complex relationships among neurodevelopment, emotion processing, and quality of life. I trust that the work presented here will contribute to the continued advancement of knowledge and, ultimately, to improving the care, opportunities, and well-being of children with neurodevelopmental disorders and their families.

I would like to dedicate this book to my family especially to the memory of my late mother Margarita Megari whose love, unwavering support, and enduring belief in me shaped the person I am today.

Dr. Kalliopi Megari

Chapter 1

Neuropsychological and Social-Emotional Development in Early Childhood: Typical and Atypical Pathways

Kalliopi Megari
http://orcid.org/0000-0002-5861-7199
University of York Europe Campus, Greece & University of Western Macedonia, Greece

Maria-Eleni Palioura
University of Western Macedonia, Greece

Stylianos Parasxiakos
University of Western Macedonia, Greece

Aglaia Skoutara
University of Western Macedonia, Greece

Panagiota Stougioude
University of Western Macedonia, Greece

Evangelos Mantsos
University of Thessaly, Greece

Efthymia Efthymiou
http://orcid.org/0000-0003-0411-1720
College of Interdisciplinary Studies, Zayed University, Dubai, UAE

Maria Sofologi
http://orcid.org/0000-0003-0380-2220
University of Ioannina, Greece

Maria Theodoratou
http://orcid.org/0000-0003-4200-4643
School of Social Sciences, Hellenic Open University, Patra, Greece

Georgios A. Kougioumtzis
http://orcid.org/0000-0002-2362-2094
Faculty of Economic and Political Sciences, National and Kapodistrian University of Athens, Greece

Dimitra V. Katsarou
http://orcid.org/0000-0001-8690-0314
University of the Aegean, Rhodes, Greece

DOI: 10.4018/979-8-3373-7072-9.ch001

ABSTRACT

Early childhood is a critical developmental period during which rapid changes occur in children's neuropsychological and socioemotional development, which lay the foundations for its later sentimental, social and cognitive function and behaviour. Disability is now defined from a biopsychological model which recognizes that limitations are a result of the interaction of biological malfunction and environmental factors.The majority of disabilities are associated with atypical brain development and differentiations in cognitive function such as memory, social information processing and attention. Additionally neurodevelopmental disabilities affect intensively socio-emotional growth and skills since they are often accompanied by difficulties in emotional regulation, social interaction, and communication. It is important to note that these difficulties are not a static situation. They are influenced by the context in which the child lives, which indicates the importance of early recognition of symptoms and planning appropriate intervention

INTRODUCTION

Neuropsychological Development in Early Childhood

Between the ages of two and six, children's brains grow from 70% of their adult weight to 90%, allowing them to master a wide range of skills, such as physical coordination, perception, attention, memory, language, logical thinking, and imagination. By the age of five, many parts of the cerebral cortex, such as the prefrontal cortex, have created a large number of synapses, almost double that of adults, which, combined with the growth and myelination of neuronal fibers, result in a peak in energy metabolism in the cerebral cortex. (Nelson et al., 2006). During early childhood, synaptic pruning occurs, whereby neurons that are not frequently stimulated lose their connecting fibers, resulting in a reduction in synapses.

Neural plasticity is the brain's ability to change its architecture in response to experience. Studies show that neural plasticity is particularly enhanced in early childhood, where developmental changes in neural networks are not static but extend from infancy to adulthood. To better understand critical periods, these are specific age phases where the brain is extra sensitive to certain stimuli. A lack of appropriate experiences during these age phases can lead to permanent impairments in abilities such as language and social perception. (Shaw et al., 2018) In conclusion, plasticity in early childhood allows children who have suffered brain damage to reorganize and recover after neurological injury (Stiles, 2000).

By the age of ten, the energy consumption of most cortical areas is greatly reduced, resulting in reaching adult levels (Lebel & Beaulieu, 2011). Electroencephalographic spectroscopy, near infrared and functional magnetic resonance imaging measurements have shown that during middle childhood the prefrontal cortex, as well as other brain areas responsible for executive function, have rapid development. Some of the executive function abilities that increase particularly are working memory, flexibility of thought, planning, and inhibition. At the age of 3 to 6 years, the left cerebral hemisphere of children is quite active, which then differentiates, as its activity begins to stabilize. Unlike the left cerebral hemisphere, the right hemisphere continues to be active throughout early and middle childhood. (Thatcher et al., 1987)

The Influence of the Environment on the Neuropsychological Development of Children

The interaction between the nervous system and the environment plays an important role in human development. Various experiences, such as play, social interaction, and educational activities, strengthen neural network connections and encourage the development of executive functions. The existence of a positive and pleasant environment. This results in better school readiness and cognitive performance in later stages of life. Conversely, adverse experiences in early childhood, such as trauma or parental neglect, can disrupt the development of executive functions and lead to long-term difficulties in attention and self-regulation (Blair, C. 2016).

A particular aspect in the study of neuropsychological development in early childhood is neurodevelopmental disorders, the most important of which is autism spectrum disorder. Children with autism are characterized by qualitative difficulties in their social life and especially in interaction with other people, uneven development of cognitive functions, difficulty in processing information and difficulties in communicating with others (Megari, 2025). In addition, children with autism often show dysfunctions in executive functions, attention skills, understanding of everyday events and situations, as well as in theory of mind (Baron-Cohen et al., 2000). Following studies by Ozonoff (1999), it was shown that executive dysfunction is the primary deficit presented in children with autism spectrum disorder. This is because the prefrontal cortex and its connections form the basis of executive skills. In typically developing children, maturation of the frontal regions is completed slowly and steadily during adolescence, after a developmental burst in infancy and early childhood. However, this developmental burst is reduced in children on the autism spectrum (Dawson & Guare, 2004).

During early childhood, rapid changes occur in both the structure and function of the brain, which are reflected in executive functions, memory, attention, and language development. Early childhood is a critical period for acquiring basic cognitive and social skills that will support the child's academic and social development. According to neuropsychological research, the combination of biological maturation and external experiences interactively contributes to brain development, resulting in practical implications for the design of early intervention and education programs.

Cognitive Functions of Attention and Memory in Early Childhood

Selective and sustained attention are critical functions for successful learning and social interaction in children. In preschool age, the ability to sustain attention on a stimulus for a long period of time increases significantly. In addition, working memory allows for short-term retention and processing of information as it is linked to the brain maturation of the prefrontal and prefrontal cortex. The development of memory and attention plays an important role in school readiness and effective performance in school activities such as reading and math (Espinet et al., 2013).

Selective and sustained forms of attention and concentration develop gradually during early childhood. Selective attention is defined as the child's ability to focus on specific information while ignoring irrelevant stimuli from the environment. In contrast, sustained attention refers to the process of maintaining focus for a long period of time on a specific stimulus (Posner & Rothbart, 2007). Neuroimaging through functional magnetic resonance imaging and electroencephalography demonstrates the participation of areas such as the anterior prefrontal cortex and other areas in the regulation of attention. As these areas mature, the child acquires the ability to better organize his behavior (Rueda, et al., 2005).

In addition to the forms of attention during early childhood, memory is also formed and developed. Between the ages of three and seven, both short-term and episodic memory show significant improvements, which are related to the neuronal maturation of the hippocampus and its connections with the prefrontal cortex. During early childhood, children begin to form ways of storing and recalling information, resulting in improvements in the learning and problem-solving process (Bauer, 2007).

Language skills and speech development constitute a key pillar of cognitive and social development during early childhood. In particular, during preschool age, children's vocabulary increases rapidly, as linguistic skills, which are located in the left hemisphere of the brain, expand at an impressive rate, while at the same time grammar, syntax and pragmatics of speech are strengthened (Bates et al., 1995). However, spatial skills, which are located in the right hemisphere of the brain, such as giving directions, drawing pictures, and recognizing geometric shapes, develop primarily in childhood and adolescence (Berk, 2019)

Executive functions include a set of cognitive processes that enable planning, control, and adaptation of a child's behavior. Executive functions have three dimensions: inhibitory control, working memory, and cognitive flexibility. These dimensions support problem solving, attention, self-regulation, and social control. During infancy, inhibition and working memory appear in children and develop rapidly during preschool age, while cognitive flexibility continues to develop until early school age. (Anderson, P. 2002). According to studies, cognitive flexibility increases steadily throughout preschool age and is associated with the development of neural networks in the frontal cortex. This results in the individual's ability to adapt between different tasks or rules (Buttelmann & Karbach, 2017).

During early brain activity or neuropsychological development and activity of children is possible through techniques such as EEG and fMRI. These two techniques have provided important data for understanding the mechanisms that support the developmental course of the functions mentioned above. In particular, it is observed that the maturity of cognitive functions and the development of executive function are associated with specific rhythms of brain activity such as theta and alpha numbers (Bell & Wolfe, 2007). Finally, the connectivity between the frontal and parietal regions is strengthened over time and age, related to increased ability to concentrate and self-regulation (Fair et al., 2009).

Relationship between Neuropsychological Development and School Readiness

School readiness is defined as a combination of academic knowledge and the set of neuropsychological skills that enable a child to respond to the cognitive, emotional, and social demands of the school environment. School readiness includes abilities such as maintaining and controlling attention, working memory, inhibiting impulsive reactions, cognitive flexibility, and emotional self-regulation (Blair & Razza, 2007, Diamond, 20130).

The development of these skills is based on the gradual maturation of the prefrontal cortex and its connections to other brain areas, such as the parietal cortex, hippocampus, and amygdala. The prefrontal cortex plays a central role in executive functions, which are considered critical for organizing behavior and adapting to the demands of the classroom. A child with well-developed executive functions can follow multi-step instructions, control impulsive behaviors, and remain focused on an activity for a long period of time (Fair et al., 2009).

The ability to pay attention plays a central role in the school learning process. Selective and sustained attention allow children to focus on information and ignore irrelevant stimuli, which is essential for successful participation in school activities. In addition, working memory allows for temporary storage and processing of information, which significantly predicts performance in areas such as reading and mathematics. (Gathercole et al., 2004).

The relationship between executive functions and school readiness has been documented in the international literature, as research shows that children with higher levels of executive functions in preschool age show better adaptation to the school environment, resulting in greater academic success. In terms of social behavior, inhibition has been linked to impulse control and compliance with school rules, while cognitive flexibility is related to the ability to adapt to new learning situations (Diamond, 2013).

In conclusion, school readiness is the result of the interaction of multiple neuropsychological systems, which enable the child to participate effectively in the learning environment. Understanding this relationship is crucial for the early detection of difficulties and the design of specific interventions aimed at strengthening the child's attention, memory, executive functions, and emotional self-regulation in preschool age (Diamond, 2013).

SOCIO-EMOTIONAL DEVELOPMENT IN EARLY CHIDHOOD

Emotional Regulation and Self-Regulation

Socio-emotional development during early childhood is cornerstone of shaping a child's personality and mental resilience. During this period, children develop skills related to regulating emotions, empathy, creating secure attachments, interacting with significant others, as well as coping strategies.

Emotional regulation and self-regulation are critical components of social-emotional development during early childhood. These processes enable children to manage their emotional experiences and behaviors in socially acceptable ways, forming the basis for late academic and interpersonal success (Κωσταρίδου-Ευκλείδη, Α., 2011).

To begin with, emotional regulation refers to the ability to monitor, evaluate and modify emotional reactions to achieve ones' s goals. In early childhood, children begin to transition from relying on external sources (e.g. caregivers) to internal strategies for managing their emotions. This development is closely linked with self-regulation, a broader construct that includes cognitive and behavioral control (Κωσταρίδου-Ευκλείδη, Α., 2011).

Moreover, the role of effortful controls, that is the ability to inhibit a dominant response and activate a subdominant one, constitutes a fundamental self-regulation mechanism. Children with higher levels of effortful control are better able to manage frustration and engage in goal-directed behavior, which facilitates adaptive emotional responses (Rothbart et al., 2011). Nevertheless, the development of self-regulatory abilities is strongly influenced by early social experiences, particularly caregiver responsiveness and modeling (Edossa et al., 2017).

In summary, self-regulation and emotional regulation are not only essential for emotional well-being but are also predictive of long-term outcomes such as school readiness, peer relationships and mental health. Therefore, fostering these abilities in childhood through supportive environments is of paramount importance.

Self-Concept and Identity

Self-concept and identity development constitute central components of socio-emotional development during early childhood, shaping how children perceive themselves and relate to others. Self-concept refers to the organized set of beliefs and evaluations children hold about their own abilities, traits and social value, while identity reflects the emerging sense of continuity and meaning of self across contexts. During the preschool and early school years, these constructs undergo rapid development and are closely intertwined with emotional regulation, empathy and social behavior.

In early childhood, self-concept is largely concrete and experience-based, emerging through everyday interactions with caregivers, peers and educators. Children gradually internalize feedback fro significant others, forming self-evaluations that influence emotional responses and behavior. Positive social experience support the development of a coherent and adaptive self-concept, whereas inconsistent or negative feedback may contribute to self-doubt and emotional vulnerability. As children become more self-aware, their self-concept increasingly guides emotional regulation and social decision making.

Recent research highlights the importance of moral self-concept as a key dimension of early identity development. Longitudinal studies demonstrate that preschool children who perspective themselves as “moral” or “helpful” are more likely to engage in prosocial behaviors such as sharing and cooperation over time (Schiele et al., 2024). Similarly, Söldner and Paulus(2024) found bidirectional relations between moral self concept and prosocial behavior, suggesting that children not only act in accordance with their self-views, but also update their self-concept based on their social behavior. These findings emphasize that identity development in early childhood is dynamic and shaped ongoing social experiences.

Self-concept also plays a critical role in children's emotional adjustment and academic pathways. Early self-evaluations influence motivation, persistence, and responses to challenges. Research indicates that children with a more positive academic self-concept demonstrate stronger long term achievement trajectories, with gender and linguistic context further moderating these outcomes (Yu et al., 2025).

Such findings underline the close connection between social emotional identity development and later educational success.

Overall, self concept and identity development serve as foundational mechanisms through which children interpret social experiences, regulate emotions, and engage with their environment. Supporting positive self concept formation through responsive caregiving, emotionally supportive educational settings and opportunities for prosocial engagement is therefore essential for healthy socio-emotional development in early childhood.

Developing Empathy

Empathy is the ability to understand and share the feelings of others, is a crucial component of social and emotional development during early childhood. Between the ages of 2 and 6, children begin to demonstrate increased emotional awareness and the capacity to respond to others' emotional states. This process is closely tied to cognitive development, self-awareness and the emerging understanding of others' perspectives (Lightfoot et al. 2015).

In the early years, empathy often begins as emotional contagion, but gradually evolves into more complex forms. For example children may cry when they see another child cry. By age 3 or 4, children start to differentiate their own emotions from those of others and can express concern or offer comfort, indicating the emerge of affective empathy (Lightfoot et al., 2015). This development is influenced by parenting style, language exposure and opportunities for social interaction.

Neuroscientific research supports this developmental trajectory, showing that brain networks involved in empathy- such as the mirror neuron system and prefrontal cortex- undergo significant maturation during early childhood (Decety et al., 2021). Social experiences, particularly in emotionally rich environments, further enhance this neural development and emotional responsiveness.

Moreover, many studies have highlighted the role of early childhood education in fostering empathy through play-based learning storytelling, and collaborative activities (Soliman et al., 2020). These experiences not only promote prosocial behavior but also help children internalize moral reasoning and emotional regulation. Empathy development in early childhood thus lays the foundation for meaningful social relationships and later moral understanding.

Theory of Mind (ToM)

Theory of Mind (ToM) refers to the ability to attribute mental states - Such as beliefs, desires, emotions, and intentions to oneself and others. And to understand that those mental states may be different across individuals and situations. This capacity is a foundational component of socio-emotional development, particularly during early childhood, when children begin to navigate complex social interactions and emotional experiences (Legg, 2023).

During early childhood, the development of theory of mind plays a crucial role in children's emerging understanding of emotions and social relationships. According to literature socio-emotional development involves learning to interpret other's behaviors, regulate one's own emotions and engage in meaningful social exchanges. ToM supports these processes by enabling children to recognize that others have independent thoughts and feelings which may not align with their own. For example, understanding that another child may feel sad despite an apparently positive situation reflects an early form of perspective-taking rooted in ToM (Lightfoot, et al., 2014).

Empirical research highlights that ToM development is closely linked to emotional understanding and regulation. Legg (2023) emphasizes that recent studies demonstrate the strong association between children's Theory of Mind abilities and their capacity for empathy, prosocial behavior, and conflict resolution. As children gain a more sophisticated understanding of mental states, they become better equipped to anticipate others' emotional reactions and adjust their behavior, accordingly, fostering positive peer relationships.

Neuroscientific evidence further supports the centrality of Theory of Mind in socio-emotional functioning. Specifically, scientific research shows that ToM related neural networks are actively involved when individuals process emotional stimuli within social contexts. Their findings suggest that the integration of emotional and mental-state information is supported by specific brain mechanisms, underscoring the biological foundations of ToM. Although their study focuses on neural responses, the applications extend to early development, as these neural systems begin forming in childhood and are saved through social interaction (Biró et al., 2025).

In early childhood, social experience such as pretend play, parent-child conversations, and peer interactions provides essential context for the development of Theory of Mind. Lightfoot et al. (2014) argue that these interactions allow children to practice interpreting intentions and emotions, thereby strengthening socio-emotional competence. Consequently, the Theory of Mind is not merely a cognitive milestone by a dynamic process deeply embedded in children's emotional social worlds. Overall, Theory of Mind is a core mechanism through which young children develop socio-emotional understanding, empathy and effective social communication. Its development reflects the continuous interplay between cognitive growth, emotional awareness, and social experience.

Attachment Theory

Attachment plays a crucial role in the social-emotional development of children during early childhood. Rooted in the emotional bond between child and caregiver, the type of attachment that is formed [Secure, Insecure-Avoidant, Insecure- Ambivalent (or Resistant), and Disorganized Attachment] has a long-term impact on the child's emotional and social functioning. For example, children with secure attachments tend to exhibit with self-esteem, better peer relationships, and more effective self-regulation (Καφέτσιος, K., 2005).

Mary Ainsworth's pioneering work on attachment theory emphasized the importance of secure attachment in the first years of life. Through the "Strange Situation" procedure, she identified key attachment styles-secure, insecure avoidant, and insecure ambivalent- which reflect the quality of caregiving experienced by the infant (Vertel, 2023). Securely attached children tend to display greater emotional resilience, social competence and autonomy, while those with insecure attachments often face challenges in emotion regulation and interpersonal relationships.

The attachment bond serves as "secure base", from which the child explores the world, returning to the caregiver for comfort and safety. This dynamic foster trust and emotional security, which are foundational for later developmental milestones with secure attachments tend to exhibit higher self-esteem, better peer relationships, and more effective self-regulation (Vertel, 2023).

Recent studies highlight both the stability and potential for change in attachment security over time. Although early patterns of attachment can persist into adolescence and adulthood, significant life events and relational experiences can reshape attachment representations (Booth-LaForce & Roisman, 2021). Thus, early interventions and supportive caregiving environments can positively alter developmental trajectories, even for children with early insecure attachments. As a result, understanding attachemnet as a dynamic, relational process is vital for parents, educators and professionals aiming to support healthy socioemotional development in early childhood.

Resilience and Coping Strategies

Resilience during early childhood is a core element of socio-emotional development, as it determines how children adapt to challenges and stressors. The development of resilience is closely tied to a child's capacity for self-regulation and metacognitive awareness, which emerge gradually through supportive interactions with caregivers and peers. These early relational experiences lay the foundation for effective coping strategies, such as emotional expression, cognitive reframing and problem solving (Chrystovska et al, 2022).

Coping mechanism is early childhood are not innate but learned through modeling and guided practice. When children observe emotionally competent adults responding adaptively to stress, they internalize strategies such as pausing before reacting or seeking help. The role of self-regulation is critical here, it enables children to manage impulses, delay gratification and reflect on their emotional states

Metacognitive strategies also contribute to resilience. By learning to identify their own thoughts and feelings, children can begin to anticipate emotional reactions and select appropriate coping tools. Educational settings that foster emotional literacy and provide structured opportunities for decision making enhance both resilience and coping efficiency.

Ultimately, resilience in early childhood is not merely the absence of dysfunction but the presence of adaptive, self-regulated responses to everyday challenges. Supporting this process through intentional teaching and responsive caregiving is essential for long-term emotional well-being.

DISCUSSION

Interaction between Neuropsychological and Socioemotional Development

Interaction between socioemotional development and neuropsychology is very crucial because many social and sentimental skills are dependent on the correct function of certain brain structures. Brain function is very much connected with the development of feelings and social adaptation. Hence, the development of the brain is connected with the development of the child's skills to conceive and regulate and express its feelings. At the same time social skills are developing in proportion to the maturing of certain brain structures. The reverse is also true: socializing experiences turn on certain neuron connections affecting the neuroplasticity, which signifies the ability of the brain to modify based on experience. This means that the environment interacts with the brain and this shapes the ability of the child to connect to Phil and to self-regulate depending on the social stimuli it receives. It is clear that sentimental learning does not function independently from certain brain structures. Experiences turn into knowledge through the brain's ability to modify its structures and connections on their basis (Chrystovska et al, 2022).

Neuroplasticity is the changes in the brain structures that are caused by experiences of one person during his whole life with emphasis given in childhood and adolescence. This way brains that have been exposed to different environmental experiences can be shaped in a different way. Developing brain at the first stages of its life it's very sensible. The periods that brain development is the most sensible to certain experiences are called critical periods (Kolb, 2018).

Therefore, we can assume that it is not only the brain function that affects the social and sentimental behavior of a person but it is about a two-way relationship since experiences can also affect the structures, development and function of the brain (McDonald, 2017). It is useful to refer to the example of emotional challenges as presented by Chrystovska (2022) who distinguishes between the emotional brain center around the amygdala and the Olympic system and the rational brain located in the prefrontal cortex. He argues that emotional intelligence does not simply arise from the psyche but has a neuropsychological basis. That is it depends on the functional maturation of the brain and the areas related to the executive function and conscious processing and language processing. The maturation of this area is also depends on neuroplasticity meaning the child's experiences which can influence brain development. It has been assumed that sentimental stability and adequate social experiences, especially with the important others, in children, are very important for mobilizing and enhancing brain networks which are related to self-regulation and social learning (Orón et al 2024).

Particular brain structures are responsible for the development of executive functions and social sentimental behavior. The maturing of these structures throughout childhood to adulthood is a major factor that determines social adaptation, difficult judgment, self-regulation and sympathy. Incidents such as injury, genetic anomalies or sensory deprivation lead to difficulties in socializing handling feeling and judgment due to the problems in development and measuring of certain brain areas (Barasso-Catanzaro & Eslinger, 2016)

Adolescence is a period during which the brain is in the states of higher high plasticity. It is also a combination of intense levels of stress which significantly affect the brain structures. Stress is a good example to observe how emotion can influence brain function. Stress during adolescence is the result of both the brain that is in a vulnerable state of maturation and social factors due to the complex social processes characteristic of this development stage. For instance the amygdala becomes hyperactive in response to fear stimuli when a person has experienced intense early stress such as children who have faced neglect or grown up in institutions. Additionally the prefrontal cortex is affected by stress as its connections with the amygdala are weakened which worsens adults ability to regulate their emotions. The striatum is also influenced by early life stress. Its role in regulating the sense of pleasure and learning through reward becomes impaired (VanTieghem & Tottenham, 2017).

However, adolescents even in conditions of lack of stress act impulsive due to the incompatible majoring of amygdala and prefrontal cortex. This means the atomic dollar which is responsible for feelings major earlier before the majoring of prefrontal cortex which is responsible for regulating feelings (Tottenham & Galvàn, 2016).

From the interaction between your psychology and an individual's social and emotional experience, it is also possible to understand the importance of early interventions involving the family or school in ensuring ballast rain maturation and emotional regulation. Examples of such interventions include parental guidance and support programs aimed at training parents to respond to their children's needs with sensitivity, consistency and empathy. This parental attitude can help reduce cortisol levels in children and improve the connection between the prefrontal cortex and the amygdala, i.e. emotional regulation (Cruz et al., 2024). Equally important is the enhancement of predictability and the sense of safety which protect brain development. The goal of these interventions is to support the developing brain in managing its social and emotional environment. Very significance becomes even greater given the brain plasticity is high during adolescence making it the period during which the brain can be influenced both negatively and positively (Smith & Pollak, 2020).

Influence of Environmental Factors

Bronfenbrenner, developed the ecological systems theory in which he argues that human development is directly influenced by a series of interconnected environmental systems. He distinguished several systems from the microsystem, which is the immediate environment (e.g. the family and school) to the macrosystem, which is the broad social structures (e.g. culture) (Guy-Evans, 2024).

Family and Upbringing Environment

Early childhood, in terms of shaping a child's character and development, is critical period which has a long-term and decisive impact on a child's life. This fundamental stage is characterized by rapid brain development and increased neuroplasticity, making the organism extremely sensitive to environmental influences and highlighting the family as the primary determinant of developmental outcomes (Martin et al., 2025; Provenzi et al.,2023). Research shows that the first 1,000 days of life are a critical window, with early experiences in the family environment profoundly shaping neural architecture and subsequent behavioral patterns (Xu et al., 2024). The family environment is recognised as the most important influence an early development across multiple domains of functioning, serving as a critical link where biological organisms interact with the social and physical environment to shape behaviour (Fishbein et al., 2019).

In this context, the complex interaction between the family environment and upbringing significantly shapes the child's neuropsychological and socio-emotional development (Bush et al., 2020; Wang, 2023). Factors such as socioeconomic status, parental involvement, emotional climate and availability of material resources profoundly influence cognitive development and socio-emotional skills (Xi, 2025). In fact, studies show how socioeconomic factors can lead to changes in brain structure and function, linking poverty to distinct neurodevelopmental changes (Mualem et al., 2024). At the same time, family stability and composition, including single-parent versus two-parent households, have been linked to different cognitive, educational and behavioral outcomes, suggesting that the structural integrity of the family unit influences neural and behavioral development (Bush et al., 2020).

The quality of family functioning in early life is a strong predictor of healthy brain development, offering protection against the onset of behavioral disorders (Delaney et al., 2022). The family environment is the primary setting for socialization, teaching children vital interpersonal and emotional control skills. Research shows that the resilience of children exposed to environmental stress is largely related to good parenting, defined as warmth, support and effective communication (Bradley et al., 2013). Conversely, Lai et al., discovered that unfavourable home settings throughout childhood might affect teenagers for a long time, indicating that early experiences can affect social interactions and behavioural problems later in life (Lai et al., 2022). In particular, a supportive Family environment setting promotes cognitive an emotional development, whereas unfavourable family experiences may expose kids to psychiatric issues in the future (McIsaac et al., 2022).

The specific parenting style also has a significant impact on socio-emotional development. Children who grow up with authoritative parenting, tend to have greater independence, better academic achievement and adaptability (Saragih & Fuadah, 2024). According to Hughes and Ensor, authoritative parenting fosters positive social relationships in kids by striking a balance between freedom and control (Hughes and Ensor, 2022). In contrast, permissive parenting reduces the child's ability to self-regulate and follow rules, while neglectful parenting has been shown to have a negative impact on children's physical and cognitive development. Neglectful parents, often cause delays in their children's intellectual and physical development (Saragih & Fuadah, 2024). Overall, family factors interact dynamically and have a decisive influence on children's neurodevelopmental trajectories and subsequent behavioral manifestations (Thijssen et al., 2023).

Interaction with Parents and Peers

During early childhood, social interactions with parents and peers play a crucial role in shaping emotional, cognitive and moral development. Parents are primary agents of socialization, offering children not only emotional security but also the first model of interpersonal relationships. Through day to day routines and reciprocal interactions, children internalize social norms, emotional regulation strategies and communication skills (Lightfoot, et al., 2015).

Parents scaffold children's behavior by guiding their play, offering feedback, and gradually allowing greater independence. For example, verbal exchanges during shared tasks help children develop language skills and cognitive strategies. Furthermore, secure attachments to caregivers are linked to higher levels of social competence and empathy in peer relationships (Lightfoot et al., 2015).

Simultaneously. Interactions with peers offer unique opportunities for learning cooperation, conflict resolution and perspective taking. Unlike relationships with adults, peer relationships are typically egalitarian, requiring children to negotiate roles and rules on more equal terms. This dynamic foster critical socio-emotional competencies, such as compromise and mutual respect (Harrist & Bakshi, 2022).

Play is a central medium through which peer interaction occurs. Cooperative and pretend play, in particular, enhance children's capacity to understand other's thoughts and emotions, contributing to theory of mind development. Overall, the interplay between parental influence and peer experiences creates a foundation for adaptive social functioning throughout life.

Stressful Events - ACEs (Adverse Childhood Experiences)

Adverse Childhood Experiences (ACEs) significantly affect neuropsychological and socio-emotional development in early childhood, a period critical for rapid brain development and increased neuroplasticity (Aluğan, 2024). These experiences include traumatic events such as neglect, physical, sexual or emotional abuse, severe external stressful events (e.g. natural disasters, death of a loved one) and dysfunctional family environment (e.g. domestic violence, addictions) (Megari & Guanco, 2026). The accumulation of ACEs is associated with negative long-term effects on mental and physical health (Felitti et al., 1998; Bellis et al., 2019).

Neuropsychological Development and Cognitive Functions ACEs Are closely related to deficits in cognitive functioning, affecting intelligence quotient, language, attention and working memory (Bai & CAI, 2024; Tyrka et al., 2013; Xiang et al., 2022). Specifically, ACEs adversely affect executive functions (EF), such as working memory, planning, shifting attention and impulse control, which are primarily developed in the prefrontal cortex (PFC) (Zelazo et al., 2016). One study showed that individuals with more ACEs performed worse on EF measures such the Inhibition and Working Memory clinical scales and the Global Executive Composite (GEC) (Henry, 2021).

Brain Structure and Biological Mechanisms Early adversity causes alterations in critical areas such as the prefrontal cortex, amygdala, hippocampus and mesolimbic system (Aluğan, 2024; Xiang et al., 2022; Teicher et al., 2002). Chronic stress exposure causes the hypothalamic-pituitary-adrenal (HPA) axis to become too activated, which results in decreased feedback on stress, elevated release of cortisol and emotional cognitive dysfunction (McEwen, 2000). Regarding brain function, brain structure and function are impacted by persistently high cortisol levels where it occurs PFC and hippocampal dendritic connections are reduced and strengthening of the amygdala's connections, which are linked to emotional and impulsive reactions (Vyas et al., 2002; McEwen, 2000). As a result, emotional reactions take precedence over controlled social behaviours that call for executive processes. This disorder, known as “allostatic overload”, is a type of toxic stress that modifies learning and synapses (Henry, 2021).

In terms of brain plasticity, BDNF (Brain Derived Neurotrophic Factor) is a key indicator of plasticity and the development of neuronal connections. Prolonged stress causes the hippocampus and prefrontal cortex to produce less BDNF (Duman et al., 2000). Neuronal atrophy, memory loss and learning impairment are caused by decreased BDNF (Bath et al., 2013). On the other hand, giving experimental mice BDNF reverses the effects of stress. Although there was no significant ACEs-BDNF link in her group (N= 236) Henry’s (2021) study revealed that this might be because of the sample age or time point of assessment. About behaviour and social emotional development, among the consequences of a reduction in executive functioning are reactive and impulsive actions, inadequate control of emotions and social connection challenges. Behaviours are controlled with EF works correctly.

Social-Emotional Development and Resilience ACEs profoundly affect emotional regulation, which in turn may mediate the relationship between adverse experiences and subsequent mental health problems (Morris et al., 202 1). Children who have been abused or neglected may have difficulty distinguishing facial emotional expressions (Tyrka et al., 2013). The consequences of reduced executive functioning include impulsive actions and difficulties in social connections, as ACEs make the more reactive to emotions (Henry, 2021). Although ACEs carry significant risks, some individuals demonstrate resilience due to environmental enrichment or other protective factors (Bai & CAI, 2024; Tyrka et al., 2013). In conclusion, early experiences have long-term effects on children’s neural, behavioral and psychological development (Smith & Pollak, 2020).

Cultural Differences in Development

Children grow up in relationships and cultural circumstances that establish what constitutes appropriate behaviour and growth. Development is influenced by social and environmental factors in addition to biological factors. Keller contests the notion that attachment theory is universally applicable and contends that cultural differences in socio-emotional development are often disregarded (Keller, 2020; Bowlby, 1979). Culture is a collection of "scripts and values" that serve as developmental settings (Keller & Kärtner, 2013).

Learning and socialization experiences are influenced by cultural factors, including home structure, number of children end educational attainment. A search claims that the middle class in the West encourages psychological autonomy, Including independence, self-expression and emotional self-regulation (Keller, 2012). These experiences are distinguished by child centeredness, dualistic engagement and the use of voice and face (Keller, 2020). The dominant theory is attachment, which emphasizes emotional expression and views the mother as the primary caregiver (Ainsworth & Bowlby, 1991). Conversely, traditional rural communities, which are founded on action-autonomy, place a strong emphasis on communal consciousness and responsibility. Multiple caregivers (such as siblings), involvement in group activities, physical touch and bodily synchronisation are all part of their experiences (Morelli, 2014). Conformity, humility, end restraint of emotional expression are their top priorities (Otto, 2014).

Early self-consciousness and ego separation from others are traits of Western children (Kärtner et al., 2010). The notions of conformity and social sensitivity are associated with cultural norms and have distinct neurobiological foundations. Children in communal societies acquire community empathy without necessarily having a distinct sense of self (Feldman & Masalha, 2010). There exist networks of attachment with several caregivers and congested contact in many communities, challenging the limited concept of the primary caregiver (Meehan & Hawks, 2013). Social experiences form or strengthen neural networks, demonstrating the brain' s plasticity in response to cultural stimuli.

Neuropsychological Development in Early Childhood: The Case of Down Syndrome

Down syndrome also known as trisomy 21 due to the additional 21st chromosome that exists in the DNA is a genetic syndrome with definitive effects in a person's life and growing. This particular syndrome is the most common chromosomic anomaly related to mental retardation characterized by a wide range of neurological and developmental diversions. In down syndrome, children usually face difficulties regarding cognitive growth and function, language processing and concentration as well as moving or sensory perception. Children with down syndrome are also known for their emotional sensitivity and social skills. However, there is great heterogeneity in their skills and weaknesses.

The whole growing rate differs importantly since it is more late in general and some malfunctions are permanent. For instance, the most important difference is related to cognitive and physical growth which is largely affected. The growth route of down syndrome is however largely predictable and although it is slow, it can be strengthened with education, emotional support, and a supportive environment.

Brain development in children with down syndrome is also different with clear anomalies in structures such as the cerebrum and hippocampus which grow smaller than typically and function differently. Social and sentimental growth of children with down syndrome is characterised by warmth, vivid sociability and will to socialize. Some difficulties are noticed in understanding rules and feeling controlling. They are very good at following positive role models and develop strong connection with the persons who are close to them (Barumani et al, 2019).

Neuropsychological Development and Disabilities in Early Childhood

Early childhood is a critical developmental period during which rapid changes occur in children's neuropsychological and socioemotional development, which lay the foundations for its later sentimental, social and cognitive function and behaviour. During this stage, specific procedures such as neurogenesis occur inside the human brain and interact with the memories and experience of a child, shaping its functional development, sentimental regulation and social skills. Although malfunction and disabilities reform the route of development. This change necessitates a new approach to development that takes into account both biological and environmental factors (Megari, Miliadi, 2024).

Disability is now defined from a biopsychological model which recognizes that limitations are a result of the interaction of biological malfunction and environmental factors. This is in contrast to the idea that disability is just determined by biological malfunction. According to the International Classification of Functioning, Disability and Health, disability is about the limitations in functioning and taking part in everyday life activities (Barrasso-Catanzaro, C., & Eslinger, P. J. 2016).

It is most common that certain disabilities such as down syndrome, autism spectrum disorder or intellectual disabilities appear in early childhood (Megari, & Genova, 2025). The majority of these disabilities are associated with atypical brain development and differentiations in cognitive function such as memory, social information processing and attention. Additionally neurodevelopmental disabilities affect intensively socio-emotional growth and skills since they are often accompanied by difficulties in emotional regulation, social interaction, and communication (Megari, & Genova, 2025). It is important to note that these difficulties are not a static situation. They are influenced by the context in which the child lives, which indicates the importance of early recognition of symptoms and planning appropriate intervention.

Disability in early childhood does not affect socioemotional or neuropsychological development separately but it works both ways, creating a link between brain function and behavior. Neuropsychological disabilities are associated with problems in the maturation of brain structures responsible for the development of executive functions and social perception. Such structures are the prefrontal cortex, amygdala and the links between them.

Neuropsychological deficits such as difficulties in memory, attention, and inhibitory control may affect a child's ability to regulate their behavior and their ability to react to the social stimuli of its environment. This results in a burden on social skills and interactions, making relationships with others and understanding social forms difficult. All of this leads to emotional dysregulation and emotional withdrawal that has its roots in dysfunctions of brain structures.

At the same time, socio-emotional experiences do actively affect sociopsychological development through neuroplasticity. A supportive family environment and systematic personalized education that ensures predictability on a daily basis, emotional security without strong fluctuations and can improve the functional links of the brain and limit the effects of disability. On the contrary in contexts characterized by high levels of stress and lacking adequate emotional stimulation, children with disabilities may experience deterioration and developmental difficulties may arise

Early intervention programs are they are usually multifactorial and interdisciplinary, involving the collaboration of many scientists such as psychologists, special educators, neurologists, and others. In addition, family is very important as well as supporting parents in order to achieve the enhancement of children's capabilities in their natural environment. Supporting parents also improves the sense of sentimental security in children and increases positive interactions which are very important for socio-emotional development

At the same time, creating inclusive environments ensures that children's individual needs are met. Carefully structured activities that combine self-regulation and social interaction contribute to increasing the functionality and participation of the child with a disability. Overall, early intervention ensures the improvement of children's situation and the cultivation of skills useful for everyday life that would not develop in other circumstances..

Early infancy is a very important period of time for the neurocognitive and neuropsychological development of a person since in this particular time the basic sociosentimental skills of a person are shaped. Disabilities and neurodevelopmental disorders have a large impact on the development of a person but they do not negate the individual's potential and ability to adapt. The interaction between the environment and biological factors shows the importance of early diagnosis, detection of difficulties and selection of appropriate intervention at an early stage. Additionally, creating a supporting and inclusive framework is vital for enhancing the functioning, social interaction and development of these children, finally affecting their whole well-being (Steed, Kranski,2020).

In conclusion, disability should be considered as a part of a relationship between biological factors and experiences which determines the course of development at a neuropsychological and socioemotional level. Hence, the value of early detection and definition of interventions are key. Early intervention is a key pillar in supporting children with disabilities since it can use the chance of neuroplasticity of the young brain. Recognizing in time the symptoms of developmental difficulties can positively affect the route of development in children, reducing the severity of the symptoms and enhancing the functioning of the young people thanks to the rebuilding of the brain links.

REFERENCES

Ainsworth, M. S., & Bowlby, J. (1991). An ethological approach to personality development. *The American Psychologist, 46*(4), 333–341. DOI: 10.1037/0003-066X.46.4.333

Aluğan, Z. (2024). The Impact of Early Childhood Adversity on Neurodevelopment A Comprehensive Review. Üha, 11(2), 45–59. https://doi.org/DOI: 10.32739/uha.jnbs.11.1539116

Anderson, P. (2002). Assessment and development of executive function (EF) during childhood. *Child Neuropsychology : A Journal on Normal and Abnormal Development in Childhood and Adolescence, 8*(2), 71–82. DOI: 10.1076/chin.8.2.71.8724 PMID: 12638061

Baron-Cohen, S., Tager-Flusberg, H., & Cohen, D. J. (2000). *Understanding other minds: Perspectives from developmental cognitive neuroscience*. Oxford University Press.

Barrasso-Catanzaro, C., & Eslinger, P. J. (2016). Neurobiological bases of executive function and social-emotional development: Typical and atypical brain changes. *Family Relations, 65*(1), 108–119. DOI: 10.1111/fare.12175

Bates, E., Dale, P. S., & Thal, D. (1995). Individual differences and their implications for theories of language development. In *Handbook of child language* (pp. 96–151). Cambridge University Press.

Bath, K. G., Schilit, A., & Lee, F. S. (2013). Stress effects on BDNF expression: Effects of age, sex, and form of stress. *Neuroscience, 239*, 149–156. DOI: 10.1016/j.neuroscience.2013.01.074 PMID: 23402850

Bauer, P. J. (2007). *Remembering the times of our lives: Memory in infancy and beyond*. Lawrence Erlbaum Associates.

Bell, M. A., & Wolfe, C. D. (2007). Changes in brain functioning from infancy to early childhood: Evidence from EEG power and coherence during working memory tasks. *Developmental Neuropsychology, 31*(1), 21–38. DOI: 10.1080/87565640709336885 PMID: 17305436

Bellis, M. A., Hughes, K., Ford, K., Rodriguez, G. R., Sethi, D., & Passmore, J. (2019). Life course health consequences and associated annual costs of adverse childhood experiences across Europe and North America: A systematic review and meta-analysis. *The Lancet. Public Health, 4*(10), e517–e528. DOI: 10.1016/S2468-2667(19)30145-8 PMID: 31492648

Berk, L. (2019). *Development Through the Lifespan*. Pearson Education Inc.

Biró, B., Cserjési, R., Kocsel, N., Galambos, A., Gecse, K., Kovács, L. N., Baksa, D., Dobos, D., Juhász, G., & Kökönyei, G. (2025). Unveiling the Role of Theory of Mind: Neural Response to Emotional Stimuli in Context. *Affective Science*, *6*(2), 1–16. DOI: 10.1007/s42761-025-00293-1 PMID: 40605950

Blair, C. (2016). Executive function and early childhood education. *Current Opinion in Behavioral Sciences*, *10*, 102–107. DOI: 10.1016/j.cobeha.2016.05.009 PMID: 30035205

Bowlby, J. (1979). The bowlby-ainsworth attachment theory. *The Behavioral and Brain Sciences*, *2*(4), 637–638. DOI: 10.1017/S0140525X00064955

Bradley, B., Davis, T. A., Wingo, A. P., Mercer, K. B., & Ressler, K. J. (2013). Family environment and adult resilience: contributions of positive parenting and the oxytocin receptor gene. European journal of psychotraumatology, 4, . https://doi.org/DOI: 10.3402/ejpt.v4i0.21659

Bush, N. R., Wakschlag, L. S., LeWinn, K. Z., Hertz-Picciotto, I., Nozadi, S. S., Pieper, S., Lewis, J., Biezonski, D., Blair, C., Deardorff, J., Neiderhiser, J. M., Leve, L. D., Elliott, A. J., Duarte, C. S., Lugo-Candelas, C., O'Shea, T. M., Avalos, L. A., Page, G. P., & Posner, J. (2020). Family Environment, Neurodevelopmental Risk, and the Environmental Influences on Child Health Outcomes (ECHO) Initiative: Looking Back and Moving Forward. *Frontiers in Psychiatry*, *11*, 547. DOI: 10.3389/fpsyt.2020.00547 PMID: 32636769

Buttelmann, F., & Karbach, J. (2017). Development and plasticity of cognitive flexibility in early and middle childhood. *Frontiers in Psychology*, *8*, 1040. DOI: 10.3389/fpsyg.2017.01040 PMID: 28676784

Cai, X., Bai, X., & Zhou, S. (2024). Childhood adversities and memory function in later life: The mediating role of activity participation. *BMC Geriatrics*, *24*(1), 536. DOI: 10.1186/s12877-024-05145-4 PMID: 38902657

Cruz, S., Sousa, M., & Mateus, V. (2024). *Emotion Regulation and Cognitive and Social Functioning in Early Development: The Interface Between Neurophysiological and Behavioural Perspectives*. IntechOpen., DOI: 10.5772/intechopen.1004233

Dawson, G., & Guare, R. (2004). *Executive skills in children and adolescents: A practical guide to assessment and intervention*. Guilford Press.

Decety, J., Steinbeis, N., & Cowell, J. M. (2021). The neurodevelopment of social preferences in early childhood! *Current Opinion in Neurobiology*, *68*, 23–28. DOI: 10.1016/j.conb.2020.12.009 PMID: 33418273

Diamond, A. (2013). Executive functions. *Annual Review of Psychology*, *64*(1), 135–168. DOI: 10.1146/annurev-psych-113011-143750 PMID: 23020641

Duman, R. S., Malberg, J., Nakagawa, S., & D'Sa, C. (2000). Neuronal plasticity and survival in mood disorders. *Biological Psychiatry*, *48*(8), 732–739. DOI: 10.1016/S0006-3223(00)00935-5 PMID: 11063970

Edossa, A. K., Shroeders, U., Weinert, S., & Artelt, C. (2017). The development of emotional and behavioral self-regulation and their effects on academic achievement in childhood. *International Journal of Behavioral Development*, *42*(2), 192–202. DOI: 10.1177/0165025416687412

Espinet, S. D., Anderson, J. E., & Zelazo, P. D. (2013). Executive function and early education. *Current Opinion in Behavioral Sciences*, *10*, 102–109. DOI: 10.1016/j.cobeha.2016.05.009 PMID: 30035205

Fair, D. A., Cohen, A. L., Power, J. D., Dosenbach, N. U. F., Church, J. A., Miezin, F. M., Schlaggar, B. L., & Petersen, S. E. (2009). Functional brain networks develop from a "local to distributed" organization. *PLoS Computational Biology*, *5*(5), e1000381. DOI: 10.1371/journal.pcbi.1000381 PMID: 19412534

Fair, D. A., Cohen, A. L., Power, J. D., Dosenbach, N. U. F., Church, J. A., Miezin, F. M., Schlaggar, B. L., & Petersen, S. E. (2009). Functional brain networks develop from a "local to distributed" organization. *PLoS Computational Biology*, *5*(5), e1000381. DOI: 10.1371/journal.pcbi.1000381 PMID: 19412534

Feldman, R., & Masalha, S. (2010). Parent–child and triadic antecedents of children's social competence: Cultural specificity, shared process. *Developmental Psychology*, *46*(2), 455–467. DOI: 10.1037/a0017415 PMID: 20210505

Felitti, V. J., Anda, R. F., Nordenberg, D., Williamson, D. F., Spitz, A. M., Edwards, V., Koss, M. P., & Marks, J. S. (1998). Relationship of childhood abuse and household dysfunction to many of the leading causes of death in adults. The Adverse Childhood Experiences (ACE) Study. *American Journal of Preventive Medicine*, *14*(4), 245–258. DOI: 10.1016/S0749-3797(98)00017-8 PMID: 9635069

Fishbein, D. H., Michael, L., Guthrie, C., Carr, C., & Raymer, J. (2019). Associations Between Environmental Conditions and Executive Cognitive Functioning and Behavior During Late Childhood: A Pilot Study. *Frontiers in Psychology*, *10*, 1263. DOI: 10.3389/fpsyg.2019.01263 PMID: 31231280

Gathercole, S. E., Pickering, S. J., Knight, C., & Stegmann, Z. (2004). Working memory skills and educational attainment: Evidence from national curriculum assessments. *Applied Cognitive Psychology*, *18*(1), 1–16. DOI: 10.1002/acp.934

Guy-Evans, O. (2024). *Bronfenbrenner's Ecological Systems Theory*. ResearchGate.

Harrist, A. W., & Bakshi, A. J. (2022). The Interplay of Parent and Peer Influences on Children's Social Development! *The Wiley-Blackwell Handbook of Childhood Social Development,* 459-481.

Henry, M. (2021). Examining the Effect of Adverse Childhood Experiences (ACEs) on Executive Functioning and Brain Plasticity.

Hughes, C., & Ensor, R. (2022). Social Development in Early Childhood. *The Journal of Social Psychology*, *45*(2), 321–335.

Kärtner, J., Keller, H., & Chaudhary, N. (2010). Cognitive and social influences on early prosocial behavior in two sociocultural contexts. *Developmental Psychology*, *46*(4), 905–914. DOI: 10.1037/a0019718 PMID: 20604610

Keller, H. (2012). Autonomy And Relatedness Revisited: Cultural Manifestations Of Universal Human Needs. *Child Development Perspectives*, *6*(1), 12–18. DOI: 10.1111/j.1750-8606.2011.00208.x

Keller, H. (2020). Children's Socioemotional Development Across Cultures. *Annual Review of Developmental Psychology*, *2*(1), 27–46. DOI: 10.1146/annurev-devpsych-033020-031552

Keller, H., & Kärtner, J. (2013). Development – The culture-specific solution of universal developmental tasks. In M. L. Gelfand, C.-Y., Chiu, & Hong, Y. Y. (Eds.), Advances in culture and psychology, Vol. 3 (pp. 63-116). Oxford, NY: Oxford University Press.

Kolb, B. (2018). Overview of factors influencing brain development. In *The neurobiology of brain and behavioral development* (pp. 51–79). Academic Press. DOI: 10.1016/B978-0-12-804036-2.00003-0

Lai, X., Huang, S., Nie, C., Yan, J. J., Li, Y., Wang, Y., & Luo, Y. (2022). Trajectory of problematic smartphone use among adolescents aged 10-18 years: The roles of childhood family environment and concurrent parent-child relationships. *Journal of Behavioral Addictions*, *11*(2), 577–587. DOI: 10.1556/2006.2022.00047 PMID: 35895472

Lebel, C., & Beaulieu, C. (2011). Longitudinal development of human brain wiring continues from childhood into adulthood. *The Journal of Neuroscience : The Official Journal of the Society for Neuroscience*, *31*(30), 10937–10947. DOI: 10.1523/JNEUROSCI.5302-10.2011 PMID: 21795544

Legg, E. W. (2023). Theory of Mind: A Review of Recent Empirical Results and Main Theoretical Explanations. *Psihologijske Teme, 32*(3), 635–661. DOI: 10.31820/pt.32.3.12

Lightfoot, C., Cole, M., & Cole, S. (2015). Early Childhood. In Bablekou, Z. (Ed.), *The development of children* (pp. 345–479). Gutenberg.

Martin, A., Galeris, M.-G., Theil, M. K., Sele, S., Cavelti, M., Keil, J., Kaess, M., von Polier, G. G., & Schlensog-Schuster, F. (2025). Early Struggles—The Relationship of Psychopathology and Development in Early Childhood. *Children (Basel, Switzerland), 12*(3), 265. DOI: 10.3390/children12030265 PMID: 40150548

McDonald, S. (2017). "Emotions are rising: the growing field of affect neuropsychology." Journal of the International Neuropsychological Society 23.9-10: 719-731.-09337-y McEwen B. S. (2000). The neurobiology of stress: from serendipity to clinical relevance. *Brain Research, 886*(1-2), 172–189. DOI: 10.1016/S0006-8993(00)02950-4

McIsaac, J. D., Lamptey, D. L., Harley, J., MacQuarrie, M., Cummings, R., Rossiter, M. D., Janus, M., & Turner, J. (2022). Early pandemic impacts on family environments that shape childhood development and health: A Canadian study. *Child: Care, Health and Development, 48*(6), 1122–1133. DOI: 10.1111/cch.13046 PMID: 35997511

Meehan, C. L., & Hawks, S. (2013). Cooperative breeding and attachment among the Aka foragers. In *Attachment reconsidered: Cultural perspectives on a Western theory* (pp. 85–113). Palgrave Macmillan US. DOI: 10.1057/9781137386724_4

Megari, K. (2025). *Clinical Applications of Pediatric Neuropsychology from Infancy to Adolescence*. IGI Global., DOI: 10.4018/979-8-3693-9689-6

Megari, K., & Genova, K. D. (2025). The Neurocognitive Characteristics of Children with Neurodevelopmental Disabilities and Their Clinical Implications (Chapter 6 pages 119-142). Clinical Applications of Pediatric Neuropsychology from Infancy to Adolescence. Pennsylvania / USA: IGI Global.

Megari, K., & Guanco, R. J. (2026, January 01). Pediatric Brain Development and Adverse Childhood Experiences: Cognitive, Emotional, and Behavioral Outcomes. [BOSN]. *Brain Organoid & Systems Neuroscience Journal, 4*, 0007. DOI: 10.34133/bosn.0007

Megari, K., & Miliadi, V. (2024). The neuropsychology of early childhood and infancy. *International Journal of Developmental Neuroscience : The Official Journal of the International Society for Developmental Neuroscience, 84*(8), 1–10. DOI: 10.1002/jdn.10381 PMID: 39323063

Morelli, G. (2014). The evolution of attachment theory and cultures of human attachment in infancy and early childhood.

Morris, A. S., Hays-Grudo, J., Kerr, K. L., & Beasley, L. O. (2021). The heart of the matter: Developing the whole child through community resources and caregiver relationships. *Development and Psychopathology*, *33*(2), 533–544. DOI: 10.1017/S0954579420001595 PMID: 33955346

Mualem, R., Morales-Quezada, L., Farraj, R. H., Shance, S., Bernshtein, D. H., Cohen, S., Mualem, L., Salem, N., Yehuda, R. R., Zbedat, Y., Waksman, I., & Biswas, S. (2024). Econeurobiology and brain development in children: Key factors affecting development, behavioral outcomes, and school interventions. *Frontiers in Public Health*, *12*, 1376075. DOI: 10.3389/fpubh.2024.1376075 PMID: 39391155

Nelson, C. A., Thomas, K. M., & de Haan, M. (2006). Neural Basis of cognitive development. In Kuuhn, D., & Siegler, R. (Eds.), Handbook of child psychology: Vol. 2. *Cognition, perception, and language* (6th ed., pp. 3–57). Wiley.

Otto, H. (2014). Don't show your emotions! Emotion regulation and attachment in the Cameroonian Nso. *Different faces of attachment*, 215-229.

Ozonoff, S., & Jensen, J. (1999). Brief report: Specific executive function profiles in three neuro-de velopmental disorders. *Journal of Autism and Developmental Disorders*, *29*(2), 171–177. DOI: 10.1023/A:1023052913110 PMID: 10382139

Posner, M. I., & Rothbart, M. K. (2007). Research on attention networks as a model for the integration of psychological science. *Annual Review of Psychology*, *58*(1), 1–23. DOI: 10.1146/annurev.psych.58.110405.085516 PMID: 17029565

Provenzi, L., Bussu, G., & Riva, V. (2023). Editorial: Risk and protective factors, family environment and (a)typical neurodevelopmental outcomes. *Frontiers in Psychology*, *14*, 1221338. DOI: 10.3389/fpsyg.2023.1221338 PMID: 37408973

Rothbart, M. K., Sheese, B. E., Rosario Rueda, M., & Posner, M. I. (2011). Developing Mechanisms of Self-Regulation in Early Life! *Emotion Review*, *3*(2), 207–213. DOI: 10.1177/1754073910387943 PMID: 21892360

Rueda, M. R., Posner, M. I., & Rothbart, M. K. (2005). The development of executive attention: Contributions to the emergence of self-regulation. *Developmental Neuropsychology*, *28*(2), 573–594. DOI: 10.1207/s15326942dn2802_2 PMID: 16144428

Saragih, B. D., & Fuadah, F. (2024). The Influence of Parenting Styles on the Early Childhood Development at TKK Kasih Mulia Cimahi. Int. J. Pharm. *Bio-Medical Sci*, *4*(10), 861–864. DOI: 10.47191/ijpbms/v4-i10-12

Schiele, T., Mues, A., Wirth, A., Christner, N., Paulus, M., Birtwistle, E., & Niklas, F. (2024). Bridging the gap: A longitudinal study on the relation between preschool children's moral self-concept, normative stances, and sharing behavior. *Social and Emotional Learning: Research, Practice, and Policy*, *3*, 100027. DOI: 10.1016/j.sel.2024.100027

Shaw, P.. (2018). *Opportunities for neurodevelopmental plasticity from infancy through early adulthood*. Society for Research in Child Development., DOI: 10.1111/cdev.13073

Smith, K. E., & Pollak, S. D. (2020). Early life stress and development: Potential mechanisms for adverse outcomes. *Journal of Neurodevelopmental Disorders*, *12*(1), 34. DOI: 10.1186/s11689-020-09337-y PMID: 33327939

Söldner, L., & Paulus, M. (2024). I help, therefore, I am?–A registered report on longitudinal inter-relations of the three-dimensional moral self-concept and prosocial behaviours in preschool children. *The British Journal of Developmental Psychology*, *42*(2), 257–284. DOI: 10.1111/bjdp.12481 PMID: 38483075

Soliman, D., Frydenberg, E., Liang, R., & Deans, J. (2020). Enhancing empathy in preschoolers: A comparison of social and emotional learning approaches! *Educational and Developmental Psychologist*, *38*(1), 64–76. DOI: 10.1080/20590776.2020.1839883

Steed, E. A., & Kranski, T. A. (2020). Participant characteristics in research on interventions for young children with challenging behavior: A systematic review. *Topics in Early Childhood Special Education*, *40*(2), 110–123. DOI: 10.1177/0271121419832969

Stiles, J. (2000). Neural plasticity and cognitive development. *Developmental Neuropsychology*, *18*(2), 237–272. DOI: 10.1207/S15326942DN1802_5 PMID: 11280966

Teicher, M. H., Andersen, S. L., Polcari, A., Anderson, C. M., & Navalta, C. P. (2002). Developmental neurobiology of childhood stress and trauma. *The Psychiatric Clinics of North America*, *25*(2), 397–viii. DOI: 10.1016/S0193-953X(01)00003-X PMID: 12136507

Thatcher, R. W., Walker, R. A., & Giudice, S. (1987). Human, cerebral, hemispheris develop at different rates and ages. *Science*, *236*(4805), 1110–1113. DOI: 10.1126/science.3576224 PMID: 3576224

Thijssen, S., Riem, M. M. E., Vijayakumar, N., Cima, M. J., & Whittle, S. (2023). Editorial: Nurturing the brain: Associations between family environment and child brain development. *Frontiers in Neuroscience*, *17*, 1119838. Advance online publication. DOI: 10.3389/fnins.2023.1119838 PMID: 36798461

Tottenham, N., & Galván, A. (2016). Stress and the adolescent brain: Amygdala-prefrontal cortex circuitry and ventral striatum as developmental targets. *Neuroscience and Biobehavioral Reviews, 70*, 217–227. Advance online publication. DOI: 10.1016/j.neubiorev.2016.07.030 PMID: 27473936

Tyrka, A. R., Burgers, D. E., Philip, N. S., Price, L. H., & Carpenter, L. L. (2013). The neurobiological correlates of childhood adversity and implications for treatment. *Acta Psychiatrica Scandinavica, 128*(6), 434–447. DOI: 10.1111/acps.12143 PMID: 23662634

VanTieghem, M. R., & Tottenham, N. (2017). Neurobiological programming of early life stress: functional development of amygdala-prefrontal circuitry and vulnerability for stress-related psychopathology. Behavioral neurobiology of PTSD, 117-136.

Vertel, A. (2023) Mary Ainsworth's attachment theory and its significance for understanding a child's early social-emotional development! *Humanities science current issues,* 1, 304-310. DOI https://doi.org/DOI: 10.24919/2308-4863/70-1-46

Vyas, A., Mitra, R., Shankaranarayana Rao, B. S., & Chattarji, S. (2002). Chronic stress induces contrasting patterns of dendritic remodeling in hippocampal and amygdaloid neurons. *The Journal of Neuroscience : The Official Journal of the Society for Neuroscience, 22*(15), 6810–6818. DOI: 10.1523/JNEUROSCI.22-15-06810.2002 PMID: 12151561

Wang, Y. (2023). Influence of Early Family Nurturing Environment on Children's Psychological and Emotional Social Development. *Iranian Journal of Public Health, 52*(10), 2138–2147. DOI: 10.18502/ijph.v52i10.13852 PMID: 37899924

Xi, D. (2025). The Impact of Family Environment on Children's Education: An Analytical Study. *Lecture Notes in Education Psychology and Public Media, 86*(1), 12–15. DOI: 10.54254/2753-7048/2025.21814

Xiang, X., Cho, J., Sun, Y., & Wang, X. (2022). Childhood adversity and cognitive impairment in later life. *Frontiers in Psychology, 13*, 935254. DOI: 10.3389/fpsyg.2022.935254 PMID: 36051218

Xu, Y., Meng, Y., Dong, X., Wang, S., & Yu, L. (2024). Relationship between family socioeconomic status and toddlers' social-emotional development: the mediation effects of home rearing environment. *Research Square*. https://doi.org/DOI: 10.21203/rs.3.rs-4725276/v1

Yu, Y., & Bailey, A. L. (2025). Self-concept in first grade and academic performance trajectories: Roles of gender and dual-language immersion versus English-medium Program Enrollment. *International Multilingual Research Journal, 19*(4), 1–20. DOI: 10.1080/19313152.2024.2387990

Zelazo, P. D., Müller, U., Frye, D., Marcovitch, S., Argitis, G., Boseovski, J., Chiang, J. K., Hongwanishkul, D., Schuster, B. V., & Sutherland, A. (2003). The development of executive function in early childhood. *Monographs of the Society for Research in Child Development, 68*(3), vii–137. DOI: 10.1111/j.0037-976X.2003.00269.x PMID: 14723273

Chapter 2
Definitions and classification of NDDs: Conceptual, Diagnostic, and Developmental Perspectives

Anuj Srivastava
http://orcid.org/0000-0003-2861-7769
Institute of Advanced Studies in Education, Jamia Millia Islamia, India

Sara Begum
Institute of Advanced studies in Education, Jamia Millia Islamia, India

Veera Gupta
National Institute of Educational Planning and Administration, India

Mohd. Faijullah Khan
Institute of Advanced studies in Education, Jamia Millia Islamia, India

ABSTRACT

Neurodevelopmental Disorders represents heterogeneous group of developmental disorders characterized by impairments in cognitive, communicative, behavioural, motor and adaptive development, emerging during the developmental period with lifelong persistence. Over successive decades, there has been marked significant progress in conceptualizations of these disorders, moving beyond narrowly defined views of childhood psychopathology to multidimensional developmental conditions influenced by neurobiological, genetic, environmental and sociocultural factors. Drawing primarily on the Diagnostic and Statistical Manual of Mental Disorders (DSM-I through DSM-5-TR) and complementary international frameworks, the chapter traces historical shifts in diagnostic thinking, addresses neurobiological and

DOI: 10.4018/979-8-3373-7072-9.ch002

genetic bases of NDDs, highlights cultural and cross-cultural issues in diagnosis. The current chapter brings together developmental, clinical and policy perspectives that can help researchers, educators, clinicians and policymakers.

1. INTRODUCTION

Neurodevelopmental disorders represent one of the most clinically and scientifically complex domains within contemporary mental health, education and disability studies. Originating during the development period, they are characterized by persistent difficulties in cognitive development, speech and language difficulties, motor coordination and adaptive functioning that significantly affect everyday life. Although the clinical presentation across neurodevelopmental disorders varies in severity, its long-term implication is certainly very great and enduring across various dimensions such as educational attainment, employment opportunities, social participation, quality of life and throughout life (Thapar et al., 2016).

Historically, conditions now classified under the collective term of neurodevelopmental disorders were defined in a disorganized and varying manner. Earlier psychiatric and medical concepts used broad, imprecisely defined categories, termed as 'mental deficiency,' 'childhood psychosis,' or 'minimal brain dysfunction,' reflecting lack of understanding about brain development, as well as an absence of standardized procedures (American Psychiatric Association, 1952; 1968). These constructs were rather narrow, static and deficit-based, failing to incorporate the dynamic role by environmental context and intervention.

In the second half of the twentieth century, advancements in developmental psychology, psychometrics, neuroscience and genetics led to a growing recognition that shared developmental mechanisms underlie of conditions that impair attention, learning, language, social interaction and intellectual functioning; and that most commonly co-occur. These observations challenged traditional categorical boundaries and led to a progressive combination of conditions that appeared during childhood into more balanced diagnostic categories (Rutter, 2011). These scientific shifts have not resolved all debates; the boundaries of diagnostic categories, the cultural validity of classification systems, and the balance between categorical and dimensional approaches continue to be contested (Hyman, 2010; Insel et al., 2010).

Modern classification systems, especially the DSM-5 and DSM-5-TR (American Psychiatric Association [APA], 2013, 2022) and the ICD-11 (World Health Organization [WHO], 2019) specifically identify neurodevelopmental disorders as a specific group of conditions that have common developmental patterns, emphasizing functional impairment, heterogeneity and lifespan continuity. Similar dimensions are provided by the American Association on Intellectual and Developmental

Disabilities (AAIDD) which focuses on adaptive behavior, contextual aspects and individualized supports (AAIDD, 2023).

Although there are emerging similarities across the various classification systems, there are also important scholarly controversies surrounding diagnostic boundary-setting, the cultural validity of the Western derived criteria, the degree of comorbidity and the duality of categorical and dimensional approaches. These are not merely theoretical concerns, but also practical ones for issues of diagnostic equity, access to services, research design and policy making (Hyman, 2010; Rutter, 2011). Further, the emergence of the paradigm of neurodiversity has introduced value-based reframing of developmental difference which challenges deficit model-oriented classification frameworks (Armstrong, 2011; Chapman, 2020).

The next section places these conceptual debates in a global epidemiological context and conceptualizes neurodevelopmental disorders before exploring definitional and classificatory foundations in greater depth.

2. PREVALENCE OF NEURODEVELOPMENTAL DISORDERS

The *Global Report on Children with Developmental Disabilities* released by the World Health Organization holds that the number of neurodevelopmental disorders is the most estimated prevalence rate of all developmental conditions in children under the age of 15 (World Health Organization [WHO], 2023).

2.1 Global Prevalence of Neurodevelopmental Disorders in Childhood

According to estimates of Global Burden of Disease (GBD) 2019 compiled in the WHO report, neurodevelopmental disorders are highly prevalent, as they are at any age, but are consistently high throughout childhood and adolescence. The prevalence of neurodevelopmental disorders is 4.1 percent among children aged below five years, 6.3 percent in children aged between 5-9 years and 7.0 percent among children aged between 10-14 years. The prevalence is still high in later adolescence as estimates are 6.3% among people aged 15-19 years (WHO, 2023).

According to these estimates, almost one in every fourteen children worldwide suffer a neurodevelopmental condition in mid-childhood, making it important to highlight the position of neurodevelopmental conditions in the global health and development agenda of child health.

2.2 Key Neurodevelopmental Disorders Prevalence

Among neurodevelopmental conditions, idiopathic developmental intellectual disability has one of the highest prevalence rates of about 2.0% at the age of 5-9 years and 10-14 years. Attention-deficit/hyperactivity disorder (ADHD) also shows a rising prevalence rate, with a range of about 0.2% in children younger than five years, and 2.3% in adolescents aged 15–19 years. Among all age categories, prevalence rate was highest at 2.9% in 10-14 years (WHO, 2023).

3. CONCEPTUAL FOUNDATIONS OF NEURODEVELOPMENTAL DISORDERS

Neurodevelopmental disorders are linked to atypical brain development and early emerging functional impairments. Contemporary frameworks conceptualize that such conditions develop as a result of a complex and probabilistic interactions among genetic susceptibility, neurobiological processes and environmental factors that acts within specific developmental timeframes (Karmiloff-Smith, 1998). Unlike disorders that arise in later life as a result of traumas, infections or neurodegeneration, neurodevelopmental disorders indicate the deviations in developmental trajectories instead of the loss of previously obtained abilities.

Figure 1. Conceptual Foundations of Neurodevelopmental Disorders

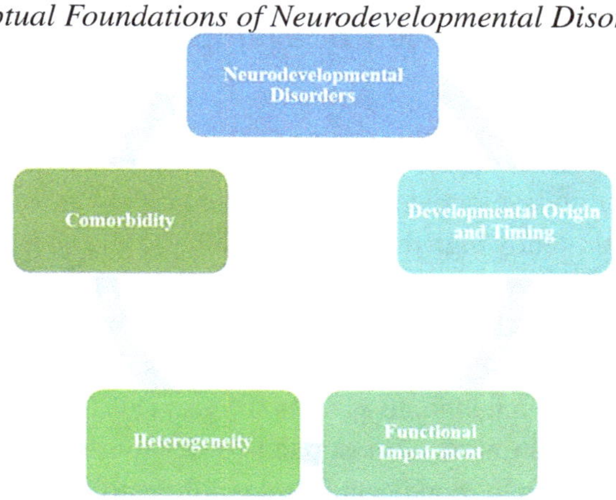

A. Developmental Origin and Timing

A defining characteristic of neurodevelopmental disorders is their occurrence during the developmental period. Both DSM-5-TR and ICD-11 emphasize that symptoms typically manifest during infancy or childhood, but complete manifestations may not be visible until the environmental requirements exceed the individual's capacities (APA, 2022; WHO, 2019). For example, specific learning disorder may not be evident until formal academic training is involved. This developmental timing complicates diagnosis because early symptoms can be mild, non-specific or misattributed to environmental factors. Modern frameworks therefore emphasize on the importance of developmental screening, longitudinal assessment and contextual interpretation rather than reliance on single-point evaluations.

B. Functional Impairment

Current diagnostic models specify that the deficits should be accompanied by the development of the clinically significant impairment in any one of the domains personal, social, academic or occupational. This functional approach shifts the orientation of classification from a purely symptomatic or psychometric approach towards practical functioning and participation (APA, 2022). The focus on the functional impairment of classification is also consistent with educational and disability assistance approaches, where it does not matter whether someone has signs or symptoms, as long as they do not have effects on learning, independent living and social inclusion. As an example of such is evident in the AAIDD model, which defines intellectual disability as deficits in adaptive behavior, not cognitive deficits (AAIDD, 2023).

C. Developmental Variability and Heterogeneity

Neurodevelopmental disorders are clinically highly heterogeneous in terms of their features, severity and developmental course. Individuals can be very different from each other in their intellectual function, language development and adaptive functioning and responses to intervention, despite having the exact same diagnosis. For instance, Autism Spectrum Disorder (ASD) encompasses individuals who have severe intellectual and language skills as well as a large number who have average or above-average intelligence and expressive language fluency (Lord et al., 2018). Such heterogeneity has criticized deficit models and highlighted the limitations of rigid diagnostic categories. It also highlights the need to assess and intervene individually and come up with plans that not only address the challenges but also capitalize on the strengths. Developmental trajectories are not solely genetically determined; rather, they emerge from ongoing, dynamic interactions between the individual potential and environmental factors, such as the family background, education and accessibility of services.

D. Comorbidity

Empirical studies consistently demonstrated a lot of overlapping among Autism Spectrum Disorder (ASD), Attention-Deficit/Hyperactivity Disorder (ADHD), Specific Learning Disorder and Intellectual Disability (Gillberg, 2010; Thapar et al., 2016). These overlaps reflect shared neurodevelopmental pathways rather than diagnostic error and thus the need to adopt integrative and transdiagnostic approaches becomes even more important. From a development psychopathology perspective, neurodevelopmental disorders are probabilistic rather than deterministic phenomena. Early vulnerabilities can lead to various paths, with final outcome depends on protective factors, the intervention timing and environmental factors.

3.1 Neurobiological and Genetic Underpinnings

Contemporary research has established that neurodevelopmental disorders arise from complex interactions between genetic predispositions and neurobiological processes unfolding during critical windows of brain development. Genome-wide association studies (GWAS) have identified numerous common genetic variants as well as rare copy number variants (CNVs) such as 16p11.2 and 22q11.2 deletions, that substantially increase risk for ASD, ADHD and intellectual disability (Sandin et al., 2017; Grove et al., 2019). Genetic risk is often trans-diagnostic: genetic vulnerability that exists in autism spectrum disorder (ASD), attention deficit hyperactivity disorder (ADHD) and schizophrenia suggests that the nature of the susceptibility to neurodevelopmental disorders is polygenic in a dimensional perspective (Lee et al., 2019). The use of neuroimaging methods to detect structural and functional differences among individuals with NDDs has shown abnormalities in cortico-striatal circuit in ADHD, decreased long-distance connectivity in ASD and aberrant development of the cerebellum in dyslexia (Castellanos & Proal, 2012; Maenner et al., 2023). These results further justify abandoning behavioural-based symptom classification and adopting biological approaches such as the RDoC system by the NIMH which organizes psychopathology along neuroscience-relevant dimensions (Insel et al., 2010).

3.2 Cultural and Cross-Cultural Considerations in Diagnosis

The development of both DSM-5-TR and ICD-11 occurred in Western high-income health-care systems, thus the application of these systems in other cultures is associated with concerns regarding the validity and equity of interpretation. Cultural considerations include differentiating between what level of behaviour is seen as being a problem, what terms can be used to a child's developmental issue, as well as how likely the family would be to seek out a formal diagnosis (Norbury & Sparks, 2013). While high levels of activity may not be considered problematic in some cultures, resulting in under-identification of attention deficit hyperactivity disorder (ADHD); in other cases, certain behaviours characteristic of higher functioning ASD may simply be a product of cultural and social norms. The ICD-11 acknowledges the need to take cultural considerations into account when diagnosing individuals, and thus represents an advance over ICD-10; however, it still poses the challenge of implementing this aspect into the system. A number of suggestions include developing culturally-specific instruments for screening, taking part in community-based participatory approach to diagnosis, as well as using indigenous understandings in defining disability in LMICs (Seligman & Kirmayer, 2008; Trani et al., 2016). Diagnostic infrastructure is often inadequate in low- and middle-income countries (LMICs) and classification systems are based not on standardized instruments, but on clinical judgement and informants provided by people from the community (Seligman & Kirmayer, 2008; Trani et al., 2016).

3.3 Early Identification and Developmental Screening

Even though individuals with NDDs exhibit significant deficits and dysfunction, the early symptoms may be hard to detect as they are similar to the normative developmental process. Therefore, early identification plays a pivotal role, as the results of interventions are far superior compared to late intervention, especially when it comes to the crucial stages of development (Zwaigenbaum et al., 2015). The use of developmental assessments such as Ages and Stages Questionnaire (ASQ), Modified Checklist for Autism in Toddlers (M-CHAT) and Strengths and Difficulties Questionnaire (SDQ) serve as first-level filters enabling timely referral. It is important to mention that universal screening does not take place worldwide. As the result, due to differences associated with socioeconomic status, geography and linguistic backgrounds, some children have their problems detected much later than others (Magana et al., 2015).

3.4 The Neurodiversity Perspective and its Implications for Classification

Neurodiversity Movement, emerging from the autistic advocacy groups, followed later in application to other NDDs, argues that autism, attention-deficit hyperactivity disorder (ADHD), and dyslexia, among others, are natural differences within the human cognition rather than pathology requiring remediation (Armstrong, 2025; Chapman, 2020). Neurodiversity theory does not make diagnostic classification obsolete, rather, it invites a reconceptualization of classification's purpose. In cases where classification serves as an entry point into support services, accommodation and legal protection without turning the person into their diagnosis, classification serves both neurodiversity and disability rights well. The greater focus on the individual's functioning that DSM-5-TR shows may be considered a step towards that direction. However, future revisions of the DSM will have to reconcile the conflicting positions further, given neurodiverse individual's growing stakeholder role in research and policymaking (Milton, 2012).

4. HISTORICAL EVOLUTION OF NEURODEVELOPMENTAL DISORDER CLASSIFICATION SYSTEMS

Modern-day NDDs owe their existence to a lengthy period of conceptual evolution influenced by changing scientific knowledge, sociocultural values and professional demands. The early classifications were affected by the lack of scientific knowledge on brain development and were based on either the same adult diagnoses as those used for psychological disorders, moral and educational considerations.

4.1 Early Psychiatric Classifications and Pre-DSM Foundations

Prior to the standardization of diagnosis manual, childhood developmental conditions have been discussed under different names from psychiatric, neurological and educational perspectives. Such terms like 'feeble-mindedness', 'mental deficiency' and 'childhood insanity' were used inconsistently and heavily criticized due to the use of derogatory and moral connotations (APA, 1952; Rutter, 2011; Trent, 1994). The above-mentioned conceptual focused on intellectual deficiency and disruptive behaviour with little attention to specific patterns of in cognitive, linguistic or social development and children with different needs were segregated or institutionalized without being evaluated or provided with individualized treatment.

4.2 DSM-I and DSM-II: Limited Recognition of Developmental Disorders

The first edition of the Diagnostic and Statistical Manual of Mental Disorders (DSM-I) (1952) reflected post-war psychiatric paradigms, with only a few mentions of childhood disorders put under broad categories, i.e. mental deficiency and behaviour disorders. However, intellectual impairment was seen as a permanent state determined since birth. DSM-II (1968) although expanded the diagnostic categories but retained mostly similar concepts and limitations.

4.3 DSM-III and DSM-III-R: The Operational Diagnostic Revolution

DSM-III (1980) was developed to introduce more structured diagnostic criteria and a multiaxial classification system. Childhood onset disorders received more attention with Infantile Autism, Attention Deficit Disorder as well as Specific Developmental Disorders have been recognized by then (APA, 1980). It marked a shift from psychoanalytic to symptoms-based diagnostic system significantly improving inter-rater reliability. In addition, DSM-III helped in establishing categories that often did not reflect developmental processes. The next publication, DSM-III-R (1987) introduced additional criteria and classifications but retained the core categorical diagnostic approach.

4.4 DSM-IV and DSM-IV-TR: Expansion and Emerging Critiques

The DSM-IV (1994) and its text-revision (DSM-IV-TR, 2000) incorporated extensive empirical research and field-trial data. Pervasive developmental disorders were categorized under autism related disorders which include Autistic Disorder, Asperger Disorders and Pervasive Developmental Disorder - Not Otherwise Specified. The criteria of learning disorders were divided in accordance with the academic domain and Attention-Deficit/Hyperactivity Disorder (ADHD) criteria were also clarified (APA, 1994; APA, 2000). However, poor subtype reliability and high comorbidity undermined categorical purity.

4.5 DSM-5 and DSM-5-TR: Emergence of the Neurodevelopmental Framework

DSM-5 (2013) introduced a significant conceptual restructuring. Conditions involving early developmental onset were first time grouped together under a specific chapter, which is called Neurodevelopmental Disorders. This restructuring reflected growing consensus that disorders like Autism Spectrum Disorder (ASD), Attention-Deficit/Hyperactivity Disorder (ADHD), Specific Learning Disorder and Intellectual Disability have common developmental antecedents and often occur co-morbidly (APA, 2013).

Among the major changes where the autism subtypes were combined to a single Autism Spectrum Disorder, Specific Learning Disorder was reconceptualized and made into one diagnosis with domain specific specifications and the clear understanding that Attention-Deficit/Hyperactivity Disorder (ADHD) as a lifelong condition. DSM-5-TR (2022) refined its descriptive text, prevalence estimates and cultural considerations, further emphasized on the adaptive functioning in the diagnosis of intellectual disability (APA, 2022).

4.6 Summary Table

Table 1. Conceptual and Diagnostic Shifts in Neurodevelopmental Disorders Across DSM Editions

Edition	Year	Key Change	Limitation
DSM-I	1952	Introduced formal psychiatric classification; childhood conditions subsumed under broad categories	No distinct developmental framework; stigmatizing terminology
DSM-II	1968	Expanded categories; ASD-like conditions classified as childhood psychosis	Conflation of developmental and psychotic presentations
DSM-III	1980	Operationalized criteria; Infantile Autism and Attention Deficit Disorder recognized	Rigid categorical boundaries; psychoanalytic legacy partially retained
DSM-III-R	1987	Refined criteria and terminology	Retained categorical structure despite emerging evidence of dimensional overlap
DSM-IV/IV-TR	1994/2000	Expanded autism subtypes (PDD-NOS, Asperger's); SLD criteria clarified	Poor subtype reliability; high comorbidity undermined categorical purity
DSM-5	2013	First introduction of "Neurodevelopmental Disorders" as a unified diagnostic chapter; autism subtypes collapsed into a single ASD spectrum; ADHD recognized as a lifespan condition; SLD reconceptualized as a single diagnosis with domain-specific specifiers; Intellectual Disability severity based on adaptive functioning rather than IQ thresholds	Retained categorical structure despite mounting dimensional evidence; clinician resistance to removal of Asperger's subtype; neurobiological biomarkers not incorporated into diagnostic criteria
DSM-5-TR	2022	Updated prevalence estimates, cultural formulations, and diagnostic specifiers across NDD categories; strengthened emphasis on adaptive functioning in Intellectual Disability; improved cultural sensitivity guidance; clarified gender differences in ASD and ADHD presentation	Primarily an incremental text revision; unresolved categorical versus dimensional classification debate; genomic and neuroimaging advances remain outside formal diagnostic criteria

4.7 Parallel Developments in ICD Classification

The DSM was developed mainly in North American psychiatric setting whereas the International Classification of Diseases (ICD) was developed as an international health classification system. In Chapter V (F) of ICD-10, the developmental disorders were distributed across multiple categories and these included mental retardation (F70-F79), specific developmental disorder of speech and scholastic skills (F80-F81), and pervasive developmental disorders (F84) (WHO, 1992). While ICD-10 acknowledged development onset, the absence of an overarching neurodevelopmental construct limited conceptual integrity.

This shortcoming was addressed in ICD-11, which added Neurodevelopmental Disorders as a distinct top-level block to Chapter 06: Mental, Behavioural or Neurodevelopmental Disorders. ICD-11 defines neurodevelopmental disorders as conditions arising during the developmental period that involve significant impairment of the acquisition and execution of intellectual, motor or social functions (WHO, 2019). This restructuring facilitated the ICD-11 closer to the conceptual similarity to DSM-5-TR, with the ability to remain flexible to global application.

4.8 Ethical and Conceptual Shifts

Across successive revisions of DSM and ICD, the evolution in terms and classification reflect the greater shift of ethical and conceptual dimensions. The replacement of stigmatization terms like ‘mental retardation’ with ‘intellectual disability’ or ‘disorders of intellectual development’ is an indication of the shift towards respect and person-centred language. On the same note, the growing focus on adaptive functioning, contextual assessment and support needs reflects alignment with contemporary disability rights frameworks and the social model of disability.

5. CLASSIFICATION OF NEURODEVELOPMENTAL DISORDERS AS PER DSM-5-TR

Neurodevelopmental disorders are operationally defined as “Neurodevelopmental disorders are a group of disorders that are characterized by displays in the developmental period and result in deficits in cognition, communication, behavior, motor function and adaptive behavior, leading to impairment in personal, social, academic or occupational functioning” (American Psychiatric Association [APA], 2022). Although the DSM-5-TR is mainly psychiatric and research-oriented, in recent years, its classification has become more aligned with ICD-11 that focuses on using more functional descriptors and ensuring a broader clinical applicability

(World Health Organization [WHO], 2019). All categories of DSM-5-TR disorders are thus addressed below with their ICD-11 counterpart to draw upon similar and distinct points.

5.1 Intellectual Disability (Intellectual Developmental Disorder)

Definition and Core Features

The Intellectual Disability (Intellectual Developmental Disorder) is a neurodevelopmental disorder whose three key characteristics include:

i. Criterion A - deficits in intellectual functioning, i.e. reasoning, problem solving, planning, abstract thinking, judgement, academic learning and learning through experience;
ii. Criterion B - deficits result in impairment of adaptive functioning that failure to meet the developmental and sociocultural criteria of personal independence and social responsibility; and
iii. Criterion C - onset during the developmental period (APA, 2022).

A notable change in DSM-5 and DSM-5-TR is prioritisation of adaptive functioning over IQ scores in the establishment of severity, recognizing the fact that psychometric scores are not sufficient to reflect real-world functioning, independence or support needs.

Classification

DSM-5-TR categories intellectual disability into six classifications:

i. F70 - Mild.
ii. F71 - Moderate.
iii. F72 - Severe.
iv. F73 - Profound.
v. F70 - Global Developmental Delay.
vi. F70 - Unspecified Intellectual Developmental Disorder.

DSM-5-TR categories intellectual disability into four levels of severity depending on adaptive functioning on conceptual, social and practical levels such as mild, moderate, severe and profound. Severity determination is based on everyday functioning and not numerical IQ thresholds which fits diagnostic practice with educational and disability-support models.

5.2 Autism Spectrum Disorder

Definition and Core Features

Autism Spectrum Disorder (ASD) is a neurodevelopmental disorder that is characterized by:

i. persistent deficits in social communication and social interaction across multiple contexts; and
ii. restricted and repetitive behaviors, interests, or activities, with symptoms that were present in the early developmental stages and led to the clinically significant impairment (APA, 2022).

The merging of the earlier distinct diagnoses like autistic disorder and Asperger's disorder into a single spectrum reflects empirical evidence of poor subtype reliability and extensive symptom overlap.

Classification

DSM-5-TR categories autism spectrum disorder into four classifications

i. F84.0 - Autism Spectrum Disorder
   a. Indicate current severity level: very substantial support is required, substantial support is required, support is required.
   b. Indicate whether: with or without additional intellectual impairment, with or without additional language impairment.
   c. Indicate whether: Allied with a known genetic or other medical condition or environmental factor (Coding note: Use additional code can identify the related genetic or other medical condition); Allied with a neurodevelopmental, mental or behavioural problem.
   d. Indicate whether: with catatonia (use additional code F06.1)

DSM-5-TR defines the severity in two areas (social communication and restricted behaviors) depending on the level of support required. The severity level is classified in level 1 - very substantial support is required, level 2 - substantial support is required, level 3 - support is required. Other specifiers include presence or absence of intellectual impairment, language impairment and associated medical or genetic conditions and co-occurring neurodevelopmental or mental disorders. These specifiers can be used for individualized characterization and support planning.

5.3 Specific Learning Disorder

Definition and Core Features

Specific Learning Disorder (SLD) is a type of neurodevelopmental disorder, which involves persistent difficulties in learning and applying academic skills, even with the specific interventions, the emergence of which occurs in the school-age years (APA, 2022).

Classification

SLD has been diagnosed as a single disorder having domain-specific specifications:

i. F81.0 - With impairment in reading (indicate whether there is word reading accuracy, reading rate or fluency, reading comprehension).
ii. F81.1 - Having impairment in written expression (indicate whether with spelling accuracy, grammar and punctuation accuracy, clarity or organization of written expression).
iii. F81.2 - Having impairment in mathematics (indicate whether in level of number sense, accurately memorizing arithmetic data, accurately or fluently calculating, accurately reasoning in math).

Based on severity of functional impact, severity is rated as mild, moderate or severe.

5.4 Attention-Deficit/Hyperactivity Disorder (ADHD)

Definition and Core Features

Attention-Deficit/Hyperactivity Disorder (ADHD) is a chronic pattern of lack of concentration and/or hyperactivity-impulsivity which disrupts functioning or development with symptoms manifested in two or more environments and diagnosed before the age of 12 (APA, 2022). Notably, DSM-5-TR is based on the conceptualization of ADHD as a lifespan neurodevelopmental disorder, which remains into adolescence and adulthood.

Diagnostic Criteria

Criterion A: A persistent pattern of inattention and/or hyperactivity-impulsivity that interferes with functioning or development, as characterized by (1) and/or (2):

i. **Inattention:** Six (or more) of the following symptoms have continued for at least 6 months to a degree. Children and adolescents to the age of 16 years must have six (or more) of the following symptoms; individuals aged 17 years and above must have five or more of the symptoms:
   a) Often do not pay close attention to details or do careless mistakes.

b) Problems with maintenance of attention in activities or in play.
c) Seeming to be not listening to the speaker.
d) Inability to adhere to instructions or get things done.
e) Problem with organizing of tasks and activities.
f) Avoids, dislikes or is reluctant to engage in tasks requiring sustained mental effort.
g) Frequently forgets things needed to accomplish tasks or activities.
h) Prone to distractions by extraneous factors.
i) Forgetful in day-to-day activities.

ii. **Hyperactivity and Impulsivity:** Six (or more) of the following symptoms have continued for at least 6 months to a degree. Children and adolescents to the age of 16 years must have six (or more) of the following symptoms; individuals aged 17 years and above must have five or more of the symptoms:
a) Often fidgets with or taps hands or feet or squirms in seat.
b) Often leaves seat in the situations where one is supposed to be seated.
c) Frequently running or climbing in the wrong occasions.
d) Frequently unable to play and engage in leisure activities in silence.
e) Always active, acting as if "driven by a motor"
f) Excessive talking
g) Giving answers too fast before questions have been asked.
h) Inability to wait his/her turn.
i) Many times, interrupts or intrudes on others.

Criterion B: Age of Onset: Several number of inattentive or hyperactive-impulsive symptoms should have existed by the age of 12 years.

Criterion C: Pervasiveness in Different Situations: The number of settings where the several symptoms occur has to be two or more (home, school, work or even social activities).

Criterion D: Functional Impairment: It has to have definite indications that the symptoms disrupt or impair the quality of, social, academic or occupational functioning.

Criterion E: Differential Diagnosis: The symptoms are not supposed to occur only in the course of the schizophrenia or another form of psychotic disorder and should not be more explicable by another mental disorder, including anxiety disorders, mood disorders, dissociative disorders or personality disorders.

Classification

There are three presentations which are identified:

i. F90.0 - Predominantly inattentive presentation: If Criterion A1 (inattention) is met but Criterion A2 (hyperactivity-impulsivity) is not met for the past 6 months.
ii. F90.1 - Predominantly hyperactive/impulsive presentation: If Criterion A2 (hyperactivity-impulsivity) is met and Criterion A1 (inattention) is not met for the past 6 months.
iii. F90.2 - Combined presentation: If both Criterion A1 (inattention) and Criterion A2 (hyperactivity-impulsivity) are met for the past 6 months.
iv. F90.8 - Other specified Attention-Deficit/Hyperactivity Disorder.
v. F90.9 - Unspecified Attention-Deficit/Hyperactivity Disorder.

Attention-Deficit/Hyperactivity Disorder can be specified as mild, moderate or severe depending on the number of symptoms that are present beyond the criteria for diagnosis and the level of functional impairment (APA, 2022).

5.5 Communication Disorders

Definition and Core Features

Communication disorders as neurodevelopmental disorders characterized by ineffective speech, language or social communication that interferes effective communication and functioning (APA, 2022).

Classification

The manual recognizes five primary disorders:

i. F80.2 - Language Disorder: Language disorder is a perennial problem of acquisition and use of language in its various modalities that is caused by impairment in comprehension or production, including low vocabulary, poor sentence structure and poor discourse. These complications are significantly below expectations for age and are not attributable to hearing impairment, intellectual disabilities, and neurological problems.
ii. F80.0 - Speech Sound Disorder: Speech sound disorder is a condition where speech production of specific sounds continue to be difficult enough to disrupt intelligibility or verbal communication, even in comparison to the expected developmental level.
iii. F80.81 - Childhood-Onset Fluency Disorder (Stuttering): It is a speech disorder that includes the problems in the normal fluency and time patterning of speech including sound and syllable repetitions, prolongations, circumlocutions, broken words, monosyllabic whole-word repetitions and speech blocks. Note: Later-onset cases are diagnosed as F98.5 adult-onset fluency disorder.

iv. F80.82 - Social (Pragmatic) Communication Disorder: The condition known as social (pragmatic) communication disorder is typified by continuing social communication challenges, such as impaired utilisation of communication to social purposes, adapting communication to context and comprehension of the implicit meaning. Most importantly, the diagnosis demands that there is no restricted or repetitive behaviour, which is the difference between this and autism spectrum disorder.
v. F80.9 - Unspecified Communication Disorder.

5.6 Motor Disorders

Motor Disorders are grouped under Neurodevelopmental Disorders are marked by early onset disturbances in motor functioning that are significantly below what is expected for age and level of development (APA, 2022). Motor Disorders occur during the developmental stage, usually in early childhood, and are marked by persistent difficulties in motor coordination, control or execution. The motor difficulties cause significant interference with academic, daily, play or self-care activities. The difficulties are not due to a general medical condition, neurological condition or substance use and are not better explained by intellectual disability or visual impairment.

Classification

DSM-5-TR has a number of motor disorders in the neurodevelopmental disorders section:

i. F98.4 - Stereotypic Movement Disorder: which is repetitive and nonfunctional motor behaviour.
    a. Indicate whether with self-injury behaviour, without self-injury behaviour.
    b. Indicate whether linked to known genetic or other medical disease, neurodevelopmental disorder or environmental determinant.
    c. Indicate severity of the present condition: Mild, Moderate, Severe.
ii. Tic Disorders.
    a. F95.2 - Tourette's Disorder.
    b. F95.1 - Chronic (Persistent) Motor / Vocal Tic Disorder.
        i. Indicate whether: With motor tics only, With vocal tics only
iii. F95.0 - Provisional Tic Disorder
iv. F95.8 - Other specified Tic Disorder.
v. F95.9 - Unspecified Tic Disorder

The disorders are covered by early onset and development course; despite they have different phenomenology.

5.7 Other Specified and Unspecified Neurodevelopmental Disorders

DSM-5-TR also incorporates other specified and unspecified neurodevelopmental disorder to record clinically significant developmental impairment that falls short of full criteria to qualify for a specific diagnosis. ICD-11 has similar residual categories, both preserve diagnostic flexibility while maintaining clinical documentation standards.

Classification

i. F88 - Other Specified Neurodevelopmental Disorder.
ii. F89 - Unspecified Neurodevelopmental Disorder.

6. CLASSIFICATION OF NEURODEVELOPMENTAL DISORDERS AS PER ICD-10 AND ICD-11

The International Classification of Diseases (ICD), maintained by the WHO, is designed to support international comparability in diagnosis, epidemiology and health service planning and policy development. Unlike the DSM, which is primarily psychiatric diagnosis focused and research-oriented, the ICD is designed to represent a wide range of cultural, linguistic and healthcare environments globally (World Health Organization [WHO], 2019).

The transition of ICD-10 to ICD-11 is one of the most radical theoretical and structural changes in the neurodevelopmental disorder's classification. Unlike ICD-10, which spread developmental conditions over several diagnostic groups to which there is no overarching conceptual framework, Chapter 06: Mental, Behavioural or Neurodevelopmental Disorders in ICD-11 presents Neurodevelopmental Disorders as a block in its own right at the top level of the hierarchy of diagnoses. Such reorganization is an indication of the advanced developmental science and the position the ICD has moved in accordance with DSM-5-TR without losing the global focus.

6.1 Neurodevelopmental Disorder in ICD-10

Structure and Limitations

In ICD-10, Neurodevelopmental conditions were not conceptualised as a unified group instead they were scattered throughout some diagnostic groupings in Chapter 5 (F) of which:

i. Mental Retardation (F70-F79).

ii. Special Developmental Disorders of Speech and Language (F80).
iii. Certain Developmental Disorders of Scholastic Skills (F81).
iv. Pervasive Developmental Disorders (F84).
v. Hyperkinetic Disorders (F90).

The absence of an overarching neurodevelopmental construct limited conceptual integrity. Disorders were characterized primarily by symptom clusters rather than developmental processes, and diagnostic boundaries were often ambiguous. For example, pervasive developmental disorders included autism related conditions which were poorly reliable and limited in clinical practice (WHO, 1992).

6.2 Conceptual restructuring in ICD-11

ICD-11 addresses many conceptual and practical shortcomings of the ICD-10 by introducing Neurodevelopmental Disorders as a new block (Block L1-6A0) in Chapter 06. In this context, neurodevelopmental disorders can be described as behavioural and cognitive abnormalities that appear during the developmental period and involve significant difficulties in the acquisition and execution of certain intellectual, motor or social capabilities (WHO, 2019).

This definition prefigured three fundamental core principles:

i. **Developmental Origin:** Occurs in the infancy or childhood period despite full appearance delayed.
ii. **Functional Impairment:** The problems should disrupt personal, social, educational or working functioning.
iii. **Etiological Complexity:** Multifactorial origins and are often unknown, discouraging reductionist explanations.

6.3 Disorders of Intellectual Development (6A00)

Definition and Core Features

ICD-11 replaces the pejorative term 'mental retardation' with 'Disorders of Intellectual Development (6A00)', not only due to ethical concerns, but also because of functional assessment progress. Intellectual development disorders are described as intellectual functioning and adaptive behavior that are significantly below average, about two or more standard deviations below the mean, and manifest during the developmental period (WHO, 2019).

Classification

The level of severity is defined as follows:

i. 6A00.0 Mild
ii. 6A00.1 Moderate
iii. 6A00.2 Severe
iv. 6A00.3 Profound
v. 6A00.4 Provisional
vi. 6A00.Z Unspecified

ICD-11 includes a provisional category (6A00.4) of young children for whom valid standardised assessment is not possible and an unspecified category (6A00.Z). The severity differentiation emphasises adaptive behaviour, but not psychometric scores alone and aligns ICD-11 with both DSM-5-TR and AAIDD frameworks.

6.4 Autism Spectrum Disorder (6A02)

Definition and Core Features

ICD-11 includes autism under sub-heading Autism Spectrum Disorder (6A02) and is a unification of the former distinct subtypes into a single spectrum diagnosis. Autism Spectrum Disorder is defined by lifelong impairments in reciprocal social interaction and communication as well as a limited, repetitive, uncompromising behavioural patterns and interests, beginning in the developmental period (WHO, 2019).

The characteristic feature of ICD-11 is that it addresses autism by functional profiling, specifying it in terms of:

i. Existence or lack of intellectual development disorder, and
ii. Level of functional language ability (mild/no impairment, impaired or absent).

Classification

Autism spectrum disorder (6A02) is specified as

i. 6A02.0 - Autism spectrum disorder in the absence of disorder of intellectual development as well as mild or no functional language impairment.
ii. 6A02.1 - Autism spectrum disorder and disorder of intellectual development and mild or no deficiency of functional language.
iii. 6A02.2 - Autism spectrum disorder in the absence of disorder of intellectual development with functional language impairment.
iv. 6A02.3 - Autism spectrum disorder in the absence of disorder of intellectual development with of functioning language impairment.
v. 6A02.4 - Autism spectrum disorder and without disorder of intellectual development and with no functional language.

vi. 6A02.5 - Autism spectrum disorder with disorder of intellectual development and absence of functional language.
vii. 6A02.Y - Autism spectrum disorder, not specified.
viii. 6A02.Z - Autism spectrum disorder, unspecified.

The approach enhances clinical utility across diverse settings and reduces the use of standardised severity scales, which might not be universally applicable. The classification of autism according to ICD-11 is conceptually similar to that of DSM-5-TR while offering greater descriptive flexibility.

6.5 Developmental Learning Disorder

Definition and Core Features

ICD-11 introduces Developmental Learning Disorder (6A03) as a neurodevelopmental disorder characterized by permanent and significant difficulties in achieving academic competence in reading, written expression or mathematics. These conditions must lead to functional impairment and cannot be occur due to intellectual disability, sensory impairment, inadequate education and language deprivation (WHO, 2019).

Classification

Subtypes of Developmental Learning Disorder include:

i. 6A03.0 - With impairment in reading.
ii. 6A03.1 - Having impairment in written expression.
iii. 6A03.2 - Having impairment in mathematics.
iv. 6A03.Y - With other specified impairment of learning.
v. 6A03.Z - Unspecified developmental learning disorder.

The ICD-11 paramount etiological exclusion of educational and psychosocial deprivation, supports the neurodevelopment model of learning disorder and is closely related to the conceptualisation of DSM-5-TR.

6.6 Attention-Deficit/Hyperactivity Disorder

Definition and Core Features

According to ICD-11, ADHD is classified under 6A05 Attention Deficit Hyperactivity Disorder, which is a chronic pattern of inattention and/or hyperactivity-impulsivity, which is developmentally inappropriate and leads to impaired functioning across multiple settings (WHO, 2019).

Classification

i. 6A05.0 - Attention-deficit/hyperactivity disorder, mostly inattentive presentation.
ii. 6A05.1 - Attention-deficit/hyperactivity disorder, mostly hyperactivity-impulsive presentation.
iii. 6A05.2 - Attention-deficit/hyperactivity disorder, mixed presentation.
iv. 6A05.Y - Attention-deficit/hyperactivity disorder, other specified.
v. 6A05.Z - Attention-deficit/hyperactivity disorder, unspecified.

ICD-11 focuses on developmental context and functional impact, making it flexible in symptom manifestation throughout the lifespan. Although the core features are quite similar to those of DSM5-TR, ICD-11 emphasizes more on the distinction between ADHD and normative developmental variability, especially in early adulthood.

6.7 Developmental speech or language disorders

Definition and Core Features

ICD-11 offers highly differentiated classification of communication disorders under 6A01 Developmental Speech or Language Disorders. These include developmental speech sound disorder, speech fluency disorder and developmental language disorder with receptive, expressive, pragmatic or mixed impairment (WHO, 2019).

Classification

i. 6A01.0 - Development speech sound disorder.
ii. 6A01.1 - Development speech fluency disorder.
iii. 6A01.2 - Development language disorder.
iv. 6A01.20 - Development language disorder with expressive and receptive language impairment.
v. 6A01.21 - Developmental language disorder with mostly impairment in expressive language.
vi. 6A01.22 - Developmental language disorder with mostly impairment in pragmatic language.
vii. 6A01.23 - Developmental language disorder, with other specified language impairment.
viii. 6A01.Y - Other specified speech or language developmental disorder.
ix. 6A01.Z - Unspecified speech or language developmental disorder.

This granularity is superior to DSM-5-TR and is more useful in differentiating language disorders and Autism Spectrum Disorder insofar as it provides more precise guidance on the latter. ICD-11 cautions clinicians against diagnosing developmental language disorder when pragmatic communication difficulties are more consistent with autism-related impairments which are more effectively attributed to autism, and this minimizes diagnostic ambiguity.

6.8 Motor Disorders and Residual Categories

Definition and Core Features

Developmental motor coordination difficulties are grouped under developmental motor coordination disorder and tic disorders are individually classified under neurological categories. Although structurally distinct from DSM-5-TR, these classifications are conceptually aligned by recognising early onset and developmental period.

Classification

i. 6A04 - Development motor coordination disorder.
ii. 6A06 - Stereotyped Movement Disorder.
iii. 6A06.0 - Stereotyped Movement Disorder with no self-injury.
iv. 6A06.1 - Stereotyped Movement Disorder with self-injury.
v. 6A06.Z - Stereotyped Movement Disorder, Unspecified.
vi. 6A0Y - Other Specified Neurodevelopmental Disorders.
vii. 6A0Z - Neurodevelopmental Disorders, unspecified.

ICD-11 also includes other specified and unspecified neurodevelopmental disorder categories, thus providing flexibility to diagnosis of the clinically significant presentation that do not meet full criteria for specific diagnoses.

7. CROSS-DISORDER COMORBIDITY AND OVERLAP IN NEURODEVELOPMENTAL DISORDERS

The concept of cross-disorder comorbidity has become a well-known characteristic of neurodevelopmental disorders as opposed to the secondary or exceptional phenomenon. Both DSM-5-TR and ICD-11 are very clear that individuals with neurodevelopmental disorders often meet the diagnostic criteria of more than one disorder, reflecting shared developmental pathways, overlapping neurocognitive processes and cumulative functional vulnerabilities (APA, 2022; WHO, 2019). This acknowledgement is a fundamental break with previous classification models that were based upon diagnostic mutual exclusivity.

In terms of developmental neuroscience, comorbidity among neurodevelopmental disorders is theoretically expected. There are cognitive, linguistic, attentional, motor and socio-emotional systems that develop simultaneously and are very much interrelated. The impairments in one area tend to spill into additional ones, leading to complicated clinical profiles that cannot be represented using a single-diagnosis paradigm (Karmiloff-Smith, 2015). Therefore, no person is likely to be exhibiting solitary impairment, especially as developmental demands increase over time.

Among the comorbid patterns with the most extensive documentation involves autism spectrum disorder and intellectual disability. Both epidemiological and clinical researches report that a significant percentage of people with autism spectrum also have deficiencies in intellectual and adaptive functioning, especially among the people requiring more support (Lord et al., 2018). The need to specify intellectual functioning status specifically in diagnosing autism in both DSM-5-TR and ICD-11 has important implications as to prognosis, educational placement and support planning due to this overlap.

The other prominent comorbidity pattern is the association between attention-deficit/hyperactivity disorder and specific learning disorder. Deficits in attention regulation, working memory, processing speed and executive functioning affect directly with academic skill acquisition, especially in reading, written expression and mathematics (Snowling and Hulme, 2012). DSM-5-TR directly allows concurrent diagnosis of ADHD and SLD whenever the disorders independently meet the diagnostic criteria, thus preventing the erroneous attribution of the academic difficulties solely to the attention problem (APA, 2022). ICD-11 follows the similar pattern where it states that developmental learning disorder should not be viewed as secondary to ADHD without clear evidence.

Communication disorders further complicate diagnosis boundaries. The language impairments can be comorbid with autism spectrum disorder, ADHD and intellectual disability, making it difficult to differentiate them. This is especially well supported by ICD-11, which cautions clinicians against the diagnosis of developmental language disorder when pragmatic communication difficulties are more compatible with autism-related social communication impairments (WHO, 2019). This focus on differential diagnosis reflects ICD-11's functional and contextualized orientation.

Comorbidity also is not confined to neurodevelopmental disorders themselves. Neurodevelopmental conditions often co-occur with anxiety disorders, mood disorders, sleep-wake disorders and behavioural regulation difficulties, especially in adolescence and in adulthood (Thapar et al., 2016). Though these conditions do not fit in the chapter of neurodevelopmental disorders, both DSM and ICD insist on the significance of the identification of co-occurring conditions to ensure a comprehensive assessment and intervention.

From a classification standpoint, pervasive comorbidity challenges the necessity of strict diagnostic boundaries and supports transdiagnostic and developmental approaches. Instead of considering comorbidity as diagnostic error, modern paradigms are beginning to think of it as the manifestation of a common neurodevelopmental vulnerability, which interacts with the developmental context. This perspective has profound implications on assessment, intervention and research which needs to rise above single-disorder models to deal with the complexity of real-world functioning.

Two emerging frameworks have formalized the transdiagnostic approach to NDD comorbidity. The Research Domain Criteria (RDoC) developed by the National Institute of Mental Health reconceptualizes psychopathology along dimensions of neuroscience constructs – such as arousal, attention and social processing – that cut across traditional diagnostic categories (Insel et al., 2010). Similarly, the Hierarchical Taxonomy of Psychopathology (HiTOP) proposes a statistically derived, dimensional model in which neurodevelopmental and internalizing/externalizing spectra represent higher-order dimensions of psychopathology (Kotov et al., 2017). While neither RDoC nor HiTOP has been adopted into clinical classification systems, both signal the direction of future diagnostic revision and are increasingly used in research designs that seek to transcend single-disorder models.

8. DIMENSIONAL VERSUS CATEGORICAL CLASSIFICATION DEBATES

The controversy over categorical and dimensional approaches lies at the core of the existing debate on the classification of neurodevelopmental disorders. The Traditional diagnostic systems like DSM and ICD are fundamentally categorical in nature and disorders are described as either present or absent based on predefined criteria. This approach offers clear benefits, such as diagnostic reliability, administrative clarity and standardized communication both in clinical and educational settings and in policy contexts.

Nonetheless, there is an accumulating body of empirical data to indicate that many neurodevelopmental traits including attentional capacity, language proficiency, social communication and academic skill acquisition are continuously distributed in the population. The diagnostic thresholds are frequently pragmatic cut-points rather than opposed to natural discontinuities, and this has led to the raise concerns that categorical models may ambiguous meaningful variability within diagnostic groups, while exaggerating differences between the diagnosed and the non-diagnosed individuals (Rutter, 2011).

Dimensional models represent neurodevelopmental characteristics as continuum with severity, frequency and functional impact rather than binary diagnostic status. These models are especially appropriate to such conditions as autism spectrum disorder when the range of intellectual ability, language use, adaptive functioning and needs of support vary significantly among people (Happé & Frith, 2020). Even the concept of a "spectrum" reflects an implicit acknowledgment of dimensionality, even within a categorical diagnostic framework.

DSM-5-TR incorporates dimensional foundations through severity specifiers, functional impairment criteria and descriptive qualifiers. ICD-11 advances dimensional thinking further by emphasizing on functional descriptors, adaptive behaviour and clinical judgement instead of strict psychometric thresholds (WHO, 2019). AAIDD framework goes further regarding the dimensionality aspect by presenting the explicit operationalization of intellectual disabilities from the standpoint of the intensity of support required, which is inconstant according to time and environmental factors (AAIDD, 2023).

In spite of such developments, full dimensional classification is not widely practiced. Legal systems, educational systems and health systems often demand the use of categorical diagnoses so that eligibility of services, accommodation and protections can be set. Therefore, modern systems adopt hybrid classification models which incorporate categorical diagnoses with dimensional modifiers. While imperfect, this trade-off reflects the tension between scientific precision and administrative practicability and administrative feasibility.

For neurodevelopmental disorders, hybrid models offer noteworthy advantages. They maintain diagnostic clarity and permit individualised characterisation, longitudinal tracking and responsiveness to developmental change. It is expected that the future classification systems will extend dimensional elements further as the understanding of neurodevelopmental continua will be tightened by genetics, neuroimaging and computation modelling.

Recent advances in computational psychiatry and precision medicine offer promising pathways for operationalizing dimensional classification in clinical settings. Machine learning algorithms trained on large-scale datasets such as the Adolescent Brain Cognitive Development (ABCD) Study have identified data-driven neurodevelopmental subtypes that cross diagnostic boundaries, suggesting that individualized profiling – rather than group-level categorical assignment – may increasingly guide intervention (Casey et al., 2018). Such approaches align with precision psychiatry's goal of matching specific interventions to specific biological and cognitive profiles. Although these methods are not yet embedded in DSM or ICD, they reinforce the trajectory toward hybrid dimensional-categorical classification systems that can accommodate both clinical practicality and scientific precision.

9. DSM VERSUS ICD PERSPECTIVES ON NEURODEVELOPMENTAL DISORDERS

Despite recent improvements in the convergence of DSM-5-TR and ICD-11 concerning neurodevelopmental disorder conceptualisation, there are still some differences in their underlying philosophy, the structure and the intended use. These differences are indicative of the different institutional mandate of the American Psychiatric Association and the world health organization.

DSM-5-TR is mainly intended to assist psychiatric diagnosis, clinical judgment and standardisation of research, mainly in North America. The focus on both detailed diagnostic criteria, the number of symptoms and operational definitions values reliability and comparability across research studies (APA, 2022). DSM revision procedures are closely associated with empirical literature and field testing, which makes the manual particularly powerful within the framework of academic and clinical research contexts.

In contrast, ICD-11 is a global health classification system to be used in a variety of cultural, linguistic and healthcare settings. As a result, ICD-11 gives greater importance to clinical utility, flexibility and contextual interpretation. It allows greater reliance on professional judgement when standardised assessment devices are not available and specifically covers the impact of sociocultural and educational context on diagnosis (WHO, 2019).

Structurally, ICD-11 includes neurodevelopmental disorders with a broader health classification framework that links mental, neurological and developmental conditions. This integration supports in epidemiological surveillance, planning of health services and international policy development. On the other hand, DSM, which is narrower in scope but provides greater depth and specificity within psychiatric domains.

The complementary nature of these frameworks is most productively understood not as a reason to avoid comparison, but as a basis for designing research and practice protocols that draw on both systems' respective strengths – with DSM anchoring research standardization and ICD enabling global epidemiological comparability.

10. IMPLICATIONS FOR RESEARCH, EDUCATION AND POLICY

10.1 Implications for Research

These evolving classification of neurodevelopmental disorders have an important impact on the research design, research method and interpretation. Traditionally, studies on childhood disorders were based on categorical diagnostic groupings which assumed the homogeneity of diagnostic categories. However, in the modern models, the focus is placed on heterogeneity, comorbidity and developmental variability, which poses a challenge to the classical case-control methods (Rutter, 2011).

Future research should prioritize developmental, longitudinal and transdiagnostic designs capable of tracking changes in symptom expression, adaptive functioning and support needs across the lifespan. Large-scale population cohorts such as the

ABCD Study (Adolescent Brain Cognitive Development Study) in the United States and the Millennium Cohort Study in the United Kingdom represent methodological models for examining neurodevelopmental trajectories in ecologically valid samples (Casey et al., 2018). The studies that analyse shared cognitive, neurobiological and environmental risk factors in disorders would provide more ecologically valid insights about the developmental pathway (Thapar et al., 2016). At the biological level, multimodal research integrating genomics, neuroimaging and cognitive profiling is needed to identify biomarkers that can bridge the gap between dimensional neuroscience and categorical clinical diagnosis. Cross-national longitudinal studies that explicitly compare DSM-5-TR and ICD-11 operationalizations of the same disorder will be particularly valuable in clarifying the impact of classification choices on prevalence estimates and treatment outcomes.

International research collaboration is also subject to the convergence of DSM-5-TR and ICD-11. The increased alignment also enhances the comparability; however, researchers should be careful to state what classification system and diagnostic criteria they use. Otherwise, it can be misinterpreted due to failure to do so, which will result in misinterpretation of the prevalence estimates, treatment outcomes, and cross-cultural comparisons. The combination of categorical diagnoses with dimensional measures of functioning, adaptive behaviour and quality of life measures may be beneficial in both explanatory and translational relevance.

10.2 Implications for Education

In educational contexts, classification systems have been a key unit in the areas of identification, eligibility and instructional planning. The diagnostic labels often serve as gateways to special services, accommodations and individualized education programs. The excessive use of categorical diagnoses, however, may confine functional needs and omit learners whose difficulties fall just below diagnostic thresholds.

Practical frameworks like Multi-Tiered Systems of Support (MTSS), Response to Intervention (RTI) and Universal Design for Learning (UDL) offer systematic ways through which the classification can be translated into effective differentiation in education without becoming too reliant on labels. Research encourages to adopt a strengths-based model of identifying the functional learning profile of the student and scaffolding instruction accordingly instead of making assistance conditional on whether or not one meets diagnostic criteria (Florian & Beaton, 2018). Furthermore, the neurodiversity paradigm has practical classroom applications in the form of inclusion, which involves accommodating diverse cognitive styles, communication preferences and sensory needs. This is now being recognized by the UN Convention on the Rights of Persons with Disabilities (CRPD).

Furthermore, recognition of comorbidity and developmental variability have significant implications on teacher training and curriculum design. Teachers need to be prepared to work with complex profiles of learners that are not easily categorised under single diagnostic categories. The educators, psychologists, speech-language pathologists and families should collaborate in the multidisciplinary manner to transform the classification into meaningful educational support.

10.3 Implications for Disability Policy

At the policy level, the classification systems make a difference in disability certification, resources allocation and the legal protections. The global orientation of ICD-11 makes it a foundation of disability policy and planning of public health, especially in low and middle-income countries. It supports more equitable access to services across diverse settings due to its focus on functional impairment and contextual judgement (WHO, 2019).

In low- and middle-income countries, where the majority of the world's children with NDDs reside, the translation of classification frameworks into policy is constrained by limited diagnostic infrastructure, shortages of trained specialists and competing health priorities (Kieling et al., 2011). The WHO's Global Report on Children with Developmental Disabilities (WHO, 2023) and the CRPD collectively call for equity-centred approaches that prioritize community-based identification, family-centred support and the elimination of diagnostic barriers related to cost and geography. ICD-11's design principle of clinical utility and contextual flexibility is particularly relevant in these settings, as it enables meaningful diagnostic activity even where formal psychometric assessment is unavailable.

The policymakers should however be conscious of the misuse of diagnostic labels which might serve to strengthen stigma or limit participation. Contemporary disability policy increasingly influenced by a rights-based approach, focusing on accessibility, reasonable accommodation, equal participation and protection of rights rather than deficit remediation alone. The adaptive behaviour and support needs are features that make the AAIDD framework provides a valuable bridge between the diagnostic classification and the policy implementation.

Finally, classification systems should function as tools for empowerment rather than exclusion. Linked to the appropriate supports and inclusive policies, diagnostic frameworks can promote education, care and community participation throughout the lifespan.

11. CONCLUSION

The definitions and classification of Neurodevelopmental disorders have been radically changed in the last century and transformed into an integrated and developmentally-based system with more focus on functioning, context and support, instead of fragmented and deficit-based systems. Recent systems, especially DSM-5-TR and ICD-11 now converge on acknowledging neurodevelopmental disorders to be arise early in life, persisting throughout the lifespan and having heterogeneity, comorbidity and dynamic interaction with environmental demands.

Introducing adaptive functioning, functional impairment and support need as fundamental elements of diagnostic frameworks is an important conceptual development, which puts classification in line with educational practice, disability policy and human rights agendas. Meanwhile, the continuing controversies of the categorical versus dimensional classification indicate the complexity of neurodevelopmental phenomena as they are and the challenging demands of scientific precision and administrative practicality.

Looking ahead, the continued refinement of NDD classification systems will be shaped by three converging forces. First, advances in genomics and neuroimaging are generating biologically grounded dimensions that may eventually replace or substantially modify symptom-based categories (Lee et al., 2019). Second, neurodiversity viewpoints incorporated in both research design and policy formulation have resulted in the reorientation of the goals of classification from deficit remediation to equity and inclusion. Third, artificial intelligence and machine learning are beginning to offer data-driven approaches to diagnosis that could reduce clinician variability and improve cross-cultural comparability (Lombardo et al., 2019). These developments suggest that the next generation of classification systems will need to be dynamic, participatory and capable of bridging scientific precision with lived-experience validity.

Combined together, DSM-5-TR, ICD-11 and the AAIDD framework are to be viewed as complementary systems, as opposed to competing systems. Their combined efforts bring a solid foundation of research, clinical practice, learning and policy formulation. The difficulty ahead is not only in the perfecting of diagnostic criteria but the ability to make classification systems meaningful support, inclusion and opportunity to individuals with neurodevelopmental disorders and their families.

REFERENCES

American Association on Intellectual and Developmental Disabilities. (2023). *Definition of intellectual disability*. https://www.aaidd.org/intellectual-disability/definition

American Psychiatric Association. (1952). *Diagnostic and statistical manual: Mental disorders*. American Psychiatric Association Mental Hospital Service. https://www.turkpsikiyatri.org/arsiv/dsm-1952.pdf

American Psychiatric Association. (1968). *Diagnostic and statistical manual of mental disorders* (2nd ed.). American Psychiatric Association. https://www.madinamerica.com/wp-content/uploads/2015/08/DSM-II.pdf

American Psychiatric Association. (1980). *Diagnostic and statistical manual of mental disorders* (3rd ed.). American Psychiatric Association.

American Psychiatric Association. (1987). *Diagnostic and statistical manual of mental disorders* (3rd ed., rev.). American Psychiatric Association.

American Psychiatric Association. (1994). *Diagnostic and statistical manual of mental disorders* (4th ed.). American Psychiatric Association.

American Psychiatric Association. (2000). *Diagnostic and statistical manual of mental disorders* (4th ed., text rev.). American Psychiatric Association.

American Psychiatric Association. (2013). *Diagnostic and statistical manual of mental disorders* (5th ed.). American Psychiatric Association.

American Psychiatric Association. (2022). *Diagnostic and statistical manual of mental disorders* (5th ed., text rev.). American Psychiatric Association.

Armstrong, T. (2011). *The Power of Neurodiversity: Unleashing the Advantages of Your Differently Wired Brain (published in Hardcover as Neurodiversity)*. Grand Central Publishing.

Armstrong, T. (2025). *The Power of Neurodiversity: Unleashing the Advantages of Your Neurodivergent Brain (Completely Revised and Updated Second Edition)*. Balance.

Casey, B., Cannonier, T., Conley, M. I., Cohen, A. O., Barch, D. M., Heitzeg, M. M., Soules, M. E., Teslovich, T., Dellarco, D. V., Garavan, H., Orr, C. A., Wager, T. D., Banich, M. T., Speer, N. K., Sutherland, M. T., Riedel, M. C., Dick, A. S., Bjork, J. M., Thomas, K. M., & Dale, A. M. (2018). The Adolescent Brain Cognitive Development (ABCD) study: Imaging acquisition across 21 sites. *Developmental Cognitive Neuroscience*, *32*, 43–54. DOI: 10.1016/j.dcn.2018.03.001 PMID: 29567376

Castellanos, F. X., & Proal, E. (2012). Large-scale brain systems in ADHD: Beyond the prefrontal–striatal model. *Trends in Cognitive Sciences*, *16*(1), 17–26. DOI: 10.1016/j.tics.2011.11.007 PMID: 22169776

Chapman, R. (2020). The reality of autism: On the metaphysics of disorder and diversity. *Philosophical Psychology*, *33*(6), 799–819. DOI: 10.1080/09515089.2020.1751103

Florian, L., & Beaton, M. (2018). Inclusive pedagogy in action: Getting it right for every child. *International Journal of Inclusive Education*, *22*(8), 870–884. DOI: 10.1080/13603116.2017.1412513

Gillberg, C. (2010). The ESSENCE in child psychiatry: Early Symptomatic Syndromes Eliciting Neurodevelopmental Clinical Examinations. *Research in Developmental Disabilities*, *31*(6), 1543–1551. DOI: 10.1016/j.ridd.2010.06.002 PMID: 20634041

Grove, J., Ripke, S., Als, T. D., Mattheisen, M., Walters, R. K., Won, H., Pallesen, J., Agerbo, E., Andreassen, O. A., Anney, R., Awashti, S., Belliveau, R., Bettella, F., Buxbaum, J. D., Bybjerg-Grauholm, J., Bækvad-Hansen, M., Cerrato, F., Chambert, K., Christensen, J. H., & Børglum, A. D. (2019). Identification of common genetic risk variants for autism spectrum disorder. *Nature Genetics*, *51*(3), 431–444. DOI: 10.1038/s41588-019-0344-8 PMID: 30804558

Happé, F., & Frith, U. (2020). Annual Research Review: Looking back to look forward - changes in the concept of autism and implications for future research. *Journal of Child Psychology and Psychiatry, and Allied Disciplines*, *61*(3), 218–232. DOI: 10.1111/jcpp.13176 PMID: 31994188

Hyman, S. E. (2010). The diagnosis of Mental Disorders: The problem of Reification. *Annual Review of Clinical Psychology*, *6*(1), 155–179. DOI: 10.1146/annurev.clinpsy.3.022806.091532 PMID: 17716032

Insel, T., Cuthbert, B., Garvey, M., Heinssen, R., Pine, D. S., Quinn, K., Sanislow, C., & Wang, P. (2010). Research domain criteria (RDoC): Toward a new classification framework for research on mental disorders. *The American Journal of Psychiatry*, *167*(7), 748–751. DOI: 10.1176/appi.ajp.2010.09091379 PMID: 20595427

Karmiloff-Smith, A. (1998). Development itself is the key to understanding developmental disorders. *Trends in Cognitive Sciences*, *2*(10), 389–398. DOI: 10.1016/S1364-6613(98)01230-3 PMID: 21227254

Kieling, C., Baker-Henningham, H., Belfer, M., Conti, G., Ertem, I., Omigbodun, O., Rohde, L. A., Srinath, S., Ulkuer, N., & Rahman, A. (2011). Child and adolescent mental health worldwide: Evidence for action. *Lancet*, *378*(9801), 1515–1525. DOI: 10.1016/S0140-6736(11)60827-1 PMID: 22008427

Kotov, R., Krueger, R. F., Watson, D., Achenbach, T. M., Althoff, R. R., Bagby, R. M., Brown, T. A., Carpenter, W. T., Caspi, A., Clark, L. A., Eaton, N. R., Forbes, M. K., Forbush, K. T., Goldberg, D., Hasin, D., Hyman, S. E., Ivanova, M. Y., Lynam, D. R., Markon, K., & Zimmerman, M. (2017). The Hierarchical Taxonomy of Psychopathology (HiTOP): A dimensional alternative to traditional nosologies. *Journal of Abnormal Psychology*, *126*(4), 454–477. DOI: 10.1037/abn0000258 PMID: 28333488

Lombardo, M. V., Lai, M., & Baron-Cohen, S. (2019). Big data approaches to decomposing heterogeneity across the autism spectrum. *Molecular Psychiatry*, *24*(10), 1435–1450. DOI: 10.1038/s41380-018-0321-0 PMID: 30617272

Lord, C., Elsabbagh, M., Baird, G., & Veenstra-Vanderweele, J. (2018). Autism spectrum disorder. *Lancet*, *392*(10146), 508–520. DOI: 10.1016/S0140-6736(18)31129-2 PMID: 30078460

Maenner, M. J., Warren, Z., Williams, A. R., Amoakohene, E., Bakian, A. V., Bilder, D. A., Durkin, M. S., Fitzgerald, R. T., Furnier, S. M., Hughes, M. M., Ladd-Acosta, C. M., McArthur, D., Pas, E. T., Salinas, A., Vehorn, A., Williams, S., Esler, A., Grzybowski, A., Hall-Lande, J., & Shaw, K. A. (2023). Prevalence and characteristics of autism spectrum disorder among children aged 8 years — Autism and Developmental Disabilities Monitoring Network, 11 sites, United States, 2020. *MMWR. Surveillance Summaries*, *72*(2), 1–14. DOI: 10.15585/mmwr.ss7202a1 PMID: 36952288

Milton, D. E. M. (2012). On the ontological status of autism: The 'double empathy problem.' *Disability & Society*, *27*(6), 883–887. DOI: 10.1080/09687599.2012.710008

Norbury, C. F., & Sparks, A. (2013). Difference or disorder? Cultural issues in understanding neurodevelopmental disorders. *Developmental Psychology*, *49*(1), 45–58. DOI: 10.1037/a0027446 PMID: 22390668

Rutter, M. (2011). Research Review: Child psychiatric diagnosis and classification: concepts, findings, challenges and potential. *Journal of Child Psychology and Psychiatry, and Allied Disciplines*, *52*(6), 647–660. DOI: 10.1111/j.1469-7610.2011.02367.x PMID: 21434914

Sandin, S., Lichtenstein, P., Kuja-Halkola, R., Hultman, C., Larsson, H., & Reichenberg, A. (2017). The heritability of autism spectrum disorder. *Journal of the American Medical Association*, *318*(12), 1182. DOI: 10.1001/jama.2017.12141 PMID: 28973605

Snowling, M. J., & Hulme, C. (2012). Annual research review: The nature and classification of reading disorders—a commentary on proposals for DSM-5. *Journal of Child Psychology and Psychiatry, and Allied Disciplines*, *53*(5), 593–607. DOI: 10.1111/j.1469-7610.2011.02495.x PMID: 22141434

Thapar, A., Cooper, M., & Rutter, M. (2016). Neurodevelopmental disorders. *The Lancet. Psychiatry*, *4*(4), 339–346. DOI: 10.1016/S2215-0366(16)30376-5 PMID: 27979720

Trent, J. W., Jr. (1994). *Inventing the feeble mind: A history of mental retardation in the United States*. University of California Press. tankona.free.fr/trent1994.pdf

World Health Organization. (1992). *The ICD-10 Classification of Mental and Behavioural Disorders: Clinical Descriptions and Diagnostic Guidelines*. https://cdn.who.int/media/docs/default-source/classification/other-classifications/9241544228_eng.pdf

World Health Organization. (2019). *Clinical descriptions and diagnostic requirements for ICD-11 mental, behavioural and neurodevelopmental disorders*. https://faculty.ksu.edu.sa/sites/default/files/icd-_11_2018.pdf

World Health Organization. (2023). *Global report on children with developmental disabilities: From the margins to the mainstream*. World Health Organization. https://iris.who.int/server/api/core/bitstreams/b699c175-08a7-4670-b757-8f6a143de6fe/content

Zwaigenbaum, L., Bauman, M. L., Stone, W. L., Yirmiya, N., Estes, A., Hansen, R. L., McPartland, J. C., Natowicz, M. R., Choueiri, R., Fein, D., Kasari, C., Pierce, K., Buie, T., Carter, A., Davis, P. A., Granpeesheh, D., Mailloux, Z., Newschaffer, C., Robins, D., Roley, S. S., … Wetherby, A. (2015). Early Identification of Autism Spectrum Disorder: Recommendations for Practice and Research. *Pediatrics, 136 Suppl 1*(Suppl 1), S10–S40. DOI: 10.1542/peds.2014-3667C

Chapter 3
Neurodevelopmental Disorders in Childhood:
Aetiology, Psychological Impact, and Therapeutic Approaches

Shirin Kulkarni
http://orcid.org/0009-0006-1444-8780
PES University, India

Shreya Ghosh
http://orcid.org/0009-0008-9309-3424
PES University, India

ABSTRACT

This chapter focuses on elucidating the causes/foundations of neurodevelopmental disorders like attention deficit hyperactivity disorder, autism spectrum disorder, Intellectual Disability, Learning disorders, Communication disorders and motor disabilities. This also focuses on delineating the biological and psychological impact of the disorders and quality of childhood and by bridging the gap of building more awareness for different interventions and therapies that bring improvements in behavioural aspects like aggression, hyperactivity; physiological aspects like stimming and providing a better and improved lifestyle for the children. Interventions like emotional and family support, and medications and therapies like occupational therapy, speech and language therapy, behavioural therapies and other developmental therapies that would help promote overall development. These therapies not only help the children but also the parents in having a better environment at home, have better communication with the children, and help solve any strenuous situations or circumstance.

DOI: 10.4018/979-8-3373-7072-9.ch003

INTRODUCTION

Neurodevelopmental disorders represent a group of conditions whose origins lie in disruptions of brain development, typically manifesting in early childhood and often persisting across the lifespan (American Psychiatric Association [APA], 2013). These disorders include attention-deficit/hyperactivity disorder (ADHD), autism spectrum. disorder (ASD), intellectual disability, learning disorders (such as dyslexia, dysgraphia, and dyscalculia), communication disorders (e.g., speech sound disorder, social (pragmatic) communication disorder), and motor disorders such as developmental coordination disorder, dystonia, and tic disorders (APA, 2013). The Diagnostic and Statistical Manual of Mental Disorders, Fifth Edition (DSM-5) places all of them under a unified "Neurodevelopmental Disorders" chapter, reflecting them. shared developmental nature and overlapping aetiologies. (APA, 2013)

The historical journey of neurodevelopmental disorders (NDDs) is a narrative of evolution moving from moral judgment and institutionalization to biological understanding and social inclusion. The following sections detail how these conditions transitioned from the margins of society to the centre of clinical and human rights discourse.

1. How Were Neurodevelopmental Disorders Recognized?

Historically, NDDs were not recognized as medical or developmental conditions but were often attributed to supernatural causes, poor parenting, or "moral insanity."

- Initial Behavioural Observation: Early recognition was purely observational. In the 19th century, clinicians like John Langdon Down first described the physical and cognitive characteristics of what we now call Down Syndrome (1866).
- The Shift to Cognitive Testing: At the turn of the 20th century, Alfred Binet developed the first intelligence tests to identify children who required alternative educational support. This shifted recognition from "moral failure" to measurable cognitive variance (APA, 2013).
- Refinement of Diagnostic Categories: It was not until the mid-20th century that specific disorders like Autism were distinguished from "childhood schizophrenia." Leo Kanner (1943) and Hans Asperger (1944) recognized that these children shared a unique pattern of social and communication differences that were distinct from other psychiatric conditions.

2. When Did They Start Giving Importance?

The "Golden Age" of importance for NDDs began in the post-World War II era, specifically the 1960s and 1970s.

- The 1960s Advocacy Movement: In the United States, President John F. Kennedy who had a sister with an intellectual disability established the President's Panel on Mental Retardation in 1961. This marked the first time NDDs were treated as a national priority, leading to federal funding for research and specialized education.
- The 1990s "Decade of the Brain": The 1990s saw a surge in Importance due to advancements in neuroimaging. Technologies like MRI allowed researchers to "see" developmental differences in the brain, proving that these conditions had a biological basis rather than being the result of "refrigerator mothers" or poor upbringing (Thapar & Cooper, 2016).

3. The History of Recognition

The history of recognition is marked by the movement from Generalization to Specification.

- Pre-1950s (Institutionalization): Children with developmental differences were often sent to large state institutions. Recognition was binary: "normal" or "feeble-minded."
- 1952–1980 (The Early DSM Era): The first editions of the *Diagnostic and Statistical Manual of Mental Disorders* (DSM) were heavily influenced by psychoanalysis. ADHD was recognized as "Minimal Brain Dysfunction," and Autism was still largely misunderstood (APA, 2013).
- 1980–2013 (Biological Specificity): DSM-III (1980) was a turning point, introducing "attention deficit disorder" and "Infantile Autism." By the time DSM-5 was released in 2013, the focus shifted to a Neurodevelopmental Continuum, recognizing that these disorders often overlap and share common genetic roots (Martinez et al., 2024).

4. How Were They Able to Destigmatize NDDs?

Destigmatization has been a hard-won battle driven by three main factors:

- The Neurodiversity Movement: This cultural shift, beginning in the late 1990s, reframed NDDs not as "broken brains" but as natural variations in the human genome. By reclaiming the narrative, neurodivergent individuals began to advocate for accommodation rather than "cures."

- The "Biological" Defence: By proving that NDDs involve measurable differences in brain structure and genetics (such as Copy Number Variants), science helped remove the "blame" from parents (Yoon et al., 2020). When a condition is seen as a medical reality, the moral stigma often fades.
- Media and Public Figures: High-profile celebrities and scientists (such as Temple Grandin) sharing their lived experiences with ASD or ADHD have humanized these labels, showing the general population that NDDs are compatible with high achievement and a meaningful life (Martinez et al., 2024).

SOME HISTORICAL FIGURES THAT HELPED US UNDERSTAND NDDS

The shift in how we understand neurodevelopmental disorders is a story of moving from mystery and shame to science and pride. In the late 1800s, pioneers like John Langdon Down began treating these conditions as medical realities rather than "moral failures," proving that children with developmental delays were capable of learning and participating in society. By the 1940s, researchers like Leo Kanner, Hans Asperger, and the often-overlooked Grunya Sukhareva provided the first detailed maps of Autism, helping doctors recognize that these children weren't "broken," but had a distinct way of relating to the world. The true revolution, however, happened when the conversation moved out of the doctor's office and into the hands of advocates and families. In the 1960s, Eunice Kennedy Shriver used the Special Olympics to show the world the physical strength and resilience of neurodivergent people, effectively shattering global stigmas. Later, in the 1990s, figures like Temple Grandin used their own lived experiences to explain that an "autistic brain" is simply a "different brain"—often one capable of incredible visual thinking and problem-solving. This era also saw sociologist Judy Singer coin the term "Neurodiversity," which fundamentally changed the goal of support. Instead of trying to "fix" a child to make them appear "normal," the focus shifted toward accepting neurological differences as a natural part of human variety and ensuring society is built to include everyone. Today, this history helps us understand that while conditions like ADHD or ASD have a biological basis—often involving genetics or brain structure—the "disability" often comes from a world that isn't yet designed for them. By looking at the work of these trailblazers, we see that the most effective way to help a child is through a mix of compassionate behavioral support, early medical screening, and a society that values their unique strengths.

Understanding the foundations and impacts of neurodevelopmental disorders is important for numerous reasons. These disorders affect a substantial proportion of children worldwide, influencing educational, social, emotional, and health aspects of childhood. Early identification and intervention can improve the path of development. and quality of life. Second, these conditions are inherently heterogeneous: they arise. from interactions between genetic, prenatal, perinatal, and environmental influences, making their aetiology complex and demanding careful, multidisciplinary inquiry (Thapar & Cooper, 2016). Third, the psychological, behavioural, and physiological impacts of these disorders often extend beyond the individual child to their families, schools, and communities. Addressing them requires more than clinical care it. demands awareness, policy support, therapeutic innovation, and social inclusion.

FOUNDATIONS AND AETIOLOGICAL FRAMEWORKS

1. Genetic Influences and Genomic Architecture

Genetics provide the "blueprint" for brain development. In NDDs, these influences are rarely simple and often involve several types of genomic variation.

- Copy Number Variants (CNVs): These occur when a person has a different number of copies of a particular gene (either deletions or duplications). For example, a deletion on chromosome 22q11.2 is strongly linked to intellectual disability and ADHD.
- De Novo Mutations: These are genetic alterations that appear for the first time in a family member because of a mutation in a germ cell (egg or sperm) or the fertilized egg itself. These mutations explain why a child may develop ASD even when there is no family history of the disorder (Thapar & Cooper, 2016).
- Polygenic Risk: Most NDDs are polygenic, meaning they result from the cumulative effect of thousands of small genetic variants, each having a tiny effect on its own.

2. Prenatal and Perinatal Risk Factors

The environment within the womb and the period immediately following birth are "critical periods" for neural tube formation and synaptogenesis.

- Prenatal Exposures: Maternal health during pregnancy is vital. Exposure to teratogens (substances like alcohol, tobacco, or certain medications), maternal infections (e.g., rubella or cytomegalovirus), and extreme maternal stress can alter foetal brain architecture.
- Perinatal Risk: This refers to the time immediately around birth. Factors such as hypoxia (oxygen deprivation), exceptionally low birth weight, and extreme prematurity are significant risk factors for cerebral palsy and intellectual disabilities.

The brain is most vulnerable during the "critical periods" of gestation and early infancy.

- Maternal Immune Activation (MIA): If a mother experiences a severe infection or chronic inflammation during pregnancy, her body releases pro-inflammatory cytokines (like IL-6 and IL-17A). These can cross the placenta and interfere with the foetus's neural migration and synaptic pruning (Frontiers in Neuroscience).
- Environmental Toxins: Exposure to endocrine-disrupting chemicals, heavy metals (like lead), or air pollution can act as a "second hit" to a genetically vulnerable system.
- Nutrition and Stress: Deficiencies in folate or exposure to elevated levels of maternal cortisol (stress hormone) can alter the epigenetic landscape of the developing foetal brain.

3. Neurobiological Pathways and Epigenetics

Understanding *how* the brain develops incorrectly involves looking at the microscopic and chemical level.

- Neurobiological Pathways: These are the functional "highways" of the brain. In ADHD, for example, there is often a disruption in the dopaminergic pathways that regulate reward and attention. In ASD, researchers often find "local over-connectivity" but "long-range under-connectivity" in the brain's white matter.

3.1 Epigenetic Mechanisms: The Link Between Environment and DNA

Epigenetics refers to chemical modifications that turn genes "on" or "off" without changing the actual DNA sequence. This is the primary way the environment "talks" to our genes.

- Epigenetic Mechanisms: Environmental factors (like toxins or trauma) can cause chemical "tags" (e.g., DNA methylation) to be added to genes, turning them "on" or "off." This explains how a child's environment can physically change how their genetic code operates.
- DNA Methylation: The addition of a methyl group to DNA, which typically acts to silence a gene. In ASD, researchers have found abnormal methylation in the dopaminergic and serotonergic pathways, which may explain differences in reward processing and mood regulation (Yoon et al., 2020).
- Histone Modification: DNA is wrapped around proteins called histones. If the wrapping is too tight, the gene cannot be "read." Dysregulation in histone deacetylases (HDACs) has been linked to social deficits and repetitive behaviours, as seen in Rett Syndrome (Thapar & Cooper, 2016)

4. Environmental Modifiers: The "Second Hit"

While genetics may create a vulnerability, environmental modifiers often determine the severity of the expression.

- Nutrition: Deficiencies in essential nutrients like folic acid or iodine during pregnancy can lead to significant cognitive deficits.
- Environmental Toxins: Exposure to heavy metals like lead or mercury has been conclusively linked to lower IQ and behavioural problems.
- Psychosocial Stress: Chronic stress or early childhood adversity (e.g., neglect) can lead to "toxic stress," which over-activates the body's stress-response system and can interfere with brain development.

5. The Gene × Environment (G × E) Interaction

The most modern understanding of NDDs is the Gene × Environment interaction. This framework suggests that genetics determine a child's *sensitivity* to the environment. For example, a child might have a genetic predisposition for ADHD, but it may only manifest severely if they are also exposed to prominent levels of lead or extreme family instability. This interaction accounts for the heterogeneity (diversity) seen in symptoms across different children. Heterogeneity why one child has mild symptoms and another has severe symptoms is explained by how a child's unique genetic profile responds to environmental stressors. A "protective" environment (good nutrition, low stress) might buffer a high genetic risk, while a "high-risk" environment might trigger it.

6. The Neurodevelopmental Continuum

Historically, disorders like ADHD, ASD, and Intellectual Disability were seen as distinct boxes. However, the neurodevelopmental continuum model emphasizes that these categories overlap significantly.

- Shared Genetic Risk: Research has shown that many of the same genes are involved in both ASD and Schizophrenia, or ADHD and Learning Disorders.
- Symptom Overlap: It is common for a child with ASD to also meet the criteria for ADHD. Rather than seeing these as "separate" problems, the continuum model views them as different manifestations of a broadly disrupted neurodevelopmental process (APA, 2013).

The Three Components of the "Triple Hit"

Why do some children develop an NDD while others with similar backgrounds do not? We look at the interaction in three layers:

1. The First Hit: Genetic Vulnerability

This is the latent predisposition. As discussed previously, this includes inherited polygenic risks, Copy Number Variants (CNVs), or de novo mutations. This "hit" does not guarantee a disorder; it simply creates a "sensitive" or "fragile" biological foundation.

- *Example:* A child born with a specific variation in the *SHANK3* gene, which is critical for synapse formation.

2. The Second Hit: Environmental Stressor (The Trigger)

This hit refers to external factors that occur during a sensitive period of development. This could be a "biological insult" like Maternal Immune Activation (MIA), prenatal exposure to toxins (like air pollution or valproate), or perinatal complications such as hypoxia (oxygen deprivation).

- *Example:* A mother contracting a severe viral infection during the second trimester, triggering an inflammatory cytokine storm that affects the vulnerable foetal brain.

3. The Third Hit: The Critical Developmental Window

The timing is the most crucial part. The brain develops in specific sequences (neurogenesis, then migration, then synaptogenesis). If the "Second Hit" occurs during a window when a specific brain region (like the prefrontal cortex or cerebellum) is under construction, the damage is far more significant.

- *Example:* If a stressor occurs during the peak of synaptic pruning (the "weeding" of the brain's connections), it can lead to the "over-connectivity" often seen in the brains of individuals with Autism.

CLASSIFICATION AND CLINICAL PROFILES OF NDD

The DSM-5 classifies NDDs into six primary categories. Each category is defined by the specific developmental domain it affects.

I. Intellectual Disabilities

The contemporary diagnostic paradigm marks a profound shift: severity is no longer determined by a rigid IQ score cutoff, but rather by the level of adaptive functioning impairment across three distinct life domains. While an IQ score of roughly two standard deviations below the population mean (IQ = 70) remains a benchmark for intellectual deficit, a formal diagnosis mandates concurrent, profound limitations in how a person manages daily life demands.

The three core clinical domains evaluated include:

- The Conceptual Domain: Involves academic competencies such as language development, reading, writing, math calculation, logic, problem-solving, and abstract reasoning.
- The Social Domain: Encompasses interpersonal communication skills, social judgment, empathy, the capacity for making and maintaining friendships, and the ability to accurately perceive and adhere to social rules.
- The Practical Domain: Relates to personal autonomy and everyday self-care, including money management, navigational independence, job performance, time organization, personal hygiene, and lifestyle safety.

1. Levels of Severity

Rather than assigning severity based on psychometric scores, clinicians assess the intensity of structural support an individual requires to navigate daily life:

- Mild: Individuals often develop functional language and academic skills up to late elementary levels with specialized instruction. They achieve independent self-care but may need minimal guidance or accommodation when handling complex tasks like tax filing or legal documentation.
- Moderate: Conceptual skills lag markedly behind peers. Individuals are capable of independent personal hygiene, household chores, and simple occupations within supported settings, but require sustained, explicit cues and structural scaffolding for conceptual and social interactions.
- Severe: Spoken language is highly restricted or entirely concrete. Structural care is required for all activities of daily living (feeding, dressing, bathing). Safety monitoring must be continuous, as independent navigation is heavily compromised.
- Profound: The individual communicates almost exclusively through nonverbal, sensory-motor channels. They require total, lifelong dependence on caregivers for physical care, health preservation, and everyday safety.

2. Global Developmental Delay (GDD)

Global Developmental Delay is explicitly reserved as a provisional, early-childhood diagnosis applied to children under the age of 5. It is deployed when a young child demonstrates an objective, significant delay in achieving expected developmental milestones across two or more core functional domains (e.g., gross or fine motor skills, speech and language, social-personal behavior, or activities of daily living).

Because standardized, norm-referenced psychometric instruments (such as the Wechsler Intelligence Scale for Children or the Stanford-Binet) cannot be reliably administered to infants and very young toddlers, a definitive diagnosis of Intellectual Disability is impossible. Therefore, GDD acts as a clinical placeholder that acknowledges significant developmental divergence while granting the child immediate access to critical early intervention programs.

3. Epidemiology and Investigative Frameworks

Research indicates that GDD affects an estimated 1% to 3% of the pediatric population under five years old globally (Mithyantha et al., 2017). The underlying causes of GDD are highly heterogeneous, presenting a complex web of exogenous, environmental, and genetic origins.

Clinical guidelines emphasize that discovering the exact etiology of a child's delay is crucial, as early targeted medical and therapeutic interventions can profoundly shift their eventual developmental trajectory. A comprehensive diagnostic workup typically addresses several major etiological pathways:

- Perinatal and Acquired Insults: Complications such as extreme prematurity, neonatal encephalopathy, birth trauma, or severe asphyxia account for a substantial percentage of documented delays, particularly in resource-limited clinical environments (Mithyantha et al., 2017).
- Genetic and Metabolic Factors: Up to half of non-environmental cases are driven by underlying genetic conditions, including chromosomal abnormalities (like Trisomy 21), copy number variants, and single-gene mutations (e.g., Fragile X syndrome). While purely metabolic disorders are rarer, investigating treatable metabolic conditions remains a vital frontline diagnostic recommendation because early medical management can halt progressive neurological damage (Mithyantha et al., 2017).
- Environmental Deprivation: Severe early environmental, maternal, or nutritional deprivation can cause profound developmental delays that mimic intrinsic neurodevelopmental pathology; however, unlike organic intellectual disabilities, these impairments are sometimes partially or fully reversible when the child's living conditions are radically enriched.

It is critical to note that a child diagnosed with GDD is not universally destined to meet criteria for an Intellectual Disability later in life. While severe delays are highly predictive of long-term cognitive impairment, milder delays are often transient and can resolve entirely through timely, domain-specific occupational, physical, and speech-language therapies (Mithyantha et al., 2017)

II. Communication Disorders

Communication Disorders comprise a core category of neurodevelopmental conditions characterized by persistent difficulties in the generation, comprehension, expression, or pragmatic application of language and speech. In contemporary clinical neuroscience and speech-language pathology, the diagnostic landscape has transitioned away from outdated discrepancy models (which required a gap between verbal and non-verbal IQ) toward a functional framework focusing on the real-world social, educational, and adaptive impact of these communicative impairments (Bishop et al., 2017).

1. Language Disorder / Developmental Language Disorder (DLD)

In clinical nosology, Language Disorder involves severe, persistent difficulties in acquiring and utilizing language across various modalities (including spoken, written, and sign language). While the DSM-5-TR utilizes the broad term *Language Disorder*, a massive international multidisciplinary consensus (the CATALISE study) introduced the term Developmental Language Disorder (DLD) to describe cases where language impairment emerges during early development without being tied to an underlying biomedical condition like a known brain injury, sensorineural hearing loss, or genetic syndrome (Bishop et al., 2017).

DLD is highly heterogeneous and is estimated to affect approximately 7% of primary-school-aged children (Bishop et al., 2017). It manifests through deficits across several core linguistic domains:

- The Lexical-Semantic Domain: Manifests as a severely restricted vocabulary size and range. Children with DLD struggle with mapping spoken words to their exact meanings, processing vocabulary, and retrieving words fluently during natural discourse.
- The Morphosyntactic Domain: Characterized by systemic difficulties with grammar, sentence structure, and word formatting (e.g., dropping tense markers, omitting auxiliary verbs, or displaying impaired syntactic comprehension).
- The Receptive vs. Expressive Divide: Difficulties can predominantly impact language production (expressive), language comprehension (receptive), or a combination of both. When receptive deficits are present, the long-term academic prognosis is typically more severely impacted.

2. Speech Sound Disorder (SSD)

Speech Sound Disorder occurs when a child's speech sound production is not age-appropriate, directly interfering with speech intelligibility and preventing effective verbal communication. It is distinct from a language disorder because the underlying cognitive formulation of language may be intact, but the execution of physical speech sounds is compromised.

SSD encompasses a range of difficulties including:

- Phonological Impairments: Cognitive-linguistic difficulties where a child struggles to master the sound system of their language and the rules governing sound combinations (e.g., consistently substituting all back-of-the-mouth sounds like /k/ with front-of-the-mouth sounds like /t/).

- Articulation Disorders: Physical or motor-based difficulties in generating specific speech sounds, resulting in omissions, distortions, or substitutions of target sounds.

3. Childhood-Onset Fluency Disorder (Stuttering)

This disorder is characterized by frequent, persistent disturbances in the normal fluency and time-patterning of speech that are inappropriate for the individual's age. These disruptions cause significant communicative anxiety and limit social or academic performance.

Core clinical manifestations include:

- Sound and syllable repetitions or sound prolongations.
- Broken words (unintended pauses within a word) and audible or silent blocking (filled or unfilled pauses in speech).
- Circumlocutions (substituting words to avoid problematic sounds) and physical tension accompanying word production.

4. Social (Pragmatic) Communication Disorder (SPCD)

Introduced as a distinct diagnostic category to bridge a critical nosological gap, SPCD is characterized by a primary, persistent deficit in the social, pragmatic use of verbal and nonverbal communication.

Unlike Autism Spectrum Disorder (ASD), a diagnosis of SPCD explicitly excludes the presence of restricted, repetitive behaviors, rituals, or fixated interests. Diagnosing SPCD requires verifying impairments across four core social pillars:

- Social Purpose: Deficits in using communication for social greetings, sharing information, and bonding in a manner appropriate to the context.
- Contextual Adaptation: An inability to match communication styles to the environment or the needs of the listener (e.g., speaking the same way to a classroom teacher as to a playground peer).
- Conversational Rules: Failure to follow the unwritten rules of engagement, such as turn-taking in conversation, rephrasing statements when misunderstood, and utilizing non-verbal cues to regulate social interaction.
- Inference and Non-literal Language: Profound difficulty deciphering what is not explicitly spoken, including struggles with idioms, metaphors, humor, or dual meanings that rely heavily on context for interpretation.

III. Autism Spectrum Disorder (ASD)

Autism Spectrum Disorder (ASD) represents a distinct category within neurodevelopmental disorders, characterized by a profound convergence of social-communicative divergence and highly structured, non-linear processing behaviors. The implementation of the DSM-5 and its subsequent Text Revision (DSM-5-TR) unified previously separate conditions—such as Autistic Disorder, Asperger's Disorder, and Pervasive Developmental Disorder Not Otherwise Specified (PDD-NOS)—into a single dimensional spectrum, acknowledging that the underlying neurobiological variations manifest along a continuum of severity and functional support requirements (American Psychiatric Association [APA], 2022).

1. Core Criterion A: Persistent Deficits in Social Communication and Social Interaction

- Deficits in Social-Emotional Reciprocity: This manifests as an atypical approach to back-and-forth social interaction. It ranges from a total reduction in conversational turn-taking and the sharing of affect, emotions, or interests, to an inability to initiate or respond to typical social overtures.
- Deficits in Nonverbal Communicative Behaviors: Individuals display differences in integrating verbal language with physical expressions. This includes atypicalities in maintaining eye gaze, anomalies in body language, impaired comprehension and execution of kinetic gestures, or a reduced range of facial expressions during interactive discourse.
- Deficits in Developing, Maintaining, and Understanding Relationships: This encompasses a struggle to flexibly adapt behavioral responses to match diverse social landscapes. It can present as challenges in navigating imaginative play, difficulties forming peer connections, or a complete absence of overt interest in peers (APA, 2022)

2. Core Criterion B: Restricted, Repetitive Patterns of Behavior, Interests, or Activities

- Stereotyped or Repetitive Motor Movements, Use of Objects, or Speech: This includes classic motor stereotypies (e.g., hand-flapping, body-rocking), idiosyncratic object manipulation (e.g., lining up toys by color, spinning wheel mechanisms), and linguistic variations such as immediate or delayed echolalia (repeating vocal phrases verbatim) and highly specific, repetitive phrasing.
- Insistence on Sameness, Inflexible Adherence to Routines, or Ritualized Behavior: Marked by profound emotional distress when encountering mi-

nor environmental transitions, rigid cognitive processing patterns, or highly structured behavioral rituals (e.g., taking identical geographic routes daily, demanding specific food preparations).

- Highly Restricted, Fixated Interests with Abnormal Intensity or Focus: Characterized by hyper-focused preoccupations with highly specific subjects, objects, or data systems that are atypical in their depth, duration, or focus.
- Hyper- or Hypo-reactivity to Sensory Input: Involves an atypical neural response to environmental stimuli. This may manifest as sensory avoidance (e.g., extreme aversion to specific acoustic frequencies or textures) or sensory seeking (e.g., excessive touching or smelling of objects, fascination with visual movement and lights).

3. Dimensional Severity Specifiers

The contemporary diagnostic paradigm requires clinicians to assign distinct severity levels to Criterion A (Social Communication) and Criterion B (Repetitive Behaviors) independently, based on the level of environmental scaffolding required:

Table 1. Shows the severity levels of clinical descriptions in ASD

Severity Level	Clinical Description	Structural Support Requirement
Level 1	"Requiring support"	Without support in place, deficits in social communication cause noticeable impairments. Inflexible behavior causes significant interference with functioning in one or more contexts.
Level 2	"Requiring substantial support"	Marked deficits in verbal and nonverbal social communication skills are apparent even with supports in place. Inflexible behaviors appear frequently enough to be obvious to the casual observer.
Level 3	"Requiring very substantial support"	Severe deficits in verbal and nonverbal social communication skills cause severe impairments in functioning. Inflexible behaviors markedly interfere with functioning in all domains.

IV. Attention-Deficit/Hyperactivity Disorder (ADHD)

1. Core Symptom Dimensions

ADHD is a lifelong neurodevelopmental condition marked by persistent, developmentally inappropriate levels of inattention and/or hyperactivity-impulsivity that compromise social, academic, or occupational functioning (American Psychiatric Association [APA], 2022). Diagnostically, children up to age 16 require ≥ 6

symptoms, while individuals aged 17 and older require ≥ 5 symptoms across either domain (APA, 2022).

- Inattention: Reflects executive dysfunction. Manifests as careless errors, difficulty sustaining focus during long lectures or tasks, poor organization, procrastination of mentally effortful work, losing essential items, and high distractibility.
- Hyperactivity-Impulsivity: Reflects behavioral and motor disinhibition. Manifests as physical fidgeting, inability to remain seated, excessive talking, extreme restlessness, blurting out answers before questions are finished, and interrupting others.

2. Presentations and Contextual Criteria

Symptoms must persist for at least 6 months, manifest across two or more settings (e.g., home and work/school), cause clear functional impairment, and not be better explained by another mental health disorder. Additionally, multiple symptoms must have been present prior to age 12 (APA, 2022).

- Predominantly Inattentive Presentation: Criteria met for Inattention only. Often under-identified due to a lack of overt disruptive behaviors.
- Predominantly Hyperactive/Impulsive Presentation: Criteria met for Hyperactivity-Impulsivity only. Most common in early childhood.
- Combined Presentation: Criteria met for both dimensions. The most prevalent clinical presentation in pediatric populations.

3. Global Epidemiology and Lifespan Trends

A comprehensive systematic review and meta-analysis across global cohorts established that the overall pooled prevalence of ADHD stands at approximately 10.3% (Al-Wardat et al., 2024).

- Sex Ratios: Diagnosed prevalence is higher in males (11.1%) than in females (7.0%) (Al-Wardat et al., 2024). However, females are frequently diagnosed later in life because they commonly present with the less disruptive, inattentive subtype.
- Lifespan & Identification Trends: While overt motor hyperactivity often declines linearly into adulthood, core executive deficits usually persist. Longitudinal tracking from 2016 to 2023 demonstrates a rising trend in clin-

ical identification, showing a 15.2% average annual increase in adult diagnoses after 2020 (Paul et al., 2025)

V. Specific Learning Disorder (SLD)

Specific Learning Disorder (SLD) represents a foundational diagnostic class within neurodevelopmental disorders. It is defined as a persistent, domain-specific impediment in the acquisition and execution of basic academic skills. Crucially, an SLD diagnosis requires that these difficulties occur in individuals who possess at least average general intellectual functioning, explicitly distinguishing it from global Intellectual Disabilities (American Psychiatric Association [APA], 2022).

The modern clinical framework treats SLD as a single overarching umbrella condition containing distinct, cross-cutting academic specifiers. It has moved entirely away from the historical "IQ-achievement discrepancy model," prioritizing instead the persistence of the learning deficits over time and their resistance to targeted educational interventions (Jabeen, 2026).

1. Core Diagnostic Criteria (The Four Pillars)

To establish a formal diagnosis of SLD under contemporary clinical guidelines, an individual must fulfill four rigid, non-negotiable diagnostic criteria (APA, 2022):

- Criterion A: Symptom Persistence. The individual must exhibit at least one documented symptom of academic difficulty for a minimum of 6 months, despite the provision of targeted, evidence-based remedial interventions.
- Criterion B: Substantial Functional Discrepancy. The affected academic skills must be substantially and quantifiably below those expected for the individual's chronological age. This must be verified via a comprehensive clinical assessment alongside individually administered, norm-referenced standardized achievement measures.
- Criterion C: Age of Onset. The learning difficulties must manifest during the early school-age years. However, the functional impairment may not fully crystallize until later in development, when academic, occupational, or daily time demands exceed the individual's limited capacity or outpace their compensatory mechanisms.
- Criterion D: Differential Exclusion. The cognitive and learning difficulties must not be better accounted for by global intellectual disabilities, uncorrected visual or auditory acuity impairments, other underlying neurological or motor disorders, psychosocial adversity, a lack of proficiency in the language of instruction, or inadequate educational instruction.

2. Academic Specifiers (Phenotypic Subtypes)

Clinicians are required to specify every precise academic domain and sub-skill showing impairment. An individual can be diagnosed with multiple overlapping specifiers simultaneously.

A. With Impairment in Reading (Dyslexia)

This sub-type is characterized by profound differences in neurological language processing, specifically impacting the accurate decoding of written text. It represents the most common presentation of SLD in literature. Impairments include:

- Word Reading Accuracy: Frequent misreadings, letter omissions, or word substitutions.
- Reading Rate or Fluency: Exceptionally slow, hesitant, and labor-intensive decoding that requires conscious mental effort.
- Reading Comprehension: Severe difficulty drawing inferences, remembering facts, or constructing meaning from a read passage, often due to the cognitive energy exhausted purely on decoding individual words.

B. With Impairment in Written Expression (Dysgraphia)

This domain reflects impairments in transitioning cognitive concepts onto paper, requiring both linguistic formulation and structural organization. Impairments include:

- Spelling Accuracy: Consistent orthographic processing difficulties, such as adding, omitting, or mixing up vowels and consonants.
- Grammar and Punctuation Accuracy: Continual errors in sentence structure, verb tenses, and standard punctuation rules.
- Clarity or Organization of Written Expression: Marked difficulties arranging paragraphs logically, resulting in disjointed or structurally confusing written communication.

C. With Impairment in Mathematics (Dyscalculia)

This sub-type involves core differences in how the brain processes numerical values, quantities, and abstract mathematical relationships. Impairments include:

- Number Sense: Profound difficulty grasping how numbers interact, visualizing spatial magnitudes, or understanding that a symbol represents an explicit quantity.

- Memorization of Arithmetic Facts: An inability to fluently retain or recall foundational equations (e.g., simple addition or multiplication tables).
- Accurate or Fluent Calculation: Heavy reliance on primitive strategies (such as counting on fingers) long after peers have internalized computational sequences.
- Accurate Math Reasoning: Severe difficulty translating linguistic story problems into actionable algebraic or mathematical operations.

4. Global Prevalence and Psychiatric Comorbidities

Large-scale systematic reviews indicate that SLDs represent a highly prevalent international educational concern, affecting approximately 5% to 15% of school-age children globally across diverse language systems and cultures (APA, 2022).

Psychological and Behavioral Comorbidities

Because SLD functions as an "invisible disability," affected individuals are highly vulnerable to systematic academic frustration, institutional stigmatization, and peer alienation. Meta-analytic data reveals a pronounced cross-disorder vulnerability profile:

- Internalizing and Externalizing Vulnerabilities: A comprehensive systematic review and meta-analysis confirmed that children diagnosed with learning disorders exhibit significantly higher rates of both internalizing psychiatric problems (such as generalized anxiety and major depressive symptoms) and externalizing behavioral challenges compared to neurotypical control groups (Donolato et al., 2021).
- The Domain Vulnerability Split: Interestingly, the severity of internalizing distress is heavily moderated by the primary nature of the developmental diagnosis. Children presenting with broader, receptive communication and language disorders frequently experience a higher magnitude of internalizing psychological distress than those whose impairments are strictly isolated to reading sub-skills (Donolato et al., 2021). This suggests that generalized communicative barriers place an even heavier burden on socio-emotional self-regulation than domain-specific academic challenges.

VI. Motor Disorders

Motor Disorders constitute a prominent diagnostic category within neurodevelopmental conditions, characterized by structural and functional divergence in the acquisition, execution, and neurological coordination of movement. The DSM-5-TR categorizes these conditions based on whether the motor impairment stems from coordinated motor planning deficits, purposeless rhythmic behaviors, or sudden, involuntary neuromuscular contractions (American Psychiatric Association [APA], 2022).

Modern clinical frameworks emphasize that motor disorders are highly comorbid with other neurodevelopmental conditions, such as ADHD and Autism Spectrum Disorder (ASD), and often carry a profound burden of socio-emotional and internalizing psychological distress (Blank et al., 2019).

1. Developmental Coordination Disorder (DCD)

Developmental Coordination Disorder (historically referred to as *dyspraxia*) is a persistent neurodevelopmental condition characterized by a marked impairment in the acquisition and execution of motor skills. Crucially, the motor deficits must be substantially below what is expected given the individual's chronological age and opportunities for skill acquisition (APA, 2022).

Diagnostic Criteria and Manifestations

To fulfill the standard clinical guidelines for DCD, four core parameters must be satisfied:

- Criterion A (Motor Execution Deficits): The manifestation of motor clumsiness (e.g., dropping or bumping into objects), slowness, and structural inaccuracy in the performance of gross or fine motor skills (e.g., catching an object, handwriting, using utensils, or riding a bicycle).
- Criterion B (Functional Interference): The motor skills deficit must significantly and persistently interfere with activities of daily living appropriate to chronological age (e.g., self-care, home maintenance) and negatively impact academic, vocational, pre-vocational, or leisure activities.
- Criterion C (Early Onset): Symptoms must emerge during the early developmental period.
- Criterion D (Differential Exclusion): The deficits must not be better explained by global intellectual disabilities, uncorrected visual impairments, or progressive neurological conditions affecting movement (such as cerebral palsy, muscular dystrophy, or a degenerative disorder).

Clinical Guidelines and Interventions

According to the international clinical consensus recommendations, the identification and treatment of DCD require a multidisciplinary approach focusing on functional, real-world adaptation rather than primitive reflex integration (Blank et al., 2019).

- Evidence-Based Interventions: Task-oriented approaches, such as Cognitive Orientation to daily Occupational Performance (CO-OP) and Task-Specific Training, are recommended as frontline therapies. These methods actively engage the individual in problem-solving motor strategies, which significantly outperforms traditional, passive sensorimotor therapies (Blank et al., 2019).
- Socio-Emotional Comorbidities: Longitudinal tracking shows that children with DCD face a secondary risk for physical inactivity, cardiovascular obesity, low physical self-worth, and elevated internalizing symptoms such as generalized anxiety and depression, caused by systematic peer exclusion in play and sports environments.

2. Stereotypic Movement Disorder (SMD)

Stereotypic Movement Disorder is distinguished by repetitive, driven, seemingly purposeless, and highly rhythmic motor behaviors. Unlike typical motor tics, stereotypic movements are often coordinated, voluntary in initiation, and can last for extended periods, though they can be stopped by external distraction or conscious effort (APA, 2022).

Behavioral Typologies and Functional Scaffolding

- Phenotypic Expressions: Common manifestations include rhythmic hand-waving, body-rocking, head-banging, finger-flicking, biting oneself, or hitting one's own body.
- The Diagnostic Split (Self-Injurious Specifier): The diagnostic guidelines mandate specifying whether the condition is with self-injurious behavior (e.g., head-banging that causes structural retinal detachment or tissue injury) or without self-injurious behavior (APA, 2022). If self-injury occurs, the behavioral intervention framework immediately pivots to include mechanical barriers (such as protective helmets) alongside functional behavioral analysis to limit permanent physical harm.
- Etiological Overlap: While SMD can occur as a primary diagnosis in neurotypical individuals, it is highly comorbid with severe global intellectual disabilities and ASD. When occurring alongside ASD, a secondary diagnosis of SMD is only warranted if the stereotypic movements cause clear functional impairment or become a primary target of clinical treatment.

3. Tic Disorders

Tic Disorders represent a spectrum of childhood-onset neurodevelopmental conditions characterized by sudden, rapid, recurrent, non-rhythmic motor movements and/or vocalizations. Tics are neurobiologically driven and are often preceded by a premonitory urge—an uncomfortable somatic sensation (such as a muscle itch or tension) that is temporarily relieved by executing the tic.

The DSM-5-TR stratifies Tic Disorders into three distinct diagnostic categories based on the duration, type, and stability of the symptoms (APA, 2022):

A. Tourette's Disorder

- Diagnostic Threshold: Both multiple motor tics AND at least one vocal tic must be present at some point during the illness, though not necessarily concurrently.
- Chronological Guardrail: The tics must persist for more than 1 year since the first tic onset, and the age of onset must be prior to 18 years.

B. Persistent (Chronic) Motor or Vocal Tic Disorder

- Diagnostic Threshold: Single or multiple motor tics OR vocal tics have been present during the illness, but not both.
- Chronological Guardrail: The tics have persisted for more than 1 year since the initial onset, beginning before age 18.

C. Provisional Tic Disorder

- Diagnostic Threshold: Single or multiple motor and/or vocal tics are present.
- Chronological Guardrail: The symptoms have been present for less than 1 year since the initial onset, serving as a critical provisional marker during early clinical evaluations.

Psychosocial Impacts and Quality of Life

The behavioural consequences of NDDs ripple through every aspect of a child's ecosystem:

1. Self-Esteem: Repeated failure in social or academic settings leads to a damaged self-concept.
2. Peer Relations: Impulsivity (ADHD) or lack of social cues (ASD) can lead to peer rejection or bullying.

3. Emotional Regulation: Many NDDs share a deficit in "Executive Function," making it difficult for children to "pause" and manage intense emotions, leading to frequent outbursts.

IMPACT ON QUALITY OF CHILDHOOD

1. Impact on Schooling and Academic Attainment

School is the primary "workplace" of a child. NDDs often create a mismatch between a child's potential and their performance.

- Executive Dysfunction: Children with ADHD or ASD often struggle with "executive functicns" the brain's ability to plan, organize, and transition between tasks. This leads to incomplete assignments and chronic academic frustration (APA, 2013).
- The "Hidden" Struggle: In Specific Learning Disorders (SLD), the child may exert double the effort for half the result. Martinez et al. (2024) note that without proper support, this leads to "school refusal" and a long-term decline in vocational aspirations.

2. Social Interaction and Peer Relations

The "social currency" of childhood is the ability to play and communicate.

- Peer Rejection: Children with ADHD may be viewed as "too intense" or intrusive, while those with ASD may be seen as "aloof." This often leads to social exclusion or bullying.
- Social Fatigue: For many children with NDDs, social interaction is not intuitive; it is an exhausting manual process. This can lead to social withdrawal as a defence mechanism to avoid the "cost" of failure in peer groups.

3. Behavioural Expressions: The Internalizing-Externalizing Duality

behaviour in NDDs is often a form of "unspoken communication." When a child lacks the executive function or language skills to express frustration, their distress manifests in two primary ways:

- Externalizing Behaviours (The "Overt" Impact): These include hyperactivity, impulsivity, aggression, and oppositional defiance. In the context of ADHD or ASD, these behaviours are often triggered by an inability to inhibit impulses or a "fight-or-flight" response to overwhelming demands. Because these behaviours are disruptive to classrooms and households, they often result in social stigma and punitive discipline rather than therapeutic support (APA, 2013).
- Internalizing Behaviours (The "Covert" Impact): These include anxiety, withdrawal, and depression. A child with a Specific Learning Disorder (SLD) may not act out but may instead "shut down" due to chronic failure. Over time, these children develop secondary emotional disorders, where the weight of "not fitting in" leads to clinical levels of anxiety or a sense of hopelessness (Thapar & Cooper, 2016).

4. Sensory Regulation and Stimming

Sensory processing is the brain's ability to organize and interpret information from the senses. In many NDDs, particularly ASD, this "filter" is dysfunctional.

- Sensory Dysregulation: This involves Hyper-reactivity (over-sensitivity) or Hypo-reactivity (under-sensitivity). A child experiencing hyper-reactivity may find the hum of a refrigerator as painful as a siren, leading to a "sensory meltdown" which is an involuntary neurological collapse, not a behavioural "tantrum."
- Stimming (Self-Stimulatory behaviour): Stimming refers to repetitive physical movements or sounds (e.g., hand-flapping, rocking, repeating words).
- Regulatory Function: Stimming is often a tool for homeostasis. For an overstimulated child, it provides a predictable rhythm to focus on. For an understimulated child, it provides the "sensory hits" the brain needs to feel alert.
- Clinical Shift: Modern therapy has moved away from "extinguishing" stimming, recognizing that for many, it is a vital coping mechanism for maintaining emotional stability (Martinez et al., 2024).

5. Systemic Impact: Family Dynamics and Siblings

The impact of an NDD is systemic, meaning it affects every member of the household.

- Parental Stress: Parents of children with NDDs report significantly higher levels of "caregiver strain" compared to parents of typically developing children. This includes financial strain from therapies and emotional exhaustion from navigating "advocacy" for their child in school systems.

- The Sibling Experience: Siblings may experience "glass child" syndrome feeling invisible because most of the parental energy and resources are directed toward the child with the NDD. However, they may also develop higher levels of empathy and resilience (Martinez et al., 2024).

3. Self-Concept and Quality of Life (QoL)

The "Quality of Childhood" is intrinsically linked to how a child perceives themselves in relation to their environment.

- Development of Self-Concept: A child's self-concept is built through "reflected appraisals" how they see themselves mirrored in the eyes of parents, teachers, and peers. When a child constantly receives feedback that they are "too loud," "slow," or "difficult," they internalize a negative self-schema. They may begin to view their identity as synonymous with their diagnosis.
- Quality of Life (QoL): QoL in NDDs is not defined by the absence of symptoms, but by the presence of autonomy and belonging.
- The Systemic Ripple: As Martinez et al. (2024) argue, a child's QoL is tethered to family functioning. If parental stress is high and sibling relationships are strained, the child's environment becomes a source of tension rather than a sanctuary.
- Self-Efficacy: The most critical factor in a positive QoL is "self-efficacy" the belief that one has the agency to navigate challenges. Targeted interventions that celebrate "neuro-diverse" strengths (like the creative problem-solving often seen in ADHD) are essential for fostering a healthy adult identity.

INTERVENTIONS AND THERAPEUTIC APPROACHES

1. Behavioural and Psychosocial Interventions

These interventions focus on modifying the environment and teaching the child new coping mechanisms to improve functional outcomes.

- Parent Training (PT): Often cited as the "first-line" treatment for preschool-aged children with ADHD and behavioural challenges. PT empowers parents with techniques like positive reinforcement and "contingency management" to reduce oppositional behaviours and improve the parent-child bond.

- behaviour Therapy & Social Skills Training (SST): For children with ASD, SST involves structured groups where they practice social cues, turn-taking, and perspective-taking. Davis et al. (2012) emphasize that behavioural interventions are most effective when they are generalized meaning the skills learned in the clinic are reinforced at home and school.
- Cognitive Interventions: For older children, Cognitive Behavioural Therapy (CBT) is used to treat comorbid anxiety or to improve "Metacognition" (thinking about one's own thinking), helping them manage impulsivity.

2. Developmental and Allied Health Therapies

These therapies target specific developmental delays in communication, motor skills, and sensory processing.

- Speech and Language Therapy (SLT): Focuses on both expressive language and Augmentative and Alternative Communication (AAC). For non-verbal children with ASD or Intellectual Disability, AAC tools (like tablet-based icons) provide a vital "voice" to reduce frustration-driven aggression.
- Occupational Therapy (OT) and Sensory Integration: OTs address Developmental Coordination Disorder and sensory dysregulation. They often use "Sensory Diets" a curated set of physical activities (like weighted vests or swinging) to help a child maintain an optimal level of arousal.
- Assistive Technology: This includes specialized software for children with Specific Learning Disorders, such as text-to-speech for dyslexia or graphic organizers for dysgraphia.

3. Pharmacological Approaches

Medication is typically used to manage specific symptoms rather than "cure" the underlying disorder.

- Stimulants vs. Non-stimulants: Stimulants (e.g., Methylphenidate) are highly effective for ADHD, increasing dopamine and norepinephrine levels in the prefrontal cortex to improve focus. Non-stimulants (e.g., Atomoxetine) are used when side effects like insomnia or appetite suppression are too severe.
- Comorbidity Management: SSRIs may be prescribed for comorbid anxiety or depression, while atypical antipsychotics (in low doses) are sometimes used to manage severe irritability or aggression in ASD (APA, 2013).

- Considerations: Prescribing for NDDs requires careful "titration" (adjusting doses) and monitoring of long-term growth and cardiovascular health, particularly in young children.

4. Family, Emotional, and Supportive Strategies

Recognizing the Systemic Nature of NDDs, these strategies support the child's entire ecosystem.

- Psychoeducation: This involves teaching families the "why" behind a child's behaviour. Understanding that a meltdown is a sensory crisis rather than a "naughty" act reduces parental guilt and improves caregiving quality.
- Family Systems Approach: Focuses on the health of the marriage and the well-being of siblings. Sibling Support Groups are essential to ensure that siblings of children with NDDs do not feel neglected.
- Home Environment Adaptation: Simple changes like using visual schedules, reducing clutter, or creating "quiet zones" can significantly lower the daily stress levels for a child with sensory or executive function challenges.

5. Evidence Strength and Practical Constraints

Evidence from Randomized Controlled Trials (RCTs) and meta-analyses consistently demonstrates that Combined Therapy (e.g., medication + behaviour therapy) yields superior results compared to any single treatment alone (Davis et al., 2012).

However, significant barriers remain:

- Cost and Accessibility: Intensive behavioural therapies (like ABA) or specialized OT can be prohibitively expensive and often have long waiting lists.
- Cultural Adaptation: Interventions must be culturally sensitive. A "parent-led" approach may need to be adapted in cultures that prioritize collective or elder-led decision-making.

WHY ARE THERAPIES RECOMMENDED AND HOW ARE THEY DIFFERENT?

1. The Emergence of Behavioral and Cognitive Therapies

The current emphasis on these therapies stems from a growing body of longitudinal research indicating that children with neurodevelopmental disorders (NDDs) are at a significantly higher risk for secondary mental health issues like anxiety and depression (Martinez et al., 2024).

Modern science has recognized that improving a child's academic or motor skills is insufficient if the child remains in a state of chronic emotional distress. Consequently, these therapies have come to the forefront to address the executive function and emotional regulation deficits that underpin many NDDs.

2. Defining the Therapies

Behavioural Therapy (BT)

Behavioural therapy is rooted in the principle of contingency management. It assumes that behaviours (both helpful and unhelpful) are learned and can be modified through reinforcement.

- Mechanism: It identifies the "triggers" for a behaviour and replaces maladaptive responses with functional ones. For a child with ADHD, this might involve a reward system for sustaining attention (Davis & Kollins, 2012).
- Applied Behaviour Analysis (ABA): Frequently used in ASD, this structured approach breaks down complex social or life skills into small, teachable steps.

Cognitive Behavioural Therapy (CBT)

CBT focuses on the "cognitive triad": the relationship between thoughts, feelings, and behaviours.

- Mechanism: It helps children identify "cognitive distortions" (e.g., "I am stupid because I can't read this word"). By challenging these thoughts, the child can reduce the resulting anxiety or frustration.
- Modification for NDDs: For younger children or those with ASD, CBT is often modified to be more visual and concrete, focusing on "social thinking" and identifying physical "warning signs" of anger or overwhelm (Davis & Kollins, 2012).

3. Impact on Life Satisfaction

Life satisfaction for a child with an NDD is tied to their sense of self-efficacy the belief that they can handle what happens to them.

- Emotional Regulation: These therapies provide a "toolkit" for managing sensory overload or social rejection, preventing the "meltdowns" that lead to social isolation.
- Autonomy: By learning to monitor their own thoughts and actions, children transition from being "managed" by adults to managing themselves, which significantly boosts self-esteem and quality of life (Martinez et al., 2024).

5. Why Public Awareness is Essential

Specific knowledge of behavioural and cognitive therapies is important for several reasons:

1. Reducing "Blame" Culture: When the public understands these therapies, they stop viewing a child's outburst as "bad parenting" and start seeing it as a deficit in emotional regulation that requires a specific therapeutic skill set (Thapar & Cooper, 2016).
2. Informed Advocacy: Parents who know the difference between these therapies can advocate for "wraparound" services in schools, ensuring their child does not just get help with reading (SLT/OT) but also help with the anxiety of being in a classroom (CBT).
3. Holistic Success: Awareness promotes the idea that a "successful" outcome for a neurodivergent child is not "becoming normal," but becoming a happy, regulated, and self-aware individual.

CHALLENGES, GAPS, AND FUTURE DIRECTIONS

Current Challenges and Knowledge Gaps

The primary obstacle in contemporary NDD management is the sheer heterogeneity of these conditions. As Thapar and Cooper (2016) observe, two children with the same diagnosis can have vastly different neurobiological profiles, leading to inconsistent responses to standardized treatments.

- Diagnostic Delays: While symptoms of ASD and ADHD often appear in infancy or toddlerhood, the average age of diagnosis remains significantly higher than the optimal window for early intervention. This is exacerbated by inequitable access to specialized care, particularly in rural or low-socioeconomic regions where "wait-and-see" approaches persist (APA, 2013).

- The Search for Biomarkers: Currently, NDDs are diagnosed via behavioural observation. The field lacks objective biomarkers (such as specific blood tests or neural signatures) that can predict a disorder before behavioural symptoms manifest. Without these, early intervention is reactive rather than proactive.
- Need for Longitudinal Research: Most studies focus on childhood. There is a profound lack of longitudinal data regarding how NDDs evolve into older adulthood, particularly concerning the interaction between neurodevelopment and age-related cognitive decline (Martinez et al., 2024).

Research Priorities: The Path Forward

Future research must shift toward Precision Medicine, which tailors' interventions to the individual's unique genetic and epigenetic signature.

- Personalized Interventions: Instead of "one-size-fits-all" behavioural plans, research is moving toward identifying which subtypes of children respond best to specific therapies (e.g., matching a specific sensory profile with a specific occupational therapy protocol).
- Neurobiological Markers: High-priority research is currently focused on using functional MRI (fMRI) and EEG to identify "neural endophenotypes" internal biological patterns that are more closely related to the underlying genetics than external behaviour (Yoon et al., 2020).
- Scalable Therapies: To address the lack of specialists, researchers are developing and testing digital therapeutics and telehealth-delivered parent training modules. These "scalable" models are essential for reaching underserved populations globally.

Policy Recommendations and Integrated Services

To bridge the gap between science and society, policy changes must focus on the systemic "ecosystem" of the child.

- Universal Early Screening: Policies should mandate neurodevelopmental screenings during routine paediatric visits starting at 18 months. Early detection is the single most effective way to improve long-term Quality of Life (QoL).
- Integrated Service Models: Families currently navigate a fragmented system of schools, clinics, and social services. Policy should Favor "one-stop" integrated care models where paediatricians, therapists, and educators collaborate on a single unified plan (Martinez et al., 2024).

- Caregiver Support and Mental Health: Policy must recognize the systemic impact of NDDs. This includes providing funded respite care, mental health counselling for parents, and support systems for siblings to prevent family burnout and improve the home environment.

WHY IS IT IMPORTANT FOR US TO LEARN AND BE AWARE ABOUT NDDS?

The study of neurodevelopmental disorders (NDDs) has evolved from a niche clinical interest into a critical pillar of public health and social policy. Understanding these conditions is not merely an academic exercise for clinicians; it is a fundamental requirement for building equitable and functional societies. Knowledge of NDDs transforms how the general population interacts with, educates, and supports a sizeable portion of its members.

The primary reason for studying NDDs is the neuroplasticity of the developing brain. Research consistently shows that the human brain undergoes its most rapid and critical development during the first few years of life.

- Early Intervention: According to the American Psychiatric Association (2013), identifying deficits early before they become entrenched allows for targeted therapies that can significantly improve a child's developmental trajectory. Studying NDDs allows researchers to identify the specific "critical windows" where therapy is most effective.
- The Biosocial Connection: Studying NDDs helps us understand the "Triple Hit" of genetics, environment, and timing. As noted by Yoon et al. (2020), understanding epigenetic mechanisms (how the environment turns genes on or off) allows for preventative strategies, such as improving prenatal nutrition or reducing environmental toxin exposure.

2. Benefits to the General Population

Knowledge of neurodevelopmental disorders does not only benefit those with a diagnosis; it provides the general population with tools to create more efficient and compassionate systems.

- Educational Innovation: Strategies originally developed for children with NDDs such as Universal Design for Learning (UDL) often benefit all students. For example, using visual schedules or breaking tasks into smaller steps (essential for ADHD and ASD) helps typically developing children improve their executive functioning as well (Davis & Kollins, 2012).

- Economic Impact: Early identification and support reduce the long-term economic burden on the state. By providing vocational training and social support early, individuals with NDDs are more likely to achieve independent living and contribute to the workforce, reducing the need for lifelong intensive care (Thapar & Cooper, 2016).
- Workplace Diversity: Knowledge of NDDs allows employers to tap into "neuro-divergent" strengths. Many individuals with ASD or ADHD possess elevated levels of hyper-focus, pattern recognition, and creative problem-solving that are highly valuable in industries like technology and the arts (Martinez et al., 2024).

3. The Power of Awareness

Awareness acts as a catalyst for cultural and systemic change, moving society from a model of "fixing" to a model of "inclusion."

- Reducing Stigma: Awareness replaces the perception of "bad behaviour" with an understanding of "neurological difference." For example, when the general population understands that stimming (repetitive movement) is a regulatory tool for sensory processing, it reduces the social isolation and bullying faced by neurodivergent individuals (Martinez et al., 2024).
- Systemic Policy and Advocacy: Awareness drives the demand for integrated services. As awareness grows, parents and advocates can lobby for policies that mandate early screening and classroom accommodations, ensuring that every child, regardless of their neurological profile, can succeed (APA, 2013).
- Enhanced Social Empathy: On a human level, awareness fosters neuro-harmony. It encourages a shift toward the "social model of disability," which posits that people are disabled more by a lack of societal accommodation than by their medical condition.

WHY THIS CHAPTER MATTERS?

The significance of this chapter lies in its role as a bridge between cold clinical data and the lived human experience. As global awareness of neurodevelopmental disorders (NDDs) increases, society faces the "paradox of visibility": while more children are being identified, the support they receive is often disjointed or overly focused on suppressing symptoms rather than fostering growth.

The following elaboration explains why an integrated, person-cantered approach is essential for modern clinical and social practice.

1. Counteracting Fragmentation and Over-Medicalization

In many modern healthcare systems, NDDs are treated through a fragmented lens. A child might see a psychiatrist for medication, a speech therapist for language, and a special educator for schooling, with little communication between these parties. When interventions focus solely on the medicines, the goal often becomes the reduction of "disruptive" symptoms (e.g., using medication to stop a child from fidgeting). This chapter argues for a shift toward the Neurodiversity Paradigm, which views neurological differences not just as pathologies to be cured, but as variations to be supported (APA, 2013). By understanding that a "meltdown" is rooted in a measurable neurobiological sensory crisis or a genetic predisposition, caregivers can move from frustration to informed compassion.

2. Humanizing the Diagnostic Category

A diagnosis is a tool for access, not a definition of a person. This chapter emphasizes that children with ADHD, ASD, or Learning Disorders are "whole persons" with unique strengths, interests, and emotional needs.

- Whole-Child Perspective: According to Martinez et al. (2024), focusing exclusively on deficits ignores the "spiky profile" of NDDs where a child may struggle with basic motor coordination but possess extraordinary mathematical or creative abilities.
- Context-Sensitive Support: A child does not exist in a vacuum. Their development is dictated by their family dynamics, cultural background, and school environment. This chapter highlights that "fixing" the child is often less effective than "fixing" the environment to better accommodate the child's needs.

3. A Pathway Toward Improved Quality of Childhood

The ultimate metric of success for any intervention is not the disappearance of a diagnosis, but the improvement of the child's Quality of Life (QoL). Compassionate Support: This involves moving away from "compliance-based" therapies that force children to mask their traits (such as forced eye contact) and moving toward support that builds self-efficacy and self-advocacy.

Timely and Timeless Insight: As research evolves, this chapter provides a “map” that is both timely (incorporating the latest genomic and epigenetic data) and timeless (emphasizing the fundamental human need for belonging and understanding).

CONCLUSION

The chapter serves as a call to action for clinicians, educators, and policymakers to move toward Integrated Service Models. By viewing NDDs through a multidisciplinary lens, we can ensure that interventions are:

1. Evidence-Based: Rooted in the biological realities.
2. Developmentally Aligned: Respectful of the child’s natural growth trajectory.
3. Human-Centred: Prioritizing the child’s dignity and the family’s stability.
4. Avoiding over or misdiagnosing children for normal behaviour.

ACKNOWLEDGMENT

An AI-assisted tool was used during the drafting process to enhance the clarity and linguistic flow of this chapter.

REFERENCES

Al-Wardat, M., Etoom, M., Almhdawi, K. A., Hawamdeh, Z., & Khader, Y. (2024). Prevalence of attention-deficit hyperactivity disorder in children, adolescents and adults in the Middle East and North Africa region: A systematic review and meta-analysis. *BMJ Open, 14*(1), e078849. Advance online publication. DOI: 10.1136/bmjopen-2023-078849 PMID: 38238059

American Psychiatric Association. (2013). *Diagnostic and statistical manual of mental disorders* (5th ed.)., DOI: 10.1176/appi.books.9780890425596

American Psychiatric Association. (2022). *Diagnostic and statistical manual of mental disorders* (5th ed., text rev.)., DOI: 10.1176/appi.books.9780890425787

Bishop, D. V. M., Snowling, M. J., Thompson, P. A., & Greenhalgh, T.The CATALISE Consortium. (2017). Phase 2 of CATALISE: A multinational and multidisciplinary consensus study of problems with language development: Terminology. *Journal of Child Psychology and Psychiatry, and Allied Disciplines, 58*(10), 1068–1080. DOI: 10.1111/jcpp.12721 PMID: 28369935

Blank, R., Barnett, A. L., Cairney, J., Green, D., Kirby, A., Polatajko, H., Rosenblum, S., Smits-Engelsman, B., Sugden, D., Wilson, P., & Vinçon, S. (2019). International clinical DSM-5 recommendations on definition, diagnosis, assessment, intervention, and care of developmental coordination disorder (DCD). *Developmental Medicine and Child Neurology, 61*(3), 242–285. DOI: 10.1111/dmcn.14132 PMID: 30671947

Davis, N. O., & Kollins, S. H. (2012). Psychosocial and behavioural interventions for children and adolescents with attention-deficit/hyperactivity disorder and autism spectrum disorder. *Current Psychiatry Reports, 14*(5), 510–517. DOI: 10.1007/s11920-012-0306-0

Donolato, E., Cardillo, R., Mammarella, I. C., & Melby-Lervag, M. (2022). Research Review: Language and specific learning disorders in children and their co-occurrence with internalizing and externalizing problems: A systematic review and meta-analysis. *Journal of Child Psychology and Psychiatry, and Allied Disciplines, 63*(5), 503–518.DOI: 10.1111/jcpp.12521 PMID: 34747025

Jabeen, A. (2026). Invisible Twice: India's unjust and inadequate policy response to students with specific learning disabilities and borderline intellectual functioning. *Cureus*, *18*(4), e12861. Advance online publication. DOI: 10.7759/cureus.12861 PMID: 41630856

Kanner, L. (1943). Autistic disturbances of affective contact. *Nervous Child*, *2*(3), 217–250.

Martinez, S., Stoyanov, K., & Carcache, L. (2024). Unraveling the spectrum: Overlap, distinctions, and nuances of ADHD and ASD in children. *Frontiers in Psychiatry*, *15*, 1387179. Advance online publication. DOI: 10.3389/fpsyt.2024.1387179 PMID: 39345916

Mithyantha, R., Kneen, R., McCann, E., & Gladstone, M. (2017). Current evidence-based recommendations on investigating children with global developmental delay. *Archives of Disease in Childhood*, *102*(11), 1071–1076. DOI: 10.1136/archdischild-2016-311271 PMID: 29054862

Paul, M. L., Sheth, P., Davis, R., Chrusciel, T., & Messias, E. (2025). Incidence of attention-deficit/hyperactivity disorder between 2016 and 2023: A retrospective cohort. *Psychiatric Research and Clinical Practice*, *7*(1), 18–24. Advance online publication. DOI: 10.1176/appi.prcp.20240121 PMID: 40171065

Singer, J. (2017). *NeuroDiversity: The birth of an idea*. Judy Singer.

Thapar, A., & Cooper, M. (2016, March 19). Attention deficit hyperactivity disorder. *Lancet*, *387*(10024), 1240–1250. DOI: 10.1016/S0140-6736(15)00238-X PMID: 26386541

Yoon, S., Choi, J., Lee, W., & Do, J. (2020). Genetic and epigenetic etiology underlying autism spectrum disorder. *Journal of Clinical Medicine*, *9*(4), 966. Advance online publication. DOI: 10.3390/jcm9040966 PMID: 32244359

Chapter 4
Parallel Circles: Living With Neurodiversity Within the Family

Kyriaki Tasiou
http://orcid.org/0000-0001-8144-8090
University of the Aegean, Greece

Eleni Nikolaou
http://orcid.org/0000-0003-1840-3433
University of the Aegean, Greece

ABSTRACT

This study is a literature review that attempts to understand the parenting experiences of neurodivergent people. It focuses on quantitative and qualitative studies describing thoughts and feelings of neurodivergent parents, the difficulties and challenges of parenting and managing these in everyday life. Reference is also made to research examining anxiety, acceptance or rejection, parental self-regulation and self-efficacy, family functioning, the impact of parenting on the above and the provision of support to parents. Finally, findings from research related to the impact of parents' characteristics on supportive programs for parents and children are presented. The findings of this study highlight the importance of understanding and the need for support for neurodivergent parents in order to improve their lives and daily routines in both crisis and normal times.

INTRODUCTION

Neurodivergence is a term that encompasses certain neurological forms such as autism, Attention-Deficit/Hyperactivity Disorder (ADHD), dyslexia and others and

DOI: 10.4018/979-8-3373-7072-9.ch004

advocates understanding and respecting these differences in the individual, rather than treating them as deficits or weaknesses of the individual (Argyriadis et al., 2025).

Neurodivergence can affect a person's attitudes and behaviour, communication and learning, and neurodivergent people may experience social isolation and inequality. Obtaining a formal diagnosis contributes to understanding and acceptance of difficulties, differences and support (Koi, 2021). Qualitative and quantitative evidence demonstrates that attempts by autistic people to 'camouflage' or 'mask' their autism to appear that they have more 'neurotypical' characteristics lead to exhaustion, burnout, anxiety, depression, reduced wellbeing and even suicidality (Cage & Troxell-Whitman, 2019; Cassidy et al., 2018; Hull et al., 2017, 2019; Livingston et al., 2019; Raymaker et al., 2020). It is therefore understood that the inclusion of neurodivergent people in mental health practices is considered necessary to promote an inclusive society (Argyriadis et al., 2025).

In this chapter, the concept of neurodiversity is explored, aiming to clarify the term and describe various neurotypes (such as autism, ADHD, dyslexia, and Tourette syndrome). The chapter also addresses the difficulties individuals may encounter, including challenges related to communication, social interaction, sensory processing, and organization, while highlighting the unique challenges that neurodivergent parents often face in raising their children. It also describes the effects of the difficulties of neurodivergent parents on the behaviour of their children and the degree and type of support they receive. Finally, reference is made to difficulties in accessing information and appropriate support services, and the need to promote educational support programmes.

Although this literature review initially aimed to investigate the experiences and challenges of neurodivergent parents more broadly, the available evidence was limited to studies involving autistic parents and parents with Attention-Deficit/Hyperactivity Disorder (ADHD), as no relevant studies examining other forms of neurodivergence were identified.

The concept of neurodiversity, further developed and adopted by the individuals themselves, has now gained wide acceptance (Botha et al., 2024). Argyriadis et al. (2025) identified an underrepresentation of certain neurodivergent populations in research, a pattern that was also evident in the present review. The available literature was predominantly focused on autism and ADHD, with little to no research addressing other forms of neurodivergence, including dyslexia, dyspraxia, intellectual disabilities, and Tourette syndrome. Future research is important to target a broader range of neurodivergent types in order for strategies and practices to be responsive to different needs (Argyriadis et al., 2025).

Most of the existing research focuses on the mental health and well-being of parents raising autistic children; however, autistic parents themselves have received very limited attention in the literature (Adams et al., 2021). This reflects a broader limitation in the parenting literature, which has predominantly been developed on neurotypical samples and may therefore not fully capture the specific cognitive, sensory, and executive functioning-related needs of neurodivergent parents. As a result, experiences related to daily regulation, emotional burden, and parent–child interaction may differ in meaningful ways among neurodivergent individuals, suggesting that the current evidence base may not adequately reflect the diversity of parental experiences across neurodivergent populations. This gap is evident across several neurodivergent groups, including autism, where research has largely focused on non-autistic parents raising autistic children, while the perspectives of autistic parents themselves remain underexplored. Furthermore, previous reviews have primarily examined pregnancy, childbirth, and infant feeding, leaving limited understanding of how autistic parents navigate later stages of parenthood as their children grow and develop (Thom-Jones et al., 2026).

This article aims to foster greater understanding and sensitivity towards autistic parents and parents with ADHD, advocating for a more inclusive society that acknowledges and supports the diverse ways in which individuals and families navigate the world. Through this, we hope to encourage further research and dialogue to ensure that the voices of neurodivergent parents are heard and valued.

METHODOLOGY

This chapter is based on a narrative literature review approach. The literature was identified through searches in major academic databases, including PsycINFO, ScienceDirect, ERIC, PubMed, Scopus, and Google Scholar, using relevant keywords related to neurodivergent parenting, neurodivergent parents/caregivers, autism, ADHD, learning difficulties, developmental coordination disorder, Dyspraxia, Tourette syndrome, parenting experiences, neurodivergence and neurodiversity. The review focused on peer-reviewed empirical and theoretical studies published in English, with a particular emphasis on studies published in the last 15 years, while also including a limited number of earlier seminal studies to support the theoretical foundations of the topic. Studies were included based on their relevance to the topic, while non-academic or irrelevant sources were excluded. The selected literature was screened and synthesised thematically in order to identify key patterns and findings.

THEORETICAL FRAMEWORK

The present chapter contributes to the existing literature by situating its findings within a broader family-centred perspective informed by Bowen's Family Systems

Theory. This theoretical framework conceptualises the family as an interdependent emotional system in which individual behaviours and experiences are shaped by ongoing interactions among family members. From this perspective, the experiences of neurodivergent parents cannot be fully understood in isolation but rather as products of the dynamic interplay between parental characteristics, child needs, family relationships, and the broader social environment. Integrating Bowen's Family Systems Theory into the interpretation of the findings provides a more comprehensive understanding of the systemic and relational factors that influence parenting experiences within neurodivergent families (Bowen, 1978; Brown & Errington, 2024).

NEURODIVERGENT INDIVIDUALS

The term "neurodiversity" describes the presence of many different ways in which people live and interact. It was first proposed by Judy Singer and refers to differences in cognitive or neurological functioning compared to what is considered typical or normal and includes autism, ADHD and Tourette's syndrome, dyslexia and dyspraxia (Singer, 2016). Chapman highlights that the concept of neurodiversity is continuously developing (2020). Some contemporary views on neurodiversity approaches suggest that they align with the social model (Bölte et al., 2021; Krcek, 2013), other authors challenge this claim (Kapp et al., 2013). Singer (2016) was not only reacting against the medical model when she introduced the term neurodiversity in her thesis. Specifically, she argued that: "*there is a need to move beyond the construction of binary oppositions such as medical model vs social model*" (pp. 555-557).

The term also describes the difference in the way information is processed and the way the world is understood compared to what is called "typical". The compound "neuro-" refers to the brain therefore neurodiverse means different brain (Hendrickx, 2010). Neurodiversity holds that inherent differences in brain development and cognitive function are natural variations in human biology rather than pathological deficits that need to be 'corrected'.

The concept of neurodiversity has been linked to the social model of disability, in contrast to the medical model, which locates disability within the individual's underlying difficulties. This is related to issues of 'ableism', according to which the absence of physical, mental or sensory divergences is better than having such differences in the individual. 'Ableism' stems from implicit stigma that may lead to discrimination and prejudice (Gerlach-Houck & Constantino, 2022).

The neurodiversity approach aims to provide an intermediate condition. One of the key principles of this approach is a cautious attitude towards the language used for people, as it requires acceptance of the neurodivergent person and the respectful use of language to describe their difficulties. Even if the person with the difficulties is to receive support such as teaching new skills, they should not feel inadequate, but accepted and respected (Dwyer, 2022).

Nick Walker (2021) made an important distinction between the 'neurodiversity movement' and the 'neurodiversity paradigm'. The 'neurodiversity movement' advocates for social justice, civil rights, equality, and the social inclusion of minority groups, while recognizing that neurodivergent individuals may assert their rights in different ways. In contrast, the 'neurodiversity paradigm' views neurodiversity as a natural and significant aspect of human diversity, rejecting the idea that there is a singular 'correct' way of neurocognitive functioning.

Neurodivergence (ND) or neurodivergent states (Doyle, 2020) include: (a) applied neurodevelopmental difficulties, such as dyslexia, dyspraxia and learning difficulties (usually referred to as general developmental delays), (b) clinical and neurodevelopmental differences, such as autism and ADHD and (c) mental illness as an acquired ND condition (Doyle, 2020). A fourth category of acquired neurodivergence has been identified that arises through neurological disease or brain damage. The term ND is used for individuals who identify with or experience the corresponding conditions (Walker, 2021). Neurodivergent individuals are those who identify as having neurodevelopmental differences such as dyslexia, dyscalculia, dyspraxia, ADHD, epilepsy, hyperlexia, autism, obsessive-compulsive disorder (OCD), pure O, Meares-Irlene syndrome, Tourette's syndrome, synesthesia and mental health conditions (Walker, 2021).

Although neurodiversity encompasses a broad range of neurodevelopmental profiles, the empirical literature identified in the present review primarily concerns autism and ADHD. The brief descriptions below are therefore provided to contextualize the broader neurodiversity framework within which this review is situated.

Autism Spectrum Disorder (ASD) and Attention Deficit Hyperactivity Disorder (ADHD) are classified as behavioural difficulties with genetic and neurological etiology, labeled as 'neurodevelopmental disorders'.

ASD referred to as "autism" according to the language preference community (Monk et al., 2022) is a neurodevelopmental condition characterized by qualitative barriers in communication and reciprocity in social interactions, repetitive and restricted behavioral patterns, and sensorimotor and perceptual difficulties (American Psychiatric Association, 2013).

ADHD includes three subtypes: attention deficit hyperactivity disorder with: (a) a predominantly inattentive type, (b) a predominantly hyperactive/impulsive type, and (c) combined type (American Psychiatric Association, 2013). Children with ADHD have difficulties in regulating their emotions and activities, maintaining attention and controlling their impulsivity (Tasiou & Nikolaou, 2023).

Dyslexia and developmental coordination disorder (DCD, also referred to as dyspraxia), are diagnosed in about 4-5% of adults. However, there is little research evidence on the evaluative knowledge of adults with these difficulties, although they have been shown to significantly affect their psychosocial and emotional functioning in adulthood (Potard et al, 2022). The above outlines the challenges encountered individuals in cognitive functioning (without intellectual difficulties) that affect their learning skills and other life activities. Dyslexia refers to difficulties in accuracy and fluency when decoding (APA, 2013). It has been suggested that wider cognitive challenges related to dyslexia (Facoetti et al., 2000; Jorm, 1983; Tallal, 1985) and that their effects on cognition persist into adulthood.

Dyspraxia describes motor coordination dysfunction (not due to learning difficulties or medical conditions) that affects activities of daily living and/or academic performance. Approximately 26% of the population experiences DCD-related difficulties (APA, 2013).

Tourette syndrome (TS) is a neurological condition that occurs in childhood and involves several motor tics and at least one vocal tic, with a symptom duration of more than one year (American Psychiatric Association, 2022). The first characteristics of the Tourette syndrome are usually simple motor tics (blinking or facial grimacing), but over time they develop into more complex tics and vocal tics over time. Adult cases are associated with more complex conditions with persistent and complex tics (Cheung et al., 2007). Comorbidity of the syndrome with ADHD has been found and approximately half of individuals with Tourette syndrome experience obsessive-compulsive disorder (OCD) throughout their lifetime (Hirschtritt et al, 2015). Adult individuals with these difficulties usually experience psychological challenges, such as severe mood swings, sleep difficulties (Altman et al., 2009) and an increased risk of suicide (Fernández del la Cruz et al., 2017).

Given the diversity of features and characteristics, it is challenging to establish a single set of criteria, and diagnostic approaches may vary depending on the condition in question. For example, autism should be diagnosed by a specialist professional (e.g. a psychiatrist or psychologist), Tourette's syndrome and anxiety disorder by a general practitioner preferably with specialist expertise, while dyslexia, since it is a learning difficulty, is recognised in the educational context and someone with expertise in educational psychology is the most appropriate. In addition, the process of identifying neurodevelopmental conditions varies across countries (Hendrickx, 2010).

Beyond Diagnosis: The Rise of Neurodiversity

The neurodiversity movement originated from the autistic advocacy movement, which emerged in the 1990s. This movement began to promote the rights of autistic individuals and advocate for their societal acceptance, particularly in response to the marginalization they faced from professionals and organizations led by the parents of autistic people (Chamak, 2008; Kapp, 2020; Pripas-Kapit, 2020; Sinclair, 2005, 2010).

The neurodiversity movement emerged from the desire of autistic people to gain recognition for their difference rather than being "cured" of something that is core to their identity. The term was originally intended to address other types of neurodivergence and not just autism (Koi, 2021). Supporters of the neurodiversity movement contest the pathologization of less common cognitive styles and argue that neurocognitive diversity should be viewed as a normal and healthy expression of biodiversity (Chapman, 2021). Silverman (2015) further explained that an effective way to understand neurodiversity is to view human functional systems instead of diagnostic labels like autism, dyslexia, or ADHD. In this chapter, an effort is made to avoid pathologizing, acknowledging that certain terms, such as ADHD and OCD, may be overly pathologizing and do not fully capture the nuances of these conditions. The aim of this article is to explore the experiences and perspectives of neurodivergent parents, validating their experiences and, potentially, the challenges they face, thereby highlighting the necessity of providing them with the appropriate support.

CHALLENGES AND DIFFICULTIES OF NEURODIVERGENT PARENTS

Regarding the difficulties and challenges that neurodivergent parents face, there is a lot of research data and a number of studies that have been published examining various aspects of the issue.

More specifically for individuals diagnosed with ADHD, Johnston et al. (2012) argue that approximately half of children with ADHD have at least one parent who also presents with ADHD characteristics. Adults with ADHD share many characteristics with children with ADHD. In particular, they may exhibit barriers in interpersonal relationships, as well as in occupational and cognitive difficulties (Biederman et al., 1990; Dinn et al., 2001; Murphy & Barkley, 1996; Schweitzer et al., 2000). It is also expected that up to a quarter of mothers of children with ADHD will themselves have ADHD (Faraone et al., 2000).

Research has shown that parents of children with ADHD face numerous challenges (Tasiou & Nikolaou, 2025). Indeed, in the case of parents who themselves identify as having ADHD, the stress of parenting is compounded by their own condition. While their parenting style may not always align with their children's needs, it is crucial to recognize that a determining factor in effective parenting is calm, consistent, and clear guidance, with appropriately structured boundaries (Sonuga-

Barke et al., 2002). Several parameters of ADHD have been proposed that may have an impact on parental functioning (Weiss et al., 2000; Arnold et al., 1997), such as traits of impulsivity, hyperactivity and inattention that may lead to parental inconsistency, reactivity and lack of reflection on the parental role (inattention). In addition, difficulties with executive functions, such as difficulties in organising daily routine-care activities are likely to degrade the level of care experienced by children. These difficulties may negatively affect parents' sense of efficacy, affect their self-esteem, and cause turmoil and uncertainty in the family.

Some of the challenges faced by parents with ADHD, such as difficulties in managing parenting strategies, disruption and inconsistency in establishing routines, poor monitoring of child behavior, ineffective problem-solving, inconsistent discipline, and overreactivity, have also been reported (Johnston et al., 2012; Theule et al., 2011).

In addition, more ineffective, less positive and harsh behaviours (Park et al., 2017) of parents with ADHD and greater household disruption have been reported (Mokrova et al., 2010). More family conflict (Biederman et al., 2002), lower parental self-efficacy and higher parental stress (Williamson & Johnston, 2019) have even been reported by parents with ADHD compared to neurotypical parents. This is also confirmed by findings that show that conflict and divorce between parents is more common in couples with ADHD partners (Wymbs et al, 2017).

In the same direction, Edel et al. (2010) found in their study that the prevalence of ADHD traits in the mother, and less so in the father, of adults with ADHD was significantly associated with an unfavourable parenting style, challenges in attachment and emotion regulation difficulties compared to adults with ADHD without a parent with ADHD. It also appeared that the ADHD traits in parents of children with ADHD may potentially affect attachment relationships and emotion regulation negatively during adulthood in children. In the same study, adults with persistent ADHD with a mother with ADHD differed considerably from those without possible maternal ADHD, reporting more rejection and punishment from their mother and more emotional warmth from their father. No statistically significant differences were observed in current attachment patterns and emotion processing in proportion to the presence of ADHD traits in fathers. A statistically significant association (relatively weak) was also identified between possible parental ADHD traits and parenting styles that may need further support and between dysfunctional attachment profiles and difficulty in emotion processing. Across the included studies, parental ADHD characteristics appear to be differentially associated with parenting behaviours and child outcomes. Overall, maternal ADHD traits are more consistently linked to attachment-related difficulties and more controlling or hyperprotective parenting behaviours, whereas paternal ADHD traits are more often associated with emotion processing and regulation difficulties.

Evidence from Ahçi et al. (2022), based on a large sample of parents with ADHD, suggests that children of ADHD parents show lower self-regulation compared to children of non-ADHD parents, with parental emotion-oriented socialisation strategies playing a more significant role in shaping self-regulation outcomes within the ADHD group. In contrast, no comparable effect of emotion regulation strategies was observed among non-ADHD parents, indicating potential differences in the mechanisms underlying child self-regulation across groups.

Similarly, Breaux and Harvey (2018) reported small to moderate associations between parental ADHD and harsh parenting, alongside weaker associations with flexible parenting and minimal associations with warm parenting, suggesting that ADHD-related parenting differences may vary in magnitude depending on the specific parenting dimension examined.

Further supporting these patterns, Dugdale et al. (2021) found that maternal hyperactivity, control, and hyperprotection were inversely associated with externally oriented cognitive styles, while adults with ADHD retrospectively reported more dismissive and punitive paternal behaviours but did not indicate persistent attachment or affective disturbances. Taken together, these findings suggest a heterogeneous pattern in which ADHD-related parenting characteristics are associated with specific emotional and behavioural processes rather than uniform deficits across parenting domains. The same researchers found an association between possible parental ADHD traits and parenting styles that may present challenges (as described by their children), attachment difficulties and difficulties in processing emotions. According to Tung et al. (2015), negative parenting (such as corporal punishment, inconsistent discipline, and poor monitoring) is a mediating factor between parent-child ADHD.

Similarly, in a study of mothers of 8- to 12-year-old children, the largest associations were found between maternal ADHD traits and harsh parenting and the smallest associations between maternal ADHD and positive parenting (Zaidman-Zait & Shilo, 2018). Aligned with the above, Woods et al. (2019) found that maternal ADHD was associated with harsh parenting and non-positive parenting behaviours in a sample of mothers of 5 to 10 year old children with and without ADHD. However, it is evident that the parenting mechanisms in mothers and fathers operate differently (Parke & Bornstein, 2002) yet studies on parenting tend to focus predominantly on mothers (Mokrova et al., 2010).

STRENGTHS AND BENEFITS ASSOCIATED WITH ADHD PARENTING

In the opposite direction, Biederman et al. (2002) report that a diagnosis of ADHD in parents is not associated with an increased risk of dysfunction (except in cases where the children are also diagnosed with ADHD) but is associated with poor school performance in children without ADHD. However, according to the study by Psychogiou et al. (2008), maternal ADHD characteristics may positively influence the child's traits in a negative parental behavior ("similarity hypothesis").

Johnston and colleagues (2012) note the possibility that parental ADHD traits may contribute to mitigating or buffering a child's developmental difficulties, suggesting a potentially adaptive role of these traits within the parent–child context. For example, parents with ADHD may be more in sync with their child's preferences for fast-paced activities or more sensitive to their children's attention difficulties. Therefore, it is important to consider how parental characteristics of ADHD are able to influence the child's socialization environment (Harold et al., 2013). Parents with ADHD traits have reported that these characteristics may influence their parenting in various ways, particularly through their impact on self-esteem and experiences of stigma associated with the diagnosis. This may involve challenges such as not conforming to the typical image of someone with ADHD, which can lead to doubts about their diagnosis, along with feelings of shame stemming from societal stigma (Hansson Hallerod et al., 2015).

Overall, the existing literature indicates that ADHD-related characteristics in adulthood may have important implications for parenting behaviours. Although the presence of these traits may negatively affect the ability of parents to fulfill their parental responsibilities successfully (such as involvement, responsiveness, punctuality, organization and routine), much less is known about how these difficulties impacts children at home. The few qualitative studies addressing this issue are limited in scope and often include either vague interpretations of the analysis or samples consisting of children under 18 years old (Alvey et al., 2024).

In fact, although the negative impacts of adult ADHD traits on parent-child relationships have been well-documented, there are also positive aspects of how ADHD appears within the family dynamic. Parents with ADHD may find it easier to connect with their children, especially when the children share ADHD- related traits. For instance, adults who were raised by a parent with ADHD often reported feeling a stronger sense of connection with that parent, being better able to understand and relate to each other's struggles, experiencing increased empathy in their relationship, and engaging in more enjoyable, playful interactions, which were attributed to the child-like behaviors that ADHD can bring out (Belo-Tomic et al., 2021). A similar study conducted in Ireland revealed that children with ADHD felt a greater sense of belonging when they had the same diagnosis as their parent (Carr-Fanning & McGuckin, 2022).

These findings are noteworthy, as they challenge the predominantly deficit-oriented perspective on ADHD within the family context. While ADHD-related difficulties are often viewed through a lens of dysfunction, recognizing these potential positive aspects emphasizes the need for a more nuanced perspective. This presents a refreshing counterpoint to the stigmatization of individuals with ADHD, suggesting that their unique traits can also foster connection and understanding within the family.

EXPERIENCES OF AUTISTIC PARENTS

Regarding the cases of autistic people, according to Marriot et al (2022), there is not enough research examining the experiences of autistic parents of autistic children. It has been found that autistic mothers face a wide range of life challenges (Bargiela et al., 2016; Leedham et al., 2020). Pohl et al. (2020) explore the experiences of 355 autistic mothers and 132 non-autistic mothers, each with at least one autistic child. They highlight that autistic mothers are more likely to experience mental health challenges and face greater parenting difficulties compared to neurotypical mothers. These challenges include managing multiple tasks, handling household responsibilities, and creating social opportunities for their children. The study also reveals that these mothers often feel misunderstood by professionals due to communication barriers. Furthermore, they are more likely to perceive motherhood as an isolating experience, express concerns about potential criticism of their parenting, and struggle with seeking support.

It has been suggested that autistic mothers need to navigate stereotypical perceptions (Rosqvist & Lövgren, 2013), face barriers to appropriate maternity care (Hampton et al., 2022), may experience increased sensory sensitivities during pregnancy (Gardner et al, 2016; Rogers et al., 2017; Talcer et al., 2021), undergo the intense experience of motherhood and need to advocate for their autistic children (Dugdale et al., 2021). They may also feel anxiety, distress, overload (Heyworth et al., 2023; Pellicano et al., 2022), reduced executive functions when communication becomes unclear (Shokrkon & Nicoladis, 2022), and even avoidance of supportive strategies and services. The risk of severe self-harm has also been identified in autistic women (Veenstra-VanderWeele, 2018). In addition, social and communication difficulties during maternity care (difficulty expressing needs and understanding information during childbirth) (Donovan, 2020) and feelings of criticism from maternity care professionals have been reported (Gardner et al., 2016; Rogers et al., 2017).

The experience of motherhood may really be different in autistic women compared to those without autistic features (Dugdale et al., 2021). On the other hand, some characteristics and values exhibited by autistic individuals are high performance standards such as increased focus on detail and strong work ideals (Lorenz et al., 2016), which may lead to increased resilience and commitment to the challenge of motherhood.

To further confirm the above, Dugdale et al. (2021) found in their study that autistic parents experienced greater misunderstandings and difficulties with professionals who took care of their autistic children, compared to neurotypical parents. Typically, some of the difficulties experienced by professionals working with autistic parents and children include a lack of awareness of masking (Hull et al., 2017), the assumption by some professionals that autistic individuals struggle with parenting, and the differential expression of their emotions, which may lead professionals to question the speech of autistic individuals (Dugdale et al., 2021).

Similar to the above-mentioned, Marriott et al. (2022) through their qualitative study highlighted parents' thoughts, which revealed that the interaction of autistic characteristics of parents and children both helps and hinders parent-child relationships. It was also articulated by parents that the home is a place where both they and their autistic children are approved members, and the complexity of professional services and parents' struggle for understanding, support and trust was acknowledged. Marriot et al. (2022), by examining the impact of parenting on autistic parents, reported as advantages: the acquisition of skills, such as engagement in situations that previously may have been difficult for parents and avoided (e.g., social conversations), the acquisition of social skills, the development of self-awareness, tolerance and the ability to be flexible to change. As negative elements, a dominant attitude, chaos, lack of control and the constant need to adapt to their child's needs have been reported by parents.

A survey by Dissanayake and colleagues (2020), involving 58 autistic parents with neurotypical children, reported that significant difficulties were highlighted in areas such as modelling and teaching positive behaviours, understanding their child's needs, controlling their emotions, feeling connected to their child, and managing the sensory needs arising from parenting. However, the parental autistic traits did not appear to affect parents' psychological well-being.

STRENGTHS OF AUTISTIC PARENTS

In contrast, Pohl et al. (2020) found that autistic mothers reported greater parenting-related difficulties compared to neurotypical mothers, while also demonstrating adaptive coping strategies, such as prioritising their child’s needs. This suggests that, despite increased challenges, autistic parents may employ compensatory or adaptive mechanisms to manage parenting demands. Indeed, it has been suggested that although autistic people may have difficulties with cognitive empathy (perspective taking), they appear to have increased emotional empathy (directly feeling the emotions of others)(Smith, 2009). Milton et al. (2022) describe the difficulty of parents to understand and be understood as the 'problem of dual empathy'.

Along the same lines, Marriot et al. (2022) reported the 'comforting effect' of identifying the characteristics of autistic parent-child that may increase mutual understanding and connection between them. On the other hand, a possible 'mismatch' of these characteristics may lead to conflict and tension between them. Heyworth et al. (2023) showed similar findings in the study where many of the participating parents described that a sense of shared autistic identity with their children increased their connection with each other. The parents themselves reported open and transparent communication and also that they were empathetic to their children's needs and as a result responded flexibly towards meeting these needs, even prioritising their children's wellbeing due to their perceived vulnerability.

In their literature review, Thom-Jones et al. (2026) identified communication challenges as a recurring theme across the majority of included studies, both qualitative and quantitative, suggesting that these difficulties may represent a consistent area of concern within the experiences of autistic parents. In particular, difficulties in communicating with healthcare and other services were highlighted in relation to participants' children. Additional issues raised by parents were sensory issues related to pregnancy, childbirth, and parenting. Several studies identified the strengths of autistic parents, such as empathy with their children, a high degree of focus and commitment to the well-being of their child and family. For these same authors, the biggest challenge is not the difficulties that come from the very nature of autism, but from the fact that parents and their autistic children are poorly understood and supported by systems designed for neurotypical parents.

Rosqvist and Lövgren (2013) analyzing words of autistic adults observed some similarities in their parenting experiences compared to neurotypical parenting (e.g., connecting and trying to achieve "good enough" parenting).

PARENTS WITH LEARNING DIFFICULTIES: BEYOND DEFICIT MODELS

Concerning parents with learning difficulties some research suggests that children of parents with such difficulties are at risk of developmental delay, maltreatment, neglect and abuse (Schilling et al., 1982). This evidence has led to the view that people with learning difficulties are not characterized by adequate parenting skills. However, such views have been challenged by arguments of unrepresentative sampling, inadequate research design and other methodological weaknesses (e.g. outcome measures) that limit the possibility of reliable generalizations (Tymchuk, 1992). Indeed, according to Tymchuk & Feldman (1991), no longitudinal research has been conducted on the effects of having parents with learning difficulties, nor has there been a record of children's progress over the years from adolescence to adulthood (Dowdney & Skuse 1993). Research findings report that there are no differences between the parenting styles of parents with learning difficulties from the styles of other parents in similar circumstances (Andron & Tymchuk, 1987), but that the obstacles they face are similar to those of other parents of similar socio-economic status (Unger & Howes 1988). For Booth & Booth (1998) most research has adopted a model that focuses on skills and abilities (ableist). The concept of competence is considered socially constructed as it is shaped by normative standards and value judgements imposed by the wider society, formal agencies and their representatives. This approach has at times led researchers to interpret inadequate childcare or poor outcomes as reflecting perceived parenting difficulties. Indeed, parents with learning difficulties are perceived to lack the skills needed to ensure their children's well-being and development. Research by the same authors challenges such formulations, arguing that the 'label' of parents alone cannot predict children's outcomes.

Alongside these findings, further attention has been given to parents' experiences in relation to service accessibility and the impact of these factors on parental mental health.

Support and Challenges in Accessing Services

The lack of a social support system is often likely in the group of parents of autistic children (Punshon et al., 2009). Typically, Hampton et al. (2022) reported that autistic mothers felt that the lack of knowledge and lack of awareness of autism-related issues by professionals prevented their needs from being met and also created issues of trust between them. Participants in the qualitative study by Marriott et al. (2022) described the reported difficulties of autistic parents (due to their own autistic characteristics) in navigating professional services and indeed parents in this study expressed feelings of isolation they experienced. For the same authors, it is very important that these experiences of parents are taken into account by government funding agencies in order to coordinate support services. On the contrary, Hernández González et al. (2024), in their systematic review, identified studies suggesting that autistic mothers can receive similar levels of social support and experience family satisfaction, which may indicate more positive social and familial outcomes than often assumed.

With regard to families where parents have ADHD, teaching strategies to foster calm and structured environments at home could play a crucial role in mitigating the potential negative impacts of parental ADHD traits, thereby contributing to a more stable and organized family dynamic (Mokrova et al., 2010).

Impact on Parents' Mental Health

Lau & Peterson (2011) observed in their study that among the 157 parent respondents who had a self-diagnosed 'Asperger's Syndrome' diagnosis, there was a predominant insecure avoidance towards romantic attachment, in contrast to the predominant secure attachment in all other groups. In the same study, the presence of a child with 'Asperger's Syndrome' led to reduced parental (but not marital) satisfaction, regardless of whether either the parents or the husband had been diagnosed with 'Asperger's Syndrome.' In contrast, Dugdale et al. (2021) demonstrated that a diagnosis of 'Asperger's Syndrome' in autistic parents did not significantly reduce their parental satisfaction, nor did it affect their secure attachment style with their child.

However, other evidence suggests a more complex picture, as Talcer et al. (2021) reported that autistic mothers may experience elevated levels of anxiety and stress, particularly in relation to sensory processing difficulties, indicating that well-being outcomes may vary depending on the specific challenges considered. These challenges arise from increased sensory reactivity and the difficulty in managing sensory overload after becoming mothers. These findings are consistent with those of Hampton et al. (2022), who found that autistic parents scored significantly higher than non-autistic participants in terms of stress and depression. However, there were no significant differences between the two groups regarding life satisfaction. Additionally, no differences were observed between the groups in parental confidence, stress, caregiving, involvement, or routine. Nonetheless, autistic parents reported lower scores in terms of discipline. This is a noteworthy result, as it indicates that autistic parents, despite facing certain challenges, exhibit levels of parental involvement and parenting self-efficacy comparable to those of non-autistic parents. These findings contribute to the growing body of evidence highlighting the parenting strengths and capabilities of autistic individuals.

Furthermore, Lau et al. (2016) compared self-reported parental efficacy among three groups (109 autistic parents-children, 128 neurotypical parents - autistic children, and 109 neurotypical parents-children). The results revealed that autistic mothers reported levels of parental efficacy comparable to those of neurotypical mothers in both groups, suggesting similar levels of perceived parenting competence across groups. However, fathers of autistic children reported significantly lower levels of parental efficacy compared to neurotypical fathers in the other two groups. For the authors, parenting for autistic parents may be differentiated; indeed, the diagnosis of autism in a child is associated with the impact of parenting on family experience.

Dugdale et al. (2021) showed that a diagnosis of 'Asperger's Syndrome' for parents did not significantly reduce the parental satisfaction they felt nor did it affect their secure attachment style with their child.

Turning Challenges into Strengths: The Role of Support Services

With regard to supportive strategies and services for children with ADHD, it has been argued that parents' ADHD traits can negatively affect the outcomes of these strategies for their children (Evans et al., 1994), with the greatest difficulties being found in parent education. In particular, Weiss et al. (2000) highlight as key factors that may affect the effectiveness of supportive services for childhood ADHD: the difficulty of parents with ADHD to consistently follow programs and instructions, lower levels of adherence, impulsivity of parents that may lead them to seek quick treatments, disruptive, argumentative attitudes and lack of organization among parents, difficulties in consistency of payment and fees among parents and reduced tendency to cooperate during these services.

Along the same lines, other researchers have described the difficulty of parents with ADHD to adhere to supportive strategies protocols. Parents' engagement with the treatments and active participation in sessions are crucial elements for the effectiveness of the these strategies (Chacko et al., 2016; Lindsey et al., 2019).

Furthermore, time management, organization and planning skills are considered necessary for monitoring sessions, designing behaviour plans and planning the teaching of skills. In addition, the ability to self-regulate (to manage stress and control emotional reactions) and the ability to maintain attention for learning new skills and for monitoring their children's behaviour are positive for the effectiveness of the supportive services. Difficulties in attention and executive functions experienced by adult parents with ADHD (Alderson et al., 2013; Boonstra et al., 2005; Nigg et al., 2005) may impede the effectiveness of supportive strategies for their children with ADHD. Many of these require parents with ADHD to use executive function skills, such as working memory and cognitive flexibility, which are typically limited in individuals with ADHD (Azar et al., 2008; Crandall et al, 2015). Similarly, several authors acknowledge the difficulties of planning, organization and time management (Alderson et al., 2013; Barkley & Murphy, 2010; Boonstra et al., 2005) that impede parents' ability to apply skills learned from their children's supportive services at home.

In a recent study by Ros-DeMarize et al. (2022), the findings indicated that parental ADHD traits were associated with increased negative parenting behaviors and decreased positive parenting behaviors following Parent–Child Interaction Therapy (PCIT) in parents of children with ADHD and co-occurring externalizing behaviors. In contrast, no such association was identified among parents of children without ADHD. Furthermore, there appeared to be a significant indirect effect of parental ADHD characteristics on supportive parenting but also on parenting approaches with more challenging dynamics, through parental stress for parents of children with

ADHD and co-existing externalizing difficulties. The impact of parental ADHD traits on treatment outcomes for parents of children with co-occurring characteristics is therefore discussed, and indeed this effect appeared to be mediated to some extent by parental stress. It is possible that parental difficulties with attention maintenance may influence perceived stress levels and therefore parenting practices (Pinderhughes et al., 2000). Similarly, Sonuga-Barke (2002) and colleagues found in their study that elevated levels of maternal ADHD traits limit the improvement that children with ADHD show after a program of intervention (PT). In the same vein are the views of several authors in which parental ADHD characteristics appeared to be associated with worse outcomes of behavioural approaches for parents (Chronis-Tuscano et al., 2011; Griggs & Mikami, 2011; Jensen et al., 2007).

Contrary to the above, several studies have found no associations between parental ADHD traits and treatment outcomes in children (Sibley et al., 2013; Thompson et al., 2009; van den Hoofdakker et al., 2009).

Despite the challenges faced by parents with ADHD, the likelihood of disengaging from services may be influenced by stigma, feelings of not fitting in within support groups, and experiences that differ from those of neurotypical individuals (Smith et al., 2015).

According to Sonuga-Barke (2002), managing parental ADHD characteristics may bring about positive effects on psychosocial strategies for childhood ADHD. Such supportive strategies aim to educate parents about ADHD, improve the quality of parent-child relationships, and teach behavioral strategies to improve attention, disruptive behavior, and behavioral organization. Support services may benefit from being tailored to the needs of parents with ADHD, including adjustments such as shorter sessions, simplified instructions, and reduced demands on executive functioning. In addition, beneficial modifications to supportive strategies for parents include the use of behavioral language, facilitating active participation, and addressing the needs and difficulties of the parents themselves in order to achieve change (Johnston et al., 2012). Dawson et al. (2016) suggest that supportive, non-directive and psychoeducational strategies may be appropriate for parents with ADHD characteristics. In addition to the above-mentioned benefits, the findings of the study by Hautmann et al. (2018) highlight that intensive support for parental ADHD traits, behavioral parenting education, and counseling can reduce the difficulties faced by children of mothers with ADHD.

CONCLUSIONS AND FUTURE DIRECTIONS

In relation to supportive services for people with ADHD, for Park and Johnston (2019) it is of paramount importance to identify the difficulties that parents with

ADHD are expected to experience and to identify their potential strengths in relation to parenting. However, it is also important to give voice to the wishes of parents with ADHD themselves regarding cognitive-behavioural therapy approaches for adult ADHD (Ramsay & Rostain, 2008; Safren et al., 2005) that include compensatory teaching strategies such as organization and planning skills, reducing distraction, and enhancing adaptive thinking (positive self-practice, identifying and challenging negative thoughts).

For autistic adults, there is a clear need for improved versions of supportive programmes, education, training and understanding of autism by health services. Some areas that need further improvement are knowledge about autism in adulthood, masking, mismatch of facial expressions with emotional state, sensory needs and the problem of dual empathy (Dugdale et al., 2021). It is important for Dugdale et al. (2021) to adopt a narrative about diversity rather than the deficit or weaknesses associated with autism, but which difficulties should be acknowledged and supported. There is no shortage of research examining the experiences of autistic parents that perpetuates stigmatizing and negative views and messages about parents.

It is also crucial that autistic people themselves are involved in the planning of autism parent education. It is also necessary to include autistic parents to identify the supports that would be most acceptable to them and that would help them with the challenges of everyday life (Dugdale et al., 2021). Developing self-compassion, understanding without criticism and recognizing pain as part of the human experience work beneficially in this direction (MacBeth & Gumley, 2012).

Although there is growing emphasis in the literature on strengths-based approaches to autism and neurodiversity, the present discussion does not fully apply a structured strengths-based framework. As a result, the analysis may place greater emphasis on difficulties rather than on the strengths, resources, and adaptive strategies of neurodivergent parents. However, the findings also align with calls in the literature for more balanced, participatory, and less deficit-focused perspectives in research and practice. Overall, this study highlights the importance of adopting more inclusive and balanced frameworks in future research on neurodivergent parenting.

Future research should further prioritise the voices and lived experiences of neurodivergent parents, adopting approaches that more fully capture both their challenges and strengths. Such an approach would contribute to a more holistic understanding of parenting experiences and align with family-centred frameworks, such as Family Systems Theory, which emphasise the interconnected and relational nature of parenting within the broader family context.

REFERENCES

Ahçi, Z. G., Akdeniz, S., & Harmanci, H. (2022). A Study of the Effects of Parental Attention Deficit and Hyperactivity Disorder (ADHD) and Parental Emotion Regulation Processes on Adolescent Self-Regulation Skills. *International Journal of Progressive Education, 18*(1), 435–447. DOI: 10.29329/ijpe.2022.426.24

Alderson, R. M., Kasper, L. J., Hudec, K. L., & Patros, C. H. G. (2013). Attention deficit/hyperactivity disorder (ADHD) and working memory in adults: A meta-analytic review. *Neuropsychology, 27*(3), 287–302. DOI: 10.1037/a0032371 PMID: 23688211

Alvey, H. M., Walters, A. S., & Noll, L. K. (2024). "Mom Just Forgot Me at a Gas Station": A Qualitative Study of Parental ADHD in the Home. *Contemporary Family Therapy*, •••, 1–19.

American Psychiatric Association. (2013). *Diagnostic and statistical manual of mental disorders* (5th ed.). American Psychiatric Association.

American Psychiatric Association. (2022). *Diagnostic and statistical manual of mental disorders: DSM-5 text revision* (5th ed.). American Psychiatric Association.

Andron, L., & Tymchuk, A. (1987). Parents who are mentally retarded. In Craft, A. (Ed.), *Mental Handicap and Sexuality: Issues and Perspectives*. D.J. Costello.

Argyriadis, A., Drakopoulou, O., Argyriadi, A., Mantsos, E., Katsarou, D. V., & Patsiaouras, A. (2025). *Towards Holistic Wellness: Strategies for Managing Mental Health and Embracing Neurodiversity. Exploring Cognitive and Psychosocial Dynamics Across Childhood and Adolescence*. IGIGlobal.

Arnold, E. H., O'Leary, S. G., & Edwards, G. H. (1997). Father involvement and self reported parenting of children with attention deficit hyperactivity disorder. *Journal of Consulting and Clinical Psychology, 65*(65), 337–342. DOI: 10.1037/0022-006X.65.2.337 PMID: 9086700

Azar, S. T., Reitz, E. B., & Goslin, M. C. (2008). Mothering: Thinking is part of the job description: Application of cognitive views to understanding maladaptive parenting and doing intervention and prevention work. *Journal of Applied Developmental Psychology, 29*(4), 295–304. DOI: 10.1016/j.appdev.2008.04.009

Bargiela, S., Steward, R., & Mandy, W. (2016). The experiences of late-diagnosed women with autism spectrum conditions: An investigation of the female autism phenotype. *Journal of Autism and Developmental Disorders, 46*(10), 3281–3294. DOI: 10.1007/s10803-016-2872-8 PMID: 27457364

Barkley, R. A., & Murphy, K. R. (2010). Impairment in occupational functioning and adult ADHD: The predictive utility of executive function (EF) ratings versus EF tests. *Archives of Clinical Neuropsychology : The Official Journal of the National Academy of Neuropsychologists*, *25*(3), 157–173. DOI: 10.1093/arclin/acq014 PMID: 20197297

Belo-Tomic, S., Quinlan, E., & Read, E. (2021). Young adult's perception of their relationship with an ADHD parent: A qualitative study. *Contemporary Family Therapy*, *43*(3), 298–304. DOI: 10.1007/s10591-021-09566-w

Biederman, J., Faraone, S. V., Knee, D., & Munir, K. (1990). Retrospective assessment of *DSM-III* attention deficit disorder in non-referred individuals. *The Journal of Clinical Psychiatry*, *51*, 102–106. PMID: 2307663

Biederman, J., Faraone, S. V., & Monuteaux, M. C. (2002). Impact of exposure to parental attention-deficit hyperactivity disorder on clinical features and dysfunction in the offspring. *Psychological Medicine*, *32*(5), 817–827. DOI: 10.1017/S0033291702005652 PMID: 12171376

Bölte, S., Lawson, W. B., Marschik, P. B., & Girdler, S. (2021). Reconciling the seemingly irreconcilable: The WHO's ICF system integrates biological and psychosocial environmental determinants of autism and ADHD – The International Classification of Functioning ICF) allows to model opposed biomedical and neurodiverse views of autism and ADHD within one framework. *BioEssays : News and Reviews in Molecular, Cellular and Developmental Biology*, *43*(9), 2000254. DOI: 10.1002/bies.202000254 PMID: 33797095

Boonstra, A. M., Oosterlaan, J., Sergeant, J. A., & Buitelaar, J. K. (2005). Executive functioning in adult ADHD: A meta-analytic review. *Psychological Medicine*, *35*(8), 1097–1108. DOI: 10.1017/S003329170500499X PMID: 16116936

Booth, T., & Booth, W. (1998). Risk, resilience and competence: parents with learning difficulties and their children. *Questions of competence: Culture, classification and intellectual disability*, 76-101.

Botha, M., Chapman, R., Giwa Onaiwu, M., Kapp, S. K., Stannard Ashley, A., & Walker, N. (2024). The neurodiversity concept was developed collectively: An overdue correction on the origins of neurodiversity theory. *Autism : The International Journal of Research and Practice*, *28*(6), 1591–1594. DOI: 10.1177/13623613241237871 PMID: 38470140

Bowen, M. (1978). *Family therapy in clinical practice*. Jason Aronson.

Breaux, R. P., & Harvey, E. A. (2018). A longitudinal study of the relation between family functioning and preschool ADHD symptoms. *Journal of Clinical Child and Adolescent Psychology : The Official Journal for the Society of Clinical Child and Adolescent Psychology, American Psychological Association, Division 53*. Advance online publication. DOI: 10.1080/15374416.2018.1437737 PMID: 29578799

Brown, J., & Errington, L. (2024). Bowen family systems theory and practice: Illustration and critique revisited. *Australian and New Zealand Journal of Family Therapy*, *45*(2), 135–155. DOI: 10.1002/anzf.1589

Cage, E., & Troxell-Whitman, Z. (2019). Understanding the reasons, contexts and costs of camouflaging for autistic adults. *Journal of Autism and Developmental Disorders*, *49*(5), 1899–1911. DOI: 10.1007/s10803-018-03878-x PMID: 30627892

Carr-Fanning, K., & McGuckin, C. (2022). I find it really difficult to control myself too: A qualitative study of the effects on the family dynamic when parent and child have ADHD. *Education Sciences*, *12*(11), 758. DOI: 10.3390/educsci12110758

Cassidy, S., Bradley, L., Shaw, R., & Baron-Cohen, S. (2018). Risk markers for suicidality in autistic adults. *Molecular Autism*, *9*(1), 42. DOI: 10.1186/s13229-018-0226-4 PMID: 30083306

Chacko, A., Jensen, S. A., Lowry, L. S., Cornwell, M., Chimklis, A., Chan, E., Lee, D., & Pulgarin, B. (2016). Engagement in behavioral parent training: Review of the literature and implications for practice. *Clinical Child and Family Psychology Review*, *19*(3), 204–215. DOI: 10.1007/s10567-016-0205-2 PMID: 27311693

Chapman, R. (2021). Neurodiversity and the social ecology of mental functions. *Perspectives on Psychological Science : A Journal of the Association for Psychological Science*, *16*(6), 1360–1372. DOI: 10.1177/1745691620959833 PMID: 33577400

Cheung, M. C., Shahed, J., & Jankovic, J. (2007). Malignant Tourette syndrome. *Movement Disorders : Official Journal of the Movement Disorder Society*, *22*(12), 1743–1750. DOI: 10.1002/mds.21599 PMID: 17566119

Chronis-Tuscano, A., O'Brien, K. A., Johnston, C., Jones, H. A., Clarke, T. L., Raggi, V. L., Rooney, M. E., Diaz, Y., Pian, J., & Seymour, K. E. (2011). The relation between maternal ADHD symptoms & improvement in child behavior following brief behavioral parent training is mediated by change in negative parenting. *Journal of Abnormal Child Psychology*, *39*(7), 1047–1057. DOI: 10.1007/s10802-011-9518-2 PMID: 21537894

Crandall, A., Deater-Deckard, K., & Riley, A. W. (2015). Maternal emotion and cognitive control capacities and parenting: A conceptual framework. *Developmental Review*, *36*, 105–126. DOI: 10.1016/j.dr.2015.01.004 PMID: 26028796

Dawson, A. E., Wymbs, B. T., Marshall, S. A., Mautone, J. A., & Power, T. J. (2016). The role of parental ADHD in sustaining the effects of a family-school intervention for ADHD. *Journal of Clinical Child and Adolescent Psychology : The Official Journal for the Society of Clinical Child and Adolescent Psychology, American Psychological Association, Division 53*, *45*(3), 305–319. DOI: 10.1080/15374416.2014.963858 PMID: 25496523

Dinn, W. M., Robbins, N. C., & Harris, C. L. (2001). Adult attention-deficit/hyperactivity disorder: Neuropsychological correlates and clinical presentation. *Brain and Cognition*, *46*(1-2), 114–121. DOI: 10.1016/S0278-2626(01)80046-4 PMID: 11527308

Dissanayake, C., Richdale, A., Kolivas, N., & Pamment, L. (2020). An exploratory study of autism traits and parenting. *Journal of Autism and Developmental Disorders*, *50*(7), 2593–2606. DOI: 10.1007/s10803-019-03984-4 PMID: 30877419

Donovan, J. (2020). Childbirth experiences of women with autism spectrum disorder in an acute care setting. *Nursing for Women's Health*, *24*(3), 165–174. DOI: 10.1016/j.nwh.2020.04.001 PMID: 32389581

Dowdney, L., & Skuse, D. (1993). Parenting provided by adults with mental retardation. *Journal of Child Psychology and Psychiatry, and Allied Disciplines*, *34*(1), 25–47. DOI: 10.1111/j.1469-7610.1993.tb00966.x PMID: 8421068

Doyle, N. (2020). Neurodiversity at work: A biopsychosocial model and the impact on working adults. *British Medical Bulletin*, *135*(1), 1–18. DOI: 10.1093/bmb/ldaa021 PMID: 32996572

Dugdale, A.-S., Thompson, A. R., Leedham, A., Beail, N., & Freeth, M. (2021). Intense connection and love: The experiences of autistic mothers. *Autism : The International Journal of Research and Practice*, *25*(7), 1973–1984. DOI: 10.1177/13623613211005987 PMID: 33840262

Dwyer, P. (2022). The neurodiversity approach (es): What are they and what do they mean for researchers? *Human Development*, *66*(2), 73–92. DOI: 10.1159/000523723 PMID: 36158596

Edel, M. A., Juckel, G., & Brüne, M. (2010). Interaction of recalled parental ADHD symptoms and rearing behavior with current attachment and emotional dysfunction in adult offspring with ADHD. *Psychiatry Research, 178*(1), 137–141. DOI: 10.1016/j.psychres.2010.04.004 PMID: 20452044

Evans, S. W., Vallano, G., & Pelham, W. (1994). Treatment of parenting behavior with a psychostimulant: A case study of an adult with attention-deficit hyperactivity disorder. *Journal of Child and Adolescent Psychopharmacology, 4*(1), 63–69. DOI: 10.1089/cap.1994.4.63

Facoetti, A., Paganoni, P., Turatto, M., Marzola, V., & Mascetti, G. G. (2000). Visual-spatial attention in developmental dyslexia. *Cortex; A Journal Devoted to the Study of the Nervous System and Behavior, 36*(1), 109–123. DOI: 10.1016/S0010-9452(08)70840-2 PMID: 10728901

Faraone, S. V., Biederman, J., Spencer, T., Wilens, T., Seidman, L. J., Mick, E., & Doyle, A. E. (2000). Attention-deficit/hyperactivity disorder in adults: An overview. *Biological Psychiatry, 48*(1), 9–20. DOI: 10.1016/S0006-3223(00)00889-1 PMID: 10913503

Fernández de la Cruz, L., Rydell, M., Runeson, B., Brander, G., Rück, C., D'Onofrio, B. M., Larsson, H., Lichtenstein, P., & Mataix-Cols, D. (2017). Suicide in Tourette's and chronic tic disorders. *Biological Psychiatry, 82*(2), 111–118. DOI: 10.1016/j.biopsych.2016.08.023 PMID: 27773353

Gardner, M., Suplee, P. D., Bloch, J., & Lecks, K. (2016). Exploratory study of childbearing experiences of women with Asperger syndrome. *Nursing for Women's Health, 20*(1), 28–P37. DOI: 10.1016/j.nwh.2015.12.001 PMID: 26902438

Gerlach-Houck, H., & Constantino, C. D. (2022). Interrupting ableism in stuttering therapy and research: Practical suggestions. *Perspectives of the ASHA Special Interest Groups, 7*(2), 357–374. DOI: 10.1044/2021_PERSP-21-00109

Griggs, M. S., & Mikami, A. Y. (2011). The role of maternal and child ADHD symptoms in shaping interpersonal relationships. [PubMed: 20931275]. *Journal of Abnormal Child Psychology, 39*(3), 437–449. DOI: 10.1007/s10802-010-9464-4 PMID: 20931275

Hampton, S., Allison, C., Aydin, E., Baron-Cohen, S., & Holt, R. (2022). Autistic mothers' perinatal well-being and parenting styles. *Autism : The International Journal of Research and Practice, 26*(7), 1805–1820. DOI: 10.1177/13623613211065544 PMID: 35105233

Hansson Hallerod, S. L., Anckarsater, H., Rastam, M., & Hansson Scherman, M. (2015). Experienced consequences of being diagnosed with ADHD as an adult: A qualitative study. *BMC Psychiatry*, *15*(31), 1–13. DOI: 10.1186/s12888-015-0410-4 PMID: 25884685

Harold, G. T., Leve, L. D., Barrett, D., Elam, K., Neiderhiser, J. M., Natsuaki, M. N., Shaw, D. S., Reiss, D., & Thapar, A. (2013). Biological and rearing mother influences on child ADHD symptoms: Revisiting the developmental interface between nature and nurture. *Journal of Child Psychology and Psychiatry, and Allied Disciplines*, *54*(10), 1038–1046. DOI: 10.1111/jcpp.12100 PMID: 24007415

Hautmann, C., Döpfner, M., Katzmann, J., Schürmann, S., Metternich-Kaizman, T., Jaite, C., & Kappel, J. (2018). Sequential treatment of ADHD in mother and child (AIMAC study): Importance of the treatment phases for intervention success in a randomized trial. *BMC Psychiatry*, *18*(1), 388. Advance online publication. DOI: 10.1186/s12888-018-1963-9 PMID: 30545333

Hendrickx, S. (2010). *The adolescent and adult neuro-diversity handbook: Asperger's syndrome, ADHD, dyslexia, dyspraxia, and related conditions*. Jessica Kingsley Publishers.

Hernández González, O., González Fernández, D., Spencer Contreras, R., Gillespie-Smith, K., & Jara Rojas, E. (2024). The childbearing and mental health experiences of autistic mothers: A systematic review. *International Journal of Developmental Disabilities*, •••, 1–15.

Heyworth, M., Brett, S., den Houting, J., Magiati, I., Steward, R., Urbanowicz, A., Stears, M., & Pellicano, E. (2023). "I'm the Family Ringmaster and Juggler": Autistic parents' experiences of parenting during the COVID-19 pandemic. *Autism in Adulthood: Challenges and Management*, *5*(1), 24–36. DOI: 10.1089/aut.2021.0097 PMID: 36941857

Hirschtritt, M. E., Lee, P. C., Pauls, D. L., Dion, Y., Grados, M. A., Illmann, C., King, R. A., Sandor, P., McMahon, W. M., Lyon, G. J., Cath, D. C., Kurlan, R., Robertson, M. M., Osiecki, L., Scharf, J. M., & Mathews, C. A. (2015). Lifetime prevalence, age of risk, and genetic relationships of comorbid psychiatric disorders in Tourette syndrome. *JAMA Psychiatry*, *72*(4), 325–333. DOI: 10.1001/jamapsychiatry.2014.2650 PMID: 25671412

Hull, L., Mandy, W., Lai, M. C., Baron-Cohen, S., Allison, C., Smith, P., & Petrides, K. V. (2019). Development and validation of the camouflaging autistic traits questionnaire (CAT-Q). *Journal of Autism and Developmental Disorders*, *49*(3), 819–833. DOI: 10.1007/s10803-018-3792-6 PMID: 30361940

Hull, L., Petrides, K. V., Allison, C., Smith, P., Baron-Cohen, S., Lai, M. C., & Mandy, W. (2017). 'Putting on my best normal': Social camouflaging in adults with autism spectrum conditions. *Journal of Autism and Developmental Disorders*, *47*(8), 2519–2534. DOI: 10.1007/s10803-017-3166-5 PMID: 28527095

Jensen, P. S., Arnold, L. E., Swanson, J. M., Vitiello, B., Abikoff, H. B., Greenhill, L. L., Hechtman, L., Hinshaw, S. P., Pelham, W., Wells, K. C., Conners, C. K., Elliott, G. R., Epstein, J. N., Hoza, B., March, J. S., Molina, B. S. G., Newcorn, J. H., Severe, J. B., Wigal, T., & Hur, K. (2007). Three-year follow-up of the NIMH MTA study. *Journal of the American Academy of Child and Adolescent Psychiatry*, *46*(8), 989–1002. DOI: 10.1097/CHI.0b013e3180686d48 PMID: 17667478

Johnston, C., Mash, E. J., Miller, N., & Ninowski, J. E. (2012). Parenting in adults with attention-deficit/hyperactivity disorder (ADHD). *Clinical Psychology Review*, *32*(4), 215–228. DOI: 10.1016/j.cpr.2012.01.007 PMID: 22459785

Jorm, A. F. (1983). Specific reading retardation and working memory: A review. *British Journal of Psychology*, *74*(3), 311–342. DOI: 10.1111/j.2044-8295.1983.tb01865.x PMID: 6616125

Kapp, S. K., Gillespie-Lynch, K., Sherman, L. E., & Hutman, T. (2013). Deficit, difference, or both? Autism and neurodiversity. *Developmental Psychology*, *49*(1), 59–71. DOI: 10.1037/a0028353 PMID: 22545843

Koi, P. (2021). Genetics on the neurodiversity spectrum: Genetic, phenotypic and endophenotypic continua in autism and ADHD. *Studies in History and Philosophy of Science*, *89*, 52–62. DOI: 10.1016/j.shpsa.2021.07.006 PMID: 34365317

Krcek, T. E. (2013). Deconstructing disability and neurodiversity: Controversial issues for autism and implications for social work. *Journal of Progressive Human Services*, *24*(1), 4–22. DOI: 10.1080/10428232.2013.740406

Lau, W., & Peterson, C. C. (2011). Adults and children with Asperger syndrome: Exploring adult attachment style, marital satisfaction and satisfaction with parenthood. *Research in Autism Spectrum Disorders*, *5*(1), 392–399. DOI: 10.1016/j.rasd.2010.06.001

Lau, W. Y. P., Peterson, C. C., Attwood, T., Garnett, M. S., & Kelly, A. B. (2016). Parents on the autism continuum: Links with parenting efficacy. *Research in Autism Spectrum Disorders*, *26*, 57–64. DOI: 10.1016/j.rasd.2016.02.007

Leedham, A., Thompson, A. R., Smith, R., & Freeth, M. (2020). 'I was exhausted trying to figure it out': The experiences of females receiving an autism diagnosis in middle to late adulthood. *Autism : The International Journal of Research and Practice*, *24*(1), 135–146. DOI: 10.1177/1362361319853442 PMID: 31144507

Lindsey, M. A., Romanelli, M., Ellis, M. L., Barker, E. D., Boxmeyer, C. L., & Lochman, J. E. (2019). The influence of treatment engagement on positive outcomes in the context of a school-based intervention for students with externalizing behavior problems. [PubMed: 29654540]. *Journal of Abnormal Child Psychology*, *47*(9), 1–18. DOI: 10.1007/s10802-019-00525-6 PMID: 30848415

Livingston, L. A., Shah, P., & Happé, F. (2019). Compensatory strategies below the behavioural surface in autism: A qualitative study. *The Lancet. Psychiatry*, *6*(9), 766–777. DOI: 10.1016/S2215-0366(19)30224-X PMID: 31350208

Lorenz, T., Frischling, C., Cuadros, R., & Heinitz, K. (2016). Autism and overcoming job barriers: Comparing job-related barriers and possible solutions in and outside of autism specific employment. *PLoS One*, *11*(1), e0147040. Advance online publication. DOI: 10.1371/journal.pone.0147040 PMID: 26766183

MacBeth, A., & Gumley, A. (2012). Exploring compassion: A meta-analysis of the association between self-compassion and psychopathology. *Clinical Psychology Review*, *32*(6), 545–552. DOI: 10.1016/j.cpr.2012.06.003 PMID: 22796446

Marriott, E., Stacey, J., Hewitt, O. M., & Verkuijl, N. E. (2022). Parenting an autistic child: Experiences of parents with significant autistic traits. *Journal of Autism and Developmental Disorders*, *52*(7), 3182–3193. DOI: 10.1007/s10803-021-05182-7 PMID: 34322826

Milton, D., Gurbuz, E., & López, B. (2022). The 'double empathy problem': *Ten years on. Autism : The International Journal of Research and Practice*, *26*(8), 1901–1903. DOI: 10.1177/13623613221129123 PMID: 36263746

Mokrova, I., O'Brien, M., Calkins, S., & Keane, S. (2010). Parental ADHD symptomology and ineffective parenting: The connecting link of home chaos. *Parenting, Science and Practice*, *10*(2), 119–135. DOI: 10.1080/15295190903212844 PMID: 20454604

Murphy, K. R., & Barkley, R. A. (1996). Attention deficit hyperactivity disorder in adults: Comorbidities and adaptive impairments. *Comprehensive Psychiatry*, *37*(6), 393–401. DOI: 10.1016/S0010-440X(96)90022-X PMID: 8932963

Nigg, J. T., Stavro, G., Ettenhofer, M., Hambrick, D. Z., Miller, T., & Henderson, J. M. (2005). Executive functions and ADHD in adults: Evidence for selective effects on ADHD symptom domains. *Journal of Abnormal Psychology, 114*(4), 706–717. DOI: 10.1037/0021-843X.114.3.706 PMID: 16351391

Park, J. L., Hudec, K. L., & Johnston, C. (2017). Parental ADHD symptoms and parenting behaviors: A meta-analytic review. *Clinical Psychology Review, 56*, 25–39. DOI: 10.1016/j.cpr.2017.05.003 PMID: 28601690

Park, J. L., & Johnston, C. (2019). Parental ADHD symptoms and parenting behaviors. *The ADHD Report, 27*(3), 1–7. DOI: 10.1521/adhd.2019.27.3.1

Parke, R. D., & Bornstein, M. H. (2002). Handbook of parenting: Vol. 3: Being and becoming a parent.

Pellicano, E., Lawson, W., Hall, G., Mahony, J., Lilley, R., Heyworth, M., Clapham, H., & Yudell, M. (2022). "I Knew She'd Get It, and Get Me": Participants' Perspectives of a Participatory Autism Research Project. *Autism in Adulthood: Challenges and Management, 4*(2), 120–129. DOI: 10.1089/aut.2021.0039 PMID: 36605972

Pinderhughes, E. E., Dodge, K. A., Bates, J. E., Pettit, G. S., & Zelli, A. (2000). Discipline responses: Influences of parents' socioeconomic status, ethnicity, beliefs about parenting, stress, and cognitiveemotional processes. *Journal of Family Psychology : JFP : Journal of the Division of Family Psychology of the American Psychological Association (Division 43), 14*(3), 380–400. DOI: 10.1037/0893-3200.14.3.380 PMID: 11025931

Pohl, A. L., Crockford, S. K., Blakemore, M., Allison, C., & Baron-Cohen, S. (2020). A comparative study of autistic and non-autistic women's experience of motherhood. *Molecular Autism, 11*(1), 1–12. DOI: 10.1186/s13229-019-0304-2 PMID: 31911826

Potard, C., Auger, A. C., Lenoir-Perrotel, S., & Jarry, C. (2022). Examining frustration intolerance beliefs among adults with dyslexia or developmental coordination disorder. *Research in Developmental Disabilities, 123*, 104184. DOI: 10.1016/j.ridd.2022.104184 PMID: 35121415

Psychogiou, L., Daley, D. M., Thompson, M. J., & Sonuga-Barke, E. J. S. (2008). Do maternal attention-deficit/hyperactivity disorder symptoms exacerbate or ameliorate the negative effect of child attention-deficit/hyperactivity disorder symptoms on parenting? *Development and Psychopathology, 20*(1), 121–137. DOI: 10.1017/S0954579408000060 PMID: 18211731

Punshon, C., Skirrow, P., & Murphy, G. (2009). The not guilty verdict' Psychological reactions to a diagnosis of Asperger syndrome in adulthood. *Autism : The International Journal of Research and Practice*, *13*(3), 265–283. DOI: 10.1177/1362361309103795 PMID: 19369388

Ramsay, J. R., & Rostain, A. (2008). *Cognitive-behavioral therapy for adult ADHD: An integrative psychosocial and medical approach*. Routledge/Taylor & Francis Group. New York, NY: Routledge.

Raymaker, D. M., Teo, A. R., Steckler, N. A., Lentz, B., Scharer, M., Santos, A. D., Kapp, S. K., Hunter, M., Joyce, A., & Nicolaidis, C. (2020). "Having all of your internal resources exhausted beyond measure and being left with no clean-up crew": Defining autistic burnout. *Autism in Adulthood: Challenges and Management*, *2*(2), 1–12. DOI: 10.1089/aut.2019.0079 PMID: 32851204

Rogers, C., Lepherd, L., Ganguly, R., & Jacob-Rogers, S. (2017). Perinatal issues for women with high functioning autism spectrum disorder. *Women and Birth : Journal of the Australian College of Midwives*, *30*(2), e89–e95. DOI: 10.1016/j.wombi.2016.09.009 PMID: 27751685

Ros-DeMarize, R., Garcia, A., & Graziano, P. A. (2022). The impact of parental ADHD symptoms on Parenting practices and stress after behavioral intervention: Comparisons across co-occurring presentations. *Journal of Child and Family Studies*, *31*(7), 1869–1879. DOI: 10.1007/s10826-021-02217-6

Rosqvist, H. B., & Lövgren, V. (2013). Doing adulthood through parenthood: Notions of parenthood among people with cognitive disabilities. *Alter (Paris)*, *7*(1), 56–68. DOI: 10.1016/j.alter.2012.11.002

Safren, S. A., Perlman, C. A., Sprich, S., & Otto, M. W. (2005). *Mastering your adult ADHD: A cognitive-behavioral treatment program*. Oxford University Press.

Schilling, R. F., Schinke, S. P., Blythe, B. J., & Barth, R. P. (1982). Child maltreatment and mentally retarded parents: Is there a relationship? *Mental Retardation*, *20*(5), 201. PMID: 6757649

Schweitzer, J. B., Faber, T. L., Grafton, S. T., Tune, L. E., Hoffman, J. M., & Kilts, C. D. (2000). Alterations in the functional anatomy of working memory in adult attention deficit hyperactivity disorder. *The American Journal of Psychiatry*, *157*(2), 278–280. DOI: 10.1176/appi.ajp.157.2.278 PMID: 10671402

Shokrkon, A., & Nicoladis, E. (2022). The directionality of the relationship between executive functions and language skills: A literature review. *Frontiers in Psychology*, *13*, 848696. DOI: 10.3389/fpsyg.2022.848696 PMID: 35928417

Sibley, M. H., Ross, J. M., Gnagy, E. M., Dixon, L. J., Conn, B., & Pelham, W. E.Jr. (2013). An intensive summer treatment program for ADHD reduces parent–adolescent conflict. *Journal of Psychopathology and Behavioral Assessment*, *35*(1), 10–19. DOI: 10.1007/s10862-012-9314-5

Silverman, C. (2015). Steve Silberman, NeuroTribes: The Legacy of Autism and the Future of Neurodiversity. *Anthropological Quarterly*, *88*(4), 1111–1122. DOI: 10.1353/anq.2015.0057

Singer, J. (2016). *Neurodiversity: The birth of an idea.* [Kindle edition].

Smith, A. (2009). The empathy imbalance hypothesis of autism: A theoretical approach to cognitive and emotional empathy in autistic development. *The Psychological Record*, *59*(3), 489–510. DOI: 10.1007/BF03395675

Smith, E., Koerting, J., Latter, S., Knowles, M. M., McCann, D. C., Thompson, M., & Sonuga-Barke, E. J. (2015). Overcoming barriers to effective early parenting interventions for attention-deficit hyperactivity disorder (ADHD): Parent and practitioner views. *Child: Care, Health and Development*, *41*(1), 93–102. DOI: 10.1111/cch.12146 PMID: 24814640

Sonuga-Barke, E. J., Daley, D., & Thompson, M. (2002). Does maternal ADHD reduce the effectiveness of parent training for preschool children's ADHD? *Journal of the American Academy of Child and Adolescent Psychiatry*, *41*(6), 696–702. DOI: 10.1097/00004583-200206000-00009 PMID: 12049444

Talcer, M. C., Duffy, O., & Pedlow, K. (2021). A qualitative exploration into the sensory experiences of autistic mothers. *Journal of Autism and Developmental Disorders*. Advance online publication. DOI: 10.1007/s10803-021-05188-1 PMID: 34251566

Tallal, P. (1985). Auditory temporal perception, phonics and reading disabilities in children. *Brain and Language*, *9*(2), 182–198. DOI: 10.1016/0093-934X(80)90139-X PMID: 7363063

Tasiou, K., & Nikolaou, E. N. (2023). Psychological resilience of families of children with attention deficit hyperactivity disorder. In *New trends and approaches in child and adult psychopathology and mental health* (pp. 99–121). Gutenberg.

Tasiou, K., & Nikolaou, E. N. (2025). Well-Being Among Parents Raising a Child Diagnosed With Attention Deficit Hyperactivity Disorder (ADHD) and Intervention Programs: A Literature Review. In *Exploring Cognitive and Psychosocial Dynamics Across Childhood and Adolescence*, (pp. 229-248). IGI Global.

Theule, J., Wiener, J., Rogers, M. A., & Marton, I. (2011). Predicting parenting stress in families of children with ADHD: Parent and contextual factors. *Journal of Child and Family Studies*, *20*(5), 640–647. DOI: 10.1007/s10826-010-9439-7

Thom-Jones, S., Brownlow, C., & Abel, S. (2026). Experiences of autistic parents, from conception to raising adult children: A systematic review of the literature. *Autism in Adulthood: Challenges and Management*, *8*(3), 284–304. DOI: 10.1089/aut.2024.0181

Thompson, M. J. J., Laver-Bradbury, C., Ayres, M., Le Poidevin, E., Mead, S., Dodds, C., & Weeks, A. (2009). A small-scale randomized controlled trial of the revised new forest parenting programme for preschoolers with attention deficit hyperactivity disorder. *European Child & Adolescent Psychiatry*, *18*(10), 605–616. DOI: 10.1007/s00787-009-0020-0 PMID: 19404717

Tung, I., Brammer, W. A., Li, J. J., & Lee, S. S. (2015). Parenting behaviour mediates the intergenerational association of parent and child offspring ADHD symptoms. *Journal of Clinical Child and Adolescent Psychology : The Official Journal for the Society of Clinical Child and Adolescent Psychology, American Psychological Association, Division 53*, *44*(5), 787–799. DOI: 10.1080/15374416.2014.913250 PMID: 24926775

Tymchuk, A. J. (1992). Predicting adequacy of parenting by people with mental retardation. *Child Abuse & Neglect*, *16*(2), 165–178. DOI: 10.1016/0145-2134(92)90025-M PMID: 1559166

Tymchuk, A. J., & Feldman, M. A. (1991). Parents with mental retardation and their children: Review of research relevant to professional practice. *Canadian Psychology = Psychologie Canadienne*, *32*(3), 486–496. DOI: 10.1037/h0079023

Unger, O., & Howes, C. (1988). Mother-Child Interactions and Symbolic Play between Toddlers and Their Adolescent or Mentally Retarded Mothers. *The Occupational Therapy Journal of Research*, *8*(4), 237–249. DOI: 10.1177/153944928800800405

van den Hoofdakker, B. J., Nauta, M. H., Veen-Mulders, L., van der Sytema, S., Emmelkamp, P. M. G., Minderaa, R. B., & Hoekstra, P. J. (2009). Behavioral parent training as an adjunct to routine care in children with attention-deficit/hyperactivity disorder: Moderators of treatment response. [PubMed: 19633060]. *Journal of Pediatric Psychology*, *35*(3), 317–326. DOI: 10.1093/jpepsy/jsp060 PMID: 19633060

Veenstra-VanderWeele, J. (2018). Recognizing the problem of suicidality in autism spectrum disorder. *Journal of the American Academy of Child and Adolescent Psychiatry*, *57*(5), 302–303. DOI: 10.1016/j.jaac.2018.03.003 PMID: 29706156

Walker, N. (2021). *Neuroqueer heresies: Notes on the neurodiversity paradigm, autistic empowerment, and postnormal possibilities*. Autonomous Press. Weird Books for Weird People.

Weiss, M., Hechtman, L., & Weiss, G. (2000). ADHD in parents. *Journal of the American Academy of Child and Adolescent Psychiatry*, *39*(8), 1059–1061. DOI: 10.1097/00004583-200008000-00023 PMID: 10939236

Williamson, D., & Johnston, C. (2019). Maternal ADHD symptoms and parenting stress: The roles of parenting self-efficacy beliefs and neuroticism. *Journal of Attention Disorders*, *23*(5), 493–505. DOI: 10.1177/1087054717693373 PMID: 28201945

Woods, K. E., Mazursky-Horowitz, H., Thomas, S. R., Dougherty, L. R., & Chronis-Tuscano, A. (2019). The unique effects of maternal ADHD symptoms and emotion dysregulation on parenting behavior. *Journal of Attention Disorders*. Advance online publication. DOI: 10.1177/1087054719829820 PMID: 30762448

Wymbs, B. T., Dawson, A. E., Egan, T. E., Sacchetti, G. M., Tams, S. T., & Wymbs, F. A. (2017). ADHD and depression symptoms in parent couples predict response to child ADHD and ODD behavior. *Journal of Abnormal Child Psychology*, *45*(3), 471–484. DOI: 10.1007/s10802-016-0220-2 PMID: 27796690

Zaidman-Zait, A., & Shilo, I. (2018). Parental ADHD symptoms and inhibitory control in relation to parenting among mothers of children with and without ADHD. *Journal of Attention Disorders*, *39*. Advance online publication. DOI: 10.1177/1087054718808063 PMID: 30442044

Chapter 5
Interconnected Minds:
Executive Function, Memory, and Learning in Neurodiverse Childhoods

Phillip James Marais
http://orcid.org/0000-0002-2872-6220
Independent Researcher, Ireland

ABSTRACT

This chapter examines inclusive education through the lens of cognitive architecture, focusing on how neurodiverse learners interact with learning environments that implicitly assume tightly integrated executive, attentional, linguistic, and memory systems. Drawing on contemporary models of executive function, memory and retrieval, attention regulation, and mutualistic coupling, it argues that many educational barriers arise not from deficits in ability, but from persistent mismatches between instructional design and the internal coordination demands placed on learners. The chapter critically evaluates prominent inclusive and neuro-affirming frameworks, including Universal Design for Learning (UDL), FEDIS+R, and dignity-oriented approaches, acknowledging their ethical and structural contributions while highlighting limitations in cognitive specificity. In so doing, the chapter positions inclusive education as an evidence-informed reconfiguration of learning environments – one that supports durable, transferable, and meaningful engagement for cognitively diverse learners.

DOI: 10.4018/979-8-3373-7072-9.ch005

INTRODUCTION

Learning – during childhood or adulthood – is neither a singular act nor simply the passive accumulation of information (Kievit et al., 2017; Peng & Kievit, 2019). Rather, learning emerges through the coordinated activity of at least six – attention, executive function (EF), memory, language, motor control, and social cognition (American Psychiatric Association, 2013) – different cognitive domains which, together, allow an individual to attend, interpret, understand, retain, and react to select information (Arciuli, 2017; Davidson & Souza, 2024; Demetriou et al., 2018; Desaunay et al., 2020; Duan et al., 2025; Geng et al., 2024; Holmes et al., 2021; Leung et al., 2016).

Combined, these systems form a kind of dynamic cognitive architecture which underpins not only semantic, somatic, and behavioural learning but also emotional regulation, social participation, and adaptive functioning (Demetriou et al., 2019; Kievit et al., 2017; Leung et al., 2016; Powell et al., 2022). In neurodevelopmental disorders, variation within the proverbial architecture becomes particularly apparent, revealing forms of cognition that diverge from more normative expectations, though – and this is important – may remain internally coherent and developmentally meaningful (Astle et al., 2022; Florian & Black-Hawkins, 2011; Holmes et al., 2021; Praslova, 2024).

When this architecture meets the ever-increasing demands of the classroom, learners find themselves needing to attend to verbal instruction, integrate new information with previously developed schema, manage competing task demands, as well as regulate the sensory demands present within the setting (Anderson, 2002; Astle et al., 2022; Davidson & Souza, 2024; Demetriou et al., 2019; Schmitt et al., 2018). Such demands are often challenging for children – neurotypical or neurodiverse – but can be particularly so for children who might otherwise express these architectural variations (Geng et al., 2024; Leung et al., 2016; Powell et al., 2022; Schmitt et al., 2018).

When these systems and structures operate in concert, learning can proceed with relative efficiency (Anderson, 2002; Holmes et al., 2021; Kievit et al., 2017). However, when these systems are instead unevenly developed, contextually fragile, function in isolation, or have simply developed within a context based on alternative assumptions, learning can become effortful and highly dependent on environmental conditions – a phenomenon regularly observed in individuals with neurodiverse needs, where attention and regulation are often particularly sensitive to interest, sensory load, emotional state, and where executive functioning varies markedly across task contexts, or where the internal use of language for self-guidance may be similarly inconsistent (Donahoe & Palmer, 2022; Eigsti & Irvine, 2022; Joseph et al., 2005; Mareva et al., 2024).

With such needs in mind, it is important to note that neurodevelopmental conditions such as Autism Spectrum Disorder (ASD), Attention-Deficit/Hyperactivity Disorder (ADHD), Developmental Language Disorder (DLD), and Specific Learning Disorders (SLD) – to name a few – are often discussed as discrete diagnostic entities (Demetriou et al., 2018; Holmes et al., 2021). However, such categorical distinctions can obscure the extent to which these conditions share overlapping cognitive features – particularly when mapped onto the six cognitive domains (Demetriou et al., 2018; Holmes et al., 2021; Ullman et al., 2020). Children who differ diagnostically may nonetheless encounter similar challenges in sustaining attention, organising information, or flexibly adapting to changing task demands (Akbar et al., 2013; Geurts et al., 2005; Holmes et al., 2021; Ullman et al., 2020). On the other hand, children who share a diagnosis may display strikingly different cognitive profiles (Bal et al., 2022; Demetriou et al., 2019; Holmes et al., 2021).

In acknowledgement of this, ongoing discourse regarding neurodevelopmental needs has begun to reflect a move toward more transdiagnostic and dimensional approaches (Demetriou et al., 2019; Holmes et al., 2021; Sokolova et al., 2017). Rather than diagnostic categories, such approaches emphasise the various dimensional criteria and characteristics shared amongst these disorders (Demetriou et al., 2019; Holmes et al., 2021; Kushki et al., 2019; Sokolova et al., 2017). In turn, this has prompted a shift in how neurocognitive diversity is understood and how learning difficulties are conceptualised (Florian & Black-Hawkins, 2011; Holmes et al., 2021).

The notion of Mutualistic Coupling provides one framework through which this might be better understood (Holmes et al., 2021; Kievit et al., 2017). Mutualistic Coupling argues that these six cognitive domains do not develop in isolation, but rather that each domain has a bidirectional relationship with each other domain (Holmes et al., 2021; Kievit et al., 2017, 2019; Peng & Kievit, 2019). In other words, while a given task might rely more heavily on one domain over the others, no singular task is likely to rely exclusively on one domain and – as a result, these cognitive domains are trained and developed in tandem (Anderson, 2002; Davidson & Souza, 2024; Holmes et al., 2021; Kievit et al., 2017).

At its foundation, the Mutualistic Coupling Framework explains neurodiversity as a kind of atypical variation in the relationship between the domains – a variation which might allow for a domain to be activated without the otherwise necessary support of others, or without sufficient regulation of the interaction between domains (Desaunay et al., 2020; Eigsti & Irvine, 2022; Joseph et al., 2005; Kozunova et al., 2023; Williams et al., 2006). This might, for example, explain why individuals with neurodiverse tendencies are more likely to remember seemingly arbitrary pieces of information – or why interest is often so necessary to maintain attention (Bal et al., 2022; Desaunay et al., 2020; Friedman & Sterling, 2019).

Holmes et al. (2021) – among others such as Kievit et al. (2019) – included within this framework more external and environmental considerations. More specifically, they argue that the environment can be treated as a kind of moderating or mediating domain, one which might influence the relationship between each of the six cognitive domains. Essentially, they argue that the environment can prevent or detract from the appropriate activation of any of these domains – a simple example might be that a classroom that is too loud, might make it challenging for an individual to appropriately attend to verbal instruction or other executive functions. Likewise, they argue that a sufficiently enriched environment could promote the coupling effect seen between the cognitive domains, which, in turn, benefits school outcomes as well as the developmental needs of the children within the environment (Donahoe & Palmer, 2022; Duan et al., 2025; Holmes et al., 2021; Kievit et al., 2019).

Through this lens, educational success or difficulty is not attributed solely to individual capacity, but rather reflects the degree to which classrooms support – or fail to support – the coordination of these domains (Florian & Black-Hawkins, 2011). This, in turn, invites a re-examination of educational practice, and extends inclusive education beyond placement or accommodation to consider the very assumptions of cognition otherwise embedded within curricula, pedagogy, and assessment (Paas et al., 2003). When educational practices presume uniformity in cognitive functioning, neurodiverse learners are required to adapt to systems not designed with their profiles in mind. When, however, cognitive variability is anticipated and valued, teaching can be structured to support multiple routes to mutualistic coupling and, in so doing, promote engagement and learning (Paas et al., 2003). Such approaches recognise that neurodiversity is not peripheral to education but must be central to its design.

Then, by examining several of the domains – EF, Memory, Attention, and Language – intrinsic to the learning process as interdependent, this chapter places learning within a broader neurocognitive and developmental context. In so doing, it also advances an account of inclusion grounded not in standardisation but in responsiveness to cognitive diversity, recognising that educational environments shape, and are shaped by, the ways children think, learn, and engage with the world.

NEUROCOGNITIVE DIVERSITY IN INCLUSIVE EDUCATION

The discourse and practice of inclusive education is inextricably linked to the understanding of the "need" – as the very foundation of inclusive education is aimed at addressing special or additional needs (Florian & Black-Hawkins, 2011; Hamilton & Petty, 2023). These additional needs represent complex challenges to an individual's ability learn or engage with their environment, and – at least through the lens of mutualistic coupling – emerge at the point of contact between a learner's neurocognitive profile and the educational environment (Donahoe & Palmer, 2022; Holmes et al., 2021; Kievit et al., 2017; Praslova, 2024). Issues arise, then, when that same environment has been designed upon more narrow assumptions regarding attention, regulation, communication, and pace (Hamilton & Petty, 2023; Kozunova et al., 2023).

With this in mind, the purpose of inclusive education is, then, to create a system capable of meeting a multidimensional array of cognitive, sensory, relational, and psychological needs – many of which might, ironically, only be noticed when the system fails to accommodate (Geng et al., 2024; Praslova, 2024; Powell et al., 2022; Syriopoulou-Delli & Filiou, 2022).

Cognitive Needs

At the cognitive level, inclusive education must account for variation across the six cognitive domains – attention, EF, memory, language, motor control, and social cognition (Arciuli, 2017; Davidson & Souza, 2024; Demetriou et al., 2018; Holmes et al., 2021). While evidence exists to argue that these domains tend to be linked, it is important to remember that many neurodivergent learners may exhibit or express a kind of "spiky" cognitive profile – one where the association between these domains can vary in atypical ways (Almeida et al., 2019; Eigsti & Irvine, 2022; Holmes et al., 2021; Joseph et al., 2005; Kievit et al., 2017). In other words, many neurodiverse learners may experience areas of pronounced strength alongside significant challenges in working memory, inhibitory control, cognitive flexibility, or temporal processing (Adams & Jarrold, 2012; Bal et al., 2022; Davidson & Souza, 2024; Demetriou et al., 2019; Schmitt et al., 2018).

Within more traditional classrooms, these differences are frequently misinterpreted as either poor effort or inconsistent ability. Yet from a cognitive load perspective, such environments often impose excessive extraneous load – mental effort expended navigating instructions that are interpreted as unclear, a space that is experienced as cluttered, pacing that feels unpredictable, and sensory demands which might be distracting (Kozunova et al., 2023; Le Cunff et al., 2025b; Mayer & Moreno, 2003).

To account for this, inclusive practice requires the deliberate management of cognitive load by providing a clear structure, visual supports, appropriately chunked instructions, and external scaffolds for time blindness and task initiation (Mayer & Pilegard, 2005; Powell et al., 2022). Models such as FEDIS+R provide a kind of guideline, allowing those involved in inclusive practices to more easily identify and reduce design-related cognitive burdens so that learners' executive resources can prioritise learning (Le Cunff et al., 2025b).

This framework deals broadly with six interlocking pillars (Le Cunff et al., 2025b). The first of these, Format, emphasises multimodal presentation – and can be achieved by ensuring that content is delivered using multiple different forms of media (Le Cunff et al., 2025b). The second pillar, Environment, targets attentional regulation by reducing visual noise and extraneous stimuli in both physical and digital spaces (Le Cunff et al., 2025b; Mokhtari & Parchini, 2024). In other words, attention can be supported by maintaining an appropriate level of stimuli, though this can be challenging when different learners within the same space have different levels of requisite stimulus and different maximum thresholds of stimulus (Kozunova et al., 2023). Delivery addresses temporal load through the Segmenting Principle, ensuring that information is presented in digestible units with adequate processing time. Instruction reduces executive ambiguity by making expectations explicit through advance organisers, clear curricula, and transparent assessment criteria (Root et al., 2021). Support recognises the prevalence of masked difficulty, embedding regular check-ins, timely feedback, and equitable access to assistive technologies (Le Cunff et al., 2025b). Finally, Research (+R) commits the model to participatory evaluation, positioning neurodivergent learners as co-creators and using empirical indicators of cognitive effort to guide ongoing refinement (Le Cunff et al., 2025b).

In other words, Cognitive accessibility cannot be separated from sensory and physiological regulation (Kozunova et al., 2023). For many neurodivergent children, the classroom is not merely distracting but actively dysregulating. Fluorescent lighting, background noise, visual clutter, or restricted opportunities for movement may trigger sensory overload or shutdown long before academic engagement even becomes possible (Kozunova et al., 2023). Inclusive environments must therefore treat sensory safety as foundational rather than supplementary, and this, in turn, involves more intentional environmental architecture – designated zones for differing levels of stimulation, more simplified visual displays, and potentially providing access to movement.

Communication

Relational and communicative needs further complicate the picture, particularly when inclusion is conflated with social compliance (Demetriou et al., 2018; Leung et al., 2016). The Double Empathy Problem challenges more traditional approaches to expression and neurotypical communication, suggesting that social difficulty arises from a reciprocal misunderstanding between neurotypes rather than from unilateral deficits.

Inclusive education must therefore reconceptualise communication as a shared responsibility, validating multiple communicative modalities – speech, writing, gesture, Augmentative and Alternative Communication (AAC) – and prioritising clarity, directness, and predictability (Almeida et al., 2019). It must also, then, dismantle the expectation of masking. There is a sufficiently robust body of literature which has linked the sustained suppression of natural regulatory behaviours to anxiety, burnout, and diminished quality of life (Bal et al., 2022). Put simply, psychological safety must be treated as a prerequisite for genuine inclusion.

These relational dynamics highlight the importance of psychological safety as a precondition for learning, and as such, the presence of emotionally attuned, self-regulated adults serves as a powerful co-regulatory resource, particularly for children who struggle with emotional modulation (Demetriou et al., 2018). In a similar fashion, predictable routines, transparent expectations, and consistent responses reduce the cognitive and emotional load required for learning in a diverse classroom (Demetriou et al., 2018).

Building on this emphasis on regulation and predictability, Universal Design for Learning (UDL) highlights the importance of learning environments as intentionally structured environments, which must support cognitive and emotional readiness for diverse learners (Gilbert, 2019; Schuck & Fung, 2024). UDL's central premise is that learner variability is both inevitable and predictable, and that curricula should therefore be designed to accommodate a wide range of cognitive, sensory, and motivational profiles from the outset (Gilbert, 2019; Schuck & Fung, 2024).

Functionally, UDL operates through three interdependent principles: multiple means of engagement, representation, and action or expression (Kennette & Wilson, 2019; Root et al., 2021). Together, these principles address why learners engage, how information is encountered, and how understanding is demonstrated, to reduce unnecessary cognitive friction (Kennette & Wilson, 2019). By providing varied routes into content, ensuring information remains perceptible and interpretable across processing differences, and decoupling assessment from narrow modes of performance, UDL redirects limited executive and emotional resources toward meaning-making rather than task navigation (Kennette & Wilson, 2019; Root et al., 2021).

Instructional design represents the point at which these diverse needs converge most visibly (Kennette & Wilson, 2019). UDL offers a principled framework for translating neuro-affirming values into concrete pedagogical practice (Hamilton & Petty, 2023; Syriopoulou-Delli & Filiou, 2022). By providing multiple means of engagement, representation, and action or expression, UDL seeks to decouple learning outcomes from narrow formats (Gilbert, 2019; Kennette & Wilson, 2019). In doing so, it addresses a persistent inequity in education: the tendency to mistake difficulty with a medium for difficulty with content (Kennette & Wilson, 2019). When learners are offered meaningful choices in how they access material and demonstrate understanding—whether through written work, oral presentation, visual artefact, or creative project—the curriculum becomes a site of access rather than exclusion (Gilbert, 2019; Root et al., 2021).

When compared to UDL, FEDIS+R is arguably more specific - at least as far as the actual mechanics of instructional design are concerned. While UDL operates through three broad principles to meet predictable learner variability, the FEDIS+R pillars such as "Delivery" and "Environment" are arguably more sensitive to attentional loads that often overwhelm neurodiverse learners. For instance, while UDL might suggest "representation" through various media, FEDIS+R's "Delivery" pillar specifically applies the Segmenting Principle to ensure information is presented in discrete units, each allocated adequate processing time. In many ways, FEDIS+R acts as a functional extension of UDL, translating its values into a model that explicitly accounts for the limited executive resources of neurodivergent students.

However, both models risk superficial application if they are not appropriately understood in relation to the way in which cognitive systems like memory and language interact. Moreover, both models require significant institutional flexibility and educator training to be implemented effectively. While UDL focuses on creating a learning community for everybody from the outset, the strength of FEDIS+R lies in its commitment to using empirical research to bridge the gap between theoretical inclusive principles and the functional cognitive needs of neurodiverse learners.

Inclusive Pedagogy extends this logic further, rejecting the notion that such flexibility should be reserved for a subset of students (Hamilton & Petty, 2023). Instead, it argues for an "everybody" approach, in which what is ordinarily available is sufficiently rich, flexible, and varied to accommodate all learners without stigma (Hamilton & Petty, 2023).

Finally, inclusive education must be understood as inherently systemic and intersectional (Hamilton & Petty, 2023; Praslova, 2024). Neurodivergent learners do not encounter educational systems as abstract individuals; their experiences are shaped by race, gender, socioeconomic status, and cultural context (Austin et al., 2014; Demetriou et al., 2019; Kennette & Wilson, 2019). Behaviour interpreted as defiance or disengagement is often filtered through these lenses, leading to disproportionate exclusion and misidentification (Florian & Black-Hawkins, 2011; Mareva et al., 2024). A genuinely inclusive framework must therefore remain attentive to how power, bias, and access intersect with neurodiversity, and must resist deterministic narratives that place artificial limits on learning potential (Hamilton & Petty, 2023).

EXECUTIVE FUNCTION IN NEURODEVELOPMENTAL DISORDERS

Within classroom settings, some of the most consequential barriers to learning are not rooted in knowledge, ability, or indeed, within the deficit thereof – but rather in the capacity to organise and regulate behaviour across time (Anderson, 2002; Demetriou et al., 2018; Le Cunff et al., 2025). Beginning a task without external prompting, holding multiple instructions in mind, inhibiting impulsive responses, adapting when an initial strategy fails, and persisting through frustration all require the coordination of executive resources (Anderson, 2002; Austin et al., 2014; Demetriou et al., 2019; Schmitt et al., 2018).

These demands are continuous, and often implicit, while still influencing whether learning can be initiated, sustained, and brought to completion (Arciuli, 2017; Batterink et al., 2019; Davidson & Souza, 2024; Holmes et al., 2021). Executive function occupies this organising role, operating as a set of higher-order processes that support goal-directed behaviour through the regulation of attention, working memory, inhibition, cognitive flexibility, emotional modulation, and self-monitoring (Anderson, 2002; Demetriou et al., 2018, 2019; Holmes et al., 2021). Because these processes unfold in constant interaction with sensory, linguistic, and affective systems, executive functioning has become central to both neurocognitive accounts of learning and to inclusive educational practice (Davidson & Souza, 2024; Demetriou et al., 2018; Mareva et al., 2024).

Early models conceptualised EF as a unitary "central executive," often associated with frontal lobe functioning (Anderson, 2002; Demetriou et al., 2019; Luria, 1966). Contemporary accounts, however, have largely abandoned this view in favour of fractionated models that recognise EF as a constellation of partially independent but interrelated processes (Anderson, 2002; Demetriou et al., 2019; Miyake et al., 2000). This shift has been particularly important for understanding neurodivergent profiles, where executive strengths and challenges rarely move in lockstep – see previous discussion regarding the mutualistic coupling framework (Demetriou et al., 2018; Holmes et al., 2021; Kievit et al., 2017; Peng & Kievit, 2019).

Unity and Diversity Model

One of the early but most influential frameworks in this regard is the Unity and Diversity model proposed by Miyake et al. (2000). This model identifies three distinct, yet correlated, core executive components – shifting (cognitive flexibility), updating (working memory), and inhibition (Austin et al., 2014; Demetriou et al., 2019; Friedman & Sterling, 2019; Holmes et al., 2021; Miyake et al., 2000). In neurotypical development, these components tend to integrate over time, supporting increasingly flexible and efficient goal-directed behaviour (Anderson, 2002; Demetriou et al., 2018; Holmes et al., 2021; Kozunova et al., 2023; Schmitt et al., 2018). In neurodivergent populations, however, this integration is often attenuated (Demetriou et al., 2018, 2019; Kozunova et al., 2023). For example, autistic individuals frequently show pronounced difficulties with set-shifting and flexibility, while basic inhibitory control may remain relatively intact (Adams & Jarrold, 2012; Barron-Linnankoski et al., 2015; Demetriou et al., 2019; Joseph et al., 2005; Schmitt et al., 2018). Individuals with ADHD, by comparison, often exhibit marked challenges with inhibition and working memory (Demetriou et al., 2018; Friedman & Sterling, 2019; Geurts et al., 2005; Kozunova et al., 2023; Schmitt et al., 2018).

A distinction between "hot" and "cold" EFs arises within existing literature, which might further refine such an approach by accounting for both emotional arousal, and motivation (Austin et al., 2014; Demetriou et al., 2019; Kozunova et al., 2023). Cold EFs refer to those regulatory operations that support goal-directed behaviour in the absence of relevant emotional or motivational cues (Kozunova et al., 2023). On the other hand, hot executive functions are engaged when regulation must occur in contexts imbued with personal significance, reward, risk, or social consequence (Demetriou et al., 2019; Kozunova et al., 2023). These include affective decision-making, delay of gratification, emotional regulation, and the capacity to navigate social situations that require rapid interpretation of others' intentions or responses (Demetriou et al., 2019; Kozunova et al., 2023).

Within such contexts, executive control must integrate cognitive evaluation with emotional and motivational signals, rendering performance more sensitive to stress, uncertainty, and relational dynamics (Demetriou et al., 2019; Kozunova et al., 2023). For many neurodivergent individuals – particularly those with autism, or those who experience difficulties with reciprocal communication – cool EFs may appear relatively intact under structured conditions, while hot EFs may present with challenges (Demetriou et al., 2019; Kozunova et al., 2023; Leung et al., 2016). Difficulties with delay of gratification, affective decision-making, or emotional regulation often persist even when formal problem-solving skills are strong (Demetriou et al., 2019; Kozunova et al., 2023).

Proactive-Reactive Control Model

Such vulnerabilities are especially observable when considered alongside the Proactive–Reactive Control model (Schmitt et al., 2018). This framework distinguishes between reactive control, which involves stopping or correcting behaviour after a cue appears, and proactive control, which involves strategically slowing or modulating behaviour in anticipation of potential conflict (Schmitt et al., 2018). Research suggests that many autistic individuals demonstrate intact reactive control – they can stop a response as efficiently as neurotypical peers when explicitly cued – but show impairments in proactive control (Adams & Jarrold, 2012; Schmitt et al., 2018). This leads to an "all-or-nothing" behavioural profile, where responses are either fully engaged or abruptly halted, with limited anticipatory modulation (Schmitt et al., 2018). In classroom settings, this pattern may appear as rigidity, difficulty with transitions, or apparent impulsivity, particularly under conditions of uncertainty (Anderson, 2002; Barron-Linnankoski et al., 2015; Demetriou et al., 2019; Schmitt et al., 2018).

To provide a precise account of these challenges, practitioners must distinguish between reactive and proactive control. For instance, Adams and Jarrold (2012) found that children with ASD often demonstrate more limited reactive control - that is the ability to stop an action in response to an immediate and external signal - but show significant deficits in proactive control - the anticipatory slowing of behavior in preparation for difficulty. In more simplified terms, Adams and Jarrold (2012) found that autistic children often struggled with impulsivity and intrusive thoughts.

This does explain why neurodiverse learners may struggle with distractors even when they can follow a direct "stop" command. Inclusive design must therefore provide explicit - and multimodal - chronometric supports, such as visual timers or countdowns, now-then signs, visual schedules, auditory confirmations. These supports help provide the proactive management with which the learner may otherwise struggle.

Hierarchical Competing Systems Model

The Hierarchical Competing Systems Model offers a complementary lens by emphasising the interaction between automatic, habit-based systems and higher-level, language-mediated control (Friedman & Sterling, 2019; Marcovitch & Zelazo, 2009). In neurotypical development, internalised language increasingly supports the regulation of behaviour, allowing reflective processes to override habitual responses with minimal effort (Eigsti & Irvine, 2022; Friedman & Sterling, 2019). In some neurodivergent individuals, however, access to automatic social-cognitive processes is reduced, necessitating heavier reliance on explicit, verbally mediated strategies (Eigsti & Irvine, 2022; Joseph et al., 2005; Russell, 1997). While this can support high-level reasoning, it also renders executive control vulnerable to overload when the verbal channel is simultaneously required for instruction, social navigation, or emotional processing (Almeida et al., 2019; Eigsti & Irvine, 2022). Educational environments that rely heavily on rapid verbal instruction without visual or structural supports may therefore inadvertently exhaust the very system neurodivergent learners depend upon most (Almeida et al., 2019; Jain et al., 2024; Le Cunff et al., 2025; Root et al., 2021).

Task Supporting Hypothesis

Finally, the Task Support Hypothesis draws attention to the role of environmental scaffolding at the point of retrieval (Almeida et al., 2019; Desaunay et al., 2020). Neurodivergent learners, particularly those with autism, often show marked difficulties with unsupported tasks such as free recall, which require self-initiated organisation and planning (Almeida et al., 2019; Barron-Linnankoski et al., 2015; Desaunay et al., 2020; Joseph et al., 2005). When appropriate cues, prompts, or recognition formats are provided, performance frequently approaches neurotypical levels (Almeida et al., 2018; Almeida et al., 2019; Desaunay et al., 2020). This pattern reinforces a central theme of inclusive education: executive "deficits" often reflect insufficient task support rather than intrinsic limitation (Almeida et al., 2018; Desaunay et al., 2020). When environments are designed to cue, structure, and prompt executive processes externally – as advocated by UDL and FEDIS+R frameworks – differences in outcome narrow substantially (Almeida et al., 2019; Kennette & Wilson, 2019; Root et al., 2021).

Almeida et al. (2019) actually provide a good example of exactly this. In their paper, they find that "cued invitations" targeting previously mentioned details as contextual clues help autistic children recall more detail, especially compared to more broad and open-ended questions.

Across these accounts, executive functioning arises as a context-sensitive system rather than a fixed internal capacity (Anderson, 2002; Demetriou et al., 2018, 2019; Holmes et al., 2021). Differences in regulation are shaped by how cognitive, emotional, linguistic, and environmental demands are configured, with performance varying accordingly across task types and settings (Demetriou et al., 2019; Kozunova et al., 2023). What appears as executive difficulty is often better understood as a mismatch between internal regulatory resources and external expectations, particularly where demands for anticipation, self-initiation, or emotional modulation are left implicit (Sayers et al., 2011; Schmitt et al., 2018). From this perspective, inclusive education is not concerned with remediating executive function as an isolated trait, but with designing environments that make organisational demands visible, shared, and supportable (Hamilton & Petty, 2023). By externalising structure, providing meaningful task support, and reducing unnecessary cognitive and affective load, educational practice can align more closely with the ways executive processes are differentially organised, allowing learning to be judged by understanding rather than by endurance (Desaunay et al., 2020; Le Cunff et al., 2025; Root et al., 2021).

MEMORY AND RETRIEVAL SYSTEMS

Memory is not a singular faculty but a dynamic system of encoding, consolidation, and retrieval processes that together enable learning to persist beyond the moment of instruction (Arciuli, 2017; Batterink et al., 2019; Desaunay et al., 2020; Earle & Ullman, 2020; Foti et al., 2015). In educational contexts, memory determines whether information can be held long enough to be manipulated, integrated with prior knowledge, and later accessed in meaningful ways (Davidson & Souza, 2024; Desaunay et al., 2020; Le Cunff et al., 2025). Crucially, many of the difficulties experienced by neurodiverse learners do not arise from failures of storage, but from misalignments between how memory is organised in the learner and how retrieval is demanded by the environment (Almeida et al., 2018; Desaunay et al., 2020; Geng et al., 2024; Joseph et al., 2005). Understanding memory through contemporary theoretical models, therefore, offers a powerful lens for inclusive education, one that reframes apparent "forgetting" as a problem of access rather than capacity (Almeida et al., 2018; Desaunay et al., 2020; Geng et al., 2024).

Atkinson-Shiffrin Model of Memory

Traditional structural models of memory, such as the Atkinson–Shiffrin framework, distinguish between short-term memory (STM) and long-term memory (LTM) (Desaunay et al., 2020). In neurotypical cognition, these systems operate mutualistically: information is held temporarily within the STM as it is rehearsed, elaborated, and consolidated into LTM (Desaunay et al., 2020). In neurodiverse populations, however, this integration is often disrupted (Desaunay et al., 2020; Massand & Bowler, 2015). Autistic individuals, for example, frequently demonstrate reduced short-term or immediate memory capacity alongside relatively preserved long-term storage, particularly for semantic information (Desaunay et al., 2020; Geng et al., 2024; Massand & Bowler, 2015). This dissociation produces the often-observed paradox of learners who can recall extensive factual detail yet struggle to follow multi-step instructions or retain information presented rapidly in class (Barron-Linnankoski et al., 2015; Desaunay et al., 2020; Geng et al., 2024; Jain et al., 2024).

Working Memory Models

The limitations of structural models become clearer when memory is examined through working memory and information processing frameworks (Desaunay et al., 2020). Baddeley's multi-component model conceptualises working memory as a system comprising a central executive and modality-specific subsystems for phonological and visuospatial information (Davidson & Souza, 2024; Desaunay et al., 2020; Holmes et al., 2021).

While neurotypical learners tend to distribute processing demands flexibly across these components, neurodivergent learners often display domain-specific vulnerabilities (Barron-Linnankoski et al., 2015; Desaunay et al., 2020; Le Cunff et al., 2025). Some children with ASD, DLD, or specific learning disorders exhibit marked visuospatial working memory limitations alongside relatively intact verbal working memory; others show a more inverted pattern (Barron-Linnankoski et al.,

2015; Desaunay et al., 2020; Holmes et al., 2021; Jain et al., 2024). Such inversions are further exacerbated when sensory or auditory processing differences are present (Davidson & Souza, 2024; Jain et al., 2024). For example, difficulties parsing spoken language place additional strain on working memory, creating a negative feedback loop in which effortful decoding consumes the very resources needed to retain meaning (Davidson & Souza, 2024; Jain et al., 2024).

Retrieval processes introduce a further layer of complexity (Desaunay et al., 2020; Geng et al., 2024; Massand & Bowler, 2015). Dual-process theories of memory distinguish between recollection – a context-rich, conscious re-experiencing of an event – and familiarity – an automatic sense that something has been encountered before without access to contextual detail (Desaunay et al., 2020; Massand & Bowler, 2015). Neurotypical memory retrieval typically draws on both processes in tandem (Massand & Bowler, 2015). By comparison, research suggests that many autistic individuals show reduced recollection alongside preserved, or even enhanced, familiarity-based retrieval (Desaunay et al., 2020; Geng et al., 2024; Massand & Bowler, 2015). This profile explains why neurodiverse learners may recognise correct answers in multiple-choice formats yet struggle with open-ended questions requiring narrative reconstruction or autobiographical detail (Almeida et al., 2019; Desaunay et al., 2020; Geng et al., 2024; Massand & Bowler, 2015).

Task Support Hypothesis

This distinction is made explicit within the Task Support Hypothesis, which has particular relevance for inclusive education as it focuses on memory functionality in individuals with ASD (Bowler et al., 2004, 2010; Desaunay et al., 2020). The hypothesis contrasts unsupported retrieval tasks, such as free recall, with supported retrieval tasks that provide cues, prompts, or recognition options (Almeida et al., 2019; Bowler et al., 2004, 2010; Desaunay et al., 2020). According to Almeida et al. (2019) and Desaunay et al. (2020) – among a small litany of others – neurotypical learners often self-generate organisational strategies during unsupported recall (Almeida et al., 2019; Bowler et al., 2008a; Desaunay et al., 2020; Unsworth, 2016).

Neurodiverse learners, especially those with ASD, frequently do not, despite having intact stored representations (Almeida et al., 2019; Bowler et al., 1997; Desaunay et al., 2020; Minshew & Goldstein, 2001). When appropriate task support is introduced, performance differences narrow dramatically (Almeida et al., 2019; Bowler et al., 2004; Desaunay et al., 2020; Phelan et al., 2011). This finding has profound implications and does suggest that educational failure often reflects insufficient environmental support rather than deficient memory (Almeida et al., 2019; Bowler et al., 2004; Desaunay et al., 2020).

Fuzzy Trace Theory

Moving, then, from how memory is accessed to what memories are actually retrieved, the Fuzzy Trace Theory claims that experiences are encoded simultaneously as verbatim traces, capturing precise surface details, gist traces, and abstract meaning (Almeida et al., 2018; Geng et al., 2024). Neurotypical development involves a gradual shift toward prioritising gist-based retrieval, enabling flexible generalisation and inferential reasoning (Almeida et al., 2019; Geng et al., 2024). Neurodiverse learners, however, may rely more heavily on verbatim traces (Almeida et al., 2019; Geng et al., 2024). Autistic children, for instance, may recall exact phrases, dates, or perceptual details while missing the overarching theme of a narrative or lesson (Desaunay et al., 2020; Geng et al., 2024; Massand & Bowler, 2015). Educational approaches that assume spontaneous gist extraction risk misinterpreting the nature of such miscommunications (Geng et al., 2024).

Memory systems also differ in their degree of conscious accessibility (Batterink et al., 2019; Desaunay et al., 2020). Implicit and explicit learning frameworks distinguish between automatic, unconscious acquisition of patterns and intentional, verbally reportable memory (Arciuli, 2017; Cier et al., 2024; Foti et al., 2015). In neurotypical cognition, implicit learning often feeds into explicit awareness over time (Arciuli, 2017; Cier et al., 2024). In neurodiverse populations, this transfer is less reliable (Cier et al., 2024; Eigsti & Irvine, 2022). Individuals with ASD and DLD frequently demonstrate intact implicit statistical learning – picking up regularities in language or patterns through exposure – while struggling with explicit recall or verbal explanation (Arciuli, 2017; Cier et al., 2024; Earle & Ullman, 2020; Foti et al., 2015). This dissociation is particularly salient in language learning, where children may "know how" to use a structure without being able to articulate it (Arciuli, 2017; Cier et al., 2024; Eigsti & Irvine, 2022). Inclusive education must therefore avoid equating verbal explanation with understanding and should provide opportunities for demonstration through action, modelling, or application rather than solely through declarative recall (Eigsti & Irvine, 2022; Foti et al., 2015; Le Cunff et al., 2025).

Procedural-Declarative Models of Memory

Procedural–declarative memory models highlight compensatory strategies commonly observed in neurodiverse learners (Cier et al., 2024; Earle & Ullman, 2020). Where procedural learning is less efficient – as proposed in the Procedural Deficit Hypothesis for DLD – learners may rely heavily on declarative memory to consciously acquire rules and facts (Cier et al., 2024; Earle & Ullman, 2020). While this strategy can support performance, it does create a system wherein which the individual may be more susceptible to cognitive overload, particularly in fast-paced or language-heavy environments (Cier et al., 2024). Educational systems that reward speed, spontaneity, and automaticity do, as such, penalise learners who are engaging in effortful compensatory processing (Le Cunff et al., 2025). Allowing additional time, reducing linguistic complexity, and supporting automatisation through repetition without penalty are therefore critical inclusion practices.

Finally, memory performance in neurodiverse populations is often modality dependent (Desaunay et al., 2020; Jain et al., 2024). Verbal reporting frequently imposes a disproportionate load, whereas visual, motoric, or recognition-based responses reveal preserved memory (Desaunay et al., 2020; Geng et al., 2024). Autistic individuals, for example, may perform better when memory is expressed through selection, construction, or action rather than speech (Geng et al., 2024; Mokhtari & Parchini, 2024). This reinforces the principle that memory should be understood as distributed across representational systems, not confined to verbal recall (Desaunay et al., 2020; Geng et al., 2024). Inclusive education must therefore legitimise multiple modes of remembering and responding, ensuring that assessment measures memory itself rather than proficiency in a particular output channel (Hamilton & Petty, 2023).

Across these models, a coherent picture arises (Almeida et al., 2019; Baddeley, 1996; Desaunay et al., 2020; Miyake et al., 2000; Wang et al., 2017). Memory difficulties in neurodiverse learners are rarely global or absolute; they are selective, context-sensitive, and deeply influenced by task design (Bal et al., 2022; Boucher & Bowler, 2008; Desaunay et al., 2020; Geng et al., 2024; Narzisi et al., 2012). When educational environments demand unsupported retrieval, transient working memory, verbal reconstruction, and rapid gist extraction simultaneously, they amplify these vulnerabilities (Almeida et al., 2019; Bowler et al., 2004; Brainerd & Reyna, 1990; Desaunay et al., 2020; Eigsti & Irvine, 2022). Conversely, when environments provide structure, cueing, multimodal input, and flexible expression, memory strengths become visible and usable (Almeida et al., 2019; Bowler et al., 2004; Le Cunff et al., 2025; Root et al., 2021; Syriopoulou-Delli & Filiou, 2022). Inclusive education, then, is not a matter of lowering expectations, but of redesigning the conditions under which memory is asked to perform – so that remembering becomes an act of access rather than endurance (Florian & Black-Hawkins, 2011; Hamilton & Petty, 2023).

ATTENTION REGULATION AND LANGUAGE

Attention regulation occupies a central position in learning, serving as the gateway through which information is selected, sustained, and integrated (Anderson, 2002; Davidson & Souza, 2024; Demetriou et al., 2019). Without some degree of attentional stability, memory cannot consolidate, executive control cannot be deployed effectively, and language cannot scaffold higher-order reasoning (Anderson, 2002; Arciuli, 2017; Davidson & Souza, 2024; Eigsti & Irvine, 2022). Attention is not, however, a unitary resource but, rather, reflects the coordinated operation of multiple systems that differ in their sensitivity to novelty, salience, effort, and meaning (Anderson, 2002; Demetriou et al., 2019; Kozunova et al., 2023). For neurodiverse learners, difficulties in education often emerge not because attention is absent, but because it is distributed, regulated, and sustained according to principles that diverge from those implicitly assumed by mainstream classrooms (Joseph et al., 2005; Kozunova et al., 2023; Schmitt et al., 2018).

Posner's Attentional Control Model

More contemporary models of attention regulation reflect this architecture (Anderson, 2002; Demetriou et al., 2019; Kozunova et al., 2023). Posner's attentional control model distinguishes between alerting, orienting, and executive attention (Demetriou et al., 2019; Kozunova et al., 2023). The alerting network supports the maintenance of arousal and readiness, regulating sensitivity to incoming stimuli (Demetriou et al., 2019; Kozunova et al., 2023). In neurodivergent learners, particularly those with autism, this system may be characterised by elevated tonic arousal – that is, a kind of base level of arousal or vigilance – alongside reduced phasic – or temporary alertness following some kind of arousing stimulus – responsiveness (Kozunova et al., 2023).

In more practical terms, this can manifest as a persistent background state of stress or vigilance, coupled with difficulty mobilising attention in response to specific cues. Such patterns help explain why environments that are continuously stimulating may exhaust attentional resources, even when overt demands appear minimal.

The orienting network, by comparison, governs the selection of sensory input, directing attention toward particular locations or features while deprioritising others (Demetriou et al., 2019; Kozunova et al., 2023). In neurodiverse individuals, atypical functioning within this network has been observed from early development, including heightened sensory responsivity (Demetriou et al., 2019; Kozunova et al., 2023; Le Cunff et al., 2025). While such sensitivity may support detailed perception, it can also render environments dense with competing stimuli particularly demanding, as attention is repeatedly drawn toward potentially task-irrelevant features (Adams & Jarrold, 2012; Kozunova et al., 2023; Le Cunff et al., 2025; Mokhtari & Parchini, 2024).

The executive attention network occupies a more explicitly regulatory role, resolving conflict between competing responses and supporting goal-directed behaviour (Demetriou et al., 2019; Kozunova et al., 2023). This system enables the inhibition of habitual responses, the maintenance of task goals, and the prioritisation of information based on contextual relevance (Anderson, 2002; Demetriou et al., 2019; Kozunova et al., 2023). In neurodivergent learners, difficulties within this network are often expressed as challenges with behavioural regulation, particularly under conditions of uncertainty or high cognitive load (Demetriou et al., 2019; Kozunova et al., 2023; Schmitt et al., 2018). Rather than modulating responses proactively, some autistic individuals rely more heavily on reactive control, resulting in patterns of engagement that appear abrupt, rigid, or inconsistent (Adams & Jarrold, 2012; Schmitt et al., 2018).

Shallice's Supervisory Attentional System

Shallice's Supervisory Attentional System (SAS) further clarifies the role of attention in non-routine behaviour (Anderson, 2002; Demetriou et al., 2019). Routine actions are governed by well-learned schemas, requiring little conscious oversight (Demetriou et al., 2019). By comparison, more novel or ambiguous situations demand supervisory control to inhibit habitual responses and select contextually appropriate alternatives (Anderson, 2002; Demetriou et al., 2019). This process is effortful and resource-dependent, requiring the individual to hold task goals in mind while resisting competing cues (Anderson, 2002; Demetriou et al., 2019).

Classrooms, perhaps unintentionally, are rich in such non-routine demands: unexpected transitions, implicit rules, shifting expectations, and socially contingent cues (Barron-Linnankoski et al., 2015; Le Cunff et al., 2025; Sayers et al., 2011). For learners who require greater supervisory input to manage these situations, attention is consumed not by learning itself but by the act of staying oriented within the task environment (Barron-Linnankoski et al., 2015).

Vygotsky and Luria

While the SAS describes how behaviour is interrupted and redirected under non-routine demands, Vygotskian and Lurian accounts clarify instead how such redirection is internally organised (Anderson, 2002; Demetriou et al., 2019). Within these models, language is less of an auxiliary system, and more of a primary medium through which action is represented, monitored, and regulated (Eigsti & Irvine, 2022; Joseph et al., 2005). Inner speech functions as a cognitive scaffold, allowing individuals to hold goals in mind, sequence behaviour, and suppress automatic responses in favour of planned action (Eigsti & Irvine, 2022; Friedman & Sterling, 2019; Joseph et al., 2005). Luria located this capacity within the frontal systems responsible for the programming and verification of activity, arguing that self-directed speech enables the shift from instinctive responding to deliberate control (Anderson, 2002; Demetriou et al., 2019; Joseph et al., 2005).

Vygotsky's developmental account further situates this regulatory function within the internalisation of language. Early overt self-talk gradually becomes silent inner speech, supporting working memory, planning, and flexible problem-solving (Eigsti & Irvine, 2022; Friedman & Sterling, 2019; Joseph et al., 2005. Contemporary extensions, such as the Hierarchical Competing Systems Model, describe this process as a dynamic negotiation between a lower-level habit system and a higher-level representational system guided by language and reflection.

Within neurotypical development, these systems become tightly coupled – language and executive function show robust associations, and internal speech is used effortlessly to rehearse rules, anticipate outcomes, and guide behaviour (Akbar et al., 2013; Austin, 2014; Barron-Linnankosi et al., 2015; Friedman & Sterling, 2019). In neurodivergent profiles – most notably autism – the feedback system between language and executive function may be attenuated or even wholly decoupled. Executive performance may bear little relation to language ability, even when structural language is well developed, suggesting a functional difficulty in deploying language as a tool for self-regulation rather than a deficit in language itself (Austin, 2014; Barron-Linnankosi et al., 2015; Friedman & Sterling, 2019).

This decoupling does have important practical consequences. Verbal individuals with autism often compensate by relying heavily on explicit, language-mediated reasoning to navigate tasks that others manage through automatic, non-verbal systems, particularly in social contexts (Gilbert, 2019; Le Cunff et al., 2025). This means that, while this strategy can support accurate performance, it is cognitively taxing and remains vulnerable to interference. When the verbal channel is taxed – by concurrent instruction, social demands, or articulatory load – regulatory efficiency declines sharply. A similar pattern is often observed in DLD, where successful acquisition of linguistic forms may obscure persistent irregularities in the memory systems that support fluent retrieval and procedural learning (Earle & Ullman, 2020; Friedman & Sterling, 2019; Cier et al., 2024). Cier et al. (2024) go so far as to emphasise that, across these profiles, difficulties arise not from the absence of language, but from its uneven availability as an internal regulatory resource. In classrooms that assume fluent verbal self-guidance, learners may appear disorganised or inattentive precisely because the system they must rely upon most is already saturated.

Russel's Hypothesis of Verbal Self-Regulation

However, the relationship between language and regulation diverges in important ways for neurodiverse individuals (Akbar et al., 2013; Friedman & Sterling, 2019; Joseph et al., 2005; Le Cunff et al., 2025). Russell's hypothesis of a verbal self-regulation deficit suggests that autistic individuals may struggle to use internal language to guide non-routine behaviour, even when their expressive and receptive language skills are otherwise well developed (Austin et al., 2014; Eigsti & Irvine, 2022; Joseph et al., 2005). This difficulty becomes most visible in situations that demand resistance to a prepotent response – that is, responses that might demand priority over other responses (Adams & Jarrold, 2012; Austin et al., 2014; Joseph et al., 2005; Schmitt et al., 2018).

This does not imply an absence of regulation, but rather a different regulatory pathway (Demetriou et al., 2019; Eigsti & Irvine, 2022; Joseph et al., 2005). Interestingly, many verbally fluent autistic individuals rely more, not less, on explicit verbal reasoning to compensate for less accessible intuitive or automatic systems (Eigsti & Irvine, 2022; Fisher et al., 2005; Friedman & Sterling, 2019; Joseph et al., 2005; Tager-Flusberg, 2001). Tasks that neurotypical peers complete implicitly may require conscious, language-mediated problem solving for neurodivergent learners (Eigsti & Irvine, 2022; Foti et al., 2015; Joseph et al., 2005; Tager-Flusberg, 2001).

This compensatory strategy carries cognitive costs (Eigsti & Irvine, 2022; Joseph et al., 2005). Because explicit verbal mediation is effortful, it is highly susceptible to overload (Eigsti & Irvine, 2022; Joseph et al., 2005). When the verbal channel is occupied, performance can degrade rapidly (Eigsti & Irvine, 2022; Joseph et al., 2005). Experimental work demonstrates that autistic individuals' performance on tasks such as false-belief reasoning slows significantly under dual-task conditions that tax verbal resources, whereas neurotypical performance remains comparatively stable (Eigsti & Irvine, 2022; Joseph et al., 2005).

These regulatory differences have direct implications for inclusive education (Florian & Black-Hawkins, 2011; Praslova, 2024). Classrooms frequently assume that attention can be sustained through verbal instruction alone, that transitions require minimal preparation, and that self-regulation will emerge through exposure rather than support (Praslova, 2024; Sayers et al., 2011). For neurodiverse learners, such assumptions translate into chronic attentional fatigue (Davidson & Souza, 2024; Praslova, 2024). Inclusive environments must therefore externalise regulation: providing visual schedules, written instructions, predictable routines, and advance warnings of change (Root et al., 2021; Syriopoulou-Delli & Filiou, 2022).

Language regulation must likewise be treated as variable rather than universal. Clear, literal communication reduces the burden of inference and frees attentional resources for learning (Praslova, 2024; Root et al., 2021; Syriopoulou-Delli & Filiou, 2022). Multimodal instruction allows learners to bypass overloaded verbal channels, while alternative forms of expression acknowledge that regulation and understanding need not be demonstrated through speech alone. Social expectations, in particular, benefit from explicit articulation. Relying on implicit norms may foster efficiency for some, but it fosters confusion for others – and confusion is a remarkably effective way to divert attention from the curriculum (Root et al., 2021; Syriopoulou-Delli & Filiou, 2022).

COGNITIVE COUPLING FRAMEWORK

The concept of mutualistic coupling offers a useful developmental account of why cognitive abilities tend to correlate across domains (Kievit et al., 2017, 2019; Van Der Maas et al., 2006). Rather than reflecting a single latent capacity, the positive manifold of intelligence is increasingly understood as an consequence of reciprocal interactions between cognitive systems over time (Kievit et al., 2017, 2019; Van Der Maas et al., 2006). Language supports executive control; executive control stabilises memory; memory consolidation enhances learning efficiency; and these gains, in turn, refine language and reasoning (Anderson, 2002; Austin et al., 2014; Batterink et al., 2019; Earle & Ullman, 2020; Joseph et al., 2005). In neurotypical development, these systems are not merely co-present but functionally integrated, such that growth in one domain reliably feeds forward into others (Kievit et al., 2017, 2019).

However, evidence within the neurodiversity literature suggests that this integration cannot be assumed universally (Desaunay et al., 2020; Joseph et al., 2005; Massand & Bowler, 2015). In several neurodiverse populations, cognitive systems that are typically tightly coupled appear to function as partially dissociated or decoupled processes (Desaunay et al., 2020; Joseph et al., 2005; Massand & Bowler, 2015; Williams et al., 2012). These decouplings do not imply the absence of ability, but rather a disruption in the developmental feedback loops that ordinarily allow skills to reinforce one another (Donahoe & Palmer, 2022; Joseph et al., 2005). As a result, learning becomes less self-propagating and more dependent on external structure – a point sometimes only discovered after significant and unnecessary frustration (Almeida et al., 2019; Bowler et al., 2004; Desaunay et al., 2020; Hill, 2004; Phelan et al., 2011).

Decoupling of Language and Attention Regulation

One of the clearest examples of disrupted mutualism appears in the relationship between language and executive regulation (Friedman & Sterling, 2019; Joseph et al., 2005). In neurotypical development, inner speech serves as a scaffold for attentional control, planning, and behavioural regulation (Austin et al., 2014; Eigsti & Irvine, 2022; Joseph et al., 2005). Language and EF are positively correlated, reflecting a coupled system in which verbal mediation supports goal-directed behaviour, particularly in non-routine contexts (Austin et al., 2014; Eigsti & Irvine, 2022; Friedman & Sterling, 2019; Joseph et al., 2005).

In neurodiverse individuals, this coupling often appears markedly weakened (Eigsti & Irvine, 2022; Joseph et al., 2005). Research indicates a verbal self-regulation deficit, whereby structural language ability and executive performance are no longer reliably associated (Austin et al., 2014; Eigsti & Irvine, 2022; Joseph et al., 2005). Autistic individuals, for example, may possess functional expressive and receptive language skills, yet experience difficulty deploying language internally to maintain response rules, inhibit prepotent actions, or flexibly redirect attention (Eigsti & Irvine, 2022; Friedman & Sterling, 2019; Joseph et al., 2005). In effect, the tool is present, but it is not automatically recruited when regulation is required (Eigsti & Irvine, 2022; Friedman & Sterling, 2019; Joseph et al., 2005).

Decoupling of Memory Storage and Self-Initiated Recall

A second disruption to mutualistic development is observed in the relationship between memory storage and retrieval, particularly in episodic memory (Desaunay et al., 2020; Massand & Bowler, 2015). The Task Support Hypothesis provides compelling evidence that, in neurodiverse individuals, memory representations are often intact but functionally inaccessible without external support (Almeida et al., 2019a; Bowler et al., 2004; Desaunay et al., 2020). Neurodiverse individuals frequently perform poorly on unsupported retrieval tasks such as free recall yet demonstrate age-appropriate performance when retrieval is scaffolded through cues, structured questioning, or recognition formats (Almeida et al., 2019a; Desaunay et al., 2020; Geng et al., 2024). This pattern suggests a decoupling between memory storage and the self-initiated search processes required for retrieval, rather than a global memory deficit (Desaunay et al., 2020; Geng et al., 2024; Massand & Bowler, 2015).

Further dissociation is evident in dual-process accounts of retrieval (Desaunay et al., 2020; Massand & Bowler, 2015). Familiarity-based processes are often preserved or even enhanced in individuals with neurodiverse needs, while recollection is diminished (Desaunay et al., 2020; Geng et al., 2024; Massand & Bowler, 2015). This imbalance contributes to difficulties with narrative coherence and autobiographical recall, despite intact recognition of previously encountered material (Desaunay et al., 2020; Geng et al., 2024; Massand & Bowler, 2015). Neuroimaging and eye-tracking studies reinforce this interpretation, showing that while neurotypical adults exhibit strong similarity between encoding and retrieval patterns, this linkage is attenuated in autistic adults (Desaunay et al., 2020; Geng et al., 2024; Massand & Bowler, 2015). Encoding and retrieval appear to occur, but not as parts of a smoothly coordinated sequence (Desaunay et al., 2020; Massand & Bowler, 2015).

Decoupling of Learning and Consolidation in DLD

In DLD, the disruption to mutualistic coupling is particularly evident in the relationship between learning and consolidation (Arciuli, 2017; Earle & Ullman, 2020). Adults with DLD often demonstrate typical-like performance during initial learning phases, suggesting intact encoding mechanisms (Earle & Ullman, 2020). However, they frequently fail to exhibit the offline consolidation gains – such as overnight improvements in retrieval – that are characteristic of neurotypical learners (Earle & Ullman, 2020).

This pattern reflects a dissociation between procedural learning and declarative retrieval (Cier et al., 2024; Earle & Ullman, 2020). While individuals with DLD may improve through repeated task engagement, their ability to later retrieve or explicitly report what has been learned is typically impaired (Cier et al., 2024; Earle & Ullman, 2020). As a result, learning does not reliably accumulate over time, weakening the reciprocal reinforcement between memory, language, and executive systems (Arciuli, 2017; Earle & Ullman, 2020). Educationally, this creates the misleading impression that progress has "evaporated," when in fact it was never allowed to stabilise (Earle & Ullman, 2020).

Implications for Inclusive Education

From a mutualistic perspective, neurodiverse learning profiles are not defined by isolated deficits, but by altered system dynamics (Kievit et al., 2017, 2019; Van Der Maas et al., 2006). When language no longer scaffolds regulation, memory does not reliably support recall, and learning fails to consolidate, the developmental architecture which ordinarily supports cognitive growth loses efficiency (Austin et al., 2014; Earle & Ullman, 2020; Joseph et al., 2005; Kievit et al., 2017). Skills may still develop, but they do so unevenly, slowly, and with limited transfer across domains (Barron-Linnankoski et al., 2015; Demetriou et al., 2018; Desaunay et al., 2020; Williams et al., 2006).

Inclusive education must therefore prioritise the *external* coupling of systems that are - otherwise - internally decoupled (Bowler et al., 2004; Desaunay et al., 2020; Massand & Bowler, 2015). This includes explicit scaffolding of retrieval, structured use of language for regulation, visual and environmental supports to reduce executive load, and repeated opportunities for consolidation across time (Almeida et al., 2019a; Bowler et al., 2004; Earle & Ullman, 2020; Joseph et al., 2005; Root et al., 2021). Support structures should not be withdrawn simply because surface performance appears adequate; mutualistic growth requires sustained reinforcement, not brief demonstrations of competence (Florian & Black-Hawkins, 2011; Hamilton & Petty, 2023; Syriopoulou-Delli & Filiou, 2022).

One functional example of this would be in the implementation of a work choice approach - that is, the students should have a voice in deciding how they are learning. This is not to say that teachers must forgo or forfeit their contribution to the classroom - far from it - but rather that the teacher could - and arguably should - provide multiple avenues through which to scaffold to the learning objective so that students may choose which avenue they might pursue.

Moreover, as explained by Root et al. (2021), educators can help reduce the cognitive load of more complex and procedural tasks by engaging in multi-modal, stimulating, and priming techniques - many of which are as simple as making use of colour coded visual aids.

In short inclusive practice succeeds when it recognises that neurodiverse children do not resist integration, but are instead operating within a world that has simply does not interface automatically - like driving a car on the wrong (right) side of the road, reading something in a language you have only practiced slightly, or dealing with an operating system that might be otherwise alien.

CONCLUSION

The models examined across this chapter converge on a shared insight: learning is not the product of isolated cognitive capacities, but of their coordination over time (Anderson, 2002; Kievit et al., 2017). Memory, attention, language, and executive control do not merely coexist; they typically develop in mutual dependence, each relying upon – and simultaneously bolstering – the effects of the others (Kievit et al., 2017; van der Maas et al., 2006). Where this coupling is intact, learning tends to be self-reinforcing (Kievit et al., 2019). Where it is disrupted, progress becomes fragile, uneven, and highly contingent on context (Desaunay et al., 2020; Massand & Bowler, 2015).

Language may exist without reliably regulating behaviour; memory may be stored without being readily retrieved; learning may occur without consolidating into durable knowledge (Bowler et al., 2004; Earle & Ullman, 2020; Joseph et al., 2005). These dissociations complicate educational participation not because learners lack capacity, but because the environments in which they are expected to function presume forms of internal coordination that cannot be taken for granted (Sayers et al., 2011). The difficulty, then, lies less in cognition itself than in the invisible assumptions embedded within pedagogical design (Florian & Black-Hawkins, 2011).

The inclusive models reviewed – ranging from neuro-affirming social perspectives to applied frameworks such as UDL, FEDIS+R – offer important corrections to these assumptions (Carrington et al., 2020; Root et al., 2021; Schuck & Fung, 2024; Waisman et al., 2022). Their shared strength lies in a shift away from remediation and toward design (Florian & Black-Hawkins, 2011; Waisman et al., 2022). Thus, by externalising structure, and reducing unnecessary cognitive load, these models begin to supply the scaffolding that decoupled systems require (Almeida et al., 2019a; Bowler et al., 2004; Desaunay et al., 2020; Root et al., 2021).

Yet these frameworks are not without limitations (Gilbert, 2019). Many rest upon broad principles that risk abstraction unless anchored in cognitive specificity (Demetriou et al., 2018; Geng et al., 2024; Joseph et al., 2005). Others assume levels of institutional flexibility, time, and training that are unevenly available in practice (Gilbert, 2019; Waisman et al., 2022). Most critically, inclusive design can drift into procedural compliance if it is not guided by a nuanced understanding of how different cognitive systems interact – and sometimes fail to interact – across neurodiverse profiles (Arciuli, 2017; Earle & Ullman, 2020; Kievit et al., 2017).

Moreover, and in the interest of clarity, the models and frameworks discussed in this section have been described using organising concepts such as inclusion, regulation, psychological safety, and universal design. These terms function as fairly broad heuristic labels, and do offer a more concise way to capture complex and interacting educational dynamics rather than implying a fixed or exhaustive mapping between theory and practice. However, as with any applied framework, their effects are contingent on context: institutional culture, resource availability, staff training, and the interpretive lenses brought by educators all shape how such models are enacted (Florian & Black-Hawkins, 2011; Waisman et al., 2022). Variability in implementation can therefore produce markedly different outcomes, even when nominally similar approaches are adopted. These limitations complicate straightforward evaluation, but they do not negate the utility of theory-informed frameworks as tools for interpreting patterns of engagement, exclusion, and support within diverse classrooms (Demetriou et al., 2019).

Be that as it may, what the cognitive evidence ultimately demands is not a rejection of existing models, but further refinement (Desaunay et al., 2020). Inclusive education must be informed not only by values of equity and belonging, but by precise accounts of how attention is regulated, how memory is retrieved, how language mediates control, and how learning consolidates over time (Anderson, 2002; Earle & Ullman, 2020; Eigsti & Irvine, 2022). Without this grounding, well-intentioned practices may remain supportive in appearance while leaving underlying barriers intact (Hamilton & Petty, 2023).

REFERENCES

Adams, N. C., & Jarrold, C. (2012). Inhibition in Autism. Children with autism have difficulty inhibiting irrelevant distractors but not prepotent responses. *Journal of Autism and Developmental Disorders*, *42*(6), 1052–1063. DOI: 10.1007/s10803-011-1345-3 PMID: 21830170

Akbar, M., Loomis, R., & Paul, R. (2013). The interplay of language on executive functions in children with ASD. *Research in Autism Spectrum Disorders*, *7*(3), 494–501. DOI: 10.1016/j.rasd.2012.09.001

Almeida, T. S., Lamb, M. E., & Weisblatt, E. J. (2019). Effects of delay on episodic memory retrieval by children with autism spectrum disorder. *Applied Cognitive Psychology*, *33*(5), 814–827. DOI: 10.1002/acp.3524 PMID: 30406912

Almeida, T. S., Lamb, M. E., & Weisblatt, E. J. (2019). a. Effects of delay, question type, and socioemotional support on episodic memory retrieval by children with ASD. *Journal of Autism and Developmental Disorders*, *49*(5), 1845–1858.

American Psychiatric Association. (2013). *Diagnostic and statistical manual of mental disorders* (5th ed.)., DOI: 10.1176/appi.books.9780890425596

Anderson, P. (2002). Assessment and development of executive function (EF) during childhood. *Child Neuropsychology : A Journal on Normal and Abnormal Development in Childhood and Adolescence*, *8*(2), 71–82. DOI: 10.1076/chin.8.2.71.8724 PMID: 12638061

Arciuli, J. (2017). The multi-component nature of statistical learning. *Philosophical Transactions of the Royal Society B: Biological Sciences, 372*(1711), 20160058.

Austin, G., Groppe, K., & Elsner, B. (2014). The reciprocal relationship between executive function and theory of mind in middle childhood: A 1-year longitudinal perspective. *Frontiers in Psychology*, *5*, 655. DOI: 10.3389/fpsyg.2014.00655 PMID: 25009527

Baddeley, A. (1996). Exploring the central executive. *The Quarterly Journal of Experimental Psychology. A, Human Experimental Psychology*, *49*(1), 5–28. DOI: 10.1080/713755608

Bal, V. H., Goin-Kochel, R. P., McEachern, A. D., Jelenic, P., Nader, A. M., & Soulières, I. (2022). Cognitive profiles of children with ASD with parent-reported extraordinary talents and personal strengths. *Journal of Autism and Developmental Disorders*, *52*(2), 585–599.

Barron-Linnankoski, S., Kortesluoma, S., Ehlers, S., Hietala, R., & Pihlaja, P. (2015). Neurocognitive performance of children with higher functioning ASD on the NEPSY-2. *Child Neuropsychology : A Journal on Normal and Abnormal Development in Childhood and Adolescence, 21*(1), 58–77. DOI: 10.1080/09297049.2013.873781 PMID: 24397431

Batterink, L. J., Paller, K. A., & Reber, P. J. (2019). Understanding the neural bases of implicit and statistical learning. *Topics in Cognitive Science, 11*(3), 481–506. DOI: 10.1111/tops.12420 PMID: 30942536

Bowler, D. M., Gardiner, J. M., & Berthollier, N. (2004). Source memory in adolescents and adults with Asperger's syndrome. *Journal of Autism and Developmental Disorders, 34*(5), 533–542. DOI: 10.1007/s10803-004-2548-7 PMID: 15628607

Brainerd, C. J., & Reyna, V. F. (1990). Gist is the grist: Fuzzy-trace theory and the new intuitionism. *Developmental Review, 10*(1), 3–47. DOI: 10.1016/0273-2297(90)90003-M

Carrington, S., Saggers, B., Webster, A., Harper-Hill, K., & Nickerson, J. (2020). What Universal Design for Learning principles, guidelines, and checkpoints are evident in educators' descriptions of their practice when supporting students on the autism spectrum? *International Journal of Educational Research, 102*, 101583. DOI: 10.1016/j.ijer.2020.101583

Cier, G. J., Bartolo, S., Kim, J., Nolan, A., & Banel, S. (2024). Implicit and Explicit Sequence Learning in Adults With Developmental Language Disorder. *Journal of Speech, Language, and Hearing Research: JSLHR, 67*(5), 1540–1552. PMID: 39024517

Davidson, A., & Souza, P. (2024). Relationships Between Auditory Processing and Cognitive Abilities in Adults: A Systematic Review. *Journal of Speech, Language, and Hearing Research: JSLHR, 67*(1), 316–336. DOI: 10.1044/2023_JSLHR-22-00716 PMID: 38147487

Demetriou, E. A., DeMayo, M. M., & Guastella, A. J. (2019). Executive function in autism spectrum disorder: History, theoretical models, empirical findings and potential as an endophenotype. *Frontiers in Psychiatry, 10*, 753. DOI: 10.3389/fpsyt.2019.00753 PMID: 31780959

Demetriou, E. A., Lampit, A., Quintana, D. S., Naismith, S. L., Song, Y. J. C., Pye, J. E., Hickie, I., & Guastella, A. J. (2018). Autism spectrum disorders: A meta-analysis of executive function. *Molecular Psychiatry, 23*(5), 1198–1204. DOI: 10.1038/mp.2017.75 PMID: 28439105

Desaunay, P., Briant, A. R., Bowler, D. M., Ring, M., Gérardin, P., Baleyte, J.-M., Guénolé, F., Eustache, F., Parienti, J.-J., & Guillery-Girard, B. (2020). Memory in autism spectrum disorder: A meta-analysis of experimental studies. *Psychological Bulletin*, *146*(5), 377–410. DOI: 10.1037/bul0000225 PMID: 32191044

Donahoe, J. W., & Palmer, D. C. (2022). Acquired Reinforcement: Implications for Autism. *The American Psychologist*, *77*(2), 295–307. PMID: 35201786

Duan, Y., Xie, H., Tan, W., & Zeng, Y. (2025). Neural connections and molecular mechanisms underlying motor skill deficits in genetic models of ASD. *Progress in Neurobiology*, •••, 102759. DOI: 10.1016/j.pneurobio.2025.102759 PMID: 40254176

Earle, F. S., & Ullman, M. T. (2020). Deficits of learning in procedural memory and consolidation in declarative memory in adults with developmental language disorder. *Journal of Speech, Language, and Hearing Research: JSLHR*, *63*(10), 3290–3305. PMID: 33524264

Eigsti, I. M., & Irvine, C. A. (2022). Verbal mediation of theory of mind in verbal adolescents with ASD. *Language Acquisition*, *29*(1), 1–25. PMID: 35281590

Fisher, N., Happé, F., & Dunn, J. (2005). The relationship between vocabulary, grammar, and false belief task performance in children with autistic spectrum disorders and children with moderate learning difficulties. *Journal of Child Psychology and Psychiatry, and Allied Disciplines*, *46*(4), 409–419. DOI: 10.1111/j.1469-7610.2004.00371.x PMID: 15819650

Florian, L., & Black-Hawkins, K. (2011). Exploring inclusive pedagogy. *British Educational Research Journal*, *37*(5), 813–828. DOI: 10.1080/01411926.2010.501096

Foti, F., De Crescenzo, F., Vivanti, G., & Fadda, S. (2015). Implicit learning in individuals with autism spectrum disorders: A meta-analysis. *Psychological Medicine*, *45*(5), 897–910. DOI: 10.1017/S0033291714001950 PMID: 25126858

Friedman, L., & Sterling, A. A. (2019). A review of language, executive function, and intervention in autism spectrum disorder. *Seminars in Speech and Language*, *40*(4), 291–304. DOI: 10.1055/s-0039-1692964 PMID: 31311054

Geng, K., Wang, Y., Fu, W., Chen, S., & Yang, Y. (2024). Episodic memory impairment and its influencing factors in individuals with autism spectrum disorder: Systematic review and meta-analysis. *European Archives of Psychiatry and Clinical Neuroscience*. PMID: 39269621

Geurts, H. M., Oosterlaan, J., & Sergeant, J. A. (2005). Is there a clinical utility of executive function measures in the assessment of ADHD subtypes? *Archives of Clinical Neuropsychology : The Official Journal of the National Academy of Neuropsychologists, 20*(4), 457–477. DOI: 10.1016/j.acn.2004.11.001 PMID: 15896560

Gilbert, E. N. (2019). Designing inclusive physical education with Universal Design for Learning. *Journal of Physical Education, Recreation & Dance, 90*(7), 15–21. DOI: 10.1080/07303084.2019.1637305

Hamilton, L. G., & Petty, S. (2023). Compassionate pedagogy for neurodiversity in higher education: A conceptual analysis. *Frontiers in Psychology, 14*, 1093290. DOI: 10.3389/fpsyg.2023.1093290 PMID: 36874864

Hill, E. L. (2004). Evaluating the theory of executive dysfunction in autism. *Developmental Review, 24*(2), 189–233. DOI: 10.1016/j.dr.2004.01.001

Holmes, J., Guy, J., Kievit, R. A., Bryant, A., Mareva, S., & Gathercole, S. E.CALM Team. (2021). Cognitive dimensions of learning in children with problems in attention, learning, and memory. *Journal of Educational Psychology, 113*(7), 1454–1480. DOI: 10.1037/edu0000644 PMID: 35855686

Jain, J., Dwarakanath, S., & Sharda, S. (2024). The relationship between auditory and cognitive processing abilities in children with specific learning disorders. *American Journal of Audiology, 33*(1), 118–129. DOI: 10.1044/2024_AJA-24-00001 PMID: 38959167

Joseph, R. M., McGrath, L. M., & Tager-Flusberg, H. (2005). Executive dysfunction and its relation to language ability in verbal school-age children with autism. *Developmental Neuropsychology, 27*(3), 361–378. DOI: 10.1207/s15326942dn2703_4 PMID: 15843102

Kennette, L. N., & Wilson, N. A. (2019). Universal Design for Learning (UDL): Student and Faculty Perceptions. *Journal of Effective Teaching in Higher Education, 2*(1), 1–26. DOI: 10.36021/jethe.v2i1.17

Kievit, R. A., Hofman, A. D., & Nation, K. (2019). Mutualistic coupling between vocabulary and reasoning in young children: A replication and extension of the study by Kievit et al. (2017). *Psychological Science, 30*(8), 1245–1252. DOI: 10.1177/0956797619841265 PMID: 31100049

Kievit, R. A., Lindenberger, U., Goodyer, I. M., Jones, P. B., Fonagy, P., Bullmore, E. T., & Dolan, R. J. (2017). Mutualistic coupling between vocabulary and reasoning supports cognitive development during late adolescence and early adulthood. *Psychological Science*, *28*(10), 1419–1431. DOI: 10.1177/0956797617710785 PMID: 28787239

Kozunova, Y. O., Zakirov, D. R., Rytikova, M. P., Sarsenova, N. B., & Vaganov, O. G. (2023). Neurobiological factors of executive dysfunction in ASD. *Neuroscience and Behavioral Physiology*, *53*(10), 1168–1180.

Le Cunff, A. L., Martis, B.-L., Glover, C., Ahmed, E., Ford, R., Giampietro, V., & Dommett, E. J. (2025b). Cognitive load and neurodiversity in online education: A preliminary framework for educational research and policy. *Frontiers in Education*, *9*, 9. DOI: 10.3389/feduc.2024.1437673

Leung, R. C., Vogan, V. M., Powell, T. L., Anagnostou, E., & Taylor, M. J. (2016). The role of executive functions in social impairment in autism spectrum disorder. *Child Neuropsychology : A Journal on Normal and Abnormal Development in Childhood and Adolescence*, *22*(3), 336–344. DOI: 10.1080/09297049.2015.1005066 PMID: 25731979

Luria, A. R. (1966). *Higher cortical functions in man*. Basic Books.

Marcovitch, S., & Zelazo, P. D. (2009). A hierarchical competing systems model of the emergence and early development of executive function. *Developmental Science*, *12*(1), 1–25. DOI: 10.1111/j.1467-7687.2008.00754.x PMID: 19120405

Mareva, S., Astle, D., Baker, K., Gathercole, S., Holmes, J., Kievit, R., Manly, T., Akarca, D., Bathelt, J., Bettencourt, M., Bennett, M., Bignardi, G., Bishop, S., Bottacin, E., Bridge, L., Brkic, D., Bryant, A., Butterfield, S., Byrne, E., & Holmes, J.Lead InvestigatorsTeam of Researchers and PhD Students. (2024). Mapping neurodevelopmental diversity in executive function. *Cortex; A Journal Devoted to the Study of the Nervous System and Behavior*, *172*, 204–221. DOI: 10.1016/j.cortex.2023.11.021 PMID: 38354470

Massand, E., & Bowler, D. M. (2015). Atypical neurophysiology underlying episodic and semantic memory in adults with autism spectrum disorder: An ERP review. *Journal of Autism and Developmental Disorders*, *45*(2), 298–315. DOI: 10.1007/s10803-013-1869-9 PMID: 23754340

Minshew, N. J., & Goldstein, G. (2001). The pattern of intact and impaired memory functions in autism. *Journal of Child Psychology and Psychiatry, and Allied Disciplines*, *42*(8), 1095–1101. DOI: 10.1111/1469-7610.00808 PMID: 11806691

Miyake, A., Friedman, N. P., Emerson, M. J., Witzki, A. H., Howerter, A., & Wager, T. D. (2000). The unity and diversity of executive functions and their contributions to complex "frontal lobe" tasks: A latent variable analysis. *Cognitive Psychology*, *41*(1), 49–100. DOI: 10.1006/cogp.1999.0734 PMID: 10945922

Mokhtari, S., & Parchini, P. (2024). The application of drawing tasks in studying cognitive functions in Autism Spectrum Disorder: A systematic review. *Review Journal of Autism and Developmental Disorders*, *11*(2), 180–193.

Paas, F., Renkl, A., & Sweller, J. (2003). Cognitive load theory and instructional design: Recent developments. *Educational Psychologist*, *38*(1), 1–4. DOI: 10.1207/S15326985EP3801_1

Peng, P., & Kievit, R. A. (2019). The development of academic achievement and cognitive abilities: A bidirectional perspective. *Child Development Perspectives*, *14*(1), 15–20. DOI: 10.1111/cdep.12352 PMID: 35909387

Phelan, H. L., Filliter, J. H., & Johnson, S. A. (2011). Brief report: Memory performance on the California Verbal Learning Test – Children's Version in autism spectrum disorder. *Journal of Autism and Developmental Disorders*, *41*(4), 518–523. DOI: 10.1007/s10803-010-1069-9 PMID: 20652387

Powell, K., O'Brien, S. E., Chawarska, K., & Klin, A. (2022). Elevated symptoms of executive dysfunction predict lower adaptive functioning in 3-year-olds with ASD. *Autism Research : Official Journal of the International Society for Autism Research*, *15*(7), 1336–1347. DOI: 10.1002/aur.2715 PMID: 35388596

Praslova, L. N. (2024). *The canary code: A guide to neurodiversity, dignity, and intersectional belonging at work*. Berrett-Koehler Publishers.

Root, J. R., Jimenez, B., & Saunders, A. (2021). Leveraging the UDL framework to plan grade-aligned mathematics in inclusive settings. *In Practice*, *1*(1), 13–2. PMID: 33039648

Russell, J. (1997). How executive disorders can bring about an inadequate "theory of mind.". In Russell, J. (Ed.), *Autism as an executive disorder* (pp. 256–304). Oxford University Press.

Sayers, N., Sayers, E., & O'Brien, S. (2011). Stereotyped behaviour in children with autism and intellectual disability: An examination of the executive dysfunction hypothesis. *Journal of Intellectual Disability Research : JIDR*, *55*(7), 701–710. DOI: 10.1111/j.1365-2788.2010.01370.x PMID: 21199048

Schmitt, L. M., Herrington, T. M., & Mosconi, M. W. (2018). Cognitive mechanisms of inhibitory control deficits in autism spectrum disorder. *Journal of Child Psychology and Psychiatry, and Allied Disciplines*, *59*(5), 586–595. DOI: 10.1111/jcpp.12837 PMID: 29052841

Schuck, R. K., & Fung, L. K. (2024). A dual design thinking – universal design approach to catalyze neurodiversity advocacy through collaboration among highschoolers. *Frontiers in Psychiatry*, *14*, 1250895. DOI: 10.3389/fpsyt.2023.1250895 PMID: 38268559

Syriopoulou-Delli, C. K., & Filiou, A. (2022). A systematic review of dysfunctional thoughts, feelings and phobias of children and adolescents with autism. Solutions and therapeutic methods. *International Journal of Developmental Disabilities*, *69*(5), 756–776. PMID: 36210890

Tager-Flusberg, H. (2001). Neuropsychological components of language acquisition in autism. *The Journal of Developmental and Learning Disorders*, *5*, 57–80.

Ullman, M. T., Earle, F. S., Walenski, M., & Janacsek, K. (2020). The neurocognition of developmental disorders of language. *Annual Review of Psychology*, *71*(1), 389–417. DOI: 10.1146/annurev-psych-122216-011555 PMID: 31337273

Unsworth, N. (2016). Working memory capacity and recall from long-term memory: Examining the influences of encoding strategies, study time allocation, search efficiency, and monitoring abilities. *Journal of Experimental Psychology. Learning, Memory, and Cognition*, *42*(1), 50–61. DOI: 10.1037/xlm0000148 PMID: 26076331

Van Der Maas, H. L. J., Dolan, C. V., Grasman, R. P. P. P., Wicherts, J. M., Huizenga, H. M., & Raijmakers, M. E. J. (2006). A dynamical model of general intelligence: The positive manifold of intelligence by mutualism. *Psychological Review*, *113*(4), 842–861. DOI: 10.1037/0033-295X.113.4.842 PMID: 17014305

Vygotsky, L. S. (1987). *Thinking and speech*. Plenum Press.

Waisman, T. C., Williams, Z. J., Cage, E., Santhanam, S. P., Magiati, I., Dwyer, P., Stockwell, K. M., Kofner, B., Brown, H., Davidson, D., Herrell, J., Shore, S. M., Caudel, D., Gurbuz, E., & Gillespie-Lynch, K. (2022). Learning from the experts: Evaluating a participatory autism and universal design training for university educators. *Autism : The International Journal of Research and Practice*, *27*(2), 356–370. DOI: 10.1177/13623613221097207 PMID: 35652315

Wang, Y., Zhang, Y. B., Liu, L. L., Cui, J. F., Wang, J., Shum, D. H. K., & Chan, R. C. K. (2017). A meta-analysis of working memory impairments in autism spectrum disorders. *Neuropsychology Review*, *27*(1), 46–61. DOI: 10.1007/s11065-016-9336-y PMID: 28102493

Williams, D. L., Goldstein, G., Kojkowski, N., & Minshew, N. J. (2008). Do individuals with high functioning autism have the IQ profile associated with nonverbal learning disability. *Research in Autism Spectrum Disorders*, *2*(2), 353–361. DOI: 10.1016/j.rasd.2007.08.005 PMID: 18516234

Williams, D. L., Hultman, C. I., Haxby, J. V., & Minshew, N. J. (2012). Brief report: Verbal mediation and planning ability in adolescents with autism spectrum disorder. *Journal of Autism and Developmental Disorders*, *42*(7), 1530–1534.

Williams, D. L., Minshew, N. J., & Goldstein, G. (2006). Visual short-term memory in autism. *Neuropsychology*, *20*(4), 458–461.

Chapter 6
The Role of Neuropsychological Assessment and Biomarkers Towards Accurate Diagnosis and Quality of Life in Attention-Deficit/Hyperactivity Disorder

Kalliopi Megari
http://orcid.org/0000-0002-5861-7199
University of York Europe Campus, Greece & University of Western Macedonia, Greece

ABSTRACT

Attention-deficit/hyperactivity disorder (ADHD) is a common neurodevelopmental condition characterized by persistent inattention, hyperactivity, and impulsivity, which can lead to considerable functional difficulties. ADHD exhibits a high degree of variability, presenting in various forms across individuals and age groups, thereby complicating the diagnostic process significantly. However, the increasing recognition of the neurobiological foundations of ADHD has driven researchers to identify biomarkers that enhance the diagnostic precision. This review aims to provide a comprehensive overview of the latest advancements in biomarkers and neuropsychological assessment for ADHD diagnosis. More specifically, it will place

DOI: 10.4018/979-8-3373-7072-9.ch006

an emphasis on the importance of early diagnosis, the necessity for enhanced diagnostic criteria, and the use of biomarkers and cognitive assessments in directing tailored interventions and optimizing patient outcomes.

I. INTRODUCTION

Attention-Deficit/Hyperactivity Disorder (ADHD) is characterized in the DSM-V as a condition marked by persistent and disruptive symptoms of inattention and/or hyperactivity/impulsivity which are not adequate for the individual's age (Megari & Genova, 2025). It is among the most common neurodevelopmental disorders, affecting around 5–7% of children globally (Rubia et al., 2021). The challenges continue into adulthood and are linked to other coexisting conditions as well as negative social and academic consequences (Hurjui et al., 2025). Children with ADHD also exhibit executive functioning deficits, which are facilitated by the late developing fronto-striato-parietal and fronto-cerebellar networks (Megari & Genova, 2025). However, the most persistent challenges are observed in motor response inhibition, working memory, cognitive flexibility, sustained attention and intraindividual response variability, and timing functions. Children exhibit greater cognitive impairments than adults with ADHD (Megari & Genova, 2025; Rubia et al., 2021; Hurjui et al., 2025).

In fact, ADHD exhibits a high degree of variability, presenting in various forms across individuals and age groups, thereby complicating the diagnostic process significantly (Gilbert et al., 2025). While hyperactivity diminishes with maturity, attentional difficulties may endure, and this makes diagnosing ADHD in adulthood even more complicated (Gondek, 2021). Therefore, early treatment and diagnosis are crucial for enhancing the long-term influences on children diagnosed with ADHD. Failure to address ADHD can lead to significant challenges in academic performance and social interactions, and may contribute to the emergence of other coexisting issues, like depression and anxiety (French et al., 2023). Early interventions can significantly reduce the ADHD symptoms and foster more effective coping strategies, ultimately enhancing the quality of life for children affected by ADHD (Hurjui et al., 2025).

While there is increasing awareness of the effects of ADHD, a troubling concern persists regarding the accuracy of its diagnosis (Theodoratou, Kougioumtzis, Yotsidi, Andriopoulou, Megari, et al., 2025). Fortes et al. (2020) reported that approximately 35% of the children who are diagnosed with ADHD exhibited minimal or no deficits in activities of daily living, raising concerns about the validity and reliability of certain diagnostic tools and suggesting that ADHD may often be overdiagnosed based solely on symptom checklists. This is crucial because excessive diagnosis results in unnecessary interventions and treatments, while insufficient diagnosis denies individuals the essential support and care that they require. As a matter of fact, the routine ADHD diagnostic process involves primarily clinical interviews and behavioral evaluations, such as self-reports, parent feedback, and teacher questionnaires (e.g., the Conners' Rating Scales and the Vanderbilt ADHD Diagnostic Rating Scale) (Hurjui et al., 2025). While they serve as valuable tools for preliminary assessment, they are often hindered by significant observer bias (Veenman et al., 2017).

Furthermore, the growing identification of the shortcomings of traditional diagnostic approaches has sparked considerable interest in the establishment of biomarkers and objective neuropsychological assessments (Megari et al., 2025) that could enhance the diagnosis of ADHD. For instance, lots of research has explored neuroimaging and electrophysiological markers as objective methods for diagnosing ADHD. Recent neuroimaging studies have revealed atrophic changes in the prefrontal cortex (PFC) and certain areas related to attention and executive functioning, which are often impaired in children diagnosed with ADHD (Meghji et al., 2024; Friedman & Robbins, 2022; Long et al., 2022). Other studies have also indicated that individuals with ADHD exhibit notably greater structural changes in the cognitive control network, with the dorsolateral prefrontal cortex (DLPFC), serving as a crucial area for attention regulation (Parlatini et al., 2024; Berberat et al., 2021).

The diagnosis of ADHD may also involve the utilization of EEG markers, including the theta/beta ratio. The oscillatory processes observed here serve as indicators of ADHD, highlighting the deficiencies in attention and cognitive control. Numerous studies have shown that individuals with ADHD exhibit higher theta/beta ratios, suggesting sustained and focused attention (Hurjui et al., 2025). Additionally, the P300 component of event-related potentials (ERPs) serves as a measure of cognitive resource allocation/execution speed, and attention. Research indicates that individuals with ADHD exhibit delays in this component, suggesting it may function as a potential electrophysiological marker for the condition (Mehta et al., 2020). Alongside the electrophysiological and neuroimaging markers, biochemical markers are also significant in the identification of ADHD. Some inflammatory cytokines, including IL-6, IL-10, and TNF-α, are proposed to play a role in the underlying mechanisms of ADHD (Elsadek et al., 2020). Research indicates that there is a corresponding connection between salivary cortisol, a stress biomarker, and the severity of the ADHD symptoms (Chang et al., 2021).

Moreover, innovative instruments for neuropsychological evaluation provide a clear and objective measurement of ADHD symptoms. The establishment of computerized tasks and game-based assessments allows for the continuous evaluation of different cognitive functions, including working memory, attention, and executive functioning (Takahashi et al., 2024). These technological advancements facilitate precise standardization and much more objective evaluations, aiding professionals in effectively grasping the evolving characteristics of ADHD symptoms. An ongoing observation offers a longitudinal perspective rather than a mere momentary glimpse, as well as notes the complex and evolving aspects of cognitive activity throughout a time period (Hurjui et al., 2025).

This review aims to provide a comprehensive overview of the latest advancements in biomarkers (e.g., neuroimaging, electrophysiological recordings, biochemical and inflammatory markers, eye-tracking and pupillometry) and neuropsychological assessment for ADHD diagnosis. More specifically, it will place an emphasis on the importance of early diagnosis, the necessity for enhanced diagnostic criteria, and the use of biomarkers and cognitive assessments in directing tailored interventions and optimizing patient outcomes (Figure 1).

Figure 1. The connection of the studied variables

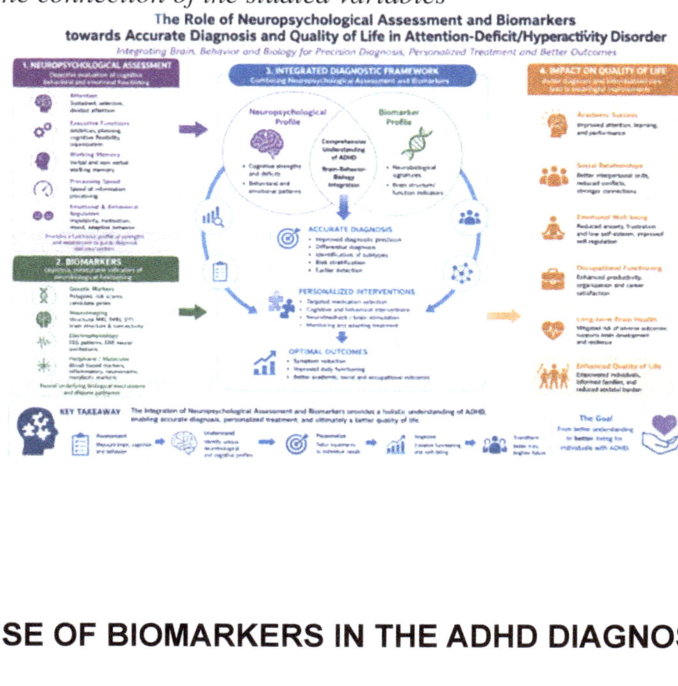

II. THE USE OF BIOMARKERS IN THE ADHD DIAGNOSTICS

2. 1. Neuroimaging Markers of ADHD

Neuroimaging approaches, such as ***Magnetic resonance imaging (MRI), functional Magnetic resonance imaging (fMRI)***, and ***Diffusion tensor imaging (DTI)***, have yielded significant insights into the structural and functional challenges associated with ADHD (Yan, 2025; Firouzabadi et al., 2021; Hurjui et al., 2025). Individuals diagnosed with ADHD often exhibit slight but extensive decreases in grey matter volume, especially within the prefrontal and subcortical areas of the brain (Long et al., 2023; Hurjui et al., 2025). With voxel-based morphometry, Long et al. (2023) observed noticeable decreases in grey matter volume in the bilateral dorsolateral prefrontal cortex (DLPFC), the anterior cingulate cortex (ACC), and the putamen. These brain areas are essential for managing attention and response inhibition, indicating that structural immaturity or underdevelopment in these areas could be a fundamental factor contributing to key symptoms of inattention and impulsivity (Long et al., 2023). Also, the cognitive and affective traits observed in individuals with ADHD were elucidated by more significant reductions in volumes in the left precentral gyrus, the left inferior frontal gyrus, and the right superior frontal gyrus (Long et al., 2023). Schulze et al. (2024) utilized quantitative susceptibility mapping (QSM) to investigate the levels of iron in the brain, revealing that children with ADHD exhibit diminished iron levels in the basal ganglia, a biomarker potentially associated with dopaminergic dysfunction, a recognized neurochemical feature of ADHD.

Functional MRI research has demonstrated significant changes in functional networks. For instance, in a study utilizing graph theory on resting-state fMRI data from adolescents, Kim et al. (2023) observed alterations in global efficiency and modularity within key networks - the default mode and salience networks. This finding aligns with previous studies suggesting that there is a dysregulation in internally directed cognition and the assignment of significance in individuals with ADHD (Schulze et al., 2024; Dupont et al., 2022; Kim et al., 2023).

Furthermore, individual-level analyses have focused on the significance of inter-individual variability in enhancing tailored approaches in mental health. Li et al. (2022), for instance, utilized individualised functional connectomes to differentiate ADHD from healthy controls with greater accuracy. On the other hand, Segura et al. (2024) used machine learning and connectome-based symptom mapping to identify specific functional circuits linked to the intensity of the symptoms of the condition. They proposed tailored objectives for prospective interventions, including transcranial magnetic stimulation (TMS) by demonstrating the effects of neuromodulation and indicating that neuroimaging-guided treatment personalisation could be an encouraging avenue. Wu et al. (2022) also classified ADHD into inattentive and mixed subtypes, revealing that patients with the combined-type displayed poorer cognitive performance and more significant functional abnormalities. However, to apply all these strategies in a clinical setting, translational validation, standardization, and replication with larger cohorts are very much still needed (Yen, 2025).

Likewise, research utilizing DTI indicates differences in the white matter in ADHD. However, the outcomes from the DTI studies are more diverse in children compared to adults, likely due to the ongoing myelination alterations occurring in the developing brain. (Firouzabadi et al., 2021). Much of the variation observed in children with ADHD, including the reduced volumes in the isthmus and splenic areas of the corpus callosum tends to normalize, for instance, in adulthood (Dramsdahl et al., 2012). DTI studies have also explored the links with key hyperactivity and impulsivity symptoms of ADHD. Impulsivity is not related to motor regions; rather, it shows a negative correlation with the fractional anisotropy (FA) of the bilateral anterior and posterior corona radiata, right superior and left inferior longitudinal fasciculus, bilateral internal capsules, left external capsule, and corticospinal tracts (Aoki et al., 2017; Aoki et al., 2018). This negative correlation aligns with the assessments of impulsivity in children who lack an ADHD diagnosis (Aoki et al., 2017). While certain research suggests that behavioral challenges stem from issues with motor inhibition, these findings support the notion that both motor functions and reward systems play a role in ADHD.

Research utilizing DTI has predominantly concentrated on the correlations between anisotropy metrics and behavioral modifications in individuals with ADHD. Sudre et al. (2020) introduced the concept of "developmental dysconnectome" to suggest that atypical connections contribute to the developmental challenges in ADHD (Theodoratou, Katsarou, Megari et al., 2025). Several white matter tracts play a significant role in cognitive control and attention systems of the brain - the right uncinate fasciculus, the left cingulum, the anterior thalamic radiations, the right superior longitudinal fasciculus, and various sections of the corpus callosum (Sudre et al., 2020; Chiang et al., 2016). Even with the differences observed among the groups, individual patients can present with varied outcomes due to the significant variability involved.

2.2. Electrophysiological Measures and Biochemical and Inflammatory Markers: Tools Utilized in the ADHD Diagnosis

Electrophysiological measures, including ***electroenchephalography (EEG)*** and ***event-related potentials (ERPs)***, are also another potential way for diagnosing ADHD. EEG studies, especially those utilizing the theta/beta ratio, revealed that individuals with ADHD show increased theta activity and decreased beta activity during cognitive tasks (van Son et al., 2019). The abnormal ratio is believed to reveal the lack of sustained attention. The P300 ERP component, indicative of cognitive processing speed and attention, shows delays in individuals with ADHD, reinforcing the potential of electrophysiological assessments as valuable diagnostic instruments for this disorder (Demirayak et al., 2023; Zhong et al., 2019).

Furthermore, ***biochemical markers***, including cortisol, vitamin D, and pro-inflammatory cytokines are more widely recognized as significant contributors to the ADHD pathophysiology. Salivary cortisol, serving as an indicator of stress response, has been associated with the intensity of ADHD symptoms (Fortes et al.,

2020). Increased levels of pro-inflammatory markers, including IL-6 and TNF-α, have also been observed in individuals with ADHD, suggesting a potential link to neuroinflammation (Elsadek et al., 2020). This indicates that biochemical testing may offer further objective indicators to enhance existing diagnostic procedures.

2.3. Eye-Tracking and Pupillometry: Novel Tools Used in Diagnosing ADHD

Other promising avenues for diagnosing ADHD include: ***eye-tracking*** and ***pupillometry***. Monitoring eye movement is recognized as a non-invasive approach to evaluate interest and cognitive control in individuals with ADHD. Utilizing eye-tracking technology, researchers can observe and quantify eye movements and gaze patterns in reaction to visual stimuli, providing insights into the attention span of individuals with ADHD (Janmohammadi et al., 2020). Studies show that individuals with ADHD demonstrate slower gaze shifts, heightened fixation, and more frequent attention lapses compared to normal controls. A study indicated that individuals diagnosed with ADHD exhibited a longer-than-anticipated gaze duration with a shorter-than-expected gaze shift during a visual search task. These findings emphasize the attention challenges which are typical for ADHD. Additionally, eye-tracking offers the benefit of delivering objective, real-time, quantifiable data on attention-related processes. This is particularly advantageous in settings, where traditional behavioral assessments rely on clinical observations (Stobernack et al., 2019). Consequently, monitoring eye movement can be beneficial in evaluating attention control in individuals with ADHD, providing insights into both the extent and nature of the challenges with attention.

The measurement of pupil dilation in response to cognitive and emotional stimuli, or pupillometry is an emerging laboratory test being utilized in research related to ADHD. It has been proposed that pupillometry could act as an indicator of cognitive effort or engagement during tasks, making it a suitable measure for exploring attentional processes in ADHD (van der Wel & van Steenbergen, 2018). In a study, Kleberg et al. (2021) revealed that children diagnosed with ADHD exhibited prolonged pupil dilation during tasks that required significant attention, in contrast to their healthy counterparts. This indicates that children with ADHD may be investing greater cognitive effort compared to those without the condition. The results highlight the ability to measure attention in real-time through pupillometry and suggest that phenomenology can serve as a practical diagnostic tool for assessing attention dysfunction in practice.

The use of eye-tracking and pupillometry biomarkers aims to improve existing diagnostic techniques and signifies a significant advancement toward a more objective and personalized approach to ADHD diagnosis. Both of these approaches uncover essential cognitive processes related to ADHD and have the potential to enhance diagnostic accuracy, especially in challenging cases where traditional behavioral assessments may fall short. With further research, it is reasonable to assume that ADHD will incorporate these instruments as integral parts of practice, enabling professionals to deliver more precise, effective, and targeted interventions.

III. NEUROPSYCHOLOGICAL EVALUATION AND COGNITIVE FUNCTIONING IN ADHD

As previously stated, ADHD is linked to difficulties in various cognitive areas, including attention, executive functions, working memory, and response inhibition. The cognitive deficits associated with ADHD significantly influence everyday activities in educational, social, and professional environments. ***Neuropsychological evaluation*** plays a crucial role in identifying ADHD and understanding its underlying cognitive factors. The rise of computerized tasks, gamification, and continuous data tracking has led to a transformation in ADHD assessments, making them more objective, valid, and dynamic than ever before.

3.1. Key Cognitive Deficits of ADHD Patients

A defining symptom of ADHD is the difficulty in sustaining attention, especially in activities that demand prolonged focus. Studies indicate that individuals with ADHD often experience challenges in sustained and selective attention, which can negatively impact their performance on tasks that necessitate the suppression of external cues (Roberts et al., 2018). A meta-analysis by Smith et al. (2020) indicated that children with ADHD exhibited significantly higher rates of inattention errors than control groups in sustained attention assessments, such as the Continuous Performance Test (CPT).

The manifestations of ADHD encompass daily executive functioning abilities, which include setting goals, shifting actions, planning, organizing, and self-regulation. In the context of executive functions significantly impacted by ADHD, it appears that inhibition control and working memory are particularly noteworthy. Individuals with ADHD exhibit challenges in managing automatic response intervals and also in mental process organization (Kofler et al., 2024). The previously mentioned deficits are most effectively detected through the Stroop Test and the Wisconsin Card Sorting Test (WCST), which are among the various assessments that evaluate executive functions (Torralva et al., 2013).

Working memory is another aspect that is particularly important in monitoring ADHD. Individuals with ADHD often experience challenges in both verbal and visual-spatial working memory, which can hinder their capacity to retain and manipulate information over short periods (Kofler et al., 2020). Consequently, children with ADHD demonstrated notably poorer performance compared to the control group on the Digit Span and Spatial Working Memory tasks (Westwood et al., 2023). Response inhibition is often considered as the most significant challenge associated with ADHD. Impairment in this area can be seen in the results of the Go/No-Go test and Stop-Signal Task (SST), where individuals with ADHD struggle to suppress dominant responses (Raud et al., 2020). Pasini et al. (2007) highlights that children with ADHD, particularly those exhibiting combined subtypes, demonstrate challenges in response inhibition that are closely associated with heightened impulsivity and hyperactivity.

3.2. Computerized Tasks and Gamification in ADHD Evaluation

The evaluation of ADHD has recently progressed through the integration of ***computerized assessments*** and gamified components, enhancing both the sensitivity of the diagnosis and its ecological validity. The Cambridge Neuropsychological Test Automated Battery (CANTAB), with its adaptive and dynamic form, facilitates the assessment of cognitive functions like working memory, attention, and response inhibition in individuals with ADHD. This method tends to provide a more precise evaluation compared to traditional manual tests and often exhibits greater creativity (Aoki et al., 2023). The components of CANTAB, including Stockings of Cambridge (SOC), Intra/Extra-Dimensional Shift (IED), and Spatial Working Memory (SWM), indicate cognitive differences between the ADHD group and the control group (Aoki et al., 2023). Studies have shown that individuals with ADHD completed these tasks notably less effectively than those without the condition, reinforcing the increasing evidence for the diagnostic capabilities of computerized neuropsychological assessments for ADHD (Claesdotter et al., 2018).

Alongside computerized assessments, the use of ***gamification***, and especially the use of serious games, for measuring ADHD symptoms has gained significant traction as an engaging approach, especially among children. For instance, Cogmed Working Memory Training (WMT) is a gamified task aimed at improving working memory and cognitive control in those with ADHD (Almarzouki et al., 2023). Children with ADHD are more motivated and want to do the task when the activities are structured as games. They not only show superior performance in working memory training compared to traditional approaches, but also exceed the clinician's expectations in various other tasks (Song et al., 2025). In addition, Park et al. (2018) studied reading difficulty through "Fairly-tale" - a narrative-driven interactive interface aimed at assisting individuals in dealing with this challenge. They employed an adaptive behavior training game platform (ABTGP) alongside brain–computer interface (BCI) and motion sensing technology. This intricate platform fosters an engaging environment for playing. As a result, there was an enhancement in the individuals' attention span and a reduction in their hyperactive behavior, leading to a favorable outcome on their reading skills (Park et al., 2018).

Additionally, Retalis et al. (2014) presented and analyzed two games - "Mathloons" and "Space Motif" - to evaluate their impact on ADHD. "Mathloons" is an engaging game designed to enhance skills in basic math skills, such as addition, subtraction, multiplication, and division, all within a manageable range of numbers."Space Motif" fosters players' organizational and spatiotemporal skills by engaging them in ordering, sorting, and pattern-matching tasks. In both games, the enhancement in individuals' executive functions was statistically significant, accompanied by a notable level of interest and motivation. Similarly, Dovis et al. (2015) also observed how incorporating game components can enhance executive functions in individuals with ADHD. The researchers assessed both the immediate and lasting impacts of gamified training on various executive functions, such as visual spatial working memory, inhibition, and cognitive flexibility, employing a range of evaluation methods. Different contexts are utilized to develop three executive functions: full-active mode, where all three are engaged at once; partially active mode, focusing on inhibition and cognitive flexibility; and placebo mode, which concentrates solely on working memory (Dovis et al., 2015). The serious game that is used is "BrainGame Brian (BGB)," which comprises 25 sessions. Each session is approximately 40 to 50 minutes long and includes a sequence of three structured training activities designed to enhance the three executive functions mentioned previously. The researchers determined that training various executive functions at the same time through the game proved to be an effective approach; additionally, they associated the observed improvements with the specific type of therapeutic intervention employed (Dovis et al., 2015).

Shaw et al. (2005), for instance, also examined how inhibitory performance influenced individuals with ADHD as they completed identical tasks in various environments, (e.g., a commercial gaming environment ("The Revenge of Frogger" and "Crash Bandicoot II"), a standard computerized environment, and a game-like environment), contrasting their findings with those of normal participants. The findings indicated improved inhibitory performance, with individuals exhibiting ADHD demonstrating performance on par with typical participants; this performance was notably superior in a game-like environment. Shaw et al. (2005) highlighted the importance of incorporating game or game-like environments for learning in individuals with ADHD, aiming to enhance their motivation and minimize the errors often associated with conventional computer-based learning.

In a separate study, Bul et al. (2015) created a serious game called "Plan-It Commander" aimed at enhancing behavioral learning and strategies essential for everyday functioning. It employs various psychological frameworks, such as the self-regulation model and social cognitive and learning theory, to achieve its goals. This online game consists of three mini-games, each designed to help players achieve their individual objectives while developing specific skills. In addition, each game consists of 10 primary missions, with various optional and special features incorporated to enhance motivation. The researchers collected feedback from participants and their parents regarding this serious game through a survey questionnaire method, resulting in favorable acceptance.

Last but not least, videogames represent a type of serious games that incorporate animation and 3D models. They have been utilized as a therapeutic tool for individuals with ADHD. One example of this is "aTenDerAH" (Mancera et al., 2017). It incorporates a 3D videogame within the ATutor e-learning platform to enhance the individuals' learning skills through the development of cognitive skills. The evaluation of this game was conducted within an e-learning course, where the participating students were highly interested and provided favorable feedback. Colombo et al. (2017) developed a serious game called "Antonyms," aimed at enhancing education and rehabilitation. This framework includes three interconnected mini-games, each designed with a variety of activities aimed at enhancing learning, fostering self-control of impulsive behaviors, and minimizing distractions from irrelevant thoughts. The outcomes from the initial pilot study suggested promising benefits in enhancing the attention of individuals with ADHD.

3.3. Real-Time Data Monitoring for ADHD Evaluation

Moreover, the assessment of ADHD through ***real-time data monitoring*** represents an innovative and developing approach that observes cognitive performance during task completion. This approach offers a greater level of precision and accuracy in detecting every time the different aspects of cognitive functioning, including the dynamics of attention, working memory, and inhibition (deBettencourt et al., 2019). Hyperactivity and heightened motor activity, which are defining symptoms of ADHD, can be assessed through movement using a method called actigraphy (Earnest et al., 2020). Recent studies have shown that the objective assessment of behavior in daily life can now be enhanced by integrating continuous neuropsychological testing with traditional methods, utilizing actigraphy data (Smith et al., 2020). Tracking cognitive data in real-time can reveal the gradually developing cognitive challenges in individuals with ADHD, thereby enhancing the accuracy of diagnosing the condition. Table 1 summarizes the comparison of new objective biomarkers and the gold standard methods for diagnosing ADHD.

Table 1. Comparison of new objective biomarkers and the gold standard methods for diagnosing ADHD.

Diagnostic Domain	Current Gold-Standard Traditional Methods	Key Limitations	Proposed Objective Markers
Clinical Diagnosis	Structured clinical interview based on **DSM-5** criteria, developmental history, and symptom assessment from multiple settings	Subjective; dependent on clinician expertise and patient/parent recall; vulnerable to reporting bias	Multimodal biomarker panels integrating biological and cognitive data
Behavioral Assessment	Parent-, teacher-, and self-report rating scales (e.g., ADHD symptom questionnaires)	Informant discrepancies; cultural influences; symptom overlap with other disorders	Digital behavioral metrics and objective performance measures
Neuropsychological Evaluation	Tests of attention, executive function, working memory, inhibitory control, and processing speed	Performance can vary with motivation, fatigue, and testing conditions; not ADHD-specific	Quantitative cognitive profiles combined with biological markers for individualized assessment
Neuroimaging	Primarily used for research or differential diagnosis; not routinely used diagnostically	High cost; lack of standardized diagnostic thresholds	Structural and functional MRI markers identifying ADHD-related brain network alterations
Electrophysiological Assessment	Limited clinical use; EEG occasionally employed as an adjunctive tool	Variable findings across studies; insufficient diagnostic specificity	EEG-derived biomarkers (e.g., altered neural oscillations, connectivity patterns, event-related potentials)
Genetic Assessment	Not routinely recommended for diagnosis; family history considered clinically	ADHD is highly polygenic; individual variants have limited predictive value	Polygenic risk scores and integrated genetic susceptibility profiles
Treatment Selection	Trial-and-error approach based on symptom presentation and clinical judgment	Variable treatment response; delayed optimization of care	Biomarker-informed personalized treatment strategies predicting response and outcomes
Longitudinal Monitoring	Periodic clinical follow-up and symptom rating scales	Relies heavily on subjective symptom reporting	Developmental biomarker trajectories tracking symptom progression and treatment effects across the lifespan

IV. THE IMPACT OF ADHD SYMPTOMS ON EMOTIONAL WELL-BEING AND QUALITY OF LIFE

ADHD encompasses more than just inattention, hyperactivity, and impulsivity. A significant issue associated with ADHD is the reduced quality of life that individuals may encounter. ADHD influences various dimensions of an individual's life, including their emotional well-being, social development, and daily routines. The growing emphasis on research related to ADHD highlights the importance of assessing quality of life indicators. This evaluation is essential for understanding the overall impact of ADHD, particularly in children and adolescents.

The emotional well-being of someone with ADHD is often overlooked, leading to diminished self-esteem compared to peers who do not have ADHD. Studies have shown that children with ADHD face a significant risk of developing co-occurring mood disorders, which can interfere with treatment and adversely affect their overall prognosis. The emotional challenges are intensified by shortcomings in academic and social performance associated with ADHD, as children with this condition often fall short of academic expectations (Drechsler et al., 2020). Studies indicate that individuals with ADHD often struggle with organizing tasks, finishing assignments, and being present in class, leading to lower performance and academic setbacks (Smith et al., 2020). The academic challenges faced by these students could lead to deteriorating life situations, likely serving as a crucial factor in their overall happiness and ability to connect socially. Schoeman et al. (2018) illustrate the prevalence of bullying and social exclusion in children with ADHD, highlighting a complex cycle characterized by difficulties in emotional regulation and increased anxiety.

ADHD has an impact on social functioning as well as on academic work. Individuals with ADHD often exhibit heightened social impulsivity and difficulties with self-regulation during social interactions, which can lead to challenges in developing appropriate social skills and engaging with peers. Children with ADHD frequently encounter difficulties in social interactions, leading to experiences of peer rejection and challenges in participating in group activities (Chen & Jiang, 2024). Fortes et al. (2020) stated that children with ADHD expressed dissatisfaction in their social relationships, which led to increased anxiety and depression. These issues may continue into adulthood, where an individual with ADHD might struggle to maintain or foster intimate relationships, as well as exhibit challenges in collaboration and efficiency in the workplace.

Furthermore, the influence of ADHD on everyday functioning is significant as it hinders the person's capacity to engage in daily activities. For individuals with ADHD, tasks like keeping track of time, staying organized, and handling finances can often feel quite daunting (Kofler et al., 2018). People with ADHD often experience ongoing disorganization and struggle with time management, leading to heightened, persistent stress and a sense of dissatisfaction in their daily lives. The impact of ADHD on a person's everyday life is significant, extending beyond the realm of healthcare and severely restricting daily activities.

To assess these various aspects of quality of life, a range of scales and tools have been developed to measure the multifaceted impacts of ADHD. Several commonly used assessments encompass WHOQOL-BREF, which assesses an individual's overall quality of life across various domains (Ramji et al., 2023). Another measure is the ADHD-QOL, which examines the impact of ADHD on academic, familial, and social interactions (Wanni Arachchige Dona et al., 2023). These tools empower professionals and researchers to concentrate on a thorough evaluation of ADHD's effects on an individual's life, ultimately enhancing the customization of treatment plans and delivering more complete individualized care.

V. IMPROVEMENTS IN ADHD ASSESSMENT AND TREATMENT METHODS

The application of objective, non-invasive techniques for assessing ADHD, along with its growing multidimensionality, provides optimism for the best possible management and improved long-term care of the condition. Recent studies emphasize the importance of early intervention initiatives that concentrate on behavioral therapy, cognitive skill enhancement, and educational support. These approaches have demonstrated effectiveness in alleviating symptom severity and fostering better long-term academic and social outcomes (Duan et al., 2021). Biomarkers, such as those derived from neuroimaging and electrophysiology, have the potential to enhance the accuracy of early ADHD diagnosis, by detecting individuals at risk prior to the onset of clinically significant symptoms.

A significant advancement will be tailored therapy for ADHD, moving away from a uniform approach. Given the diverse nature of ADHD, individuals will exhibit varying responses to different therapeutic approaches, influenced by their unique genetic, neurobiological, and environmental characteristics. The enhanced use of neuroimaging and electrophysiological biomarkers can help pinpoint patients who are most likely to gain from particular treatment approaches. For instance, the EEG theta/beta ratio serves as a biomarker that reflects treatment response to neurofeedback, while various genetic biomarkers can foresee the response to stimulant medications. These treatment options may improve the effectiveness of therapy, minimize negative side effects, and lead to better results as a whole (Mehta et al., 2020).

Given the growing awareness of ADHD, it is evident that interventions will be significantly influenced by biomarker data and cognitive profiling. Neuroimaging and genetic profiling progressively clarify the individual differences in the manifestation of ADHD. For instance, individuals with ADHD often demonstrate difficulties with attention and executive functioning; research has indicated that some may have structural and functional brain abnormalities, including reduced grey matter in the prefrontal cortex (Duan et al., 2021). Gaining insight into the condition from this perspective allows professionals to customize treatment plans by focusing on particular neuroanatomical areas or pathways linked to the symptoms exhibited by individuals with ADHD.

Furthermore, assessing cognitive strengths and weaknesses across different areas of an individual's profile can guide the development of customized treatment approaches that address the unique needs of each individual. Cognitive assessments like CANTAB and Cogmed Working Memory Training Diagnostics can identify cognitive impairment, and interventions focused on enhancing executive functions can be designed (Almarzouki et al., 2023; Aoki et al., 2023). For instance, individuals experiencing significant challenges with working memory may benefit from specialized cognitive training, while those facing difficulties with inhibitory control could find support through neurofeedback interventions. Tailoring treatment to fit unique cognitive profiles can improve the prompt handling of symptoms and support ongoing recovery.

Research is being conducted that highlights the importance of lifestyle modifications, such as diet, exercise, and sleep, in effectively managing symptoms associated with ADHD. For example, the DASH diet, combined with magnesium and vitamin D, has shown some effectiveness in enhancing behavioral outcomes related to ADHD in children (Abhishek et al., 2024). The integration of these nutritional strategies with behavioral supports offers a proactive approach for early intervention, reducing the necessity for medication and thereby lessening dependence on pharmacological treatments in instances of mild ADHD. Additionally, neurostimulation methods, including transcranial magnetic stimulation (TMS) and neurofeedback, represent innovative approaches for addressing ADHD symptoms by influencing particular neural pathways related to attention and impulse regulation (Yen et al., 2024). These methods have demonstrated the potential to foster neural adaptability and enhance cognitive abilities, serving as a valuable complement to pharmacological interventions. Nonetheless, additional studies are necessary to elucidate the long-term efficacy and optimal implementation of these interventions, especially in children (Michelini et al., 2022).

VI. CONCLUDING REMARKS AND FUTURE DIRECTION

This thorough literature review highlights significant advancements in understanding the neurobiological frameworks of ADHD, as well as the promising role of biomarkers and neuropsychological evaluations in improving diagnosis and treatment strategies. Although traditional diagnostic approaches remain significant, a growing body of research on biomarkers signals a shift towards more objective, precise, and personalized assessments. Timely action using biomarkers and neuropsychological assessments is essential to reduce the lasting impacts of ADHD on educational, emotional, and social development. The integration of biomarkers into practice can enhance personalized treatment, reducing the trial-and-error approach in ADHD management.

Future investigations into ADHD should concentrate on several crucial domains. Initially, it is essential to conduct developmental follow-up studies that track the progression of ADHD symptoms from childhood into adulthood. This will help in understanding the natural history of the condition and in recognizing its earliest indicators. These studies may prove valuable in pinpointing the most predictive long-term outcome indicators and the most impactful interventions across an individual's lifespan. It is essential to adopt comprehensive strategies that integrate genetic, neuroimaging, and electrophysiological indicators alongside cognitive assessments to tailor treatment methods effectively. These methods will identify the precise biological and cognitive factors contributing to an individual's ADHD, facilitating the development of more tailored treatment options. Moreover, given the evolving nature of research related to the diagnosis and treatment of ADHD, it is essential for professionals, researchers, and policymakers to work together more closely to effectively implement new insights into practice. The exploration of biomarkers and the development of personalized treatment protocols will significantly enhance the quality of care for adults with ADHD.

REFERENCES

Abhishek, F., Gugnani, J. S., Kaur, H., Damera, A. R., Mane, R., Sekhri, A., Singh, G., & Kaur, G. (2024). Dietary Interventions and Supplements for Managing Attention-Deficit/Hyperactivity Disorder (ADHD): A Systematic Review of Efficacy and Recommendations. *Cureus*, *16*(9), e69804. DOI: 10.7759/cureus.69804 PMID: 39429382

Almarzouki, A. F., Bellato, A., Al-Saad, M. S., & Al-Jabri, B. (2023). COGMED working memory training in children with Attention Deficit/Hyperactivity Disorder (ADHD): A feasibility study in Saudi Arabia. *Applied Neuropsychology. Child*, *12*(3), 202–213. DOI: 10.1080/21622965.2022.2070020 PMID: 35549563

Aoki, S., Nagatani, F., Kagitani-Shimono, K., Ohno, Y., Taniike, M., & Mohri, I. (2023). Examining normative values using the Cambridge neuropsychological test automated battery and developmental traits of executive functions among elementary school-aged children in Japan. *Frontiers in Psychology*, *14*, 1141628. DOI: 10.3389/fpsyg.2023.1141628 PMID: 37663362

Aoki, Y., Cortese, S., & Castellanos, F. X. (2018). Research Review: Diffusion tensor imaging studies of attention-deficit/hyperactivity disorder: meta-analyses and reflections on head motion. *Journal of Child Psychology and Psychiatry, and Allied Disciplines*, *59*(3), 193–202. DOI: 10.1111/jcpp.12778 PMID: 28671333

Aoki, Y., Yoncheva, Y. N., Chen, B., Nath, T., Sharp, D., Lazar, M., Velasco, P., Milham, M. P., & Di Martino, A. (2017). Association of White Matter Structure With Autism Spectrum Disorder and Attention-Deficit/Hyperactivity Disorder. *JAMA Psychiatry*, *74*(11), 1120–1128. DOI: 10.1001/jamapsychiatry.2017.2573 PMID: 28877317

Berberat, J., Huggenberger, R., Montali, M., Gruber, P., Pircher, A., Lövblad, K. O., Killer, H. E., & Remonda, L. (2021). Brain activation patterns in medicated versus medication-naïve adults with attention-deficit hyperactivity disorder during fMRI tasks of motor inhibition and cognitive switching. *BMC Medical Imaging*, *21*(1), 53. DOI: 10.1186/s12880-021-00579-3 PMID: 33740903

Bul, K. C., Franken, I. H., Van Der Oord, S., Kato, P. M., Danckaerts, M., Vreeke, L. J., Willems, A., Van Oers, H. J., Van Den Heuvel, R., Van Slagmaat, R., & Maras, A. (2015). Development and User Satisfaction of "Plan-It Commander," a Serious Game for Children with ADHD. *Games for Health Journal*, *4*(6), 502–512. DOI: 10.1089/g4h.2015.0021 PMID: 26325247

Chang, J. P., Su, K. P., Mondelli, V., & Pariante, C. M. (2021). Cortisol and inflammatory biomarker levels in youths with attention deficit hyperactivity disorder (ADHD): Evidence from a systematic review with meta-analysis. *Translational Psychiatry*, *11*(1), 430. DOI: 10.1038/s41398-021-01550-0 PMID: 34413283

Chen, M., & Jiang, X. (2024). The impact of modified Cognitive-Behavioral Group Therapy in social adjustment functions of children with attention deficit hyperactivity disorder and their parents' stress levels: A nonrandomized clinical trial. *Journal of Clinical Psychology*, *80*(9), 1969–1980. DOI: 10.1002/jclp.23704 PMID: 38747969

Chiang, H. L., Chen, Y. J., Shang, C. Y., Tseng, W. Y., & Gau, S. S. (2016). Different neural substrates for executive functions in youths with ADHD: A diffusion spectrum imaging tractography study. *Psychological Medicine*, *46*(6), 1225–1238. DOI: 10.1017/S0033291715002767 PMID: 26744120

Claesdotter, E., Cervin, M., Åkerlund, S., Råstam, M., & Lindvall, M. (2018). The effects of ADHD on cognitive performance. *Nordic Journal of Psychiatry*, *72*(3), 158–163. DOI: 10.1080/08039488.2017.1402951 PMID: 29161919

Colombo, V., Baldassini, D., Mottura, S., Sacco, M., Crepaldi, M., & Antonietti, A. (2017). Antonyms: A serious game for enhancing inhibition mechanisms in children with Attention Deficit/Hyperactivity Disorder (ADHD). In *International Conference on Virtual Rehabilitation, ICVR* (Vol. 2017-June, pp. 10–11). https://doi.org/DOI: 10.1109/ICVR.2017.8007457

deBettencourt, M. T., Keene, P. A., Awh, E., & Vogel, E. K. (2019). Real-time triggering reveals concurrent lapses of attention and working memory. *Nature Human Behaviour*, *3*(8), 808–816. DOI: 10.1038/s41562-019-0606-6 PMID: 31110335

Demirayak, P., Kıyı, İ., İşbitiren, Y. Ö., & Yener, G. (2023). Cognitive load associates prolonged P300 latency during target stimulus processing in individuals with mild cognitive impairment. *Scientific Reports*, *13*(1), 15956. DOI: 10.1038/s41598-023-43132-8 PMID: 37743392

Dovis, S., Van Der Oord, S., Wiers, R. W., & Prins, P. J. M. (2015). Improving Executive Functioning in Children with ADHD: Training Multiple Executive Functions within the Context of a Computer Game. A Randomized Double-Blind Placebo Controlled Trial. *PLoS One*, *10*(4), e0121651. DOI: 10.1371/journal.pone.0121651 PMID: 25844638

Dramsdahl, M., Westerhausen, R., Haavik, J., Hugdahl, K., & Plessen, K. J. (2012). Adults with attention-deficit/hyperactivity disorder - a diffusion-tensor imaging study of the corpus callosum. *Psychiatry Research*, *201*(2), 168–173. DOI: 10.1016/j.pscychresns.2011.08.005 PMID: 22386969

Drechsler, R., Brem, S., Brandeis, D., Grünblatt, E., Berger, G., & Walitza, S. (2020). ADHD: Current Concepts and Treatments in Children and Adolescents. *Neuropediatrics*, *51*(5), 315–335. DOI: 10.1055/s-0040-1701658 PMID: 32559806

Duan, K., Jiang, W., Rootes-Murdy, K., Schoenmacker, G. H., Arias-Vasquez, A., Buitelaar, J. K., Hoogman, M., Oosterlaan, J., Hoekstra, P. J., Heslenfeld, D. J., Hartman, C. A., Calhoun, V. D., Turner, J. A., & Liu, J. (2021). Gray matter networks associated with attention and working memory deficit in ADHD across adolescence and adulthood. *Translational Psychiatry*, *11*(1), 184. DOI: 10.1038/s41398-021-01301-1 PMID: 33767139

Dupont, G., Van Rooij, D., Buitelaar, J. K., Reif, A., & Grimm, O. (2022). Sex-related differences in adult attention-deficit hyperactivity disorder patients – An analysis of external globus pallidus functional connectivity in resting-state functional MRI. *Frontiers in Psychiatry*, *13*, 962911. Advance online publication. DOI: 10.3389/fpsyt.2022.962911 PMID: 36117656

Earnest, T., Shephard, E., Tye, C., McEwen, F., Woodhouse, E., Liang, H., Sheerin, F., & Bolton, P. F. (2020). Actigraph-Measured Movement Correlates of Attention-Deficit/Hyperactivity Disorder (ADHD) Symptoms in Young People with Tuberous Sclerosis Complex (TSC) with and without Intellectual Disability and Autism Spectrum Disorder (ASD). *Brain Sciences*, *10*(8), 491. DOI: 10.3390/brainsci10080491 PMID: 32731531

Elsadek, A. E., Al-Shokary, A. H., Abdelghani, W. E., Kamal, N. M., Ibrahim, A. O., El-Shorbagy, H. H., Suliman, H. A., Barseem, N. F., Abdel Maksoud, Y. H., Azab, S. M., & Nour El Din, D. M. (2020). Serum Levels of Interleukin-6 and Tumor Necrosis Factor Alpha in Children With Attention-Deficit Hyperactivity Disorder. *Journal of Pediatric Neurosciences*, *15*(4), 402–408. DOI: 10.4103/JPN.JPN_1_20 PMID: 33936305

Firouzabadi, F. D., Ramezanpour, S., Firouzabadi, M. D., Yousem, I. J., Puts, N. J., & Yousem, D. M. (2021). Neuroimaging in Attention-Deficit/Hyperactivity Disorder: Recent Advances. *AJR. American Journal of Roentgenology*, *218*(2), 321–332. DOI: 10.2214/AJR.21.26316 PMID: 34406053

Fortes, D., Figueiredo, T., Lima, G., Segenreich, D., Serra-Pinheiro, M. A., & Mattos, P. (2020). Disregarding Impairment in ADHD Diagnosis Inflates Its Prevalence. *Journal of Attention Disorders*, *25*(11), 1529–1533. DOI: 10.1177/1087054720911969 PMID: 32329397

French, B., Daley, D., Groom, M., & Cassidy, S. (2023). Risks Associated With Undiagnosed ADHD and/or Autism: A Mixed-Method Systematic Review. *Journal of Attention Disorders*, *27*(12), 1393–1410. DOI: 10.1177/10870547231176862 PMID: 37341291

Friedman, N. P., & Robbins, T. W. (2022). The role of prefrontal cortex in cognitive control and executive function. *Neuropsychopharmacology : Official Publication of the American College of Neuropsychopharmacology*, *47*(1), 72–89. DOI: 10.1038/s41386-021-01132-0 PMID: 34408280

Gilbert, M., Boecker, M., Reiss, F., Kaman, A., Erhart, M., Schlack, R., Westenhöfer, J., Döpfner, M., & Ravens-Sieberer, U. (2025). Gender and Age Differences in ADHD Symptoms and Co-occurring Depression and Anxiety Symptoms Among Children and Adolescents in the BELLA Study. *Child Psychiatry and Human Development*, *56*(4), 1162–1172. DOI: 10.1007/s10578-023-01622-w PMID: 37851158

Gondek, T. (2021). Diagnosing ADHD in adults: Diagnostic tools and differential diagnosis. *European Psychiatry : The Journal of the Association of European Psychiatrists*, *64*(S1), S72–S73. DOI: 10.1192/j.eurpsy.2021.226

Hurjui, I. A., Hurjui, R. M., Hurjui, L. L., Serban, I. L., Dobrin, I., Apostu, M., & Dobrin, R. P. (2025). Biomarkers and Neuropsychological Tools in Attention-Deficit/Hyperactivity Disorder: From Subjectivity to Precision Diagnosis. *Medicina (Kaunas, Lithuania)*, *61*(7), 1211. DOI: 10.3390/medicina61071211 PMID: 40731840

Janmohammadi, S., Haghgoo, H. A., Farahbod, M., Overton, P. G., & Pishyareh, E. (2020). Effect of a visual tracking intervention on attention and behavior of children with Attention Deficit Hyperactivity Disorder. *Journal of eye movement research*, *12*(8), . https://doi.org/DOI: 10.16910/jemr.12.8.6

Kim, B., Niu, X., & Zhang, F. (2023). Functional connectivity strength and topology differences in social phobia adolescents with and without ADHD comorbidity. *Neuropsychologia*, *178*, 108418. DOI: 10.1016/j.neuropsychologia.2022.108418 PMID: 36403658

Kleberg, J. L., Frick, M. A., & Brocki, K. C. (2021). Increased pupil dilation to happy faces in children with hyperactive/impulsive symptoms of ADHD. *Development and Psychopathology*, *33*(3), 767–777. DOI: 10.1017/S0954579420000036 PMID: 32102703

Kofler, M. J., Sarver, D. E., Harmon, S. L., Moltisanti, A., Aduen, P. A., Soto, E. F., & Ferretti, N. (2018). Working memory and organizational skills problems in ADHD. *Journal of Child Psychology and Psychiatry, and Allied Disciplines*, *59*(1), 57–67. DOI: 10.1111/jcpp.12773 PMID: 28714075

Kofler, M. J., Singh, L. J., Soto, E. F., Chan, E. S. M., Miller, C. E., Harmon, S. L., & Spiegel, J. A. (2020). Working memory and short-term memory deficits in ADHD: A bifactor modeling approach. *Neuropsychology*, *34*(6), 686–698. DOI: 10.1037/neu0000641 PMID: 32437194

Li, M., Dahmani, L., Hubbard, C. S., Hu, Y., Wang, M., Wang, D., & Liu, H. (2022). Individualized functional connectome identified generalizable biomarkers for psychiatric symptoms in transdiagnostic patients. *Neuropsychopharmacology : Official Publication of the American College of Neuropsychopharmacology*, *48*(4), 633–641. DOI: 10.1038/s41386-022-01500-4 PMID: 36402836

Long, Y., Pan, N., Ji, S., Qin, K., Chen, Y., Zhang, X., He, M., Suo, X., Yu, Y., Wang, S., & Gong, Q. (2022). Distinct brain structural abnormalities in attention-deficit/hyperactivity disorder and substance use disorders: A comparative meta-analysis. *Translational Psychiatry*, *12*(1), 368. DOI: 10.1038/s41398-022-02130-6 PMID: 36068207

Mancera, L., Baldiris, S., Fabregat, R., Gomez, S., & Mejia, C. (2017). ATenDerAH: A Videogame to Support e-Learning Students with ADHD. In *Proceedings - IEEE 17th International Conference on Advanced Learning Technologies, ICALT 2017* (pp. 438–440). https://doi.org/DOI: 10.1109/ICALT.2017.157

Megari, K., & Genova, K. D. (2025). The Neurocognitive Characteristics of Children With Neurodevelopmental Disabilities and Their Clinical Implications. In *IGI Global eBooks* (pp. 119–142). https://doi.org/DOI: 10.4018/979-8-3693-9689-6.ch006

Megari, K., Sofologi, M., Kougioumtzis, G., Thomaidou, E., Thomaidis, G., Katsarou, D., ... & Theodoratou, M. (2025). Neurocognitive and psycho-emotional profile of children with disabilities. Applied Neuropsychology: Child, 14(3), 323-328.

Meghji, S., Hilderley, A. J., Murias, K., Brooks, B. L., Andersen, J., Fehlings, D., Dlamini, N., Kirton, A., & Carlson, H. L. (2024). Executive functioning, ADHD symptoms and resting state functional connectivity in children with perinatal stroke. *Brain Imaging and Behavior*, *18*(2), 263–278. DOI: 10.1007/s11682-023-00827-w PMID: 38038867

Mehta, T., Mannem, N., Yarasi, N. K., & Bollu, P. C. (2020). Biomarkers for ADHD: The Present and Future Directions. *Current Developmental Disorders Reports*, *7*(3), 85–92. DOI: 10.1007/s40474-020-00196-9

Michelini, G., Norman, L. J., Shaw, P., & Loo, S. K. (2022). Treatment biomarkers for ADHD: Taking stock and moving forward. *Translational Psychiatry*, *12*(1), 444. DOI: 10.1038/s41398-022-02207-2 PMID: 36224169

Park, K., Kihl, T., Park, S., Kim, M., & Chang, J. (2018). Fairy tale directed game-based training system for children with ADHD using BCI and motion sensing technologies. *Behaviour & Information Technology*, *38*(6), 564–577. DOI: 10.1080/0144929X.2018.1544276

Parlatini, V., Bellato, A., Gabellone, A., Margari, L., Marzulli, L., Matera, E., Petruzzelli, M. G., Solmi, M., Correll, C. U., & Cortese, S. (2024). A state-of-the-art overview of candidate diagnostic biomarkers for Attention-deficit/hyperactivity disorder (ADHD). *Expert Review of Molecular Diagnostics*, *24*(4), 259–271. DOI: 10.1080/14737159.2024.2333277 PMID: 38506617

Pasini, A., Paloscia, C., Alessandrelli, R., Porfirio, M. C., & Curatolo, P. (2007). Attention and executive functions profile in drug naive ADHD subtypes. *Brain & Development*, *29*(7), 400–408. DOI: 10.1016/j.braindev.2006.11.010 PMID: 17207595

Ramji, R., Rämgård, M., & Kottorp, A. (2023). Psychometric properties of the WHOQOL-BREF in citizens from a disadvantaged neighborhood in Southern Sweden. *Frontiers in Psychology*, *14*, 1118575. DOI: 10.3389/fpsyg.2023.1118575 PMID: 37113124

Raud, L., Westerhausen, R., Dooley, N., & Huster, R. J. (2020). Differences in unity: The go/no-go and stop signal tasks rely on different mechanisms. *NeuroImage*, *210*, 116582. DOI: 10.1016/j.neuroimage.2020.116582 PMID: 31987997

Retalis, S., Korpa, T., Skaloumpakas, C., Boloudakis, M., Kourakli, M., Altanis, I., & Pervanidou, P. (2014). Empowering children with ADHD learning disabilities with the kinems kinect learning games. In *8th European Conference on Games Based Learning* (pp. 469–477).

Roberts, M., Ashinoff, B. K., Castellanos, F. X., & Carrasco, M. (2018). When attention is intact in adults with ADHD. *Psychonomic Bulletin & Review*, *25*(4), 1423–1434. DOI: 10.3758/s13423-017-1407-4 PMID: 29181782

Rubia, K., Westwood, S., Aggensteiner, P. M., & Brandeis, D. (2021). Neurotherapeutics for Attention Deficit/Hyperactivity Disorder (ADHD): A Review. *Cells*, *10*(8), 2156. DOI: 10.3390/cells10082156 PMID: 34440925

Schoeman, R., Enright, J., James, A., Vermeulen, C., & De Beer, N. (2018). Removing mental health barriers to education: A community project. *South African Journal of Psychiatry*, *24*. Advance online publication. DOI: 10.4102/sajpsychiatry.v24i0.1293

Schulze, M., Coghill, D., Lux, S., Philipsen, A., & Silk, T. (2024). Assessing brain iron and its relationship to cognition and comorbidity in children with Attention-Deficit/Hyperactivity Disorder with quantitative susceptibility mapping. *Biological Psychiatry. Cognitive Neuroscience and Neuroimaging*. Advance online publication. DOI: 10.1016/j.bpsc.2024.08.015 PMID: 39218036

Segura, P., Pagani, M., Bishop, S. L., Thomson, P., Colcombe, S., Xu, T., Factor, Z. Z., Hector, E. C., Kim, S. H., Lombardo, M. V., Gozzi, A., Castellanos, X. F., Lord, C., Milham, M. P., & Di Martino, A. (2024). Connectome-based symptom mapping andin silicorelated gene expression in children with autism and/or attention-deficit/ hyperactivity disorder. medRxiv *(Cold Spring Harbor Laboratory)*. https://doi.org/ DOI: 10.1101/2024.12.09.24318621

Shaw, R., Grayson, A., & Lewis, V. (2005). Inhibition, ADHD, and Computer Games: The Inhibitory Performance of Children with ADHD on Computerized Tasks and Games. *Journal of Attention Disorders*, *8*(4), 160–168. DOI: 10.1177/1087054705278771 PMID: 16110046

Smith, J. N., Raiker, J. S., Fosco, W. D., Jusko, M. L., Campez, M., Little, K., Mattfeld, A., Espinal, K., Sanchez, G., Merrill, B., Musser, E. D., Gnagy, E., Greiner, A., Coles, E., & Pelham, W. E.Jr. (2020). Executive Functioning and Activity in Children: A Multimethod Examination of Working Memory, Inhibition, and Hyperactivity. *Journal of Abnormal Child Psychology*, *48*(9), 1143–1153. DOI: 10.1007/ s10802-020-00665-0 PMID: 32557161

Song, X., Hou, Y., Shi, W., Wang, Y., Fan, F., & Hong, L. (2025). Exploring the impact of different types of exercise on working memory in children with ADHD: A network meta-analysis. *Frontiers in Psychology*, *16*, 1522944. DOI: 10.3389/ fpsyg.2025.1522944 PMID: 39931282

Stobernack, T., de Vries, S. P. W., Rodrigues Pereira, R., Pelsser, L. M., Ter Braak, C. J. F., Aarts, E., van Baarlen, P., Kleerebezem, M., Frankena, K., & Hontelez, S. (2019). Biomarker Research in ADHD: The Impact of Nutrition (BRAIN) - study protocol of an open-label trial to investigate the mechanisms underlying the effects of a few-foods diet on ADHD symptoms in children. *BMJ Open*, *9*(11), e029422. DOI: 10.1136/bmjopen-2019-029422 PMID: 31694844

Sudre, G., Frederick, J., Sharp, W., Ishii-Takahashi, A., Mangalmurti, A., Choudhury, S., & Shaw, P. (2020). Mapping associations between polygenic risks for childhood neuropsychiatric disorders, symptoms of attention deficit hyperactivity disorder, cognition, and the brain. *Molecular Psychiatry*, *25*(10), 2482–2492. DOI: 10.1038/ s41380-019-0350-3 PMID: 30700802

Takahashi, N., Ono, T., Omori, Y., Iizumi, M., Kato, H., Kasuno, S., Persing, B., & Tsuchiya, K. J. (2024). Assessment of executive functions using a 3D-video game in children and adolescents with ADHD. *Frontiers in Psychiatry*, *15*, 1407703. DOI: 10.3389/fpsyt.2024.1407703 PMID: 39238936

Theodoratou, M., Katsarou, D. V., Megari, K., Papadopoulou, S. L., Efthymiou, E., Sofologi, M., Kougioumtzis, G. A., Yotsidi, V., Koundourou, C., Toki, E. I., Argyrides, M., & Mantsos, E. (2025). Innovative Neuropsychological Interventions for ADHD and Asperger's Syndrome and Clinical Implications for Practitioners: Integrating Traditional Approaches With Emerging Technologies (Chapter 19, pages 391-410). *Clinical Applications of Pediatric Neuropsychology from Infancy to Adolescence.* Pennsylvania / USA: IGI Global.

Theodoratou, M., Kougioumtzis, G. A., Yotsidi, V., Andriopoulou, P., Megari, K., Koundourou, C., Siouti, Z., & Argyrides, M. (2025). Clinical Neuropsychological Profile and Interventions for Co-Occurrence of ADHD and ASD. In Sofologi, M., Katsarou, D., & Efthymiou, E. (Eds.), *Exploring Cognitive and Psychosocial Dynamics Across Childhood and Adolescence* (pp. 211–228). IGI Global., DOI: 10.4018/979-8-3693-4022-6.ch011

Torralva, T., Gleichgerrcht, E., Lischinsky, A., Roca, M., & Manes, F. (2013). "Ecological" and highly demanding executive tasks detect real-life deficits in high-functioning adult ADHD patients. *Journal of Attention Disorders*, *17*(1), 11–19. DOI: 10.1177/1087054710389988 PMID: 22826512

van der Wel, P., & van Steenbergen, H. (2018). Pupil dilation as an index of effort in cognitive control tasks: A review. *Psychonomic Bulletin & Review*, *25*(6), 2005–2015. DOI: 10.3758/s13423-018-1432-y PMID: 29435963

van Son, D., de Rover, M., De Blasio, F. M., van der Does, W., Barry, R. J., & Putman, P. (2019). Electroencephalography theta/beta ratio covaries with mind wandering and functional connectivity in the executive control network. *Annals of the New York Academy of Sciences*, *1452*(1), 52–64. DOI: 10.1111/nyas.14180 PMID: 31310007

Veenman, B., Luman, M., & Oosterlaan, J. (2017). Further Insight into the Effectiveness of a Behavioral Teacher Program Targeting ADHD Symptoms Using Actigraphy, Classroom Observations and Peer Ratings. *Frontiers in Psychology*, *8*, 1157. DOI: 10.3389/fpsyg.2017.01157 PMID: 28744244

Wanni Arachchige Dona, S., Badloe, N., Sciberras, E., Gold, L., Coghill, D., & Le, H. N. D. (2023). The Impact of Childhood Attention-Deficit/Hyperactivity Disorder (ADHD) on Children's Health-Related Quality of Life: A Systematic Review and Meta-Analysis. *Journal of Attention Disorders, 27*(6), 598–611. DOI: 10.1177/10870547231155438 PMID: 36800919

Westwood, S. J., Parlatini, V., Rubia, K., Cortese, S., Sonuga-Barke, E. J. S., Banaschewski, T., Baeyens, D., Bölte, S., Brandeis, D., Buitelaar, J., Carucci, S., Coghill, D., Daley, D., Döpfner, M., Ferrin, M., Galera, C., Hollis, C., Holtmann, M., Purper-Ouakil, D., & Zuddas, A. (2023). Computerized cognitive training in attention-deficit/hyperactivity disorder (ADHD): A meta-analysis of randomized controlled trials with blinded and objective outcomes. *Molecular Psychiatry, 28*(4), 1402–1414. DOI: 10.1038/s41380-023-02000-7 PMID: 36977764

Wu, Z., Wang, P., Liu, L., Liu, J., Cao, X., Sun, L., Cao, Q., Yang, L., Wang, Y., & Yang, B. (2022). ADHD-inattentive versus ADHD-Combined subtypes: A severity continuum or two distinct entities? A comprehensive analysis of clinical, cognitive and neuroimaging data. *Journal of Psychiatric Research, 149*, 28–36. DOI: 10.1016/j.jpsychires.2022.02.012 PMID: 35219873

Yan, H. (2025). Neuroimaging Biomarkers for ADHD and ASD: Recent advances, transdiagnostic overlaps, and implications for precision Psychiatry. *Lecture Notes in Education Psychology and Public Media, 111*(1), 31–44. DOI: 10.54254/2753-7048/2025.ND26282

Yen, C., Valentine, E. P., & Chiang, M. C. (2024). The Use of Transcranial Magnetic Stimulation in Attention Optimization Research: A Review from Basic Theory to Findings in Attention-Deficit/Hyperactivity Disorder and Depression. *Life (Basel, Switzerland), 14*(3), 329. DOI: 10.3390/life14030329 PMID: 38541654

Zhong, R., Li, M., Chen, Q., Li, J., Li, G., & Lin, W. (2019). The P300 Event-Related Potential Component and Cognitive Impairment in Epilepsy: A Systematic Review and Meta-analysis. *Frontiers in Neurology, 10*, 943. DOI: 10.3389/fneur.2019.00943 PMID: 31543861

Chapter 7
Understanding the Inside:
The Biological and Genetic Underpinnings of ASD and ADHD and Their Effects on Children

Kiara Tiwari
http://orcid.org/0009-0002-6728-344X
PES University, India

Jessica Arun Robert
http://orcid.org/0009-0000-3641-4131
PES University, India

Deepti Swamy
http://orcid.org/0000-0003-1167-9947
PES University, India

ABSTRACT

This chapter investigates the biological and genetic foundations of Autism Spectrum Disorder (ASD) and Attention-Deficit Hyperactivity Disorder (ADHD) in children, framing them as neurodevelopmental conditions with evolving trajectories affecting learning, socialisation, and quality of life (QoL). It details polygenic architectures, shared risks in synaptic signalling and rare variants (e.g., SHANK3, CHD8 in ASD; DRD4, SLC6A3 in ADHD), alongside unique profiles impacting cortical development and striatal function. Neurobiological models reveal overlapping fronto-striatal disruptions, neurotransmitter imbalances (dopamine, serotonin, GABA), and connectivity variances: ASD's social under-connectivity versus ADHD's executive deficits. Intersections in emotion regulation, sensory processing, and executive functions contrast with divergences in social cognition and reward systems. Developmental

DOI: 10.4018/979-8-3373-7072-9.ch007

outcomes include comorbid maladaptive behaviours, peer challenges, and adaptive gaps, underscoring needs for epigenetic research, biomarkers, and neurodiversity-aligned interventions.

INTRODUCTION

In recent years, a growing number of children have been diagnosed with some form of neurodivergence–brain functioning that differs from the pattern most common in the general population (Legault et al., 2021). Autism spectrum disorder (ASD) and attention-deficit/hyperactivity disorder (ADHD) are neurodevelopmental conditions that emerge early in life and shape trajectories of learning, social participation, and health-related quality of life (QoL) through interactions among genetic liability, biological mechanisms, and environment. This chapter treats ASD and ADHD as distinct diagnostic entities while examining where their biology overlaps and diverges, keeping the focus on how these mechanisms affect children's everyday functioning and quality of life.

ASD and ADHD as Neurodevelopmental Conditions

ASD refers to relatively stable differences in social interaction and communication compared with neurotypical peers. Children with ASD show restricted and repetitive patterns of behavior, interests, and activities, along with differences in language development, cognitive profile, sensory reactivity, and adaptive functioning (Braconnier & Siper, 2021; Lai et al., 2016). Longitudinal studies of preschoolers and high-risk infant siblings reveal a varied developmental course (Sacrey et al., 2018; Szatmari et al., 2015). Some children improve and adapt well over time, whereas others show persistent or widening gaps in functioning. Symptom severity and adaptive functioning are therefore not fixed but dynamic. In practical terms, two children with the same diagnosis can follow very different paths–one steadily gaining independence in daily routines and friendships, another needing sustained support–so the label itself predicts little about an individual child's future.

Atypical trajectories of brain activity and feeding also emerge over time, suggesting ASD is an ongoing developmental process rather than a fixed state (Guo et al., 2017; Peverill et al., 2019). Lundstrom et al. (2015) found that autistic traits remained stable over a decade even as registered diagnoses rose, showing how service systems and diagnostic practices shape which profiles are recognized.

ADHD, in turn, is defined by impairing patterns of inattention and/or hyperactivity and impulsivity. Children with ADHD commonly experience difficulties with executive functioning, emotion regulation, and peer relationships, which can stem from underlying attentional differences. Recent studies show that ADHD-related outcomes are strongly shaped by family, environmental, and social factors, as well as by broader contextual risk (Huang et al., 2018; Tercan & Bayhan, 2025). Many children with ADHD also show emotional dysregulation, peer difficulties, and academic underachievement, suggesting that the condition involves broad regulatory and relational challenges rather than isolated attention deficits alone (Binti Marsus et al., 2022; van Stralen, 2016). For a child, these difficulties often surface first in the classroom and on the playground–trouble waiting for a turn, staying with a task, or settling after a setback–rather than as "inattention" in isolation.

Both are associated with variation in brain development and can create barriers to social participation and well-being, especially when the environment is not adapted to the child's needs (Leblond et al., 2024; Wan et al., 2025; Wang et al., 2023).

When they co-occur, children may face greater impairment across attention, social communication, sensory sensitivity, academics, peer inclusion, and family relationships, which can foster maladaptive coping (Cai et al., 2018; van Stralen, 2016). Studying the two together clarifies which mechanisms are shared and which are condition-specific.

For example, Tye et al. (2014) showed that neurophysiological responses to emotional faces distinguish ASD, ADHD, and combined groups—evidence of partially overlapping but distinct pathways to socioemotional difficulty.

Genetic and neurobiological research indicates that ASD and ADHD share aspects of polygenic architecture and neurodevelopmental risk while retaining disorder-specific signatures, reflecting interactions among common and rare variants, environment, and developmental timing (Kim & Leventhal, 2015; Šulc et al., 2025; Woodbury-Smith & Scherer, 2018). Identifying these shared, transdiagnostic mechanisms can improve prediction and intervention.

Risk Architecture to Mechanisms: Genetic and Biological Underpinnings

Research on the genetic and biological basis of ASD has grown rapidly, showing that both common variants of small effect and rare, highly penetrant variants contribute to risk (that is, many common variants that each nudge risk only slightly, together with a smaller number of rare changes that individually have a much larger effect) (Kim & Leventhal, 2015; Woodbury-Smith & Scherer, 2018). At the cellular level, ASD involves converging disruptions in synaptic function, neuronal connectivity, neuroimmune signaling, and activity-dependent transcription; Masini et al. (2020) identify synaptic activity as a central hub linking molecular risk to altered network dynamics, and Ch'ng et al. (2015) found reproducible gene-expression differences in postmortem ASD brains.

Differences in neurotransmitter and neuromodulator systems–GABA, glutamate, serotonin, dopamine, histamine, and oxytocin–influence sensory processing, arousal, inhibition, and social motivation, and are central to emotion regulation and behavior (Marotta et al., 2020; Wagner & Harony-Nicolas, 2017; Wright et al., 2017).

Neurodiversity-informed frameworks aim to interpret genetic findings while respecting autistic identities and supporting precision care (Leblond et al., 2024). Interactions among genetic variation, developmental timing, and environment help explain the wide range of children's outcomes, and circuit-level evidence suggests ASD reflects disruptions in specific networks and developmental windows (Willsey & State, 2015).

Neurodevelopment also extends beyond the brain: immune, metabolic, and environmental factors interact with genetic susceptibility to shape brain development and behavior (Matelski & Van de Water, 2016), informing interventions tailored to the individual child (Wang et al., 2023).

Early ADHD research emphasized dopamine, noradrenaline, and fronto-striatal circuits, but EEG and network studies show broader regulatory and connectivity differences spanning emotion- and cognitive-control networks (Ansari Nasab et al., 2021; Banaschewski et al., 2004; Shimizu et al., 2014).

Overall, genetic and biological research on ASD and ADHD converges on several principles. First, risk is highly polygenic and probabilistic. Polygenic simply means that many genes each contribute a small amount to risk, rather than a single gene determining the outcome. Second, developmental timing and environmental context–including prenatal exposures, family environment, and broader social determinants–shape how that risk is expressed. Third, biological influences act through intermediate systems such as synaptic function, neuromodulation, and network-level connectivity, which together support regulation, learning, and social functioning (Kim & Leventhal, 2015; Masini et al., 2020; Wang et al., 2023).

Theoretical and Conceptual Models

Theoretical models of ASD and ADHD increasingly integrate genetic liability, neurocircuitry, and environmental context to explain why outcomes vary so widely among children with the same diagnosis: biological differences give rise to characteristic patterns of cognition, behavior, and emotion (Kim & Leventhal, 2015; Wang et al., 2023).

Neurobiological and Genetic Models of ASD

Polygenic and Systems-Level Genetic Models

Genetic models describe ASD risk as highly polygenic and multifactorial rather than the product of a single "autism gene." Family, twin, and molecular studies indicate that both common variants of small effect and rare, highly penetrant variants contribute to susceptibility, often within pathways governing synaptic development and plasticity, neuronal connectivity, and neuroimmune function (Kim & Leventhal, 2015; Masini et al., 2020; Woodbury-Smith & Scherer, 2018). Heritability helps account for the variation in traits seen across individuals with ASD; importantly, it describes a population-level estimate rather than a fixed genetic "share" for any one child (Kim & Leventhal, 2015). A continuing puzzle, however, is that twin-based heritability estimates are high, yet the specific variants identified so far explain only a fraction of that risk–a "missing heritability" gap that cautions against over-interpreting any single genetic finding.

Systems-biology work identifies coordinated dysregulation of synaptic and neuronal signaling genes (Ch'ng et al., 2015), with synaptic activity as a convergence point for genetic and environmental factors (Masini et al., 2020). Rylaarsdam and Guemez-Gamboa (2019) distinguish variants that sharply increase risk from those that modify how the condition presents, so the same condition can manifest differently across children.

Leblond et al. (2024) frame genetic findings as describing variation in developmental pathways rather than pathology in itself, using genetic architecture to identify biologically informed subtypes and support needs.

Neurocircuitry and Neurochemical Models

Neurobiological models examine how molecular and genetic differences shape brain connectivity–that is, the connections among cortical and subcortical regions. Willsey and State (2015) proposed that ASD may arise from disruptions to circuits that support social-cognitive development, language, and planning. A related model suggests that the brain's local activity patterns develop atypically, indicating differences in how intrinsic (resting) activity is organized. Disruptions in these circuits can make everyday social tasks–following a back-and-forth conversation, reading facial expressions, or changing plans–more effortful for a child.

Neurochemical theories add another layer by focusing on neurotransmitter and neuromodulator systems. Marotta et al. (2020) reviewed altered GABAergic, glutamatergic, serotonergic, and dopaminergic systems in ASD and proposed that an imbalance between excitation and inhibition (the balance between brain signals that increase neural activity and those that dampen it) could underlie sensory sensitivities, altered arousal, and differences in social behavior. Wright et al. (2017) reported changes in the expression of histamine-signaling genes in ASD brains, suggesting these genes help regulate arousal and cognition. Oxytocin-based theories, often tested in animal models, examine how changes in the oxytocin system may shape social motivation, bonding, and repetitive behavior; Wagner and Harony-Nicolas (2017) summarized this work in relation to neuromodulation and social cognition.

Neurodevelopment also depends on feedback from immune, metabolic, and other bodily systems, not the brain alone (Matelski & Van de Water, 2016).

Emotion Regulation and Developmental Neurobiology

Emotion regulation sits at the intersection of neurocircuitry and outcomes. Autistic individuals often find monitoring and adjusting emotional responses difficult (Cai et al., 2018), with atypically high prefrontal and limbic recruitment during regulation (Richey et al., 2015). Individual differences in arousal and caregiver-supported regulation relate to later self-regulation (Berkovits et al., 2016; Laurent & Gorman, 2017; Zantinge et al., 2017), as neurochemistry sets arousal thresholds that interact with the environment from early life (Wan et al., 2025).

Neurobiological and Cognitive Models of ADHD

Frontostriatal and Network-Based Models

Traditional models of ADHD emphasize disruptions in dopaminergic and noradrenergic systems and in fronto-striatal circuits, which are central to attention, inhibition, and motivation. Fronto-striatal loops connect the prefrontal cortex (PFC) with the basal ganglia and support response inhibition, reward processing, and the ability to wait for delayed rewards. Banaschewski et al. (2004) and Rubia (2018) noted that disruptions in these loops can make it hard for children with ADHD to sustain attention, delay gratification, and inhibit inappropriate responses. More recent findings, however, describe ADHD as a distributed pattern of altered functioning across several circuits–fronto-striatal, fronto-parietal, and fronto-cerebellar–which better fits the range of executive and timing difficulties that children experience (Rubia, 2018; Tseng et al., 2004). In daily life, this can look like difficulty waiting for a turn, leaving tasks unfinished, or reacting strongly to small frustrations.

Atypical connectivity in emotion- and control-networks and atypical sensory processing further point to an integrated view of ADHD spanning sensory, affective, executive, and neural systems (Ansari Nasab et al., 2021; Shimizu et al., 2014).

Executive-Function and Self-Regulation Models

Executive function links brain activity to ADHD symptoms, with separable impairments across fronto-striatal, fronto-parietal, and fronto-cerebellar circuits affecting inhibition, working memory, timing, and motivational control (Rubia, 2018). These higher-order processes–working memory, inhibition, planning–support goal-directed behavior.

Emotional dysregulation is a common, major source of impairment in ADHD–rapid mood shifts, high intensity, difficulty returning to baseline–reflecting both emotional control and broader executive functioning via striato-amygdalo-medial-prefrontal circuits (van Stralen, 2016).

Meta-analytic and earlier evidence shows that children with ADHD have difficulty recognizing emotional cues, attending to them, and modulating responses–each interacting with cognitive-control systems (Da Fonseca et al., 2008; Shapiro et al., 1993; Soler-Gutiérrez et al., 2025; van Stralen, 2016).

Intersection and Divergence Between ASD and ADHD Frameworks

The leading models converge on several points. Both conditions show substantial heritability, though the specific profile differs from child to child.

Both are shaped by gene–environment interaction, in which genetic liability influences sensitivity to prenatal, immune, family, and occupational exposures (Huang et al., 2018; Man et al., 2015; Matelski & Van de Water, 2016; Šulc et al., 2025; Tercan & Bayhan, 2025; Wang et al., 2023).

Both are modeled as more than "attention" or "social behavior" alone: ASD frameworks emphasize networks for social cognition, language, and executive control (Guo et al., 2017; Richey et al., 2015; Willsey & State, 2015), and ADHD frameworks emphasize fronto-striatal and executive networks affecting reward, sensory integration, and emotion (Ansari Nasab et al., 2021; Shimizu et al., 2014).

Emotion regulation is a shared point: difficulties are clinically significant in both ASD and ADHD (Cai et al., 2018; van Stralen, 2016), arising from interactions among circuitry, arousal, and environmental support (Berkovits et al., 2016; Laurent & Gorman, 2017). Yet Tye et al. (2014) show that a shared difficulty can have distinct neurophysiological signatures.

The frameworks nonetheless diverge in emphasis. ASD models focus on social cognition, motivation, and sensory-perceptual processing and how early differences change across development (Marotta et al., 2020; Wan et al., 2025; Willsey & State, 2015).

ADHD models focus on attentional control, reward, and the timing of behavior in fronto-striatal and fronto-cortical circuits, asking why children struggle to sustain attention, inhibit responses, and adjust to delayed consequences (Ansari Nasab et al., 2021; Tseng et al., 2004).

GENETIC UNDERPINNINGS OF ASD AND ADHD

Genetic studies provide the strongest evidence for high heritability in ASD and ADHD, both of which have a polygenic architecture of common and rare variants. Twin studies place heritability at roughly 70–90% (Kim & Leventhal, 2015), and family studies show elevated risk among relatives (Woodbury-Smith & Scherer, 2018). Heritability here refers to how much of the variation in a trait across a population is linked to genetic differences; it does not mean that 70–90% of any one child's outcome is fixed by genes. GWAS and exome sequencing implicate shared pathways in synaptic signaling and connectivity alongside condition-specific loci, and cross-disorder analyses confirm moderate pleiotropy–shared genetic influence–between ASD and ADHD (Leblond et al., 2024; Rylaarsdam & Guemez-Gamboa, 2019). For families, this shared-but-distinct picture helps explain why ASD and ADHD so often co-occur in the same child or family, even though they call for different kinds of support.

Significant Genetic Findings in ASD

The genetic architecture of ASD shows substantial locus heterogeneity–many different genes can be involved–and includes both rare variants of large effect and common polygenic risk. Rare de novo mutations (new genetic changes that appear in the child but are not inherited from either parent) and copy-number variants (CNVs) (stretches of DNA that are duplicated or deleted) account for roughly 10–20% of cases, often disrupting genes essential for forming synapses and for chromatin remodeling (the packaging and regulation of DNA). For example, loss-of-function variants in high-confidence ASD genes such as SHANK3, CHD8, and SCN2A strongly raise risk by disrupting postsynaptic structures, transcriptional regulation, and neuronal activity. Large-scale exome sequencing supports these findings, showing converging disruptions in "constrained" genes–those that normally tolerate little variation–particularly genes active during prenatal cortical development.

Common-variant polygenic risk, measured with GWAS polygenic risk scores (PRS) (a single score that adds up the small effects of many common variants to estimate a person's genetic liability), accounts for an additional 5–11% of liability for ASD and involves thousands of loci that are especially active prenatally in excitatory neurons and interneurons (Grove et al., 2019). It is worth emphasizing that such scores explain only a small portion of overall heritability and are not accurate enough to diagnose or predict outcomes for an individual child; they describe group-level tendencies, not destinies. Transcriptional meta-analyses converge on synaptic signaling–including the PSD-95 complex and the mTOR pathway–as central (Ch'ng et al., 2015; Masini et al., 2020).

Histamine-signaling genes (HTR1E, HNMT) are downregulated in the ASD prefrontal cortex, implicating arousal circuits (Wright et al., 2017), and risk variants preferentially disrupt early-developing social-cognition and language circuits, consistent with wide phenotypic variation (Willsey & State, 2015). Neurodiversity-informed models use molecular stratification to identify biologically similar subgroups (Leblond et al., 2024).

Significant Genetic Findings in ADHD

ADHD is even more polygenically complex than ASD but emphasizes somewhat different biology. The first ADHD GWAS implicated loci involving dopaminergic transmission (DRD4, SLC6A3), neuronal migration, and target recognition (Demontis et al., 2019). CNVs, particularly 16p11.2 deletions and duplications, confer a roughly 2- to 5-fold increase in risk and overlap with ASD (Martin et al., 2019), while de novo mutation rates are elevated but less pronounced than in ASD (Satterstrom et al., 2020).

Unlike ASD, ADHD polygenic risk is associated with intelligence (about $r = -0.25$) and educational attainment, suggesting broader cognitive effects (Lee et al., 2018), with pathway enrichment for neurotransmitter release, postsynaptic density, and forebrain development (Demontis et al., 2019).

Shared Genetic Risk Factors

Family and twin studies provide strong evidence of shared genetic liability. Concordance in identical (monozygotic) twins is about 4 to 10 times higher than in fraternal (dizygotic) twins for both conditions, and full siblings of children with ASD have a 2- to 4-fold increased risk of ADHD (Ghirardi et al., 2019). Cross-disorder GWAS show a moderate genetic correlation ($rg \approx 0.30$–0.40) (rg estimates how much the genetic influences on one condition overlap with those on another, where 0 means no overlap and 1 means complete overlap) and suggest roughly 10–15% genetic overlap (Demontis et al., 2019; Grove et al., 2019).

Shared risk factors include SHANK2 (a postsynaptic scaffolding gene), 16p11.2 CNVs, and KDM6B (an epigenetic regulator), identified by whole-exome sequencing of families affected by both conditions (Niarchou et al., 2023), with additional loci in neuronal migration and synaptic pruning (Cao et al., 2022). Polygenic scores predict bidirectionally–ASD scores predict ADHD inattention, and ADHD scores predict ASD-related social difficulties (Grove et al., 2019).

Unique Genetic Profiles Differentiating ASD and ADHD

Each condition also has a distinct signature: ASD shows higher rates of rare de novo mutations in chromatin modifiers (CHD8) and ion channels (SCN2A) and enrichment for prenatal interneuron markers (Rylaarsdam & Guemez-Gamboa, 2019; Willsey & State, 2015), whereas ADHD is driven more by common-variant risk, and the histamine downregulation seen in ASD is absent in ADHD (Wright et al., 2017). Broadly, ASD risk ties to early circuit formation and ADHD to later cognitive maturation (Grove et al., 2019).

Inheritance Patterns From Twin and Family Studies

Classical twin studies quantify heritability: for ASD, monozygotic concordance of about 60–90% versus dizygotic 0–20% ($h^2 \approx 80\%$); for ADHD, monozygotic 70–80% versus dizygotic 20–30% ($h^2 \approx 75\%$) (Tick et al., 2016). Cross-trait co-occurrence in identical twins far exceeds that in fraternal twins (Ghirardi et al., 2019). Family studies show a dose–response pattern: relatives of children with both ASD and ADHD carry the highest risk, followed by relatives of children with a single condition (Leblond et al., 2024). Parent and child symptoms also tend to track together, with parental ADHD and ASD symptoms relating to ADHD and ASD symptoms in their children (Liljenwall et al., 2022).

Taken together, these patterns support a model of additive polygenic inheritance modified by gene–environment interplay: shared genetic liability accounts for the frequent comorbidity of the two conditions, while distinct genetic profiles drive their divergence. Molecular findings consistently converge on synapse- and circuit-level mechanisms, providing a bridge to the neurobiological and quality-of-life outcomes examined later in this chapter. For a child, this means inherited risk is rarely deterministic–it raises or lowers the likelihood of certain difficulties, but timing, environment, and support all shape how those difficulties actually unfold.

BIOLOGICAL AND NEURAL MECHANISMS

Neuroimaging reveals both overlap and divergence in the biological pathways of ASD and ADHD. They overlap in fronto-striatal systems, dopaminergic and serotonergic signaling, and network connectivity (Ansari Nasab et al., 2021; Guo et al., 2017; Rubia, 2018), with structural, fMRI, and EEG differences in cortical thickness, connectivity, and task-related activation that shape executive planning, emotion regulation, and social communication (Ansari Nasab et al., 2021; Guo et al., 2017).

Shared Neurobiological Pathways

Fronto-striatal circuits are a key point of convergence, linking prefrontal regions to the striatum to support executive function, reward, and motor control; both conditions show reduced fronto-striatal connectivity during response suppression and cognitive flexibility (Rubia, 2018). Genetic risk affects dopamine genes–DRD2 in ASD, and DRD4 and SLC6A3 in ADHD (Demontis et al., 2019)–and prenatal SSRI exposure suggests lasting serotonergic effects relevant to both (Man et al., 2015).

Recent meta-analyses confirm similar structural patterns: Bedford et al. (2023) found comparable thickness increases in the superior temporal gyrus and precuneus across ASD and ADHD. A parallel functional finding involves the frontoparietal network (FPN) and default mode network (DMN): both show reduced anti-correlation (less separation) between the FPN and DMN during executive tasks, linked to attention difficulties and to shifting between self-focused and externally focused processing (Segura et al., 2025). Histamine signaling is another shared pathway, with reduced histamine-gene expression in the ASD prefrontal cortex and histamine dysregulation in ADHD tied to arousal and sensory difficulties (Marotta et al., 2020; Wright et al., 2017).

Structural Brain Differences

Structural MRI reveals convergent and divergent gray-matter effects. ASD shows early cortical overgrowth (ages 2–5) followed by thinning of social-brain areas and amygdala enlargement (Willsey & State, 2015), with an atypical course of local spontaneous activity and persistent posterior default-mode hyperconnectivity (Guo et al., 2017). ADHD instead shows more global prefrontal and cingulate thinning, smaller caudate and putamen, and a smaller cerebellar vermis, tied to executive and timing difficulties (Rubia, 2018).

Co-occurring ASD+ADHD shows a distinct pattern: increased cortical thickness with reduced surface area, suggesting altered gyrification rather than volume loss (Bedford et al., 2023). Caudate volumes are elevated in both–bilaterally in ASD, more right-sided in ADHD–and white-matter differences overlap in the corpus callosum and superior longitudinal fasciculus (Guo et al., 2017).

Sex moderates these findings–cortical-thickness differences in ASD are more pronounced in males, while ADHD differences are less sex-differentiated (Bedford et al., 2023)–and ADHD cerebellar and striatal differences are clearer in childhood than adolescence (Rubia, 2018).

Functional Brain Differences

Functional neuroimaging points to network disorganization rather than discrete lesions. In ASD, the social-brain network shows under-connectivity alongside local sensory over-connectivity during theory-of-mind and face-processing tasks (Richey et al., 2015; Willsey & State, 2015), and the reduced FPN–DMN anti-correlation is consistent with social and communication difficulties (Segura et al., 2025).

In ADHD, functional patterns center on fronto-striato-cerebellar circuits, with task-related underactivation in the right inferior frontal cortex and pre-supplementary motor area and under-recruitment of frontoparietal networks (Rubia, 2018). Ansari Nasab et al. (2021) found altered emotion–cognition networks, with lower amygdala–PFC connectivity tracking emotional lability.

Cross-diagnostic comparisons reveal both similarities and differences. Tye et al. (2014) recorded event-related potentials (ERPs)—electrical brain responses measured by EEG—while participants viewed emotional faces, and found that early visual responses (the P1 and N170 components) differed across ASD, ADHD, and ASD+ADHD groups: ADHD was marked by an anterior attentional bias, and ASD by difficulties with the holistic ("configural") processing of faces in posterior regions. At rest, the conditions share disrupted connectivity in the salience network but differ in default-mode activity: ASD shows persistent posterior DMN activity, whereas ADHD shows anterior DMN over-activation (Segura et al., 2025).

Cognitive and Behavioral Influences

These biological endophenotypes—measurable biological traits that sit between genes and observable behavior—directly shape cognitive and behavioral outcomes. Fronto-striatal under-connectivity strongly predicts executive difficulties in both conditions: children with ASD tend to show rigidity on set-shifting tasks (e.g., the Wisconsin Card Sorting Test), while children with ADHD struggle with response inhibition on stop-signal tasks (Lai et al., 2016; Rubia, 2018). Altered dopaminergic regulation underlies reward hypersensitivity in ADHD (reflected in steeper delay-discounting, or a stronger pull toward immediate rewards) and reduced sensitivity to social rewards in ASD (reflected in less gaze-following) (Demontis et al., 2019).

Emotion regulation provides another mechanistic link. In ASD, atypical dorsolateral PFC–amygdala connectivity during reappraisal correlates with difficulty suppressing emotion (Richey et al., 2015); in ADHD, reduced ventromedial PFC–striatum connectivity during emotional conflict is linked to irritability (Ansari

Nasab et al., 2021). Shared FPN–DMN dissociation impairs executive control and mentalizing, while sensory over-connectivity unique to ASD underlies its sensory sensitivities (Guo et al., 2017; Shimizu et al., 2014).

Social cognition shows condition-specific translation: reduced fusiform face-area activity tied to temporal-lobe thinning in ASD (Willsey & State, 2015), and prefrontal underactivation impairing social response-monitoring in ADHD (Rubia, 2018).

Developmental trajectories qualify these effects. Guo et al. (2017) reported that ASD hyperconnectivity partly normalizes by adolescence, whereas fronto-striatal differences in ADHD remain more stable over time. Age and sex interact in more nuanced ways–for example, females with ASD may show some protective effects, possibly due to later symptom onset, while sex differences in ADHD appear more stable (Bedford et al., 2023). Translated into daily life, these patterns help explain why a child with ASD may find unstructured social play especially hard, while a child with ADHD may do well one-on-one yet struggle to monitor their behavior in a busy classroom.

DEVELOPMENTAL AND PSYCHOSOCIAL IMPLICATIONS

Genetic and biological risk factors shape how ASD and ADHD develop, including socialization and executive functioning. The two share origins in genetic variation, neurochemical differences, and gene–environment interactions, yet diverge through condition-specific mechanisms.

Developmental Trajectories and Adaptive Functioning

In ASD, de novo mutations and polygenic risk disrupt synapse formation and connectivity from early childhood, producing diverse pathways in symptom intensity and adaptive skills (Rylaarsdam & Guemez-Gamboa, 2019; Willsey & State, 2015; Woodbury-Smith & Scherer, 2018).

In a longitudinal study of preschool children with autism, Szatmari et al. (2015) identified diverse developmental pathways: some children showed persistent mild symptoms with gradual gains in socialization and communication, while others faced sustained, substantial challenges in daily-living and motor skills. This diversity is partly biological, reflecting variation in synaptic gene expression–meta-analyses have found hundreds of genes differentially expressed in postmortem autistic brain tissue (Ch'ng et al., 2015). Sacrey et al. (2018) corroborated this in high-risk infant-sibling samples, where slower early adaptation was associated with an accumulation of difficulties over time. This variability carries a central message for practitioners and families: the same diagnosis is compatible with very different developmental outcomes, so support is best matched to the individual child rather than to the label.

In ADHD, genetic models emphasize delayed motor and executive development from polygenic–environmental interaction; Tseng et al. (2004) found motor difficulties tied to inattention and impulsivity that affect academics and self-care, with dopaminergic disruption contributing to impulsivity-related delays that compound over time rather than plateauing as in ASD.

Lundstrom et al. (2015) found autistic traits stable over a decade even as diagnoses rose, suggesting stable biology with diagnostic broadening driven by service and environmental factors; in ADHD, family and peer environments contribute to variability in severity and comorbidity (Buschgens et al., 2008).

Overlapping risks affecting excitation–inhibition balance yield different outcomes–plateauing skills in ASD versus inconsistent functioning in ADHD (Kim & Leventhal, 2015; Matelski & Van de Water, 2016)–so precision therapy must target these shared yet divergent factors (Wang et al., 2023).

Emotional Regulation and Executive Control

Shared neurochemical and prefrontal differences affect emotion regulation and executive function, but play out differently. In ASD, children often show heightened arousal and less cognitive reappraisal, shaped partly by oxytocin-system differences (Berkovits et al., 2016; Cai et al., 2018; Wagner & Harony-Nicolas, 2017; Zantinge et al., 2017), with reduced prefrontal activation and weaker amygdala–prefrontal connectivity during regulation (Richey et al., 2015); executive-function deficits in working memory and inhibition can worsen emotional lability (Lai et al., 2016).

In ADHD, emotional dysregulation is a core feature–hyperreactivity and poor modulation tied to fronto-striatal dopaminergic differences (van Stralen, 2016). EEG responses to emotional faces partly resemble ASD but diverge in the combined group (Ansari Nasab et al., 2021; Da Fonseca et al., 2008; Tye et al., 2014), and atypical processing of emotional material links to control and inhibitory failures (Banaschewski et al., 2004; Braaten & Rosén, 2000; Shapiro et al., 1993).

Shared features such as prefrontal hypoactivation have divergent developmental effects. In ASD, they tend toward internalizing patterns such as avoidance and rigidity (Marotta et al., 2020), whereas in ADHD they tend toward externalizing patterns such as outbursts, along with a slowed cognitive tempo in some children (Becker & Langberg, 2012; Soler-Gutiérrez et al., 2025). (Internalizing difficulties are turned inward, such as anxiety and withdrawal, whereas externalizing difficulties are turned outward, such as outbursts and overactivity.) Shared involvement of serotonin and histamine transmission may amplify these difficulties and contribute to comorbidity risk (Man et al., 2015; Wright et al., 2017).

Socialization With Peers and Family

Social engagement also shows condition-specific patterns. In ASD, restricted interests and pragmatic-communication differences can limit peer acceptance and family interaction (Baird & Norbury, 2015; Sterrett et al., 2017). In ADHD, impulsivity lowers peer status (Hoza et al., 2005), with parenting a mediating factor and family styles differing across the two conditions (Buschgens et al., 2008; Laurent & Gorman, 2017; Mikami et al., 2010).

Friendship problems in ASD often stem from inflexibility, whereas in ADHD they involve conflict-laden friendships (Binti Marsus et al., 2022; Greenway et al., 2023; Mikami & Normand, 2015). Family beliefs and biological influences such as prenatal SSRI exposure can intensify these difficulties (Chou et al., 2020; Šulc et al., 2025), and sociodemographic risks in ADHD can compound co-occurring ASD difficulties (Tercan & Bayhan, 2025).

These pathways yield distinct outcomes: withdrawal and solitude in ASD (Masini et al., 2020) versus hyperactivity-driven peer rejection in ADHD (Dipeolu et al., 2023). Connecting biological understanding to family-based, neurodiversity-affirming intervention is a promising response (Leblond et al., 2024).

Overlapping Traits and Distinct Developmental Outcomes

Shared vulnerabilities–synaptic dysregulation, epigenetic influences, and environmental factors–produce overlapping traits like impulsivity, rigidity, and dysregulation that diverge by condition (Ch'ng et al., 2015; Guo et al., 2017; Richey et al., 2015): rigidity and withdrawal in ASD (Braconnier & Siper, 2021; Peverill et al., 2019) versus externalizing difficulties in ADHD (Hampshire et al., 2015; Nowell et al., 2019). Prenatal and occupational exposures sharpen these differences (Man et al., 2015; Šulc et al., 2025), which begin in infancy (Wan et al., 2025) and point to tailored strategies–synaptic stability for ASD, dopaminergic modulation for ADHD (Baribeau & Anagnostou, 2021; Sassone-Corsi & Christen, 2016)–improving diagnosis and treatment (Leblond et al., 2024; Wang et al., 2023).

MALADAPTIVE BEHAVIOR AND COMORBIDITY

In both conditions, maladaptive behaviors and comorbidities arise from interrelated genetic, biological, and environmental risks, producing shared challenges–impulsivity, rigidity, emotional dysregulation–and high rates of comorbid anxiety and learning disorders, while condition-specific mechanisms yield distinct profiles: internalized rigidity in ASD, externalized impulsivity in ADHD.

Overlapping Behavioral Challenges

Impulsivity, rigidity, and emotional instability are core overlapping challenges with shared bases (Banaschewski et al., 2004; Tseng et al., 2004). Impulsivity, central to ADHD and frequent in ASD, reflects prefrontal–striatal dopaminergic dysregulation and weak inhibitory control and contributes to poor peer relationships in both (Hoza et al., 2005; Sterrett et al., 2017). ASD rigidity–repetition and reduced flexibility–relates to perseverative errors and, in both conditions, to excitatory–inhibitory imbalance in cortical circuits (Guo et al., 2017; Matelski & Van de Water, 2016).

Emotional dysregulation clearly links the two: heightened reactivity and poor modulation in ADHD (van Stralen, 2016), and more reliance on suppression than reappraisal in ASD (Berkovits et al., 2016; Cai et al., 2018). Tye et al. (2014) found shared but not identical arousal patterns (Da Fonseca et al., 2008; Zantinge et al., 2017). Prenatal SSRI exposure and altered histamine expression may add to these risks (Man et al., 2015; Wright et al., 2017), and meta-analysis confirms emotion-processing difficulties spanning both conditions (Richey et al., 2015; Soler-Gutiérrez et al., 2025).

These difficulties share roots in polygenic risk affecting synaptic plasticity (Ch'ng et al., 2015; Woodbury-Smith & Scherer, 2018) and environmental contributors such as maternal occupational exposures (Šulc et al., 2025), with caregivers' beliefs about behavior shaping responses in both conditions (Buschgens et al., 2008; Chou et al., 2020).

Comorbidities From Shared Etiological Roots

Anxiety–reported in roughly 40–50% of children with ASD or ADHD–arises partly from genetic tendencies disrupting amygdala–prefrontal regulation (Cai et al., 2018; van Stralen, 2016), with shared serotonin and oxytocin pathways heightening threat vigilance (prenatal exposures more predictive of ASD, familial factors of ADHD; Huang et al., 2018; Man et al., 2015). Learning disorders intersect through executive dysfunction and slowed processing (Becker & Langberg, 2012; Lai et al., 2016).

Feeding and sleep difficulties linked to sensory processing also co-occur (Peverill et al., 2019; Shimizu et al., 2014), and rare synaptic-gene variants underlie ASD–ADHD comorbidity (Leblond et al., 2024; Rylaarsdam & Guemez-Gamboa, 2019). Epigenetic modifiers may add to anxiety (Kim & Leventhal, 2015; Masini et al., 2020), and longitudinal studies show anxiety-compounded declines in adaptive functioning in ASD that parallel ADHD (Lingineni et al., 2012; Sacrey et al., 2018; Szatmari et al., 2015).

Unique Maladaptive Patterns in ASD vs. ADHD

Although they share features, the maladaptive behaviors of ASD and ADHD differ in their biological emphasis. In ASD, difficulties are more inwardly directed: rigidity appears as repetitive behaviors and heightened sensory sensitivity, thought to reflect GABA/glutamate imbalances and reduced oxytocin signaling (Marotta et al., 2020; Matelski & Van de Water, 2016; Wagner & Harony-Nicolas, 2017). Practical social difficulties can lead to reduced interaction and, over time, isolation (Baird & Norbury, 2015; Braconnier & Siper, 2021). Emotional dysregulation in ASD may present either as outward reactivity (such as tantrums or meltdowns) or as withdrawal and shutting down (Berkovits et al., 2016).

In contrast, ADHD is expressed more outwardly and through differences in arousal and activity. Many children with ADHD experience conflict in peer relationships rather than withdrawal, often related to impulsivity and overactivity (Binti Marsus et al., 2022; Hoza et al., 2005). Some children, however, show the opposite profile–a slowed, hypoaroused pattern sometimes described as "sluggish cognitive tempo," marked by passivity and disengagement rather than aggression, and not typically seen in ASD (Becker & Langberg, 2012). Emotional lability in ADHD tends to appear as rapid mood shifts, in contrast to the emotion suppression more common in ASD (Braaten & Rosén, 2000; Shapiro et al., 1993).

Co-occurring ASD and ADHD can blend into a hybrid presentation. ASD is more often associated with synaptic under-connectivity (Guo et al., 2017) and ADHD with over-connectivity in some networks (Tye et al., 2014); prenatal factors push ASD toward inflexibility and ADHD toward impulsivity (Man et al., 2015; Tercan & Bayhan, 2025), mapping onto interventions that build flexibility in ASD and inhibitory control in ADHD (Hampshire et al., 2015; Nowell et al., 2019).

In summary, despite shared origins, biological differences produce distinct profiles that shape how comorbidities are managed (Baribeau & Anagnostou, 2021; Wang et al., 2023), and future research must refine these models (Leblond et al., 2024).

CURRENT GAPS AND FUTURE DIRECTIONS

Research on ASD and ADHD has deepened understanding of shared vulnerabilities, but its translational impact is limited by insufficiently diverse samples and a reliance on cross-sectional designs. Emerging methods–epigenetics and neurodevelopmental biomarkers–may help bridge these gaps and improve treatment and early intervention.

Limitations in Genetic Research

Genetic studies lack sample diversity–most participants are of European descent–so allele-frequency differences make findings hard to replicate elsewhere (Woodbury-Smith & Scherer, 2018), and rare variants explain only about 10–20% of heritability, leaving polygenic effects underexamined across populations (Rylaarsdam & Guemez-Gamboa, 2019). Research has also skewed toward higher-functioning individuals, overlooking low-SES and minority groups for whom environmental risk may be greater (Leblond et al., 2024; Šulc et al., 2025; Tercan & Bayhan, 2025).

Cross-sectional designs dominate, offering snapshots rather than trajectories: postmortem gene-expression work spans ages and skips prenatal periods (Ch'ng et al., 2015; Willsey & State, 2015), and inception cohorts for tracking adaptive change are scarce (Sacrey et al., 2018; Szatmari et al., 2015). ADHD prevalence surveys cannot establish causality (Chou et al., 2020; Huang et al., 2018; Lingineni et al., 2012).

These limitations can lead researchers to treat comorbidities like anxiety and learning disabilities as static, underplaying gene–environment interactions (Kim & Leventhal, 2015; Man et al., 2015).

Limitations in Neurobiological Research

Neurobiological research faces similar constraints: fMRI emotion-regulation studies in ASD used small, higher-functioning, non-longitudinal samples (Cai et al., 2018; Richey et al., 2015), and EEG work on ASD–ADHD overlap is cross-sectional, omitting maturation (Guo et al., 2017; Tye et al., 2014); rigidity and impulsivity tasks also overlook cultural differences (Matelski & Van de Water, 2016; van Stralen, 2016).

Sensory and motor assessments in ADHD are likewise cross-sectional (Shimizu et al., 2014; Tseng et al., 2004), and peer-socialization studies, though longitudinal, do not capture genetic–neural mechanisms (Hoza et al., 2005; Sterrett et al., 2017). The diversity gap persists, with peer research often Eurocentric despite cultural variation in parenting (Binti Marsus et al., 2022; Buschgens et al., 2008; Mikami et al., 2010).

Emerging Approaches: Epigenetics

Epigenetics helps bridge these gaps by making gene–environment interactions visible. Epigenetic changes alter how genes are switched on or off–often through chemical tags such as DNA methylation–without changing the DNA sequence itself. Masini et al. (2020) examined modifiers of synaptic activity and suggested that prenatal exposures may produce methylation changes that help explain ASD–ADHD co-occurrence (Man et al., 2015; Šulc et al., 2025). Sassone-Corsi and Christen (2016) linked metabolic hormones to epigenomic regulation, offering mechanistic insight beyond fixed genetics. Kim and Leventhal (2015) support interactive models in which epigenetic processes help account for differences in heritability (Rylaarsdam & Guemez-Gamboa, 2019). Longitudinal epigenomic studies in diverse populations could map these pathways and improve polygenic scores (Ch'ng et al., 2015; Leblond et al., 2024).

Emerging Approaches: Neurodevelopmental Biomarkers

Biomarker research targets earlier identification: synaptic and inflammatory markers may guide treatment selection (Wang et al., 2023), and infant eye-tracking and EEG identify early signs of neurodivergence (Wan et al., 2025). Neurochemical assays distinguish histamine and serotonin patterns (Marotta et al., 2020; Wright et al., 2017), oxytocin indexes regulation (Wagner & Harony-Nicolas, 2017), and high-risk sibling studies and international collaborations support time-tracked, more diverse data (Lundstrom et al., 2015; Sacrey et al., 2018).

Implications for Therapeutic Models

These advances are shaping therapy: epigenetic research informs targeted approaches–HDAC inhibitors for synaptic plasticity in ASD-related rigidity (Baribeau & Anagnostou, 2021; Masini et al., 2020) and dopamine modulators for ADHD impulsivity–while biomarkers allow earlier, tailored support in social communication and self-management matched to infancy screening (Brignell et al., 2018; Hampshire et al., 2015; Nowell et al., 2019; Wan et al., 2025).

Diversity-focused designs support fairer outcomes, such as culturally specific family therapies (Laurent & Gorman, 2017; Mikami & Normand, 2015), and comorbidity can be addressed through shared targets like emotion-regulation skills (Nowell et al., 2019; Watkins et al., 2015).

Implications for Early Intervention

Early intervention improves when biomarkers predict developmental pathways (Peverill et al., 2019; Szatmari et al., 2015) and when longitudinal epigenetics guides timing–monitoring prenatal risk (Man et al., 2015) and triggering graduated infant support (Sacrey et al., 2018). Emerging combinations include oxytocin-based approaches for ASD and peer-focused behavioral intervention for ADHD (Hoza et al., 2005; Sterrett et al., 2017), shifting care from symptoms toward causes (Leblond et al., 2024; Wang et al., 2023).

Summary and Transition

This chapter has examined the genetic and biological factors underlying ASD and ADHD, revealing both similarities and differences across developmental, psychosocial, and neurobiological domains. Shared factors–polygenic risk, synaptic dysregulation, and gene–environment interplay–produce common challenges such as emotional dysregulation, impulsivity, and social difficulty, while condition-specific mechanisms produce divergent outcomes that call for tailored approaches (Kim & Leventhal, 2015; Leblond et al., 2024; Matelski & Van de Water, 2016).

Synthesized Understanding of Shared and Unique Mechanisms

At a basic level, ASD and ADHD share genetic influences that disrupt typical neurodevelopment (softened from the original, which stated the conditions are caused by the same genetic defects). Meta-analyses of postmortem brain tissue indicate that de novo mutations and polygenic risk affect synaptic pruning, gene expression, and the balance of excitatory and inhibitory activity, and hundreds of differentially expressed genes are shared across the two conditions (Ch'ng et al., 2015; Rylaarsdam & Guemez-Gamboa, 2019; Woodbury-Smith & Scherer, 2018). Prenatal factors such as SSRI exposure and maternal occupational hazards may add to risk through effects on serotonin and inflammation, contributing to the impulsivity and emotional dysregulation common to both conditions (Man et al., 2015; Šulc et al., 2025). Neurochemically, altered histamine signaling and reduced oxytocin can impede emotion regulation, while prefrontal hypoactivation affects executive control (Richey et al., 2015; Wagner & Harony-Nicolas, 2017; Wright et al., 2017).

These mechanisms help explain overlapping difficulties. Emotional dysregulation is a key link–emotion suppression in ASD paralleling more impulsive reactions in ADHD (Berkovits et al., 2016; Cai et al., 2018; van Stralen, 2016)–while impulsivity and inflexibility share an imbalance involving dopamine and GABA/glutamate that heightens peer rejection and family stress (Binti Marsus et al., 2022; Hoza et al., 2005; Sterrett et al., 2017). Comorbid anxiety and learning difficulties also arise from these factors (Lai et al., 2016; Sacrey et al., 2018; Szatmari et al., 2015).

Yet each condition's biology leads to a distinct path. In ASD, synaptic underconnectivity and neurochemical rigidity favor stable, internalizing patterns such as withdrawal and repetition (Guo et al., 2017; Marotta et al., 2020; Matelski & Van de Water, 2016), with stable trait prevalence pointing to excitatory–inhibitory differences (Lundstrom et al., 2015). In ADHD, over-connectivity, dopaminergic dysregulation, and motor difficulties favor externalizing patterns and conflict-prone peer interactions (Becker & Langberg, 2012; Tseng et al., 2004; Tye et al., 2014).

Socially, ASD rigidity can limit friendship formation while ADHD impulsivity leads to peer rejection (Laurent & Gorman, 2017; Mikami et al., 2010), reflecting condition-specific factors–synaptic genes more central to ASD, fronto-striatal pathways to ADHD (Banaschewski et al., 2004; Da Fonseca et al., 2008; Willsey & State, 2015).

Emerging Directions as Unifiers

Epigenetics and biomarkers point toward a more unified approach: methylation shows how environment acts on shared genes, and infant EEG and eye-tracking can help predict development (Masini et al., 2020; Wan et al., 2025; Wang et al., 2023), supporting personalized treatment that distinguishes ASD rigidity from ADHD disinhibition (Baribeau & Anagnostou, 2021; Sassone-Corsi & Christen, 2016).

This picture can guide intervention. Shared pathways support transdiagnostic strategies such as emotion-regulation training (Nowell et al., 2019; Watkins et al., 2015) and family-based approaches (Hampshire et al., 2015; Laurent & Gorman, 2017), while distinct mechanisms call for specificity–synaptic stability in ASD, dopaminergic regulation in ADHD (Baribeau & Anagnostou, 2021). Early biomarkers support stratified models and well-timed, prenatally informed prevention (Brignell et al., 2018; Man et al., 2015; Sacrey et al., 2018).

These themes bear on diagnosis. Overlapping features raise misdiagnosis risk (Soler-Gutiérrez et al., 2025; Tye et al., 2014), but genetic scores and early indicators may add specificity (Leblond et al., 2024; Wan et al., 2025), and dimensional assessments incorporating executive-function and peer profiles tend to outperform rigid categories (Braconnier & Siper, 2021; Lai et al., 2016). Attention to cultural diversity in diagnostic standards is essential for fairness (Chou et al., 2020; Tercan & Bayhan, 2025).

In sum, shared mechanisms underlie ASD–ADHD comorbidity, while each condition's distinct biology defines pathways toward new interventions and improved diagnostics. Later chapters translate this etiology into practical care (Wang et al., 2023).

REFERENCES

Ansari Nasab, S., Panahi, S., Ghassemi, F., Jafari, S., Rajagopal, K., Ghosh, D., & Perc, M. (2021). Functional neuronal networks reveal emotional processing differences in children with ADHD. *Cognitive Neurodynamics*, *16*(1), 91–100. DOI: 10.1007/s11571-021-09699-6 PMID: 35126772

Baird, G., & Norbury, C. F. (2015). Social (pragmatic) communication disorders and autism spectrum disorder. *Archives of Disease in Childhood*, *101*(8), 745–751. DOI: 10.1136/archdischild-2014-306944 PMID: 26699538

Banaschewski, T., Brandeis, D., Heinrich, H., Albrecht, B., Brunner, E., & Rothenberger, A. (2004). Questioning inhibitory control as the specific deficit of ADHD: Evidence from brain electrical activity. *Journal of Neural Transmission*, *111*(7), 841–864. https://pmc.ncbi.nlm.nih.gov/articles/PMC3472099/. DOI: 10.1007/s00702-003-0040-8 PMID: 15206002

Baribeau, D., & Anagnostou, E. (2021). Novel treatments for autism spectrum disorder based on genomics and systems biology. *Pharmacology & Therapeutics*, *107939*. Advance online publication. DOI: 10.1016/j.pharmthera.2021.107939 PMID: 34174273

Becker, S. P., & Langberg, J. M. (2012). Sluggish cognitive tempo among young adolescents with ADHD. *Journal of Attention Disorders*, *17*(8), 681–689. DOI: 10.1177/1087054711435411 PMID: 22441891

Bedford, S. A.. (2023). Brain-charting autism and attention deficit hyperactivity disorder: A mega-analysis of structural MRI. *Molecular Psychiatry*. Advance online publication. DOI: 10.1038/s41380-023-02290-7

Berkovits, L., Eisenhower, A., & Blacher, J. (2016). Emotion regulation in young children with autism spectrum disorders. *Journal of Autism and Developmental Disorders*, *47*(1), 68–79. DOI: 10.1007/s10803-016-2922-2 PMID: 27838805

Binti Marsus, N., Sook Huey, L., Saffari, N., & Motevalli, S. (2022). Peer relationship difficulties among children with ADHD: A systematic review. *International Journal of Academic Research in Business & Social Sciences*, *12*(6). Advance online publication. DOI: 10.6007/IJARBSS/v12-i6/13352

Braaten, E. B., & Rosén, L. A. (2000). Self-regulation of affect in attention deficit-hyperactivity disorder (ADHD) and non-ADHD boys: Differences in empathic responding. *Journal of Consulting and Clinical Psychology*, *68*(2), 313–321. DOI: 10.1037/0022-006X.68.2.313 PMID: 10780132

Braconnier, M. L., & Siper, P. M. (2021). Neuropsychological assessment in autism spectrum disorder. *Current Psychiatry Reports, 23*(10), 63. Advance online publication. DOI: 10.1007/s11920-021-01277-1 PMID: 34331144

Brignell, A., Chenausky, K. V., Song, H., Zhu, J., Suo, C., & Morgan, A. T. (2018). Communication interventions for autism spectrum disorder in minimally verbal children. *Cochrane Database of Systematic Reviews, 5*(11). Advance online publication. DOI: 10.1002/14651858.CD012324.pub2 PMID: 30395694

Buschgens, C. J. M., van Aken, M. A. G., Swinkels, S. H. N., Altink, M. E., Fliers, E. A., Rommelse, N. N. J., Minderaa, R. B., Sergeant, J. A., Faraone, S. V., & Buitelaar, J. K. (2008). Differential family and peer environmental factors are related to severity and comorbidity in children with ADHD. *Journal of Neural Transmission, 115*(2), 177–186. DOI: 10.1007/s00702-007-0838-x PMID: 18200433

Cai, R. Y., Richdale, A. L., Uljarević, M., Dissanayake, C., & Samson, A. C. (2018). Emotion regulation in autism spectrum disorder: Where we are and where we need to go. *Autism Research : Official Journal of the International Society for Autism Research, 11*(7), 962–978. DOI: 10.1002/aur.1968 PMID: 29979494

Cao, C., He, Q., Zhao, X., Wang, L., Ma, L., & Jiang, L. (2022). Shared genetics between autism spectrum disorder and attention-deficit/hyperactivity disorder and their association with extraversion. *Psychiatry Research, 315*, 114711. Advance online publication. DOI: 10.1016/j.psychres.2022.114711

Ch'ng, C., Kwok, W., Rogic, S., & Pavlidis, P. (2015). Meta-analysis of gene expression in autism spectrum disorder. *Autism Research : Official Journal of the International Society for Autism Research, 8*(5), 593–608. DOI: 10.1002/aur.1475 PMID: 25720351

Chou, W.-J., Liu, T.-L., Hsiao, R. C., Chen, Y.-M., Chang, C.-C., & Yen, C.-F. (2020). Caregiver-attributed etiologies of children's attention-deficit/hyperactivity disorder: A study in Taiwan. *International Journal of Environmental Research and Public Health, 17*(5), 1652. DOI: 10.3390/ijerph17051652 PMID: 32143281

Da Fonseca, D., Seguier, V., Santos, A., Poinso, F., & Deruelle, C. (2008). Emotion understanding in children with ADHD. *Child Psychiatry and Human Development, 40*(1), 111–121. DOI: 10.1007/s10578-008-0114-9 PMID: 18663570

Demontis, D., Walters, R. K., Martin, J., Mattheisen, M., Als, T. D., Agerbo, E., Baldursson, G., Belliveau, R., Bybjerg-Grauholm, J., Bækvad-Hansen, M., Cerrato, F., Chambert, K., Churchhouse, C., Dumont, A., Eriksson, N., Gandal, M., Goldstein, J. I., Grasby, K. L., Grove, J., & Neale, B. M. (2019). Discovery of the first genome-wide significant risk loci for attention deficit/hyperactivity disorder. *Nature Genetics*, *51*(1), 63–75. DOI: 10.1038/s41588-018-0269-7 PMID: 30478444

Dipeolu, A., Hargrave, S., Cabrera, Y. A., Longoria, A., & Escalante, M. (2023). Dysfunctional career thoughts and peer relationships in adolescents with ADHD. *International Journal for Educational and Vocational Guidance*. Advance online publication. DOI: 10.1007/s10775-023-09612-z

Ghirardi, L., Brikell, I., Kuja-Halkola, R., Freitag, C. M., Franke, B., Asherson, P., & Larsson, H. (2019). The familial co-aggregation of ASD and ADHD: A register-based cohort study. *Molecular Psychiatry*, *24*(11), 1732–1737. DOI: 10.1038/s41380-019-0555-z PMID: 29703945

Greenway, C. W., Robinson, A., & King, J. M. (2023). The effect of social devaluation, labelling, and familiarity on children's attitudes and behavioral intentions toward a peer with symptoms of ADHD. *Psychology in the Schools*, *60*(11), 4452–4465. Advance online publication. DOI: 10.1002/pits.23004

Grove, J., Ripke, S., Als, T. D., Mattheisen, M., Walters, R. K., Won, H., Pallesen, J., Agerbo, E., Andreassen, O. A., Anney, R., Awashti, S., Belliveau, R., Bettella, F., Buxbaum, J. D., Bybjerg-Grauholm, J., Bækvad-Hansen, M., Cerrato, F., Chambert, K., Christensen, J. H., & Børglum, A. D. (2019). Identification of common genetic risk variants for autism spectrum disorder. *Nature Genetics*, *51*(3), 431–444. DOI: 10.1038/s41588-019-0344-8 PMID: 30804558

Guo, X., Chen, H., Long, Z., Duan, X., Zhang, Y., & Chen, H. (2017). Atypical developmental trajectory of local spontaneous brain activity in autism spectrum disorder. *Scientific Reports*, *7*(1), 39822. Advance online publication. DOI: 10.1038/srep39822 PMID: 28057930

Hampshire, P. K., Butera, G. D., & Bellini, S. (2015). Self-management and parents as interventionists to improve homework independence in students with autism spectrum disorders. *Preventing School Failure*, *60*(1), 22–34. DOI: 10.1080/1045988X.2014.954515

Hoza, B., Mrug, S., Gerdes, A. C., Hinshaw, S. P., Bukowski, W. M., Gold, J. A., Kraemer, H. C., Pelham, W. E., Wigal, T., & Arnold, L. E. (2005). What aspects of peer relationships are impaired in children with attention-deficit/hyperactivity disorder? *Journal of Consulting and Clinical Psychology, 73*(3), 411–423. DOI: 10.1037/0022-006X.73.3.411 PMID: 15982139

Huang, Y., Xu, H., Au, W., Xu, C., & Wu, K. (2018). Involvement of family environmental, behavioral, and social functional factors in children with attention-deficit/hyperactivity disorder. *Psychology Research and Behavior Management, 11*, 447–457. DOI: 10.2147/PRBM.S178080 PMID: 30349411

Kim, Y. S., & Leventhal, B. L. (2015). Genetic epidemiology and insights into interactive genetic and environmental effects in autism spectrum disorders. *Biological Psychiatry, 77*(1), 66–74. DOI: 10.1016/j.biopsych.2014.11.001 PMID: 25483344

Lai, C. L. E., Lau, Z., Lui, S. S. Y., Lok, E., Tam, V., Chan, Q., Cheng, K. M., Lam, S. M., & Cheung, E. F. C. (2016). Meta-analysis of neuropsychological measures of executive functioning in children and adolescents with high-functioning autism spectrum disorder. *Autism Research : Official Journal of the International Society for Autism Research, 10*(5), 911–939. DOI: 10.1002/aur.1723 PMID: 27874266

Laurent, A. C., & Gorman, K. (2017). Development of emotion self-regulation among young children with autism spectrum disorders: The role of parents. *Journal of Autism and Developmental Disorders, 48*(4), 1249–1260. DOI: 10.1007/s10803-017-3430-8 PMID: 29249011

Leblond, C. S., Rolland, T., Barthome, E., Mougin, Z., Fleury, M., Ecker, C., Bonnot-Briey, S., Cliquet, F., Tabet, A.-C., Maruani, A., Chaumette, B., Green, J., Delorme, R., & Bourgeron, T. (2024). A genetic bridge between medicine and neurodiversity for autism. *Annual Review of Genetics, 58*(1), 487–512. DOI: 10.1146/annurev-genet-111523-102614 PMID: 39585908

Lee, J. J., Wedow, R., Okbay, A., Kong, E., Maghzian, O., Zacher, M., Nguyen-Viet, T. A., Bowers, P., Sidorenko, J., Karlsson Linnér, R., Fontana, M. A., Kundu, T., Lee, C., Li, H., Li, R., Royer, R., Timshel, P. N., Walters, R. K., Willoughby, E. A., & Cesarini, D. (2018). Gene discovery and polygenic prediction from a genome-wide association study of educational attainment in 1.1 million individuals. *Nature Genetics, 50*(8), 1112–1121. DOI: 10.1038/s41588-018-0147-3 PMID: 30038396

Liljenwall, H., Lean, R. E., Smyser, T. A., Smyser, C. D., & Rogers, C. E. (2022). Parental ADHD and ASD symptoms and contributions of psychosocial risk to childhood ADHD and ASD symptoms in children born very preterm. *Journal of Perinatology : Official Journal of the California Perinatal Association*. Advance online publication. DOI: 10.1038/s41372-022-01463-w PMID: 35840709

Lingineni, R. K., Biswas, S., Ahmad, N., Jackson, B. E., Bae, S., & Singh, K. P. (2012). Factors associated with attention deficit/hyperactivity disorder among US children: Results from a national survey. *BMC Pediatrics*, *12*(1), 50. Advance online publication. DOI: 10.1186/1471-2431-12-50 PMID: 22583686

Lundstrom, S., Reichenberg, A., Anckarsater, H., Lichtenstein, P., & Gillberg, C. (2015). Autism phenotype versus registered diagnosis in Swedish children: Prevalence trends over 10 years in general population samples. *BMJ (Clinical Research Ed.)*, *350*(apr28 2), h1961. DOI: 10.1136/bmj.h1961 PMID: 25922345

Man, K. K. C., Tong, H. H. Y., Wong, L. Y. L., Chan, E. W., Simonoff, E., & Wong, I. C. K. (2015). Exposure to selective serotonin reuptake inhibitors during pregnancy and risk of autism spectrum disorder in children: A systematic review and meta-analysis of observational studies. *Neuroscience and Biobehavioral Reviews*, *49*, 82–89. DOI: 10.1016/j.neubiorev.2014.11.020 PMID: 25498856

Marotta, R., Risoleo, M. C., Messina, G., Parisi, L., Carotenuto, M., Vetri, L., & Roccella, M. (2020). The neurochemistry of autism. *Brain Sciences*, *10*(3), 163. DOI: 10.3390/brainsci10030163 PMID: 32182969

Martin, J., Taylor, M. J., & Lichtenstein, P. (2019). Assessing the evidence for shared genetic risks across psychiatric disorders and traits. *Psychological Medicine*, *49*(7), 1067–1077. DOI: 10.1017/S0033291718004214 PMID: 29198204

Masini, E., Loi, E., Vega-Benedetti, A. F., Carta, M., Doneddu, G., Fadda, R., & Zavattari, P. (2020). An overview of the main genetic, epigenetic and environmental factors involved in autism spectrum disorder focusing on synaptic activity. *International Journal of Molecular Sciences*, *21*(21), 8290. DOI: 10.3390/ijms21218290 PMID: 33167418

Matelski, L., & Van de Water, J. (2016). Risk factors in autism: Thinking outside the brain. *Journal of Autoimmunity*, *67*, 1–7. DOI: 10.1016/j.jaut.2015.11.003 PMID: 26725748

Mikami, A. Y., Jack, A., Emeh, C. C., & Stephens, H. F. (2010). Parental influence on children with attention-deficit/hyperactivity disorder: I. Relationships between parent behaviors and child peer status. *Journal of Abnormal Child Psychology*, *38*(6), 721–736. DOI: 10.1007/s10802-010-9393-2 PMID: 20339912

Mikami, A. Y., & Normand, S. (2015). The importance of social contextual factors in peer relationships of children with ADHD. *Current Developmental Disorders Reports*, *2*(1), 30–37. DOI: 10.1007/s40474-014-0036-0

Niarchou, M., Lazary, J., Zhou, R., & Reichenberg, A. (2023). Common genetic risk factors in ASD and ADHD co-occurring families. *Psychiatry Research*, *327*, 115384. Advance online publication. DOI: 10.1016/j.psychres.2023.115384

Nowell, S. W., Watson, L. R., Boyd, B., & Klinger, L. G. (2019). Efficacy study of a social communication and self-regulation intervention for school-age children with autism spectrum disorder: A randomized controlled trial. *Language, Speech, and Hearing Services in Schools*, *50*(3), 416–433. DOI: 10.1044/2019_LSHSS-18-0093 PMID: 31287766

Peverill, S., Smith, I. M., Duku, E., Szatmari, P., Mirenda, P., Vaillancourt, T., Volden, J., Zwaigenbaum, L., Bennett, T., Elsabbagh, M., Georgiades, S., & Ungar, W. J. (2019). Developmental trajectories of feeding problems in children with autism spectrum disorder. *Journal of Pediatric Psychology*, *44*(8), 988–998. DOI: 10.1093/jpepsy/jsz033 PMID: 31089730

Richey, J. A., Damiano, C. R., Sabatino, A., Rittenberg, A., Petty, C., Bizzell, J., Voyvodic, J., Heller, A., Coffman, M. C., Smoski, M., Davidson, R. J., & Dichter, G. S. (2015). Neural mechanisms of emotion regulation in autism spectrum disorder. *Journal of Autism and Developmental Disorders*, *45*(11), 3409–3423. DOI: 10.1007/s10803-015-2359-z PMID: 25618212

Rubia, K. (2018). Cognitive neuroscience of attention deficit hyperactivity disorder (ADHD) and its clinical translation. *Frontiers in Human Neuroscience*, *12*, 100. DOI: 10.3389/fnhum.2018.00100 PMID: 29651240

Rylaarsdam, L., & Guemez-Gamboa, A. (2019). Genetic causes and modifiers of autism spectrum disorder. *Frontiers in Cellular Neuroscience*, *13*, 385. DOI: 10.3389/fncel.2019.00385 PMID: 31481879

Sacrey, L. R., Zwaigenbaum, L., Bryson, S., Brian, J., Smith, I. M., Raza, S., Roberts, W., Szatmari, P., Vaillancourt, T., Roncadin, C., & Garon, N. (2018). Developmental trajectories of adaptive behavior in autism spectrum disorder: A high-risk sibling cohort. *Journal of Child Psychology and Psychiatry, and Allied Disciplines*, *60*(6), 697–706. DOI: 10.1111/jcpp.12985 PMID: 30295313

Sassone-Corsi, P., & Christen, Y. (2016). *Research and perspectives in endocrine interactions: A time for metabolism and hormones*. https://library.oapen.org/bitstream/handle/20.500.12657/27865/1/1002139.pdf

Satterstrom, F. K., Kosmicki, J. A., Wang, J., Breen, M. S., De Rubeis, S., An, J.-Y., Peng, M., Collins, R., Grove, J., Klei, L., Stevens, C., Reichert, J., Mulhern, M. S., Artomov, M., Gerges, S., Sheppard, B., Xu, X., Bhaduri, A., Norman, U., & Buxbaum, J. D. (2020). Large-scale exome sequencing study implicates both developmental and functional changes in the neurobiology of autism. *Cell*, *180*(3), 568–584.e23. DOI: 10.1016/j.cell.2019.12.036 PMID: 31981491

Segura, P.. (2025). Connectome-based symptom mapping and in silico related gene expression in neurodevelopmental conditions. *Molecular Psychiatry*. Advance online publication. DOI: 10.1038/s41380-025-03205-8 PMID: 41131279

Shapiro, E. G., Hughes, S. J., August, G. J., & Bloomquist, M. L. (1993). Processing of emotional information in children with attention-deficit hyperactivity disorder. *Developmental Neuropsychology*, *9*(3–4), 207–224. DOI: 10.1080/87565649309540553

Shimizu, V. T., Bueno, O. F. A., & Miranda, M. C. (2014). Sensory processing abilities of children with ADHD. *Brazilian Journal of Physical Therapy*, *18*(4), 343–352. DOI: 10.1590/bjpt-rbf.2014.0043 PMID: 25076000

Soler-Gutiérrez, A.-M., Sánchez-Carmona, A. J., Albert, J., Hinojosa, J. A., Cortese, S., Bellato, A., & Mayas, J. (2025). Emotion processing difficulties in ADHD: A Bayesian meta-analysis study. *European Child & Adolescent Psychiatry*, *34*(8), 2369–2390. Advance online publication. DOI: 10.1007/s00787-025-02647-3 PMID: 39853403

Sterrett, K., Shire, S., & Kasari, C. (2017). Peer relationships among children with ASD: Interventions targeting social acceptance, friendships, and peer networks. *International Review of Research in Developmental Disabilities*, *52*, 37–74. DOI: 10.1016/bs.irrdd.2017.07.006

Šulc, L., Wu, F., Lashari, A., Remnélius, K. L., Pyko, A., Nevriana, A., Lissåker, C., Sjöström, M., Wiebert, P., Bölte, S., Gustavsson, P., Albin, M., & Selander, J. (2025). The impact of maternal occupational exposure on ADHD and autism diagnoses in children. *Occupational and Environmental Medicine*, *A31*, 2–A32. DOI: 10.1136/oemed-2025-EPICOHabstracts.77

Szatmari, P., Georgiades, S., Duku, E., Bennett, T. A., Bryson, S., Fombonne, E., Mirenda, P., Roberts, W., Smith, I. M., Vaillancourt, T., Volden, J., Waddell, C., Zwaigenbaum, L., Elsabbagh, M., & Thompson, A. (2015). Developmental trajectories of symptom severity and adaptive functioning in an inception cohort of preschool children with autism spectrum disorder. *JAMA Psychiatry*, *72*(3), 276. DOI: 10.1001/jamapsychiatry.2014.2463 PMID: 25629657

Tercan, H., & Bayhan, P. (2025). The interplay of family dynamics, lifestyle, and ADHD: A case–control study on sociodemographic risk factors. *Brain and Behavior, 15*(9), e70830. Advance online publication. DOI: 10.1002/brb3.70830 PMID: 40916512

Tick, B., Bolton, P., Happé, F., Rutter, M., & Rijsdijk, F. (2016). Heritability of autism spectrum disorders: A meta-analysis of twin studies. *Journal of Child Psychology and Psychiatry, and Allied Disciplines, 57*(5), 585–595. DOI: 10.1111/jcpp.12499 PMID: 26709141

Tseng, M. H., Henderson, A., Chow, S. M., & Yao, G. (2004). Relationship between motor proficiency, attention, impulse, and activity in children with ADHD. *Developmental Medicine and Child Neurology, 46*(6), 381–388. Advance online publication. DOI: 10.1017/S0012162204000623 PMID: 15174529

Tye, C., Battaglia, M., Bertoletti, E., Ashwood, K. L., Azadi, B., Asherson, P., Bolton, P., & McLoughlin, G. (2014). Altered neurophysiological responses to emotional faces discriminate children with ASD, ADHD and ASD+ADHD. *Biological Psychology, 103*, 125–134. DOI: 10.1016/j.biopsycho.2014.08.013 PMID: 25179537

van Stralen, J. (2016). Emotional dysregulation in children with attention-deficit/hyperactivity disorder. *Attention Deficit and Hyperactivity Disorders, 8*(4), 175–187. DOI: 10.1007/s12402-016-0199-0 PMID: 27299358

Wagner, S., & Harony-Nicolas, H. (2017). Oxytocin and animal models for autism spectrum disorder. In *Behavioral pharmacology of neuropeptides* (pp. 213–237). Oxytocin., DOI: 10.1007/7854_2017_15

Wan, M. W., Meera, S. S., & Swanson, M. R. (2025). Emerging neurodivergence in infancy and toddlerhood. *Infant Behavior & Development, 80*, 102133. DOI: 10.1016/j.infbeh.2025.102133 PMID: 40903314

Wang, L., Wang, B., Wu, C., Wang, J., & Sun, M. (2023). Autism spectrum disorder: Neurodevelopmental risk factors, biological mechanism, and precision therapy. *International Journal of Molecular Sciences, 24*(3), 1819. DOI: 10.3390/ijms24031819 PMID: 36768153

Watkins, L., Kuhn, M., Ledbetter-Cho, K., Gevarter, C., & O'Reilly, M. (2015). Evidence-based social communication interventions for children with autism spectrum disorder. *Indian Journal of Pediatrics, 84*(1), 68–75. DOI: 10.1007/s12098-015-1938-5 PMID: 26581197

Willsey, A. J., & State, M. W. (2015). Autism spectrum disorders: From genes to neurobiology. *Current Opinion in Neurobiology*, *30*, 92–99. DOI: 10.1016/j.conb.2014.10.015 PMID: 25464374

Woodbury-Smith, M., & Scherer, S. W. (2018). Progress in the genetics of autism spectrum disorder. *Developmental Medicine and Child Neurology*, *60*(5), 445–451. DOI: 10.1111/dmcn.13717 PMID: 29574884

Wright, C., Shin, J. H., Rajpurohit, A., Deep-Soboslay, A., Collado-Torres, L., Brandon, N. J., Hyde, T. M., Kleinman, J. E., Jaffe, A. E., Cross, A. J., & Weinberger, D. R. (2017). Altered expression of histamine signaling genes in autism spectrum disorder. *Translational Psychiatry*, *7*(5), e1126. Advance online publication. DOI: 10.1038/tp.2017.87 PMID: 28485729

Zantinge, G., van Rijn, S., Stockmann, L., & Swaab, H. (2017). Physiological arousal and emotion regulation strategies in young children with autism spectrum disorders. *Journal of Autism and Developmental Disorders*, *47*(9), 2648–2657. DOI: 10.1007/s10803-017-3181-6 PMID: 28593596

Chapter 8
Foundations of Typical Development and Neurodevelopment Disorders:
Definitions, Classification, Conceptual Frameworks, and Indian Context

B. N. Bhumika
http://orcid.org/0009-0006-7042-4935
PES University, India

ABSTRACT

Understanding typical development alongside neurodevelopmental disorders offers an integrative framework for appreciating the full spectrum of human developmental diversity. Typical developmental milestone provides essential reference points, while the study of neurodevelopmental disorders illuminates atypical trajectories shaped by dynamic gene-environment interactions, neural plasticity and contextual influences. Contemporary perspectives such as developmental psychopathology, neurodiversity and dimensional models challenge deficit- based views and emphasize continuity, individual variability and strengths-based understanding. The chapter highlights the importance of early identification, culturally responsive assessment and individualized, family-centered interventions, with education systems playing a central role in inclusion. Within the Indian context, alignment with the Rights of Persons with Disabilities Act (2016) and the National Education Policy (2020) supports a shift toward rights based, inclusive and sustainable practices across the lifespan.

DOI: 10.4018/979-8-3373-7072-9.ch008

INTRODUCTION

Human development is a dynamic and lifelong process, shaped by the continuous and reciprocal interaction of biological maturation, psychological processes and environmental influences. From conception through old age, individuals undergo systematic changes in physical growth, brain development, cognition, emotion and social functioning. Developmental psychology seeks to understand not only how individuals grow and change across the lifespan, but also why developmental patterns differ across individuals and contexts. Typical development provides an essential framework for understanding normative patterns of growth across physical, cognitive, language, emotional and social domains. These developmental milestones serve as important reference points for identifying additional support or intervention. These differences reflect variations in genetic endowment, neural development, family environments, cultural practices, educational experiences and broader socio-economic conditions. Within this broad framework, the study of typical development plays a foundational role by outlining expected patterns of growth and age-appropriate milestones across developmental domains. Typical development does not imply uniformity or an idealized standard, rather, it represents a range of normative variations that occur within particular cultural and contextual settings. These developmental benchmarks serve as reference points that enable professionals to recognize when developmental trajectories diverge in ways that may indicate risk or difficulty.

In contrast, neurodevelopmental disorders (NDDs) refer to conditions that arise from atypical brain development and manifest early in life, often during infancy or childhood. These disorders are characterized by persistent impairments in cognition, communication, behaviour, motor functioning and adaptive skills that interfere with everyday functioning across home, school and community settings. Neurodevelopmental disorders include conditions such as Autism Spectrum Disorder (ASD), Attention-Deficit/ Hyperactivity Disorder (ADHD), Intellectual Disability (ID), Communication Disorders and Specific Learning Disorders (SLD). Importantly, these conditions are not isolated or static impairments confined to childhood, rather, they are dynamic developmental conditions whose manifestations evolve across the lifespan in interaction with changing environmental demands, educational expectations, family systems and social contexts. For example, difficulties in attention or social communication that appear manageable during early childhood may become more pronounces during adolescence or adulthood when academic, occupational and interpersonal demands increase.

Understanding the foundations of typical development alongside neurodevelopmental disorders is therefore essential for psychologists, educators, clinicians and policymakers. Typical development provides the necessary framework for identifying deviations, while the study of neurodevelopmental disorder offers deeper insights into brain-behaviour relationships, developmental plasticity and the diversity of human functioning, integrating these perspectives allows for more accurate assessment, earlier intervention and more inclusive educational and social practices.

Recent epidemiological research indicates a substantial global increase in the identification and recognition of neurodevelopmental disorders, partly due to improved awareness, expanded diagnostic criteria and better screening practices. According to the World Health Organization (WHO, 2023), Autism Spectrum Disorder affects approximately 1 in 100 children worldwide, while Attention- Deficit/ Hyperactivity Disorder is estimated to affect nearly 5-7% of children and adolescents globally. Similarly, Specific Learning Disorders, including dyslexia, dysgraphia and dyscalculia, affect approximately 5-15% of school-aged children across different educational contexts. Within the Indian context. Emerging epidemiological evidence from organizations such as the National Institute of Mental Health and Neurosciences (NIMHANS) and the Indian Council of Medical Research (ICMR) suggest that developmental disabilities affect approximately 2-3% of children, while ADHD prevalence estimates range from 1.6% to 7.2%, depending on diagnostic methods and population samples. School-based studies further estimate that Specific Learning Disorders affect nearly 6-10% of Indian students. However, these figures likely underestimate the true prevalence due to limited awareness, stigma, shortage of trained professionals and unequal access to diagnostic and intervention services, especially in rural and underserved regions. Children in low-resource settings frequently experience delayed diagnosis, inadequate educational support and reduced access to multidisciplinary interventions.

Longitudinal studies published in journals such as *The Lancet Psychiatry* (2022-2024) further demonstrate that neurodevelopmental disorders frequently persist into adolescence and adulthood, influencing multiple domains of functioning across the lifespan. Individuals with neurodevelopmental disorders are increased risk of co-occurring mental health conditions such as anxiety disorders depression and emotional dysregulation. They may also experience challenges related to academic achievement, vocational adjustment, independent living and social relationships. Adults with neurodevelopmental disorders often encounter barriers to higher education, employment opportunities and community participation, particularly in societies with limited inclusive infrastructure and workplace accommodations. These findings underscore the importance of viewing neurodevelopmental disorders not merely as childhood conditions, but as lifelong developmental conditions with significant educational, psychological, social and economic implications. Consequently, there is a growing need for early screening, culturally responsive assessment, interdisciplinary interventions and long-term support systems that extent beyond childhood into adulthood and community life.

Accordingly, this chapter presents an integrated overview of typical development and neurodevelopmental disorders, examining key definitions, classification systems and conceptual frameworks that guide contemporary research and practice. By situating developmental differences within biological, psychological, cultural and ethical contexts, this chapter aims to promote a comprehensive and inclusive understanding of developmental diversity across the lifespan.

1. CONCEPTUALIZING TYPICAL DEVELOPMENT

Development is best understood as a lifelong, multidimensional, multidirectional, plastic and contextual proves, a view strongly supported by lifespan developmental theories (Baltes, 1987; Lerner, 2006). This perspective emphasizes that development does not conclude at the end of childhood or adolescence but continues from conception through adulthood and into old age. Erikson's psychological theory, for example, explicitly conceptualizes development as a sequence of age-related crises extending across the entire lifespan, from trust versus mistrust in infancy to integrity versus despair in late adulthood (Erikson, 1950). Across the lifespan, individuals experience continuous changes that reflect both biological maturation and accumulated experience, underscoring the dynamic nature of development.

Development is multidimensional, involving interconnected domains such as physical growth, cognitive functioning, emotional regulation, social relationships and moral reasoning (Baltes, Lindenberger & Staudinger, 2006). Physical development includes processes such as brain maturation, motor development, hormonal changes and overall physiological growth. Cognitive development refers to changes in mental processes including attention, memory, language, reasoning, problem- solving and executive functioning, while socio-emotional development encompasses emotional regulation, attachment, identity formation, interpersonal relationships and moral understanding (Berk, 2021; Papalia & Martorell, 2021). Theories of human development increasingly recognize that these domains do not operate independently. For instance, Piaget's theory highlights how advances in cognitive structures facilitate more complex moral reasoning and social understanding, while Vygotsky's sociocultural theory emphasizes the role of social interaction in shaping cognitive development (Piaget, 1952; Vygotsky, 1978). Similarly, emotional regulation has been shown influence learning, peer relationships and mental health outcomes, illustrating the reciprocal influence among developmental domains.

It is also multidirectional, meaning that development involves patterns of both growth and decline across the lifespan. According to Baltes' lifespan theory, development is characterized by simultaneously gains and losses, rather than a single trajectory of continuous improvement (Baltes, 1987). While abilities such as language acquisition, sensory processing and processing speed tend to peak in early life, other capacities, such as crystallized intelligence, emotional regulation, wisdom and social competence that may remain stable or even improve during adulthood and later life (Schaie, 1996; Carstensen, 2006). This multidirectional view challenges stage-based and linear models of development and highlights adaptive reorganization across life stages.

A key feature of development is its plasticity, or the capacity for change in response to experience and environmental conditions. Plasticity enables individuals to adapt to challenges, recover from adversity and benefit from learning and intervention (Lerner, 2006). Although plasticity is generally grater during early childhood due to heightened neural sensitivity, research in cognitive aging and rehabilitation demonstrates that developmental change remains possible across adulthood, particularly when enriched environments and targeted interventions are provided (Kolb & Gibb, 2011)). This principle forms the foundation for early intervention programs as well as lifelong learning initiatives.

Finally, development is deeply contextual, shaped by the multiple environments in which individuals are embedded. Bronfenbrenner's ecological systems theory emphasizes that development is influenced by interactions across nested systems, including the microsystem (family, peers), mesosystem, eco-system and macrosystem (culture, social policies) (Bronfenbrenner, 1979). Cultural values, educational opportunities, historical timing and socio-economic conditions interact with biological predispositions to produce probabilistic rather than predetermined outcomes (Lerner,2006). Consequently, development cannot be understood as a rigid or universal pathway but rather as a range of possible trajectories shaped by continuous person-environment interactions across time.

Several major developmental theories further contribute to understanding typical development. Piaget's cognitive developmental theory emphasizes qualitive changes in children's thinking as they progress through distinct stages of cognitive growth (Piaget, 1952). Vygotsky's sociocultural theory highlights the role of social interaction, language and cultural tool shaping cognitive development, particularly through guided participation and the zone of proximal development (Vygotsky, 1978). Erikson's psychosocial theory conceptualizes development as a series of psychosocial crises extending across the lifespan, with each stage involving specific developmental tasks related to identity, relationships and psychological well-being (Erikson, 1968). Together, these perspectives reinforce the understanding that typical development is a complex, interactive and contextually shaped process influenced by biological, psychological, social and cultural factors across the lifespan.

1.1 Domains of Typical Development

Typical development unfolds across three broad and interrelated domains, that is, physical, cognitive and socio-emotional development. Although these domains are described separately for conceptual clarity, they function in close interaction throughout the lifespan. Development in each domain both influences and is influenced by changes in the others, underscoring the integrated and holistic nature of human growth (Lerner, 2006)

Physical Development

Physical development encompasses changes In body size and proportions, growth in height and weight, maturation of the nervous system, development of motor skills and pubertal changes. Early physical development is characterized by rapid brain growth, including processes such as synaptogenesis, synaptic pruning and myelination, which enhance neural efficiency and support increasingly complex behaviour (Nelson, de Haan & Thomas, 2006: Kolb & Whishaw, 2015). These neurobiological changes provide the foundation for later cognitive, emotional and behavioural capacities. Motor development progresses from simple reflexes in infancy to increasingly coordinated gross and fine motor skills, enabling children to explore their environments and engage in social interaction (Thelen & Smith, 1994). Puberty represents another major phase of physical development, marked by hormonal changes and sexual maturation. These changes are associated not only with physical growth but also with shifts in emotional regulation, self-concept and peer relationship (Susman &Dorn. 2009). Thus, physical development both directly and indirectly shapes development in other domains.

Cognitive Development

Cognitive development refers to age-related changes in mental processes such as perception, attention, memory, language, reasoning and problem-solving. During early childhood, rapid gains in language and symbolic thought support communication and learning, while later childhood and adolescence are characterized by improvements in logical reasoning, abstract thinking and executive functions (Bjorklund & Causey, 2018). Several theoretical frameworks have contributed to understanding cognitive development cognitive development. Piaget's theory of cognitive development emphasizes qualitative changes in thinking, proposing that children progress through stages marked by distinct cognitive structures (Piaget, 1952). In contrast, information-processing approaches focus on gradual, quantitative changes in cognitive efficiency, including improvements in processing speed, working memory, and strategy use (Case, 1998; Siegler, 2016). Together, these perspectives suggest that cognitive development involves both structural reorganization and continuous refinement of mental processes. Cognitive development plays a critical role in academic achievement, decision- making and adaptive functioning across the lifespan.

Social-Emotional Development

Socio-emotional development involves changes in emotional experience and regulation, attachment patterns, self-concept, identity formation moral reasoning and interpersonal relationships. Early socio-emotional development is closely linked to caregiver-child relationships, with secure attachment serving as a foundation for emotional security and later social competence (Bowlby, 1969-1982; Ainsworth et al., 1978). As children mature, they develop greater self-awareness, empathy and the ability to regulate emotions in socially appropriate ways. Several theoretical perspectives inform this domain. Erikson's psychosocial theory emphasizes age-specific developmental tasks and highlights the role of social relationships in shaping identity and personality across the lifespan (Erikson, 1968). Bandura's social learning theory underscores the importance of observational learning, modelling and reinforcement in the acquisition of social and emotional behaviours (Bandura, 1977). Socio-emotional development is also deeply influenced by cultural values, family structures and peer contexts, making it a highly contextual and culturally embedded process.

Interconnectedness of Developmental Domains

The domains of physical, cognitive and socio-emotional development are deeply interconnected and changes in one domain often produce cascading effects in others. For example, advances in language and cognitive skills facilitate more complex social interactions and emotional expression, while effective emotional regulation supports attention, learning and academic engagement (Denham et al., 2012). Similarly, physical maturation and motor competence influence opportunities for exploration and social participation, which in turn promote cognitive and emotional growth. Recognizing this interdependence is essential for understanding both typical and atypical development. Developmental challenges rarely occur in isolation and effective assessment and intervention must adopt a whole-child, lifespan and contextual perspective (Baltes, Lindenberger & Staudinger, 2006).

Table 1. Selected Developmental Milestones Across Early Childhood

Age	Gross motor	Fine motor	Language	Socio-emotional
6 months	Rolls over, sits with support	Transfers objects between hands	Babbles	Recognizes familiar people
12 months	Walks with support	Pincer grasp	Says 1-2 words	Waves goodbye
18 months	Walks independently	Scribbles	Uses 10-20 words	Shows affection
2 years	Runs, climbs stairs	Builds tower of blocks	Two-word sentences	Parallel play
3 years	Pedals tricycle	Draws simple shapes	Uses short conversations	Cooperative play begins
4 years	Hops on one foot	Uses scissors	Speaks clearly	Engages in imaginative play
5 years	Skips, balances	Writes some letters	Tells stories	Understands social rules

1.2 Genetic Influences, Prenatal Development and Early Brain Growth

Human development begins at conception with the combination of genetic materials from both parents, resulting in a unique genetic makeup that provides the biological foundation development. Genes influence a wide range of physical and psychological characteristics, including height, neurological organization (Berk,2021; Papalia & Martorell, 2021). Many traits such as intelligence and emotional reactivity are polygenic, meaning they are influenced by multiple genes rather than a single genetic factor (Plomin et al., 2016).

Importantly, genes do not function in isolation or determine outcomes in a fixed manner. Contemporary research emphasizes the role of gene-environment interaction, wherein genetic predispositions are expressed differently depending on environmental conditions (Rutter,2012). Through processes such as epigenetics, environmental factors can regulate gene expression without altering the DNA sequence itself. Experiences such as prenatal stress, nutrition, caregiving quality and exposure to toxins can activate or silence certain genes, thereby influencing developmental trajectories (Meaney, 2010; Moore et al., 2017). This interaction helps explain why individuals with similar genetic vulnerabilities may show widely different developmental outcomes.

Prenatal development represents a critical and highly sensitive period in human development, during which major organ systems and neural structures are formed. The prenatal period is commonly divided into the germinal, embryonic and foetal stages, each characterized by distinct developmental processes (Papalia & Martorell, 2021).

During this time, the developing foetus is particularly vulnerable to environmental influences. Factors such as maternal nutrition, exposure to substances (e.g., alcohol, drugs, environmental toxins), infections, chronic illness and psychological stress can significantly affect foetal growth and brain development, potentially increasing the risk for neurodevelopmental disorders (Berk, 2021; Shonkoff et al., 2012).

The early postnatal period is marked by rapid brain growth and neural reorganization, often referred to as a period of heightened neural plasticity. Processes such as synaptogenesis, synaptic pruning and myelination occur at an accelerated pace, enabling the brain to adapt to environmental experiences, sensory stimulation and early learning opportunities, thereby laying the foundation for cognitive, emotional, language and social development across the lifespan.

2. UNDERSTANDING NEURODEVELOPMENTAL DISORDERS

2.1 Definition and Core Characteristics

Neurodevelopmental disorders (NDDs) are a group of conditions that involve early-onset disruptions in brain development, affecting cognitive, social, emotional and behavioural functioning. These disorders are typically reorganized during infancy, childhood or adolescences, although their effects often persist into adulthood. They reflect atypical development of the central nervous system, leading to long-term difficulties in learning, behaviour, communication and adaptive functioning (American Psychiatric Association [APA], 2022).

Both the DSM-5-TR (Diagnostic and Statistical Manual of Mental Disorders, 5th Edition, Text Revision) and the ICD-11 (International Classification of Diseases, 11th Revision) classify neurodevelopmental disorders as conditions with a developmental origin, emphasizing that they are lifelong conditions rather than transient developmental delays (APA,2022; World Health Organization [WHO], 2019). Contemporary developmental psychopathology perspectives emphasizes that neurodevelopmental disorders are not isolated deficits but reflect complex interactions among genetic vulnerability, brain maturation, environmental influences and developmental experiences over time. Increasingly, research conceptualizes neurodevelopmental disorders dimensionally rather than categorically, recognizing overlapping symptoms, shared genetic mechanisms and common neurobiological pathways across disorders (Astle et al., 2022).

Although specific disorders within this category vary, several core characteristics are commonly observed;

1. Early developmental onset

One of the defining characteristics of NDDs is that symptoms emerge during the developmental period, often before formal schooling. Developmental delays in speech, motor coordination, attention or social interaction are often among the earliest signs. For instance, longitudinal studies on autism spectrum disorder, atypical social communication, reduced eye contact and restricted or repetitive behaviours may be evident before the age of three years (APA, 2022; Lord et al., 2020). Similarly, prospective cohort studies of ADHD indicate that early difficulties in self-regulation, inhibitory control and temperament during preschool years predict later attentional and behavioural problems (Campbell et al., 2014).

Recent developmental neuroscience research suggests that early symptoms emerge because neurodevelopmental differences affect foundational processes such as sensory integration, executive control and social information processing during critical periods of brain maturation. Meta- analytic evidence also indicates that earlier symptom recognition and intervention are associated with significantly improved long-term outcomes in language development, adaptive functioning and academic achievement (Fuller & Kaiser, 2020).

Importantly, contemporary longitudinal studies emphasizes that developmental trajectories are highly variable. Some children show stable symptoms over time, whereas others exhibit changing patterns depending on environmental supports, intervention quality and co-occurring conditions (Johnson et al., 2015).

2. Atypical brain development and neurobiological mechanisms

Neurodevelopment disorders are associated with structural and functional differences in the brain. Research indicated alterations in neural connectivity, synaptic functioning, neurotransmitter systems and the development of cortical and subcortical regions. These neurobiological differences can disrupt information processing, attention regulation, memory, emotional control and social cognition (Johnson et al., 2015).

Research using magnetic resonance imaging (MRI), diffusion tensor imaging (DTI) and functional MRI (fMRI) has identified alterations in cortical thickness and brain volume, white matter connectivity, synaptic pruning processes, neural network organization and functional connectivity between brain regions. For instance, studies of ADHD consistently report abnormalities in frontostriatal circuits involved in attention regulation, inhibitory control and executive functioning (Faraone et al., 2021). Similarly, autism research highlights atypical connectivity within social brain networks, including the amygdala, superior temporal sulcus and medial prefrontal cortex (Richter et al., 2019).

Contemporary genomic research demonstrates strong heritability across many neurodevelopmental disorders. Twin and family studies estimate heritability rates of approximately:

- 70-80% for ADHD
- 60-90% for autism spectrum disorder
- 40-70% for specific learning disorders.

Genome- wide association studies (GWAS) and meta-analyses have identified hundreds of genetic variants associated with NDDs, many of which affect synaptic functioning, neuronal migration and neurotransmitter regulation (Grove et al., 2019). However, current research emphasizes that no single gene causes most NDDs. Instead, disorders arise through polygenic and multifactorial mechanisms involving interactions between genes and environmental influences. Epigenetic research further demonstrates that prenatal stress, maternal nutrition, toxin exposure, inflammation and early adversity may alter gene expression related to neural development. These findings support developmental systems models emphasizing dynamic interaction between biology and environment.

3. Deficits in cognition, communication, behaviour or adaptive functioning

Neurodevelopmental disorders often involve impairments across multiple domains of functioning, although the specific profile varies between disorders and individuals. Cognitive impairments may include difficulties in learning, memory, executive functioning or problem-solving. Communication challenges are especially prominent in autism spectrum disorder and communication disorders and can involve expressive or receptive language deficits, pragmatic language difficulties or impaired nonverbal communication. Behavioural symptoms may include hyperactivity, impulsivity, repetitive behaviours, emotional dysregulation or social withdrawal. Additionally, adaptive functioning refers to practical, conceptual and social skills necessary for independent living. Deficits in adaptive functioning affect everyday skills as self-care, academic performance and peer relationships and more (APA,2022; Schalock et al., 2021). Meta-analytic evidence consistently identifies executive dysfunction as a transdiagnostic feature across several NDDs, particularly ADHD, ASD and learning disorders (Craig et al., 2016). Difficulties in planning, inhibitory control and cognitive flexibility significantly affect academic and social functioning.

4. Functional impairment across multiple settings

A defining feature of NDDs is that symptoms interfere significantly with functioning across settings such as home, school, workplace and community environments. The difficulties associated with neurodevelopmental disorders are pervasive and evident across different contexts, including home, school and community environments. For example, a child with attention-deficit/hyperactivity disorder (ADHD) may show inattention and impulsivity in the classroom, poor organizational skills at home and difficulties in maintaining peer relationships, indication widespread functional impairment (Barkley, 2015; APA,2022). Longitudinal studies consistently demonstrate that functional impairment often extends into adulthood. Adults with childhood ADHD, for example, show increased risk for occupational difficulties, relationship problems, substance misuse and mental health disorders (Sibley et al., 2022). Similarly, long-term follow-up studies of autism indicate variability in adult outcomes, with social support, adaptive skills and early intervention significantly influencing employment, independence and wellbeing (Lord et al., 2020).

5. Environmental and psychosocial influences

Although NDDs have strong biological foundations, environmental factors significantly influence symptom expression, severity and developmental outcomes. Important environmental influences include prenatal exposure to toxins or infections. Premature birth and low birth weight, chronic stress, parenting quality, peer relationships etc. Longitudinal resilience research indicates that supportive caregiving, inclusive educational settings and strong social relationships can substantially improve developmental outcomes despite neurodevelopmental vulnerabilities. Recent ecological and developmental systems theories emphasizes that disability emerges not only from individual impairments but also from barriers within social and environmental contexts.

Overall, neurodevelopmental disorders represent enduring patterns of atypical development shaped by complex interactions among genetic, neurobiological and environmental factor. Contemporary research demonstrates that these conditions involve dynamic developmental trajectories rather than fixed deficits. Advances in neuroscience, longitudinal research and meta-analytic evidence have improved understanding of the mechanisms underlying NDDs, while also highlighting the importance of early interventions, environmental support and individualized care. Increasingly, researchers and clinicians adopt dimensional and neurodiversity- informed approaches that recognizes both challenges and strengths among neurodivergent individuals.

Understanding these disorders within a developmental and ecological framework is essential for promoting early identification, affecting intervention, social inclusion and long-term support across the lifespan.

2.2 Etiology of Neurodevelopmental Disorders

The etiology of neurodevelopmental disorders in multifactorial, arising from the complex interplay of genetic, biological and environmental factors. Genetic influences play a significant role, with many disorders such as autism spectrum disorder and attention-deficit/hyperactivity disorder (ADHD) demonstrating high heritability (APA, 2022). Specific gene variations or chromosomal abnormalities can affect brain development, neuronal connectivity and neurotransmitter systems, thereby creating a biological vulnerability. At the same time, environmental factors such as prenatal complications, perinatal injuries, early deprivation and psychosocial stressors can influence the severity and expression of these disorders (Bronfenbrenner & Morris, 2006; Sameroff, 2010). Advances in neuroscience have shown that disruptions in neural connectivity, neurotransmitter regulations and large-scale brain network organization are common mechanisms underlying many neurodevelopmental conditions (Johnson et al., 2015). The interaction between genetic predispositions and environmental influences is best understood through the biopsychosocial model, which emphasizes that biological vulnerabilities interact with psychological processes and social contexts to shape developmental outcomes (Engel,1977). This perspective highlights why early identification, supportive environments and targeted interventions can significantly improve functioning in individuals with neurodevelopmental disorder (Shonkoff et al., 2012).

A child with a strong family history of ADHD showed early difficulties with impulse control and emotional regulation. However, consistent parental support, structured routines, early behavioural intervention and supportive schooling helped the child develop effective coping skills and academic competence. In contrast, untreated stress and punitive educational responses might have intensified behavioural difficulties. This example illustrates how biological vulnerability interacts dynamically with environmental experiences in shaping developmental outcomes. Current research therefore supports viewing neurodevelopmental disorders not as fixed deficits but as dynamic developmental conditions influenced by ongoing interactions among genes, brain development, experience and social context. This perspective reinforces the importance of early identification, inclusive policies, family support and evidence-based interventions in improving functioning and quality of life across the lifespan.

2.3 Classification of Neurodevelopmental Disorders

The two main systems used worldwide to classify and diagnose neurodevelopmental disorders are the Diagnostic and Statistical Manual of Mental Disorders (DSM-5) and the International Classification and Diseases (ICD-11). The DSM-5, published by the American Psychiatric Association, is widely used in clinical and research settings, particularly in the United States. It provides detailed diagnostic criteria, symptom descriptions and severity specifiers, which help clinicians identify disorders such as autism spectrum disorder, ADHD, intellectual disability and specific learning disorders. The ICD-11, published by the World Health Organization, is used internationally for health reporting and epidemiological purposes. It categorizes disorders based on broader medical and mental health classifications, facilitating consistency in diagnosis across countries. While both systems aim to standardize the identification of neurodevelopmental disorders, the DSM-5 is often more detailed in clinical criteria, whereas the ICD-11 emphasizes global applicability and public health use. Together, these systems guide assessment, research and treatment planning, ensuring that individuals with neurodevelopmental disorders receive appropriate diagnosis and support.

Table 2. DSM-5-TR vs ICD-11: Comparison of Neurodevelopmental Disorder Classification

Feature	DSM-5-TR	ICD-11
Publisher	American Psychiatric Association	World Health Organization
Primary purpose	Clinical diagnosis and research	Global health classification and epidemiology
Scope	Mental disorders only	All medical and mental health conditions
Diagnostic style	Detailed symptom-based criteria	Broader clinical descriptions
Global usage	Common in the United States and research settings	Used internationally across healthcare systems
Coding system	Compatible with ICD codes	Universal international coding system
Approach to ASD	Spectrum-based with severity levels	Spectrum-based with functional descriptions
Use in research	Highly influential in psychiatric research	Useful for public health and cross-national data
Clinical detail	More specific diagnostic thresholds	Greater flexibility for diverse healthcare contexts

Both the DSM-5 and ICD-11 classify neurodevelopmental disorder as a group of conditions that share common defining features, most notably early onset during the developmental period and persistent impairments in cognitive, communicative, behavioural or motor functioning. These disorders typically emerge in infancy or childhood and interfere with everyday functioning across educational, social and occupational domains. Grouping these conditions together underscored their developmental origins and highlights the importance of early identification and intervention.

Within this category, several key diagnostic groups are recognized. Intellectual disability is characterized by significant limitations in intellectual functioning and adaptive behaviour, affecting conceptual, social and practical skills. Communication disorders include difficulties in speech sound production, language comprehension or expression and social use of language, which may significantly impact academic performance and social interaction. Autism spectrum disorder (ASD) is defined by persistent deficits in social communication and social interaction, alongside restricted, repetitive patterns of behaviour, interests or activities.

Attention deficit/hyperactivity disorder (ADHD) is characterised by developmentally inappropriate levels of inattention, hyperactivity and/or impulsivity that interfere with functioning across multiple settings. Specific learning disorders involve persistent difficulties in acquiring and using academic skills such as reading, writing or mathematics, despite adequate instruction and normal intelligence. Motor disorders, including developmental coordination disorder and tic disorders, involve impairments in motor coordination or involuntary movements that affect daily activities.

Table 3. Major Neurodevelopmental Disorders in DSM-5-TR and ICD-11

Disorder category	Core characteristics	Functional impact
Intellectual disability	Deficits in intellectual and adaptive functioning	Difficulties in independent living, learning and social functioning
Communication disorders	Problems in speech, language or communication	Academic and interpersonal difficulties
Autism Spectrum Disorder	Social communication deficits and repetitive behaviours	Challenges in social interaction, flexibility and daily functioning
ADHD	Inattention, hyperactivity and impulsivity	Impaired academic, occupational and behavioural functioning
Specific Learning Disorder	Difficulties in reading, writing or mathematics	Reduced academic achievement
Motor disorders	Coordination problems or involuntary movements	Difficulties in motor tasks and daily activities

A key strength of the DSM-5 classification lied in its dimensional approach, particularly in the conceptualization of autism spectrum disorder. Rather than viewing autism as a set of discrete subtypes, the DSM-5 recognizes autism as a spectrum, withs symptoms varying in severity and functional impact across individuals. Specifiers related to language ability, intellectual functioning and level of support required allow for a more nuanced and individualized understanding of the condition. This dimensional emphasis reflects growing recognition of heterogeneity within neurodevelopmental disorders and supports more personalized assessment, intervention and support planning.

2.4 Common Examples of Neurodevelopmental Disorders

Neurodevelopmental disorders encompass as diverse group of conditions that emerge during the developmental period and affect cognitive, behavioural, social, emotional and adaptive functioning. Although these disorders differ in symptom presentation and severity, they frequently involve atypical brain development, persistent functional impairments and challenges across educational, social and occupational domains. Contemporary research increasingly highlights the dimensional and overlapping nature of neurodevelopmental disorders, with many individuals experiencing co-occurring conditions and shared neurobiological mechanisms (APA, 20220; Astle et al., 2022).

Some of the most recognized neurodevelopmental disorders include:

1. Autism Spectrum Disorder (ASD)

Autism spectral disorder (ASD) is a neurodevelopmental condition characterised by difficulties in social communication and interaction, along with restricted and repetitive patterns of behaviour interests or activities. The term "spectrum" reflects the substantial variability in symptom presentation, cognitive abilities, language development and adaptive functioning observed among autistic individuals. Some individuals may require minimal support, while others experience significant impairments affecting communication, learning and independent living.

Recent neurodevelopmental research indicates that ASD is associated with atypical neural connectivity and differences in the functioning of social brain networks, including the amygdala, temporal cortex and prefrontal regions (Richter et al., 2019). Genome-wide association studies and large-scale meta-analyses demonstrate strong genetic influences, with heritability estimates ranging from 60% to 90% (Grove et al., 2019). However, contemporary evidence suggest that autism arises through complex interactions among genetic susceptibility, prenatal influences and environmental factors rather than a single causal mechanisms.

2. Attention-Deficit/ Hyperactivity Disorder (ADHD)

Attention Deficit/ Hyperactive Disorder (ADHD) is marked by persistent patterns of inattention, hyperactivity and impulsivity that interfere with functioning and development. It is often identified in childhood, particularly when difficulties in school performance, classroom behaviour or peer relationships become evident.

The inattentive dimension includes difficulties sustaining attention, forgetfulness, distractibility and problems with organization and task completion. Hyperactivity and impulsivity may involve excessive movement, restlessness, interrupting others and difficulty waiting or controlling impulses. ADHD symptoms must be present across multiple settings, such as home and school and significantly impair social, academic or occupational functioning.

Genetic research shows ADHD to be highly heritable, with heritability estimates around 70-80%. Environmental risk factors such as prenatal exposure to tobacco or alcohol, prematurity, low birth weight and psychosocial adversity may also contribute to symptom development and severity.

Contemporary approaches to ADHD emphasize multimodal intervention, including behavioural therapy, educational accommodations, parent training and pharmacological treatment. Meta- analyses support stimulant medications and behavioural interventions as evidence-based approaches for reducing symptoms and improving functioning (Cortese et al., 2018).

3. Intellectual Disability (ID)

Intellectual disability is defined by significant limitations in intellectual functioning and adaptive behaviour, affecting abilities such as reasoning, problem-solving, learning and judgement, as well as practical life skills related to communication, self-care and social responsibility. These limitations typically emerge during the developmentary and can vary in severity, influencing an individual's capacity for independent living, academic achievement and social participation.

Individuals with ID may experience difficulties in communication, academic learning, self-care, decision-making, social participation and occupational functioning. Severity levels range from mild to profound and are primarily determined by adaptive functioning rather than IQ scores alone (Schalock et al., 2021).

4. Communication Disorder

Communication disorders include conditions such as language disorder, speech sound disorder and social pragmatic communication disorder, which affect the development and use of verbal and non-verbal communication. Children with these disorders may experience difficulties with vocabulary, grammar, speech clarity or the appropriate social use of language, impacting academic learning, social interactions and overall communication effectiveness (APA, 2022).

Children with communication disorders may experience difficulties with vocabulary acquisition, grammar, sentence formation, speech clarity, fluency or the social use of language. Problems in pragmatic communication may include difficulty understanding conversational rules, interpreting social cue or adjusting communication according to context.

Longitudinal studies demonstrate that communication disorder can have significant long-term effects on academic achievement, literacy development, peer relationships and emotional wellbeing (Conti- Ramsden et al., 2018). Children with persistent language difficulties are also at increased risk for anxiety, low self-esteem and social exclusion. Meta-analytic supports early speech-language interventions, parent-mediated communication programs and classroom-based language support in improving expressive and receptive language outcomes (Law et al., 2017). Increasingly, researchers emphasize the importance of identifying communication difficulties during preschool years, as early intervention is associated with better developmental outcomes.

5. Specific Learning Disorder (SLD)

Specific learning disorders are characterised by persistent difficulties in learning and using academic skills such as reading (dyslexia), writing (dysgraphia) or mathematics (dyscalculia), despite adequate intelligence, motivation and access to schooling. These difficulties interfere with academic achievement and everyday functioning and often become evident during early school years when formal learning demands increase.

Children with dyslexia may struggle with word recognition, decoding, spelling and reading fluency. Dysgraphia affects handwriting, spelling and written organization, whereas dyscalculia involves difficulties understanding numerical concepts, arithmetic operations and mathematical reasoning. Research indicates that SLDs are associated with atypical neural processing in brain regions involved in language, phonological processing and numerical cognition. Neuroimaging studies of dyslexia, for example, consistently reveal differences in left hemisphere reading networks, particularly in temporoparietal and occipitotemporal regions (Peterson & Pennington, 2015).

Major neurodevelopmental disorders such as ASD, ADHD, Intellectual disability, communication disorder and specific earning disorders represent complex conditions arising from interactions among genetic, neurobiological and environmental influences. Contemporary research increasingly emphasizes developmental variability, comorbidity and dimensional approaches to understanding these disorders. Longitudinal studies and meta-analytic evidence demonstrate that early identification, evidence-based intervention, family support and inclusive educational environments significantly improve developmental outcomes and quality of life. At the same time, modern neurodiversity perspectives encourage recognition of individual strengths, autonomy and social inclusion, shifting the focus from deficit-based models toward holistic and person-centred approaches to neurodevelopmental differences.

3. CONTEMPORARY CONCEPTUAL FRAMEWORKS

3.1 Developmental Psychopathology Perspective

The developmental psychopathology approach seeks to understand maladaptive behaviour and psychological disorders by examining them in relation to typical developmental processes. Rather than viewing psychopathology as a static or isolated condition, this perspective conceptualizes it as the outcome of developmental pathways that unfold over time through continuous interactions between biological, psychological and environmental factors (Cicchetti & Rogosch, 2002; Sroufe, 1997). A core assumption of this approach is that normal and abnormal development are not fundamentally separate, but exist along a continuum, sharing common mechanisms and processes (Cicchetti,1984).

One central concept within this framework is continuity and discontinuity. Continuity refers to the persistence of certain behavioural or emotional patterns across developmental stages, such as early difficulties in attention regulation continuing into adolescence or adulthood (Sroufe, Egeland, Carlson & Collins, 2005). Discontinuity, on the other hand, recognizes that developmental change can occur and early problems may diminish or transform dur to maturation, environmental support or intervention (Rutter, 1989). This highlights the importance of longitudinal perspectives in understanding how developmental outcomes evolve over time.

Another key focus of developmental psychopathology is the identification of risk and protective factors. Risk factors may include genetic vulnerability, prenatal complications, early deprivation, inconsistent parenting or socio-economic adversity, all of which increase the likelihood of maladaptive outcomes (Sameroff, 2000; Rutter, 2006). In contrast, protective factors such as secure attachment, supportive family environments, effective schooling and early interventions can buffer against risk and promote resilience (Masten, 2001). Importantly, the impact of these factors is probabilistic rather than deterministic, meaning that risk does not inevitability lead to disorder.

The concepts of equifinality and multifinality further illustrate the complexity of developmental pathways. Equifinality refers to the phenomenon where different developmental pathways or risk factors lead to the same outcome, such as diverse genetic, environmental or experiential influences resulting in similar behavioural difficulties (Cicchetti & Rogosch, 1996). Multifinality, conversely describes how similar early risk factors can lead to different outcomes, depending on the timing, intensity and context of experiences (Cicchetti & Blender, 2006). For example, early language delay may resolve completely in some children, contribute to learning difficulties in others or be associated with broader neurodevelopmental disorders in a subset of cases.

Overall, the developmental psychopathology perspective provides a nuanced and dynamic framework for understanding neurodevelopmental disorders. It emphasizes developmental timing, individual differences and contextual influences, offering valuable insights for assessment, prevention and intervention (Cicchetti & Toth, 2009). By integrating knowledge of typical development with the study of maladaptation, this approach supports early identification, individualized intervention and a strength- based understanding of developmental diversity.

3.2 Neurodiversity Perspective

The neurodiversity movement represents a paradigm shift in the understanding of neurodevelopmental disorders by challenging traditional deficit-based and pathology- oriented models, particularly in relation to autism spectrum disorder. Rooted in disability studies and self-advocacy movements, the neurodiversity perspective proposes that variations in neurological functioning such as differences in social communication, sensory processing, attention and cognition are natural forms of human diversity rather than inherently disordered or deficient (Singer, 1999; Kapp et al., 2013). From this viewpoint, conditions such as autism, attention-deficit/hyperactivity disorder (ADHD) and dyslexia are understood neurodevelopmental differences that reflect alternative cognitive styles and ways to interacting with the world, rather than solely medical pathologies (Armstrong, 2010). Individuals may exhibit distinctive strengths, including heightened attention to detail, strong visual-spatial abilities, creativity, pattern recognition or intense focus on areas of interest (Baron-Cohen, 2009). The neurodiversity framework therefore encourages a strengths-based approach, emphasizing capabilities and adaptive potential alongside challenges, rather than focusing exclusively on impairments (Kapp et al., 2013).

Importantly, the neurodiversity movement does not deny the presences of functional difficulties or the need for support. Instead, it argues that many challenges faced by neurodivergent individuals arise from a mismatch between individual differences and societal expectations, such as rigid educational systems, sensory-unfriendly environments and limited acceptance of behavioural diversity (Milton, 2012). Consequently, the focus shifts from "normalizing" the individual to modifying environments, providing reasonable accommodations and fostering inclusive practices that enable participation and psychological well-being. This perspective has significant implications for assessment, intervention and policy. In educational settings, it supports inclusive classrooms, universal design for learning and individualized accommodations rather than segregated or exclusionary models (Rose & Meyer, 2002). Clinically, it encourages collaborative goal-setting that respects individual identity, autonomy and quality of life, alongside evidence-based supports (APA,2022). Ethically, it aligns with rights-based frameworks such as the Rights of

Persons with Disabilities Act (2016) in India, which emphasizes dignity, equality, non-discrimination and social inclusion. At the same time, the neurodiversity perspective invites critical reflection and balance. While it promotes acceptance and empowerment, it must be integrated with developmental and clinical approaches to address substantial support needs, particularly for individuals with significant communication, adaptive or behavioural challenges (Volkmar & McPartland, 2014). When combined thoughtfully with evidence-based interventions, the neurodiversity approach offers a more humane, inclusive and holistic understanding of neurodevelopment diversity.

3.3 RDoC and Dimensional Models

The Research Domain Criteria (RDoC) framework, developed by the National Institute of Mental Health (NIMH), represents an alternative approach to understanding mental disorders by moving beyond traditional categorical diagnostic systems such as the DSM and ICD. Instead of classifying disorders based solely on clusters of observable symptoms, RDoC emphasizes the study of fundamental neurobiological and psychological systems that underlie behaviour, emotion and cognition. These systems are examined across multiple levels of analysis, including genes, neural circuits, physiology, behaviour self-report (Insel et al., 2010, Cuthbert & Insel, 2013). A central premise of the RDoC framework is that many psychiatric and neurodevelopmental conditions share common underlying mechanisms, even when they are assigned different diagnostic labels. For example, difficulties in attention regulation, reward processing or emotional reactivity may be present across disorders such as ADHD, ASD, anxiety disorders and mood disorders (Insel, 2014). By focusing on core functional domains such as cognitive systems, negative and positive valence systems, social processes and arousal/regulatory systems. RDoC enables researchers to identify patterns of dysfunction that cut across diagnostic categories (Cuthbert, 2014). This dimensional and transdiagnostic approach supports a more nuanced understanding of brain-behaviour relationships, recognizing that psychological functioning exists along continua rather than as discrete categories. It also allows for the study of individual differences in neural functioning, which may help explain why individuals with the same diagnosis respond differently to interventions (Casey et al., 2014). From a developmental perspective, RDoC is particularly valuable because it facilitates the examination of how neural systems emerge, interact and change across developmental stages, offering insights into early risk markers and trajectories of adaptation or maladaptation (Beauchaine & Cicchetti, 2019).

While RDoC is primarily a research framework rather than a clinical diagnostic tool, its implications for practice are substantial. It encourages the development of targeted interventions that address specific functional domains rather than broad diagnostic categories, paving the way for more personalized and precision-based approaches to mental health care (Insel & Cuthbert, 2015). When integrated with developmental psychopathology and neurodiversity perspectives, the RDoC framework contributes to a more comprehensive and biologically informed understanding of neurodevelopmental disorders (Cicchetti & Toth, 2009).

3.4 Comorbidity and Transdiagnostic Perspectives

One of the most important findings in recent neurodevelopmental research is the high rate of comorbidity among disorder. Meta-analytic studies show that ADHD and autism frequently co-occur, learning disorders commonly coexist with ADHD, anxiety and depression are highly prevalent in adolescents and adults with NDDs and motor coordination problems often accompany communication and attentional difficulties. These findings challenge rigid diagnostic boundaries and support transdiagnostic models that focus on shared cognitive, emotional and neurobiological mechanisms across disorders rather than viewing each condition as entirely separate (Astle et al., 2022). Neuroimaging and genetic studies further support this perspective by showing overlapping neural networks and shared genetic risk factors across ADHD, ASD, dyslexia and other developmental disorders (Siugzdaite et al., 2020). For example, disruptions in large-scale brain networks involved in attention, salience detection and cognitive control have been observed across several neurodevelopmental and psychiatric conditions, suggesting common underlying pathways rather than disorder-specific deficits (Jones et al., 2022).

The transdiagnostic approach has important implications for assessment and intervention. Instead of focusing solely on categorical diagnoses, clinicians increasingly examine dimensions of functioning such as executive skills, sensory processing, adaptive behaviour and emotional regulation. This approach promotes individualized and strengths-based interventions tailored to the specific needs of the person rather than rigid diagnostic labels. Furthermore, transdiagnostic frameworks align closely with the neurodiversity paradigm, which emphasizes understanding and supporting diverse patterns of brain functioning rather than viewing all differences solely as deficits (Fletcher-Watson, 2022).

4. LIFESPAN AND SOCIOCULTURAL PERSPECTIVES

4.1 Lifespan Perspective and Adult Outcomes

Modern research increasingly recognizes neurodevelopmental disorders as lifelong conditions rather than childhood-limited disorders. Longitudinal studies show that many individuals continue to experience challenges in adulthood related to employment, independent living, relationships, mental health and executive functioning (Astle et al., 2022). Adults with ADHD may continue to struggle with organizations, time management and occupational stability, while autistic adults may experience difficulties in social communication, sensory regulation and navigating workplace environments.

At the same time, outcomes are highly heterogenous. Many individuals with NDDs lead successful and fulfilling lives, particularly when supported through inclusive environments, accommodations and strengths-based approaches. Strengths commonly associated with neurodivergent individuals such as, creativity, attention to detail, persistence, innovation and unique problem-solving abilities can contribute significantly to personal and professional success, increasing advocacy for neurodiversity has also shifted societal perspectives from a deficit-focused model toward a strengths-based and inclusive approach that values individual differences (Fletcher-Watson, 2022).

Research further highlights the importance of contextual and environmental factors in shaping adult outcomes. Access to healthcare, family support, educational opportunities, vocational training and social acceptance strongly influence quality of life for individuals with NDDs. Conversely, stigma, lack of accommodations and limited mental health support may increase the risk of secondary difficulties such as anxiety, depression and social isolation. Transition periods, particularly the movement from school to higher education. Employment or independent living, are often associated with increased vulnerability and require structured support services (Astle et al., 2022). Overall, the lifespan perspective emphasizes that neurodevelopmental disorders are dynamic conditions influenced by developmental changed and environmental contexts. Contemporary approaches therefore advocate continuous support across the lifespan, focusing not only on symptom reduction but also on well-being, participation, autonomy and quality of life.

4.2 Cultural and Contextual Considerations

Developmental norms and perceptions of a typicality are not universal but our socially culturally constructed (Super & Harkness, 1986). What is considered typical or problematic behaviour in one cultural context may be viewed as acceptable, adaptive or even desirable in another. Cultural belief systems shape parenting practices, child-rearing goals, expectations for independence, emotional expression, communication styles and social behaviour, all of which influences how children's development is interpreted and evaluated (Bornstein, 2012; Keller, 2018). For instance, cultural variations in expectations regarding eye contact, obedience, activity level or verbal expressiveness can affect the recognition of neurodevelopmental concerns such as autism or ADHD (Daley,2004; Mandell & Novak, 2005). Behaviours interpreted as inattentive or hyperactive in structured classroom environments may be perceived as normal exuberance or creativity in less formal or community-based settings (Timimi & Taylor, 2004). Similarly, delays in language development may not be viewed as concerning in multilingual or orally rich cultural contexts where formal literacy in emphasized later in childhood (Toppelberg & Collins, 2010). Access to diagnostic and intervention services further complicates identification, particularly in low-resourced and rural settings. Limited availability of trained professionals, standardized assessment tools and early screening programs can result in delayed or missed diagnoses (Patel et al., 2018; WHO, 2013). In many contexts, including parts of India, families may rely on informal explanations rooted in cultural or spiritual beliefs, seeking support from community elders or traditional healers before approaching formal healthcare systems (Daley & Singhal, 2010).

Stigma associated with disability remains a significant barrier to early identification and intervention. Concerns about social labelling, marriage prospects, academic exclusion or family reputation may lead caregivers to minimize or conceal developmental difficulties (Groce et al., 2011; Kalyanpur, 2011). This stigma can also influence educators' and professionals' responses, resulting in under-referral or misinterpretation of children's needs (Corrigan & Watson, 2002). Understanding neurodevelopmental disorders therefor require cultural sensitivity and contextual awareness. Clinicians and educators must adopt culturally responsive assessment practices, interpret behaviours within socio-cultural contexts and engage families in respectful, collaborative ways (APA, 2022). Strengths-based and community-oriented approaches, along with culturally adapted interventions are particularly essential in diverse and low-resource settings (Patel et al., 2011). By integrating developmental science with cultural understanding, professionals can promote more equitable, accurate and effective identification and support for neurodivergent individuals (WHO, 2013).

Globally, inclusive education has become a central educational policy objective following the Salamanca Statement and subsequent international commitments to educational equity. Recent reviews indicate substantial growth in the adoption of inclusive education policies across countries; however, implementation remains uneven. While many nations have formally embraced inclusive schooling, challenges persist in teacher preparation, resource allocation, classroom accommodations and support services. Low and middle income countries often face additional barriers related to workforce shortages and limited infrastructure. These findings suggest that policy adoption alone is insufficient and must be accompanied by sustained investment in implementation and capacity- building efforts

Socioeconomic Inequality, Health-System Disparities and Neurodevelopmental Disorders

Poverty is one of the strongest social predictors of adverse neurodevelopmental outcomes. Chronic socioeconomic disadvantage affects children through multiple pathways, including malnutrition, environmental stress, inadequate prenatal care, toxin exposure, poor housing conditions and limited access to stimulating educational environments. Developmental neuroscience research describes poverty as influencing neurodevelopment through interconnected biological, psychological and environmental systems that shape early brain architecture (Johnson et al., 2016; Farah, 2017; Ursache & Noble, 2016).

Neuroimaging and longitudinal studies demonstrate that children from lower socioeconomic backgrounds often show differences in brain regions associated with language, executive functioning, emotional regulation and memory. Lower household income and reduced parental education have been linked with altered cortical development, reduced hippocampal volume and weaker neural connectivity related to cognitive processing (Noble et al., 2015; McLaughlin et al., 2021).

Research further indicates that chronic poverty-related stress elevates cortisol and inflammatory responses, negatively affecting neural plasticity and socioemotional development during sensitive developmental periods. These effects are particularly significant during the first 1000 days of life, a critical period for synaptic growth and brain maturation.

Children living in poverty are also more likely to experience educational disadvantage and reduced access to developmental screening services, contributing to delayed identification of conditions such as autism spectrum disorder (ASD), ADHD and specific learning disorders. In many low-resource communities, symptoms may be misunderstood as behavioural problems, poor parenting or lack of academic motivation rather than neurodevelopmental differences.

Role of Parental education

Parental education, particularly maternal education, is consistently identified as a protective factor in neurodevelopmental outcomes. Higher parental education is associated with:

- Batter prenatal and postnatal healthcare utilization
- Increased awareness of developmental milestones
- Earlier recognition of developmental delays
- Greater access to intervention services

- More cognitively stimulating home environments

Large-scale international studies and systematic reviews have shown that low maternal education is associated with increased developmental risk, poorer language outcome and reduced access to early intervention services.

Longitudinal research further indicates that parental education can buffer some negative effects of poverty on cognitive and language development. Parents with higher educational attainment are more likely to engage in responsive caregiving, language-rick interactions and educational advocacy within healthcare and school systems (Bradley & Corwyn, 2002).

In contrast, families with limited educational opportunities may face difficulties recognizing developmental symptoms, navigating diagnostic systems or accessing specialized support services. Stigma, low mental health literacy and lack of awareness may further delay help-seeking behaviours, especially in rural and underserved communities (Patel et al., 2018).

Health-system Disparities and Unequal Access to Diagnosis

Access to early diagnosis and intervention remains highly unequal across socioeconomic and geographic contexts. Children from economically disadvantaged families frequently encounter:

- Limited availability of developmental specialists
- Long waiting periods for assessment
- Financial barriers to therapy
- Lack of insurance coverage
- Poor transportation infrastructure
- Shortages of trained professionals in rural regions

Health- system disparities are especially evident in low and middle income countries (LMICs), where child developmental and mental health services are often underfunded and concentrated in urban centres (Patel et al., 2018; Olusanya et al., 2018). Many LMICs lack universal developmental screening systems, resulting in underdiagnosis or delayed diagnosis of NDDs.

In India, disparities exist between urban private healthcare systems and rural public health infrastructure. Families in metropolitan areas may access multidisciplinary assessments and therapy services relatively early, whereas children in rural or low-income settings may remain undiagnosed for several years. India also faces substantial shortages of child psychiatrists, developmental paediatricians, speech-language therapists and occupational therapists, particularly in semi-urban and rural regions (Sharma & Juneja, 2022).

Socioeconomic inequality additionally affects intervention quality. Evidence-based therapies such as behavioural interventions, speech therapy and specialized educational support are often expensive and inaccessible for marginalized populations. Consequently, children from lower socioeconomic backgrounds may experience poorer educational attainment, reduced adaptive functioning and increased long-term social exclusion.

Global South comparative perspective

Although the Indian context reflects many challenges associated with neurodevelopmental disorders in LMICs, similar patterns are observed across Africa, Southeast Asia and Latin America. Comparative Global South perspectives reveal common structural barriers including poverty, stigma, inadequate healthcare infrastructure and shortages of trained professionals (Patel et al., 2018; Olusanya et al.,2018).

Across the Global South, neurodevelopmental disorders (NDDs) are increasingly recognized as major public health concerns; however, substantial disparities in healthcare infrastructure, socioeconomic resources and educational access continue to affect early identification and intervention. Research from African countries indicates particularly high neurodevelopmental risk associated with poverty, malnutrition, infectious diseases, perinatal complications and limited maternal healthcare access. Developmental disorders across many African regions remain significantly underidentified because of insufficient screening systems, scarcity of specialists and concentration of serviced within urban centres. Cultural stigma and misconceptions surrounding disability frequently delay diagnosis, with many families initially seeking traditional or religious healing before medical assessment.

Similarly, Southeast Asian countries such as Thailand, Malaysia and Indonesia show growing awareness regarding autism spectrum disorder (ASD) and ADHD in urban settings, while rural populations continue to experience major service gaps, delayed diagnosis, limited school accommodations and significant financial burden due to reliance on private therapies (Ha et al., 2014; Sun et al., 2013). Social stigma and low awareness further discourage early help-seeking behaviours, although recent inclusive education initiatives and parent-led advocacy movements have improved awareness and intervention access across the region (UNICEF, 2021).

In Latin America, countries such as Brazil and Mexico increasingly recognize NDDs as important developmental and mental health priorities, yet socioeconomic inequality, maternal stress, nutritional deficiencies, community violence exposure and reduced educational opportunities continue to negatively influence neurodevelopmental outcomes (Black et al., 2017). Longitudinal studies from Brazil further demonstrate that neighbourhood disadvantage and parental educational inequality significantly affect cognitive development, emotional regulation and school readiness.

Across these regions, urban-rural healthcare disparities shortage of trained professionals and inconsistent intervention access remain persistent barriers. Consequently, many low and middle income countries are increasingly adopting community- based rehabilitation, task-shifting approaches and family-centred intervention models to improve developmental screening, early identification and support services in low-resource settings (Patel et al., 2018).

Toward Equity- Oriented Neurodevelopmental Care

Across Global South contexts, contemporary research increasingly emphasizes the importance of equity- oriented and culturally responsive approaches to neuro-developmental care. International evidence supports:

- Universal developmental screening within primary healthcare
- Parent education and awareness initiatives
- Integration of developmental services into community health systems
- Training non-specialist healthcare workers
- Reducing stigma through awareness campaigns
- Strengthening maternal and child healthcare services
- Improving affordability and accessibility of interventions

Global health researchers argue that effective neurodevelopmental care requires moving beyond narrowly biomedical models toward broader developmental and social frameworks that address poverty, educational inequality and structural healthcare disparities alongside clinical intervention (Patel et al., 2018; Ritcher et al., 2019).

Table 4. Recent Epidemiological Evidence of Neurodevelopmental Disorders

Disorder	Global prevalence	Indian estimates	Key sources
ASD	~1%	0.15-1.5%	WHO, ICMR, NIMHANS
ADHD	5-7%	1.6-7.2%	Meta-analyses
SLD	5-15%	5-15%	School-based studies
ID	~1%	1-3%	National surveys

5. ADVANCES IN IDENTIFICATION AND INTERVENTION

5.1 Advances in Early Identification and Intervention

One of the most significant developments in recent decades is the emphasis on early screening and intervention. Meta- analyses demonstrate that early behavioural, educational and family-based interventions can improve language development, social communication, emotional regulation, academic skills and adaptive functioning. Interventions are increasingly individualised and multidisciplinary, involving psychologist, speech-language therapists, occupational therapists, educators and families. Current evidence-based approaches include Applied Behaviour Analysis (ABA), Naturalistic developmental behavioural interventions, Paret-mediated interventions, Cognitive- behavioural approaches, Executive functioning training, School-based supports. However, contemporary neurodiversity advocates emphasizes that interventions should focus on enhancing wellbeing, autonomy and participation rather than attempting to "normalize" neurodivergent individuals.

Recent advances in digital health technologies have expanded opportunities for early identification of neurodevelopmental disorders. Machine learning algorithms, electronic health records, computer-assisted behavioural assessments, eye-tracking technologies, and digital screening platforms are increasingly being investigated as tools for supporting earlier detection of Autism Spectrum Disorder and ADHD. Although these technologies are not intended to replace comprehensive clinical assessment, emerging evidence suggest that AI-assisted screening systems may improve scalability, reduce diagnostic delays, and facilitate identification in underserved populations. However, concerns remain regarding algorithmic bias, generalizability across cultural contexts, data privacy and the need for clinical validation before widespread implementation.

5.2 Principles of Interventions for Neurodevelopmental Disorders

Interventions for neurodevelopmental disorders are guided by several core principles that ensure they are effective, meaningful and sustainable. Early identification and intervention is crucial, as it takes advantage of the brain's plasticity, allowing children to make significant gains in cognitive, language and socio-emotional skills (Shonkoff & Phillips, 2000; Kolb & Gibb, 2011). Interventions must also be developmentally appropriate, focusing on the child's current abilities and stage of development rather than strictly their chronological age, to ensure that goals are realistic and achievable (Vygotsky, 1978; Guralnick, 2011).

Interventions must have ecological validity, meaning the skills taught should generalize beyond therapy sessions to everyday environments such as home, school and community, ensuring that improvements translate into real-life functional gains (Bronfenbrenner & Morris, 2006; WHO, 2013). Together, these principles create a framework for interventions that are personalized, practical and aligned with both the child's needs and the family's context.

5.3 Intervention Models for Neurodevelopmental Disorders

Intervention for neurodevelopmental disorders is based on the principle of neuroplasticity, the brain's ability to adapt and reorganize, which is especially pronounced during early childhood (Kolb & Gibb, 2011; Shonkoff & Phillips, 2000). Effective interventions focus not only on reducing deficits but also on enhancing strengths, fostering adaptive skills and improving overall quality of life (WHO, 2013). Modern approaches are early individualized and family centered, recognizing that each child has unique needs and that family involvement is crucial for generalization of skills across settings. (Dunst, Trivette & Hamby, 2007; Guralnick, 2011).

Interventions are often multidisciplinary, combing inputs from psychologists, special educators, speech and language therapists, occupational therapists and medical professionals to provide comprehensive support. Globally, evidence-based models such as behavioural therapy, cognitive- behavioural therapy and developmental approaches are recommended (NRC, 2001; Weisz et al., 2017), while in India, interventions are increasingly aligned with policy frameworks like the *Right to Education Act* (2009) and the *National Trust Act* (1999), which emphasizes inclusion, accessibility and support services for children with neurodevelopmental disorders (Government of India, 1999 & 2009). By combing early intervention, tailored strategies and family engagement, these approaches aim to maximize functional outcomes and help individuals lead meaningful, independent lives (Guralnick, 2011; WHO, 2013).

Developmental and Naturalistic Interventions

1. Early Start Denver Model (ESDM)

The Early Start Denver Model (ESDM) is an evidence-based early intervention approach developed for young children with Autism Spectrum Disorder, typically between 12 and 48 months of age. It integrates principles of Applied Behaviour Analysis (ABA) within a naturalistic, play-based and relationship-focused framework, emphasizing learning through everyday social interactions rather than highly structured drill-based teaching (Rogers & Dawson, 2010). ESDM places strong emphasis on the developmental of joint attention, reciprocal social engagement, early language and communication skills and shared positive affect with adults actively following the child's interests and embedding learning opportunities within play, caregiving routines and daily activities. Intervention is delivered in a warm, responsive and developmentally appropriate manner, promoting social motivation and active participation by the child (Rogers et al., 2012). In the Indian context, ESDM is particularly relevant due to its compatibility with family-centered caregiving practices, where children use closely supported by parents, grandparents and extended family members. The model's focus on learning through routine activities such as feeding, dressing, play and storytelling aligns well with typical Indian home environments. Additionally, it's adaptability for home-based intervention makes ESDM a practical and accessible approach in semi-urban and rural areas where specialized autism intervention services may be limited.

2. DIR/Floortime Approach

The Developmental, Individual Differences, Relationship-Based (DIR/Floortime) approach is a developmental intervention that prioritizes emotional regulation, social communication and the formation of meaningful relationships as the foundation for learning and development. It focuses on understanding the child's unique sensory profile, emotional capacities and functional developmental level and interventions tailored accordingly. A core principle of this approach is engaging the child at their current developmental stage and following the child's lead during play, thereby fostering intrinsic motivation and active participation. Through warm, responsive caregiver-child interactions, the approach strengthens emotional connections while promoting shared attention, symbolic play, problem-solving and increasingly complex social communication, Floortime sessions typically involve caregivers joining the child's play at eye level, responding sensitively to verbal and nonverbal cues and gradually expanding interactions into longer, more reciprocal communicative exchanges (Greenspan & Wieder, 1998; Greenspan & Wieder, 2006). In the Indian context, DIR/Floortime is particularly relevant as it aligns well with cultural values that emphasizes emotional bonding, nurturance and interdependence within families. The strong involvement of parents and extended family members in children's daily routines facilitates the natural implementation of relationship-based interventions. Moreover, the flexibility of DIR/Floortime allows it be adapted across diverse linguistic, cultural and socioeconomic settings, making it a practical and culturally responsive intervention without reliance on expensive materials or highly structured programs.

Academic and Cognitive Interventions

1. Individualized Education Plans (IEPs)

Individualized education Plans (IEPs) are structured, learner-centres educational frameworks designed to address the specific academic and developmental needs of children with disabilities. Developed through a collaborative process involving general teachers, special educators psychologists, parents and where appropriate, the child, IEPs aim to ensure meaningful participation and progress within the educational system (Friend & Bursuck, 2019). An IEP clearly outlines achievable and measurable learning goals that are tailored to the child's academic, social, emotional and functional needs. It also specifies appropriate accommodations and adjustments such as extended time, modified instructions or assistive technology that enable the child to access the curriculum without altering expected learning outcomes (Turbull et al., 2015). Furthermore, IEPs incorporate individualized teaching strategies aligned with the learner's profile, including multisensory instruction, task breakdown, repetition, peer-assisted learning and the use of visual supports. Continuous and flexible evaluation methods are integral to IEPs with progress monitored through formative assessments, portfolios, observations and periodic reviews, allowing timely modifications to instructional approaches (Hallahan et al., 2018).

2. Inclusive education and Universal Design for Learning (UDL)

Inclusive education emphasizes educating children with disabilities within mainstream classrooms, ensuring equal participation and meaningful learning opportunities. Within this framework, Universal Design for Learning (UDL) provides a proactive and flexible framework for inclusion by designing curricula that are accessible to all learners from the outset, rather than relying exclusively on individualized accommodations after barriers arise. UDL promotes multiple means of representation by presenting information through varied formats such as text, audio, visuals, demonstrations and digital media to accommodate differences in perception, language and comprehension. It also emphasizes multiple means of engagement, encouraging learner motivation and involvement through collaborative activities, choice-based tasks, culturally responsive content and interactive teaching strategies. In addition, UDL supports multiple means of expression by allowing students to demonstrate their learning in diverse ways, including written assignments, oral presentations, projects, artistic expressions, role-play or digital outputs. By addressing learner variability in a systematic and inclusive manner, UDL strengthens participations, equity and learning outcomes within inclusive educational settings (CAST, 2018; Florian & Black-Hawkins, 2011).

3. Speech and Language Therapy (SLT)

Speech and language therapy focuses on improving communication abilities that are fundamental to academic learning, social interaction and emotional expression. It targets expressive language by enhancing a child's ability to communicate thoughts, needs, emotions and ideas through words, sentences, gestures or alternative and augmentative communication systems such as picture exchange and AAC devices. Receptive language skills are also addressed by improving the child's understanding of spoken language, including instructions, questions, vocabulary, sentence structure and social cues. In addition, speech and language therapy emphasizes pragmatic communication, which involves developing the social use of language such as turn-taking, maintaining conversations, appropriate eye contact, interpreting non-verbal cues and adapting language across different social contexts. The therapy further focuses on articulation and fluency, aiming to correct speech and language therapy supports academic readiness, strengthens peer relationships, promotes emotional regulation and reduces frustration associated with communication difficulties (American Speech Language- Hearing Association [ASHA, 2021; Paul & Norbury, 2012).

4. Occupational Therapy (OT)

Occupational Therapy focuses on enabling individuals to participate independently in meaningful daily activities, commonly referred to as "occupation", with particular emphasis on self-care, school performance and play. It addresses key areas such as sensory integration by helping children regulate their responses to sensory input including touch, sound, movement and visual stimuli, which is especially beneficial for those who are hypersensitive or hyposensitive to sensory experiences. Occupational therapy also targets the development of fine motos skills, enhancing hand-eye coordination grip strength, bilateral coordination and precision required for tasks such as writing, drawing, buttoning and using classroom tools. In addition, it supports activities of daily living (ADLs) by training children in essential slf-care skills like dressing, eating, grooming, toileting and managing personal belongings, thereby fostering independence and self-confidence. Overall, occupational therapy contributes significantly to improved school participation, attention, self- regulation and functional autonomy across home and educational settings (American Occupational Therapy Association [AOTA], 2020).

5. Executive Function Training

Executive functions are higher-order cognitive processes that regulate goal-oriented behaviour. Deficits in executive functioning are commonly observed in children with ADHD and learning disorders, significantly affecting academic and classroom performance (Barkley, 2012; Diamond, 2013). One core executive function is working memory, which involves the ability to hold and manipulate information over short periods, weaknesses in working memory interfere with tasks such as following multistep instructions, mental arithmetic and reading comprehension and can be addressed through interventions such as memory games, sequencing activities, chunking strategies and computer-based cognitive training programs (Baddeley, 2012). Another critical area is planning and organization, where executive dysfunction manifests as difficulty in task initiation, time management and organization of schoolwork, training in task-breakdown techniques, the use of planners, checklists and visual schedules, as well as structured goal-setting and progress-monitoring exercises, has been shown to improve functional outcomes (Dawson & Guare,2018). Additionally, self-regulation and inhibitory control are essential for managing impulses, emotions and behaviour and deficits in these areas often result in distractibility, hyperactivity and disruptive classroom behaviour, interventions such as behavioural self-monitoring, mindfulness-based attention training and cognitive- behavioural strategies are effective in enhancing impulse control and emotional regulation (Barkley, 2015; Zelazo & Lyons, 2012).

6. Remedial education for children with learning disabilities

Remedial education for children with learning disabilities (LD) involves systematic, individualized and skill-focused instructional aimed at addressing specific academic deficits through structured and repetitive practice delivered by trained special educators or psychologists (APA,2013). Core areas targeted include phonological awareness, reading fluency, written expression and mathematical reasoning. Phonological awareness refers to the ability to recognize and manipulate speech sounds and deficits in this domain are a hallmark of dyslexia. Remedial interventions therefore emphasize sound-letter correspondence, phenome blending and segmentation and rhyming activities to strengthen decoding skills (Lyon, Shaywitz & Shaywitz, 2003). Reading fluency, defined by speed, accuracy and prosody is often impaired in children with LD and is addressed through repeated reading, guided oral reading and time practice with corrective feedback, which in turn supports reading comprehension and academic confidence (Rasinski, 2012). Difficulties in written expression, such as poor spelling, grammar, sentence construction and organization are managed using structured writing frameworks, explicit phonics and morphology-based spelling instruction and guided practice in sentence expansion and coherence (Graham & Harris, 2013). Mathematical reasoning deficits, commonly seen in dyscalculia are addressed through the use of concrete materials, visual representations, step-by-step problem-solving strategies and real-life applications to promote conceptual understanding rather than role memorization (Butterworth, Varma & Laurillard, 2011). In the Indian context, the NIMHANS Specific Learning Disability Battery plays a crucial role in assessing reading, writing, spelling and arithmetic skills, identifying specific academic weaknesses and guiding individualized remedial intervention plans, particularly for certification, accommodations and educational planning within the school system (NIMHANS,2019).

Pharmacological Interventions

Pharmacological interventions refer to the use of medications to manage the core symptoms of neurodevelopmental disorders and are most commonly applied in the treatment of Attention Deficit/ Hyperactivity Disorder (ADHD), where neurobiological factors play a central role. Medication is not considered a standalone treatment, rather, it forms an essential component of a multimodal intervention approach that also includes behavioural, educational and psychosocial strategies (APA, 2022). In ADHD, pharmacological treatment primarily aims to reduces symptoms of inattention, impulsivity and hyperactivity, thereby improving concentration, task persistence and behavioural self-regulation. By stabilizing these core symptoms, medication enhances he child's capacity to benefit from educational instruction, behavioural therapy and social interactions, creating a more supportive environment for learning and psychosocial development (Barkley, 2015).

Pharmacological treatment must be prescribed and closely supervised by qualified medical professionals such as psychiatrists, paediatricians or neurologists with training in child and adolescent mental health. Accurate diagnosis, individualized dosage and regular follow-up are crucial to ensure both safety and therapeutic effectiveness. Medications used in ADHD are most effective when combined with psychosocial interventions including behavioural therapy, parent management training, classroom accommodations and executive function or remedial interventions. This integrated approach addresses not only symptom reduction but also the development of adaptive skills and functional competence, leading to better long-term academic, social and emotional outcomes (Hinshaw & Ellison, 2016).

Ongoing monitoring for side effects is a critical principle of pharmacological management. Common areas of concern include changes in appetite, sleep disturbances, mood fluctuations, irritability and potential effects on growth in children. Continuous evaluation allows clinicians to adjust dosages or modify treatment plans as needed, thereby minimizing adverse effects while maximizing benefits (Faraone et al., 2014). The most commonly prescribed medications for ADHD include stimulants, such as methylphenidate, which enhance dopaminergic and noradrenergic activity in the brain and have strong empirical support for improving attention and impulse control. Non-stimulant medications, such as atomoxetine, are often used when stimulants are contraindicated, poorly tolerated, or ineffective, particularly in cases involving comorbid anxiety or tic disorders. The selection of medication depends on the child's individual profile, comorbid conditions and clinical judgment. When carefully prescribed, monitored and combined with psychosocial strategies, pharmacological interventions significantly improve functional outcomes and quality of life for children with ADHD and their families.

Psychosocial and Mental Health Interventions

Children in adolescence with neurodevelopmental disorders such as ADHD autism spectrum disorder and learning disabilities often face chronic academic struggles, peer difficulties and negative feedback from adults. As a result, they are at a significantly increased risk for internalising problems including anxiety, depression, low self-esteem and emotional dysregulation. Psychosocial and mental health interventions aim to promote emotional wellbeing, resilience and adaptive functioning.

1. Cognitive behavioural therapy CBT

Cognitive behavioural therapy is an evidence-based psychological interventions that focuses on the relationship between thoughts, emotions and behaviours. For children and adolescents with neurodevelopmental disorders, CBT is adapted to match their developmental level, cognitive abilities and attention span.

Adaptations in CBT for neurodevelopmental disorders are use of simple language and concrete examples, visual aids, stories and role plays, shorter structured sessions, active involvement of parents and caregivers and emphasis on skill practise in real-life situations. Therapeutic goals and benefits of adapted CBT are managing anxiety which helps in reducing avoidance behaviour and builds confidence, improving emotional regulation which leads to better classroom behaviour and peer relationships, enhancing coping skills which promotes resilience in psychological well-being. Adapted Cognitive Behavioural Therapy plays a crucial role in addressing the emotional and mental health needs of children and adolescents with neurodevelopmental disorders. When integrated with educational, behavioural and family based interventions, CBT provides a holistic and sustainable approach to care.

2. Family and Parent Training Programs

Family and parent training programs recognize that parents and caregivers are the primary agents of change, as they interact with the child across multiple settings and over long periods of time. Parent-mediated interventions aim to empower caregivers with knowledge, skills and confidence, enabling them to support the child's development consistently and effectively. In parent training programs, parents are trained to create a structured and supportive home environments that reinforces academic and cognitive skills learned at school or during therapy, managing behaviours effectively through positive reinforcements and reward systems, clear instructions and consistent consequences, managing tantrums, aggression and emotional dysregulations, and finally advocating for services and accommodations.

3. Community Based Rehabilitation (CRB)

Community Based Rehabilitation (CRB) is a holistic, rights-based approach to rehabilitation that aims to enhance the quality of life, independence and social inclusion of persons with disabilities, including children and adolescents with neurodevelopmental disorders. Rather than relying solely on specialized institutions,

CBR emphasizes community participation, local resources and empowerments of families. This model is particularly relevant in rural and low-resource Indian settings, where access to specialized professionals and institutional services is limited. There are four core focus areas in this, which are accessibility, inclusion, skill development and social participation.

While the interventions discussed above are widely supported in research, their effectiveness varies depending on the child's developmental profile, family involvement, resource availability and cultural context. Developmental and naturalistic models such as the ESDM and DIR/Floortime emphasize social engagement, emotional connection and learning through everyday interactions, making the more flexible and culturally adaptable in family-oriented contexts like India. Meta-analytic evidence indicates that ESDM produces moderate improvements in cognition and language development in young autistic children, although effects on core autism symptoms and adaptive functioning are comparatively limited (Fuller & Keiser, 2020; McGlade et al., 2023). However these approaches often require intensive caregiver participation and long-term consistency, which may not always be feasible for families with limited time or resources. In contrast, highly structured short-term gains in intellectual functioning and adaption behaviour, yet critics argue that rigid behavioural approaches may insufficiently address emotional reciprocity, autonomy and cultural responsiveness (Eckes et al., 2023).

Similarly, educational interventions such as Individualized Education Plans (IEPs) and Universal Design for Learning (UDL) promote inclusion and learner accessibility. Recent meta analyses suggest that UDL-based instruction moderately improves academic achievement and participation in inclusive classrooms (Almeqdad et al., 2023). Nevertheless, the effectiveness of these models depends heavily on teacher training, classroom resources and institutional support, which remain inconsistent in many low-resource educational settings. Research further indicates that professional development significantly influences successful implementation of inclusive practices (Donath et al., 2023).

Pharmacological interventions for ADHD show strong evidence for reducing inattention, impulsivity and hyperactivity, but medication alone does not address broader academic, social or emotional difficulties and require careful monitoring for side effects. In comparison psychosocial interventions such as Cognitive Behavioural Therapy (CBT) and parent-training programs contribute more substantially to long-term emotional regulation, coping skills and family functioning, though access to trained professionals may limit their availability in rural and undeserved regions. Therefore, current evidence increasingly supports multimodal and context-sensitive approaches that integrate developmental, educational, behavioural and psychosocial interventions tailored to the child's individual and sociocultural needs.

5.4 Indian Policy Alignment with Intervention

Effective intervention for children and adolescents with neurodevelopmental disorders must be aligned with national disability and education policies. In India, the Rights of Persons with Disabilities (RPwD) Act, 2016 and the National Education Policy (NEP), 2020 provide a strong legal and institutional framework to support inclusive, accessible and holistic interventions.

Rights of Persons with Disabilities (RPwD) Act, 2016

The Rights of Persons with Disabilities (RPwD) Act, 2016 adopts a rights-based approach that shifts the understanding of disability from charity to empowerment, inclusion and equal opportunity. It emphasizes inclusive education by enduring that children with disabilities can study in mainstream schools with reasonable accommodations, individualised educational planning and access to special educators and support services, thereby promoting dignity and social integration. The Act also mandates barrier free physical, sensory and digital environments through accessible infrastructure, assistive technologies and inclusive communication systems to enable independent functioning. Additionally, it highlights skill development and vocational training for adolescents and young adults focusing on life skills, ability-based vocational education and linkages with employment initiatives to support independent living and employability.

National Education Policy (NEP), 2020

National Education Policy (NEP) 2020 reinforces inclusive and equitable education by emphasising early identification, teacher preparedness and coordinated support systems for diverse learners. It highlights the importance of early screening for developmental delays and learning difficulties to enable timely intervention, prevent secondary academic and emotional problems and improve long term outcomes. This policy also stresses capacity building through teacher training in inclusive practises, classroom adaptations, differentiated instruction and collaboration with mental health and special education profession professionals. Additionally, NEP 2020 promotes multidisciplinary support systems involving psychologists, special educators, counsellors and health care professionals to ensure comprehensive assessment, intervention and follow up addressing learner's academic, cognitive, emotional and social needs.

The RPwD Act, 2016 and the NEP 2020 together form an integrated policy intervention framework that provides strong legal and educational support for inclusive practises in addressing neurodevelopmental disorders. These policies promote early, preventive and holistic interventions while strengthening coordination among education, health and social service systems. By aligning interventions with these frameworks, support strategies become not only clinically effective but also legally mandated, socially just and sustainable ultimately benefiting children with neuro-developmental disorders, their families and the wider community.

6. EDUCATIONAL, CLINICAL AND ETHICAL IMPLICATIONS

6.1 Educational and Applied Implications

Schools occupy a pivotal position in the early identification and support of children with developmental difficulties. Because children spend a significant portion of their time in educational settings, teachers are often the first professionals to observe patterns of learning, attention, behaviour or social interaction that deviate from age-appropriate expectations (Lindsay & Dockrell,2012; Shonkoff & Phillips, 2000). Difficulties such as persistent inattention, poor academic progress despite adequate instruction, challenged in peer relationships or atypical communication styles may become evident within classroom environments, prompting further evaluation (DuPaul & Stoner, 2014). Early identification within schools is particularly important, as timely intervention can capitalize on developmental plasticity and prevent secondary difficulties such as academic failure, emotional distress or low self-esteem (Hechman,2008; Shonkoff et al., 2012). Once concerns are identified, individualized educational planning becomes central to effective support. Individualized Education Plans (IEPs) or equivalent accommodations outline specific learning goals, instructional strategies, environmental modifications and evaluation procedures tailored to the child's needs (Friend & Bursuck, 2019). The effectiveness of school-based support is greatly enhanced through interdisciplinary collaboration. Educators, school psychologists, special educators, counsellors, parents and healthcare professionals each contribute unique perspectives and expertise (Power et al., 2013). Teachers provide insights into classroom functioning and learning demands, psychologists assist with assessment and intervention planning, healthcare professionals address medical or developmental factors and parents offer critical knowledge of the child's strengths, challenges and home environment (Christenson & Sheridan, 2001).

Within the Indian context, initiatives under the *Samagra Shiksha Abhiyan* and the *National Education Policy (NEP), 2020* emphasizes inclusive schooling, teacher training and early screening (Government of India, 2018; Ministry of Education, 2020). However, successful implementation requires ongoing capacity building, resource allocation and attitudinal change (Kalyanpur, 2011).

6.2 Clinical and Social Implications

Early identification and timely intervention are crucial for improving developmental, academic and psychosocial outcomes in individuals with new developmental disorders NDDs. Evidence suggests that early targeted support can reduce the severity of functional impairments and prevent secondary emotional and behavioural difficulties (APA,2013). Contemporary research demonstrates that interventions during early childhood when the brain shows heightened neuroplasticity can significantly enhance communication, adaptive functioning, emotional regulation and social participation (Dawson et al., 2010; WHO, 2023). Evidence-based early support reduces the severity of functional impairments and may prevent secondary difficulties such as anxiety, depression, school refusal and behavioural dysregulation that frequently emerge when developmental needs remain unaddressed (APA, 2022).

Recent longitudinal; studies also emphasizes that developmental outcomes improve substantially when intervention is individualized, family-centered and sustained across developmental transitions rather than limited to early childhood alone. For example, children receiving coordinated behavioural, educational and speech-language interventions before the age of five demonstrate better long-term academic achievement and adaptive functioning that those identified later (Zwaigdenbaum et al., 2021). Increasingly, researcher advocate for neurodiversity- informed approached that focus not only on reducing deficits but also on enhancing strengths, autonomy and quality of life.

Interventions typically involve a multidisciplinary approach including behavioural therapy, speech and language therapy, occupational therapy, educational accommodations and in some cases pharmacological treatment depending on individual needs. As NDDs often persist across lifespan, they may influence higher education, employment opportunities, social relationships and independent living in adulthood, highlighting the need for ongoing and flexible support systems (WHO,2019). Increased awareness, inclusive attitudes and appropriate accommodations in schools, workplaces and communities can significantly enhance participation, autonomy and overall quality of life for individuals with entities and their families.

Emerging technological advances are also reshaping intervention practices globally. Digital therapeutics, AI-assisted screening tools, telehealth-based parent training and virtual learning supports have increased accessibility of care, particularly after the COVID-19 pandemic. Research from countries such as Canada, Australia and the United Kingdom shows that tele-intervention models can effectively improve parental engagement and early developmental monitoring in rural or underserved populations (WHO, 2023). Similarly, Scandinavian countries have increasingly adopted inclusive education models emphasizing universal classroom accommodations rather that segregated special education systems.

Case example 1- Early Autism Intervention

A four-year- old in an urban Indian setting showed limited eye contact, delayed speech and repetitive play behaviours. Initially, family members believed the child was simply "slow to talk". Following developmental screening and multidisciplinary assessment, the child received speech therapy. Parent-mediated behavioural intervention and structured preschool support. Over two years, significantly improvements were observed in communication, emotional regulation and peer interaction. The case illustrates how early identification combined with family involvement can improve adaptive functioning and reduce parental stress.

Case example 2- Transition to Adulthood in ASD

A young adult with ASD completed secondary education successfully but struggled during the transition to employment due to sensory sensitivities and social communication difficulties. Participation in a supported vocational training program and workplace mentoring initiative improved- occupational adjustment and independent living skills. The case reflects current findings that structured transition planning and inclusive workplaces are essential for long-term outcomes in adulthood.

Despite shared diagnostic features, the clinical presentation of neurodevelopmental disorders varies considerably across individuals due to differences in cognitive abilities, environmental experiences, family support and comorbid conditions. Therefore, interventions must remain individualized, culturally sensitive and developmentally appropriate. Understanding NDDs through developmental, neurological and social perspective enabled professionals, families and communities to support individuals in achieving meaningful participation and reaching their full potential.

6.3 Ethical Considerations in Diagnosis and Intervention

Diagnosis plays a complex and often paradoxical role in the lives of individuals with neurodevelopmental disorders. On one hand, receiving a diagnosis can be empowering, as it provides a framework for understanding difficulties, validates lived experiences and enables access to essential services, accommodations and legal protections (Hacking, 1999; Singh, 2011). For families and individuals, diagnostic clarity can reduce self-blame, guide intervention planning and facilitate advocacy within educational, clinical and social systems (National Research Council, 2001). At the same time, diagnostic labels carry the risk of stigmatization and social exclusion. Labels may lead to lowered expectations from teachers, caregivers or peers, resulting in reduced opportunities for learning, autonomy and participation (Rosenthal & Jacobson, 1968; Link & Phelan, 2001). In some cases, individuals may be defined primarily by their diagnosis rather than their abilities, interests and potential (Goffman, 1963). This risk is heightened in contexts where disability is associated with negative stereotypes, fear or social marginalization. (Corrigan &

Watson, 2002). Ethical practice in diagnosis therefore requires a careful balance between accurate identification and respect for individual dignity. Professionals must adopt a person-centered and strengths-based approach, ensuring that assessment processes highlight competencies alongside challenges (APA,2017). Diagnostic feedback should be communicated sensitively, using language that is non-pathologizing and culturally appropriate and emphasizing that a diagnosis describes patterns of functioning rather than fixed limitations (DSM-5-TR; APA,2022).

Cultural contexts play a critical role in ethical diagnosis. Beliefs about disability, child development and mental health vary widely across cultures and influence how diagnoses are perceived and accepted (Kirmayer, 2012). Ethical practitioners must be mindful of these perspectives, engage families collaboratively and avoid imposing culturally incongruent interpretations (Bernal et al., 2009). In the Indian context, this includes addressing stigma, supporting family understanding and aligning diagnostic practices with rights-based frameworks such as the *Rights of Persons with Disabilities Act* (2016) Government of India, 2016).

Ultimately, ethical diagnosis should serve as a tool for inclusion and support, not a source of marginalization. When grounded in developmental understanding, cultural sensitivity and respect for individual identity, diagnostic practices can promote empowerment, self-advocacy and meaningful participation across educational and social contexts (WHO,2013; UNICEF, 2019).

CONCLUSION

Understanding typical development alongside neurodevelopmental disorders offers a comprehensive and integrative framework for appreciating the full spectrum of human developmental diversity. Typical development provides essential reference points for recognising age-appropriate milestones across physical, cognitive and socio emotional domains, while the study of neurodevelopmental disorders deepens insight into atypical developmental pathways shaped by complex interactions among biological, psychological and environmental factors. Viewing these processes together reinforces the idea that development is dynamic, probabilistic and context dependent rather than linear or uniform.

Critics chapter has highlighted that neurodevelopmental disorders are not isolated clinical entities but developmental condition that unfold overtime and across context. Advances in neuroscience, genetics and developmental psychology underscores the role of early brain development, gene-environment interactions and neural plasticity in shaping outcomes. Contemporary frameworks such as developmental psychopathology, neurodiversity and dimensional models challenge purely deficit-based perspectives and emphasise continuity between typical and atypical development, individual variability and the importance of strength-based understanding.

Equally important are the applied and ethical implications of this knowledge. Early identification, culturally responsive assessment and individualised family centred interventions are critical for optimising developmental outcomes. Educational systems play a pivotal role in fostering inclusion through individualised education plans, universal designs for learning and interdisciplinary collaboration. Interventional models ranging from developmental and behavioural approaches to psychosocial educational and community-based rehabilitation strategies demonstrate that meaningful improvement and participation are achievable when support systems are timely coordinated and contextually grounded.

Within the Indian context alignment with rights-based policies such as the Rights of Persons with Disability Act 2016 and the National Education Policy 2020 reinforces the shift from segregation and remediation toward inclusion, accessibility and empowerment. These frameworks emphasise early screening, teacher training, multidisciplinary support and community participation ensuring that intervention offers efforts are not only evidence-based but also socially just and sustainable.

In conclusion, integrating knowledge of typical development with an informed understanding of neurodevelopmental disorders enables professionals to move beyond labels toward holistic, ethical and inclusive practise. Such an approach recognises neurodevelopmental differences as a part of human diversity while addressing genuine support needs, ultimately promoting dignity, participation and ultimately quality of life across the lifespan.

REFERENCES

Ainsworth, M. D. S., Blehar, M. C., Waters, E., & Wall, S. (1978). *Patterns of attachment: A psychological study of the strange situation*. Lawrence Erlbaum Associates.

American Occupational Therapy Association. (2020). Occupational therapy practice framework: Domain and process (4th ed.). *American Journal of Occupational Therapy, 74*(Suppl. 2), Article 7412410010. https://doi.org/DOI: 10.5014/ajot.2020.74S2001

American Psychiatric Association. (2013). *Diagnostic and statistical manual of mental disorders* (5th ed.). American Psychiatric Publishing.

American Psychiatric Association. (2017). *Multicultural guidelines: An ecological approach to context, identity, and intersectionality*. American Psychological Association.

American Psychiatric Association. (2022). *Diagnostic and statistical manual of mental disorders* (5th ed., text rev.). American Psychiatric Publishing.

American Speech-Language-Hearing Association. (2021). Speech and language disorders. *ASHA*.

Armstrong, T. (2010). *The power of neurodiversity: Unleashing the advantages of your differently wired brain*. Da Capo Press.

Astle, D. E., Holmes, J., Kievit, R., & Gathercole, S. (2022). Annual research review: Transdiagnostic approaches to neurodevelopmental disorders. *Journal of Child Psychology and Psychiatry, and Allied Disciplines*, *63*(4), 397–417. DOI: 10.1111/jcpp.13481 PMID: 34296774

Baddeley, A. (2012). Working memory: Theories, models, and controversies. *Annual Review of Psychology*, *63*(1), 1–29. DOI: 10.1146/annurev-psych-120710-100422 PMID: 21961947

Baltes, P. B. (1987). Theoretical propositions of life-span developmental psychology: On the dynamics between growth and decline. *Developmental Psychology*, *23*(5), 611–626. DOI: 10.1037/0012-1649.23.5.611

Baltes, P. B., Lindenberger, U., & Staudinger, U. M. (2006). Life span theory in developmental psychology. In Lerner, R. M. (Ed.),; 6th ed., pp. 569–664). Handbook of child psychology. Wiley.

Bandura, A. (1977). *Social learning theory*. Prentice Hall.

Barkley, R. A. (2012). *Executive functions: What they are, how they work, and why they evolved*. Guilford Press.

Barkley, R. A. (2015). *Attention-deficit hyperactivity disorder: A handbook for diagnosis and treatment* (4th ed.). Guilford Press.

Baron-Cohen, S. (2009). Autism: The empathizing–systemizing (E-S) theory. *Annals of the New York Academy of Sciences*, *1156*(1), 68–80. DOI: 10.1111/j.1749-6632.2009.04467.x PMID: 19338503

Beauchaine, T. P., & Cicchetti, D. (2019). Emotion dysregulation and emerging psychopathology. *Journal of Child Psychology and Psychiatry, and Allied Disciplines*, *60*(4), 361–363. DOI: 10.1111/jcpp.13031 PMID: 31290735

Berk, L. E. (2021). *Development through the lifespan* (8th ed.). Pearson.

Bernal, G., Jiménez-Chafey, M. I., & Domenech Rodríguez, M. M. (2009). Cultural adaptation of treatments: A resource for considering culture in evidence-based practice. *Professional Psychology, Research and Practice*, *40*(4), 361–368. DOI: 10.1037/a0016401

Bjorklund, D. F., & Causey, K. B. (2018). *Children's thinking: Cognitive development and individual differences* (6th ed.). Sage.

Black, M. M., Walker, S. P., Fernald, L. C. H., Andersen, C. T., DiGirolamo, A. M., Lu, C., McCoy, D. C., Fink, G., Shawar, Y. R., Shiffman, J., Devercelli, A. E., Wodon, Q. T., Vargas-Barón, E., & Grantham-McGregor, S. (2017). Early childhood development coming of age: Science through the life course. *Lancet*, *389*(10064), 77–90. DOI: 10.1016/S0140-6736(16)31389-7 PMID: 27717614

Bornstein, M. H. (2012). Cultural approaches to parenting. *Parenting, Science and Practice*, *12*(2–3), 212–221. DOI: 10.1080/15295192.2012.683359 PMID: 22962544

Bowlby, J. (1982). Attachment and loss: Vol. 1. *Attachment* (2nd ed.). Basic Books. (Original work published 1969)

Bradley, R. H., & Corwyn, R. F. (2002). Socioeconomic status and child development. *Annual Review of Psychology*, *53*(1), 371–399. DOI: 10.1146/annurev.psych.53.100901.135233 PMID: 11752490

Bronfenbrenner, U. (1979). *The ecology of human development*. Harvard University Press. DOI: 10.4159/9780674028845

Bronfenbrenner, U., & Morris, P. A. (2006). The bioecological model of human development. In Lerner, R. M. (Ed.),; 6th ed.). Handbook of child psychology. Wiley.

Butterworth, B., Varma, S., & Laurillard, D. (2011). Dyscalculia: From brain to education. *Science, 332*(6033), 1049–1053. DOI: 10.1126/science.1201536 PMID: 21617068

Campbell, S. B., von Stauffenberg, C., & Center, N. (2014). Early predictors of attention-deficit/hyperactivity disorder symptoms. *Development and Psychopathology, 26*(2), 555–569.

Carstensen, L. L. (2006). The influence of a sense of time on human development. *Science, 312*(5782), 1913–1915. DOI: 10.1126/science.1127488 PMID: 16809530

Case, R. (1998). The development of conceptual structures. In Kuhn, D., & Siegler, R. S. (Eds.),; 5th ed.). Handbook of child psychology. Wiley.

Casey, B. J., Oliveri, M. E., & Insel, T. (2014). A neurodevelopmental perspective on the Research Domain Criteria (RDoC) framework. *Biological Psychiatry, 76*(5), 350–353. DOI: 10.1016/j.biopsych.2014.01.006 PMID: 25103538

Centers for Disease Control and Prevention. (2024). *Developmental milestones.* https://www.cdc.gov

Christenson, S. L., & Sheridan, S. M. (2001). *Schools and families: Creating essential connections for learning*. Guilford Press.

Cicchetti, D. (1984). The emergence of developmental psychopathology. *Child Development, 55*(1), 1–7. DOI: 10.2307/1129830 PMID: 6705613

Cicchetti, D., & Blender, J. A. (2006). A multiple-levels-of-analysis approach to resilience. *Development and Psychopathology Russo, 18*(3), 767–773.

Cicchetti, D., & Rogosch, F. A. (1996). Equifinality and multifinality in developmental psychopathology. *Development and Psychopathology, 8*(4), 597–600. DOI: 10.1017/S0954579400007318

Cicchetti, D., & Rogosch, F. A. (2002). A developmental psychopathology perspective on adolescence. *Journal of Consulting and Clinical Psychology, 70*(1), 6–20. DOI: 10.1037/0022-006X.70.1.6 PMID: 11860057

Cicchetti, D., & Toth, S. L. (2009). A developmental psychopathology perspective on child maltreatment. *Journal of the American Academy of Child and Adolescent Psychiatry, 48*(6), 592–594. DOI: 10.1097/CHI.0b013e3181a2b30c

Conti-Ramsden, G., Durkin, K., Toseeb, U., Botting, N., & Pickles, A. (2018). Developmental language disorder: A consensus approach. *Journal of Child Psychology and Psychiatry, and Allied Disciplines, 59*(10), 1068–1080. DOI: 10.1111/jcpp.12893

Corrigan, P. W., & Watson, A. C. (2002). Understanding the impact of stigma on people with mental illness. *World Psychiatry; Official Journal of the World Psychiatric Association (WPA), 1*(1), 16–20. PMID: 16946807

Cortese, S., Adamo, N., Del Giovane, C., Mohr-Jensen, C., Hayes, A. J., Carucci, S., Atkinson, L. Z., Tessari, L., Banaschewski, T., Coghill, D., Hollis, C., Simonoff, E., Zuddas, A., & Barbui, C., Panz , M., Agnoli, A., Restenziale, A., Brignere, M., & Cipriani, A. (. (2018). Comparative efficacy and tolerability of medications for ADHD. *The Lancet. Psychiatry, 5*(9), 727–738. DOI: 10.1016/S2215-0366(18)30269-4 PMID: 30097390

Craig, F., Margari, F., Legrottaglie, A. R., Palumbi, R., de Giambattista, C., & Margari, L. (2016). A systematic review of executive function deficits in autism spectrum disorder and ADHD. *Neuropsychiatric Disease and Treatment, 12*, 1191–1202. DOI: 10.2147/NDT.S104620 PMID: 27274255

Cuthbert, B. N. (2014). The RDoC framework: Facilitating transition from ICD/DSM to dimensional approaches. *World Psychiatry; Official Journal of the World Psychiatric Association (WPA), 13*(1), 28–35. DOI: 10.1002/wps.20087 PMID: 24497240

Cuthbert, B. N., & Insel, T. R. (2013). Toward the future of psychiatric diagnosis: The seven pillars of RDoC. *BMC Medicine, 11*(1), 126. Advance online publication. DOI: 10.1186/1741-7015-11-126 PMID: 23672542

Daley, T. C. (2004). From symptom recognition to diagnosis: Children with autism in urban India. *Social Science & Medicine, 58*(7), 1323–1335. DOI: 10.1016/S0277-9536(03)00330-7 PMID: 14759679

Daley, T. C., & Singhal, N. (2010). Understanding autism in India. *Indian Journal of Pediatrics, 77*(3), 313–319. DOI: 10.1007/s12098-010-0033-0 PMID: 20091358

Dawson, G., Rogers, S., Munson, J., Smith, M., Winter, J., Greenson, J., Donaldson, A., & Varley, J. (2010). Randomized controlled trial of an intervention for toddlers with autism: The Early Start Denver Model. *Pediatrics, 125*(1), e17–e23. DOI: 10.1542/peds.2009-0958 PMID: 19948568

Dawson, P., & Guare, R. (2018). *Executive skills in children and adolescents* (3rd ed.). Guilford Press.

Denham, S. A., Bassett, H. H., Thayer, S. K., Mincic, M. S., Sirotkin, Y. S., & Zinsser, K. (2012). Social-emotional learning and academic success. *Early Education and Development, 23*(5), 652–680. DOI: 10.1080/10409289.2010.497450

Diamond, A. (2013). Executive functions. *Annual Review of Psychology*, *64*(1), 135–168. DOI: 10.1146/annurev-psych-113011-143750 PMID: 23020641

Dunst, C. J., Trivette, C. M., & Hamby, D. W. (2007). Meta-analysis of family-centered helpgiving practices. *Mental Retardation and Developmental Disabilities Research Reviews*, *13*(4), 370–378. DOI: 10.1002/mrdd.20176 PMID: 17979208

DuPaul, G. J., & Stoner, G. (2014). *ADHD in the schools* (3rd ed.). Guilford Press.

Engel, G. L. (1977). The need for a new medical model: A challenge for biomedicine. *Science*, *196*(4286), 129–136. DOI: 10.1126/science.847460 PMID: 847460

Erikson, E. H. (1950). *Childhood and society*. Norton.

Erikson, E. H. (1968). *Identity: Youth and crisis*. Norton.

Farah, M. J. (2017). The neuroscience of socioeconomic status: Correlates, causes and consequences. *Neuron*, *96*(1), 56–71. DOI: 10.1016/j.neuron.2017.08.034 PMID: 28957676

Faraone, S. V., Banaschewski, T., Coghill, D., Zheng, Y., Biederman, J., Bellgrove, M. A., Newcorn, J. H., Mattos, P., Solanto, M. V., Andrade, E. N., Asherson, P., Franke, B., Luo, Y., Schulz, K. P., Swanson, J. M., Thapar, A., Wang, Y., & Wang, J. (2014). The pharmacology of ADHD medications. *Journal of Child Psychology and Psychiatry, and Allied Disciplines*, *55*(1), 3–14. DOI: 10.1111/jcpp.12132 PMID: 24117606

Faraone, S. V., Banaschewski, T., Coghill, D., Zheng, Y., Biederman, J., Bellgrove, M. A., & Wang, Y. (2021). The World Federation of ADHD international consensus statement. *Neuroscience and Biobehavioral Reviews*, *128*, 789–818. DOI: 10.1016/j.neubiorev.2021.01.022 PMID: 33549739

Fletcher-Watson, S. (2022). Neurodiversity and autism research. *Autism : The International Journal of Research and Practice*, *26*(1), 3–5. DOI: 10.1177/1362361319883506 PMID: 35000419

Florian, L., & Black-Hawkins, K. (2011). Exploring inclusive pedagogy. *Cambridge Journal of Education*, *41*(4), 813–828.

Friend, M., & Bursuck, W. D. (2019). *Including students with special needs* (8th ed.). Pearson.

Fuller, E. A., & Kaiser, A. P. (2020). The effects of early intervention on social communication outcomes for children with autism spectrum disorder. *Journal of Autism and Developmental Disorders*, *50*(5), 1683–1700. DOI: 10.1007/s10803-019-03927-z PMID: 30805766

Goffman, E. (1963). *Stigma: Notes on the management of spoiled identity*. Prentice Hall.

Government of India. (1999). *The National Trust Act*. Ministry of Social Justice and Empowerment.

Government of India. (2009). *Right of Children to Free and Compulsory Education Act*. Ministry of Law and Justice.

Government of India. (2016). *Rights of Persons with Disabilities Act*. Ministry of Law and Justice.

Government of India. (2018). *Samagra Shiksha Abhiyan framework*. Ministry of Education.

Graham, S., & Harris, K. R. (2013). Designing an effective writing program. *Focus on Exceptional Children*, *45*(7), 1–14.

Greenspan, S. I., & Wieder, S. (1998). *The child with special needs*. Perseus Books.

Greenspan, S. I., & Wieder, S. (2006). *Engaging autism*. Da Capo Press.

Groce, N., Kett, M., Lang, R., & Trani, J. F. (2011). Disability and poverty. *Lancet*, *374*(9704), 1801–1802.

Grove, J., Ripke, S., Als, T. D., Mattheisen, M., Walters, R. K., Won, H., Pallesen, J., Agerbo, E., Andreassen, O. A., Anney, R., Lane, E. K., & Børglum, A. D. (2019). Identification of common genetic risk variants for autism spectrum disorder. *Nature Genetics*, *51*(3), 431–444. DOI: 10.1038/s41588-019-0344-8 PMID: 30804558

Guralnick, M. J. (2011). Why early intervention works. *Infants and Young Children*, *24*(1), 6–28. DOI: 10.1097/IYC.0b013e3182002cfe PMID: 21532932

Hacking, I. (1999). *The social construction of what?* Harvard University Press.

Hallahan, D. P., Kauffman, J. M., & Pullen, P. C. (2018). *Exceptional learners* (14th ed.). Pearson.

Hinshaw, S. P., & Ellison, K. (2016). *ADHD: What everyone needs to know*. Oxford University Press.

Insel, T., Cuthbert, B., Garvey, M., Heinssen, R., Pine, D. S., Quinn, K., Sanislow, C., & Wang, P. (2010). Research Domain Criteria (RDoC): Toward a new classification framework for research on mental disorders. *The American Journal of Psychiatry*, *167*(7), 748–751. DOI: 10.1176/appi.ajp.2010.09091379 PMID: 20595427

Insel, T. R. (2014). The NIMH Research Domain Criteria (RDoC) project. *The American Journal of Psychiatry*, *171*(4), 395–397. DOI: 10.1176/appi.ajp.2014.14020138 PMID: 24687194

Insel, T. R., & Cuthbert, B. N. (2015). Brain disorders? Precisely. *Science*, *348*(6234), 499–500. DOI: 10.1126/science.aab2358 PMID: 25931539

Johnson, M. H., Gliga, T., Jones, E., & Charman, T. (2015). Neurodevelopmental disorders and developmental neuroscience. *Current Opinion in Neurobiology*, *30*, 1–7. DOI: 10.1016/j.conb.2014.08.004

Johnson, S. B., Riis, J. L., & Noble, K. G. (2016). State of the art review: Poverty and the developing brain. *Pediatrics*, *137*(4), e20153075. DOI: 10.1542/peds.2015-3075 PMID: 26952506

Jones, E. J. H., Guild, J., & McPartland, J. (2022). Shared neural pathways in neurodevelopmental disorders. *Nature Reviews. Neurology*, *18*(8), 495–507.

Kalyanpur, M. (2011). Paradigm and paradox: Education for all and the inclusion of children with disabilities in Cambodia. *International Journal of Inclusive Education*, *15*(10), 1053–1071. DOI: 10.1080/13603116.2011.555069

Kapp, S. K., Gillespie-Lynch, K., Sherman, L. E., & Hutman, T. (2013). Deficit, difference, or both? Autism and neurodiversity. *Developmental Psychology*, *49*(1), 59–71. DOI: 10.1037/a0028353 PMID: 22545843

Keller, H. (2018). Universality claim of attachment theory. *Human Development*, *61*(5–6), 254–264. PMID: 30397121

Kirmayer, L. J. (2012). Cultural competence and evidence-based practice in mental health. *Social Science & Medicine*, *75*(2), 249–256. DOI: 10.1016/j.socscimed.2012.03.018 PMID: 22575699

Kolb, B., & Gibb, R. (2011). Brain plasticity and behaviour in the developing brain. *Journal of the Canadian Academy of Child and Adolescent Psychiatry = Journal de l'Académie Canadienne de Psychiatrie de l'Enfant et de l'Adolescent*, *20*(4), 265–276. PMID: 22114608

Kolb, B., & Whishaw, I. Q. (2015). *An introduction to brain and behavior* (4th ed.). Worth Publishers.

Law, J., Garrett, Z., & Nye, C. (2017). Interventions for children with speech and language difficulties. *International Journal of Language & Communication Disorders*, *52*(1), 3–15. PMID: 27184439

Lerner, R. M. (2006). Developmental science, developmental systems, and contemporary theories of human development. In Lerner, R. M. (Ed.),; 6th ed.). Handbook of child psychology. Wiley.

Lindsay, G., & Dockrell, J. (2012). Longitudinal patterns of behavior problems in children with specific speech and language difficulties. *Child Language Teaching and Therapy*, *28*(2), 135–150. DOI: 10.1177/0265659010396608

Link, B. G., & Phelan, J. C. (2001). Conceptualizing stigma. *Annual Review of Sociology*, *27*(1), 363–385. DOI: 10.1146/annurev.soc.27.1.363

Lord, C., Brugha, T. S., Charman, T., Cusack, J., Fuentes, J., Jones, E. J. H., Jones, R. M., Pickles, A., Rogers, S. J., Siracusano, M., & Veenstra-VanderWeele, J. (2020). Autism spectrum disorder. *Nature Reviews. Disease Primers*, *6*(1), 5. Advance online publication. DOI: 10.1038/s41572-019-0138-4 PMID: 31949163

Lyon, G. R., Shaywitz, S. E., & Shaywitz, B. A. (2003). Defining dyslexia. *Annals of Dyslexia*, *53*(1), 1–14. DOI: 10.1007/s11881-003-0001-9

Mandell, D., & Novak, M. (2005). The role of culture in families' treatment decisions for autism spectrum disorders. *Mental Retardation and Developmental Disabilities Research Reviews*, *11*(2), 110–115. DOI: 10.1002/mrdd.20061 PMID: 15977313

Masten, A. S. (2001). Ordinary magic: Resilience processes in development. *The American Psychologist*, *56*(3), 227–238. DOI: 10.1037/0003-066X.56.3.227 PMID: 11315249

McLaughlin, K. A., Weissman, D., & Bitrán, D. (2021). Childhood adversity and neural development: A systematic review. *Annual Review of Developmental Psychology*, *3*, 277–312. DOI: 10.1146/annurev-devpsych-060320-051114 PMID: 32455344

Meaney, M. J. (2010). Epigenetics and the biological definition of gene × environment interactions. *Child Development*, *81*(1), 41–79. DOI: 10.1111/j.1467-8624.2009.01381.x PMID: 20331654

Milton, D. (2012). On the ontological status of autism. *Disability & Society*, *27*(6), 883–887. DOI: 10.1080/09687599.2012.710008

Ministry of Education. (2020). National [Government of India.]. *Educational Policy*, •••, 2020.

Moore, D. S.. (2017). *The developing genome*. Oxford University Press.

National Institute of Mental Health and Neurosciences. (2019). *NIMHANS index for specific learning disabilities*. NIMHANS.

National Research Council. (2001). *Educating children with autism*. National Academy Press.

Nelson, C. A., de Haan, M., & Thomas, K. M. (2006). *Neuroscience of cognitive development*. Wiley.

Noble, K. G., Houston, S. M., Brito, N. H., Bartsch, H., Kan, E., Kuperman, J. M., Akshoomoff, N., Amaral, D. G., Bloss, C. S., Libiger, O., Schork, N. J., Murray, S. S., Casey, B. J., Chang, L., Ernst, T. M., Frazier, J. A., Gruen, J. R., Kennedy, D. N., Van Zijl, P., & Sowell, E. R. (2015). Family income, parental education and brain structure in children and adolescents. *Nature Neuroscience*, *18*(5), 773–778. DOI: 10.1038/nn.3983 PMID: 25821911

Olusanya, B. O., Davis, A. C., Wertlieb, D., Boo, N. Y., Nair, M. K. C., Halpern, R., & Kofumn, G.Global Research on Developmental Disabilities Collaborators. (2018). Developmental disabilities among children younger than five years in low- and middle-income countries. *The Lancet. Global Health*, *6*(10), e1100–e1121. DOI: 10.1016/S2214-109X(18)30309-7 PMID: 30172774

Papalia, D. E., & Martorell, G. (2021). *Experience human development* (15th ed.). McGraw-Hill.

Patel, V., Belkin, G. S., Chockalingam, A., Cooper, J., Saxena, S., & Unützer, J. (2011). Grand challenges: Integrating mental health services into priority health care platforms. *PLoS Medicine*, *8*(5), e1001448. DOI: 10.1371/journal.pmed.1001448 PMID: 23737736

Patel, V., Saxena, S., Lund, C., Thornicroft, G., Baingana, F., Bolton, P., Chisholm, D., Collins, P. Y., Cooper, J. L., Eaton, J., Herrman, H., & Lomola, S.. (2018). The Lancet Commission on global mental health and sustainable development. *Lancet*, *392*(10157), 1553–1598. DOI: 10.1016/S0140-6736(18)31612-X PMID: 30314863

Peterson, R. L., & Pennington, B. F. (2015). Developmental dyslexia. *Lancet*, *379*(9830), 1997–2007. DOI: 10.1016/S0140-6736(12)60198-6 PMID: 22513218

Piaget, J. (1952). *The origins of intelligence in children*. International Universities Press. DOI: 10.1037/11494-000

Plomin, R., DeFries, J. C., Knopik, V. S., & Neiderhiser, J. M. (2016). Top 10 replicated findings from behavioral genetics. *Perspectives on Psychological Science : A Journal of the Association for Psychological Science*, *11*(1), 3–23. DOI: 10.1177/1745691615617439 PMID: 26817721

Power, T. J., Soffer, S. L., Fives, C. J., & Nissley-Tsiopinis, J. (2013). Family-school intervention for children with ADHD. *School Psychology Review*, *42*(3), 251–271.

Rasinski, T. V. (2012). Why reading fluency should be hot. *The Reading Teacher, 65*(8), 516–522. DOI: 10.1002/TRTR.01077

Richter, L. M., Daelmans, B., Lombardi, J., Heymann, J., Boo, F. L., Behrman, J. R., Lu, C., Lucas, J. E., Perez-Escamilla, R., Dua, T., Bhutta, Z. A., Stenberg, K., Gertler, P., & Darmstadt, G. L.Paper Steering Committee. (2019). Investing in the foundation of sustainable development: Pathways to scale up for early childhood development. *Lancet, 389*(10064), 103–118. DOI: 10.1016/S0140-6736(16)31698-1 PMID: 27717610

Rogers, S. J., & Dawson, G. (2010). *Early Start Denver Model for young children with autism*. Guilford Press.

Rogers, S. J., Estes, A., Lord, C., Vismara, L., Winter, J., Fitzpatrick, A., Guo, Y., & Dawson, G. (2012). Early Start Denver Model intervention for young children with autism. *Journal of the American Academy of Child and Adolescent Psychiatry, 51*(1), 105–115.

Rose, D. H., & Meyer, A. (2002). *Teaching every student in the digital age*. ASCD.

Rosenthal, R., & Jacobson, L. (1968). *Pygmalion in the classroom*. Holt, Rinehart & Winston. DOI: 10.1007/BF02322211

Rutter, M. (1989). Pathways from childhood to adult life. *Journal of Child Psychology and Psychiatry, and Allied Disciplines, 30*(1), 23–51. DOI: 10.1111/j.1469-7610.1989.tb00768.x PMID: 2647779

Rutter, M. (2006). Genes and behavior. *Nature, 443*(7114), 924–925. PMID: 17066023

Rutter, M. (2012). Resilience as a dynamic concept. *Development and Psychopathology, 24*(2), 335–344. DOI: 10.1017/S0954579412000028 PMID: 22559117

Sameroff, A. J. (2000). Developmental systems and psychopathology. *Development and Psychopathology, 12*(3), 297–312. DOI: 10.1017/S0954579400003035 PMID: 11014740

Sameroff, A. J. (2010). A unified theory of development. *Child Development, 81*(1), 6–22. DOI: 10.1111/j.1467-8624.2009.01378.x PMID: 20331651

Schaie, K. W. (1996). *Intellectual development in adulthood*. Cambridge University Press.

Schalock, R. L.. (2021). *Intellectual disability: Definition, diagnosis, classification, and systems of supports* (12th ed.). AAIDD.

Shonkoff, J. P., Garner, A. S., Siegel, B. S., Dobbins, M. I., Earls, M. F., Garner, A. S., McGuinn, L., Pascoe, J., & Wood, D. L. (2012). The lifelong effects of early childhood adversity and toxic stress. *Pediatrics, 129*(1), e232–e246. DOI: 10.1542/peds.2011-2663 PMID: 22201156

Shonkoff, J. P., & Phillips, D. A. (2000). *From neurons to neighborhoods*. National Academy Press.

Sibley, M. H., Arnold, L. E., Swanson, J. M., Hechtman, L. T., Kennedy, T. M., & Owens, E.MTA Cooperative Group. (2022). Defining ADHD symptom persistence in adulthood. *Journal of Child Psychology and Psychiatry, and Allied Disciplines, 63*(2), 123–135. DOI: 10.1111/jcpp.13449 PMID: 27642116

Siegler, R. S. (2016). *Cognitive development* (4th ed.). Pearson.

Singer, J. (1999). Why can't you be normal for once in your life? In Corker, M., & French, S. (Eds.), *Disability discourse* (pp. 59–67). Open University Press.

Siugzdaite, R., Bathelt, J., Holmes, J., & Astle, D. E. (2020). Transdiagnostic brain mapping in developmental disorders. *Current Biology : CB, 30*(7), 1245–1257. DOI: 10.1016/j.cub.2020.01.078 PMID: 32109389

Sroufe, L. A. (1997). Psychopathology as an outcome of development. *Development and Psychopathology, 9*(2), 251–268. DOI: 10.1017/S0954579497002046 PMID: 9201444

Sroufe, L. A., Egeland, B., Carlson, E., & Collins, W. A. (2005). *The development of the person*. Guilford Press.

Super, C. M., & Harkness, S. (1986). The developmental niche. *International Journal of Behavioral Development, 9*(4), 545–569. DOI: 10.1177/016502548600900409

Susman, E. J., & Dorn, L. D. (2009). Puberty: Its role in development. In Lerner, R. M., & Steinberg, L. (Eds.),; 3rd ed.). Handbook of adolescent psychology. Wiley. DOI: 10.1002/9780470479193.adlpsy001006

Thapar, A., Cooper, M., & Rutter, M. (2017). Neurodevelopmental disorders. *The Lancet. Psychiatry, 4*(4), 339–346. DOI: 10.1016/S2215-0366(16)30376-5 PMID: 27979720

Thapar, A., Cooper, M., & Rutter, M. (2021). Neurodevelopmental disorders. *The Lancet Psychiatry, 8*(4), 339–346. *(Note: This reference is an alternative entry or updated correspondence to the 2017 iteration included in the original text).*

Thelen, E., & Smith, L. B. (1994). *A dynamic systems approach to the development of cognition and action*. MIT Press. DOI: 10.7551/mitpress/2524.001.0001

Timimi, S., & Taylor, E. (2004). ADHD is best understood as a cultural construct. *The British Journal of Psychiatry : The Journal of Mental Science, 184*(1), 8–9. DOI: 10.1192/bjp.184.1.8 PMID: 14702221

Toppelberg, C. O., & Collins, B. A. (2010). Language, culture, and adaptation in immigrant children. *Child and Adolescent Psychiatric Clinics of North America, 19*(4), 697–717. DOI: 10.1016/j.chc.2010.07.003 PMID: 21056342

Turnbull, A., Turnbull, R., Wehmeyer, M., & Shogren, K. (2015). *Exceptional lives* (8th ed.). Pearson.

Uher, R. (2022). Gene–environment interactions in severe mental illness. *World Psychiatry; Official Journal of the World Psychiatric Association (WPA), 21*(1), 72–73.

UNICEF. (2019). *Children with disabilities: Ensuring inclusion and equity*. UNICEF.

United Nations Educational, Scientific and Cultural Organization. (2024). *Q&A: How inclusion in education has evolved*. UNESCO. https://www.unesco.org/en/articles/qa-what-you-need-know-about-inclusion-education

Ursache, A., & Noble, K. G. (2016). Socioeconomic status, white matter and executive function in children. *Developmental Science, 19*(5), 672–685. DOI: 10.1111/desc.12334 PMID: 27781144

Volkmar, F., & McPartland, J. C. (2014). From Kanner to DSM-5. *Annual Review of Clinical Psychology, 10* , 193–212.

Vygotsky, L. S. (1978). *Mind in society*. Harvard University Press.

Weisz, J. R., Kuppens, S., Ng, M. Y., Eckshtain, D., Ugueto, A. M., Vaughn-Coaxum, R., Jensen-Doss, A., Marchette, L. K., Fordwood, S. R., & Cortés, R. C. (2017). Psychotherapy for children and adolescents. *Annual Review of Clinical Psychology, 13*, 337–363. PMID: 27442352

World Health Organization. (2013). *Mental health action plan 2013–2020*. WHO.

World Health Organization. (2019). *International classification of diseases for mortality and morbidity statistics* (11th rev.). WHO.

World Health Organization. (2023). *Autism spectrum disorders*. WHO.

World Health Organization. (2023). *Nurturing care for early childhood development*. WHO.

Zelazo, P. D., & Lyons, K. E. (2012). The potential benefits of mindfulness training in early childhood. *Child Development Perspectives, 6*(2), 154–160. DOI: 10.1111/j.1750-8606.2012.00241.x

Zwaigenbaum, L., Bauman, M. L., Choueiri, R., Kasari, C., Carter, A., Granpeesheh, D., Mailloux, Z., Smith-Roley, S., Wagner, S., Fein, D., Pierce, K., Buie, T., Davis, P. A., Newschaffer, C., Robins, D., Wetherby, A., Stone, W. L., Yirmiya, N., Estes, A., & Natowicz, M. R. (2021). Early intervention for children with autism spectrum disorder under 3 years of age. *Pediatrics*, *136*(Suppl. 1), S60–S81. DOI: 10.1542/peds.2014-3667E PMID: 26430170

Chapter 9
Attentional Control in Co-Occurring Separation Anxiety Among Children With Autism Spectrum Disorder:
A Narrative Review

Alana Jeni
http://orcid.org/0000-0003-1360-3903
Christ (Deemed to be) University, India

Payal Sharma
Christ (Deemed to be) University, India

ABSTRACT

Separation Anxiety Disorder (SAD) is highly prevalent in children with Autism Spectrum Disorder (ASD), with attentional control deficits increasing vulnerability to anxiety, particularly SAD and phobias. These difficulties often intensify emotional dysregulation, hyper-responsivity, avoidance, and social withdrawal. This chapter integrates current research on SAD in ASD and reviews neuropsychological frameworks underlying its development. It highlights the role of attentional control in anxiety, SAD, and impairments in emotional regulation and self-control. Findings underscore the involvement of the amygdala, hippocampus, and prefrontal cortex in regulating responses to separation-related cues, as well as the negative impact of oxytocin network dysregulation on SAD symptoms in ASD. Overall, attentional control emerges as a key factor in the development and maintenance of SAD. The

DOI: 10.4018/979-8-3373-7072-9.ch009

review emphasizes the need for anxiety-specific assessment tools for ASD, attention-based interventions, and further research to improve functional outcomes for children with co-occurring ASD and SAD.

INTRODUCTION

Background

Autism spectrum disorder (ASD) is characterized by challenges in social interaction, communication, and restricted, repetitive patterns of behavior (Supekar et al., 2017). Children with ASD are at a greater risk for co-occurring psychiatric conditions, including anxiety disorders, which diminishes their behavioral, social, and cognitive functioning (Stadnick et al., 2016). For instance, separation anxiety disorder (SAD) is notably prevalent among children with ASD. It exacerbates emotional dysregulation due to difficulties in managing fear related to separation from primary caregivers (Renno & Wood, 2013).

SAD is characterized by excessive fear or anxiety about separation from attachment figures, most commonly primary caregivers, which can significantly interfere with a child's daily life (Rodgers et al., 2016). Younger children with ASD show a tendency toward separation anxiety symptoms that may persist as they grow older. However, this manifestation may evolve into other anxiety disorders, such as specific phobias or social anxiety, as they transition into different developmental stages (Guerrera et al., 2022).

Attentional control, the ability to shift attention flexibly and disengage from irrelevant stimuli, has an impact on anxiety experienced by children with ASD. Research has demonstrated that when children with ASD experience separation, their attentional control deficits may lead to heightened fear responses. Their limited ability to focus on supportive thoughts or coping strategies when separated from caregivers can result in heightened behavioral response to the situation, thereby amplifying their distress (Johnston et al., 2013). This emotional dysregulation can be especially pronounced in unfamiliar environments, where children may have to cope without the immediate support of their caregivers (Duker et al., 2011).

Emotional dysregulation may also stem from authoritarian or overly protective parenting style which fosters dependency and separation anxiety in children (Rostami & Saadati, 2018). Heightened anxiety can result in attentional avoidance of socially salient stimuli, promoting social disengagement and reinforcing self-control deficits (Kanat et al., 2017). As a result, children get fixated on problem-solving tasks and have difficulties adopting alternative strategies when confronted with separation related cues (Faja & Darling, 2018; Lecavalier et al., 2020; Peters-Scheffer et al.,

2013). Such attentional biases (inflexibility in attention) toward threat-related cues (e.g., reminders of caregiver absence) further slowed the disengagement from separation cues, contributing to withdrawal from social or classroom activities during separation contexts (Hollocks et al., 2021; Pouretemad et al., 2022).

Children with ASD experience deficits in set-shifting and flexible problem-solving that contribute to both anxiety about separation and outward frustration or irritability when flexible coping is required (Faja & Darling, 2018; Lecavalier et al., 2020; Shaffer et al., 2022). Increased rumination regarding separation scenarios are common, leading to intolerance of uncertainty (e.g., not knowing what will happen during a separation). These processes increase the likelihood of separation anxiety, worry, irritability, and other internalizing symptoms (Burrows et al., 2017; Costescu et al., 2023; Ozsivadjian et al., 2020; Shaffer et al., 2022).

At an affective level, the avoidance behaviors are fueled by attachment insecurity (feeling unsafe or anxious about their bonds with caregivers), alexithymia (struggling to recognize or put words to what they are feeling physically and emotionally), and an intolerance of uncertainty. Due to reduced mentalization or understanding of others' emotions, separation related cues trigger stronger stress responses and anxiety (Komoróczy et al., 2024; Ozsivadjian et al., 2020; Vincenzo, 2026). Maladaptive avoidance of anxiety-provoking stimuli offers immediate, short-term reinforcement through distress reduction. However, this avoidance pattern creates a clinical paradox: it precludes opportunities for exposure-based learning, a mechanism essential for disconfirming catastrophic expectations and fostering cognitive flexibility (Pouretemad et al., 2022; Sethi et al., 2018; Shaffer et al., 2022). Therefore, this attentional inflexibility presents a barrier to effective self-regulation in children with ASD.

Need and Significance

A study estimated that nearly 40% of children with ASD had clinically elevated anxiety or at least one anxiety disorder, with specific phobias alone affecting around 30% (van Steensel et al., 2011). As part of these anxiety disorders, SAD prevalence has been emphasized in various studies. A systematic review indicated that rates of SAD range from 9% to 38% among children with ASD (Ung et al., 2013). Children with higher cognitive abilities displayed an increased prevalence of generalized anxiety and SAD, underscoring the complexity of autism and its associated disorders (Gjevik et al., 2010). It was also found that early childhood poses a higher risk for the development of SAD, aligning with patterns observed in typically developing populations (Wijnhoven et al., 2018). This showcases the need to understand SAD in depth, and for early interventions to alleviate distress related to SAD in the ASD population.

Children may display overwhelming panic or tantrums when faced with separation (Farrow et al., 2024). Distress during separation may further complicate social interactions. Children might withdraw from peer relationships due to fears about separation that arise in social situations, making them more prone to social isolation (Sowden et al., 2015). When children with ASD experience heightened anxiety due to separation, they may struggle with cognitive tasks necessary for learning and social engagement. The resultant lack of focus can interfere with their ability to participate in classroom activities or structured play with peers (Solomon et al., 2009). The emotional strain resulting from these difficulties can exacerbate the risk of developing comorbid mental health issues, such as Generalised Anxiety Disorder (GAD) or depression (Farrow et al., 2024; Horiuchi et al., 2014). Therefore, SAD in children with ASD can lead to an enduring negative impact on their emotional health and overall well-being.

Anxiety symptoms in ASD have substantial neurobiological underpinnings rather than being purely psychologically derived (Bertollo et al., 2025). There's a scope for synthesizing how neurobiological research such as the oxytocin system and atypical neural connectivity in fear-processing circuits are connected to cognitive deficits like "sticky attention." This integrative approach is significant as it throws light on the neuropsychological roots of challenges faced by the ASD population. Since the existing diagnostic paradigms often overlook the biological "proximal responsivity" unique to ASD, this study showcases how immense the regulatory burden placed on caregivers truly is. Ultimately, this work is essential for shifting therapeutic focus from generic anxiety management to targeted interventions that address the underlying attentional and neurobiological mechanisms, offering a pathway to improve adaptive functioning and prevent the developmental stagnation often caused by untreated avoidance behaviors.

Objectives

1. To examine how separation anxiety manifests in children with ASD.
2. To understand the neuropsychological factors underlying separation anxiety in children with ASD.
3. To outline how attentional control deficits influence separation anxiety in children with ASD.
4. To explore how attentional control deficits can affect emotional dysregulation and self-control in children with ASD.

METHODS

Design

The chapter will employ conceptual review methodology, a subtype of narrative review (Misra & Agarwal, 2018), to synthesize existing literature on the intersection of ASD, attentional control, and separation anxiety. This methodology was adopted considering the heterogeneity of the literature on the topic (Cranston et al., 2008).

Search Terms

Key search terms and their combinations included, but not limited to: "Autism Spectrum Disorder," "ASD," "Children with ASD," "Anxiety in ASD," "Attention in ASD," "Neuropsychology of ASD," "Separation Anxiety," "Emotional Regulation," "Self-Control," "Attentional Control," "Attentional Deficits," "Neuropsychology" and "Comorbidity."

Databases and Sources

The review primarily focused on peer-reviewed articles from major psychological and medical databases (e.g., PsycINFO, PubMed/MEDLINE, Google Scholar, Frontiers) up to the year 2026.

Inclusion Criteria

Empirical studies (quantitative and qualitative), systematic reviews, meta-analyses, and other reviews that discuss at least two of the three core constructs (ASD/Anxiety/ Separation anxiety/Attentional Control/Attention) or the mechanisms (Emotional Regulation/ Self-Control/ Avoidance) that link them.

Exclusion Criteria

Studies that aren't in English were excluded.

Literature Selection

The selection process was iterative, starting with broad searches and then refining the scope based on the relevance to the specific link between variables.

DISCUSSION

Manifestation of Separation Anxiety in Children with ASD

Anxiety in ASD is both "traditional" (DSM diagnoses) and "distinct" (ASD-specific fears). Nearly half of autistic children had distinct, non-DSM types of fears, such as; fear of change, fear of specific odd items (e.g., toilets, songs), confusion in social situations rather than fear of judgment, anxiety tied to special interests, and compulsive behaviors that don't fit typical Obsessive Compulsive Disorder (OCD) patterns (Kerns et al., 2021). In comparison to the typically developing children, ASD children displayed distinct fears suggesting children with autism have a unique profile of anxiety, not just more anxiety.

Examples of distinct ASD anxieties include "uncommon phobias" (e.g., intense fear of specific sounds or textures (Cascio et al., 2012; Johnston et al., 2022; Williams et al., 2021), distress over minor disruptions to routine (intolerance of uncertainty) (South & Rodgers, 2017), and fear of losing access to special interests (Kerns et al., 2014; South & Rodgers, 2017). In contrast, traditional anxieties in the Typically Developing (TD) population, such as social anxiety, are typically driven by fear of negative evaluation. However, in ASD, social avoidance may stem from confusion over social rules or sensory overload rather than fear of judgment (Montaser et al., 2023).

Symptoms of separation anxiety are frequently seen in people with ASD and in those who show subthreshold autistic traits (ATs). Research suggests that anxiety in ASD is a separate condition, not just a byproduct of ASD traits (Kerns et al., 2021). Individuals with ASD tend to display strong attachment responses, but mainly toward a limited group of significant caregivers (Pini et al., 2025). Attachment security is generally lower in ASD than in neurotypical populations, and greater AT burden tends to be associated with more insecure attachment patterns, particularly avoidance and reduced security with caregivers (Cochran et al., 2015; Kahane & El-Tahir, 2015; Komoróczy et al., 2024). For example, cross-sectional and meta-analytic work indicates that higher core autism characteristics correlate with more insecure attachment in childhood, with several studies reporting lower rates of secure attachment in higher-functioning and more severely affected groups alike, although the magnitude can vary by sample and measure (Cochran et al., 2015; Kahane & El-Tahir, 2015; Komoróczy et al., 2024).

Effect of IQ

Separation anxiety patterns may vary with IQ and ASD severity. Some reviews and synthesis papers note that separation anxiety is a component of anxiety disorders in ASD but its prevalence and magnitude vary with IQ and related cognitive functioning. However, items measuring separation anxiety—such as statements like *"is easily upset when separation is expected"*—were frequently endorsed across all IQ groups in ASD (Hallett et al., 2013). Even children with higher levels of IQ showed a full range of anxiety (Kerns et al., 2021).

Higher IQ may be linked with higher endorsement of certain anxiety items, including those related to separation, in some samples (Hallett et al., 2013), and higher IQ may interact with other factors to shape internalizing symptoms, including separation anxiety (Edirisooriya et al., 2020). Higher IQ can coincide with increased self-awareness and social concerns that amplify separation-related worries in some youths (Eussen et al., 2012; Horwitz et al., 2023). Other studies emphasize measurement challenges (informant differences, ASD symptom overlap) that can influence observed separation anxiety levels in relation to IQ, rather than a simple linear effect of IQ alone (Cochran et al., 2015; Hallett et al., 2013; Schiltz & Magnus, 2021). Separation anxiety scores might be over- or under-estimated rather than the true risk depending on the child's cognitive and communicative profile (Schiltz & Magnus, 2021). This reinforces the need for multiple measures and informants when assessing separation anxiety in ASD. This suggests that SAD may occur across all IQ levels, though its specific manifestations in different groups warrant further investigation.

Whereas, in ASD with low IQ, SAD manifestations may be less readily distinguished from global anxiety and mood problems or from behavior problems tied to communication limitations and cognitive rigidity. Some evidence suggests higher rates of comorbid anxiety in ASD with low IQ, yet the specific fraction presenting as SAD is less consistently reported (Mingins et al., 2020). Therefore, there's a need for innovative tools to measure comorbidity of anxiety disorders in low IQ ASD groups.

Responsivity

How one responds to a separation related cue depends on responsivity, as individuals with ASD often exhibit exaggerated responses to sensory stimuli, resulting in feelings of unease and distress in seemingly benign situations (Green et al., 2015). Researchers distinguish between *proximal responsivity*—responses to emotional situations within close relationships—and *peripheral responsivity*—responses to emotional situations in more distant or less personal contexts. A recent study found that people with ASD had significantly reduced peripheral responsivity, while their levels of emotion contagion (automatic mirroring of others' emotions) and proximal responsivity were similar to those of neurotypical individuals. This suggests that individuals with ASD are especially attuned to emotional dynamics within their family environment. As a result, any disruption to family harmony may heighten separation anxiety responses, including possibly increased suicidality as shown in figure 1 (Pini et al., 2025). For children, disruptions to family dynamics or routines may be more distressing than disruptions in other areas of life, highlighting the need for further research on this topic.

Figure 1. Conceptual pathway from responsivity to suicidality in ASD

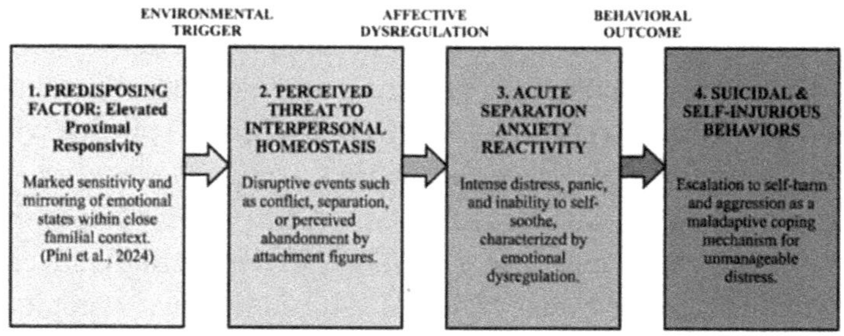

Furthermore, like children with SAD, borderline personality disorder (BPD), or eating disorders, children with ASD may also be at increased risk of developing insecure attachment patterns. This may stem from challenges in communication and social interaction, or from similar subthreshold ATs in their parents. Such factors can contribute to the emergence of SAD symptoms and create areas of overlap not only between ASD and SAD but also with BPD and Anorexia Nervosa, which themselves often co-occur (Pini et al., 2025).

Alexithymia and Mentalization Challenges

Alexithymia and reduced mentalization can amplify internal distress, complicate separation experiences, and drive avoidance or heightened anxiety in separation contexts (Caine et al., 2020; Kinnaird et al., 2019; Maisel et al., 2016; Oakley et al., 2020). Alexithymia is associated with difficulties recognising negative facial expressions, low detection of emotions conveyed in vocalisation, reduced empathy, and lower motivation to offer altruistic support to those in distress (Bird & Cook, 2013). Alexithymia disrupts emotional awareness and labeling, which impairs emotion regulation and heightens distress in situations involving separation from caregiver or routine changes. This pathway has been supported by mediation models showing alexithymia mediating the relationship between autistic features and anxiety/depression severity in ASD samples (Albantakis et al., 2020; Maisel et al., 2016; Morie et al., 2019; Oakley et al., 2020). In children and adolescents, higher alexithymia levels correlate with greater self-reported or parent-reported anxiety, including separation-related concerns, particularly when tasks require labeling or describing emotions during separations (Costa et al., 2020; Fietz et al., 2018; Milosavljevic et al., 2015).

Impairments in mentalization linked to both ASD traits and insecure attachment patterns. Reduced mentalization can contribute to misinterpreting a caregiver's intentions during departures. Neurocognitive models propose that deficits in social cognition, theory of mind, and emotion recognition—common in ASD and amplified by alexithymia—underlie heightened separation anxiety in separations from caregivers (Caine et al., 2020; Cochran et al., 2015; Mul et al., 2018; Sörnyei et al., 2023). Longitudinal and cross-sectional work points to mentalizing as a mediator of attachment security and anxiety in ASD contexts, suggesting that improving mentalization could reduce separation distress indirectly by enhancing caregiver–child attunement during departures (Maisel et al., 2016; Sörnyei et al., 2023).

The presentation of separation anxiety in youth with ASD is shaped by diverse factors. Dissecting these influences allows clinicians to better isolate the risk factors and protective mechanisms involved in the onset and maintenance of comorbid SAD. Future research could explore the proactive mechanisms that underlie reduction of SAD symptoms in the ASD population.

What does SAD Look Like in Children with ASD?

Cognitive characteristics of SAD in children with ASD often include persistent, excessive fears concerning separation from primary caregivers. These fears may manifest as preoccupations with the potential harm befalling on the caregiver or the child's own distress upon separation. Children may also display maladaptive thought patterns, such as catastrophic thinking regarding separation events. This cognitive anxiety can lead to a heightened state of alertness and avoidance behaviors (Hallett et al., 2013; Rodgers et al., 2016).

Emotionally, children with ASD and comorbid SAD may experience heightened levels of fear and worry specifically surrounding separation from caregivers. Symptoms often include increased irritability, mood swings, and episodes of crying or tantrums when separation is imminent or during transitions into new environments (Renno & Wood, 2013; van Steensel et al., 2011). Furthermore, emotional regulation may be impaired, children may struggle to express their anxiety verbally, leading to frustration and potential behavioral outbursts (Hallett et al., 2013; Wu et al., 2023).

Behaviorally, children presenting with SAD in the context of ASD may exhibit several hallmark symptoms, such as clinging to caregivers, refusing to engage in activities that do not involve their primary attachment figure, and even physical symptoms like stomachaches or headaches during anticipated separations (Shear, 2006; Renno & Wood, 2013; Rodgers et al., 2016) . These behaviors are often exacerbated in unfamiliar settings or during changes to routine—traits that are characteristic of ASD. Children may also engage in avoidance behaviors, resisting school attendance, avoiding staying away from home, or social interactions (Hallett et al., 2013; Kossowsky et al., 2013; Lebowitz et al., 2016; Tsang et al., 2012).

It is essential to recognize that children with ASD may display anxiety-related behaviors that overlap with core ASD features—such as rigidity and resistance to change—which can complicate the diagnosis of SAD. A child's reluctance to engage in new situations may stem from anxiety and SAD rather than a lack of interest, which is often interpreted as social withdrawal in ASD (Hallett et al., 2013; Rodgers et al., 2016; Tsang et al., 2012). Hence, caregivers and clinicians must differentiate between behaviors stemming from separation anxiety and those rooted in broader autism spectrum characteristics (Renno & Wood, 2013; Wu et al., 2023).

How is SAD in ASD Different from SAD in the Neurotypical Population?

Both children with ASD and neurotypical children experience symptoms common to SAD, such as excessive fear of separation from primary caregivers, distress during separations, and physical symptoms (Shear, 2006). Clinically, both groups may exhibit avoidance behaviors, where the child refuses to participate in activities that involve separation (Kossowsky et al., 2013). Additionally, mood disturbances can be observed in both populations when facing potential separation from caregivers (Renno & Wood, 2013). However, there are differences in manifestations of SAD symptoms in the ASD population versus the neurotypical population (Pini et al., 2025).

While the core feeling of fear regarding separation is shared, the timing, triggers, and behavioral expressions differ significantly due to the specific nature of autism. In neurotypical population, SAD symptoms typically arise during the late infancy developmental stages. Individuals with ASD may exhibit SAD signs later in life due to the developmental delays in ASD. In neurotypical adults, SAD is often driven by worry about the attachment figure's safety or fear of being alone. In ASD, the anxiety is compounded by core autistic traits such as insistence for sameness and reliance on the caregiving environment for safety and sameness. Additionally, the distress from separation anxiety can "amplify nuclear symptoms" of autism (e.g., more intense stimming or rigidity). The competing anxiety symptoms in ASD can cause the onset of "aggressive and self-injurious behaviors," which is a severe manifestation not typically highlighted as a primary symptom of SAD in neurotypical adults (Pini et al., 2025).

In neurotypical children with SAD, cognitive apprehensions are often directly linked to familiar social situations and peer interactions, predicated on a fear of negative evaluation or the potential harm that could come during separation. Conversely, children with ASD may not express typical cognitive concerns relating to social judgments but might instead demonstrate rigidity and an overwhelming need for routine, which contributes to their anxiety around separation. Their thoughts are more likely to reflect anxiety related to changes in environment rather than peer-based evaluations, marking a divergence in cognitive patterns associated with SAD (Maddox & White, 2015; Maisel et al., 2016).

Emotionally, children with ASD may struggle to articulate their anxiety, which manifests as frustration and anger rather than verbal expression of fear, a characteristic not as prevalent in neurotypical children with SAD. Neurotypical children often show a heightened emotional awareness, allowing them to verbalize their fears about separation, whereas children with ASD might express anxiety through meltdowns or non-verbal behaviors, reflecting a challenge in recognizing and expressing emotions (Espelöer et al., 2020; Renno & Wood, 2013). Inherent difficulties in emotional processing can lead to emotional dysregulation, which in turn may intensify the individual's reaction to separation anxiety.

Behaviorally, children with ASD might display a spectrum of maladaptive behaviors that include more pronounced rituals or routines surrounding separation. For example, a child with ASD may develop specific routines that must be adhered to before a separation occurs, highlighting their struggle with flexibility—a trait often less pronounced in neurotypical peers (Belin et al., 2017). In contrast, neurotypical children may exhibit protest behaviors, such as crying or clinging, in a more straightforward manner, linked directly to the fear of being apart from their caregivers (Renno & Wood, 2013). Additionally, while both groups might experience physical complaints related to anxiety, children with ASD might also exhibit increased sensory sensitivities that come into play during separation events. For instance, a loud noise during a drop-off might exacerbate their anxiety significantly more than it would for a neurotypical peer (Belin et al., 2017).

Neuropsychological Correlates of Separation Anxiety in Children with ASD

Anxiety disorders are highly prevalent in children with ASD (estimates vary widely by sample and measurement), and separation anxiety symptoms are commonly reported in younger children with ASD (van Steensel et al., 2011). For children with autism, the processing of fear may be different from that of the typically developing children. Once the sensory organs transduce the stimulus, signals reach the thalamus. Thalamus forwards signals to primary sensory cortices and directly to the amygdala for rapid threat detection (Khalil et al., 2023). However, in the case of individuals with ASD, they may show atypical thalamic responses and thalamocortical connectivity (hyperconnectivity or hypoconnectivity). This may amplify or attenuate the incoming sensory input. Some children may have hypo or hyper responsiveness in the primary sensory cortices, leading to hypersensitive reactions or failing to register the threat altogether (Ayub et al., 2021).

Reduced functional connectivity between PFC and amygdala is commonly reported in children with autism (Ibrahim et al., 2019). Dysregulation in the amygdala activation, which is critical for processing fear and anxiety, may also lead to hyper-arousal to non-threatening exposures in children with ASD (Herrington et al., 2016). The amygdala is central to separation-related fear learning and attachment-related distress in neurotypical development; in ASD its developmental trajectory and relation to anxiety are heterogeneous. Some longitudinal and cross-sectional MRI studies report larger right amygdala volumes in children with ASD who have 'DSM anxiety' presentations, while other studies (and analyses of subnuclei) report smaller or altered subnuclear volumes in ASD subgroups with distinct anxiety phenotypes (Andrews et al., 2022; Yarger et al., 2022). The latter group also had slower emergence of right amygdala volumes, indicating a brain-behavior relationship between amygdala development and development of distinct anxieties (Andrews et al., 2022).

Salience, Sensory and Frontoparietal Networks

In the next step of fear processing, information is transferred to the salience network deep within the cerebral hemispheres. The salience network consists of ventral anterior insula which integrates interoceptive signals (heart rate, gut feelings) and frontoparietal control networks such as dorsal Anterior Cingulate Cortex (dACC) and limbic structures (Seeley, 2019). This network gates attention and interoceptive awareness, and are frequently atypical in ASD, showing greater connectivity. This in turn leads to increased arousal when exposed to salient stimuli (Green et al., 2016).

Greater resting connectivity between the salience network and primary sensory areas suggests that youth with sensory hyper-responsivity may inherently assign too much importance to basic sensory input. This idea is reinforced by the findings that stronger salience-network connectivity (between the anterior insula and amygdala) predicts stronger amygdala responses to mildly aversive sounds and touch. Likewise, tighter coupling between the anterior insula and somatosensory cortex relates to heightened somatosensory activity during these stimuli. Over time, this ongoing co-activation of salience and sensory regions may further reinforce and strengthen these neural links. Children with ASD may have increased co-activation of salience and sensory-related regions even during rest, suggesting that their brains may be "primed" to notice, attend to, and attribute salience to basic sensory information to the detriment of potentially important social information (Green et al., 2016).

For children whose separation anxiety is partly triggered by sensory overload or unpredictability, altered salience/frontoparietal signaling can amplify threat appraisal when caregivers are absent (Sarmukadam et al., 2023). Children with autism who are more sensitive to sensory input or who avoid sensory situations tend to have more anxiety. Hence, sensory seeking may be used as a coping strategy. Children may seek extra stimulation to distract themselves from feeling anxious (Sarmukadam et al., 2023).

Research has shown that connectivity between the frontoparietal network and the hippocampus is particularly significant during tasks that require emotional regulation and contextual processing. For instance, during states of anxiety, alterations in the functional connectivity between the frontoparietal network and the amygdala and hippocampus can affect how children with ASD encode and respond to anxiety-provoking situations (Uddin et al., 2013; Yuan et al., 2022). The hippocampus, when developed normally, allows children to contextualize their experiences, helping them differentiate between past trauma and present situations, a process that is often disrupted in those with ASD due to atypical neural circuitry (Duan et al., 2020; Uddin et al., 2013).

Recent meta-analyses and connectivity studies point out that the frontoparietal network, in conjunction with the default mode network (neural network responsible for higher order cognition at rest and consists of anterior medial frontal cortex, ventral medial prefrontal cortex, posterior cingulate cortex, precuneus, inferior parietal lobule, and middle temporal gyrus), supports goal-directed cognition and emotional processing (Azarias et al., 2025; Spreng et al., 2010; Xu et al., 2019). The interconnection between these networks, especially in states of emotional distress, suggests that a robust link between the frontoparietal network and hippocampus could serve as an adaptive mechanism for navigating anxiety. Individuals with enhanced connectivity between these networks may experience more effective emotional regulation, reducing the likelihood of heightened anxiety during separation or unfamiliar scenarios (Uddin et al., 2013; Yuan et al., 2022). Conversely, reduced connectivity may lead to maladaptive responses, reinforcing patterns of anxiety when faced with social or environmental challenges.

The maturation of the hippocampus is integral to children's learning processes, particularly in the context of contextualizing and remembering separation-related experiences. As the hippocampus develops, it acquires the capacity to modulate the amygdala-driven fear responses, embedding these responses within a larger spatial, temporal, and emotional framework. This embedding is essential in helping children differentiate genuine cues of separation from harmless situations, mitigating inappropriate distress responses (Greenwood et al., 2008; Wiltgen et al., 2006). The collaboration between the hippocampus and medial-temporal structures—including the entorhinal cortex and parahippocampal regions—plays a significant role in memory consolidation and contextual prediction, which are crucial for attachment learning (Greenwood et al., 2008).

While there is limited direct examination of hippocampal functioning in SAD within ASD, animal research and studies of human neuropsychology suggest that atypical or delayed maturation of the hippocampus may impair contextual learning (Murphy et al., 2011). Specifically, such deficits can lead to the consolidation of separation experiences as persistent fear memories, thereby intensifying inflexible distress responses during separation events (Murphy et al., 2011). This notion is further supported by investigations that highlight the critical role hippocampus plays in conditioning responses to fearful stimuli, as it integrates contextual information and guides the appropriate emotional response through feedback loops involving the amygdala and prefrontal cortex (Greenwood et al., 2008; Wiltgen et al., 2006).

Research indicates that in conditions such as ASD, there may be impairments in how effectively the hippocampus can perform these functions, contributing to the heightened and inflexible distress responses observed in children with ASD (Murphy et al., 2011). This association suggests that the developmental progress of the hippocampus, and its interactions with other brain structures, is pivotal in shaping the emotional landscape of children, especially those with autism as they navigate experiences of separation (Murphy et al., 2011). Moreover, understanding the neuroanatomical nuances between typical and atypical development can shed light on the mechanisms at play in ASD, particularly concerning memory consolidation and contextual learning, which remain critical for attachment, social interaction and emotional regulation (Murphy et al., 2011).

Oxytocin / Social Neuropeptides

Research has increasingly focused on the role of oxytocin, a neuropeptide known for its influence on social bonding and emotional regulation, in children with ASD. A meta-analysis conducted by LoParo and Waldman (2015) concluded that oxytocin contributes to ASD in children primarily through its role in shaping social cognition, attachment, and social learning, with genetic variation in the oxytocin receptor gene (OXTR) influencing individual vulnerability.

Several OXTR polymorphisms (common variations in a gene or Deoxyribonucleic Acid (DNA) sequence that make individuals differ from one another), notably rs7632287, rs237887, rs2268491, and rs2254298, lead to lower plasma oxytocin levels, reduced receptor expression, or altered receptor functioning, ultimately adding ASD risk. This suggests that altered oxytocin signaling may disrupt core social phenotypes. Risk alleles (genetic variants associated with an increased probability of developing a particular disease) in these single nucleotide polymorphisms (SNPs) (the simplest type of polymorphism, involving a change in a single DNA base at a specific position in the genome) have been linked to reduced social skills, impaired communication, weaker attachment security, lower empathy, and diminished face-recognition memory, features central to ASD. Variants located in regulatory regions of OXTR may affect receptor expression or oxytocin sensitivity, thereby modulating the efficiency of social reward and bonding circuits during development. Importantly, the effects of OXTR variants appear to vary by ethnicity and may influence symptom severity rather than diagnosis alone, contributing to heterogeneity in social impairment, adaptive functioning, and caregiving sensitivity observed across children with ASD (LoParo & Waldman, 2015).

In a research study it was found that children with SAD showed lower levels of oxytocin than normal controls, pointing to the role of oxytocin in their ability to form secure attachments and buffer stress responses (Üstün et al., 2023). Variations in the oxytocin receptor (OXTR) gene have been linked to the social deficits characteristic of ASD, suggesting that dysregulation in this system may contribute to heightened anxiety and issues with separation from caregivers (Campbell et al., 2011). SAD in the ASD population may be exacerbated by oxytocin dysregulation. Low levels of oxytocin may correlate with increased symptoms of separation anxiety in children, possibly due to impaired attachment relationships and emotional dysregulation (Lebowitz et al., 2016). Similarly, higher serum oxytocin levels were associated with greater social deficits in children with ASD, suggesting that children experiencing social challenges may release more oxytocin as a compensatory mechanism (Yang et al., 2017).

Conversely, research by Miller highlighted that lower oxytocin levels in boys with ASD are associated with deficits in social behaviors, reinforcing the link between oxytocin signaling and social attachment issues in this population (Miller et al., 2013). This decreased peripheral oxytocin may contribute to an inability to buffer stress and enhance social interactions, thereby heightening anxiety during separation situations (Miller et al., 2013). Furthermore, Scatliffe provided insightful evidence that oxytocin plays a crucial role in early social bonding during parent-infant interactions, emphasizing the importance of this neuropeptide in attachment behaviors (Scatliffe et al., 2019). In contexts of separation, such atypical signaling could manifest as increased anxiety, as the emotional buffer normally afforded by strong social bonds is compromised.

The therapeutic potential of oxytocin has also been highlighted, with studies indicating that intranasal administration of oxytocin can enhance social behavior and emotional recognition in individuals with ASD (Andari et al., 2010; Lebowitz et al., 2016). This is underscored by findings from Andari who demonstrated improvements in social approach behaviors post-oxytocin treatment among individuals with high-functioning autism (Andari et al., 2010). Despite these promising results, the clinical evidence remains preliminary and suggests that individual variability in oxytocin responses may play a significant role in therapeutic outcomes.

In sum, low levels result in a compromised ability to "buffer stress" and form secure bonds, leading to increased symptoms of separation anxiety and weaker attachment security (Miller et al., 2013; Lebowitz et al., 2016). Genetic variants causing lower oxytocin levels or receptor expression are linked to reduced empathy, impaired communication, and diminished face-recognition memory (LoParo & Waldman, 2015)

Effect of Attentional Control on Separation Cues in Children with ASD

Attentional control is the ability to flexibly direct, shift, and inhibit attention (Chen & Barnes, 2012). This ability may be dysfunctional in children diagnosed with ASD, where neuropsychological factors contribute to persistent anxiety, including separation anxiety (Fischer et al., 2013). Structural and functional abnormalities in brain networks associated with executive functioning, including the prefrontal cortex and anterior cingulate cortex, hinder attention regulation during emotionally charged situations, such as caregiver separations (Fan et al., 2012). Some theories suggest that atypical attention in autism may explain sensory behaviors: distress and hyper-reactivity may come from heightened vigilance to unpleasant stimuli, sensory interests from intense focus on enjoyable stimuli, and hypo-reactivity from stimuli not reaching awareness. Regardless of the cause, sensory processing differences strongly affect daily life, including participation in activities, sleep, quality of life, and mental health (Dwyer et al., 2024).

Research indicates that children with ASD often exhibit "sticky attention," characterized by an inability to disengage from particular stimuli (Fischer et al., 2013; Fischer et al., 2015) and "springy attention" or the tendency to return to the previous focus of attention after briefly engaging with a new stimulus (Dwyer et al., 2024). In ASD participants with slower attention disengagement, the caregiver reports of hyper-responsiveness to sensory stimuli, enhanced perception of background stimuli and proactive sensory interest seeking were noted (Dwyer et al., 2024). In a study that assessed infants high on risk for ASD with disengagement and shift trials, it was found that infants who were later diagnosed with ASD took longer to disengage from stimuli only at 12 months of age. The disengagement pattern worsened from 6 months to 12 months of age, suggesting that it emerges during development, especially when the brain starts using more control and planning systems. Additionally, a difficulty in shifting attention to the left was also observed only in the participants later diagnosed with ASD, pointing to a right brain difference in ASD. Higher left side disengagement was also associated with increased ASD symptom severity, high irritability, increased difficulty to soothe, and lower emotional regulation. These results point to the need for early attention training interventions for children with ASD (Bryson et al., 2018).

Attention disengagement was specifically slower in children with ASD when visually threatening stimuli (picture of snakes) were used. Participants with ASD got "stuck" looking at snakes and couldn't look away from them showing that threatening stimuli hold attention and delay disengagement. This may cause avoidance and withdrawal symptoms, which are common in the population with ASD. The study also found that the connection between the emotion system and control system in the brain is weaker, therefore, making the children with ASD take longer to suppress the emotional reaction to threat (Isomura et al., 2015).

Toddlers with ASD showed higher levels of distress to social threats (stranger approaching them) and they used fewer social ways (such as seeking comfort from parents, seeking physical closeness, or communicating distress socially) to calm themselves down. Higher levels of fear of social threat in early life is linked to behavioral inhibition and social anxiety later in life (Macari et al., 2020). High-risk ASD infants show unique "acoustic signatures" in their cries during separation, indicating a different physiological state of distress compared to neurotypical peers. Toddlers who were later diagnosed with ASD had the highest-pitched cries and some of the shortest overall crying durations (Esposito et al., 2014). These results indicate that caregiver separation and encounters with unfamiliar individuals can provoke intense distress in children with ASD, suggesting that both situations are experienced as threatening. In this context, cues associated with separation may overwhelmingly capture attention, exacerbating anxiety-related distress. Such cognitive entrapment reinforces anxious states rather than fostering adaptive coping mechanisms. Cues such as a caregiver preparing to leave or changes in routine may disproportionately capture the child's attention, triggering heightened distress.

Plateaued attention development (attention develops normally early on, however stops improving (plateaus) between 10 and 25 months) was observed in infants who showed higher autism traits at age three. These children also showed reduced adaptive functioning. Low attentional control across infancy was noticed in children with mildly elevated autism traits, and this was especially linked to non-social autism traits such as repetitive behaviors. These findings suggest that when attention goes off-track, it may lead to autism-like traits (Hendry et al., 2020). Such deficits in top-down attentional control make it harder for children with ASD to override bottom-up, emotion-driven attention (Ridderinkhof et al., 2020). When anxiety-related stimuli dominate attentional resources, children are less able to redirect focus toward calming or distracting alternatives, reinforcing anxious responses rather than resolving them.

Several neuropsychological factors associated with ASD can intensify attentional control difficulties and, in turn, anxiety symptoms:

1. ***Executive Dysfunction***

Children with ASD often experience significant impairments in inhibitory control, leading to challenges in suppressing intrusive anxiety-related thoughts. Once anxiety responses are initiated, they can become cognitively "locked in," creating a feedback loop that perpetuates the anxious state (Kozunova et al., 2023; Sáez-Suanes, 2024).

2. ***Heightened Sensory Processing Differences***

Sensory hypersensitivity, prevalent in children with ASD, exacerbates attentional challenges during separation events. The emotional distress linked to sensory overload can lead to an overwhelming perception of sensory stimuli, straining limited attentional resources (Patil & Kaple, 2023).

3. ***Emotion Regulation Difficulties***

The interplay between attentional control and emotion regulation is critical. Children with ASD typically display reduced connectivity between limbic structures involved in emotional responses and prefrontal regions that regulate these responses, making it difficult to downregulate fear after an anxiety trigger emerges (South & Rodgers, 2017; White et al., 2014). This dysregulation allows anxiety to persist disproportionately.

4. ***Intolerance of Uncertainty***

The inherent uncertainty of separation events—such as not knowing when a caregiver will return—captures the attention of children with ASD in unique ways. Poor attentional control prevents these children from disengaging from uncertainties, fueling hypervigilance and anxiety through heightened threat monitoring (South & Rodgers, 2017).

Therefore, attentional control deficits do not merely trigger separation anxiety, they help maintain it over time. When a child repeatedly focuses attention on perceived threats associated with separation, anxious expectations become reinforced through learning. Each separation episode becomes an opportunity for attentional bias toward threat, rather than habituation or adaptive coping. Avoidance behaviors—such as refusing school or clinging to caregivers (Nordin et al., 2024)—are then negatively reinforced because they temporarily reduce anxiety, further limiting opportunities for the child to practice attentional flexibility and emotional regulation. Moreover, impaired attentional control reduces the effectiveness of internal coping strategies, such as self-soothing or recalling past successful separations. Without the ability to redirect attention, children remain cognitively anchored to fear, preventing anxiety from naturally subsiding.

Effect of Attentional Control on Emotion Regulation and Self-Control in Children with ASD

Research suggests that children with ASD exhibit notable impairments in attentional control compared to typically developing peers (Cañigueral et al., 2021; Corbett et al., 2009). These deficits in attentional processes may involve the alerting system, which is crucial for maintaining sustained attention across various situations. Children with ASD take longer to look away from angry faces initially. In later stages, they may avoid these faces to reduce discomfort. Slower attention in children with ASD was linked to more severe social and emotional difficulties (Sahuquillo-Leal et al., 2025).

Poor attentional control leads to difficulties regulating thoughts and emotions, increasing vulnerability to heightened negative emotions (e.g., anxiety, anger), rumination and emotional rigidity, and cognitive inflexibility. This is due to atypical functioning of prefrontal cortex regions (e.g., DLPFC, VLPFC, DMPFC), which normally exert top-down regulation over emotion-processing regions such as the amygdala (Mazefsky et al., 2013). When attentional control is weak, this top-down modulation is less effective, resulting in stronger and less regulated emotional responses. As a result, threatening stimuli capture attention and can trigger an excessively strong response in individuals with ASD (South et al., 2014; White et al., 2014).

Effect of Attentional Control on Emotional Regulation and Self-Control

Emotional regulation involves the ability to monitor and manage one's emotional experiences and responses adaptively. Deficits in this area are prevalent in children with ASD, as indicated by studies showing that these children often display heightened emotional reactivity and difficulty modulating their responses to emotional stimuli (Anastopoulos et al., 2010; Samson et al., 2014). Moreover, poor self-control, which encompasses the ability to inhibit impulsive responses and delay gratification, is closely linked with emotional dysregulation and general functioning in ASD (Hammud et al., 2023; Ni et al., 2020).

Attentional control deficits can lead to difficulties in emotional regulation by limiting the cognitive resources available for self-monitoring and emotional processing. The mechanisms underlying executive functions (EFs), which include attentional control, are critical for self-regulation and emotional control (Diamond, 2013). They face difficulty in using EFs to manage emotions leading to deficits in modulating the intensity and timing of emotional responses, controlling emotional behaviors once aroused, and maintaining goal-directed behavior when emotionally distressed (Lim, 2020). When these mechanisms are compromised, children with ASD may struggle more with impulsive behaviors, leading to elevated instances of frustration, anxiety, and other emotional disturbances (Fong & Iarocci, 2020; Nigg, 2016). Children with ASD also experience negative emotions such as anxiety and anger more often, more strongly, and more reactively than typically developing children. They also have difficulty returning to their baseline emotional state once upset. Therefore, these children tend to engage in repetitive or stereotyped behaviors, use avoidance or disengaged coping, and vent emotions inappropriately or withdraw from stressors. These strategies are linked to increased negative affect and maladaptive behavior. Emotional dysregulation may increase the severity of core ASD symptoms, and elevate the chances of persistence of emotional difficulties into adolescence and adulthood (Lim, 2020). Studies indicate that improving EF skills, particularly in attention and emotional regulation through targeted interventions, can lead to enhancements in social competence among these children (Fong & Iarocci, 2020; Vogan et al., 2018)

Children with ASD show substantial impairments in self-control across multiple dimensions, including physiological regulation (e.g., arousal, sensory and bodily regulation), emotional regulation (managing emotions and impulses), and regulation during transitions (difficulty shifting between tasks or situations). Self-control difficulties are strongly associated with poorer adaptive functioning and restrict engagement and learning opportunities. Children with ASD who struggle with self-control have fewer opportunities for social interaction, structured learning, and peer engagement (Bashshar & Elashram, 2025). Reid and colleagues introduced five types of self-regulation strategies for ASD population, which includes, self monitoring, self evaluation, goal setting, self instruction, and self reinforcement (Reid et al., 2013). The strategies may alleviate the social and behavioral challenges faced by children with ASD. All the evidence discussed suggests that fostering attentional control may subsequently improve both emotional regulation and self-control in children with ASD.

CONCLUSION & LIMITATIONS

The manifestation of SAD in children with ASD is characterized by a unique clinical profile that diverges significantly from neurotypical presentations. Anxiety in this population is often "distinct," involving non-DSM fears such as specific phobias, intolerance of uncertainty, and a rigid adherence to routine, rather than solely fear of social evaluation (Kerns et al., 2021; South & Rodgers, 2017). Unlike typically developing children, whose separation anxiety often stems from fear of harm to the caregiver, distress in children with ASD is frequently driven by sensory overload and a disruption of "sameness" (Pini et al., 2025). Furthermore, Pini et al. (2025) highlight that individuals with ASD exhibit heightened "proximal responsivity," making them acutely attuned to emotional dynamics within the family; consequently, even minor disruptions to family harmony can trigger exaggerated separation anxiety responses and maladaptive behaviors. Since SAD in ASD is characterised by greater internalization, exaggerated avoidance behaviors, emotion regulation, and self control deficits, an immense psychological and physical load is placed on caregivers to provide an environment that neutralizes the triggers of anxiety.

Neuropsychologically, these behavioral manifestations are underpinned by atypical neural connectivity and structural alterations in fear-processing circuits. Research indicates a reduced functional connectivity between the prefrontal cortex (PFC) and the amygdala, resulting in a failure of top-down emotional regulation and subsequent hyper-arousal to non-threatening stimuli (Ibrahim et al., 2019; Herrington et al., 2016).

Concurrently, the salience network in children with ASD appears "primed" through increased resting connectivity with sensory regions, causing an over-assignment of importance to basic sensory inputs at the expense of relevant social information (Green et al., 2016). This neural dysregulation is compounded by atypical hippocampal maturation, which impairs contextual learning and causes separation experiences to be consolidated as persistent, inflexible fear memories rather than temporary, manageable events (Murphy et al., 2011).

At the molecular level, dysregulation of the oxytocin system plays a pivotal role in the etiology of SAD within the ASD population. Meta-analytic evidence links risk alleles in the OXTR to lower plasma oxytocin levels and reduced receptor expression (LoParo & Waldman, 2015). These deficits compromise the biological "stress buffer" required for secure attachment, thereby exacerbating separation anxiety and impairing social cognition (Miller et al., 2013; Lebowitz et al., 2016). While some evidence suggests that elevated oxytocin may occasionally appear as a compensatory mechanism (Yang et al., 2017), the prevailing consensus associates diminished oxytocin signaling with the core social and emotional vulnerabilities that hinder the formation of secure caregiver bonds (Scatliffe et al., 2019).

Finally, deficits in attentional control and executive function act as critical maintenance mechanisms for anxiety in ASD. Children with ASD exhibit "sticky attention," characterized by an inability to disengage from threatening stimuli, which cognitively entraps them in anxious states (Isomura et al., 2015; Fischer et al., 2013). This attentional rigidity, coupled with executive dysfunction in prefrontal regions, hinders effective emotion regulation, leading to heightened reactivity and maladaptive coping strategies such as avoidance or repetitive behaviors (Mazefsky et al., 2013; South et al., 2014). Consequently, the inability to flexibly shift attention and regulate impulses not only intensifies immediate distress but also restricts opportunities for adaptive learning and social engagement, potentially extending emotional difficulties into adulthood (Bashshar & Elashram, 2025).

The discussion is primarily limited by significant heterogeneity and inferential gaps in the current evidence base, particularly regarding neurobiological markers. Findings on amygdala structure remain inconsistent, varying by age and anxiety subtype, while the proposed role of the hippocampus relies largely on animal models rather than direct empirical data from children with ASD and Separation Anxiety Disorder (SAD). Clinical identification is further complicated by the phenotypic overlap between SAD symptoms and core ASD traits—such as rigidity, sensory sensitivities, and intolerance of uncertainty—which makes distinguishing true separation anxiety from autism-specific distress difficult. Additionally, evidence regarding the oxytocin system remains preliminary and contradictory, with therapeutic potential obscured by individual genetic polymorphisms, ethnic variability, and unclear causality regarding whether altered oxytocin levels represent a primary deficit or a compensatory mechanism. Finally, the directional relationship between attentional control deficits and anxiety remains unresolved, creating a "chicken-and-egg" dilemma that hinders the development of targeted interventions.

Implications

These findings can have implications for the children, their caregivers and for the researchers. The finding that anxiety in ASD is "distinct" (rooted in sensory phobias and intolerance of uncertainty rather than social evaluation) implies a high risk of clinical misinterpretation. Behaviors stemming from SAD—such as rigidity or refusal to enter a new environment—may be dismissed as "core autism traits" or "behavioral non-compliance" rather than recognized as distress. Children may be subjected to behavioral discipline for what is essentially a biological panic response, potentially worsening their "proximal responsivity" and distress.

The evidence regarding "sticky attention" and executive dysfunction suggests that standard anxiety treatments (like standard CBT) may be less effective if they rely heavily on cognitive reframing. If a child cannot physiologically disengage attention from a threat (e.g., a door closing), they cannot process cognitive strategies. Interventions must likely prioritize bottom-up regulation (sensory calming, attention shift training) before attempting top-down cognitive work. Additionally, if anxiety drives a child to avoid social situations or school, and this avoidance is accommodated, they miss critical windows for developing social skills and adaptive functioning, reinforcing the "plateau" in attention development (Hendry et al., 2020).

Parents act as the external "prefrontal cortex" for their children with ASD. Since the child's distress is triggered by disruptions in family harmony, caregivers may feel pressured to maintain an artificially perfect, conflict-free environment, leading to caregiver burnout. If parents share the same genetic risk alleles or anxiety predispositions, their own heightened anxiety could feed the child's "proximal responsivity," creating a feedback loop of mutual dysregulation. Caregivers must distinguish between behaviors rooted in rigidity (an ASD trait) versus separation fear (an SAD trait). Understanding that a meltdown during drop-off is driven by a neurobiological failure to "contextualize" the separation (due to hippocampal immaturity) rather than simple stubbornness can shift the parenting approach from punitive to supportive.

Future Directions

Future studies must stratify participants not just by ASD diagnosis, but by specific anxiety phenotypes. There is a critical lack of longitudinal studies to determine the directional relationship between attentional control deficits and anxiety, leaving it unclear whether executive dysfunction acts as a precursor to or a consequence of chronic distress. There's a need to evaluate the protective factors that aid the management of SAD in ASD. Direct empirical evidence linking hippocampal maturity to contextual learning deficits in this specific population is virtually absent, with current theories relying heavily on inferences from animal models rather than human neuroimaging in ASD cohorts. Additionally, the field lacks refined diagnostic tools that can validly differentiate between SAD symptoms and overlapping core ASD traits, such as sensory avoidance and rigidity, inhibiting accurate prevalence estimates. Finally, oxytocin research requires more rigorous stratification by genotype and ethnicity to resolve contradictory findings regarding its therapeutic efficacy and the functional role of compensatory hormone release.

REFERENCES

Albantakis, L., Brandi, M., Zillekens, I. C., Henco, L., Weindel, L., Thaler, H., Schliephake, L., Timmermans, B., & Schilbach, L. (2020). Alexithymic and autistic traits: Relevance for comorbid depression and social phobia in adults with and without autism spectrum disorder. *Autism : The International Journal of Research and Practice*, *24*(8), 2046–2056. DOI: 10.1177/1362361320936024 PMID: 32662285

Anastopoulos, A. D., Smith, T. F., Garrett, M. E., Morrissey-Kane, E., Schatz, N. K., Sommer, J. L., Kollins, S. H., & Ashley-Koch, A. E. (2010). Self-Regulation of Emotion, Functional Impairment, and Comorbidity Among ChildrenWith AD/HD. *Journal of Attention Disorders*, *15*(7), 583–592. DOI: 10.1177/1087054710370567 PMID: 20686097

Andari, E., Duhamel, J., Zalla, T., Herbrecht, E., Leboyer, M., & Sirigu, A. (2010). Promoting social behavior with oxytocin in high-functioning autism spectrum disorders. *Proceedings of the National Academy of Sciences of the United States of America*, *107*(9), 4389–4394. DOI: 10.1073/pnas.0910249107 PMID: 20160081

Andrews, D. S., Aksman, L., Kerns, C. M., Lee, J. K., Winder-Patel, B. M., Harvey, D. J., Waizbard-Bartov, E., Heath, B., Solomon, M., Rogers, S. J., Altmann, A., Nordahl, C. W., & Amaral, D. G. (2022). Association of amygdala development with different forms of anxiety in autism spectrum disorder. *Biological Psychiatry*, *91*(11), 977–987. DOI: 10.1016/j.biopsych.2022.01.016 PMID: 35341582

Ayub, R., Sun, K. L., Flores, R. E., Lam, V. T., Jo, B., Saggar, M., & Fung, L. K. (2021). Thalamocortical connectivity is associated with autism symptoms in high-functioning adults with autism and typically developing adults. *Translational Psychiatry*, *11*(1), 93. DOI: 10.1038/s41398-021-01221-0 PMID: 33536431

Azarias, F. R., Almeida, G. H. D. R., de Melo, L. F., Rici, R. E. G., & Maria, D. A. (2025). The Journey of the Default Mode Network: Development, Function, and Impact on Mental Health. *Biology (Basel)*, *14*(4), 395. DOI: 10.3390/biology14040395 PMID: 40282260

Bashshar, A. M. A. A. B., & Elashram, R. E. M. (2025). The Relationship Between Self-Regulation Difficulties and Adaptive Functioning in Children with Autism Spectrum Disorder (ASD). *International Journal of Disability Development and Education*, *72*(7), 1248–1270. DOI: 10.1080/1034912X.2024.2419871

Belin, L., Henry, L., Destays, M., Hausberger, M., & Grandgeorge, M. (2017). Simple shapes elicit different emotional responses in children with autism spectrum disorder and neurotypical children and adults. *Frontiers in Psychology, 8*. Advance online publication. DOI: 10.3389/fpsyg.2017.00091 PMID: 28194129

Bertollo, A. G., Puntel, C. F., da Silva, B. V., Martins, M. R., Bagatini, M. D., & Ignácio, Z. M. (2025). Neurobiological Relationships Between Neurodevelopmental Disorders and Mood Disorders. *Brain Sciences, 15*(3), 307. DOI: 10.3390/brainsci15030307 PMID: 40149827

Bird, G., & Cook, R. (2013). Mixed emotions: The contribution of alexithymia to the emotional symptoms of autism. *Translational Psychiatry, 3*(7), e285–e285. DOI: 10.1038/tp.2013.61 PMID: 23880881

Bryson, S., Garon, N., McMullen, T., Brian, J., Zwaigenbaum, L., Armstrong, V., Roberts, W., Smith, I., & Szatmari, P. (2018). Impaired disengagement of attention and its relationship to emotional distress in infants at high-risk for autism spectrum disorder. *Journal of Clinical and Experimental Neuropsychology, 40*(5), 487–501. DOI: 10.1080/13803395.2017.1372368 PMID: 28914144

Burrows, C. A., Timpano, K. R., & Uddin, L. Q. (2017). Putative Brain Networks Underlying Repetitive Negative Thinking and Comorbid Internalizing Problems in Autism. *Clinical Psychological Science, 5*(3), 522–536. DOI: 10.1177/2167702616683506 PMID: 28603665

Caine, J. A., Klein, B., & Edwards, S. L. (2020). Emotion Recognition in adults with ASD and Alexithymia: The impact of a Novel Mimicry Task for Therapeutic Benefit Study Protocol (Preprint). *JMIR Research Protocols*. Advance online publication. DOI: 10.2196/24543 PMID: 34170257

Campbell, J. L., Datta, D., Jones, S. T., Lee, E. B., Sutcliffe, J. S., Hammock, E. A. D., & Levitt, P. (2011). Association of oxytocin receptor (oxtr) gene variants with multiple phenotype domains of autism spectrum disorder. *Journal of Neurodevelopmental Disorders, 3*(2), 101–112. DOI: 10.1007/s11689-010-9071-2 PMID: 21484202

Cañigueral, R., Palmer, J., Ashwood, K. L., Azadi, B., Asherson, P., Bolton, P., McLoughlin, G., & Tye, C. (2021). Alpha oscillatory activity during attentional control in children with Autism Spectrum Disorder (ASD), Attention-Deficit/Hyperactivity Disorder (ADHD), and ASD+ADHD. *Journal of Child Psychology and Psychiatry, and Allied Disciplines, 63*(7), 745–761. DOI: 10.1111/jcpp.13514 PMID: 34477232

Cascio, C. J., Moana-Filho, E. J., Guest, S., Nebel, M. B., Weisner, J., Baranek, G. T., & Essick, G. K. (2012). Perceptual and neural response to affective tactile texture stimulation in adults with autism spectrum disorders. *Autism Research : Official Journal of the International Society for Autism Research*, *5*(4), 231–244. DOI: 10.1002/aur.1224 PMID: 22447729

Chen, J. Y., & Barnes, M. J. (2012). Supervisory control of multiple robots in dynamic tasking environments. *Ergonomics*, *55*(9), 1043–1058. DOI: 10.1080/00140139.2012.689013 PMID: 22676776

Cochran, D., Sikoglu, E. M., Hodge, S. M., Edden, R. A. E., Foley, A., Kennedy, D. N., Moore, C. M., & Frazier, J. A. (2015). Relationship among Glutamine, γ-Aminobutyric Acid, and Social Cognition in Autism Spectrum Disorders. *Journal of Child and Adolescent Psychopharmacology*, *25*(4), 314–322. DOI: 10.1089/cap.2014.0112 PMID: 25919578

Corbett, B. A., Constantine, L. J., Hendren, R. L., Rocke, D. M., & Ozonoff, S. (2009). Examining executive functioning in children with autism spectrum disorder, attention deficit hyperactivity disorder and typical development. *Psychiatry Research*, *166*(2-3), 210–222. DOI: 10.1016/j.psychres.2008.02.005 PMID: 19285351

Costa, A. P., Loor, C., & Steffgen, G. (2020). Suicidality in Adults with Autism Spectrum Disorder: The Role of Depressive Symptomatology, Alexithymia, and Antidepressants. *Journal of Autism and Developmental Disorders*, *50*(10), 3585–3597. DOI: 10.1007/s10803-020-04433-3 PMID: 32172508

Costescu, C., Ro an, A., David, C. C., Cozma, L., & Calota, A. (2023). The Relation between Cognitive and Emotional Processes in Children and Adolescents with Neurodevelopmental Disorders—A Meta-Analysis. *European Journal of Investigation in Health, Psychology and Education*, *13*(12), 2811–2826. DOI: 10.3390/ejihpe13120194 PMID: 38131893

Cranston, J. M., Crockett, A., Moss, J., Pegram, R. W., & Stocks, N. (2008). Models of chronic disease management in primary care for patients with mild-to-moderate asthma or COPD: A narrative review. *The Medical Journal of Australia*, *188*(S8). Advance online publication. DOI: 10.5694/j.1326-5377.2008.tb01744.x PMID: 18429736

Diamond, A. (2013). Executive Functions. *Annual Review of Psychology*, *64*(1), 135–168. DOI: 10.1146/annurev-psych-113011-143750 PMID: 23020641

Duan, X., Wang, R., Xiao, J., Li, Y., Huang, X., Guo, X., Cao, J., He, L., He, C., Ling, Z., Shan, X., Chen, H., Kang, X., & Chen, H. (2020). Subcortical structural covariance in young children with autism spectrum disorder. *Progress in Neuro-Psychopharmacology & Biological Psychiatry, 99*, 109874. DOI: 10.1016/j.pnpbp.2020.109874 PMID: 31981719

Duker, L., Polido, J., Mailloux, Z., Coleman, G., & Cermak, S. (2011). Oral care and sensory sensitivities in children with autism spectrum disorders. *Special Care in Dentistry : Official Publication of the American Association of Hospital Dentists, the Academy of Dentistry for the Handicapped, and the American Society for Geriatric Dentistry, 31*(3), 102–110. DOI: 10.1111/j.1754-4505.2011.00187.x PMID: 21592164

Dwyer, P., Sillas, A., Prieto, M., Camp, E., Nordahl, C. W., & Rivera, S. M. (2024). Hyper-focus, sticky attention, and springy attention in young autistic children: Associations with sensory behaviors and cognitive ability. *Autism Research : Official Journal of the International Society for Autism Research, 17*(8), 1677–1695. DOI: 10.1002/aur.3174 PMID: 38840328

Edirisooriya, M., Dykiert, D., & Auyeung, B. (2020). IQ and Internalising Symptoms in Adolescents with ASD. *Journal of Autism and Developmental Disorders, 51*(11), 3887–3907. DOI: 10.1007/s10803-020-04810-y PMID: 33381856

Espelöer, J., Hellmich, M., Vogeley, K., & Falter-Wagner, C. M. (2020). Brief report: Social anxiety in autism spectrum disorder is based on deficits in social competence. *Journal of Autism and Developmental Disorders, 51*(1), 315–322. DOI: 10.1007/s10803-020-04529-w PMID: 32410100

Esposito, G., Del Carmen Rostagno, M., Venuti, P., Haltigan, J. D., & Messinger, D. S. (2014). Brief Report: Atypical expression of distress during the separation phase of the strange situation procedure in infant siblings at high risk for ASD. *Journal of Autism and Developmental Disorders, 44*(4), 975–980. DOI: 10.1007/s10803-013-1940-6 PMID: 24026913

Eussen, M., Gool, A. R. V., Verheij, F., de Nijs, P. F., Verhulst, F. C., & Greaves-Lord, K. (2012). The association of quality of social relations, symptom severity and intelligence with anxiety in children with autism spectrum disorders. *Autism : The International Journal of Research and Practice, 17*(6), 723–735. DOI: 10.1177/1362361312453882 PMID: 22917843

Faja, S., & Darling, L. N. (2018). Variation in restricted and repetitive behaviors and interests relates to inhibitory control and shifting in children with autism spectrum disorder. *Autism : The International Journal of Research and Practice*, *23*(5), 1262–1272. DOI: 10.1177/1362361318804192 PMID: 30394786

Fan, J., Bernardi, S., Dam, N. T. V., Anagnostou, E., Gu, X., Martin, L., & Hof, P. R. (2012). Functional deficits of the attentional networks in autism. *Brain and Behavior*, *2*(5), 647–660. DOI: 10.1002/brb3.90 PMID: 23139910

Farrow, A., Al-Jaishi, A., O'Donnell, S., Palmeter, S., Georgiades, S., Chen, Y., McPhee, P. G., & Edjoc, R. (2024). Functional difficulties in children and youth with autism spectrum disorder: Analysis of the 2019 canadian health survey on children and youth. *Health Promotion and Chronic Disease Prevention in Canada : Research, Policy and Practice*, *44*(1), 9–20. DOI: 10.24095/hpcdp.44.1.02 PMID: 38231089

Fietz, J., Valencia, N., & Silani, G. (2018). Alexithymia and autistic traits as possible predictors for traits related to depression, anxiety, and stress: A multivariate statistical approach. *Journal of Evaluation in Clinical Practice*, *24*(4), 901–908. DOI: 10.1111/jep.12961 PMID: 29882629

Fischer, J., Koldewyn, K., Jiang, Y., & Kanwisher, N. (2013). Unimpaired Attentional Disengagement and Social Orienting in Children With Autism. *Clinical Psychological Science*, *2*(2), 214–223. DOI: 10.1177/2167702613496242 PMID: 25419497

Fischer, J., Smith, H., Martinez-Pedraza, F., Carter, A. S., Kanwisher, N., & Káldy, Z. (2015). Unimpaired attentional disengagement in toddlers with autism spectrum disorder. *Developmental Science*, *19*(6), 1095–1103. DOI: 10.1111/desc.12386 PMID: 26690733

Fong, V. C., & Iarocci, G. (2020). The Role of Executive Functioning in Predicting Social Competence in Children with and without Autism Spectrum Disorder. *Autism Research : Official Journal of the International Society for Autism Research*, *13*(11), 1856–1866. DOI: 10.1002/aur.2350 PMID: 33460309

Gjevik, E., Eldevik, S., Fjæran-Granum, T., & Sponheim, E. (2010). Kiddie-SADS Reveals High Rates of DSM-IV Disorders in Children and Adolescents with Autism Spectrum Disorders. *Journal of Autism and Developmental Disorders*, *41*(6), 761–769. DOI: 10.1007/s10803-010-1095-7 PMID: 20824493

Green, S., Hernandez, L., Tottenham, N., Krasileva, K., Bookheimer, S., & Dapretto, M. (2015). Neurobiology of sensory overresponsivity in youth with autism spectrum disorders. *Journal of the American Academy of Child and Adolescent Psychiatry*, *72*(8), 778. DOI: 10.1001/jamapsychiatry.2015.0737 PMID: 26061819

Green, S. A., Hernandez, L., Bookheimer, S. Y., & Dapretto, M. (2016). Salience Network Connectivity in Autism Is Related to Brain and Behavioral Markers of Sensory Overresponsivity. *Journal of the American Academy of Child and Adolescent Psychiatry, 55*(7), 618–626.e1. DOI: 10.1016/j.jaac.2016.04.013 PMID: 27343889

Greenwood, B. N., Strong, P. V., Foley, T. E., & Fleshner, M. (2008). A behavioral analysis of the impact of voluntary physical activity on hippocampus-dependent contextual conditioning. *Hippocampus, 19*(10), 988–1001. DOI: 10.1002/hipo.20534 PMID: 19115374

Guerrera, S., Pontillo, M., Tata, M., Vincenzo, C., Bellantoni, D., Napoli, E., & Vicari, S. (2022). Anxiety in autism spectrum disorder: Clinical characteristics and the role of the family. *Brain Sciences, 12*(12), 1597. DOI: 10.3390/brainsci12121597 PMID: 36552057

Hallett, V., Lecavalier, L., Sukhodolsky, D. G., Cipriano, N., Aman, M. G., McCracken, J. T., McDougle, C. J., Tierney, E., King, B. H., Hollander, E., Sikich, L., Bregman, J., Anagnostou, E., Donnelly, C., Katsovich, L., Dukes, K., Vitiello, B., Gadow, K., & Scahill, L. (2013). Exploring the manifestations of anxiety in children with autism spectrum disorders. *Journal of Autism and Developmental Disorders, 43*(10), 2341–2352. DOI: 10.1007/s10803-013-1775-1 PMID: 23400347

Hammud, G., Avital-Magen, A., Schusheim, G., Barzuza, I., & Engel-Yeger, B. (2023). How Self-Regulation and Executive Functions Deficits Affect Quality of Life of Children/Adolescents with Emotional Regulation Disorders. *Children (Basel, Switzerland), 10*(10), 1622. DOI: 10.3390/children10101622 PMID: 37892283

Hendry, A., Jones, E. J. H., Bedford, R., Andersson Konke, L., Begum Ali, J., B lte, S., Brocki, K. C., Demurie, E., Johnson, M., Pijl, M. K. J., Roeyers, H., & Charman, T. (2020). Atypical Development of Attentional Control Associates with Later Adaptive Functioning, Autism and ADHD Traits. *Journal of Autism and Developmental Disorders, 50*(11), 4085–4105. DOI: 10.1007/s10803-020-04465-9 PMID: 32221749

Herrington, J., Miller, J., Pandey, J., & Schultz, R. (2016). Anxiety and social deficits have distinct relationships with amygdala function in autism spectrum disorder. *Social Cognitive and Affective Neuroscience, 11*(6), 907–914. DOI: 10.1093/scan/nsw015 PMID: 26865425

Hollocks, M. J., Charman, T., Baird, G., Lord, C., Pickles, A., & Simonoff, E. (2021). Exploring the impact of adolescent cognitive inflexibility on emotional and behavioural problems experienced by autistic adults. *Autism : The International Journal of Research and Practice, 26*(5), 1229–1241. DOI: 10.1177/13623613211046160 PMID: 34579554

Horiuchi, F., Oka, Y., Uno, H., Kawabe, K., Okada, F., Saito, I., Tanigawa, T., & Ueno, S. (2014). Age- and sex-related emotional and behavioral problems in children with autism spectrum disorders: Comparison with control children. *Psychiatry and Clinical Neurosciences*, *68*(7), 542–550. DOI: 10.1111/pcn.12164 PMID: 24447342

Horwitz, E., Vos, M., de Bildt, A., Greaves-Lord, K., Rommelse, N., Schoevers, R. A., & Hartman, C. A. (2023). Sex differences in the course of autistic and co-occurring psychopathological symptoms in adolescents with and without autism spectrum disorder. *Autism : The International Journal of Research and Practice*, *27*(6), 1716–1729. DOI: 10.1177/13623613221146477 PMID: 36680498

Ibrahim, K., Eilbott, J. A., Ventola, P., He, G., Pelphrey, K. A., McCarthy, G., & Sukhodolsky, D. G. (2019). Reduced Amygdala-Prefrontal Functional Connectivity in Children With Autism Spectrum Disorder and Co-occurring Disruptive Behavior. *Biological Psychiatry. Cognitive Neuroscience and Neuroimaging*, *4*(12), 1031–1041. DOI: 10.1016/j.bpsc.2019.01.009 PMID: 30979647

Isomura, T., Ogawa, S., Shibasaki, M., & Masataka, N. (2015). Delayed disengagement of attention from snakes in children with autism. *Frontiers in Psychology*, *6*, 241. DOI: 10.3389/fpsyg.2015.00241 PMID: 25784895

Johnston, K., Dittner, A., Bramham, J., Murphy, C., Knight, A., & Russell, A. (2013). Attention deficit hyperactivity disorder symptoms in adults with autism spectrum disorders. *Autism Research : Official Journal of the International Society for Autism Research*, *6*(4), 225–236. DOI: 10.1002/aur.1283 PMID: 23788522

Kahane, L., & El-Tahir, M. O. (2015). Attachment behavior in children with Autistic Spectrum Disorders. *Advances in Mental Health and Intellectual Disabilities*, *9*(2), 79–89. DOI: 10.1108/AMHID-06-2014-0026

Kanat, M., Spenthof, I., Riedel, A., Elst, L., Heinrichs, M., & Domes, G. (2017). Restoring effects of oxytocin on the attentional preference for faces in autism. *Translational Psychiatry*, *7*(4), e1097–e1097. DOI: 10.1038/tp.2017.67 PMID: 28418399

Kerns, C. M., Kendall, P. C., Berry, L., Souders, M. C., Franklin, M. E., Schultz, R. T., Miller, J., & Herrington, J. (2014). Traditional and atypical presentations of anxiety in youth with autism spectrum disorder. *Journal of Autism and Developmental Disorders*, *44*(11), 2851–2861. DOI: 10.1007/s10803-014-2141-7 PMID: 24902932

Kerns, C. M., Winder-Patel, B., Iosif, A. M., Nordahl, C. W., Heath, B., Solomon, M., & Amaral, D. G. (2021). Clinically significant anxiety in children with autism spectrum disorder and varied intellectual functioning. *Journal of Clinical Child and Adolescent Psychology : The Official Journal for the Society of Clinical Child and Adolescent Psychology, American Psychological Association, Division 53*, *50*(6), 780–795. DOI: 10.1080/15374416.2019.1703712 PMID: 31971849

Khalil, V., Faress, I., Mermet-Joret, N., Kerwin, P., Yonehara, K., & Nabavi, S. (2023). Subcortico-amygdala pathway processes innate and learned threats. *eLife*, *12*, e85459. DOI: 10.7554/eLife.85459 PMID: 37526552

Kinnaird, E., Stewart, C., & Tchanturia, K. (2019). Investigating alexithymia in autism: A systematic review and meta-analysis. *European Psychiatry : The Journal of the Association of European Psychiatrists*, *55*, 80–89. DOI: 10.1016/j.eurpsy.2018.09.004 PMID: 30399531

Komoróczy, E., Sörnyei, D., Vass, Á., Szuromi, B., Vizin, G., Réthelyi, J., & Farkas, K. (2024). Understanding depression in autism: The mediating role of mentalization, attachment, social support, and psychological flexibility. https://doi.org/DOI: 10.1101/2024.07.12.24310324

Kossowsky, J., Pfaltz, M. C., Schneider, S., Taeymans, J., Locher, C., & Gaab, J. (2013). The separation anxiety hypothesis of panic disorder revisited: A meta-analysis. *The American Journal of Psychiatry*, *170*(7), 768–781. DOI: 10.1176/appi.ajp.2012.12070893 PMID: 23680783

Kozunova, G. L., Zakirov, F. K., Rytikova, A. M., Stroganova, T. A., & Chernyshev, B. V. (2023). Neurobiological factors of executive dysfunction in autism spectrum disorders. *Neuroscience and Behavioral Physiology*, *53*(7), 1158–1174. DOI: 10.1007/s11055-023-01512-7

Lebowitz, E. R., Leckman, J. F., Feldman, R., Zagoory-Sharon, O., McDonald, N., & Silverman, W. K. (2016). Salivary oxytocin in clinically anxious youth: Associations with separation anxiety and family accommodation. *Psychoneuroendocrinology*, *65*, 35–43. DOI: 10.1016/j.psyneuen.2015.12.007 PMID: 26716876

Lecavalier, L., Bodfish, J. W., Harrop, C., Whitten, A., Jones, D. R., Pritchett, J., Faldowski, R. A., & Boyd, B. A. (2020). Development of the Behavioral Inflexibility Scale for Children with Autism Spectrum Disorder and Other Developmental Disabilities. *Autism Research : Official Journal of the International Society for Autism Research*, *13*(3), 489–499. DOI: 10.1002/aur.2257 PMID: 31904198

Lim, J. M. (2020). Emotion regulation and intervention in adults with autism spectrum disorder: A synthesis of the literature. *Advances in Autism*, *6*(1), 48–62. DOI: 10.1108/AIA-12-2018-0050

LoParo, D., & Waldman, I. D. (2015). The oxytocin receptor gene (OXTR) is associated with autism spectrum disorder: A meta-analysis. *Molecular Psychiatry*, *20*(5), 640–646. DOI: 10.1038/mp.2014.77 PMID: 25092245

Macari, S. L., Vernetti, A., & Chawarska, K. (2020). Attend less, fear more: Elevated distress to social threat in toddlers with autism spectrum disorder. *Autism Research : Official Journal of the International Society for Autism Research*, *14*(5), 1025–1036. DOI: 10.1002/aur.2448 PMID: 33283976

Maddox, B. B., & White, S. W. (2015). Comorbid social anxiety disorder in adults with autism spectrum disorder. *Journal of Autism and Developmental Disorders*, *45*(12), 3949–3960. DOI: 10.1007/s10803-015-2531-5 PMID: 26243138

Maisel, M. E., Stephenson, K. G., South, M., Rodgers, J., Freeston, M. H., & Gaigg, S. (2016). Modeling the cognitive mechanisms linking autism symptoms and anxiety in adults. *Journal of Abnormal Psychology*, *125*(5), 692–703. DOI: 10.1037/abn0000168 PMID: 27196436

Mazefsky, C. A., Herrington, J., Siegel, M., Scarpa, A., Maddox, B. B., Scahill, L., & White, S. W. (2013). The role of emotion regulation in autism spectrum disorder. *Journal of the American Academy of Child and Adolescent Psychiatry*, *52*(7), 679–688. DOI: 10.1016/j.jaac.2013.05.006 PMID: 23800481

Miller, M., Bales, K. L., Taylor, S. L., Yoon, J. H., Hostetler, C. M., Carter, C. S., & Solomon, M. (2013). Oxytocin and vasopressin in children and adolescents with autism spectrum disorders: Sex differences and associations with symptoms. *Autism Research : Official Journal of the International Society for Autism Research*, *6*(2), 91–102. DOI: 10.1002/aur.1270 PMID: 23413037

Milosavljevic, B., Leno, V. C., Simonoff, E., Baird, G., Pickles, A., Jones, C. R. G., Erskine, C., Charman, T., & Happé, F. (2015). Alexithymia in Adolescents with Autism Spectrum Disorder: Its Relationship to Internalising Difficulties, Sensory Modulation and Social Cognition. *Journal of Autism and Developmental Disorders*, *46*(4), 1354–1367. DOI: 10.1007/s10803-015-2670-8 PMID: 26659552

Mingins, J. E., Tarver, J., Waite, J., Jones, C., & Surtees, A. (2020). Anxiety and intellectual functioning in autistic children: A systematic review and meta-analysis. *Autism : The International Journal of Research and Practice*, *25*(1), 18–32. DOI: 10.1177/1362361320953253 PMID: 33198481

Misra, D. P., & Agarwal, V. (2018). Systematic Reviews: Challenges for Their Justification, Related Comprehensive Searches, and Implications. *Journal of Korean Medical Science*, *33*(12), e92. Advance online publication. DOI: 10.3346/jkms.2018.33.e92 PMID: 29542301

Montaser, J., Umeano, L., Pujari, H. P., Nasiri, S. M. Z., Parisapogu, A., Shah, A., & Khan, S. (2023). Correlations Between the Development of Social Anxiety and Individuals With Autism Spectrum Disorder: A Systematic Review. *Cureus*, *15*(9), e44841. DOI: 10.7759/cureus.44841 PMID: 37809175

Morie, K. P., Jackson, S. L. J., Zhai, Z. W., Potenza, M. N., & Dritschel, B. (2019). Mood Disorders in High-Functioning Autism: The Importance of Alexithymia and Emotional Regulation. *Journal of Autism and Developmental Disorders*, *49*(7), 2935–2945. DOI: 10.1007/s10803-019-04020-1 PMID: 31028592

Mul, C., Stagg, S. D., Herbelin, B., & Aspell, J. E. (2018). The Feeling of Me Feeling for You: Interoception, Alexithymia and Empathy in Autism. *Journal of Autism and Developmental Disorders*, *48*(9), 2953–2967. DOI: 10.1007/s10803-018-3564-3 PMID: 29644587

Murphy, C. M., Deeley, Q., Daly, E., Ecker, C., O'Brien, F. M., Hallahan, B., Loth, E., Toal, F., Reed, S., Hales, S., Robertson, D. M., Craig, M. C., Mullins, D., Barker, G. J., Lavender, T., Johnston, P., Murphy, K. C., & Murphy, D. (2011). Anatomy and aging of the amygdala and hippocampus in autism spectrum disorder: An in vivo magnetic resonance imaging study of asperger syndrome. *Autism Research : Official Journal of the International Society for Autism Research*, *5*(1), 3–12. DOI: 10.1002/aur.227 PMID: 21948742

Ni, H., Lin, H., Tseng, W. I., & Gau, S. S. (2020). Association of self-regulation with white matter correlates in boys with and without autism spectrum disorder. *Scientific Reports*, *10*(1), 13811. Advance online publication. DOI: 10.1038/s41598-020-70836-y PMID: 32796900

Nigg, J. T. (2016). Annual Research Review: On the relations among self-regulation, self-control, executive functioning, effortful control, cognitive control, impulsivity, risk-taking, and inhibition for developmental psychopathology. *Journal of Child Psychology and Psychiatry, and Allied Disciplines*, *58*(4), 361–383. DOI: 10.1111/jcpp.12675 PMID: 28035675

Nordin, V., Palmgren, M., Lindbladh, A., Bölte, S., & Jonsson, U. (2024). School absenteeism in autistic children and adolescents: A scoping review. *Autism : The International Journal of Research and Practice*, *28*(7), 1622–1637. DOI: 10.1177/13623613231217409 PMID: 38159071

Oakley, B., Jones, E. J. H., Crawley, D., Charman, T., Buitelaar, J. K., Tillmann, J., Murphy, D., & Loth, E. (2020). Alexithymia in autism: Cross-sectional and longitudinal associations with social-communication difficulties, anxiety and depression symptoms. *Psychological Medicine*, *52*(8), 1458–1470. DOI: 10.1017/S0033291720003244 PMID: 33028432

Ozsivadjian, A., Hollocks, M. J., Magiati, I., Happé, F., Baird, G., & Absoud, M. (2020). Is cognitive inflexibility a missing link? The role of cognitive inflexibility, alexithymia and intolerance of uncertainty in externalising and internalising behaviours in young people with autism spectrum disorder. *Journal of Child Psychology and Psychiatry, and Allied Disciplines*, *62*(6), 715–724. DOI: 10.1111/jcpp.13295 PMID: 32827150

Patil, O., & Kaple, M. (2023). Sensory Processing Differences in Individuals With Autism Spectrum Disorder: A Narrative Review of Underlying Mechanisms and Sensory-Based Interventions. *Cureus*, *15*(10), e48020. DOI: 10.7759/cureus.48020 PMID: 38034138

Peters-Scheffer, N., Didden, R., Sigafoos, J., Green, V. A., & Korzilius, H. (2013). Behavioral flexibility in children with autism spectrum disorder and intellectual disability. *Research in Autism Spectrum Disorders*, *7*(6), 699–709. DOI: 10.1016/j.rasd.2013.02.016

Pini, S., Nardi, B., Carpita, B., Amatori, G., Cremone, I. M., & Dell'Osso, L. (2025). Relevance of separation anxiety in the autism spectrum and related disorders. *Journal of Psychopathology*, *31*. Advance online publication. DOI: 10.36148/2284-0249-N615

Pouretemad, H. R., Sadeghi, S., Badv, R. S., & Brand, S. (2022). Differentiating Post–Digital Nannying Autism Syndrome from Autism Spectrum Disorders in Young Children: A Comparative Cross-Sectional Study. *Journal of Clinical Medicine*, *11*(22), 6786. DOI: 10.3390/jcm11226786 PMID: 36431264

Reid, R., Mason, L., & Asaro-Saddler, K. (2013). Self-regulation strategies for students with autism spectrum disorder. In *Interventions for autism spectrum disorders: Translating science into practice* (pp. 257–281). Springer New York., DOI: 10.1007/978-1-4614-5301-7_13

Renno, P., & Wood, J. (2013). Discriminant and convergent validity of the anxiety construct in children with autism spectrum disorders. *Journal of Autism and Developmental Disorders*, *43*(9), 2135–2146. DOI: 10.1007/s10803-013-1767-1 PMID: 23354538

Ridderinkhof, A., de Bruin, E. I., van den Driesschen, S., & Bögels, S. M. (2020). Attention in Children With Autism Spectrum Disorder and the Effects of a Mindfulness-Based Program. *Journal of Attention Disorders, 24*(5), 681–692. DOI: 10.1177/1087054718797428 PMID: 30222027

Rodgers, J., Wigham, S., McConachie, H., Freeston, M., Honey, E., & Parr, J. (2016). Development of the anxiety scale for children with autism spectrum disorder (asc-asd). *Autism Research : Official Journal of the International Society for Autism Research, 9*(11), 1205–1215. DOI: 10.1002/aur.1603 PMID: 26887910

Rostami, M., & Saadati, N. (2018). Role of maternal parenting styles in predicting oppositional defiant, behavior, conduct, mood, and separation anxiety disorders among students. *Journal of Research and Health, 8*(5), 418–424. DOI: 10.29252/jrh.8.5.418

Sáez-Suanes, G. P. (2024). Mood Alternations on the Autistic Spectrum. *The Palgrave Encyclopedia of Disability*, 1-13. https://doi.org/DOI: 10.1007/978-3-031-40858-8_5-1

Sahuquillo-Leal, R., Perea, M., Moreno-Giménez, A., Salmerón, L., Andreu, J., Pons, D., Vento, M., & García-Blanco, A. (2025). Emotional face processing in autism spectrum condition: A study of attentional orienting and inhibitory control. *Journal of Autism and Developmental Disorders, 55*(2), 440–448. DOI: 10.1007/s10803-023-06200-6 PMID: 38238508

Samson, A. C., Hardan, A. Y., Podell, R. W., Phillips, J. M., & Gross, J. J. (2014). Emotion Regulation in Children and Adolescents With Autism Spectrum Disorder. *Autism Research : Official Journal of the International Society for Autism Research, 8*(1), 9–18. DOI: 10.1002/aur.1387 PMID: 24863869

Sarmukadam, K., Bitsika, V., & Sharpley, C. F. (2023). Frontoparietal connectivity, sensory features, and anxiety in children and adolescents with autism spectrum disorder. *Advances in Neurodevelopmental Disorders, 7*(1), 14–26. DOI: 10.1007/s41252-022-00271-9

Scatliffe, N., Casavant, S. G., Vittner, D., & Cong, X. (2019). Oxytocin and early parent-infant interactions: A systematic review. *International Journal of Nursing Sciences, 6*(4), 445–453. DOI: 10.1016/j.ijnss.2019.09.009 PMID: 31728399

Schiltz, H. K., & Magnus, B. E. (2021). Differential Item Functioning Based on Autism Features, IQ, and Age on the Screen for Child Anxiety Related Disorders (SCARED) Among Youth on the Autism Spectrum. *Autism Research : Official Journal of the International Society for Autism Research, 14*(6), 1220–1236. DOI: 10.1002/aur.2481 PMID: 33543824

Seeley, W. W. (2019). The salience network: A neural system for perceiving and responding to homeostatic demands. *The Journal of Neuroscience : The Official Journal of the Society for Neuroscience*, *39*(50), 9878–9882. DOI: 10.1523/JNEUROSCI.1138-17.2019 PMID: 31676604

Sethi, C., Harrop, C., Zhang, W., Pritchett, J., Whitten, A., & Boyd, B. A. (2018). Parent and professional perspectives on behavioral inflexibility in autism spectrum disorders: A qualitative study. *Autism : The International Journal of Research and Practice*, *23*(5), 1236–1248. DOI: 10.1177/1362361318810217 PMID: 30394796

Shaffer, R. C., Schmitt, L., Reisinger, D. L., Coffman, M. C., Horn, P. S., Goodwin, M. S., Mazefsky, C. A., Randall, S., & Erickson, C. A. (2022). Regulating Together: Emotion Dysregulation Group Treatment for ASD Youth and Their Caregivers. *Journal of Autism and Developmental Disorders*, *53*(5), 1942–1962. DOI: 10.1007/s10803-022-05461-x PMID: 35141815

Shear, K., Jin, R., Ruscio, A. M., Walters, E. E., & Kessler, R. C. (2006). Prevalence and correlates of estimated dsm-iv child and adult separation anxiety disorder in the national comorbidity survey replication. *The American Journal of Psychiatry*, *163*(6), 1074–1083. DOI: 10.1176/ajp.2006.163.6.1074 PMID: 16741209

Solomon, M., Ozonoff, S., Ursu, S., Ravizza, S., Cummings, N., Ly, S., & Carter, C. (2009). The neural substrates of cognitive control deficits in autism spectrum disorders. *Neuropsychologia*, *47*(12), 2515–2526. DOI: 10.1016/j.neuropsychologia.2009.04.019 PMID: 19410583

Sörnyei, D., Vass, Á., Németh, D., & Farkas, K. (2023). Autistic and schizotypal traits exhibit similarities in their impact on mentalization and adult attachment impairments. https://doi.org/DOI: 10.31234/osf.io/8ga3f

South, M., Chamberlain, P. D., Wigham, S., Newton, T., Le Couteur, A., McConachie, H., Gray, L., Freeston, M., Parr, J., Kirwan, C. B., & Rodgers, J. (2014). Enhanced decision making and risk avoidance in high-functioning autism spectrum disorder. *Neuropsychology*, *28*(2), 222–228. DOI: 10.1037/neu0000016 PMID: 24219603

South, M., & Rodgers, J. (2017). Sensory, Emotional and Cognitive Contributions to Anxiety in Autism Spectrum Disorders. *Frontiers in Human Neuroscience*, *11*, 20. DOI: 10.3389/fnhum.2017.00020 PMID: 28174531

Sowden, S., Koehne, S., Catmur, C., Dziobek, I., & Bird, G. (2015). Intact automatic imitation and typical spatial compatibility in autism spectrum disorder: Challenging the broken mirror theory. *Autism Research : Official Journal of the International Society for Autism Research*, *9*(2), 292–300. DOI: 10.1002/aur.1511 PMID: 26112060

Spreng, R. N., Stevens, W. D., Chamberlain, J., Gilmore, A. W., & Schacter, D. L. (2010). Default network activity, coupled with the frontoparietal control network, supports goal-directed cognition. *NeuroImage*, *53*(1), 303–317. DOI: 10.1016/j.neuroimage.2010.06.016 PMID: 20600998

Supekar, K., Iyer, T., & Menon, V. (2017). The influence of sex and age on prevalence rates of comorbid conditions in autism. *Autism Research : Official Journal of the International Society for Autism Research*, *10*(5), 778–789. DOI: 10.1002/aur.1741 PMID: 28188687

Tsang, T. W., Kohn, M., Efron, D., Clarke, S. D., Clark, C. R., Lamb, C., & Williams, L. M. (2012). Anxiety in young people with adhd. *Journal of Attention Disorders*, *19*(1), 18–26. DOI: 10.1177/1087054712446830 PMID: 22713359

Uddin, L. Q., Supekar, K., Lynch, C. J., Khouzam, A., Phillips, J. M., Feinstein, C., Ryali, S., & Menon, V. (2013). Salience network–based classification and prediction of symptom severity in children with autism. *JAMA Psychiatry*, *70*(8), 869. DOI: 10.1001/jamapsychiatry.2013.104 PMID: 23803651

Ung, D., Arnold, E. B., Nadai, A. S. D., Lewin, A. B., Phares, V., Murphy, T. K., & Storch, E. A. (2013). Inter-rater Reliability of the Anxiety Disorders Interview Schedule for DSM-IV in High-Functioning Youth with Autism Spectrum Disorder. *Journal of Developmental and Physical Disabilities*, *26*(1), 53–65. DOI: 10.1007/s10882-013-9343-3 PMID: 24683302

Üstün, N. S. G., Gümüş, Ş. N., & Soylu, N. (2023). Oxytocin Levels in Children with Separation Anxiety and Their Mothers before and after Treatment. *Clinical Psychopharmacology and Neuroscience : The Official Scientific Journal of the Korean College of Neuropsychopharmacology*, *21*(3), 499–515. DOI: 10.9758/cpn.22.1008 PMID: 37424418

van Steensel, F. J., Bögels, S. M., & Perrin, S. (2011). Anxiety disorders in children and adolescents with autistic spectrum disorders: A meta-analysis. *Clinical Child and Family Psychology Review*, *14*(3), 302–317. DOI: 10.1007/s10567-011-0097-0 PMID: 21735077

Vincenzo, C. D. (2026). Pediatric obsessive–compulsive disorder as a developmental disorder of cognitive–emotional control: A transdiagnostic and family-integrated perspective. *Frontiers in Psychiatry*, *16*, 1750938. Advance online publication. DOI: 10.3389/fpsyt.2025.1750938 PMID: 41625616

Vogan, V. M., Leung, R. C., Safar, K., Martinussen, R., Smith, M. L., & Taylor, M. J. (2018). Longitudinal Examination of Everyday Executive Functioning in Children With ASD: Relations With Social, Emotional, and Behavioral Functioning Over Time. *Frontiers in Psychology*, *9*, 1774. Advance online publication. DOI: 10.3389/fpsyg.2018.01774 PMID: 30364134

White, S. W., Mazefsky, C. A., Dichter, G. S., Chiu, P. H., Richey, J. A., & Ollendick, T. H. (2014). Social-cognitive, physiological, and neural mechanisms underlying emotion regulation impairments: Understanding anxiety in autism spectrum disorder. *International Journal of Developmental Neuroscience : The Official Journal of the International Society for Developmental Neuroscience*, *39*(1), 22–36. DOI: 10.1016/j.ijdevneu.2014.05.012 PMID: 24951837

Wijnhoven, L. A. M. W., Creemers, D. H. M., Vermulst, A. A., & Granic, I. (2018). Prevalence and Risk Factors of Anxiety in a Clinical Dutch Sample of Children with an Autism Spectrum Disorder. *Frontiers in Psychiatry*, *9*, 50. Advance online publication. DOI: 10.3389/fpsyt.2018.00050 PMID: 29551982

Williams, Z. J., Suzman, E., & Woynaroski, T. G. (2021). Prevalence of decreased sound tolerance (hyperacusis) in individuals with autism spectrum disorder: A meta-analysis. *Ear and Hearing*, *42*(5), 1137–1150. DOI: 10.1097/AUD.0000000000001005 PMID: 33577214

Wiltgen, B., Sanders, M., Anagnostaras, S., Sage, J., & Fanselow, M. (2006). Context fear learning in the absence of the hippocampus. *The Journal of Neuroscience : The Official Journal of the Society for Neuroscience*, *26*(20), 5484–5491. DOI: 10.1523/JNEUROSCI.2685-05.2006 PMID: 16707800

Wu, M., Joubran, E., Kumar, D., Assadi, N. D., & Nguyen, H. M. (2023). Variations in anxiety and related psychiatric comorbidity levels among youths with individual diagnoses of autism spectrum disorder or attention deficit hyperactivity disorder and those with both diagnoses. *Cureus*. Advance online publication. DOI: 10.7759/cureus.41759 PMID: 37575727

Xu, J., Dam, N. T. V., Feng, C., Luo, Y., Ai, H., Gu, R., & Xu, P. (2019). Anxious brain networks: A coordinate-based activation likelihood estimation meta-analysis of resting-state functional connectivity studies in anxiety. *Neuroscience and Biobehavioral Reviews*, *96*, 21–30. DOI: 10.1016/j.neubiorev.2018.11.005 PMID: 30452934

Yang, S., Dong, X., Guo, X., Han, Y., Song, H., Gao, L., Dai, W., Su, Y., & Zhang, X. (2017). Serum oxytocin levels and an oxytocin receptor gene polymorphism (rs2254298) indicate social deficits in children and adolescents with autism spectrum disorders. *Frontiers in Neuroscience*, *11*, 221. Advance online publication. DOI: 10.3389/fnins.2017.00221 PMID: 28484366

Yarger, H. A., Nordahl, C. W., & Redcay, E. (2022). Examining Associations Between Amygdala Volumes and Anxiety Symptoms in Autism Spectrum Disorder. *Biological Psychiatry. Cognitive Neuroscience and Neuroimaging*, *7*(9), 916–924. DOI: 10.1016/j.bpsc.2021.10.010 PMID: 34688922

Yuan, S., Wu, H., Wu, Y., Xu, H., Yu, J., Zhong, Y., Zhang, N., Li, J., Xu, Q., & Wang, C. (2022). Neural effects of cognitive behavioral therapy in psychiatric disorders: A systematic review and activation likelihood estimation meta-analysis. *Frontiers in Psychology*, *13*, 853804. Advance online publication. DOI: 10.3389/fpsyg.2022.853804 PMID: 35592157

Chapter 10

Social Cognition and Core Cognitive Processes in Neurodevelopmental Disorders:

Exploring Theory of Mind, Attention, Memory, Executive Functions, and Language

Kalliopi Megari
http://orcid.org/0000-0002-5861-7199
University of York Europe Campus, Greece & University of Western Macedonia, Greece

Nikoleta Tsompanidou
University of York Europe Campus, Greece

ABSTRACT

This chapter provides an in-depth examination of the core impairments of children with Neurodevelopmental Disorders with a particular focus on Social Cognition (Theory of Mind), Attention, Memory, Executive Functions and Language. Specifically, it presents the conceptual definitions, typical developmental trajectories and underlying neuroscientific mechanisms of these domains. Synchronously, it clarifies the deviations evident in children with NDDs and emphasizes on Social Cognition as a central transdiagnostic construct to scrutinize its bidirectional relationships with Attention, Memory, Executive Functions and Language, uncovering overall

DOI: 10.4018/979-8-3373-7072-9.ch010

and disorder-specific trends. Furtherly, this paper delineates the consequences of these impairments on children's daily, social and academic functioning, mental and physical health, as well as quality of life

1. INTRODUCTION

1.1. Background Information

Neurodevelopmental Disorders (NDDs) begin in childhood and affect brain development (Morris-Rosendahl & Crocq, 2022). They are divided into Intellectual Disorder (ID), Attention-Deficit Hyperactivity Disorder (ADHD), Autism Spectrum Disorder (ASD), Communication Disorders (CDs), Specific Learning Disorders (SLDs) and Motor Disorders (MDs) (Morris-Rosendahl & Crocq, 2022). With regards to prevalence rates, the statistics are 0.63% for ID, 5–11% for ADHD, 0.70–3% for ASD, 3–10% for SLDs, 1–3.42% for CDs and 0.76–17% for MDs (Francés et al., 2023), reflecting the importance of considering NDDs as a major public health concern that affects a substantial population of children worldwide. Overall, NDDs are more evident in males rather than females, except for the inattentive subtype of ADHD, though there is the risk of potential diagnostic biases that lead to such underdiagnosis (Morris-Rosendahl & Crocq, 2022). Important to note is that core impairments exist across all NDDs in cognitive and linguistic domains that furtherly impact the individual in multiple life areas, requiring alternative intervention approaches (Peristeri et al., 2024).

1.2 Aim of Review

The aim of this narrative review is to critically examine and summarize findings on children with Neurodevelopmental Disorders with respect to core impairments in Social Cognition (Theory of Mind), Attention, Memory, Executive Functions and Language, as converging research suggests that these domains are closely interrelated (Benallie et al., 2021). Despite the expediting literature, there are several gaps in studies; (1) they solely focus on one or two domains rather than co-occurring interactions, (2) they overemphasize on NDDs like ADHD or ASD and under-represent others, (3) they insufficiently acknowledge the impairments' everyday effects and (4) they mostly present interventions aiming at one or two domains rather than multiple. Initially, to establish a solid conceptual and empirical background, this paper delineates the operational definitions of all terms, the typical developmental trajectories in neurotypical children and the neuroscientific underpinnings. Supplementary, it looks at the impairments present in children with NDDs and the links between Social Cognition (Theory of Mind) and Attention, Memory, Executive Functions and Language, drawing on both overall and disorder-specific trends. The vitality of this topic is also insinuated by presenting how these impairments affect the children's daily, social and academic functioning, mental and physical health, as well as quality of life. Finally, in order to convert theory into practice, it outlines impairment-specific and holistic intervention approaches and concludes by proposing possible future directions with regards to research, clinical practice and policies.

1.3. Method of Review

This review entailed a structured methodological framework, consisting of a pre-defined literature search strategy, explicit study selection criteria and systematic procedures for data extraction and analysis. In the literature search strategy, multiple electronic databases were consulted, including Google Scholar and Science Direct and a diverse range of keyword variations and combinations were entailed depending on each section of the paper (Table 1). Synchronously, study selection was completed by precise inclusion criteria. Eligible research papers were required to be (1) published between 2018 and 2025, (2) written in English language and (3) peer-reviewed to maintain scientific rigor. Concurrently, the screening of the research papers was conducted by reviewing their titles, abstracts and then whole text in order to confirm their relevance with the review's objectives. Furtherly, data extraction was performed systematically by reviewers who noted the study's characteristics, including sample, design, assessments and findings and then organized and synthesized the extracted information according to the review's thematic subsections.

Table 1. Literature Search Keywords

Construct	**Keywords**
Population Group	"Children" OR "Child" OR "Youth"
Disorder Group	"Neurodevelopmental Disorder" OR "Neurodevelopmental Condition" OR "NDD", "Intellectual Disorder" OR "ID", "Communication Disorder" OR "CD", "Autism Spectrum Disorder" OR "ASD", "Attention-Deficit/Hyperactivity Disorder" OR "ADHD", "Specific Learning Disorder* OR "SLD", "Motor Disorder" OR "MD"
Definition	"Definition" OR "Meaning" OR "Term"
Typical Developmental Trajectory	"Typical Development" OR "Normal Development" OR "Developmental Trajectory" OR "Development In Healthy Children" OR "Development In Neurotypical Children"
Neuroscientific Underpinning	"Neuroscience" OR "Neurobiological Basis" OR "Neural Basis" OR "Brain Parts"
Impairment	"Impairment" OR "Deficit" Or "Dysfunction" OR "Difficulty"

continued on following page

Table 1. Continued

Construct	Keywords
Association Between Domains	"Association" OR "Link" OR "Relationship"
Social Cognition	"Social Cognition" OR "SC", "Theory of Mind" OR "ToM"
Attention	"Attention", "Selective Attention", "Sustained Attention", "Divided Attention"
Memory	"Memory", "Working Memory" OR "WM", "Short-Term Memory" OR "STM", "Long-Term Memory" OR "LTM"
Executive Functions	"Executive Function" OR "EF" OR "Cognitive Flexibility"
Daily Functioning	"Daily Functioning" OR "Daily Life" OR "Daily Task" OR "Daily Activity" OR "Instrumental Activity"
Social Functioning	"Social Functioning" OR "Psychosocial Functioning" OR "Social Life" OR "Social Interactions" OR "Social Relationships" OR "Peer Relationships"
Academic Functioning	"Academic Functioning" OR "Academic Achievements" OR "School Functioning" OR "School Achievements"
Mental Health	"Mental Health" OR "Psychological Health" OR "Emotional Well-Being"
Physical Health	"Physical Health" OR "Physical Well-Being"
Quality of Life	"Quality of Life" OR "QoL"
Intervention	"Intervention" OR "Improvement" OR "Treatment"

2. SUMMARIZED RESULTS

The summarized results are distributed into four overarching thematic topics being (1) Impairments, which detail the domain's deficit characteristics, (2) Association Between Impairments, which examines the interrelationships among domains, (3) Impact of Impairments, which addresses functional and health consequences and (4) Interventions for Impairments, which synthesize evidence-based approaches.

2.1. Social Cognition

2.1.1. Definition and Typical Developmental Trajectory

Social Cognition (SC) is conceptualized as the cognitive capacity to process, perceive, interpret and respond to a social-related stimulus such as social cues, interactions and relationships (Yaşgüçlükal et al., 2024). At the same time, Theory of Mind (ToM) is referred to as the mental capacity to explain and differentiate other people's cognitive (ex. beliefs and intentions) and affective (ex. emotions and desires) mental states from their own (Yaşgüçlükal et al., 2024). Overall, ToM is present from infancy (12–18 months), as suggested by behavioural observations and violation of expectation tasks and peaks at childhood (5–6 years), as seen by false belief tasks that require understanding of others' beliefs that may be different from own or even reality (Beaudoin et al., 2020). Then, it continues to develop and refine in adolescence and adulthood, by expediting knowledge and increasing competence on complex social reasoning like interpretation of sarcasm and white lies (Beaudoin et al., 2020). Scientifically, ToM is most associated with the activation of the temporo-parietal junction, medial prefrontal and posterior parietal cortex and supramarginal, middle temporal and inferior frontal gyrus (Boccadoro et al., 2019).

2.1.2. Impairments In Children with NDDs

Subsequently, SC and ToM are considered prominent impairments in children with Neurodevelopmental Disorders, although children with Autism Spectrum Disorder have more implicit and with Attention-Deficit/Hyperactivity Disorder explicit social cognition difficulties, highlighting the heterogeneity across NDDs and importance of considering the NDD profile (Bölte, 2025). From a broader perspective, empirical studies integrating a Naturalistic Movie for the Assessment of Social Cognition (Isaksson et al., 2019) and Stories From Everyday Life Task and Reading The Mind In The Eyes Test (Pérez-Vigil et al., 2024), indicate that NDD symptom severity directly correlates with greater social cognition impairments and co-according communication and interaction challenges (Isaksson et al., 2019). Additionally, the presence of NDD corresponds to worse emotional recognition and theory of mind skills, as demonstrated with the Developmental NEuroPSYchological Assessment Battery (Pastorino et al., 2021). Holistically, experimental paradigms using the Social Attribution Task with video stimuli reveal worse social categorization and interpretation (Amorim et al., 2025) and functional magnetic resonance imaging (fMRI), atypical activation within ToM brain areas such as middle temporal and anterior cingulate gyri, as well as the bilateral middle cingulate and right supramarginal and superior temporal gyri (Vandewouw et al., 2021).

2.2. Attention

2.2.1. Definition and Typical Developmental Trajectory

Attention is broadly defined as the cognitive ability to concentrate mental resources on a specific stimulus (Vandewouw et al., 2021). Generally, attention is relatively limited in childhood (5–12 years) due to an increased vulnerability to distractions, stabilizes in early adolescence (around 12 years) and continues developing up until late adolescence (around 17 years), which is accredited to the maturation of according neural networks (Karakaş, 2024). Neuroscientifically, attention is mostly linked with the dorsal frontoparietal network, as well as brain areas responsible for sensory information receptiveness and processing (Nobre & Gresch, 2025).

2.2.2. Impairments In Children With NDDs

Thereafter, attention is a fundamental impairment in children with Neurodevelopmental Disorders. Eye-tracking methods portray compelling evidence that children with NDDs have greater selective attention in nonsocial (ex. fractals) rather than social (ex. faces) stimuli (Wang et al., 2020). Similar methods applied to sustained attention, portray longer eye fixations to irrelevant (ex. classroom objects) rather than relevant (ex. teacher) stimuli (Demirdöğen et al., 2022), worse visual–spatial sustained attention via the Track-It Task (Smolak et al., 2020) and a decrease as the level of difficulty increases during the Computerized Continuous Performance Task (Rehman et al., 2025). Overall, worse selective (Sky Search Subtest), sustained ("Score!" Subtest) and divided (Sky Search Dual Task) attention is documented with the Test of Everyday Attention for Children (McDougal et al., 2020). Also, undergoing functional Near-Infrared Spectroscopy (fNIRS) during Go/No-Go Tasks pinpoints prefrontal cortex abnormalities with activation deficits and hyperconnectivity between the motor area and the prefrontal lobe (Cui et al., 2024), while resting-state functional Magnetic Resonance Imaging (rs-fMRI) decreased spontaneous neural activity in left middle, superior and medial frontal gyrus (Zhang et al., 2025).

2.3. Memory

2.3.1. Definition and Typical Developmental Trajectory

Memory is operationalized as a cognitive modality that enables encoding, storage and retrieval of information (Mahdi & Kherbouche, 2021). Ordinarily, memory develops in childhood and peaks in adolescence, as there is a progressive improvement in memory strategies (Čepukaitytė et al., 2023). Then, from early to late adulthood it gradually declines, with the most decline occurring in aspects of working memory (Čepukaitytė et al., 2023). Neuroscientifically, memory mostly relies on the medial temporal lobe, and more specifically the hippocampus, for cellular (renewal and enhancement of synaptic connections) and system (renewal of information into hippocampus and neocortex) consolidation, while working memory additionally incorporates the prefrontal cortex (Sridhar et al., 2023).

2.3.2. Impairments In Children With NDDs

Correspondingly, memory is a key pervasive impairment in children with Neurodevelopmental Disorders. Image-based paired association learning tasks (Bui et al., 2023) and the Opposite Meanings Task (Chalmpe & Vlachos, 2025) reveal worse long-term memory, while Memory Task With Immediate Sequence Recall of Syllables worse audiovisual phonemic short-term memory (Bryłka & Cygan, 2023). Consequently, converging evidence is illustrated via tasks under functional Near Infrared Spectroscopy (fNIRS) that imply worse short-term and phonological working memory due to reduced hemodynamic response in the dorsolateral prefrontal cortex (Friedman et al., 2023). Thereafter, epidemiologic studies exhibit that 67–71% of youth with NDDs have impairments in at least one working memory domain (Liu, 2025) and comparative studies with neurotypical children demonstrate lower indices in the Wechsler Intelligence Scale for Children (Márquez-Caraveo et al., 2021) and significant lower working memory, as indicated with the Backward Digit Span (Chalmpe & Vlachos, 2025) and Odd One Out (Smolak et al., 2020) tasks.

2.4. Executive Functions

2.4.1. Definition and Typical Developmental Trajectory

Executive Functions (EFs) are a set of cognitive skills amalgamating control, coordination, organization, flexibility, planning, goal-directed behavior and problem solving (Megari, & Genova 2026). EFs are commonly classified into Hot (simple functions activated automatically) which are mainly based on the ventro-medial prefrontal cortex, and Cool (complex functions activated with abstract concepts), based on the dorso-lateral prefrontal cortex. Comprehensively, Cool executive functions are evident from 12 weeks of age and Hot executive functions encounter developmental difficulties until 2 years of life due to a self-centered mindset that averts emotional regulation and reward delay. Respectively, in childhood and preadolescence (5–11 years old) inhibitory control, concept generation and cognitive flexibility reach maturity and in adolescence (12–16 years old) strategic planning, problem-solving, decision-making and hypothesis searching. The peak of executive functions happens at early adulthood (20–30 years old) and starts declining in middle to late adulthood (53–64 years old), reflecting age-related changes in neural plasticity (Megari, & Genova 2026).

2.4.2. Impairments In Children With NDDs

Concomitantly, executive functions are vital impairments in children with Neurodevelopmental Disorders. Greater difficulties are reported in executive functions (NIH Toolbox) and cognitive flexibility (Dimensional Change Card Sort) in children with NDDs compared to healthy controls (Anning et al., 2023). Similar findings are unfolded in inhibition and shifting (NEPSY II) and verbal/visuospatial updating (E-Prime) (Crisci et al., 2021). Also, NDD symptom severity significantly correlates with executive functioning deficits (Behavior Rating Inventory of Executive Function), though impaired attention, inhibition, working memory and planning/organization is associated more with ADHD traits and set-shifting, along with holistic deficits with ASD traits (Otterman et al., 2019; Sadozai et al., 2024). Furthermore, to complement the findings of assessment-based measures, the Behavior Rating Inventory of Executive Function - Preschool Version, including parental (Pardo-Salamanca et al., 2024) and teacher observations (Herreras, 2025) verify the impairment severity, while decreased executive functions (Amsterdam Executive Function Inventory) act as the mediator between neurodevelopmental traits and academic achievement (Southon, 2022).

2.5. Language

2.5.1. Definition and Typical Developmental Trajectory

Language is a complex communication system that integrates both lectical (ex. Spoken and written form) and non-lectical (ex. gestures) components (Oviogun & Veerdee, 2020). Usually, language acquisition begins at birth, progresses rapidly during the critical period of 1–4 years old, which is characterized by heightened exposure to language with evolving speaking skills, and matures throughout the school years up until 12 years old (Al-Harbi, 2020). At the same time the time-frame of 2–12 years old is considered particularly optimal for language development due to lack of lateralization, allowing an efficient acquisition (Sholihah, 2022). Neuroscientifically, language is predominantly lateralized in the left hemisphere, although language processing is bilaterally distributed depending on the input modality. In spoken input, the auditory information is acquired by the temporal lobe (specifically by the primary auditory cortex) and processed in the Wernicke's Area for comprehension and interpretation. Then if no response is required it is redirected to brain areas associated with memory and if a response is required to the Broca's Area for speech production (Sholihah, 2022). Simultaneously, in the case of written input, the visual information is routed to the occipital lobe (specifically to the visual cortex), then to the angular gyrus for information integration, Wernicke's Area for comprehension and Broca's Area for production (Sholihah, 2022).

2.5.2. Impairments In Children With NDDs

Correspondingly, language is a profound impairment in children with Neurodevelopmental Disorders. Children with NDDs have greater language development delays, as seen with the developmental milestones from the American Academy of Pediatrics (Zoppé et al., 2025) and poorer language skills compared to typically developing peers with executive functions mediating this relationship (Méndez-Freije et al., 2023). Following, behavioral assessments highlight worse language skills via comprehension and narrative productions (Smolak et al., 2020), as well as presence of incongruences in picture-sentence associations (Dai et al., 2022). In structural language, worse phonological skills (Test for the Detection and Investigation of Reading Difficulties), morphosyntax (Diagnostic Test of Linguistic Intelligence) and expressive vocabulary (Wechsler Intelligence Scale for Children) is demonstrated as well (Andreou et al., 2025). Functionally, these deficits are evident with an overall slower language development, decreased talking, diminished vocabulary, limited word reading strategies, less production of unique words during toy play and difficulties in inferring non-direct language (ex. humor and body language) due to worse adaptive and cognitive functioning (Filipe et al., 2023; Palumbo et al., 2024).

2.6. Association Between Social Cognition and Attention, Memory, Executive Functions and Language

2.6.1. Typical Developmental Trajectory

In typically developing children, a reciprocal dynamic relationship exists between ToM and Executive Functions, Attention, Memory and Language (Forest & Amso, 2023). More specifically, despite the fact that ToM (default-mode network) and EFs (salience network) rely on distinct neurobiological mechanisms, research pinpoints the critical developmental window of 2–6 years old, whereas a rapid increase in node development and interaction strength occurs (Wade et al., 2018). In turn, this reveals certain neural overlaps and synchronization in structural and functional maturation of these networks with increased local and global functionality (Wade et al., 2018). Additionally, ToM development appears to be predicted by the maturation of other cognitive and linguistic domains (Malik & Marwaha, 2023). Attention plays a foundational role in memory processes from early infancy as it is closely interrelated with the frontal lobes' maturation (Karakaş, 2024) and EFs correspond to language skills, especially between the ages of 2–7 years old whereas reciprocality emerges and continues in the long-term (Ebert, 2020; Shahaeian et al., 2023).

2.6.2. Overall Trends in Children with NDDs

Moving on, overall trends on the association between Social Cognition and Attention, Memory, Executive Functions and Language will be denoted in children with Neurodevelopmental Disorders. Generally, NDD symptomatology severity acts as the mediator in the correlation between ToM (Comic Strip Test) and executive functions (Tower of London) (Mazza et al., 2023). Alike, greater social pragmatic problems (Social Pragmatic Problems and Receptive/Expressive Social Communication Abilities Composite) are correlated with lower executive functions (Behavior Rating Inventory), less sustained attention (Eye-Tracking Method During Videos) and worse expressive language abilities (Vineland Adaptive Behavior Scales and Expressive One-Word Picture Vocabulary Test) (Howard et al., 2023). At the same time in a co-twin control design, children with NDDs have worse ToM (Reading The Mind In The Eyes Test) due to weaker central coherence (Fragmented Pictures Test) and executive functions (Tower Test) (Isaksson et al., 2021). Ultimately, the study of Capuozzo et al. (2024) documents that children with NDDs have worse ToM (empathy, facial expression comprehension, social emotions, emotional understanding and ToM knowledge) and social cognition related language (pragmatic skills, verbal/nonverbal communication, emotional prosody, interaction skills, sincerity and sarcasm). Though, executive functions related to social cognition (emotion matching, complex social judgments, inferences, mental–physical distinction, understanding ambiguous situations, problem solving, emotional regulation, recognition of emotional faces and gestures codification) serve as a mediator (Capuozzo et al., 2024).

2.6.3. Disorder-Specific Trends In NDDs

Respectively, disorder-specific trends on the association between Social Cognition (Theory of Mind) and Attention, Memory, Executive Functions and Language will be denoted in children with Neurodevelopmental Disorders that are displayed both with parental/teacher reports and observations, as well as assessments completed by children. In Intellectual Disabilities, worse ToM specifically interrelates to executive functions deficits that disable the prediction of adaptive behaviors (Gravråkmo et al., 2022; Jacobs et al., 2020), while in Communication Disorders to weaker executive functions and language that lead to deficits in the "inner speech" (Baron & Arbel, 2022; Choo et al., 2020). Next, in ASD the greater social pragmatic and communication problems are accredited to lower executive functions and less sustained attention (Gu et al., 2024; Howard et al., 2023) and in Attention-Deficit/Hyperactivity

Disorder to worse executive functions, processing speed, sustained attention, working memory and pragmatic language (Hernández-Torres, 2019; Singh et al., 2021). Furthermore, in Specific Learning Disorders it is mostly associated with language comprehension deficits that disrupt the understanding of others' actions depending on beliefs rather than the situation (Bailey & Im-Bolter, 2024; Drljan et al., 2024), while in Motor Disorders with executive function delays and oral language (verbal fluency) deficits (Feehan & Charest, 2023; Sadozai et al., 2024).

2.7. Impact of Impairments

2.7.1. Daily Functioning of Children with NDDs

Progressing, the aforementioned impairments greatly affect the daily functioning of children with Neurodevelopmental Disorders, as implied mainly by parental reports. The Child and Adolescent Scale of Participation presents that these children have difficulties in conducting instrumental activities with respect to self (ex. hygiene routines) and house (ex. cleaning) care (Blanco-Martínez et al., 2020). Accordingly, they have complications in participating in meaningful activities related to community (ex. volunteering) and school (ex. group projects) settings (Blanco-Martínez et al., 2020). On the same note from parental perspectives, semi-structured interviews depict that the children require daily support in all routine activities (ex. school attendance or getting dressed), irrelevant of the ranging difficulty (Materula et al., 2024). Extensively, the Bruininks-Oseretsky Test of Motor Performance and Activities of Daily Living with WeeFIM, discloses that the lack of independence in daily activities is strongly interrelated with the existing coordination, motor control and balancing problems (Volkan-Yazici et al., 2018).

2.7.2. Social Functioning of Children with NDDs

Advancing, the impairments affect the social functioning of children with Neurodevelopmental Disorders. The Strengths and Difficulties Questionnaire completed by parents, as well as teachers points out prosocial behaviour and peer relationship problems that lead to limited close interpersonal relationships (Löytömäki et al., 2022). Likewise, this is explained by the existence of extended barriers throughout the process of friendship creation and maintenance, especially with healthy peers (Douglas & Josol, 2025). Additionally, another aspect is the presence of augmented arguments due to lack of interpersonal consideration and empathy, difficulties in conflict resolution due to preference of skipping arguments or ending friendships and possibility of unintentional aggressive and bullying behaviors, as indicated by the Friendship Quality Questionnaire (Kouvava et al., 2025). Moreover, the

Multi-Response Racial Attitude Task exhibits higher implicit and explicit prejudicial attitudes due to decreased cognitive flexibility (Hoyo et al., 2019). Hence, in the long-term all these aspects may lead to loneliness and social isolation which complicates psychosocial development throughout the school years and persists in adulthood (Kwan et al., 2020).

2.7.3. Academic Functioning of Children With NDDs

Continuing, the impairments affect the academic functioning of children with Neurodevelopmental Disorders. Some highlights are poor school attendance, academic skills and achievements with the inability to achieve academic goals eliciting frustration and stress, decreasing internal motivation and worsening the NDD symptomatology severity (Abín et al., 2024; Russell, 2022). In addition, lower school achievement is linked to less classroom participation and school attendance, as well as negative relationships with teachers (Carlberg & Granlund, 2018). When delving into precise basic and complex academic skills, assessments detect worse reading (word recognition and comprehension), writing (spelling and composition) and math (calculation and problem-solving) scores (Trane & Willcutt, 2022), with standardized tests confirming worse arithmetic (Arithmetic Tests) and reading (Reading Tests) skills (Kloo et al., 2022). Longitudinally the lower grades in language and mathematics are especially evident in the start rather than the end of secondary school (Lange-Küttner et al., 2025).

2.7.4. Mental and Physical Health of Children with NDDs

Substantially, the impairments affect the mental and physical health of children with Neurodevelopmental Disorders. A longitudinal study unfolds extensive mental health problems with the Strength and Difficulties Questionnaire and worse well-being with the Mental Health Continuum (Augustine et al., 2021). Co-accordingly, a large cohort study based on parental reports of their child's official diagnoses documents that NDD diagnosis is associated with anxiety and depression and the existence of multiple NDDs with greater impairments, as well as anxiety and depression severity (Zhou et al., 2026). This is explained by the daily, social and academic functioning impairments limiting the sense of hope, coherence, self-esteem and independence in covering basic psychological needs (Kwan et al., 2020). Extensively, physical complications are evident via national surveys demonstrating chronic physical pain such as headaches and back or body pain (Xie et al., 2025) and parental interviews uncovering epilepsy, migraine, asthma, diarrhea, constipation, daytime enuresis and encopresis (Alabaf et al., 2018).

2.7.5. Quality of Life of Children with NDDs

On an extensive note, the NDD symptomatology, along with the impairments, alter the quality of life of children with Neurodevelopmental Disorders. Parent-reported quality of life measured with the Pediatric Quality of Life Inventory 4.0 Generic Core Scale (Alam et al., 2025), alongside with child self-reports using the KIDSCREEN–52 (Coales et al., 2019) consistently suggest lower physical, social, emotional and school functioning. However, essential to mention is that the quality of life level is often nuanced based on the informant's perception and interpretation. As an example, a discrepancy exists between parental and children's scores, meaning that parents of children with NDDs tend to attribute lower scores across all quality of life domains, than the actual children (Kumar et al., 2025). Analogously, parents' self-reported lower quality of life via semi-structured interviews (Faden et al., 2023) and standardized instruments like the Short Form–12 Health Survey (Lobato-Ruiz et al., 2025) furtherly mirrors the parents' state and explains the according bidirectional relationship that exists with the children' s state.

2.8. Interventions

2.8.1. Social Cognition Interventions for Children with NDDs

A 15-session Social Skills Group Training with/without parent/teacher involvement, following the Cognitive-Behavioural Therapy format of conversation, homework review, topic introduction, role play, new homework and play time, shows improvements in social functioning (Vineland Adaptive Behavior Scales) and skills (ESTIA Training-Specific Skills), as well as frequency of general social skills (Social Skills Rating Scale) (Dekke et al., 2018). Similarly, a 14-week online Programme For Education and Enrichment of Relational Skills for both NDD children and their parents with homework review, didactic lessons, role-plays and behavioral exercises also uncovers improvements in social performance (Quality of Socialization Questionnaire) and knowledge (Test of Adolescent Social Skills Knowledge) (Fatta et al., 2024). Other two 10-week group-based programmes, the Socio-Dramatic Affective-Relational Intervention with acting games and Fun Activities For Children and Teens with recreational activities, portrays amelioration in emotion recognition (Diagnostic Analyses of Nonverbal Accuracy), peer interactions (Social Interaction Observation Scale), reciprocal friendships (Peer-Reported Sociometric Interview) and social skills (Social Skills Improvement System) (Kang et al., 2025). Integrating virtual reality, a 4-week Virtual School Environment and Daily Living Skills Intervention with interactive everyday tasks within a 3D school environment prompts social skills (Social Skills Questionnaire) (Li et al., 2025).

2.8.2. Attention Interventions for Children with NDDs

Simultaneously, there are numerous interventions targeting Attention in children with Neurodevelopmental Disorders. A 5-week Digital Intervention with home-administered tasks via touchscreen tablets shows enhanced attention (Test of Variables of Attention and Attention Comparison Score) (Kirk et al., 2024), while the online Attentive Rehabilitation and Improvement of Attention Intervention based on storytelling enhanced sustained attention (Continuous Performance Test) (Nejati & Derakhshan, 2024). Similarly, a 6-week Cognitive Attention Training "Keeping Score" Intervention with an online interactive table tennis game whereas scores are kept mentally, demonstrates slight, though non-significant, sustained attention capacity enhancement (Test of Everyday Attention for Children) (Slattery et al., 2023) and a 9-session Gaze-Contingent Attention Training with training games, again slight elevation in attention, through parental reports (Infant Behavior Questionnaire), observations (Laboratory Temperament Assessment Battery) and physiological measures (Eye-Tracker) (Goodwin et al., 2021).

2.8.3. Memory Interventions for NDDs

Substantially, there are many interventions targeting Memory in children with Neurodevelopmental Disorders, though the primary focus is on working memory. The 8-week Cogmed Working Memory Training with personalized/non-personalized coaching and verbal/visual WM online tasks discloses improvement in working memory performance (Working Memory Test Battery for Children), as well as academic outcomes (Speed Reading and Math Test scores) (Roording-Ragetlie et al., 2023). The same intervention in a 5-week format also projects WM improvements via a greater range of monitoring tests; Leiter-R Spatial Memory Subtest, Stanford Binet 5 Block Span Subtest and WISC-IV Digit Span Backward Subtest (Calub et al., 2022). Continuing, a 8-week school-based Working Memory Training Intervention under teacher supervision with introduction and implementation of behavioral strategies via pencil-and-paper games, greatly ameliorates working memory, as seen with the Forward and Backward Digit Span Test, Selective Working Memory Test, Walk-No Walk Test and Matching Figures Test (Capodieci et al., 2018).

2.8.4. Executive Functions Interventions for Children with NDDs

Next, there are abundant interventions targeting Executive Functions in children with Neurodevelopmental Disorders. The 20-session Maltti Intervention with a three-phase programme of cognitive and behavioral tasks accompanied with stop and go signals, tokens and pleasant activities enhances executive functioning (ATTEX

Questionnaire) (Paananen et al., 2022). In the same manner, the 4-week Brain Fit Intervention with home-administered attention tasks via touchscreen tablets increases executive function skills (Behavior Rating Inventory of Executive Function Scale) (Zhao et al., 2024). In addition, a 8-week Executive Function Training Intervention exhibits slight, but non-significant improvement in executive functions (NEPSY Second Edition and Behavior Rating Inventory of Executive Function – Preschool Version) (Shuai et al., 2020), while the same programme at a 9-week format significant improvements via the Corsi Block-Tapping Tasks (Trinczer & Shalev, 2024).

2.8.5. Language Interventions for Children with NDDs

Eventually, there are various interventions targeting Language in children with Neurodevelopmental Disorders. A 24-session face-to-face Pragmatic Intervention Programme in educational settings using activities for children and feedback to parents highlights great parental satisfaction (Satisfaction Survey) in the programme's appropriateness and effectiveness in improving the children's pragmatic language skills (Pereira et al., 2025). Co-accordingly, a 39-session Complex Syntax Intervention (Recast Therapy and Robust Vocabulary/Phonological Awareness Intervention) also supports an improvement in language production and performance via science and language content tests (Owen et al., 2023). Analogously, a 6-month Conventional Language Intervention with pictures, flashcards, and objects, as well as a combination with the Let's Learn Computer Program with auditory, visual, and tactile inputs, shows that the combined programme improves receptive, expressive, and total language skills (Receptive Expressive Arabic Language Scale) (Sami & Tarek, 2025). Another multi-modal 3-month Early Language Intervention with tailored individual (language tasks), group (daily activities, educational play, language stimulation and practice) and parental (group/home meetings and psycho-education) programmes, depicts receptive syntax (Schlichting Receptive Language Test) and expressive language (Schlichting Expressive Language Test) improvement (Vermeij et al., 2023).

2.8.6. Holistic Interventions for Children with NDDs

Thereafter, there are holistic interventions for children with Neurodevelopmental Disorders, though most are based on multi-dimensional cognitive training. An 8-week Targeted Cognitive Training Intervention with 33 digital tasks unfolds perception (Time Selection, Paper Folding and Random Dot Motion Task), attention (Flanker and Vigilance Task), memory (K-Score and Digit Span Forward Task), executive function (Go/No-Go and Digit Span Backward Task) and social cognition (Emotion Recognition Task) improvements (Dang et al., 2025). Likewise, a 12-Week Cognitive Stimulation Program with divergent tasks validates an improvement in social cognition (Neuropsychological Evaluation Battery), attention (Nesplora Aula School), working memory (Nesplora Ice Cream), executive functions (Nesplora Aula School and Nesplora Ice Cream) and language (TOKEN Test, Test of Verbal Fluency and Inter-American Reading Series) skills (Rodríguez-Prieto et al., 2024). Alternatively, a 12-week Gymnastics Intervention with aerobic exercises scheduled 3 times/week improves inhibitory control (Stroop Task), working memory (Self-Ordered Pointing Task) and cognitive flexibility (Wisconsin Card Sorting Task) (Deng et al., 2025), while a 6-month Pivotal Response Intervention for Social Motivation, social responsiveness and expressive language as suggested by video recordings during parent-child plays (Barrett et al., 2020).

3. DISCUSSION

3.1. Findings and Observations

Respectively, the findings across the four dimensions reveal some noteworthy and subsisting tendencies. Regarding the impairments, the reviewed studies homogeneously report that children with NDDs have higher impairments than their typically developing peers in the constructs of social cognition, attention, memory, executive functions and language, as well as their subtypes. Though, when examining the association between impairments, Social Cognition appears to relate more strongly to different cognitive or linguistic domains, depending on the NDD profile. Thus, this aspect suggests the existence of disorder-specific patterns of interdependence rather than a single uniform model that fits all NDDs. Simultaneously, in terms of the impact of these impairments, it is clearly evident from the literature that the difficulties affect these children's everyday functioning and health. In turn, these challenges alter not only the children, but also their parents' overall quality of life, indicating the systemic effects that exist within the family context. Finally, in interventions, findings reveal great variability across all dimensions, both when domains are separately addressed or when targeted in an integrated and multi-dimensional manner based on the children's needs. Nevertheless, particularly within the memory domain, an important pattern of methodological convergence emerges whereas research predominantly focuses on working memory rather than short-term or long-term systems and the intervention programmes adopt a very similar training format.

3.2. Critical Analysis

The study provides strong evidence that, in both typical and atypical development, social cognition—specifically, Theory of Mind (ToM)—is intricately linked to attention, memory, executive processes, and language. ToM appears to result from the coordinated development of several cognitive systems rather than operating as a separate construct. According to developmental data, the years between the ages of two and six are particularly important because during this time, brain networks that underpin social cognition and executive functioning rapidly mature and integrate. This supports modern theories of development that see social cognition as the result of dynamic interactions between social and cognitive processes.

This viewpoint is further supported by research from children with neurodevelopmental disorders (NDDs). Executive functions regularly show up as a key pathway connecting cognitive capacities to social comprehension across illnesses. Skills including cognitive flexibility, inhibitory control, emotional management, and problem-solving may offer the basis required for deciphering and reacting to social information, according to the consistent identification of executive functions as a mediator. Similar to this, successful socio-cognitive functioning seems to be strongly correlated with language skills, especially pragmatic language and social communication, underscoring the significance of communication in comprehending the mental states of others.

Crucially, the data shows that social cognitive deficits have wide-ranging effects that go beyond social interactions. The prevalence of social-cognitive difficulties in NDDs is demonstrated by difficulty with everyday living, academic performance, mental health, and general quality of life.

When considered as a whole, these results provide credence to a comprehensive developmental framework where social, linguistic, and cognitive domains interact with one another. Because neurodevelopment is interrelated, therapies that target executive processes, language, and social cognition all at once may be more successful than those that concentrate on individual deficiencies.

3.3. Limitations

Consequently, it is crucial to acknowledge and mention several limitations that may affect the findings' interpretation and generalizability. The substantial methodological heterogeneity across the studies in terms of design (ex. cross-sectional/ longitudinal or experimental/correlational), measurement (ex. assessment type for same construct), sample (ex. participant number and gender) and diagnosis (ex. based on diagnostic criteria of ICD-10/DSM-5 or clinician's judgement) leads to inclusion study inconsistency. Simultaneously, some studies heavily rely on self-reported data measures, especially for subjective constructs such as Quality of Life. Though, this reliance could entail various forms of bias, including recall and response bias or be under the influence of social desirability, which distorts outcomes and weakens internal validity. Another issue is language bias, as the pre-dominance of studies utilizing English language could exclude significant findings and restrict cultural diversity, leading to overgeneralization without adequately capturing information from different populations. Also, contextual insensitivity is a valuable characteristic to note as not taking into consideration social, cultural and situational factors could oversimplify complex phenomena.

3.4. Implications and Future Suggestions

Ultimately, this review's findings appraise ideas with respect to research directions, clinical practice and policy enhancement. In research directions, this paper highlights that it would be immensely innovative for a study to inspect longitudinally in the same sample how different NDDs and their subtypes cause the mentioned cognitive and linguistic impairments. Similarly, it would be productive to re-inform and create tailored interventions for diverse neuropsychological profiles that target precise impairments, while providing diverse options to cover individualized needs, in order to scrutinize their effectiveness in each case scenario. Here, a possible notion could be the integration of virtual reality and digital tools for initial training and gradual application of the acquired skills in real-life settings. In clinical practice, this chapter raises awareness on the importance of the multi-disciplinary approach in early screening and intervention of cognitive and linguistic deficits in children with NDDs in order to limit the long-lasting negative outcomes. During this process, a vital aspect is the cultural adaptation and multi-faceted collaboration between the child, family, educators and clinicians for a homogenous improvement of the child's and parent's life. Eventually, in policy enhancement, a greater focus should be given on the development of awareness and psychoeducation programmes (ex. on complications and outcomes to parents and teachers), inclusive education policies (ex. in school curriculums), accessibility to services (ex. hospitals' neurodevelopmental department) and community support networks (ex. for children and parents).

4. CONCLUSION

To sum up, a comprehensive literature review was conducted to inspect the impairments in Social Cognition (Theory of Mind), Attention, Memory, Executive Functions and Language in children with Neurodevelopmental Disorders. These domains were investigated both independently through their respective subcomponents and in combination with each other, allowing an identification of overarching and disorder-specific trends. Next, an emphasis was placed on how these impairments collectively affect the children's overall functioning and health. At last, evidence-based interventions targeting specific impairments were scrutinized, alongside with more holistic approaches that target multiple domains simultaneously. Epitomizing, by synthesizing assessment and intervention research, this review paper set an informational foundation for future directions in research and clinical practice, as well as policy enhancement.

REFERENCES

Al-Harbi, S. S. (2020). Language development and acquisition in early childhood. *Journal of Education and Learning*, *14*(1), 69–73. Advance online publication. DOI: 10.11591/edulearn.v14i1.14209

Alabaf, S., Gillberg, C., Lundström, S., Lichtenstein, P., Kerekes, N., Råstam, M., & Anckarsäter, H. (2018). Physical health in children with neurodevelopmental disorders. *Journal of Autism and Developmental Disorders*, *49*(1), 83–95. DOI: 10.1007/s10803-018-3697-4 PMID: 30043349

Alam, J., Sathi, T. A., Sobi, R. A., Mahmud, M., & Hawlader, M. D. H. (2025, October). I., & Hawlader, M. D. H. (2025). Health-related quality of life in children with neurodevelopmental disorders in Bangladesh. *Journal of Public Health Research*, *14*(4), 22799036251395264. Advance online publication. DOI: 10.1177/22799036251395264 PMID: 41246194

Amorim, K., Vandewouw, M. M., Huynh, N., de Villa, K., Safati, C., Almonte, A., Nicolson, R., Kelley, E., Crosbie, J., Brian, J., Anagnostou, E., Taylor, M. J., & Sato, J. (2025). A transdiagnostic study of theory of mind in children and youth with neurodevelopmental conditions. *Molecular Autism*, *16*(1), 37. DOI: 10.1186/s13229-025-00671-3 PMID: 40685381

Andreou, G., Lymperopoulou, V., & Aslanoglou, V. (2025). Structural language in neurodevelopmental disorders: Comparison between autism spectrum disorder (ASD) and developmental language disorder (DLD). *Frontiers in Education*, *10*, 1641303. Advance online publication. DOI: 10.3389/feduc.2025.1641303

Anning, K. L., Langley, K., Hobson, C., & Van Goozen, S. H. M. (2023). Dimensional associations between executive function processes and symptoms of ADHD, ASD, oppositional defiance and anxiety in young school-referred children. *Cortex; A Journal Devoted to the Study of the Nervous System and Behavior*, *167*, 132–147. DOI: 10.1016/j.cortex.2023.06.005 PMID: 37557009

Augustine, L., Lygnegård, F., & Granlund, M. (2021). Trajectories of participation, mental health, and mental health problems in adolescents with self-reported neurodevelopmental disorders. *Disability and Rehabilitation*, *44*(9), 1595–1608. DOI: 10.1080/09638288.2021.1955304 PMID: 34353177

Bailey, K. M., & Im-Bolter, N. (2024). Social Cognitive Processes in Children With Specific Learning Disorder: The Importance of Language. *Learning Disability Quarterly*, *48*(4), 215–226. Advance online publication. DOI: 10.1177/07319487241288531 PMID: 40979616

Baron, L. S., & Arbel, Y. (2022). Inner Speech and Executive Function in Children With Developmental Language Disorder: Implications for Assessment and Intervention. *Perspectives of the ASHA Special Interest Groups*, *7*(6), 1645–1659. DOI: 10.1044/2022_PERSP-22-00042 PMID: 38957614

Barrett, A. C., Vernon, T. W., McGarry, E. S., Holden, A. N., Bradshaw, J., Ko, J. A., Horowitz, E. J., & German, T. C. (2020). Social responsiveness and language use associated with an enhanced PRT approach for young children with ASD: Results from a pilot RCT of the PRISM model. *Research in Autism Spectrum Disorders*, *71*, 101497. DOI: 10.1016/j.rasd.2019.101497

Beaudoin, C., Leblanc, É., Gagner, C., & Beauchamp, M. H. (2020). Systematic Review and Inventory of Theory of Mind Measures for Young Children. *Frontiers in Psychology*, *10*, 2905. Advance online publication. DOI: 10.3389/fpsyg.2019.02905 PMID: 32010013

Benallie, K. J., McClain, M. B., Bakner, K. E., Roanhorse, T., & Ha, J. (2021). Executive functioning in children with ASD + ADHD and ASD + ID: A systematic review. *Research in Autism Spectrum Disorders*, *86*, 101807. DOI: 10.1016/j.rasd.2021.101807

Blanco-Martínez, N., Delgado-Lobete, L., Montes-Montes, R., Ruiz-Pérez, N., Ruiz-Pérez, M., & Santos-del-Riego, S. (2020). Participation in Everyday Activities of Children with and without Neurodevelopmental Disorders: A Cross-Sectional Study in Spain. *Children (Basel, Switzerland)*, *7*(10), 157. DOI: 10.3390/children7100157 PMID: 33019630

Boccadoro, S., Cracco, E., Hudson, A. R., Bardi, L., Nijhof, A. D., Wiersema, J. R., Brass, M., & Mueller, S. C. (2019). Defining the neural correlates of spontaneous theory of mind (ToM): An fMRI multi-study investigation. *NeuroImage*, *203*, 116193. DOI: 10.1016/j.neuroimage.2019.116193 PMID: 31525499

Bölte, S. (2025). Social cognition in autism and ADHD. *Neuroscience and Biobehavioral Reviews*, *169*, 106022. DOI: 10.1016/j.neubiorev.2025.106022 PMID: 39832687

Bryłka, M., & Cygan, H. B. (2023). VISUALLY SUPPORTED SHORT-TERM AUDITORY MEMORY IN CHILDREN WITH DEVELOPMENTAL LANGUAGE DISORDER (DLD). *Journal of Hearing Science*, *13*(1), 43–52. DOI: 10.17430/jhs/163178

Bui, T. A., Rosenfelt, C., Whitlock, K. H., Weber, S. M., Leclerq, M., Droit, A., Wiebe, S. A., Pei, J., & Bolduc, F. V. (2023). Long-term Memory Testing in Children With Typical Development and Neurodevelopmental Disorders: Remote Web-based Image Task Feasibility Study. *JMIR Pediatrics and Parenting*, *6*, e39720. DOI: 10.2196/39720 PMID: 37155237

Calub, C. A., Benyakorn, S., Sun, S., Iosif, A.-M., Boyle, L. H., Solomon, M., Hessl, D., & Schweitzer, J. B. (2022). Working Memory Training in Youth With Autism, Fragile X, and Intellectual Disability: A Pilot Study. *American Journal on Intellectual and Developmental Disabilities*, *127*(5), 369–389. DOI: 10.1352/1944-7558-127.5.369 PMID: 36018768

Capodieci, A., Gola, M. L., Cornoldi, C., & Re, A. M. (2018). Effects of a working memory training program in preschoolers with symptoms of attention-deficit/hyperactivity disorder. *Journal of Clinical and Experimental Neuropsychology*, *40*(1), 17–29. DOI: 10.1080/13803395.2017.1307946 PMID: 28332914

Capuozzo, A., Rizzato, S., Grossi, G., & Strappini, F. (2024). A Systematic Review on Social Cognition in ADHD: The Role of Language, Theory of Mind, and Executive Functions. *Brain Sciences*, *14*(11), 1117. DOI: 10.3390/brainsci14111117 PMID: 39595880

Carlberg, L., & Granlund, M. (2018). Achievement and participation in schools for young adolescents with self-reported neuropsychiatric disabilities: A cross-sectional study from the southern part of Sweden. *Scandinavian Journal of Public Health*, *47*(2), 199–206. Advance online publication. DOI: 10.1177/1403494818788415 PMID: 30070167

Čepukaitytė, G., Thom, J. L., Kallmayer, M., Nobre, A. C., & Zokaei, N. (2023). The Relationship between Short- and Long-Term Memory Is Preserved across the Age Range. *Brain Sciences*, *13*(1), 106. DOI: 10.3390/brainsci13010106 PMID: 36672087

Chalmpe, M., & Vlachos, F. (2025). WORKING AND LONG-TERM MEMORY DEFICITS IN DEVELOPMENTAL DYSLEXIA. *INTED Proceedings*, **•••**, 3482–3487. DOI: 10.21125/inted.2025.0885

Choo, A. L., Smith, S. A., & Li, H. (2020). Associations between stuttering, comorbid conditions and executive function in children: A population-based study. *BMC Psychology*, *8*(1), 113. DOI: 10.1186/s40359-020-00481-7 PMID: 33129350

Coales, C., Heaney, N., Ricketts, J., Dockrell, J. E., Lindsay, G., Palikara, O., & Charman, T. (2019). Health-related quality of life in children with autism spectrum disorders and children with developmental language disorders. *Autism & Developmental Language Impairments, 4*, 2396941519851225. Advance online publication. DOI: 10.1177/2396941519851225

Crisci, G., Caviola, S., Cardillo, R., & Mammarella, I. C. (2021). Executive Functions in Neurodevelopmental Disorders: Comorbidity Overlaps Between Attention Deficit and Hyperactivity Disorder and Specific Learning Disorders. *Frontiers in Human Neuroscience, 15*, 594234. Advance online publication. DOI: 10.3389/fnhum.2021.594234 PMID: 33732121

Cui, Z., Liang, A., Huang, H., & Ni, X. (2024). Brain Function Characteristics of Children with Attention-Deficit/Hyperactivity Disorder Aged 4-9 Years During a GO/NOGO Task: An Functional Near-Infrared Spectroscopy Study. *Neuropsychiatric Disease and Treatment, 20*, 2507–2516. DOI: 10.2147/NDT.S486656 PMID: 39691630

Dai, H., He, X., Chen, L., & Yin, C. (2022). Language impairments in children with developmental language disorder and children with high-functioning autism plus language impairment: Evidence from Chinese negative sentences. [Secondary Psychology of Language]. *Frontiers in Psychology, 13*, 926897. Advance online publication. DOI: 10.3389/fpsyg.2022.926897 PMID: 36248514

Dang, C., Zhu, Y., Luo, X., Liu, L., Feng, Y., Wu, G., Zhong, S., Wang, X., Zhang, J., Zhu, Y., Liu, S., Liu, Z., Qin, L., Ma, X., Wang, Y., Wang, X., Yang, J., Wang, C., & Sun, L. (2025). The promoting effects of digital targeted cognitive training in medication treatment for children with ADHD: A randomized controlled trial. *BMC Medicine, 23*(1), 371. DOI: 10.1186/s12916-025-04192-x PMID: 40598377

Demirdöğen, E. Y., Esin, İ. S., Turan, B., & Dursun, O. B. (2022). Assessing sustained attention of children with ADHD in a class flow video task. *Nordic Journal of Psychiatry, 76*(7), 497–506. DOI: 10.1080/08039488.2022.2064545 PMID: 35521909

Deng, C., Zhu, Z., Luo, G., Zeng, H., Jiang, X., Yu, Q., & Pan, X. (2025). Effects of gymnastics exercises on executive function in children with autism spectrum disorder aged 6 to 9 years: A pilot study of a randomized controlled trial. *Frontiers in Psychology, 16*, 1660305. Advance online publication. DOI: 10.3389/fpsyg.2025.1660305 PMID: 41221190

Douglas, S. N., & Josol, C. K. (2025). Friendship Experiences of Children With Neurodevelopmental Disabilities and Their Peers: A Meta-Synthesis. *Focus on Autism and Other Developmental Disabilities*, *40*(4), 189–199. Advance online publication. DOI: 10.1177/10883576251349208

Drljan, B., Ječmenica, N., & Buha, N. (2024). Theory of mind in children with developmental language disorder: Developmental tendencies. *Inovacije U Nastavi*, *37*(1), 43–60. DOI: 10.5937/inovacije2401043D

Ebert, S. (2020). Theory of mind, language, and reading: Developmental relations from early childhood to early adolescence. *Journal of Experimental Child Psychology*, *191*, 104739. DOI: 10.1016/j.jecp.2019.104739 PMID: 31830710

Faden, S. Y., Merdad, N., & Faden, Y. A. (2023). Parents of Children With Neurodevelopmental Disorders: A Mixed Methods Approach to Understanding Quality of Life, Stress, and Perceived Social Support. *Cureus*, *15*(4), e37356. DOI: 10.7759/cureus.37356 PMID: 37182086

Fatta, L. M., Laugeson, E. A., Bianchi, D., Laghi, F., & Scattoni, M. L. (2024). Program for the Education and Enrichment of Relational Skills (PEERS®) for Italy: A Randomized Controlled Trial of a Social Skills Intervention for Autistic Adolescents. *Journal of Autism and Developmental Disorders*, *55*(1), 202–220. DOI: 10.1007/s10803-023-06211-3 PMID: 38190054

Feehan, A., & Charest, M. (2023). A scoping review of oral language and social communication abilities in children with Tourette syndrome. *International Journal of Language & Communication Disorders*. Advance online publication. DOI: 10.1111/1460-6984.12949 PMID: 37667569

Filipe, M. G., Carvalhais, L., Abbeduto, L., & Frota, S. (2023). Editorial: Language across neurodevelopmental disorders. *Frontiers in Psychology*, *13*, 1121997. Advance online publication. DOI: 10.3389/fpsyg.2022.1121997 PMID: 36687986

Forest, T. A., & Amso, D. (2023). Neurodevelopment of Attention, Learning, and Memory Systems in Infancy. *Annual Review of Developmental Psychology*, *5*(1), 45–65. DOI: 10.1146/annurev-devpsych-120321-011300

Francés, L., Ruiz, A., Virgínia Soler, C., Fernández Francés, J., & Caules, J. (2023). Prevalence, comorbidities, and profiles of neurodevelopmental disorders according to the DSM-5-TR in children aged 6 years old in a European region. *Frontiers in Psychiatry*, *14*, 1260747. Advance online publication. DOI: 10.3389/fpsyt.2023.1260747 PMID: 38025459

Friedman, L. M., Eckrich, S. J., Rapport, M. D., Bohil, C. J., & Calub, C. A. (2023). Working and short-term memory in children with ADHD: An examination of prefrontal cortical functioning using functional Near-Infrared Spectroscopy (fNIRS). *Child Neuropsychology : A Journal on Normal and Abnormal Development in Childhood and Adolescence*, *30*(3), 462–485. DOI: 10.1080/09297049.2023.2213463 PMID: 37199502

Goodwin, A., Jones, E. J. H., Salomone, S., Mason, L., Holman, R., Begum-Ali, J., Hunt, A., Ruddock, M., Vamvakas, G., Robinson, E., Holden, C. J., Taylor, C., Smith, T. J., Sonuga-Barke, E., Bolton, P., Charman, T., Pickles, A., Wass, S., & Johnson, M. H. (2021). INTERSTAARS: Attention training for infants with elevated likelihood of developing ADHD: A proof-of-concept randomised controlled trial. *Translational Psychiatry*, *11*(1), 644. DOI: 10.1038/s41398-021-01698-9 PMID: 34930893

Gravråkmo, S., Olsen, A., Lydersen, S., Ingul, J. M., Henry, L., & Øie, M. G. (2022). Associations between executive functions, intelligence and adaptive behaviour in children and adolescents with mild intellectual disability. *Journal of Intellectual Disabilities : JOID*, *27*(3), 715–727. Advance online publication. DOI: 10.1177/17446295221095951 PMID: 35543122

Gu, T., Jin, C., Lin, L., Wang, X., Li, X., Jing, J., & Cao, M. (2024). The relationship between executive function and the association of motor coordination difficulties and social communication deficits in autistic children. [Secondary Autism]. *Frontiers in Psychiatry*, *15*, 1363406. Advance online publication. DOI: 10.3389/fpsyt.2024.1363406 PMID: 38596639

Hernández-Torres, D. (2019). Executive Functions and Social Cognition in School-Aged Children with ADHD: an Assessment Proposal. *Conference: 47th Annual Meeting of the International Neuropsychological Society*. DOI: 10.13140/RG.2.2.25450.24004

Herreras, E. B. (2025, September 14). Executive Functioning Profiles in Children with Neurodevelopmental Disorders. *Behavioral Sciences (Basel, Switzerland)*, *15*(9), 1256. DOI: 10.3390/bs15091256 PMID: 41009286

Howard, J., Herold, B., Major, S., Leahy, C., Ramseur, K.II, Franz, L., Deaver, M., Vermeer, S., Carpenter, K. L., Murias, M., Huang, W. A., & Dawson, G. (2023). Associations between executive function and attention abilities and language and social communication skills in young autistic children. *Autism : The International Journal of Research and Practice*, *27*(7), 2135–2144. Advance online publication. DOI: 10.1177/13623613231154310 PMID: 36802865

Hoyo, Á., Rueda, M. R., & Rodríguez-Bailón, R. (2019). Children's Individual Differences in Executive Function and Theory of Mind in Relation to Prejudice Toward Social Minorities. [Secondary Human Developmental Psychology]. *Frontiers in Psychology, 10*, 2293. Advance online publication. DOI: 10.3389/fpsyg.2019.02293 PMID: 31681092

Isaksson, J., Neufeld, J., & Bölte, S. (2021). What's the Link Between Theory of Mind and Other Cognitive Abilities – A Co-twin Control Design of Neurodevelopmental Disorders. [Secondary Cognitive Neuroscience]. *Frontiers in Psychology, 12*, 575100. Advance online publication. DOI: 10.3389/fpsyg.2021.575100 PMID: 34168585

Isaksson, J., Westeinde, A. V., Cauvet, É., Kuja-Halkola, R., Lundin, K., Neufeld, J., Willfors, C., & Bölte, S. (2019). Social Cognition in Autism and Other Neurodevelopmental Disorders: A Co-twin Control Study. *Journal of Autism and Developmental Disorders, 49*(7), 2838–2848. DOI: 10.1007/s10803-019-04001-4 PMID: 30972652

Jacobs, E., Simon, P., & Nader-Grosbois, N. (2020). Social Cognition in Children With Non-specific Intellectual Disabilities: An Exploratory Study. [Secondary Human Developmental Psychology]. *Frontiers in Psychology, 11*, 1884. Advance online publication. DOI: 10.3389/fpsyg.2020.01884 PMID: 32849105

Kang, E., Rosen, T. E., Keifer, C. M., Gerber, A. H., & Lerner, M. D. (2025). A single-blind active-control randomized controlled trial of group-based social competence intervention. *Scientific Reports, 15*(1), 28872. DOI: 10.1038/s41598-025-12876-w PMID: 40774996

Karakaş, S. (2024). A Review of Childhood Developmental Changes in Attention as Indexed in the Electrical Activity of the Brain. *Brain Sciences, 14*(5), 458. DOI: 10.3390/brainsci14050458 PMID: 38790437

Kirk, H. E., Richmond, S., Gaunson, T., Bennett, M., Herschtal, A., Bellgrove, M., & Cornish, K. (2024). A 5-week Digital Intervention to Reduce Attention Problems in Children With ADHD: A Double-Blind Randomized Controlled Trial. *Journal of Attention Disorders, 28*(11), 1454–1466. Advance online publication. DOI: 10.1177/10870547241256269 PMID: 38804292

Kloo, D., Osterhaus, C., Kristen-Antonow, S., & Sodian, B. (2022). The impact of theory of mind and executive function on math and reading abilities: A longitudinal study. *Infant and Child Development, 31*(6), e2356. DOI: 10.1002/icd.2356

Kouvava, S., Antonopoulou, K., Kokkinos, C. M., & Ralli, A. M. (2025). Social Understanding and Friendships in Children with Attention Deficit/Hyperactivity Disorder or Dyslexia. *Behavioral Sciences (Basel, Switzerland), 15*(2), 216. DOI: 10.3390/bs15020216 PMID: 40001849

Kumar, G., Barhoun, P., Fuelscher, I., Zwicker, J. G., Bianco, K., Singh, M., Mukherjee, M., Williams, J., & Hyde, C. (2025). Quality of life in children with developmental coordination disorder (DCD): A systematic review and meta-analysis. *Research in Developmental Disabilities, 160*, 104981. DOI: 10.1016/j.ridd.2025.104981 PMID: 40121827

Kwan, C., Gitimoghaddam, M., & Collet, J.-P. (2020). Effects of Social Isolation and Loneliness in Children with Neurodevelopmental Disabilities: A Scoping Review. *Brain Sciences, 10*(11), 786. DOI: 10.3390/brainsci10110786 PMID: 33126519

Lange-Küttner, C., Lockl, K., & Gnambs, T. (2025). ADHD and secondary school grades: Evidence from two longitudinal studies. *Current Psychology, 44*(20), 16701–16717. DOI: 10.1007/s12144-025-08324-7

Li, L., Zhu, X., Wan, S., Wang, L., Pan, L., Peng, S., & Chen, J. (2025). Research on the improvement of daily living skills of children with autism in virtual campus environments. *Scientific Reports, 15*(1), 30102. DOI: 10.1038/s41598-025-08224-7 PMID: 40820136

Liu, H. (2025). The Effect of Working Memory Deficits on Academic Performances among Children with ADHD. *Communications in Humanities Research, 55*, 42–49. https://www.ewadirect.com/proceedings/chr/article/view/21250

Lobato-Ruiz, V., Romero-Ayuso, D., Toledano-González, A., & Triviño-Juárez, J. M. (2025). Quality of life and parental stress related to executive functioning, sensory processing, and activities of daily living in children and adolescents with neurodevelopmental disorders. *PeerJ, 13*, e19326. DOI: 10.7717/peerj.19326 PMID: 40292106

Löytömäki, J., Laakso, M.-L., & Huttunen, K. (2022). Social-Emotional and Behavioural Difficulties in Children with Neurodevelopmental Disorders: Emotion Perception in Daily Life and in a Formal Assessment Context. *Journal of Autism and Developmental Disorders, 53*(12), 4744–4758. DOI: 10.1007/s10803-022-05768-9 PMID: 36184695

Mahdi, N. E. H., & Kherbouche, O. (2021). *Memory Types and Mechanisms*. ResearchGate. https://www.researchgate.net/publication/357434462_Memory_Types_and_Mechanisms

Malik, F., & Marwaha, R. (2023). *Cognitive development*. National Library of Medicine; StatPearls Publishing. https://www.ncbi.nlm.nih.gov/books/NBK537095/

Márquez-Caraveo, M. E., Rodríguez-Valentín, R., Pérez-Barrón, V., Vázquez-Salas, R. A., Sánchez-Ferrer, J. C., De Castro, F., Allen-Leigh, B., & Lazcano-Ponce, E. (2021). Children and adolescents with neurodevelopmental disorders show cognitive heterogeneity and require a person-centered approach. *Scientific Reports*, *11*(1), 18463. DOI: 10.1038/s41598-021-97551-6 PMID: 34531454

Materula, D., Currie, G., Jia, X. Y., Finlay, B., Lau, A.-M., Richard, C., Yohemas, M., Estes, M., Gall, N., Dewan, T., MacEachern, S., Gibbard, W. B., & Zwicker, J. D. (2024). Needs of children with neurodevelopmental disorders and medical complexity: Caregiver perspectives. *Research in Developmental Disabilities*, *153*, 104815. DOI: 10.1016/j.ridd.2024.104815 PMID: 39142086

Mazza, M., Attanasio, M., & Bologna, A., Ilenia Le Donne, & Valenti, M. (2023). The relationship between theory of mind, executive functioning, and repetitive behavior in high functioning autism spectrum disorder. *Journal of Psychopathology*, *1–2*. Advance online publication. DOI: 10.36148/2284-0249-N284

McDougal, E., Riby, D. M., & Hanley, M. (2020). Profiles of academic achievement and attention in children with and without Autism Spectrum Disorder. *Research in Developmental Disabilities*, *106*, 103749. DOI: 10.1016/j.ridd.2020.103749 PMID: 32858397

Megari, K., & Genova, K. D. (2026). Cognitive Pathways in Atypical Development: Executive Functions in Children With Attention-Deficit/Hyperactivity Disorder and Specific Learning Disorders. *International Journal of Developmental Neuroscience : The Official Journal of the International Society for Developmental Neuroscience*, *86*(1), e70094. DOI: 10.1002/jdn.70094 PMID: 41545901

Méndez-Freije, I., Areces, D., & Pérez, C. R. (2023). Language Skills in Children with Attention Deficit Hyperactivity Disorder and Developmental Language Disorder: A Systematic Review. *Children (Basel, Switzerland)*, *11*(1), 14. DOI: 10.3390/children11010014 PMID: 38275435

Morris-Rosendahl, D. J., & Crocq, M.-A. (2022). Neurodevelopmental disorders—The history and future of a diagnostic concept. *Dialogues in Clinical Neuroscience*, *22*(1), 65–72. DOI: 10.31887/DCNS.2020.22.1/macrocq PMID: 32699506

Nejati, V., & Derakhshan, Z. (2024). Attention Training Improves Executive Functions and Ameliorates Behavioral Symptoms in Children with Attention-Deficit Hyperactivity Disorder: Implication of Tele-Cognitive-Rehabilitation in the Era of Coronavirus Disease. *Games for Health Journal*, *13*(1), 40–49. Advance online publication. DOI: 10.1089/g4h.2023.0002 PMID: 38300525

Nobre, A. C., & Gresch, D. (2025). How the brain shifts between external and internal attention. *Neuron, 113*(15), 2382–2398. DOI: 10.1016/j.neuron.2025.06.013 PMID: 40675155

Otterman, D. L., Koopman-Verhoeff, M. E., White, T. J., Tiemeier, H., Bolhuis, K., & Jansen, P. W. (2019). Executive functioning and neurodevelopmental disorders in early childhood: A prospective population-based study. *Child and Adolescent Psychiatry and Mental Health, 13*(1), 38. DOI: 10.1186/s13034-019-0299-7 PMID: 31649749

Oviogun, P. V., & Veerdee, P. S. (2020). Definition of language and linguistics: Basic competence. *Macrolinguistics and Microlinguistics, 1*(1), 1–12. DOI: 10.21744/mami.v1n1.1

Owen, A., Curran, M., Cook, S. W., Cole, R. S., & McGregor, K. K. (2023). Teaching little kids big sentences: A randomized controlled trial showing that children with DLD respond to complex syntax intervention embedded within the context of preschool/kindergarten science instruction. *International Journal of Language & Communication Disorders, 58*(5), 1551–1569. DOI: 10.1111/1460-6984.12882 PMID: 37129110

Paananen, M., Husberg, H., Katajamäki, H., & Aro, T. (2022). School-based group intervention in attention and executive functions: Intervention response and moderators. *Frontiers in Psychology, 13*, 975856. Advance online publication. DOI: 10.3389/fpsyg.2022.975856 PMID: 36186366

Palumbo, M. L., Mody, M., Klykylo, W. M., Ballard, K. J., McDougle, C. J., & Guenther, F. H. (2024). Neurodevelopmental disorders: Speech and language disorders. In Tasman, A., Riba, M. B., Alarcón, R. D., Alfonso, C. A., Kanba, S., Lecic-Tosevski, D., Ndetei, D. M., Ng, C. H., & Schulze, T. G. (Eds.), *Tasman's Psychiatry* (pp. 1533–1559). Springer Nature Switzerland AG., DOI: 10.1007/978-3-030-51366-5_86

Pardo-Salamanca, A., Paoletti, D., Pastor-Cerezuela, G., De Stasio, S., & Berenguer, C. (2024). Executive Functioning Profiles in Neurodevelopmental Disorders: Parent–Child Outcomes. *Children (Basel, Switzerland), 11*(8), 909. DOI: 10.3390/children11080909 PMID: 39201844

Pastorino, G. M. G., Operto, F. F., Padovano, C., Vivenzio, V., Scuoppo, C., Pastorino, N., Roccella, M., Vetri, L., Carotenuto, M., & Coppola, G. (2021). Social Cognition in Neurodevelopmental Disorders and Epilepsy. [Secondary Pediatric Neurology]. *Frontiers in Neurology, 12*, 658823. Advance online publication. DOI: 10.3389/fneur.2021.658823 PMID: 33935956

Pereira, T., Ramalho, A. M., & Lousada, M. (2025). Parents' and Early Childhood Educators' Perceptions after the Implementation of the Pragmatic Intervention Programme (PICP). *Autism & Developmental Language Impairments, 10*, 23969415251330465. Advance online publication. DOI: 10.1177/23969415251330465 PMID: 40370932

Pérez-Vigil, A., Ilzarbe, D., Garcia-Delgar, B., Morer, A., Pomares, M., Puig, O., Lera-Miguel, S., Rosa, M., Romero, M., Escalona, R. C., & Lázaro, L. (2024). Theory of mind in neurodevelopmental disorders: Beyond autistic spectrum disorder. *Neurología : Publicación Oficial de la Sociedad Española de Neurología, 39*(2), 117–126. DOI: 10.1016/j.nrleng.2024.01.005 PMID: 38272257

Peristeri, E., Frantzidis, C. A., & Andreou, M. (2024). Editorial: Neural mechanisms of language and cognitive performance in individuals with neurodevelopmental disorders. *Frontiers in Psychology, 15*, 1414354. Advance online publication. DOI: 10.3389/fpsyg.2024.1414354 PMID: 38741752

Rehman, A., Heldal, I., Costescu, C., David, C., & Lin, J. C.-W. (2025). *An Adaptive Scoring Framework for Attention Assessment in NDD Children via Serious Games*. IEEE Access. https://arxiv.org/pdf/2509.08353

Rodríguez-Prieto, P., Giral-Oliveros, N. A., Simpson, I. C., & Ibáñez-Alfonso, J. A. (2024). Cognitive stimulation in socioeconomically disadvantaged children with neurodevelopmental disorders: A case series. [Secondary Pediatric Psychology]. *Frontiers in Psychology, 15*, 1365697. Advance online publication. DOI: 10.3389/fpsyg.2024.1365697 PMID: 39045438

Roording-Ragetlie, S., Pieters, S., Wennekers, E., Klip, H., Buitelaar, J. K., & Slaats-Willemse, D. (2023). Working memory training in children with neurodevelopmental disorders and intellectual disabilities, the role of coaching: A double-blind randomised controlled trial. *Journal of Intellectual Disability Research : JIDR, 67*(9), 842–859. DOI: 10.1111/jir.13047 PMID: 37313626

Russell, A. E. (2022). Neurodevelopmental Disorders and Attendance at School. In Moore, D. A., Finning, K., & Ford, T. (Eds.), *Mental Health and Attendance at School* (pp. 78–105). Cambridge University Press., https://www.cambridge.org/core/books/abs/mental-health-and-attendance-at-school/neurodevelopmental-disorders-and-attendance-at-school/DC186CBEF0D46CD6D3D92129DF78EEC6 DOI: 10.1017/9781911623151.006

Sadozai, A. K., Sun, C., Demetriou, E. A., Lampit, A., Munro, M., Perry, N., Boulton, K. A., & Guastella, A. J. (2024). Executive function in children with neurodevelopmental conditions: A systematic review and meta-analysis. *Nature Human Behaviour, 8*(12), 2357–2366. DOI: 10.1038/s41562-024-02000-9 PMID: 39424962

Sami, R., & Tarek, G. (2025). Multimodal approaches in language therapy for children with developmental language delay: Enhancing engagement and outcomes using Let's Learn Program. *The Egyptian Journal of Otolaryngology*, *41*(1), 64. DOI: 10.1186/s43163-025-00804-8

Shahaeian, A., Haynes, M., & Frick, P. J. (2023). The role of language in the association between theory of mind and executive functioning in early childhood: New longitudinal evidence. *Early Childhood Research Quarterly*, *62*, 251–258. DOI: 10.1016/j.ecresq.2022.09.003

Sholihah, R. A. (2022). Language and Brain: Neurological Aspects in Language Acquisition. *MUHARRIK: Jurnal Dakwah Dan Sosial*, *5*(1), 220–230. Advance online publication. DOI: 10.37680/muharrik.v5i1.1069

Shuai, L., Wang, Y., Li, W., Wilson, A., Wang, S., Chen, R., & Zhang, J. (2020). Executive Function Training for Preschool Children With ADHD: A Randomized Controlled Trial. *Journal of Attention Disorders*, *25*(14), 2037–2047. Advance online publication. DOI: 10.1177/1087054720956723 PMID: 32964771

Singh, J., Arun, P., & Bajaj, M. K. (2021). Theory of Mind and Executive Functions in Children With Attention Deficit Hyperactivity Disorder and Specific Learning Disorder. *Indian Journal of Psychological Medicine*, *43*(5), 392–398. Advance online publication. DOI: 10.1177/0253717621999807 PMID: 34584303

Slattery, E. J., Ryan, P., Fortune, D. G., & McAvinue, L. P. (2023). Evaluation of a School-Based Attention Training Program for Improving Sustained Attention. *Mind, Brain and Education : The Official Journal of the International Mind, Brain, and Education Society*, *18*(1), 103–124. DOI: 10.1111/mbe.12396

Smolak, E., McGregor, K. K., Arbisi-Kelm, T., & Eden, N. (2020). Sustained Attention in Developmental Language Disorder and Its Relation to Working Memory and Language. *Journal of Speech, Language, and Hearing Research: JSLHR*, *63*(12), 4096–4108. DOI: 10.1044/2020_JSLHR-20-00265 PMID: 33166200

Southon, C. (2022). The relationship between executive function, neurodevelopmental disorder traits, and academic achievement in university students. *Frontiers in Psychology*, *13*, 958013. Advance online publication. DOI: 10.3389/fpsyg.2022.958013 PMID: 36118426

Sridhar, S., Khamaj, A., & Asthana, M. K. (2023). Cognitive neuroscience perspective on memory: Overview and summary. *Frontiers in Human Neuroscience*, *17*, 1217093. Advance online publication. DOI: 10.3389/fnhum.2023.1217093 PMID: 37565054

Trane, F. E., & Willcutt, E. G. (2022). Attention-Deficit/Hyperactivity Disorder and Academic Functioning: Reading, Writing, and Math Abilities in a Community Sample of Youth with and without ADHD. *Research on Child and Adolescent Psychopathology, 51*(4), 583–596. DOI: 10.1007/s10802-022-01004-1 PMID: 36480079

Trinczer, I. L., & Shalev, L. (2024). Computerised Attention Functions Training Versus Computerised Executive Functions Training for Children with Attention Deficit/Hyperactivity Disorder: A Randomised Controlled Trial. *Journal of Clinical Medicine, 13*(23), 7239. DOI: 10.3390/jcm13237239 PMID: 39685698

Vandewouw, M. M., Safar, K., Mossad, S. I., Lu, J., Lerch, J. P., Anagnostou, E., & Taylor, M. J. (2021). Do shapes have feelings? Social attribution in children with autism spectrum disorder and attention-deficit/hyperactivity disorder. *Translational Psychiatry, 11*(1), 493. DOI: 10.1038/s41398-021-01625-y PMID: 34564704

Vermeij, B., Wiefferink, C. H., Knoors, H., & Scholte, R. H. J. (2023). Effects in language development of young children with language delay during early intervention. *Journal of Communication Disorders, 103*, 106326. DOI: 10.1016/j.jcomdis.2023.106326 PMID: 37086608

Volkan-Yazici, M., Elbasan, B., & Yazici, G. (2018). Motor Performance and Activities of Daily Living in Children with Neurodevelopmental Disorders. *Iranian Journal of Pediatrics, 28*(6), e65396. DOI: 10.5812/ijp.65396

Wade, M., Prime, H., Jenkins, J. M., Yeates, K. O., Williams, T., & Lee, K. (2018). On the relation between theory of mind and executive functioning: A developmental cognitive neuroscience perspective. *Psychonomic Bulletin & Review, 25*(6), 2119–2140. DOI: 10.3758/s13423-018-1459-0 PMID: 29619648

Wang, Q., Chang, J., & Chawarska, K. (2020). Atypical Value-Driven Selective Attention in Young Children With Autism Spectrum Disorder. *JAMA Network Open, 3*(5), e204928. DOI: 10.1001/jamanetworkopen.2020.4928 PMID: 32374399

Xie, Q., Pan, N., Ou, X., Shen, S., Jing, J., Weng, X., Shi, L., Lin, L., Yang, J., Li, X., Zhang, K., Chen, F., Wang, Y., Wu, J., & Wang, X. (2025). Chronic Physical Pain in Children With and Without Autism Spectrum Disorder in the United States: Findings from the 2016 – 2021 National Survey of Children's Health. *Journal of Autism and Developmental Disorders*. Advance online publication. DOI: 10.1007/s10803-025-06846-4 PMID: 40301196

Yaşgüçlükal, M. A., Elmalı, A. D., & Korkmaz, B. (2024). Social Cognition and Theory of Mind. *Neuropsychiatric Investigation, 62*(3), 100–108. DOI: 10.5152/NeuropsychiatricInvest.2024.24016

Zhang, Q., He, Q., & Hou, Y. (2025). A resting-state functional magnetic resonance imaging meta-analysis of differences in brain activity between children and adolescents with attention-deficit/hyperactivity disorder using activation likelihood estimation. *European Child & Adolescent Psychiatry*. Advance online publication. DOI: 10.1007/s00787-025-02906-3 PMID: 41222592

Zhao, L., Agazzi, H., Du, Y., Meng, H., Maku, R., Li, K., Aspinall, P., Garvan, C. W., & Fang, S. (2024). A Digital Cognitive-Physical Intervention for Attention-Deficit/Hyperactivity Disorder: Randomized Controlled Trial. *Journal of Medical Internet Research, 26*, e55569. DOI: 10.2196/55569 PMID: 38728075

Zhou, X., Jia, F., Bambling, M., Edirippulige, S., Whiteford, H., & Lin, J. (2026). Associations between multiple neurodevelopmental disorders and mental health in children. *Journal of Affective Disorders*, *393*, 120397. DOI: 10.1016/j.jad.2025.120397 PMID: 41072876

Zoppé, H., Trocmet, L., Rambault, A., Abtroun, Y., Defresne, D., Ansoborlo, M., Hazard, M., & Bonnet-Brilhault, F. (2025). Early detection of neurodevelopmental disorders in children with delayed milestones: Navigating between overlapping trajectories and the limits of a single-diagnosis categorical approach (A Preliminary Study for the CONDOR Cohort). *Asian Journal of Psychiatry*, *109*, 104561. DOI: 10.1016/j.ajp.2025.104561 PMID: 40466582

Compilation of References

Abhishek, F., Gugnani, J. S., Kaur, H., Damera, A. R., Mane, R., Sekhri, A., Singh, G., & Kaur, G. (2024). Dietary Interventions and Supplements for Managing Attention-Deficit/Hyperactivity Disorder (ADHD): A Systematic Review of Efficacy and Recommendations. *Cureus*, *16*(9), e69804. DOI: 10.7759/cureus.69804 PMID: 39429382

Adams, N. C., & Jarrold, C. (2012). Inhibition in Autism. Children with autism have difficulty inhibiting irrelevant distractors but not prepotent responses. *Journal of Autism and Developmental Disorders*, *42*(6), 1052–1063. DOI: 10.1007/s10803-011-1345-3 PMID: 21830170

Ahçi, Z. G., Akdeniz, S., & Harmanci, H. (2022). A Study of the Effects of Parental Attention Deficit and Hyperactivity Disorder (ADHD) and Parental Emotion Regulation Processes on Adolescent Self-Regulation Skills. *International Journal of Progressive Education*, *18*(1), 435–447. DOI: 10.29329/ijpe.2022.426.24

Ainsworth, M. D. S., Blehar, M. C., Waters, E., & Wall, S. (1978). *Patterns of attachment: A psychological study of the strange situation*. Lawrence Erlbaum Associates.

Ainsworth, M. S., & Bowlby, J. (1991). An ethological approach to personality development. *The American Psychologist*, *46*(4), 333–341. DOI: 10.1037/0003-066X.46.4.333

Akbar, M., Loomis, R., & Paul, R. (2013). The interplay of language on executive functions in children with ASD. *Research in Autism Spectrum Disorders*, *7*(3), 494–501. DOI: 10.1016/j.rasd.2012.09.001

Alabaf, S., Gillberg, C., Lundström, S., Lichtenstein, P., Kerekes, N., Råstam, M., & Anckarsäter, H. (2018). Physical health in children with neurodevelopmental disorders. *Journal of Autism and Developmental Disorders*, *49*(1), 83–95. DOI: 10.1007/s10803-018-3697-4 PMID: 30043349

Alam, J., Sathi, T. A., Sobi, R. A., Mahmud, M., & Hawlader, M. D. H. (2025, October). I., & Hawlader, M. D. H. (2025). Health-related quality of life in children with neurodevelopmental disorders in Bangladesh. *Journal of Public Health Research*, *14*(4), 22799036251395264. Advance online publication. DOI: 10.1177/22799036251395264 PMID: 41246194

Albantakis, L., Brandi, M., Zillekens, I. C., Henco, L., Weindel, L., Thaler, H., Schliephake, L., Timmermans, B., & Schilbach, L. (2020). Alexithymic and autistic traits: Relevance for comorbid depression and social phobia in adults with and without autism spectrum disorder. *Autism : The International Journal of Research and Practice*, *24*(8), 2046–2056. DOI: 10.1177/1362361320936024 PMID: 32662285

Alderson, R. M., Kasper, L. J., Hudec, K. L., & Patros, C. H. G. (2013). Attention deficit/hyperactivity disorder (ADHD) and working memory in adults: A meta-analytic review. *Neuropsychology*, *27*(3), 287–302. DOI: 10.1037/a0032371 PMID: 23688211

Al-Harbi, S. S. (2020). Language development and acquisition in early childhood. *Journal of Education and Learning*, *14*(1), 69–73. Advance online publication. DOI: 10.11591/edulearn.v14i1.14209

Almarzouki, A. F., Bellato, A., Al-Saad, M. S., & Al-Jabri, B. (2023). COGMED working memory training in children with Attention Deficit/Hyperactivity Disorder (ADHD): A feasibility study in Saudi Arabia. *Applied Neuropsychology. Child*, *12*(3), 202–213. DOI: 10.1080/21622965.2022.2070020 PMID: 35549563

Almeida, T. S., Lamb, M. E., & Weisblatt, E. J. (2019). a. Effects of delay, question type, and socioemotional support on episodic memory retrieval by children with ASD. *Journal of Autism and Developmental Disorders*, *49*(5), 1845–1858.

Almeida, T. S., Lamb, M. E., & Weisblatt, E. J. (2019). Effects of delay on episodic memory retrieval by children with autism spectrum disorder. *Applied Cognitive Psychology*, *33*(5), 814–827. DOI: 10.1002/acp.3524 PMID: 30406912

Aluğan, Z. (2024). The Impact of Early Childhood Adversity on Neurodevelopment A Comprehensive Review. Üha, 11(2), 45–59. https://doi.org/DOI: 10.32739/uha.jnbs.11.1539116

Alvey, H. M., Walters, A. S., & Noll, L. K. (2024). "Mom Just Forgot Me at a Gas Station": A Qualitative Study of Parental ADHD in the Home. *Contemporary Family Therapy*, •••, 1–19.

Al-Wardat, M., Etoom, M., Almhdawi, K. A., Hawamdeh, Z., & Khader, Y. (2024). Prevalence of attention-deficit hyperactivity disorder in children, adolescents and adults in the Middle East and North Africa region: A systematic review and meta-analysis. *BMJ Open*, *14*(1), e078849. Advance online publication. DOI: 10.1136/bmjopen-2023-078849 PMID: 38238059

American Association on Intellectual and Developmental Disabilities. (2023). *Definition of intellectual disability*. https://www.aaidd.org/intellectual-disability/definition

American Occupational Therapy Association. (2020). Occupational therapy practice framework: Domain and process (4th ed.). *American Journal of Occupational Therapy*, *74*(Suppl. 2), Article 7412410010. https://doi.org/DOI: 10.5014/ajot.2020.74S2001

American Psychiatric Association. (1952). *Diagnostic and statistical manual: Mental disorders*. American Psychiatric Association Mental Hospital Service. https://www.turkpsikiyatri.org/arsiv/dsm-1952.pdf

American Psychiatric Association. (1968). *Diagnostic and statistical manual of mental disorders* (2nd ed.). American Psychiatric Association. https://www.madinamerica.com/wp-content/uploads/2015/08/DSM-II.pdf

American Psychiatric Association. (1980). *Diagnostic and statistical manual of mental disorders* (3rd ed.). American Psychiatric Association.

American Psychiatric Association. (2017). *Multicultural guidelines: An ecological approach to context, identity, and intersectionality*. American Psychological Association.

American Psychiatric Association. (2022). *Diagnostic and statistical manual of mental disorders: DSM-5 text revision* (5th ed.). American Psychiatric Association.

American Speech-Language-Hearing Association. (2021). Speech and language disorders. *ASHA*.

Amorim, K., Vandewouw, M. M., Huynh, N., de Villa, K., Safati, C., Almonte, A., Nicolson, R., Kelley, E., Crosbie, J., Brian, J., Anagnostou, E., Taylor, M. J., & Sato, J. (2025). A transdiagnostic study of theory of mind in children and youth with neurodevelopmental conditions. *Molecular Autism*, *16*(1), 37. DOI: 10.1186/s13229-025-00671-3 PMID: 40685381

Anastopoulos, A. D., Smith, T. F., Garrett, M. E., Morrissey-Kane, E., Schatz, N. K., Sommer, J. L., Kollins, S. H., & Ashley-Koch, A. E. (2010). Self-Regulation of Emotion, Functional Impairment, and Comorbidity Among ChildrenWith AD/HD. *Journal of Attention Disorders*, *15*(7), 583–592. DOI: 10.1177/1087054710370567 PMID: 20686097

Andari, E., Duhamel, J., Zalla, T., Herbrecht, E., Leboyer, M., & Sirigu, A. (2010). Promoting social behavior with oxytocin in high-functioning autism spectrum disorders. *Proceedings of the National Academy of Sciences of the United States of America*, *107*(9), 4389–4394. DOI: 10.1073/pnas.0910249107 PMID: 20160081

Anderson, P. (2002). Assessment and development of executive function (EF) during childhood. *Child Neuropsychology : A Journal on Normal and Abnormal Development in Childhood and Adolescence*, *8*(2), 71–82. DOI: 10.1076/chin.8.2.71.8724 PMID: 12638061

Andreou, G., Lymperopoulou, V., & Aslanoglou, V. (2025). Structural language in neurodevelopmental disorders: Comparison between autism spectrum disorder (ASD) and developmental language disorder (DLD). *Frontiers in Education*, *10*, 1641303. Advance online publication. DOI: 10.3389/feduc.2025.1641303

Andrews, D. S., Aksman, L., Kerns, C. M., Lee, J. K., Winder-Patel, B. M., Harvey, D. J., Waizbard-Bartov, E., Heath, B., Solomon, M., Rogers, S. J., Altmann, A., Nordahl, C. W., & Amaral, D. G. (2022). Association of amygdala development with different forms of anxiety in autism spectrum disorder. *Biological Psychiatry*, *91*(11), 977–987. DOI: 10.1016/j.biopsych.2022.01.016 PMID: 35341582

Andron, L., & Tymchuk, A. (1987). Parents who are mentally retarded. In Craft, A. (Ed.), *Mental Handicap and Sexuality: Issues and Perspectives*. D.J. Costello.

Anning, K. L., Langley, K., Hobson, C., & Van Goozen, S. H. M. (2023). Dimensional associations between executive function processes and symptoms of ADHD, ASD, oppositional defiance and anxiety in young school-referred children. *Cortex; A Journal Devoted to the Study of the Nervous System and Behavior*, *167*, 132–147. DOI: 10.1016/j.cortex.2023.06.005 PMID: 37557009

Ansari Nasab, S., Panahi, S., Ghassemi, F., Jafari, S., Rajagopal, K., Ghosh, D., & Perc, M. (2021). Functional neuronal networks reveal emotional processing differences in children with ADHD. *Cognitive Neurodynamics*, *16*(1), 91–100. DOI: 10.1007/s11571-021-09699-6 PMID: 35126772

Aoki, S., Nagatani, F., Kagitani-Shimono, K., Ohno, Y., Taniike, M., & Mohri, I. (2023). Examining normative values using the Cambridge neuropsychological test automated battery and developmental traits of executive functions among elementary school-aged children in Japan. *Frontiers in Psychology*, *14*, 1141628. DOI: 10.3389/fpsyg.2023.1141628 PMID: 37663362

Aoki, Y., Cortese, S., & Castellanos, F. X. (2018). Research Review: Diffusion tensor imaging studies of attention-deficit/hyperactivity disorder: meta-analyses and reflections on head motion. *Journal of Child Psychology and Psychiatry, and Allied Disciplines*, *59*(3), 193–202. DOI: 10.1111/jcpp.12778 PMID: 28671333

Aoki, Y., Yoncheva, Y. N., Chen, B., Nath, T., Sharp, D., Lazar, M., Velasco, P., Milham, M. P., & Di Martino, A. (2017). Association of White Matter Structure With Autism Spectrum Disorder and Attention-Deficit/Hyperactivity Disorder. *JAMA Psychiatry*, *74*(11), 1120–1128. DOI: 10.1001/jamapsychiatry.2017.2573 PMID: 28877317

Arciuli, J. (2017). The multi-component nature of statistical learning. *Philosophical Transactions of the Royal Society B: Biological Sciences, 372*(1711), 20160058.

Argyriadis, A., Drakopoulou, O., Argyriadi, A., Mantsos, E., Katsarou, D. V., & Patsiaouras, A. (2025). *Towards Holistic Wellness: Strategies for Managing Mental Health and Embracing Neurodiversity. Exploring Cognitive and Psychosocial Dynamics Across Childhood and Adolescence*. IGIGlobal.

Armstrong, T. (2025). *The Power of Neurodiversity: Unleashing the Advantages of Your Neurodivergent Brain (Completely Revised and Updated Second Edition)*. Balance.

Armstrong, T. (2010). *The power of neurodiversity: Unleashing the advantages of your differently wired brain*. Da Capo Press.

Armstrong, T. (2011). *The Power of Neurodiversity: Unleashing the Advantages of Your Differently Wired Brain (published in Hardcover as Neurodiversity)*. Grand Central Publishing.

Arnold, E. H., O'Leary, S. G., & Edwards, G. H. (1997). Father involvement and self reported parenting of children with attention deficit hyperactivity disorder. *Journal of Consulting and Clinical Psychology*, *65*(65), 337–342. DOI: 10.1037/0022-006X.65.2.337 PMID: 9086700

Astle, D. E., Holmes, J., Kievit, R., & Gathercole, S. (2022). Annual research review: Transdiagnostic approaches to neurodevelopmental disorders. *Journal of Child Psychology and Psychiatry, and Allied Disciplines*, *63*(4), 397–417. DOI: 10.1111/jcpp.13481 PMID: 34296774

Augustine, L., Lygnegård, F., & Granlund, M. (2021). Trajectories of participation, mental health, and mental health problems in adolescents with self-reported neurodevelopmental disorders. *Disability and Rehabilitation*, *44*(9), 1595–1608. DOI: 10.1080/09638288.2021.1955304 PMID: 34353177

Austin, G., Groppe, K., & Elsner, B. (2014). The reciprocal relationship between executive function and theory of mind in middle childhood: A 1-year longitudinal perspective. *Frontiers in Psychology*, *5*, 655. DOI: 10.3389/fpsyg.2014.00655 PMID: 25009527

Ayub, R., Sun, K. L., Flores, R. E., Lam, V. T., Jo, B., Saggar, M., & Fung, L. K. (2021). Thalamocortical connectivity is associated with autism symptoms in high-functioning adults with autism and typically developing adults. *Translational Psychiatry*, *11*(1), 93. DOI: 10.1038/s41398-021-01221-0 PMID: 33536431

Azarias, F. R., Almeida, G. H. D. R., de Melo, L. F., Rici, R. E. G., & Maria, D. A. (2025). The Journey of the Default Mode Network: Development, Function, and Impact on Mental Health. *Biology (Basel)*, *14*(4), 395. DOI: 10.3390/biology14040395 PMID: 40282260

Azar, S. T., Reitz, E. B., & Goslin, M. C. (2008). Mothering: Thinking is part of the job description: Application of cognitive views to understanding maladaptive parenting and doing intervention and prevention work. *Journal of Applied Developmental Psychology*, *29*(4), 295–304. DOI: 10.1016/j.appdev.2008.04.009

Baddeley, A. (1996). Exploring the central executive. *The Quarterly Journal of Experimental Psychology. A, Human Experimental Psychology*, *49*(1), 5–28. DOI: 10.1080/713755608

Baddeley, A. (2012). Working memory: Theories, models, and controversies. *Annual Review of Psychology*, *63*(1), 1–29. DOI: 10.1146/annurev-psych-120710-100422 PMID: 21961947

Bailey, K. M., & Im-Bolter, N. (2024). Social Cognitive Processes in Children With Specific Learning Disorder: The Importance of Language. *Learning Disability Quarterly*, *48*(4), 215–226. Advance online publication. DOI: 10.1177/07319487241288531 PMID: 40979616

Baird, G., & Norbury, C. F. (2015). Social (pragmatic) communication disorders and autism spectrum disorder. *Archives of Disease in Childhood*, *101*(8), 745–751. DOI: 10.1136/archdischild-2014-306944 PMID: 26699538

Baltes, P. B. (1987). Theoretical propositions of life-span developmental psychology: On the dynamics between growth and decline. *Developmental Psychology*, *23*(5), 611–626. DOI: 10.1037/0012-1649.23.5.611

Baltes, P. B., Lindenberger, U., & Staudinger, U. M. (2006). Life span theory in developmental psychology. In Lerner, R. M. (Ed.),; 6th ed., pp. 569–664). Handbook of child psychology. Wiley.

Bal, V. H., Goin-Kochel, R. P., McEachern, A. D., Jelenic, P., Nader, A. M., & Soulières, I. (2022). Cognitive profiles of children with ASD with parent-reported extraordinary talents and personal strengths. *Journal of Autism and Developmental Disorders*, *52*(2), 585–599.

Banaschewski, T., Brandeis, D., Heinrich, H., Albrecht, B., Brunner, E., & Rothenberger, A. (2004). Questioning inhibitory control as the specific deficit of ADHD: Evidence from brain electrical activity. *Journal of Neural Transmission*, *111*(7), 841–864. https://pmc.ncbi.nlm.nih.gov/articles/PMC3472099/. DOI: 10.1007/s00702-003-0040-8 PMID: 15206002

Bandura, A. (1977). *Social learning theory*. Prentice Hall.

Bargiela, S., Steward, R., & Mandy, W. (2016). The experiences of late-diagnosed women with autism spectrum conditions: An investigation of the female autism phenotype. *Journal of Autism and Developmental Disorders*, *46*(10), 3281–3294. DOI: 10.1007/s10803-016-2872-8 PMID: 27457364

Baribeau, D., & Anagnostou, E. (2021). Novel treatments for autism spectrum disorder based on genomics and systems biology. *Pharmacology & Therapeutics*, *107939*. Advance online publication. DOI: 10.1016/j.pharmthera.2021.107939 PMID: 34174273

Barkley, R. A. (2012). *Executive functions: What they are, how they work, and why they evolved*. Guilford Press.

Barkley, R. A. (2015). *Attention-deficit hyperactivity disorder: A handbook for diagnosis and treatment* (4th ed.). Guilford Press.

Barkley, R. A., & Murphy, K. R. (2010). Impairment in occupational functioning and adult ADHD: The predictive utility of executive function (EF) ratings versus EF tests. *Archives of Clinical Neuropsychology : The Official Journal of the National Academy of Neuropsychologists*, *25*(3), 157–173. DOI: 10.1093/arclin/acq014 PMID: 20197297

Baron-Cohen, S. (2009). Autism: The empathizing–systemizing (E-S) theory. *Annals of the New York Academy of Sciences*, *1156*(1), 68–80. DOI: 10.1111/j.1749-6632 2009.04467.x PMID: 19338503

Baron-Cohen, S., Tager-Flusberg, H., & Cohen, D. J. (2000). *Understanding other minds: Perspectives from developmental cognitive neuroscience*. Oxford University Press.

Baron, L. S., & Arbel, Y. (2022). Inner Speech and Executive Function in Children With Developmental Language Disorder: Implications for Assessment and Intervention. *Perspectives of the ASHA Special Interest Groups*, *7*(6), 1645–1659. DOI: 10.1044/2022_PERSP-22-00042 PMID: 38957614

Barrasso-Catanzaro, C., & Eslinger, P. J. (2016). Neurobiological bases of executive function and social-emotional development: Typical and atypical brain changes. *Family Relations*, *65*(1), 108–119. DOI: 10.1111/fare.12175

Barrett, A. C., Vernon, T. W., McGarry, E. S., Holden, A. N., Bradshaw, J., Ko, J. A., Horowitz, E. J., & German, T. C. (2020). Social responsiveness and language use associated with an enhanced PRT approach for young children with ASD: Results from a pilot RCT of the PRISM model. *Research in Autism Spectrum Disorders*, *71*, 101497. DOI: 10.1016/j.rasd.2019.101497

Barron-Linnankoski, S., Kortesluoma, S., Ehlers, S., Hietala, R., & Pihlaja, P. (2015). Neurocognitive performance of children with higher functioning ASD on the NEPSY-2. *Child Neuropsychology : A Journal on Normal and Abnormal Development in Childhood and Adolescence*, *21*(1), 58–77. DOI: 10.1080/09297049.2013.873781 PMID: 24397431

Bashshar, A. M. A. A. B., & Elashram, R. E. M. (2025). The Relationship Between Self-Regulation Difficulties and Adaptive Functioning in Children with Autism Spectrum Disorder (ASD). *International Journal of Disability Development and Education*, *72*(7), 1248–1270. DOI: 10.1080/1034912X.2024.2419871

Bates, E., Dale, P. S., & Thal, D. (1995). Individual differences and their implications for theories of language development. In *Handbook of child language* (pp. 96–151). Cambridge University Press.

Bath, K. G., Schilit, A., & Lee, F. S. (2013). Stress effects on BDNF expression: Effects of age, sex, and form of stress. *Neuroscience*, *239*, 149–156. DOI: 10.1016/j.neuroscience.2013.01.074 PMID: 23402850

Batterink, L. J., Paller, K. A., & Reber, P. J. (2019). Understanding the neural bases of implicit and statistical learning. *Topics in Cognitive Science*, *11*(3), 481–506. DOI: 10.1111/tops.12420 PMID: 30942536

Bauer, P. J. (2007). *Remembering the times of our lives: Memory in infancy and beyond*. Lawrence Erlbaum Associates.

Beauchaine, T. P., & Cicchetti, D. (2019). Emotion dysregulation and emerging psychopathology. *Journal of Child Psychology and Psychiatry, and Allied Disciplines*, *60*(4), 361–363. DOI: 10.1111/jcpp.13031 PMID: 31290735

Beaudoin, C., Leblanc, É., Gagner, C., & Beauchamp, M. H. (2020). Systematic Review and Inventory of Theory of Mind Measures for Young Children. *Frontiers in Psychology*, *10*, 2905. Advance online publication. DOI: 10.3389/fpsyg.2019.02905 PMID: 32010013

Becker, S. P., & Langberg, J. M. (2012). Sluggish cognitive tempo among young adolescents with ADHD. *Journal of Attention Disorders*, *17*(8), 681–689. DOI: 10.1177/1087054711435411 PMID: 22441891

Bedford, S. A.. (2023). Brain-charting autism and attention deficit hyperactivity disorder: A mega-analysis of structural MRI. *Molecular Psychiatry*. Advance online publication. DOI: 10.1038/s41380-023-02290-7

Belin, L., Henry, L., Destays, M., Hausberger, M., & Grandgeorge, M. (2017). Simple shapes elicit different emotional responses in children with autism spectrum disorder and neurotypical children and adults. *Frontiers in Psychology*, *8*. Advance online publication. DOI: 10.3389/fpsyg.2017.00091 PMID: 28194129

Bellis, M. A., Hughes, K., Ford, K., Rodriguez, G. R., Sethi, D., & Passmore, J. (2019). Life course health consequences and associated annual costs of adverse childhood experiences across Europe and North America: A systematic review and meta-analysis. *The Lancet. Public Health*, *4*(10), e517–e528. DOI: 10.1016/S2468-2667(19)30145-8 PMID: 31492648

Bell, M. A., & Wolfe, C. D. (2007). Changes in brain functioning from infancy to early childhood: Evidence from EEG power and coherence during working memory tasks. *Developmental Neuropsychology*, *31*(1), 21–38. DOI: 10.1080/87565640709336885 PMID: 17305436

Belo-Tomic, S., Quinlan, E., & Read, E. (2021). Young adult's perception of their relationship with an ADHD parent: A qualitative study. *Contemporary Family Therapy*, *43*(3), 298–304. DOI: 10.1007/s10591-021-09566-w

Benallie, K. J., McClain, M. B., Bakner, K. E., Roanhorse, T., & Ha, J. (2021). Executive functioning in children with ASD + ADHD and ASD + ID: A systematic review. *Research in Autism Spectrum Disorders*, *86*, 101807. DOI: 10.1016/j.rasd.2021.101807

Berberat, J., Huggenberger, R., Montali, M., Gruber, P., Pircher, A., Lövblad, K. O., Killer, H. E., & Remonda, L. (2021). Brain activation patterns in medicated versus medication-naïve adults with attention-deficit hyperactivity disorder during fMRI tasks of motor inhibition and cognitive switching. *BMC Medical Imaging*, *21*(1), 53. DOI: 10.1186/s12880-021-00579-3 PMID: 33740903

Berk, L. (2019). *Development Through the Lifespan*. Pearson Education Inc.

Berk, L. E. (2021). *Development through the lifespan* (8th ed.). Pearson.

Berkovits, L., Eisenhower, A., & Blacher, J. (2016). Emotion regulation in young children with autism spectrum disorders. *Journal of Autism and Developmental Disorders*, *47*(1), 68–79. DOI: 10.1007/s10803-016-2922-2 PMID: 27838805

Bernal, G., Jiménez-Chafey, M. I., & Domenech Rodríguez, M. M. (2009). Cultural adaptation of treatments: A resource for considering culture in evidence-based practice. *Professional Psychology, Research and Practice*, *40*(4), 361–368. DOI: 10.1037/a0016401

Bertollo, A. G., Puntel, C. F., da Silva, B. V., Martins, M. R., Bagatini, M. D., & Ignácio, Z. M. (2025). Neurobiological Relationships Between Neurodevelopmental Disorders and Mood Disorders. *Brain Sciences*, *15*(3), 307. DOI: 10.3390/brainsci15030307 PMID: 40149827

Biederman, J., Faraone, S. V., Knee, D., & Munir, K. (1990). Retrospective assessment of *DSM-III* attention deficit disorder in non-referred individuals. *The Journal of Clinical Psychiatry*, *51*, 102–106. PMID: 2307663

Biederman, J., Faraone, S. V., & Monuteaux, M. C. (2002). Impact of exposure to parental attention-deficit hyperactivity disorder on clinical features and dysfunction in the offspring. *Psychological Medicine*, *32*(5), 817–827. DOI: 10.1017/S0033291702005652 PMID: 12171376

Binti Marsus, N., Sook Huey, L., Saffari, N., & Motevalli, S. (2022). Peer relationship difficulties among children with ADHD: A systematic review. *International Journal of Academic Research in Business & Social Sciences*, *12*(6). Advance online publication. DOI: 10.6007/IJARBSS/v12-i6/13352

Bird, G., & Cook, R. (2013). Mixed emotions: The contribution of alexithymia to the emotional symptoms of autism. *Translational Psychiatry*, *3*(7), e285–e285. DOI: 10.1038/tp.2013.61 PMID: 23880881

Biró, B., Cserjési, R., Kocsel, N., Galambos, A., Gecse, K., Kovács, L. N., Baksa, D., Dobos, D., Juhász, G., & Kökönyei, G. (2025). Unveiling the Role of Theory of Mind: Neural Response to Emotional Stimuli in Context. *Affective Science*, *6*(2), 1–16. DOI: 10.1007/s42761-025-00293-1 PMID: 40605950

Bishop, D. V. M., Snowling, M. J., Thompson, P. A., & Greenhalgh, T. The CATALISE Consortium. (2017). Phase 2 of CATALISE: A multinational and multidisciplinary consensus study of problems with language development: Terminology. *Journal of Child Psychology and Psychiatry, and Allied Disciplines*, *58*(10), 1068–1080. DOI: 10.1111/jcpp.12721 PMID: 28369935

Bjorklund, D. F., & Causey, K. B. (2018). *Children's thinking: Cognitive development and individual differences* (6th ed.). Sage.

Black, M. M., Walker, S. P., Fernald, L. C. H., Andersen, C. T., DiGirolamo, A. M., Lu, C., McCoy, D. C., Fink, G., Shawar, Y. R., Shiffman, J., Devercelli, A. E., Wodon, Q. T., Vargas-Barón, E., & Grantham-McGregor, S. (2017). Early childhood development coming of age: Science through the life course. *Lancet*, *389*(10064), 77–90. DOI: 10.1016/S0140-6736(16)31389-7 PMID: 27717614

Blair, C. (2016). Executive function and early childhood education. *Current Opinion in Behavioral Sciences*, *10*, 102–107. DOI: 10.1016/j.cobeha.2016.05.009 PMID: 30035205

Blanco-Martínez, N., Delgado-Lobete, L., Montes-Montes, R., Ruiz-Pérez, N., Ruiz-Pérez, M., & Santos-del-Riego, S. (2020). Participation in Everyday Activities of Children with and without Neurodevelopmental Disorders: A Cross-Sectional Study in Spain. *Children (Basel, Switzerland)*, *7*(10), 157. DOI: 10.3390/children7100157 PMID: 33019630

Blank, R., Barnett, A. L., Cairney, J., Green, D., Kirby, A., Polatajko, H., Rosenblum, S., Smits-Engelsman, B., Sugden, D., Wilson, P., & Vinçon, S. (2019). International clinical DSM-5 recommendations on definition, diagnosis, assessment, intervention, and care of developmental coordination disorder (DCD). *Developmental Medicine and Child Neurology*, *61*(3), 242–285. DOI: 10.1111/dmcn.14132 PMID: 30671947

Boccadoro, S., Cracco, E., Hudson, A. R., Bardi, L., Nijhof, A. D., Wiersema, J. R., Brass, M., & Mueller, S. C. (2019). Defining the neural correlates of spontaneous theory of mind (ToM): An fMRI multi-study investigation. *NeuroImage*, *203*, 116193. DOI: 10.1016/j.neuroimage.2019.116193 PMID: 31525499

Bölte, S. (2025). Social cognition in autism and ADHD. *Neuroscience and Biobehavioral Reviews*, *169*, 106022. DOI: 10.1016/j.neubiorev.2025.106022 PMID: 39832687

Bölte, S., Lawson, W. B., Marschik, P. B., & Girdler, S. (2021). Reconciling the seemingly irreconcilable: The WHO's ICF system integrates biological and psychosocial environmental determinants of autism and ADHD – The International Classification of Functioning ICF) allows to model opposed biomedical and neurodiverse views of autism and ADHD within one framework. *BioEssays : News and Reviews in Molecular, Cellular and Developmental Biology*, *43*(9), 2000254. DOI: 10.1002/bies.202000254 PMID: 33797095

Boonstra, A. M., Oosterlaan, J., Sergeant, J. A., & Buitelaar, J. K. (2005). Executive functioning in adult ADHD: A meta-analytic review. *Psychological Medicine*, *35*(8), 1097–1108. DOI: 10.1017/S003329170500499X PMID: 16116936

Booth, T., & Booth, W. (1998). Risk, resilience and competence: parents with learning difficulties and their children. *Questions of competence: Culture, classification and intellectual disability*, 76-101.

Bornstein, M. H. (2012). Cultural approaches to parenting. *Parenting, Science and Practice*, *12*(2–3), 212–221. DOI: 10.1080/15295192.2012.683359 PMID: 22962544

Botha, M., Chapman, R., Giwa Onaiwu, M., Kapp, S. K., Stannard Ashley, A., & Walker, N. (2024). The neurodiversity concept was developed collectively: An overdue correction on the origins of neurodiversity theory. *Autism : The International Journal of Research and Practice*, *28*(6), 1591–1594. DOI: 10.1177/13623613241237871 PMID: 38470140

Bowen, M. (1978). *Family therapy in clinical practice*. Jason Aronson.

Bowlby, J. (1979). The bowlby-ainsworth attachment theory. *The Behavioral and Brain Sciences*, *2*(4), 637–638. DOI: 10.1017/S0140525X00064955

Bowlby, J. (1982). Attachment and loss: Vol. 1. *Attachment* (2nd ed.). Basic Books. (Original work published 1969)

Bowler, D. M., Gardiner, J. M., & Berthollier, N. (2004). Source memory in adolescents and adults with Asperger's syndrome. *Journal of Autism and Developmental Disorders*, *34*(5), 533–542. DOI: 10.1007/s10803-004-2548-7 PMID: 15628607

Braaten, E. B., & Rosén, L. A. (2000). Self-regulation of affect in attention deficit-hyperactivity disorder (ADHD) and non-ADHD boys: Differences in empathic responding. *Journal of Consulting and Clinical Psychology*, *68*(2), 313–321. DOI: 10.1037/0022-006X.68.2.313 PMID: 10780132

Braconnier, M. L., & Siper, P. M. (2021). Neuropsychological assessment in autism spectrum disorder. *Current Psychiatry Reports*, *23*(10), 63. Advance online publication. DOI: 10.1007/s11920-021-01277-1 PMID: 34331144

Bradley, B., Davis, T. A., Wingo, A. P., Mercer, K. B., & Ressler, K. J. (2013). Family environment and adult resilience: contributions of positive parenting and the oxytocin receptor gene. European journal of psychotraumatology, 4, . https://doi.org/DOI: 10.3402/ejpt.v4i0.21659

Bradley, R. H., & Corwyn, R. F. (2002). Socioeconomic status and child development. *Annual Review of Psychology, 53*(1), 371–399. DOI: 10.1146/annurev.psych.53.100901.135233 PMID: 11752490

Brainerd, C. J., & Reyna, V. F. (1990). Gist is the grist: Fuzzy-trace theory and the new intuitionism. *Developmental Review, 10*(1), 3–47. DOI: 10.1016/0273-2297(90)90003-M

Breaux, R. P., & Harvey, E. A. (2018). A longitudinal study of the relation between family functioning and preschool ADHD symptoms. *Journal of Clinical Child and Adolescent Psychology : The Official Journal for the Society of Clinical Child and Adolescent Psychology, American Psychological Association, Division 53*. Advance online publication. DOI: 10.1080/15374416.2018.1437737 PMID: 29578799

Brignell, A., Chenausky, K. V., Song, H., Zhu, J., Suo, C., & Morgan, A. T. (2018). Communication interventions for autism spectrum disorder in minimally verbal children. *Cochrane Database of Systematic Reviews, 5*(11). Advance online publication. DOI: 10.1002/14651858.CD012324.pub2 PMID: 30395694

Bronfenbrenner, U. (1979). *The ecology of human development*. Harvard University Press. DOI: 10.4159/9780674028845

Bronfenbrenner, U., & Morris, P. A. (2006). The bioecological model of human development. In Lerner, R. M. (Ed.),; 6th ed.). Handbook of child psychology. Wiley.

Brown, J., & Errington, L. (2024). Bowen family systems theory and practice: Illustration and critique revisited. *Australian and New Zealand Journal of Family Therapy, 45*(2), 135–155. DOI: 10.1002/anzf.1589

Bryłka, M., & Cygan, H. B. (2023). VISUALLY SUPPORTED SHORT-TERM AUDITORY MEMORY IN CHILDREN WITH DEVELOPMENTAL LANGUAGE DISORDER (DLD). *Journal of Hearing Science, 13*(1), 43–52. DOI: 10.17430/jhs/163178

Bryson, S., Garon, N., McMullen, T., Brian, J., Zwaigenbaum, L., Armstrong, V., Roberts, W., Smith, I., & Szatmari, P. (2018). Impaired disengagement of attention and its relationship to emotional distress in infants at high-risk for autism spectrum disorder. *Journal of Clinical and Experimental Neuropsychology, 40*(5), 487–501. DOI: 10.1080/13803395.2017.1372368 PMID: 28914144

Bui, T. A., Rosenfelt, C., Whitlock, K. H., Weber, S. M., Leclerq, M., Droit, A., Wiebe, S. A., Pei, J., & Bolduc, F. V. (2023). Long-term Memory Testing in Children With Typical Development and Neurodevelopmental Disorders: Remote Web-based Image Task Feasibility Study. *JMIR Pediatrics and Parenting*, *6*, e39720. DOI: 10.2196/39720 PMID: 37155237

Bul, K. C., Franken, I. H., Van Der Oord, S., Kato, P. M., Danckaerts, M., Vreeke, L. J., Willems, A., Van Oers, H. J., Van Den Heuvel, R., Van Slagmaat, R., & Maras, A. (2015). Development and User Satisfaction of "Plan-It Commander," a Serious Game for Children with ADHD. *Games for Health Journal*, *4*(6), 502–512. DOI: 10.1089/g4h.2015.0021 PMID: 26325247

Burrows, C. A., Timpano, K. R., & Uddin, L. Q. (2017). Putative Brain Networks Underlying Repetitive Negative Thinking and Comorbid Internalizing Problems in Autism. *Clinical Psychological Science*, *5*(3), 522–536. DOI: 10.1177/2167702616683506 PMID: 28603665

Buschgens, C. J. M., van Aken, M. A. G., Swinkels, S. H. N., Altink, M. E., Fliers, E. A., Rommelse, N. N. J., Minderaa, R. B., Sergeant, J. A., Faraone, S. V., & Buitelaar, J. K. (2008). Differential family and peer environmental factors are related to severity and comorbidity in children with ADHD. *Journal of Neural Transmission*, *115*(2), 177–186. DOI: 10.1007/s00702-007-0838-x PMID: 18200433

Bush, N. R., Wakschlag, L. S., LeWinn, K. Z., Hertz-Picciotto, I., Nozadi, S. S., Pieper, S., Lewis, J., Biezonski, D., Blair, C., Deardorff, J., Neiderhiser, J. M., Leve, L. D., Elliott, A. J., Duarte, C. S., Lugo-Candelas, C., O'Shea, T. M., Avalos, L. A., Page, G. P., & Posner, J. (2020). Family Environment, Neurodevelopmental Risk, and the Environmental Influences on Child Health Outcomes (ECHO) Initiative: Looking Back and Moving Forward. *Frontiers in Psychiatry*, *11*, 547. DOI: 10.3389/fpsyt.2020.00547 PMID: 32636769

Buttelmann, F., & Karbach, J. (2017). Development and plasticity of cognitive flexibility in early and middle childhood. *Frontiers in Psychology*, *8*, 1040. DOI: 10.3389/fpsyg.2017.01040 PMID: 28676784

Butterworth, B., Varma, S., & Laurillard, D. (2011). Dyscalculia: From brain to education. *Science*, *332*(6033), 1049–1053. DOI: 10.1126/science.1201536 PMID: 21617068

Cage, E., & Troxell-Whitman, Z. (2019). Understanding the reasons, contexts and costs of camouflaging for autistic adults. *Journal of Autism and Developmental Disorders*, *49*(5), 1899–1911. DOI: 10.1007/s10803-018-03878-x PMID: 30627892

Caine, J. A., Klein, B., & Edwards, S. L. (2020). Emotion Recognition in adults with ASD and Alexithymia: The impact of a Novel Mimicry Task for Therapeutic Benefit Study Protocol (Preprint). *JMIR Research Protocols*. Advance online publication. DOI: 10.2196/24543 PMID: 34170257

Cai, R. Y., Richdale, A. L., Uljarević, M., Dissanayake, C., & Samson, A. C. (2018). Emotion regulation in autism spectrum disorder: Where we are and where we need to go. *Autism Research : Official Journal of the International Society for Autism Research*, *11*(7), 962–978. DOI: 10.1002/aur.1968 PMID: 29979494

Cai, X., Bai, X., & Zhou, S. (2024). Childhood adversities and memory function in later life: The mediating role of activity participation. *BMC Geriatrics*, *24*(1), 536. DOI: 10.1186/s12877-024-05145-4 PMID: 38902657

Calub, C. A., Benyakorn, S., Sun, S., Iosif, A.-M., Boyle, L. H., Solomon, M., Hessl, D., & Schweitzer, J. B. (2022). Working Memory Training in Youth With Autism, Fragile X, and Intellectual Disability: A Pilot Study. *American Journal on Intellectual and Developmental Disabilities*, *127*(5), 369–389. DOI: 10.1352/1944-7558-127.5.369 PMID: 36018768

Campbell, J. L., Datta, D., Jones, S. T., Lee, E. B., Sutcliffe, J. S., Hammock, E. A. D., & Levitt, P. (2011). Association of oxytocin receptor (oxtr) gene variants with multiple phenotype domains of autism spectrum disorder. *Journal of Neurodevelopmental Disorders*, *3*(2), 101–112. DOI: 10.1007/s11689-010-9071-2 PMID: 21484202

Campbell, S. B., von Stauffenberg, C., & Center, N. (2014). Early predictors of attention-deficit/hyperactivity disorder symptoms. *Development and Psychopathology*, *26*(2), 555–569.

Cañigueral, R., Palmer, J., Ashwood, K. L., Azadi, B., Asherson, P., Bolton, P., McLoughlin, G., & Tye, C. (2021). Alpha oscillatory activity during attentional control in children with Autism Spectrum Disorder (ASD), Attention-Deficit/Hyperactivity Disorder (ADHD), and ASD+ADHD. *Journal of Child Psychology and Psychiatry, and Allied Disciplines*, *63*(7), 745–761. DOI: 10.1111/jcpp.13514 PMID: 34477232

Cao, C., He, Q., Zhao, X., Wang, L., Ma, L., & Jiang, L. (2022). Shared genetics between autism spectrum disorder and attention-deficit/hyperactivity disorder and their association with extraversion. *Psychiatry Research*, *315*, 114711. Advance online publication. DOI: 10.1016/j.psychres.2022.114711

Capodieci, A., Gola, M. L., Cornoldi, C., & Re, A. M. (2018). Effects of a working memory training program in preschoolers with symptoms of attention-deficit/hyperactivity disorder. *Journal of Clinical and Experimental Neuropsychology*, *40*(1), 17–29. DOI: 10.1080/13803395.2017.1307946 PMID: 28332914

Capuozzo, A., Rizzato, S., Grossi, G., & Strappini, F. (2024). A Systematic Review on Social Cognition in ADHD: The Role of Language, Theory of Mind, and Executive Functions. *Brain Sciences*, *14*(11), 1117. DOI: 10.3390/brainsci14111117 PMID: 39595880

Carlberg, L., & Granlund, M. (2018). Achievement and participation in schools for young adolescents with self-reported neuropsychiatric disabilities: A cross-sectional study from the southern part of Sweden. *Scandinavian Journal of Public Health*, *47*(2), 199–206. Advance online publication. DOI: 10.1177/1403494818788415 PMID: 30070167

Carr-Fanning, K., & McGuckin, C. (2022). I find it really difficult to control myself too: A qualitative study of the effects on the family dynamic when parent and child have ADHD. *Education Sciences*, *12*(11), 758. DOI: 10.3390/educsci12110758

Carrington, S., Saggers, B., Webster, A., Harper-Hill, K., & Nickerson, J. (2020). What Universal Design for Learning principles, guidelines, and checkpoints are evident in educators' descriptions of their practice when supporting students on the autism spectrum? *International Journal of Educational Research*, *102*, 101583. DOI: 10.1016/j.ijer.2020.101583

Carstensen, L. L. (2006). The influence of a sense of time on human development. *Science*, *312*(5782), 1913–1915. DOI: 10.1126/science.1127488 PMID: 16809530

Cascio, C. J., Moana-Filho, E. J., Guest, S., Nebel, M. B., Weisner, J., Baranek, G. T., & Essick, G. K. (2012). Perceptual and neural response to affective tactile texture stimulation in adults with autism spectrum disorders. *Autism Research : Official Journal of the International Society for Autism Research*, *5*(4), 231–244. DOI: 10.1002/aur.1224 PMID: 22447729

Case, R. (1998). The development of conceptual structures. In Kuhn, D., & Siegler, R. S. (Eds.),; 5th ed.). Handbook of child psychology. Wiley.

Casey, B. J., Oliveri, M. E., & Insel, T. (2014). A neurodevelopmental perspective on the Research Domain Criteria (RDoC) framework. *Biological Psychiatry*, *76*(5), 350–353. DOI: 10.1016/j.biopsych.2014.01.006 PMID: 25103538

Casey, B., Cannonier, T., Conley, M. I., Cohen, A. O., Barch, D. M., Heitzeg, M. M., Soules, M. E., Teslovich, T., Dellarco, D. V., Garavan, H., Orr, C. A., Wager, T. D., Banich, M. T., Speer, N. K., Sutherland, M. T., Riedel, M. C., Dick, A. S., Bjork, J. M., Thomas, K. M., & Dale, A. M. (2018). The Adolescent Brain Cognitive Development (ABCD) study: Imaging acquisition across 21 sites. *Developmental Cognitive Neuroscience*, *32*, 43–54. DOI: 10.1016/j.dcn.2018.03.001 PMID: 29567376

Cassidy, S., Bradley, L., Shaw, R., & Baron-Cohen, S. (2018). Risk markers for suicidality in autistic adults. *Molecular Autism*, *9*(1), 42. DOI: 10.1186/s13229-018-0226-4 PMID: 30083306

Castellanos, F. X., & Proal, E. (2012). Large-scale brain systems in ADHD: Beyond the prefrontal–striatal model. *Trends in Cognitive Sciences*, *16*(1), 17–26. DOI: 10.1016/j.tics.2011.11.007 PMID: 22169776

Centers for Disease Control and Prevention. (2024). *Developmental milestones*. https://www.cdc.gov

Čepukaitytė, G., Thom, J. L., Kallmayer, M., Nobre, A. C., & Zokaei, N. (2023). The Relationship between Short- and Long-Term Memory Is Preserved across the Age Range. *Brain Sciences*, *13*(1), 106. DOI: 10.3390/brainsci13010106 PMID: 36672087

Ch'ng, C., Kwok, W., Rogic, S., & Pavlidis, P. (2015). Meta-analysis of gene expression in autism spectrum disorder. *Autism Research : Official Journal of the International Society for Autism Research*, *8*(5), 593–608. DOI: 10.1002/aur.1475 PMID: 25720351

Chacko, A., Jensen, S. A., Lowry, L. S., Cornwell, M., Chimklis, A., Chan, E., Lee, D., & Pulgarin, B. (2016). Engagement in behavioral parent training: Review of the literature and implications for practice. *Clinical Child and Family Psychology Review*, *19*(3), 204–215. DOI: 10.1007/s10567-016-0205-2 PMID: 27311693

Chalmpe, M., & Vlachos, F. (2025). WORKING AND LONG-TERM MEMORY DEFICITS IN DEVELOPMENTAL DYSLEXIA. *INTED Proceedings*, •••, 3482–3487. DOI: 10.21125/inted.2025.0885

Chang, J. P., Su, K. P., Mondelli, V., & Pariante, C. M. (2021). Cortisol and inflammatory biomarker levels in youths with attention deficit hyperactivity disorder (ADHD): Evidence from a systematic review with meta-analysis. *Translational Psychiatry*, *11*(1), 430. DOI: 10.1038/s41398-021-01550-0 PMID: 34413283

Chapman, R. (2020). The reality of autism: On the metaphysics of disorder and diversity. *Philosophical Psychology*, *33*(6), 799–819. DOI: 10.1080/09515089.2020.1751103

Chapman, R. (2021). Neurodiversity and the social ecology of mental functions. *Perspectives on Psychological Science : A Journal of the Association for Psychological Science*, *16*(6), 1360–1372. DOI: 10.1177/1745691620959833 PMID: 33577400

Chen, J. Y., & Barnes, M. J. (2012). Supervisory control of multiple robots in dynamic tasking environments. *Ergonomics*, *55*(9), 1043–1058. DOI: 10.1080/00140139.2012.689013 PMID: 22676776

Chen, M., & Jiang, X. (2024). The impact of modified Cognitive-Behavioral Group Therapy in social adjustment functions of children with attention deficit hyperactivity disorder and their parents' stress levels: A nonrandomized clinical trial. *Journal of Clinical Psychology*, *80*(9), 1969–1980. DOI: 10.1002/jclp.23704 PMID: 38747969

Cheung, M. C., Shahed, J., & Jankovic, J. (2007). Malignant Tourette syndrome. *Movement Disorders : Official Journal of the Movement Disorder Society*, *22*(12), 1743–1750. DOI: 10.1002/mds.21599 PMID: 17566119

Chiang, H. L., Chen, Y. J., Shang, C. Y., Tseng, W. Y., & Gau, S. S. (2016). Different neural substrates for executive functions in youths with ADHD: A diffusion spectrum imaging tractography study. *Psychological Medicine*, *46*(6), 1225–1238. DOI: 10.1017/S0033291715002767 PMID: 26744120

Choo, A. L., Smith, S. A., & Li, H. (2020). Associations between stuttering, comorbid conditions and executive function in children: A population-based study. *BMC Psychology*, *8*(1), 113. DOI: 10.1186/s40359-020-00481-7 PMID: 33129350

Chou, W.-J., Liu, T.-L., Hsiao, R. C., Chen, Y.-M., Chang, C.-C., & Yen, C.-F. (2020). Caregiver-attributed etiologies of children's attention-deficit/hyperactivity disorder: A study in Taiwan. *International Journal of Environmental Research and Public Health*, *17*(5), 1652. DOI: 10.3390/ijerph17051652 PMID: 32143281

Christenson, S. L., & Sheridan, S. M. (2001). *Schools and families: Creating essential connections for learning*. Guilford Press.

Chronis-Tuscano, A., O'Brien, K. A., Johnston, C., Jones, H. A., Clarke, T. L., Raggi, V. L., Rooney, M. E., Diaz, Y., Pian, J., & Seymour, K. E. (2011). The relation between maternal ADHD symptoms & improvement in child behavior following brief behavioral parent training is mediated by change in negative parenting. *Journal of Abnormal Child Psychology*, *39*(7), 1047–1057. DOI: 10.1007/s10802-011-9518-2 PMID: 21537894

Cicchetti, D. (1984). The emergence of developmental psychopathology. *Child Development*, *55*(1), 1–7. DOI: 10.2307/1129830 PMID: 6705613

Cicchetti, D., & Blender, J. A. (2006). A multiple-levels-of-analysis approach to resilience. *Development and Psychopathology Russo*, *18*(3), 767–773.

Cicchetti, D., & Rogosch, F. A. (1996). Equifinality and multifinality in developmental psychopathology. *Development and Psychopathology*, *8*(4), 597–600. DOI: 10.1017/S0954579400007318

Cicchetti, D., & Rogosch, F. A. (2002). A developmental psychopathology perspective on adolescence. *Journal of Consulting and Clinical Psychology*, *70*(1), 6–20. DOI: 10.1037/0022-006X.70.1.6 PMID: 11860057

Cicchetti, D., & Toth, S. L. (2009). A developmental psychopathology perspective on child maltreatment. *Journal of the American Academy of Child and Adolescent Psychiatry*, *48*(6), 592–594. DOI: 10.1097/CHI.0b013e3181a2b30c

Cier, G. J., Bartolo, S., Kim, J., Nolan, A., & Banel, S. (2024). Implicit and Explicit Sequence Learning in Adults With Developmental Language Disorder. *Journal of Speech, Language, and Hearing Research: JSLHR*, *67*(5), 1540–1552. PMID: 39024517

Claesdotter, E., Cervin, M., Åkerlund, S., Råstam, M., & Lindvall, M. (2018). The effects of ADHD on cognitive performance. *Nordic Journal of Psychiatry*, *72*(3), 158–163. DOI: 10.1080/08039488.2017.1402951 PMID: 29161919

Coales, C., Heaney, N., Ricketts, J., Dockrell, J. E., Lindsay, G., Palikara, O., & Charman, T. (2019). Health-related quality of life in children with autism spectrum disorders and children with developmental language disorders. *Autism & Developmental Language Impairments*, *4*, 2396941519851225. Advance online publication. DOI: 10.1177/2396941519851225

Cochran, D., Sikoglu, E. M., Hodge, S. M., Edden, R. A. E., Foley, A., Kennedy, D. N., Moore, C. M., & Frazier, J. A. (2015). Relationship among Glutamine, γ-Aminobutyric Acid, and Social Cognition in Autism Spectrum Disorders. *Journal of Child and Adolescent Psychopharmacology*, *25*(4), 314–322. DOI: 10.1089/cap.2014.0112 PMID: 25919578

Colombo, V., Baldassini, D., Mottura, S., Sacco, M., Crepaldi, M., & Antonietti, A. (2017). Antonyms: A serious game for enhancing inhibition mechanisms in children with Attention Deficit/Hyperactivity Disorder (ADHD). In *International Conference on Virtual Rehabilitation, ICVR* (Vol. 2017-June, pp. 10–11). https://doi.org/DOI: 10.1109/ICVR.2017.8007457

Conti-Ramsden, G., Durkin, K., Toseeb, U., Botting, N., & Pickles, A. (2018). Developmental language disorder: A consensus approach. *Journal of Child Psychology and Psychiatry, and Allied Disciplines*, *59*(10), 1068–1080. DOI: 10.1111/jcpp.12893

Corbett, B. A., Constantine, L. J., Hendren, R. L., Rocke, D. M., & Ozonoff, S. (2009). Examining executive functioning in children with autism spectrum disorder, attention deficit hyperactivity disorder and typical development. *Psychiatry Research*, *166*(2-3), 210–222. DOI: 10.1016/j.psychres.2008.02.005 PMID: 19285351

Corrigan, P. W., & Watson, A. C. (2002). Understanding the impact of stigma on people with mental illness. *World Psychiatry; Official Journal of the World Psychiatric Association (WPA), 1*(1), 16–20. PMID: 16946807

Cortese, S., Adamo, N., Del Giovane, C., Mohr-Jensen, C., Hayes, A. J., Carucci, S., Atkinson, L. Z., Tessari, L., Banaschewski, T., Coghill, D., Hollis, C., Simonoff, E., Zuddas, A., & Barbui, C., Panz , M., Agnoli, A., Restenziale, A., Brignere, M., & Cipriani, A. (. (2018). Comparative efficacy and tolerability of medications for ADHD. *The Lancet. Psychiatry, 5*(9), 727–738. DOI: 10.1016/S2215-0366(18)30269-4 PMID: 30097390

Costa, A. P., Loor, C., & Steffgen, G. (2020). Suicidality in Adults with Autism Spectrum Disorder: The Role of Depressive Symptomatology, Alexithymia, and Antidepressants. *Journal of Autism and Developmental Disorders, 50*(10), 3585–3597. DOI: 10.1007/s10803-020-04433-3 PMID: 32172508

Costescu, C., Ro an, A., David, C. C., Cozma, L., & Calota, A. (2023). The Relation between Cognitive and Emotional Processes in Children and Adolescents with Neurodevelopmental Disorders—A Meta-Analysis. *European Journal of Investigation in Health, Psychology and Education, 13*(12), 2811–2826. DOI: 10.3390/ejihpe13120194 PMID: 38131893

Craig, F., Margari, F., Legrottaglie, A. R., Palumbi, R., de Giambattista, C., & Margari, L. (2016). A systematic review of executive function deficits in autism spectrum disorder and ADHD. *Neuropsychiatric Disease and Treatment, 12*, 1191–1202. DOI: 10.2147/NDT.S104620 PMID: 27274255

Crandall, A., Deater-Deckard, K., & Riley, A. W. (2015). Maternal emotion and cognitive control capacities and parenting: A conceptual framework. *Developmental Review, 36*, 105–126. DOI: 10.1016/j.dr.2015.01.004 PMID: 26028796

Cranston, J. M., Crockett, A., Moss, J., Pegram, R. W., & Stocks, N. (2008). Models of chronic disease management in primary care for patients with mild-to-moderate asthma or COPD: A narrative review. *The Medical Journal of Australia, 188*(S8). Advance online publication. DOI: 10.5694/j.1326-5377.2008.tb01744.x PMID: 18429736

Crisci, G., Caviola, S., Cardillo, R., & Mammarella, I. C. (2021). Executive Functions in Neurodevelopmental Disorders: Comorbidity Overlaps Between Attention Deficit and Hyperactivity Disorder and Specific Learning Disorders. *Frontiers in Human Neuroscience, 15*, 594234. Advance online publication. DOI: 10.3389/fnhum.2021.594234 PMID: 33732121

Cruz, S., Sousa, M., & Mateus, V. (2024). *Emotion Regulation and Cognitive and Social Functioning in Early Development: The Interface Between Neurophysiological and Behavioural Perspectives*. IntechOpen., DOI: 10.5772/intechopen.1004233

Cui, Z., Liang, A., Huang, H., & Ni, X. (2024). Brain Function Characteristics of Children with Attention-Deficit/Hyperactivity Disorder Aged 4-9 Years During a GO/NOGO Task: An Functional Near-Infrared Spectroscopy Study. *Neuropsychiatric Disease and Treatment*, *20*, 2507–2516. DOI: 10.2147/NDT.S486656 PMID: 39691630

Cuthbert, B. N. (2014). The RDoC framework: Facilitating transition from ICD/DSM to dimensional approaches. *World Psychiatry; Official Journal of the World Psychiatric Association (WPA)*, *13*(1), 28–35. DOI: 10.1002/wps.20087 PMID: 24497240

Cuthbert, B. N., & Insel, T. R. (2013). Toward the future of psychiatric diagnosis: The seven pillars of RDoC. *BMC Medicine*, *11*(1), 126. Advance online publication. DOI: 10.1186/1741-7015-11-126 PMID: 23672542

Da Fonseca, D., Seguier, V., Santos, A., Poinso, F., & Deruelle, C. (2008). Emotion understanding in children with ADHD. *Child Psychiatry and Human Development*, *40*(1), 111–121. DOI: 10.1007/s10578-008-0114-9 PMID: 18663570

Dai, H., He, X., Chen, L., & Yin, C. (2022). Language impairments in children with developmental language disorder and children with high-functioning autism plus language impairment: Evidence from Chinese negative sentences. [Secondary Psychology of Language]. *Frontiers in Psychology*, *13*, 926897. Advance online publication. DOI: 10.3389/fpsyg.2022.926897 PMID: 36248514

Daley, T. C. (2004). From symptom recognition to diagnosis: Children with autism in urban India. *Social Science & Medicine*, *58*(7), 1323–1335. DOI: 10.1016/S0277-9536(03)00330-7 PMID: 14759679

Daley, T. C., & Singhal, N. (2010). Understanding autism in India. *Indian Journal of Pediatrics*, *77*(3), 313–319. DOI: 10.1007/s12098-010-0033-0 PMID: 20091358

Dang, C., Zhu, Y., Luo, X., Liu, L., Feng, Y., Wu, G., Zhong, S., Wang, X., Zhang, J., Zhu, Y., Liu, S., Liu, Z., Qin, L., Ma, X., Wang, Y., Wang, X., Yang, J., Wang, C., & Sun, L. (2025). The promoting effects of digital targeted cognitive training in medication treatment for children with ADHD: A randomized controlled trial. *BMC Medicine*, *23*(1), 371. DOI: 10.1186/s12916-025-04192-x PMID: 40598377

Davidson, A., & Souza, P. (2024). Relationships Between Auditory Processing and Cognitive Abilities in Adults: A Systematic Review. *Journal of Speech, Language, and Hearing Research: JSLHR*, *67*(1), 316–336. DOI: 10.1044/2023_JSLHR-22-00716 PMID: 38147487

Davis, N. O., & Kollins, S. H. (2012). Psychosocial and behavioural interventions for children and adolescents with attention-deficit/hyperactivity disorder and autism spectrum disorder. *Current Psychiatry Reports*, *14*(5), 510–517. DOI: 10.1007/s11920-012-0306-0

Dawson, A. E., Wymbs, B. T., Marshall, S. A., Mautone, J. A., & Power, T. J. (2016). The role of parental ADHD in sustaining the effects of a family-school intervention for ADHD. *Journal of Clinical Child and Adolescent Psychology : The Official Journal for the Society of Clinical Child and Adolescent Psychology, American Psychological Association, Division 53*, *45*(3), 305–319. DOI: 10.1080/15374416.2014.963858 PMID: 25496523

Dawson, G., & Guare, R. (2004). *Executive skills in children and adolescents: A practical guide to assessment and intervention*. Guilford Press.

Dawson, G., Rogers, S., Munson, J., Smith, M., Winter, J., Greenson, J., Donaldson, A., & Varley, J. (2010). Randomized controlled trial of an intervention for toddlers with autism: The Early Start Denver Model. *Pediatrics*, *125*(1), e17–e23. DOI: 10.1542/peds.2009-0958 PMID: 19948568

Dawson, P., & Guare, R. (2018). *Executive skills in children and adolescents* (3rd ed.). Guilford Press.

deBettencourt, M. T., Keene, P. A., Awh, E., & Vogel, E. K. (2019). Real-time triggering reveals concurrent lapses of attention and working memory. *Nature Human Behaviour*, *3*(8), 808–816. DOI: 10.1038/s41562-019-0606-6 PMID: 31110335

Decety, J., Steinbeis, N., & Cowell, J. M. (2021). The neurodevelopment of social preferences in early childhood! *Current Opinion in Neurobiology*, *68*, 23–28. DOI: 10.1016/j.conb.2020.12.009 PMID: 33418273

Demetriou, E. A., DeMayo, M. M., & Guastella, A. J. (2019). Executive function in autism spectrum disorder: History, theoretical models, empirical findings and potential as an endophenotype. *Frontiers in Psychiatry*, *10*, 753. DOI: 10.3389/fpsyt.2019.00753 PMID: 31780959

Demetriou, E. A., Lampit, A., Quintana, D. S., Naismith, S. L., Song, Y. J. C., Pye, J. E., Hickie, I., & Guastella, A. J. (2018). Autism spectrum disorders: A meta-analysis of executive function. *Molecular Psychiatry*, *23*(5), 1198–1204. DOI: 10.1038/mp.2017.75 PMID: 28439105

Demirayak, P., Kıyı, İ., İşbitiren, Y. Ö., & Yener, G. (2023). Cognitive load associates prolonged P300 latency during target stimulus processing in individuals with mild cognitive impairment. *Scientific Reports*, *13*(1), 15956. DOI: 10.1038/s41598-023-43132-8 PMID: 37743392

Demirdöğen, E. Y., Esin, İ. S., Turan, B., & Dursun, O. B. (2022). Assessing sustained attention of children with ADHD in a class flow video task. *Nordic Journal of Psychiatry*, *76*(7), 497–506. DOI: 10.1080/08039488.2022.2064545 PMID: 35521909

Demontis, D., Walters, R. K., Martin, J., Mattheisen, M., Als, T. D., Agerbo, E., Baldursson, G., Belliveau, R., Bybjerg-Grauholm, J., Bækvad-Hansen, M., Cerrato, F., Chambert, K., Churchhouse, C., Dumont, A., Eriksson, N., Gandal, M., Goldstein, J. I., Grasby, K. L., Grove, J., & Neale, B. M. (2019). Discovery of the first genome-wide significant risk loci for attention deficit/hyperactivity disorder. *Nature Genetics*, *51*(1), 63–75. DOI: 10.1038/s41588-018-0269-7 PMID: 30478444

Deng, C., Zhu, Z., Luo, G., Zeng, H., Jiang, X., Yu, Q., & Pan, X. (2025). Effects of gymnastics exercises on executive function in children with autism spectrum disorder aged 6 to 9 years: A pilot study of a randomized controlled trial. *Frontiers in Psychology*, *16*, 1660305. Advance online publication. DOI: 10.3389/fpsyg.2025.1660305 PMID: 41221190

Denham, S. A., Bassett, H. H., Thayer, S. K., Mincic, M. S., Sirotkin, Y. S., & Zinsser, K. (2012). Social-emotional learning and academic success. *Early Education and Development*, *23*(5), 652–680. DOI: 10.1080/10409289.2010.497450

Desaunay, P., Briant, A. R., Bowler, D. M., Ring, M., Gérardin, P., Baleyte, J.-M., Guénolé, F., Eustache, F., Parienti, J.-J., & Guillery-Girard, B. (2020). Memory in autism spectrum disorder: A meta-analysis of experimental studies. *Psychological Bulletin*, *146*(5), 377–410. DOI: 10.1037/bul0000225 PMID: 32191044

Diamond, A. (2013). Executive functions. *Annual Review of Psychology*, *64*(1), 135–168. DOI: 10.1146/annurev-psych-113011-143750 PMID: 23020641

Dinn, W. M., Robbins, N. C., & Harris, C. L. (2001). Adult attention-deficit/hyperactivity disorder: Neuropsychological correlates and clinical presentation. *Brain and Cognition*, *46*(1-2), 114–121. DOI: 10.1016/S0278-2626(01)80046-4 PMID: 11527308

Dipeolu, A., Hargrave, S., Cabrera, Y. A., Longoria, A., & Escalante, M. (2023). Dysfunctional career thoughts and peer relationships in adolescents with ADHD. *International Journal for Educational and Vocational Guidance*. Advance online publication. DOI: 10.1007/s10775-023-09612-z

Dissanayake, C., Richdale, A., Kolivas, N., & Pamment, L. (2020). An exploratory study of autism traits and parenting. *Journal of Autism and Developmental Disorders*, *50*(7), 2593–2606. DOI: 10.1007/s10803-019-03984-4 PMID: 30877419

Donahoe, J. W., & Palmer, D. C. (2022). Acquired Reinforcement: Implications for Autism. *The American Psychologist*, *77*(2), 295–307. PMID: 35201786

Donolato, E., Cardillo, R., Mammarella, I. C., & Melby-Lervag, M. (2022). Research Review: Language and specific learning disorders in children and their co-occurrence with internalizing and externalizing problems: A systematic review and meta-analysis. *Journal of Child Psychology and Psychiatry, and Allied Disciplines*, *63*(5), 503–518.DOI: 10.1111/jcpp.12521 PMID: 34747025

Donovan, J. (2020). Childbirth experiences of women with autism spectrum disorder in an acute care setting. *Nursing for Women's Health*, *24*(3), 165–174. DOI: 10.1016/j.nwh.2020.04.001 PMID: 32389581

Douglas, S. N., & Josol, C. K. (2025). Friendship Experiences of Children With Neurodevelopmental Disabilities and Their Peers: A Meta-Synthesis. *Focus on Autism and Other Developmental Disabilities*, *40*(4), 189–199. Advance online publication. DOI: 10.1177/10883576251349208

Dovis, S., Van Der Oord, S., Wiers, R. W., & Prins, P. J. M. (2015). Improving Executive Functioning in Children with ADHD: Training Multiple Executive Functions within the Context of a Computer Game. A Randomized Double-Blind Placebo Controlled Trial. *PLoS One*, *10*(4), e0121651. DOI: 10.1371/journal.pone.0121651 PMID: 25844638

Dowdney, L., & Skuse, D. (1993). Parenting provided by adults with mental retardation. *Journal of Child Psychology and Psychiatry, and Allied Disciplines*, *34*(1), 25–47. DOI: 10.1111/j.1469-7610.1993.tb00966.x PMID: 8421068

Doyle, N. (2020). Neurodiversity at work: A biopsychosocial model and the impact on working adults. *British Medical Bulletin*, *135*(1), 1–18. DOI: 10.1093/bmb/ldaa021 PMID: 32996572

Dramsdahl, M., Westerhausen, R., Haavik, J., Hugdahl, K., & Plessen, K. J. (2012). Adults with attention-deficit/hyperactivity disorder - a diffusion-tensor imaging study of the corpus callosum. *Psychiatry Research, 201*(2), 168–173. DOI: 10.1016/j.pscychresns.2011.08.005 PMID: 22386969

Drechsler, R., Brem, S., Brandeis, D., Grünblatt, E., Berger, G., & Walitza, S. (2020). ADHD: Current Concepts and Treatments in Children and Adolescents. *Neuropediatrics, 51*(5), 315–335. DOI: 10.1055/s-0040-1701658 PMID: 32559806

Drljan, B., Ječmenica, N., & Buha, N. (2024). Theory of mind in children with developmental language disorder: Developmental tendencies. *Inovacije U Nastavi, 37*(1), 43–60. DOI: 10.5937/inovacije2401043D

Duan, K., Jiang, W., Rootes-Murdy, K., Schoenmacker, G. H., Arias-Vasquez, A., Buitelaar, J. K., Hoogman, M., Oosterlaan, J., Hoekstra, P. J., Heslenfeld, D. J., Hartman, C. A., Calhoun, V. D., Turner, J. A., & Liu, J. (2021). Gray matter networks associated with attention and working memory deficit in ADHD across adolescence and adulthood. *Translational Psychiatry, 11*(1), 184. DOI: 10.1038/s41398-021-01301-1 PMID: 33767139

Duan, X., Wang, R., Xiao, J., Li, Y., Huang, X., Guo, X., Cao, J., He, L., He, C., Ling, Z., Shan, X., Chen, H., Kang, X., & Chen, H. (2020). Subcortical structural covariance in young children with autism spectrum disorder. *Progress in Neuro-Psychopharmacology & Biological Psychiatry, 99*, 109874. DOI: 10.1016/j.pnpbp.2020.109874 PMID: 31981719

Duan, Y., Xie, H., Tan, W., & Zeng, Y. (2025). Neural connections and molecular mechanisms underlying motor skill deficits in genetic models of ASD. *Progress in Neurobiology*, •••, 102759. DOI: 10.1016/j.pneurobio.2025.102759 PMID: 40254176

Dugdale, A.-S., Thompson, A. R., Leedham, A., Beail, N., & Freeth, M. (2021). Intense connection and love: The experiences of autistic mothers. *Autism : The International Journal of Research and Practice, 25*(7), 1973–1984. DOI: 10.1177/13623613211005987 PMID: 33840262

Duker, L., Polido, J., Mailloux, Z., Coleman, G., & Cermak, S. (2011). Oral care and sensory sensitivities in children with autism spectrum disorders. *Special Care in Dentistry : Official Publication of the American Association of Hospital Dentists, the Academy of Dentistry for the Handicapped, and the American Society for Geriatric Dentistry, 31*(3), 102–110. DOI: 10.1111/j.1754-4505.2011.00187.x PMID: 21592164

Duman, R. S., Malberg, J., Nakagawa, S., & D'Sa, C. (2000). Neuronal plasticity and survival in mood disorders. *Biological Psychiatry*, *48*(8), 732–739. DOI: 10.1016/S0006-3223(00)00935-5 PMID: 11063970

Dunst, C. J., Trivette, C. M., & Hamby, D. W. (2007). Meta-analysis of family-centered helpgiving practices. *Mental Retardation and Developmental Disabilities Research Reviews*, *13*(4), 370–378. DOI: 10.1002/mrdd.20176 PMID: 17979208

DuPaul, G. J., & Stoner, G. (2014). *ADHD in the schools* (3rd ed.). Guilford Press.

Dupont, G., Van Rooij, D., Buitelaar, J. K., Reif, A., & Grimm, O. (2022). Sex-related differences in adult attention-deficit hyperactivity disorder patients – An analysis of external globus pallidus functional connectivity in resting-state functional MRI. *Frontiers in Psychiatry*, *13*, 962911. Advance online publication. DOI: 10.3389/fpsyt.2022.962911 PMID: 36117656

Dwyer, P. (2022). The neurodiversity approach (es): What are they and what do they mean for researchers? *Human Development*, *66*(2), 73–92. DOI: 10.1159/000523723 PMID: 36158596

Dwyer, P., Sillas, A., Prieto, M., Camp, E., Nordahl, C. W., & Rivera, S. M. (2024). Hyper-focus, sticky attention, and springy attention in young autistic children: Associations with sensory behaviors and cognitive ability. *Autism Research : Official Journal of the International Society for Autism Research*, *17*(8), 1677–1695. DOI: 10.1002/aur.3174 PMID: 38840328

Earle, F. S., & Ullman, M. T. (2020). Deficits of learning in procedural memory and consolidation in declarative memory in adults with developmental language disorder. *Journal of Speech, Language, and Hearing Research: JSLHR*, *63*(10), 3290–3305. PMID: 33524264

Earnest, T., Shephard, E., Tye, C., McEwen, F., Woodhouse, E., Liang, H., Sheerin, F., & Bolton, P. F. (2020). Actigraph-Measured Movement Correlates of Attention-Deficit/Hyperactivity Disorder (ADHD) Symptoms in Young People with Tuberous Sclerosis Complex (TSC) with and without Intellectual Disability and Autism Spectrum Disorder (ASD). *Brain Sciences*, *10*(8), 491. DOI: 10.3390/brainsci10080491 PMID: 32731531

Ebert, S. (2020). Theory of mind, language, and reading: Developmental relations from early childhood to early adolescence. *Journal of Experimental Child Psychology*, *191*, 104739. DOI: 10.1016/j.jecp.2019.104739 PMID: 31830710

Edel, M. A., Juckel, G., & Brüne, M. (2010). Interaction of recalled parental ADHD symptoms and rearing behavior with current attachment and emotional dysfunction in adult offspring with ADHD. *Psychiatry Research, 178*(1), 137–141. DOI: 10.1016/j.psychres.2010.04.004 PMID: 20452044

Edirisooriya, M., Dykiert, D., & Auyeung, B. (2020). IQ and Internalising Symptoms in Adolescents with ASD. *Journal of Autism and Developmental Disorders, 51*(11), 3887–3907. DOI: 10.1007/s10803-020-04810-y PMID: 33381856

Edossa, A. K., Shroeders, U., Weinert, S., & Artelt, C. (2017). The development of emotional and behavioral self-regulation and their effects on academic achievement in childhood. *International Journal of Behavioral Development, 42*(2), 192–202. DOI: 10.1177/0165025416687412

Eigsti, I. M., & Irvine, C. A. (2022). Verbal mediation of theory of mind in verbal adolescents with ASD. *Language Acquisition, 29*(1), 1–25. PMID: 35281590

Elsadek, A. E., Al-Shokary, A. H., Abdelghani, W. E., Kamal, N. M., Ibrahim, A. O., El-Shorbagy, H. H., Suliman, H. A., Barseem, N. F., Abdel Maksoud, Y. H., Azab, S. M., & Nour El Din, D. M. (2020). Serum Levels of Interleukin-6 and Tumor Necrosis Factor Alpha in Children With Attention-Deficit Hyperactivity Disorder. *Journal of Pediatric Neurosciences, 15*(4), 402–408. DOI: 10.4103/JPN.JPN_1_20 PMID: 33936305

Engel, G. L. (1977). The need for a new medical model: A challenge for biomedicine. *Science, 196*(4286), 129–136. DOI: 10.1126/science.847460 PMID: 847460

Erikson, E. H. (1950). *Childhood and society*. Norton.

Erikson, E. H. (1968). *Identity: Youth and crisis*. Norton.

Espelöer, J., Hellmich, M., Vogeley, K., & Falter-Wagner, C. M. (2020). Brief report: Social anxiety in autism spectrum disorder is based on deficits in social competence. *Journal of Autism and Developmental Disorders, 51*(1), 315–322. DOI: 10.1007/s10803-020-04529-w PMID: 32410100

Esposito, G., Del Carmen Rostagno, M., Venuti, P., Haltigan, J. D., & Messinger, D. S. (2014). Brief Report: Atypical expression of distress during the separation phase of the strange situation procedure in infant siblings at high risk for ASD. *Journal of Autism and Developmental Disorders, 44*(4), 975–980. DOI: 10.1007/s10803-013-1940-6 PMID: 24026913

Eussen, M., Gool, A. R. V., Verheij, F., de Nijs, P. F., Verhulst, F. C., & Greaves-Lord, K. (2012). The association of quality of social relations, symptom severity and intelligence with anxiety in children with autism spectrum disorders. *Autism : The International Journal of Research and Practice, 17*(6), 723–735. DOI: 10.1177/1362361312453882 PMID: 22917843

Evans, S. W., Vallano, G., & Pelham, W. (1994). Treatment of parenting behavior with a psychostimulant: A case study of an adult with attention-deficit hyperactivity disorder. *Journal of Child and Adolescent Psychopharmacology, 4*(1), 63–69. DOI: 10.1089/cap.1994.4.63

Facoetti, A., Paganoni, P., Turatto, M., Marzola, V., & Mascetti, G. G. (2000). Visual-spatial attention in developmental dyslexia. *Cortex; A Journal Devoted to the Study of the Nervous System and Behavior, 36*(1), 109–123. DOI: 10.1016/S0010-9452(08)70840-2 PMID: 10728901

Faden, S. Y., Merdad, N., & Faden, Y. A. (2023). Parents of Children With Neurodevelopmental Disorders: A Mixed Methods Approach to Understanding Quality of Life, Stress, and Perceived Social Support. *Cureus, 15*(4), e37356. DOI: 10.7759/cureus.37356 PMID: 37182086

Fair, D. A., Cohen, A. L., Power, J. D., Dosenbach, N. U. F., Church, J. A., Miezin, F. M., Schlaggar, B. L., & Petersen, S. E. (2009). Functional brain networks develop from a "local to distributed" organization. *PLoS Computational Biology, 5*(5), e1000381. DOI: 10.1371/journal.pcbi.1000381 PMID: 19412534

Faja, S., & Darling, L. N. (2018). Variation in restricted and repetitive behaviors and interests relates to inhibitory control and shifting in children with autism spectrum disorder. *Autism : The International Journal of Research and Practice, 23*(5), 1262–1272. DOI: 10.1177/1362361318804192 PMID: 30394786

Fan, J., Bernardi, S., Dam, N. T. V., Anagnostou, E., Gu, X., Martin, L., & Hof, P. R. (2012). Functional deficits of the attentional networks in autism. *Brain and Behavior, 2*(5), 647–660. DOI: 10.1002/brb3.90 PMID: 23139910

Farah, M. J. (2017). The neuroscience of socioeconomic status: Correlates, causes and consequences. *Neuron, 96*(1), 56–71. DOI: 10.1016/j.neuron.2017.08.034 PMID: 28957676

Faraone, S. V., Banaschewski, T., Coghill, D., Zheng, Y., Biederman, J., Bellgrove, M. A., Newcorn, J. H., Mattos, P., Solanto, M. V., Andrade, E. N., Asherson, P., Franke, B., Luo, Y., Schulz, K. P., Swanson, J. M., Thapar, A., Wang, Y., & Wang, J. (2014). The pharmacology of ADHD medications. *Journal of Child Psychology and Psychiatry, and Allied Disciplines*, *55*(1), 3–14. DOI: 10.1111/jcpp.12132 PMID: 24117606

Faraone, S. V., Banaschewski, T., Coghill, D., Zheng, Y., Biederman, J., Bellgrove, M. A., & Wang, Y. (2021). The World Federation of ADHD international consensus statement. *Neuroscience and Biobehavioral Reviews*, *128*, 789–818. DOI: 10.1016/j.neubiorev.2021.01.022 PMID: 33549739

Faraone, S. V., Biederman, J., Spencer, T., Wilens, T., Seidman, L. J., Mick, E., & Doyle, A. E. (2000). Attention-deficit/hyperactivity disorder in adults: An overview. *Biological Psychiatry*, *48*(1), 9–20. DOI: 10.1016/S0006-3223(00)00889-1 PMID: 10913503

Farrow, A., Al-Jaishi, A., O'Donnell, S., Palmeter, S., Georgiades, S., Chen, Y., McPhee, P. G., & Edjoc, R. (2024). Functional difficulties in children and youth with autism spectrum disorder: Analysis of the 2019 canadian health survey on children and youth. *Health Promotion and Chronic Disease Prevention in Canada : Research, Policy and Practice*, *44*(1), 9–20. DOI: 10.24095/hpcdp.44.1.02 PMID: 38231089

Fatta, L. M., Laugeson, E. A., Bianchi, D., Laghi, F., & Scattoni, M. L. (2024). Program for the Education and Enrichment of Relational Skills (PEERS®) for Italy: A Randomized Controlled Trial of a Social Skills Intervention for Autistic Adolescents. *Journal of Autism and Developmental Disorders*, *55*(1), 202–220. DOI: 10.1007/s10803-023-06211-3 PMID: 38190054

Feehan, A., & Charest, M. (2023). A scoping review of oral language and social communication abilities in children with Tourette syndrome. *International Journal of Language & Communication Disorders*. Advance online publication. DOI: 10.1111/1460-6984.12949 PMID: 37667569

Feldman, R., & Masalha, S. (2010). Parent–child and triadic antecedents of children's social competence: Cultural specificity, shared process. *Developmental Psychology*, *46*(2), 455–467. DOI: 10.1037/a0017415 PMID: 20210505

Felitti, V. J., Anda, R. F., Nordenberg, D., Williamson, D. F., Spitz, A. M., Edwards, V., Koss, M. P., & Marks, J. S. (1998). Relationship of childhood abuse and household dysfunction to many of the leading causes of death in adults. The Adverse Childhood Experiences (ACE) Study. *American Journal of Preventive Medicine*, *14*(4), 245–258. DOI: 10.1016/S0749-3797(98)00017-8 PMID: 9635069

Fernández de la Cruz, L., Rydell, M., Runeson, B., Brander, G., Rück, C., D'Onofrio, B. M., Larsson, H., Lichtenstein, P., & Mataix-Cols, D. (2017). Suicide in Tourette's and chronic tic disorders. *Biological Psychiatry*, *82*(2), 111–118. DOI: 10.1016/j.biopsych.2016.08.023 PMID: 27773353

Fietz, J., Valencia, N., & Silani, G. (2018). Alexithymia and autistic traits as possible predictors for traits related to depression, anxiety, and stress: A multivariate statistical approach. *Journal of Evaluation in Clinical Practice*, *24*(4), 901–908. DOI: 10.1111/jep.12961 PMID: 29882629

Filipe, M. G., Carvalhais, L., Abbeduto, L., & Frota, S. (2023). Editorial: Language across neurodevelopmental disorders. *Frontiers in Psychology*, *13*, 1121997. Advance online publication. DOI: 10.3389/fpsyg.2022.1121997 PMID: 36687986

Firouzabadi, F. D., Ramezanpour, S., Firouzabadi, M. D., Yousem, I. J., Puts, N. J., & Yousem, D. M. (2021). Neuroimaging in Attention-Deficit/Hyperactivity Disorder: Recent Advances. *AJR. American Journal of Roentgenology*, *218*(2), 321–332. DOI: 10.2214/AJR.21.26316 PMID: 34406053

Fischer, J., Koldewyn, K., Jiang, Y., & Kanwisher, N. (2013). Unimpaired Attentional Disengagement and Social Orienting in Children With Autism. *Clinical Psychological Science*, *2*(2), 214–223. DOI: 10.1177/2167702613496242 PMID: 25419497

Fischer, J., Smith, H., Martinez-Pedraza, F., Carter, A. S., Kanwisher, N., & Káldy, Z. (2015). Unimpaired attentional disengagement in toddlers with autism spectrum disorder. *Developmental Science*, *19*(6), 1095–1103. DOI: 10.1111/desc.12386 PMID: 26690733

Fishbein, D. H., Michael, L., Guthrie, C., Carr, C., & Raymer, J. (2019). Associations Between Environmental Conditions and Executive Cognitive Functioning and Behavior During Late Childhood: A Pilot Study. *Frontiers in Psychology*, *10*, 1263. DOI: 10.3389/fpsyg.2019.01263 PMID: 31231280

Fisher, N., Happé, F., & Dunn, J. (2005). The relationship between vocabulary, grammar, and false belief task performance in children with autistic spectrum disorders and children with moderate learning difficulties. *Journal of Child Psychology and Psychiatry, and Allied Disciplines*, *46*(4), 409–419. DOI: 10.1111/j.1469-7610.2004.00371.x PMID: 15819650

Fletcher-Watson, S. (2022). Neurodiversity and autism research. *Autism : The International Journal of Research and Practice*, *26*(1), 3–5. DOI: 10.1177/1362361319883506 PMID: 35000419

Florian, L., & Beaton, M. (2018). Inclusive pedagogy in action: Getting it right for every child. *International Journal of Inclusive Education, 22*(8), 870–884. DOI: 10.1080/13603116.2017.1412513

Florian, L., & Black-Hawkins, K. (2011). Exploring inclusive pedagogy. *British Educational Research Journal, 37*(5), 813–828. DOI: 10.1080/01411926.2010.501096

Florian, L., & Black-Hawkins, K. (2011). Exploring inclusive pedagogy. *Cambridge Journal of Education, 41*(4), 813–828.

Fong, V. C., & Iarocci, G. (2020). The Role of Executive Functioning in Predicting Social Competence in Children with and without Autism Spectrum Disorder. *Autism Research : Official Journal of the International Society for Autism Research, 13*(11), 1856–1866. DOI: 10.1002/aur.2350 PMID: 33460309

Forest, T. A., & Amso, D. (2023). Neurodevelopment of Attention, Learning, and Memory Systems in Infancy. *Annual Review of Developmental Psychology, 5*(1), 45–65. DOI: 10.1146/annurev-devpsych-120321-011300

Fortes, D., Figueiredo, T., Lima, G., Segenreich, D., Serra-Pinheiro, M. A., & Mattos, P. (2020). Disregarding Impairment in ADHD Diagnosis Inflates Its Prevalence. *Journal of Attention Disorders, 25*(11), 1529–1533. DOI: 10.1177/1087054720911969 PMID: 32329397

Foti, F., De Crescenzo, F., Vivanti, G., & Fadda, S. (2015). Implicit learning in individuals with autism spectrum disorders: A meta-analysis. *Psychological Medicine, 45*(5), 897–910. DOI: 10.1017/S0033291714001950 PMID: 25126858

Francés, L., Ruiz, A., Virgínia Soler, C., Fernández Francés, J., & Caules, J. (2023). Prevalence, comorbidities, and profiles of neurodevelopmental disorders according to the DSM-5-TR in children aged 6 years old in a European region. *Frontiers in Psychiatry, 14*, 1260747. Advance online publication. DOI: 10.3389/fpsyt.2023.1260747 PMID: 38025459

French, B., Daley, D., Groom, M., & Cassidy, S. (2023). Risks Associated With Undiagnosed ADHD and/or Autism: A Mixed-Method Systematic Review. *Journal of Attention Disorders, 27*(12), 1393–1410. DOI: 10.1177/10870547231176862 PMID: 37341291

Friedman, L. M., Eckrich, S. J., Rapport, M. D., Bohil, C. J., & Calub, C. A. (2023). Working and short-term memory in children with ADHD: An examination of prefrontal cortical functioning using functional Near-Infrared Spectroscopy (fNIRS). *Child Neuropsychology : A Journal on Normal and Abnormal Development in Childhood and Adolescence*, *30*(3), 462–485. DOI: 10.1080/09297049.2023.2213463 PMID: 37199502

Friedman, L., & Sterling, A. A. (2019). A review of language, executive function, and intervention in autism spectrum disorder. *Seminars in Speech and Language*, *40*(4), 291–304. DOI: 10.1055/s-0039-1692964 PMID: 31311054

Friedman, N. P., & Robbins, T. W. (2022). The role of prefrontal cortex in cognitive control and executive function. *Neuropsychopharmacology : Official Publication of the American College of Neuropsychopharmacology*, *47*(1), 72–89. DOI: 10.1038/s41386-021-01132-0 PMID: 34408280

Friend, M., & Bursuck, W. D. (2019). *Including students with special needs* (8th ed.). Pearson.

Fuller, E. A., & Kaiser, A. P. (2020). The effects of early intervention on social communication outcomes for children with autism spectrum disorder. *Journal of Autism and Developmental Disorders*, *50*(5), 1683–1700. DOI: 10.1007/s10803-019-03927-z PMID: 30805766

Gardner, M., Suplee, P. D., Bloch, J., & Lecks, K. (2016). Exploratory study of childbearing experiences of women with Asperger syndrome. *Nursing for Women's Health*, *20*(1), 28–P37. DOI: 10.1016/j.nwh.2015.12.001 PMID: 26902438

Gathercole, S. E., Pickering, S. J., Knight, C., & Stegmann, Z. (2004). Working memory skills and educational attainment: Evidence from national curriculum assessments. *Applied Cognitive Psychology*, *18*(1), 1–16. DOI: 10.1002/acp.934

Geng, K., Wang, Y., Fu, W., Chen, S., & Yang, Y. (2024). Episodic memory impairment and its influencing factors in individuals with autism spectrum disorder: Systematic review and meta-analysis. *European Archives of Psychiatry and Clinical Neuroscience*. PMID: 39269621

Gerlach-Houck, H., & Constantino, C. D. (2022). Interrupting ableism in stuttering therapy and research: Practical suggestions. *Perspectives of the ASHA Special Interest Groups*, *7*(2), 357–374. DOI: 10.1044/2021_PERSP-21-00109

Geurts, H. M., Oosterlaan, J., & Sergeant, J. A. (2005). Is there a clinical utility of executive function measures in the assessment of ADHD subtypes? *Archives of Clinical Neuropsychology : The Official Journal of the National Academy of Neuropsychologists, 20*(4), 457–477. DOI: 10.1016/j.acn.2004.11.001 PMID: 15896560

Ghirardi, L., Brikell, I., Kuja-Halkola, R., Freitag, C. M., Franke, B., Asherson, P., & Larsson, H. (2019). The familial co-aggregation of ASD and ADHD: A register-based cohort study. *Molecular Psychiatry, 24*(11), 1732–1737. DOI: 10.1038/s41380-019-0555-z PMID: 29703945

Gilbert, E. N. (2019). Designing inclusive physical education with Universal Design for Learning. *Journal of Physical Education, Recreation & Dance, 90*(7), 15–21. DOI: 10.1080/07303084.2019.1637305

Gilbert, M., Boecker, M., Reiss, F., Kaman, A., Erhart, M., Schlack, R., Westenhöfer, J., Döpfner, M., & Ravens-Sieberer, U. (2025). Gender and Age Differences in ADHD Symptoms and Co-occurring Depression and Anxiety Symptoms Among Children and Adolescents in the BELLA Study. *Child Psychiatry and Human Development, 56*(4), 1162–1172. DOI: 10.1007/s10578-023-01622-w PMID: 37851158

Gillberg, C. (2010). The ESSENCE in child psychiatry: Early Symptomatic Syndromes Eliciting Neurodevelopmental Clinical Examinations. *Research in Developmental Disabilities, 31*(6), 1543–1551. DOI: 10.1016/j.ridd.2010.06.002 PMID: 20634041

Gjevik, E., Eldevik, S., Fjæran-Granum, T., & Sponheim, E. (2010). Kiddie-SADS Reveals High Rates of DSM-IV Disorders in Children and Adolescents with Autism Spectrum Disorders. *Journal of Autism and Developmental Disorders, 41*(6), 761–769. DOI: 10.1007/s10803-010-1095-7 PMID: 20824493

Goffman, E. (1963). *Stigma: Notes on the management of spoiled identity*. Prentice Hall.

Gondek, T. (2021). Diagnosing ADHD in adults: Diagnostic tools and differential diagnosis. *European Psychiatry : The Journal of the Association of European Psychiatrists, 64*(S1), S72–S73. DOI: 10.1192/j.eurpsy.2021.226

Goodwin, A., Jones, E. J. H., Salomone, S., Mason, L., Holman, R., Begum-Ali, J., Hunt, A., Ruddock, M., Vamvakas, G., Robinson, E., Holden, C. J., Taylor, C., Smith, T. J., Sonuga-Barke, E., Bolton, P., Charman, T., Pickles, A., Wass, S., & Johnson, M. H. (2021). INTERSTAARS: Attention training for infants with elevated likelihood of developing ADHD: A proof-of-concept randomised controlled trial. *Translational Psychiatry, 11*(1), 644. DOI: 10.1038/s41398-021-01698-9 PMID: 34930893

Government of India. (1999). *The National Trust Act*. Ministry of Social Justice and Empowerment.

Government of India. (2009). *Right of Children to Free and Compulsory Education Act*. Ministry of Law and Justice.

Government of India. (2016). *Rights of Persons with Disabilities Act*. Ministry of Law and Justice.

Government of India. (2018). *Samagra Shiksha Abhiyan framework*. Ministry of Education.

Graham, S., & Harris, K. R. (2013). Designing an effective writing program. *Focus on Exceptional Children*, *45*(7), 1–14.

Gravråkmo, S., Olsen, A., Lydersen, S., Ingul, J. M., Henry, L., & Øie, M. G. (2022). Associations between executive functions, intelligence and adaptive behaviour in children and adolescents with mild intellectual disability. *Journal of Intellectual Disabilities : JOID*, *27*(3), 715–727. Advance online publication. DOI: 10.1177/17446295221095951 PMID: 35543122

Green, S. A., Hernandez, L., Bookheimer, S. Y., & Dapretto, M. (2016). Salience Network Connectivity in Autism Is Related to Brain and Behavioral Markers of Sensory Overresponsivity. *Journal of the American Academy of Child and Adolescent Psychiatry*, *55*(7), 618–626.e1. DOI: 10.1016/j.jaac.2016.04.013 PMID: 27343889

Green, S., Hernandez, L., Tottenham, N., Krasileva, K., Bookheimer, S., & Dapretto, M. (2015). Neurobiology of sensory overresponsivity in youth with autism spectrum disorders. *Journal of the American Academy of Child and Adolescent Psychiatry*, *72*(8), 778. DOI: 10.1001/jamapsychiatry.2015.0737 PMID: 26061819

Greenspan, S. I., & Wieder, S. (1998). *The child with special needs*. Perseus Books.

Greenspan, S. I., & Wieder, S. (2006). *Engaging autism*. Da Capo Press.

Greenway, C. W., Robinson, A., & King, J. M. (2023). The effect of social devaluation, labelling, and familiarity on children's attitudes and behavioral intentions toward a peer with symptoms of ADHD. *Psychology in the Schools*, *60*(11), 4452–4465. Advance online publication. DOI: 10.1002/pits.23004

Greenwood, B. N., Strong, P. V., Foley, T. E., & Fleshner, M. (2008). A behavioral analysis of the impact of voluntary physical activity on hippocampus-dependent contextual conditioning. *Hippocampus*, *19*(10), 988–1001. DOI: 10.1002/hipo.20534 PMID: 19115374

Griggs, M. S., & Mikami, A. Y. (2011). The role of maternal and child ADHD symptoms in shaping interpersonal relationships. [PubMed: 20931275]. *Journal of Abnormal Child Psychology, 39*(3), 437–449. DOI: 10.1007/s10802-010-9464-4 PMID: 20931275

Groce, N., Kett, M., Lang, R., & Trani, J. F. (2011). Disability and poverty. *Lancet, 374*(9704), 1801–1802.

Grove, J., Ripke, S., Als, T. D., Mattheisen, M., Walters, R. K., Won, H., Pallesen, J., Agerbo, E., Andreassen, O. A., Anney, R., Awashti, S., Belliveau, R., Bettella, F., Buxbaum, J. D., Bybjerg-Grauholm, J., Bækvad-Hansen, M., Cerrato, F., Chambert, K., Christensen, J. H., & Børglum, A. D. (2019). Identification of common genetic risk variants for autism spectrum disorder. *Nature Genetics, 51*(3), 431–444. DOI: 10.1038/s41588-019-0344-8 PMID: 30804558

Guerrera, S., Pontillo, M., Tata, M., Vincenzo, C., Bellantoni, D., Napoli, E., & Vicari, S. (2022). Anxiety in autism spectrum disorder: Clinical characteristics and the role of the family. *Brain Sciences, 12*(12), 1597. DOI: 10.3390/brainsci12121597 PMID: 36552057

Guo, X., Chen, H., Long, Z., Duan, X., Zhang, Y., & Chen, H. (2017). Atypical developmental trajectory of local spontaneous brain activity in autism spectrum disorder. *Scientific Reports, 7*(1), 39822. Advance online publication. DOI: 10.1038/srep39822 PMID: 28057930

Guralnick, M. J. (2011). Why early intervention works. *Infants and Young Children, 24*(1), 6–28. DOI: 10.1097/IYC.0b013e3182002cfe PMID: 21532932

Gu, T., Jin, C., Lin, L., Wang, X., Li, X., Jing, J., & Cao, M. (2024). The relationship between executive function and the association of motor coordination difficulties and social communication deficits in autistic children. [Secondary Autism]. *Frontiers in Psychiatry, 15*, 1363406. Advance online publication. DOI: 10.3389/fpsyt.2024.1363406 PMID: 38596639

Guy-Evans, O. (2024). *Bronfenbrenner's Ecological Systems Theory*. ResearchGate.

Hacking, I. (1999). *The social construction of what?* Harvard University Press.

Hallahan, D. P., Kauffman, J. M., & Pullen, P. C. (2018). *Exceptional learners* (14th ed.). Pearson.

Hallett, V., Lecavalier, L., Sukhodolsky, D. G., Cipriano, N., Aman, M. G., McCracken, J. T., McDougle, C. J., Tierney, E., King, B. H., Hollander, E., Sikich, L., Bregman, J., Anagnostou, E., Donnelly, C., Katsovich, L., Dukes, K., Vitiello, B., Gadow, K., & Scahill, L. (2013). Exploring the manifestations of anxiety in children with autism spectrum disorders. *Journal of Autism and Developmental Disorders*, *43*(10), 2341–2352. DOI: 10.1007/s10803-013-1775-1 PMID: 23400347

Hamilton, L. G., & Petty, S. (2023). Compassionate pedagogy for neurodiversity in higher education: A conceptual analysis. *Frontiers in Psychology*, *14*, 1093290. DOI: 10.3389/fpsyg.2023.1093290 PMID: 36874864

Hammud, G., Avital-Magen, A., Schusheim, G., Barzuza, I., & Engel-Yeger, B. (2023). How Self-Regulation and Executive Functions Deficits Affect Quality of Life of Children/Adolescents with Emotional Regulation Disorders. *Children (Basel, Switzerland)*, *10*(10), 1622. DOI: 10.3390/children10101622 PMID: 37892283

Hampshire, P. K., Butera, G. D., & Bellini, S. (2015). Self-management and parents as interventionists to improve homework independence in students with autism spectrum disorders. *Preventing School Failure*, *60*(1), 22–34. DOI: 10.1080/1045988X.2014.954515

Hampton, S., Allison, C., Aydin, E., Baron-Cohen, S., & Holt, R. (2022). Autistic mothers' perinatal well-being and parenting styles. *Autism : The International Journal of Research and Practice*, *26*(7), 1805–1820. DOI: 10.1177/13623613211065544 PMID: 35105233

Hansson Hallerod, S. L., Anckarsater, H., Rastam, M., & Hansson Scherman, M. (2015). Experienced consequences of being diagnosed with ADHD as an adult: A qualitative study. *BMC Psychiatry*, *15*(31), 1–13. DOI: 10.1186/s12888-015-0410-4 PMID: 25884685

Happé, F., & Frith, U. (2020). Annual Research Review: Looking back to look forward - changes in the concept of autism and implications for future research. *Journal of Child Psychology and Psychiatry, and Allied Disciplines*, *61*(3), 218–232. DOI: 10.1111/jcpp.13176 PMID: 31994188

Harold, G. T., Leve, L. D., Barrett, D., Elam, K., Neiderhiser, J. M., Natsuaki, M. N., Shaw, D. S., Reiss, D., & Thapar, A. (2013). Biological and rearing mother influences on child ADHD symptoms: Revisiting the developmental interface between nature and nurture. *Journal of Child Psychology and Psychiatry, and Allied Disciplines*, *54*(10), 1038–1046. DOI: 10.1111/jcpp.12100 PMID: 24007415

Harrist, A. W., & Bakshi, A. J. (2022). The Interplay of Parent and Peer Influences on Children's Social Development! *The Wiley-Blackwell Handbook of Childhood Social Development,* 459-481.

Hautmann, C., Döpfner, M., Katzmann, J., Schürmann, S., Metternich-Kaizman, T., Jaite, C., & Kappel, J. (2018). Sequential treatment of ADHD in mother and child (AIMAC study): Importance of the treatment phases for intervention success in a randomized trial. *BMC Psychiatry, 18*(1), 388. Advance online publication. DOI: 10.1186/s12888-018-1963-9 PMID: 30545333

Hendrickx, S. (2010). *The adolescent and adult neuro-diversity handbook: Asperger's syndrome, ADHD, dyslexia, dyspraxia, and related conditions.* Jessica Kingsley Publishers.

Hendry, A., Jones, E. J. H., Bedford, R., Andersson Konke, L., Begum Ali, J., B lte, S., Brocki, K. C., Demurie, E., Johnson, M., Pijl, M. K. J., Roeyers, H., & Charman, T. (2020). Atypical Development of Attentional Control Associates with Later Adaptive Functioning, Autism and ADHD Traits. *Journal of Autism and Developmental Disorders, 50*(11), 4085–4105. DOI: 10.1007/s10803-020-04465-9 PMID: 32221749

Henry, M. (2021). Examining the Effect of Adverse Childhood Experiences (ACEs) on Executive Functioning and Brain Plasticity.

Hernández González, O., González Fernández, D., Spencer Contreras, R., Gillespie-Smith, K., & Jara Rojas, E. (2024). The childbearing and mental health experiences of autistic mothers: A systematic review. *International Journal of Developmental Disabilities,* •••, 1–15.

Hernández-Torres, D. (2019). Executive Functions and Social Cognition in School-Aged Children with ADHD: an Assessment Proposal. *Conference: 47th Annual Meeting of the International Neuropsychological Society*. DOI: 10.13140/RG.2.2.25450.24004

Herreras, E. B. (2025, September 14). Executive Functioning Profiles in Children with Neurodevelopmental Disorders. *Behavioral Sciences (Basel, Switzerland), 15*(9), 1256. DOI: 10.3390/bs15091256 PMID: 41009286

Herrington, J., Miller, J., Pandey, J., & Schultz, R. (2016). Anxiety and social deficits have distinct relationships with amygdala function in autism spectrum disorder. *Social Cognitive and Affective Neuroscience, 11*(6), 907–914. DOI: 10.1093/scan/nsw015 PMID: 26865425

Heyworth, M., Brett, S., den Houting, J., Magiati, I., Steward, R., Urbanowicz, A., Stears, M., & Pellicano, E. (2023). "I'm the Family Ringmaster and Juggler": Autistic parents' experiences of parenting during the COVID-19 pandemic. *Autism in Adulthood: Challenges and Management*, *5*(1), 24–36. DOI: 10.1089/aut.2021.0097 PMID: 36941857

Hill, E. L. (2004). Evaluating the theory of executive dysfunction in autism. *Developmental Review*, *24*(2), 189–233. DOI: 10.1016/j.dr.2004.01.001

Hinshaw, S. P., & Ellison, K. (2016). *ADHD: What everyone needs to know*. Oxford University Press.

Hirschtritt, M. E., Lee, P. C., Pauls, D. L., Dion, Y., Grados, M. A., Illmann, C., King, R. A., Sandor, P., McMahon, W. M., Lyon, G. J., Cath, D. C., Kurlan, R., Robertson, M. M., Osiecki, L., Scharf, J. M., & Mathews, C. A. (2015). Lifetime prevalence, age of risk, and genetic relationships of comorbid psychiatric disorders in Tourette syndrome. *JAMA Psychiatry*, *72*(4), 325–333. DOI: 10.1001/jamapsychiatry.2014.2650 PMID: 25671412

Hollocks, M. J., Charman, T., Baird, G., Lord, C., Pickles, A., & Simonoff, E. (2021). Exploring the impact of adolescent cognitive inflexibility on emotional and behavioural problems experienced by autistic adults. *Autism : The International Journal of Research and Practice*, *26*(5), 1229–1241. DOI: 10.1177/13623613211046160 PMID: 34579554

Holmes, J., Guy, J., Kievit, R. A., Bryant, A., Mareva, S., & Gathercole, S. E.CALM Team. (2021). Cognitive dimensions of learning in children with problems in attention, learning, and memory. *Journal of Educational Psychology*, *113*(7), 1454–1480. DOI: 10.1037/edu0000644 PMID: 35855686

Horiuchi, F., Oka, Y., Uno, H., Kawabe, K., Okada, F., Saito, I., Tanigawa, T., & Ueno, S. (2014). Age- and sex-related emotional and behavioral problems in children with autism spectrum disorders: Comparison with control children. *Psychiatry and Clinical Neurosciences*, *68*(7), 542–550. DOI: 10.1111/pcn.12164 PMID: 24447342

Horwitz, E., Vos, M., de Bildt, A., Greaves-Lord, K., Rommelse, N., Schoevers, R. A., & Hartman, C. A. (2023). Sex differences in the course of autistic and co-occurring psychopathological symptoms in adolescents with and without autism spectrum disorder. *Autism : The International Journal of Research and Practice*, *27*(6), 1716–1729. DOI: 10.1177/13623613221146477 PMID: 36680498

Howard, J., Herold, B., Major, S., Leahy, C., Ramseur, K.II, Franz, L., Deaver, M., Vermeer, S., Carpenter, K. L., Murias, M., Huang, W. A., & Dawson, G. (2023). Associations between executive function and attention abilities and language and social communication skills in young autistic children. *Autism : The International Journal of Research and Practice*, *27*(7), 2135–2144. Advance online publication. DOI: 10.1177/13623613231154310 PMID: 36802865

Hoyo, Á., Rueda, M. R., & Rodríguez-Bailón, R. (2019). Children's Individual Differences in Executive Function and Theory of Mind in Relation to Prejudice Toward Social Minorities. [Secondary Human Developmental Psychology]. *Frontiers in Psychology*, *10*, 2293. Advance online publication. DOI: 10.3389/fpsyg.2019.02293 PMID: 31681092

Hoza, B., Mrug, S., Gerdes, A. C., Hinshaw, S. P., Bukowski, W. M., Gold, J. A., Kraemer, H. C., Pelham, W. E., Wigal, T., & Arnold, L. E. (2005). What aspects of peer relationships are impaired in children with attention-deficit/hyperactivity disorder? *Journal of Consulting and Clinical Psychology*, *73*(3), 411–423. DOI: 10.1037/0022-006X.73.3.411 PMID: 15982139

Huang, Y., Xu, H., Au, W., Xu, C., & Wu, K. (2018). Involvement of family environmental, behavioral, and social functional factors in children with attention-deficit/hyperactivity disorder. *Psychology Research and Behavior Management*, *11*, 447–457. DOI: 10.2147/PRBM.S178080 PMID: 30349411

Hughes, C., & Ensor, R. (2022). Social Development in Early Childhood. *The Journal of Social Psychology*, *45*(2), 321–335.

Hull, L., Mandy, W., Lai, M. C., Baron-Cohen, S., Allison, C., Smith, P., & Petrides, K. V. (2019). Development and validation of the camouflaging autistic traits questionnaire (CAT-Q). *Journal of Autism and Developmental Disorders*, *49*(3), 819–833. DOI: 10.1007/s10803-018-3792-6 PMID: 30361940

Hull, L., Petrides, K. V., Allison, C., Smith, P., Baron-Cohen, S., Lai, M. C., & Mandy, W. (2017). 'Putting on my best normal': Social camouflaging in adults with autism spectrum conditions. *Journal of Autism and Developmental Disorders*, *47*(8), 2519–2534. DOI: 10.1007/s10803-017-3166-5 PMID: 28527095

Hurjui, I. A., Hurjui, R. M., Hurjui, L. L., Serban, I. L., Dobrin, I., Apostu, M., & Dobrin, R. P. (2025). Biomarkers and Neuropsychological Tools in Attention-Deficit/Hyperactivity Disorder: From Subjectivity to Precision Diagnosis. *Medicina (Kaunas, Lithuania)*, *61*(7), 1211. DOI: 10.3390/medicina61071211 PMID: 40731840

Hyman, S. E. (2010). The diagnosis of Mental Disorders: The problem of Reification. *Annual Review of Clinical Psychology*, *6*(1), 155–179. DOI: 10.1146/annurev.clinpsy.3.022806.091532 PMID: 17716032

Ibrahim, K., Eilbott, J. A., Ventola, P., He, G., Pelphrey, K. A., McCarthy, G., & Sukhodolsky, D. G. (2019). Reduced Amygdala-Prefrontal Functional Connectivity in Children With Autism Spectrum Disorder and Co-occurring Disruptive Behavior. *Biological Psychiatry. Cognitive Neuroscience and Neuroimaging*, *4*(12), 1031–1041. DOI: 10.1016/j.bpsc.2019.01.009 PMID: 30979647

Insel, T. R. (2014). The NIMH Research Domain Criteria (RDoC) project. *The American Journal of Psychiatry*, *171*(4), 395–397. DOI: 10.1176/appi.ajp.2014.14020138 PMID: 24687194

Insel, T. R., & Cuthbert, B. N. (2015). Brain disorders? Precisely. *Science*, *348*(6234), 499–500. DOI: 10.1126/science.aab2358 PMID: 25931539

Insel, T., Cuthbert, B., Garvey, M., Heinssen, R., Pine, D. S., Quinn, K., Sanislow, C., & Wang, P. (2010). Research domain criteria (RDoC): Toward a new classification framework for research on mental disorders. *The American Journal of Psychiatry*, *167*(7), 748–751. DOI: 10.1176/appi.ajp.2010.09091379 PMID: 20595427

Isaksson, J., Neufeld, J., & Bölte, S. (2021). What's the Link Between Theory of Mind and Other Cognitive Abilities – A Co-twin Control Design of Neurodevelopmental Disorders. [Secondary Cognitive Neuroscience]. *Frontiers in Psychology*, *12*, 575100. Advance online publication. DOI: 10.3389/fpsyg.2021.575100 PMID: 34168585

Isaksson, J., Westeinde, A. V., Cauvet, É., Kuja-Halkola, R., Lundin, K., Neufeld, J., Willfors, C., & Bölte, S. (2019). Social Cognition in Autism and Other Neurodevelopmental Disorders: A Co-twin Control Study. *Journal of Autism and Developmental Disorders*, *49*(7), 2838–2848. DOI: 10.1007/s10803-019-04001-4 PMID: 30972652

Isomura, T., Ogawa, S., Shibasaki, M., & Masataka, N. (2015). Delayed disengagement of attention from snakes in children with autism. *Frontiers in Psychology*, *6*, 241. DOI: 10.3389/fpsyg.2015.00241 PMID: 25784895

Jabeen, A. (2026). Invisible Twice: India's unjust and inadequate policy response to students with specific learning disabilities and borderline intellectual functioning. *Cureus*, *18*(4), e12861. Advance online publication. DOI: 10.7759/cureus.12861 PMID: 41630856

Jacobs, E., Simon, P., & Nader-Grosbois, N. (2020). Social Cognition in Children With Non-specific Intellectual Disabilities: An Exploratory Study. [Secondary Human Developmental Psychology]. *Frontiers in Psychology*, *11*, 1884. Advance online publication. DOI: 10.3389/fpsyg.2020.01884 PMID: 32849105

Jain, J., Dwarakanath, S., & Sharda, S. (2024). The relationship between auditory and cognitive processing abilities in children with specific learning disorders. *American Journal of Audiology*, *33*(1), 118–129. DOI: 10.1044/2024_AJA-24-00001 PMID: 38959167

Janmohammadi, S., Haghgoo, H. A., Farahbod, M., Overton, P. G., & Pishyareh, E. (2020). Effect of a visual tracking intervention on attention and behavior of children with Attention Deficit Hyperactivity Disorder. *Journal of eye movement research*, *12*(8), . https://doi.org/DOI: 10.16910/jemr.12.8.6

Jensen, P. S., Arnold, L. E., Swanson, J. M., Vitiello, B., Abikoff, H. B., Greenhill, L. L., Hechtman, L., Hinshaw, S. P., Pelham, W., Wells, K. C., Conners, C. K., Elliott, G. R., Epstein, J. N., Hoza, B., March, J. S., Molina, B. S. G., Newcorn, J. H., Severe, J. B., Wigal, T., & Hur, K. (2007). Three-year follow-up of the NIMH MTA study. *Journal of the American Academy of Child and Adolescent Psychiatry*, *46*(8), 989–1002. DOI: 10.1097/CHI.0b013e3180686d48 PMID: 17667478

Johnson, M. H., Gliga, T., Jones, E., & Charman, T. (2015). Neurodevelopmental disorders and developmental neuroscience. *Current Opinion in Neurobiology*, *30*, 1–7. DOI: 10.1016/j.conb.2014.08.004

Johnson, S. B., Riis, J. L., & Noble, K. G. (2016). State of the art review: Poverty and the developing brain. *Pediatrics*, *137*(4), e20153075. DOI: 10.1542/peds.2015-3075 PMID: 26952506

Johnston, C., Mash, E. J., Miller, N., & Ninowski, J. E. (2012). Parenting in adults with attention-deficit/hyperactivity disorder (ADHD). *Clinical Psychology Review*, *32*(4), 215–228. DOI: 10.1016/j.cpr.2012.01.007 PMID: 22459785

Johnston, K., Dittner, A., Bramham, J., Murphy, C., Knight, A., & Russell, A. (2013). Attention deficit hyperactivity disorder symptoms in adults with autism spectrum disorders. *Autism Research : Official Journal of the International Society for Autism Research*, *6*(4), 225–236. DOI: 10.1002/aur.1283 PMID: 23788522

Jones, E. J. H., Guild, J., & McPartland, J. (2022). Shared neural pathways in neurodevelopmental disorders. *Nature Reviews. Neurology*, *18*(8), 495–507.

Jorm, A. F. (1983). Specific reading retardation and working memory: A review. *British Journal of Psychology*, *74*(3), 311–342. DOI: 10.1111/j.2044-8295.1983.tb01865.x PMID: 6616125

Joseph, R. M., McGrath, L. M., & Tager-Flusberg, H. (2005). Executive dysfunction and its relation to language ability in verbal school-age children with autism. *Developmental Neuropsychology*, *27*(3), 361–378. DOI: 10.1207/s15326942dn2703_4 PMID: 15843102

Kahane, L., & El-Tahir, M. O. (2015). Attachment behavior in children with Autistic Spectrum Disorders. *Advances in Mental Health and Intellectual Disabilities*, *9*(2), 79–89. DOI: 10.1108/AMHID-06-2014-0026

Kalyanpur, M. (2011). Paradigm and paradox: Education for all and the inclusion of children with disabilities in Cambodia. *International Journal of Inclusive Education*, *15*(10), 1053–1071. DOI: 10.1080/13603116.2011.555069

Kanat, M., Spenthof, I., Riedel, A., Elst, L., Heinrichs, M., & Domes, G. (2017). Restoring effects of oxytocin on the attentional preference for faces in autism. *Translational Psychiatry*, *7*(4), e1097–e1097. DOI: 10.1038/tp.2017.67 PMID: 28418399

Kang, E., Rosen, T. E., Keifer, C. M., Gerber, A. H., & Lerner, M. D. (2025). A single-blind active-control randomized controlled trial of group-based social competence intervention. *Scientific Reports*, *15*(1), 28872. DOI: 10.1038/s41598-025-12876-w PMID: 40774996

Kanner, L. (1943). Autistic disturbances of affective contact. *Nervous Child*, *2*(3), 217–250.

Kapp, S. K., Gillespie-Lynch, K., Sherman, L. E., & Hutman, T. (2013). Deficit, difference, or both? Autism and neurodiversity. *Developmental Psychology*, *49*(1), 59–71. DOI: 10.1037/a0028353 PMID: 22545843

Karakaş, S. (2024). A Review of Childhood Developmental Changes in Attention as Indexed in the Electrical Activity of the Brain. *Brain Sciences*, *14*(5), 458. DOI: 10.3390/brainsci14050458 PMID: 38790437

Karmiloff-Smith, A. (1998). Development itself is the key to understanding developmental disorders. *Trends in Cognitive Sciences*, *2*(10), 389–398. DOI: 10.1016/S1364-6613(98)01230-3 PMID: 21227254

Kärtner, J., Keller, H., & Chaudhary, N. (2010). Cognitive and social influences on early prosocial behavior in two sociocultural contexts. *Developmental Psychology*, *46*(4), 905–914. DOI: 10.1037/a0019718 PMID: 20604610

Keller, H., & Kärtner, J. (2013). Development – The culture-specific solution of universal developmental tasks. In M. L. Gelfand, C.-Y., Chiu, & Hong, Y. Y. (Eds.), Advances in culture and psychology, Vol. 3 (pp. 63-116). Oxford, NY: Oxford University Press.

Keller, H. (2012). Autonomy And Relatedness Revisited: Cultural Manifestations Of Universal Human Needs. *Child Development Perspectives*, *6*(1), 12–18. DOI: 10.1111/j.1750-8606.2011.00208.x

Keller, H. (2018). Universality claim of attachment theory. *Human Development*, *61*(5–6), 254–264. PMID: 30397121

Keller, H. (2020). Children's Socioemotional Development Across Cultures. *Annual Review of Developmental Psychology*, *2*(1), 27–46. DOI: 10.1146/annurev-devpsych-033020-031552

Kennette, L. N., & Wilson, N. A. (2019). Universal Design for Learning (UDL): Student and Faculty Perceptions. *Journal of Effective Teaching in Higher Education*, *2*(1), 1–26. DOI: 10.36021/jethe.v2i1.17

Kerns, C. M., Kendall, P. C., Berry, L., Souders, M. C., Franklin, M. E., Schultz, R. T., Miller, J., & Herrington, J. (2014). Traditional and atypical presentations of anxiety in youth with autism spectrum disorder. *Journal of Autism and Developmental Disorders*, *44*(11), 2851–2861. DOI: 10.1007/s10803-014-2141-7 PMID: 24902932

Kerns, C. M., Winder-Patel, B., Iosif, A. M., Nordahl, C. W., Heath, B., Solomon, M., & Amaral, D. G. (2021). Clinically significant anxiety in children with autism spectrum disorder and varied intellectual functioning. *Journal of Clinical Child and Adolescent Psychology : The Official Journal for the Society of Clinical Child and Adolescent Psychology, American Psychological Association, Division 53*, *50*(6), 780–795. DOI: 10.1080/15374416.2019.1703712 PMID: 31971849

Khalil, V., Faress, I., Mermet-Joret, N., Kerwin, P., Yonehara, K., & Nabavi, S. (2023). Subcortico-amygdala pathway processes innate and learned threats. *eLife*, *12*, e85459. DOI: 10.7554/eLife.85459 PMID: 37526552

Kieling, C., Baker-Henningham, H., Belfer, M., Conti, G., Ertem, I., Omigbodun, O., Rohde, L. A., Srinath, S., Ulkuer, N., & Rahman, A. (2011). Child and adolescent mental health worldwide: Evidence for action. *Lancet*, *378*(9801), 1515–1525. DOI: 10.1016/S0140-6736(11)60827-1 PMID: 22008427

Kievit, R. A., Hofman, A. D., & Nation, K. (2019). Mutualistic coupling between vocabulary and reasoning in young children: A replication and extension of the study by Kievit et al. (2017). *Psychological Science, 30*(8), 1245–1252. DOI: 10.1177/0956797619841265 PMID: 31100049

Kievit, R. A., Lindenberger, U., Goodyer, I. M., Jones, P. B., Fonagy, P., Bullmore, E. T., & Dolan, R. J. (2017). Mutualistic coupling between vocabulary and reasoning supports cognitive development during late adolescence and early adulthood. *Psychological Science, 28*(10), 1419–1431. DOI: 10.1177/0956797617710785 PMID: 28787239

Kim, B., Niu, X., & Zhang, F. (2023). Functional connectivity strength and topology differences in social phobia adolescents with and without ADHD comorbidity. *Neuropsychologia, 178*, 108418. DOI: 10.1016/j.neuropsychologia.2022.108418 PMID: 36403658

Kim, Y. S., & Leventhal, B. L. (2015). Genetic epidemiology and insights into interactive genetic and environmental effects in autism spectrum disorders. *Biological Psychiatry, 77*(1), 66–74. DOI: 10.1016/j.biopsych.2014.11.001 PMID: 25483344

Kinnaird, E., Stewart, C., & Tchanturia, K. (2019). Investigating alexithymia in autism: A systematic review and meta-analysis. *European Psychiatry : The Journal of the Association of European Psychiatrists, 55*, 80–89. DOI: 10.1016/j.eurpsy.2018.09.004 PMID: 30399531

Kirk, H. E., Richmond, S., Gaunson, T., Bennett, M., Herschtal, A., Bellgrove, M., & Cornish, K. (2024). A 5-week Digital Intervention to Reduce Attention Problems in Children With ADHD: A Double-Blind Randomized Controlled Trial. *Journal of Attention Disorders, 28*(11), 1454–1466. Advance online publication. DOI: 10.1177/10870547241256269 PMID: 38804292

Kirmayer, L. J. (2012). Cultural competence and evidence-based practice in mental health. *Social Science & Medicine, 75*(2), 249–256. DOI: 10.1016/j.socscimed.2012.03.018 PMID: 22575699

Kleberg, J. L., Frick, M. A., & Brocki, K. C. (2021). Increased pupil dilation to happy faces in children with hyperactive/impulsive symptoms of ADHD. *Development and Psychopathology, 33*(3), 767–777. DOI: 10.1017/S0954579420000036 PMID: 32102703

Kloo, D., Osterhaus, C., Kristen-Antonow, S., & Sodian, B. (2022). The impact of theory of mind and executive function on math and reading abilities: A longitudinal study. *Infant and Child Development, 31*(6), e2356. DOI: 10.1002/icd.2356

Kofler, M. J., Sarver, D. E., Harmon, S. L., Moltisanti, A., Aduen, P. A., Soto, E. F., & Ferretti, N. (2018). Working memory and organizational skills problems in ADHD. *Journal of Child Psychology and Psychiatry, and Allied Disciplines*, *59*(1), 57–67. DOI: 10.1111/jcpp.12773 PMID: 28714075

Kofler, M. J., Singh, L. J., Soto, E. F., Chan, E. S. M., Miller, C. E., Harmon, S. L., & Spiegel, J. A. (2020). Working memory and short-term memory deficits in ADHD: A bifactor modeling approach. *Neuropsychology*, *34*(6), 686–698. DOI: 10.1037/neu0000641 PMID: 32437194

Koi, P. (2021). Genetics on the neurodiversity spectrum: Genetic, phenotypic and endophenotypic continua in autism and ADHD. *Studies in History and Philosophy of Science*, *89*, 52–62. DOI: 10.1016/j.shpsa.2021.07.006 PMID: 34365317

Kolb, B. (2018). Overview of factors influencing brain development. In *The neurobiology of brain and behavioral development* (pp. 51–79). Academic Press. DOI: 10.1016/B978-0-12-804036-2.00003-0

Kolb, B., & Gibb, R. (2011). Brain plasticity and behaviour in the developing brain. *Journal of the Canadian Academy of Child and Adolescent Psychiatry = Journal de l'Académie Canadienne de Psychiatrie de l'Enfant et de l'Adolescent*, *20*(4), 265–276. PMID: 22114608

Kolb, B., & Whishaw, I. Q. (2015). *An introduction to brain and behavior* (4th ed.). Worth Publishers.

Komoróczy, E., Sörnyei, D., Vass, Á., Szuromi, B., Vizin, G., Réthelyi, J., & Farkas, K. (2024). Understanding depression in autism: The mediating role of mentalization, attachment, social support, and psychological flexibility. https://doi.org/DOI: 10.1101/2024.07.12.24310324

Kossowsky, J., Pfaltz, M. C., Schneider, S., Taeymans, J., Locher, C., & Gaab, J. (2013). The separation anxiety hypothesis of panic disorder revisited: A meta-analysis. *The American Journal of Psychiatry*, *170*(7), 768–781. DOI: 10.1176/appi.ajp.2012.12070893 PMID: 23680783

Kotov, R., Krueger, R. F., Watson, D., Achenbach, T. M., Althoff, R. R., Bagby, R. M., Brown, T. A., Carpenter, W. T., Caspi, A., Clark, L. A., Eaton, N. R., Forbes, M. K., Forbush, K. T., Goldberg, D., Hasin, D., Hyman, S. E., Ivanova, M. Y., Lynam, D. R., Markon, K., & Zimmerman, M. (2017). The Hierarchical Taxonomy of Psychopathology (HiTOP): A dimensional alternative to traditional nosologies. *Journal of Abnormal Psychology*, *126*(4), 454–477. DOI: 10.1037/abn0000258 PMID: 28333488

Kouvava, S., Antonopoulou, K., Kokkinos, C. M., & Ralli, A. M. (2025). Social Understanding and Friendships in Children with Attention Deficit/Hyperactivity Disorder or Dyslexia. *Behavioral Sciences (Basel, Switzerland)*, *15*(2), 216. DOI: 10.3390/bs15020216 PMID: 40001849

Kozunova, G. L., Zakirov, F. K., Rytikova, A. M., Stroganova, T. A., & Chernyshev, B. V. (2023). Neurobiological factors of executive dysfunction in autism spectrum disorders. *Neuroscience and Behavioral Physiology*, *53*(7), 1158–1174. DOI: 10.1007/s11055-023-01512-7

Kozunova, Y. O., Zakirov, D. R., Rytikova, M. P., Sarsenova, N. B., & Vaganov, O. G. (2023). Neurobiological factors of executive dysfunction in ASD. *Neuroscience and Behavioral Physiology*, *53*(10), 1168–1180.

Krcek, T. E. (2013). Deconstructing disability and neurodiversity: Controversial issues for autism and implications for social work. *Journal of Progressive Human Services*, *24*(1), 4–22. DOI: 10.1080/10428232.2013.740406

Kumar, G., Barhoun, P., Fuelscher, I., Zwicker, J. G., Bianco, K., Singh, M., Mukherjee, M., Williams, J., & Hyde, C. (2025). Quality of life in children with developmental coordination disorder (DCD): A systematic review and meta-analysis. *Research in Developmental Disabilities*, *160*, 104981. DOI: 10.1016/j.ridd.2025.104981 PMID: 40121827

Kwan, C., Gitimoghaddam, M., & Collet, J.-P. (2020). Effects of Social Isolation and Loneliness in Children with Neurodevelopmental Disabilities: A Scoping Review. *Brain Sciences*, *10*(11), 786. DOI: 10.3390/brainsci10110786 PMID: 33126519

Lai, C. L. E., Lau, Z., Lui, S. S. Y., Lok, E., Tam, V., Chan, Q., Cheng, K. M., Lam, S. M., & Cheung, E. F. C. (2016). Meta-analysis of neuropsychological measures of executive functioning in children and adolescents with high-functioning autism spectrum disorder. *Autism Research : Official Journal of the International Society for Autism Research*, *10*(5), 911–939. DOI: 10.1002/aur.1723 PMID: 27874266

Lai, X., Huang, S., Nie, C., Yan, J. J., Li, Y., Wang, Y., & Luo, Y. (2022). Trajectory of problematic smartphone use among adolescents aged 10-18 years: The roles of childhood family environment and concurrent parent-child relationships. *Journal of Behavioral Addictions*, *11*(2), 577–587. DOI: 10.1556/2006.2022.00047 PMID: 35895472

Lange-Küttner, C., Lockl, K., & Gnambs, T. (2025). ADHD and secondary school grades: Evidence from two longitudinal studies. *Current Psychology*, *44*(20), 16701–16717. DOI: 10.1007/s12144-025-08324-7

Laurent, A. C., & Gorman, K. (2017). Development of emotion self-regulation among young children with autism spectrum disorders: The role of parents. *Journal of Autism and Developmental Disorders*, *48*(4), 1249–1260. DOI: 10.1007/s10803-017-3430-8 PMID: 29249011

Lau, W. Y. P., Peterson, C. C., Attwood, T., Garnett, M. S., & Kelly, A. B. (2016). Parents on the autism continuum: Links with parenting efficacy. *Research in Autism Spectrum Disorders*, *26*, 57–64. DOI: 10.1016/j.rasd.2016.02.007

Lau, W., & Peterson, C. C. (2011). Adults and children with Asperger syndrome: Exploring adult attachment style, marital satisfaction and satisfaction with parenthood. *Research in Autism Spectrum Disorders*, *5*(1), 392–399. DOI: 10.1016/j.rasd.2010.06.001

Law, J., Garrett, Z., & Nye, C. (2017). Interventions for children with speech and language difficulties. *International Journal of Language & Communication Disorders*, *52*(1), 3–15. PMID: 27184439

Le Cunff, A. L., Martis, B.-L., Glover, C., Ahmed, E., Ford, R., Giampietro, V., & Dommett, E. J. (2025b). Cognitive load and neurodiversity in online education: A preliminary framework for educational research and policy. *Frontiers in Education*, *9*, 9. DOI: 10.3389/feduc.2024.1437673

Lebel, C., & Beaulieu, C. (2011). Longitudinal development of human brain wiring continues from childhood into adulthood. *The Journal of Neuroscience : The Official Journal of the Society for Neuroscience*, *31*(30), 10937–10947. DOI: 10.1523/JNEUROSCI.5302-10.2011 PMID: 21795544

Leblond, C. S., Rolland, T., Barthome, E., Mougin, Z., Fleury, M., Ecker, C., Bonnot-Briey, S., Cliquet, F., Tabet, A.-C., Maruani, A., Chaumette, B., Green, J., Delorme, R., & Bourgeron, T. (2024). A genetic bridge between medicine and neurodiversity for autism. *Annual Review of Genetics*, *58*(1), 487–512. DOI: 10.1146/annurev-genet-111523-102614 PMID: 39585908

Lebowitz, E. R., Leckman, J. F., Feldman, R., Zagoory-Sharon, O., McDonald, N., & Silverman, W. K. (2016). Salivary oxytocin in clinically anxious youth: Associations with separation anxiety and family accommodation. *Psychoneuroendocrinology*, *65*, 35–43. DOI: 10.1016/j.psyneuen.2015.12.007 PMID: 26716876

Lecavalier, L., Bodfish, J. W., Harrop, C., Whitten, A., Jones, D. R., Pritchett, J., Faldowski, R. A., & Boyd, B. A. (2020). Development of the Behavioral Inflexibility Scale for Children with Autism Spectrum Disorder and Other Developmental Disabilities. *Autism Research : Official Journal of the International Society for Autism Research*, *13*(3), 489–499. DOI: 10.1002/aur.2257 PMID: 31904198

Leedham, A., Thompson, A. R., Smith, R., & Freeth, M. (2020). 'I was exhausted trying to figure it out': The experiences of females receiving an autism diagnosis in middle to late adulthood. *Autism : The International Journal of Research and Practice*, *24*(1), 135–146. DOI: 10.1177/1362361319853442 PMID: 31144507

Lee, J. J., Wedow, R., Okbay, A., Kong, E., Maghzian, O., Zacher, M., Nguyen-Viet, T. A., Bowers, P., Sidorenko, J., Karlsson Linnér, R., Fontana, M. A., Kundu, T., Lee, C., Li, H., Li, R., Royer, R., Timshel, P. N., Walters, R. K., Willoughby, E. A., & Cesarini, D. (2018). Gene discovery and polygenic prediction from a genome-wide association study of educational attainment in 1.1 million individuals. *Nature Genetics*, *50*(8), 1112–1121. DOI: 10.1038/s41588-018-0147-3 PMID: 30038396

Legg, E. W. (2023). Theory of Mind: A Review of Recent Empirical Results and Main Theoretical Explanations. *Psihologijske Teme*, *32*(3), 635–661. DOI: 10.31820/pt.32.3.12

Lerner, R. M. (2006). Developmental science, developmental systems, and contemporary theories of human development. In Lerner, R. M. (Ed.),; 6th ed.). Handbook of child psychology. Wiley.

Leung, R. C., Vogan, V. M., Powell, T. L., Anagnostou, E., & Taylor, M. J. (2016). The role of executive functions in social impairment in autism spectrum disorder. *Child Neuropsychology : A Journal on Normal and Abnormal Development in Childhood and Adolescence*, *22*(3), 336–344. DOI: 10.1080/09297049.2015.1005066 PMID: 25731979

Lightfoot, C., Cole, M., & Cole, S. (2015). Early Childhood. In Bablekou, Z. (Ed.), *The development of children* (pp. 345–479). Gutenberg.

Li, L., Zhu, X., Wan, S., Wang, L., Pan, L., Peng, S., & Chen, J. (2025). Research on the improvement of daily living skills of children with autism in virtual campus environments. *Scientific Reports*, *15*(1), 30102. DOI: 10.1038/s41598-025-08224-7 PMID: 40820136

Liljenwall, H., Lean, R. E., Smyser, T. A., Smyser, C. D., & Rogers, C. E. (2022). Parental ADHD and ASD symptoms and contributions of psychosocial risk to childhood ADHD and ASD symptoms in children born very preterm. *Journal of Perinatology : Official Journal of the California Perinatal Association*. Advance online publication. DOI: 10.1038/s41372-022-01463-w PMID: 35840709

Li, M., Dahmani, L., Hubbard, C. S., Hu, Y., Wang, M., Wang, D., & Liu, H. (2022). Individualized functional connectome identified generalizable biomarkers for psychiatric symptoms in transdiagnostic patients. *Neuropsychopharmacology : Official Publication of the American College of Neuropsychopharmacology, 48*(4), 633–641. DOI: 10.1038/s41386-022-01500-4 PMID: 36402836

Lim, J. M. (2020). Emotion regulation and intervention in adults with autism spectrum disorder: A synthesis of the literature. *Advances in Autism, 6*(1), 48–62. DOI: 10.1108/AIA-12-2018-0050

Lindsay, G., & Dockrell, J. (2012). Longitudinal patterns of behavior problems in children with specific speech and language difficulties. *Child Language Teaching and Therapy, 28*(2), 135–150. DOI: 10.1177/0265659010396608

Lindsey, M. A., Romanelli, M., Ellis, M. L., Barker, E. D., Boxmeyer, C. L., & Lochman, J. E. (2019). The influence of treatment engagement on positive outcomes in the context of a school-based intervention for students with externalizing behavior problems. [PubMed: 29654540]. *Journal of Abnormal Child Psychology, 47*(9), 1–18. DOI: 10.1007/s10802-019-00525-6 PMID: 30848415

Lingineni, R. K., Biswas, S., Ahmad, N., Jackson, B. E., Bae, S., & Singh, K. P. (2012). Factors associated with attention deficit/hyperactivity disorder among US children: Results from a national survey. *BMC Pediatrics, 12*(1), 50. Advance online publication. DOI: 10.1186/1471-2431-12-50 PMID: 22583686

Link, B. G., & Phelan, J. C. (2001). Conceptualizing stigma. *Annual Review of Sociology, 27*(1), 363–385. DOI: 10.1146/annurev.soc.27.1.363

Liu, H. (2025). The Effect of Working Memory Deficits on Academic Performances among Children with ADHD. *Communications in Humanities Research, 55*, 42–49. https://www.ewadirect.com/proceedings/chr/article/view/21250

Livingston, L. A., Shah, P., & Happé, F. (2019). Compensatory strategies below the behavioural surface in autism: A qualitative study. *The Lancet. Psychiatry, 6*(9), 766–777. DOI: 10.1016/S2215-0366(19)30224-X PMID: 31350208

Lobato-Ruiz, V., Romero-Ayuso, D., Toledano-González, A., & Triviño-Juárez, J. M. (2025). Quality of life and parental stress related to executive functioning, sensory processing, and activities of daily living in children and adolescents with neurodevelopmental disorders. *PeerJ, 13*, e19326. DOI: 10.7717/peerj.19326 PMID: 40292106

Lombardo, M. V., Lai, M., & Baron-Cohen, S. (2019). Big data approaches to decomposing heterogeneity across the autism spectrum. *Molecular Psychiatry*, *24*(10), 1435–1450. DOI: 10.1038/s41380-018-0321-0 PMID: 30617272

Long, Y., Pan, N., Ji, S., Qin, K., Chen, Y., Zhang, X., He, M., Suo, X., Yu, Y., Wang, S., & Gong, Q. (2022). Distinct brain structural abnormalities in attention-deficit/hyperactivity disorder and substance use disorders: A comparative meta-analysis. *Translational Psychiatry*, *12*(1), 368. DOI: 10.1038/s41398-022-02130-6 PMID: 36068207

LoParo, D., & Waldman, I. D. (2015). The oxytocin receptor gene (OXTR) is associated with autism spectrum disorder: A meta-analysis. *Molecular Psychiatry*, *20*(5), 640–646. DOI: 10.1038/mp.2014.77 PMID: 25092245

Lord, C., Brugha, T. S., Charman, T., Cusack, J., Fuentes, J., Jones, E. J. H., Jones, R. M., Pickles, A., Rogers, S. J., Siracusano, M., & Veenstra-VanderWeele, J. (2020). Autism spectrum disorder. *Nature Reviews. Disease Primers*, *6*(1), 5. Advance online publication. DOI: 10.1038/s41572-019-0138-4 PMID: 31949163

Lord, C., Elsabbagh, M., Baird, G., & Veenstra-Vanderweele, J. (2018). Autism spectrum disorder. *Lancet*, *392*(10146), 508–520. DOI: 10.1016/S0140-6736(18)31129-2 PMID: 30078460

Lorenz, T., Frischling, C., Cuadros, R., & Heinitz, K. (2016). Autism and overcoming job barriers: Comparing job-related barriers and possible solutions in and outside of autism specific employment. *PLoS One*, *11*(1), e0147040. Advance online publication. DOI: 10.1371/journal.pone.0147040 PMID: 26766183

Löytömäki, J., Laakso, M.-L., & Huttunen, K. (2022). Social-Emotional and Behavioural Difficulties in Children with Neurodevelopmental Disorders: Emotion Perception in Daily Life and in a Formal Assessment Context. *Journal of Autism and Developmental Disorders*, *53*(12), 4744–4758. DOI: 10.1007/s10803-022-05768-9 PMID: 36184695

Lundstrom, S., Reichenberg, A., Anckarsater, H., Lichtenstein, P., & Gillberg, C. (2015). Autism phenotype versus registered diagnosis in Swedish children: Prevalence trends over 10 years in general population samples. *BMJ (Clinical Research Ed.)*, *350*(apr28 2), h1961. DOI: 10.1136/bmj.h1961 PMID: 25922345

Luria, A. R. (1966). *Higher cortical functions in man*. Basic Books.

Lyon, G. R., Shaywitz, S. E., & Shaywitz, B. A. (2003). Defining dyslexia. *Annals of Dyslexia*, *53*(1), 1–14. DOI: 10.1007/s11881-003-0001-9

Macari, S. L., Vernetti, A., & Chawarska, K. (2020). Attend less, fear more: Elevated distress to social threat in toddlers with autism spectrum disorder. *Autism Research : Official Journal of the International Society for Autism Research, 14*(5), 1025–1036. DOI: 10.1002/aur.2448 PMID: 33283976

MacBeth, A., & Gumley, A. (2012). Exploring compassion: A meta-analysis of the association between self-compassion and psychopathology. *Clinical Psychology Review, 32*(6), 545–552. DOI: 10.1016/j.cpr.2012.06.003 PMID: 22796446

Maddox, B. B., & White, S. W. (2015). Comorbid social anxiety disorder in adults with autism spectrum disorder. *Journal of Autism and Developmental Disorders, 45*(12), 3949–3960. DOI: 10.1007/s10803-015-2531-5 PMID: 26243138

Maenner, M. J., Warren, Z., Williams, A. R., Amoakohene, E., Bakian, A. V., Bilder, D. A., Durkin, M. S., Fitzgerald, R. T., Furnier, S. M., Hughes, M. M., Ladd-Acosta, C. M., McArthur, D., Pas, E. T., Salinas, A., Vehorn, A., Williams, S., Esler, A., Grzybowski, A., Hall-Lande, J., & Shaw, K. A. (2023). Prevalence and characteristics of autism spectrum disorder among children aged 8 years — Autism and Developmental Disabilities Monitoring Network, 11 sites, United States, 2020. *MMWR. Surveillance Summaries, 72*(2), 1–14. DOI: 10.15585/mmwr.ss7202a1 PMID: 36952288

Mahdi, N. E. H., & Kherbouche, O. (2021). *Memory Types and Mechanisms*. ResearchGate.https://www.researchgate.net/publication/357434462_Memory_Types_and_Mechanisms

Maisel, M. E., Stephenson, K. G., South, M., Rodgers, J., Freeston, M. H., & Gaigg, S. (2016). Modeling the cognitive mechanisms linking autism symptoms and anxiety in adults. *Journal of Abnormal Psychology, 125*(5), 692–703. DOI: 10.1037/abn0000168 PMID: 27196436

Malik, F., & Marwaha, R. (2023). *Cognitive development*. National Library of Medicine; StatPearls Publishing. https://www.ncbi.nlm.nih.gov/books/NBK537095/

Mancera, L., Baldiris, S., Fabregat, R., Gomez, S., & Mejia, C. (2017). ATenDerAH: A Videogame to Support e-Learning Students with ADHD. In *Proceedings - IEEE 17th International Conference on Advanced Learning Technologies, ICALT 2017* (pp. 438–440). https://doi.org/DOI: 10.1109/ICALT.2017.157

Mandell, D., & Novak, M. (2005). The role of culture in families' treatment decisions for autism spectrum disorders. *Mental Retardation and Developmental Disabilities Research Reviews, 11*(2), 110–115. DOI: 10.1002/mrdd.20061 PMID: 15977313

Man, K. K. C., Tong, H. H. Y., Wong, L. Y. L., Chan, E. W., Simonoff, E., & Wong, I. C. K. (2015). Exposure to selective serotonin reuptake inhibitors during pregnancy and risk of autism spectrum disorder in children: A systematic review and meta-analysis of observational studies. *Neuroscience and Biobehavioral Reviews*, *49*, 82–89. DOI: 10.1016/j.neubiorev.2014.11.020 PMID: 25498856

Marcovitch, S., & Zelazo, P. D. (2009). A hierarchical competing systems model of the emergence and early development of executive function. *Developmental Science*, *12*(1), 1–25. DOI: 10.1111/j.1467-7687.2008.00754.x PMID: 19120405

Mareva, S., Astle, D., Baker, K., Gathercole, S., Holmes, J., Kievit, R., Manly, T., Akarca, D., Bathelt, J., Bettencourt, M., Bennett, M., Bignardi, G., Bishop, S., Bottacin, E., Bridge, L., Brkic, D., Bryant, A., Butterfield, S., Byrne, E., & Holmes, J.Lead InvestigatorsTeam of Researchers and PhD Students. (2024). Mapping neurodevelopmental diversity in executive function. *Cortex; A Journal Devoted to the Study of the Nervous System and Behavior*, *172*, 204–221. DOI: 10.1016/j.cortex.2023.11.021 PMID: 38354470

Marotta, R., Risoleo, M. C., Messina, G., Parisi, L., Carotenuto, M., Vetri, L., & Roccella, M. (2020). The neurochemistry of autism. *Brain Sciences*, *10*(3), 163. DOI: 10.3390/brainsci10030163 PMID: 32182969

Márquez-Caraveo, M. E., Rodríguez-Valentín, R., Pérez-Barrón, V., Vázquez-Salas, R. A., Sánchez-Ferrer, J. C., De Castro, F., Allen-Leigh, B., & Lazcano-Ponce, E. (2021). Children and adolescents with neurodevelopmental disorders show cognitive heterogeneity and require a person-centered approach. *Scientific Reports*, *11*(1), 18463. DOI: 10.1038/s41598-021-97551-6 PMID: 34531454

Marriott, E., Stacey, J., Hewitt, O. M., & Verkuijl, N. E. (2022). Parenting an autistic child: Experiences of parents with significant autistic traits. *Journal of Autism and Developmental Disorders*, *52*(7), 3182–3193. DOI: 10.1007/s10803-021-05182-7 PMID: 34322826

Martin, A., Galeris, M.-G., Theil, M. K., Sele, S., Cavelti, M., Keil, J., Kaess, M., von Polier, G. G., & Schlensog-Schuster, F. (2025). Early Struggles—The Relationship of Psychopathology and Development in Early Childhood. *Children (Basel, Switzerland)*, *12*(3), 265. DOI: 10.3390/children12030265 PMID: 40150548

Martinez, S., Stoyanov, K., & Carcache, L. (2024). Unraveling the spectrum: Overlap, distinctions, and nuances of ADHD and ASD in children. *Frontiers in Psychiatry*, *15*, 1387179. Advance online publication. DOI: 10.3389/fpsyt.2024.1387179 PMID: 39345916

Martin, J., Taylor, M. J., & Lichtenstein, P. (2019). Assessing the evidence for shared genetic risks across psychiatric disorders and traits. *Psychological Medicine*, *49*(7), 1067–1077. DOI: 10.1017/S0033291718004214 PMID: 29198204

Masini, E., Loi, E., Vega-Benedetti, A. F., Carta, M., Doneddu, G., Fadda, R., & Zavattari, P. (2020). An overview of the main genetic, epigenetic and environmental factors involved in autism spectrum disorder focusing on synaptic activity. *International Journal of Molecular Sciences*, *21*(21), 8290. DOI: 10.3390/ijms21218290 PMID: 33167418

Massand, E., & Bowler, D. M. (2015). Atypical neurophysiology underlying episodic and semantic memory in adults with autism spectrum disorder: An ERP review. *Journal of Autism and Developmental Disorders*, *45*(2), 298–315. DOI: 10.1007/s10803-013-1869-9 PMID: 23754340

Masten, A. S. (2001). Ordinary magic: Resilience processes in development. *The American Psychologist*, *56*(3), 227–238. DOI: 10.1037/0003-066X.56.3.227 PMID: 11315249

Matelski, L., & Van de Water, J. (2016). Risk factors in autism: Thinking outside the brain. *Journal of Autoimmunity*, *67*, 1–7. DOI: 10.1016/j.jaut.2015.11.003 PMID: 26725748

Materula, D., Currie, G., Jia, X. Y., Finlay, B., Lau, A.-M., Richard, C., Yohemas, M., Estes, M., Gall, N., Dewan, T., MacEachern, S., Gibbard, W. B., & Zwicker, J. D. (2024). Needs of children with neurodevelopmental disorders and medical complexity: Caregiver perspectives. *Research in Developmental Disabilities, 153*, 104815. DOI: 10.1016/j.ridd.2024.104815 PMID: 39142086

Mazefsky, C. A., Herrington, J., Siegel, M., Scarpa, A., Maddox, B. B., Scahill, L., & White, S. W. (2013). The role of emotion regulation in autism spectrum disorder. *Journal of the American Academy of Child and Adolescent Psychiatry*, *52*(7), 679–688. DOI: 10.1016/j.jaac.2013.05.006 PMID: 23800481

Mazza, M., Attanasio, M., & Bologna, A., Ilenia Le Donne, & Valenti, M. (2023). The relationship between theory of mind, executive functioning, and repetitive behavior in high functioning autism spectrum disorder. *Journal of Psychopathology*, *1–2*. Advance online publication. DOI: 10.36148/2284-0249-N284

McDonald, S. (2017). "Emotions are rising: the growing field of affect neuropsychology." Journal of the International Neuropsychological Society 23.9-10: 719-731.-09337-y McEwen B. S. (2000). The neurobiology of stress: from serendipity to clinical relevance. *Brain Research*, *886*(1-2), 172–189. DOI: 10.1016/S0006-8993(00)02950-4

McDougal, E., Riby, D. M., & Hanley, M. (2020). Profiles of academic achievement and attention in children with and without Autism Spectrum Disorder. *Research in Developmental Disabilities*, *106*, 103749. DOI: 10.1016/j.ridd.2020.103749 PMID: 32858397

McIsaac, J. D., Lamptey, D. L., Harley, J., MacQuarrie, M., Cummings, R., Rossiter, M. D., Janus, M., & Turner, J. (2022). Early pandemic impacts on family environments that shape childhood development and health: A Canadian study. *Child: Care, Health and Development*, *48*(6), 1122–1133. DOI: 10.1111/cch.13046 PMID: 35997511

McLaughlin, K. A., Weissman, D., & Bitrán, D. (2021). Childhood adversity and neural development: A systematic review. *Annual Review of Developmental Psychology*, *3*, 277–312. DOI: 10.1146/annurev-devpsych-060320-051114 PMID: 32455344

Meaney, M. J. (2010). Epigenetics and the biological definition of gene × environment interactions. *Child Development*, *81*(1), 41–79. DOI: 10.1111/j.1467-8624.2009.01381.x PMID: 20331654

Meehan, C. L., & Hawks, S. (2013). Cooperative breeding and attachment among the Aka foragers. In *Attachment reconsidered: Cultural perspectives on a Western theory* (pp. 85–113). Palgrave Macmillan US. DOI: 10.1057/9781137386724_4

Megari, K., & Genova, K. D. (2025). The Neurocognitive Characteristics of Children with Neurodevelopmental Disabilities and Their Clinical Implications (Chapter 6 pages 119-142). Clinical Applications of Pediatric Neuropsychology from Infancy to Adolescence. Pennsylvania / USA: IGI Global.

Megari, K., & Genova, K. D. (2025). The Neurocognitive Characteristics of Children With Neurodevelopmental Disabilities and Their Clinical Implications. In *IGI Global eBooks* (pp. 119–142). https://doi.org/DOI: 10.4018/979-8-3693-9689-6.ch006

Megari, K., Sofologi, M., Kougioumtzis, G., Thomaidou, E., Thomaidis, G., Katsarou, D., ... & Theodoratou, M. (2025). Neurocognitive and psycho-emotional profile of children with disabilities. Applied Neuropsychology: Child, 14(3), 323-328.

Megari, K. (2025). *Clinical Applications of Pediatric Neuropsychology from Infancy to Adolescence*. IGI Global., DOI: 10.4018/979-8-3693-9689-6

Megari, K., & Genova, K. D. (2026). Cognitive Pathways in Atypical Development: Executive Functions in Children With Attention-Deficit/Hyperactivity Disorder and Specific Learning Disorders. *International Journal of Developmental Neuroscience : The Official Journal of the International Society for Developmental Neuroscience*, *86*(1), e70094. DOI: 10.1002/jdn.70094 PMID: 41545901

Megari, K., & Guanco, R. J. (2026, January 01). Pediatric Brain Development and Adverse Childhood Experiences: Cognitive, Emotional, and Behavioral Outcomes. [BOSN]. *Brain Organoid & Systems Neuroscience Journal*, *4*, 0007. DOI: 10.34133/bosn.0007

Megari, K., & Miliadi, V. (2024). The neuropsychology of early childhood and infancy. *International Journal of Developmental Neuroscience : The Official Journal of the International Society for Developmental Neuroscience*, *84*(8), 1–10. DOI: 10.1002/jdn.10381 PMID: 39323063

Meghji, S., Hilderley, A. J., Murias, K., Brooks, B. L., Andersen, J., Fehlings, D., Dlamini, N., Kirton, A., & Carlson, H. L. (2024). Executive functioning, ADHD symptoms and resting state functional connectivity in children with perinatal stroke. *Brain Imaging and Behavior*, *18*(2), 263–278. DOI: 10.1007/s11682-023-00827-w PMID: 38038867

Mehta, T., Mannem, N., Yarasi, N. K., & Bollu, P. C. (2020). Biomarkers for ADHD: The Present and Future Directions. *Current Developmental Disorders Reports*, *7*(3), 85–92. DOI: 10.1007/s40474-020-00196-9

Méndez-Freije, I., Areces, D., & Pérez, C. R. (2023). Language Skills in Children with Attention Deficit Hyperactivity Disorder and Developmental Language Disorder: A Systematic Review. *Children (Basel, Switzerland)*, *11*(1), 14. DOI: 10.3390/children11010014 PMID: 38275435

Michelini, G., Norman, L. J., Shaw, P., & Loo, S. K. (2022). Treatment biomarkers for ADHD: Taking stock and moving forward. *Translational Psychiatry*, *12*(1), 444. DOI: 10.1038/s41398-022-02207-2 PMID: 36224169

Mikami, A. Y., Jack, A., Emeh, C. C., & Stephens, H. F. (2010). Parental influence on children with attention-deficit/hyperactivity disorder: I. Relationships between parent behaviors and child peer status. *Journal of Abnormal Child Psychology*, *38*(6), 721–736. DOI: 10.1007/s10802-010-9393-2 PMID: 20339912

Mikami, A. Y., & Normand, S. (2015). The importance of social contextual factors in peer relationships of children with ADHD. *Current Developmental Disorders Reports*, *2*(1), 30–37. DOI: 10.1007/s40474-014-0036-0

Miller, M., Bales, K. L., Taylor, S. L., Yoon, J. H., Hostetler, C. M., Carter, C. S., & Solomon, M. (2013). Oxytocin and vasopressin in children and adolescents with autism spectrum disorders: Sex differences and associations with symptoms. *Autism Research : Official Journal of the International Society for Autism Research*, *6*(2), 91–102. DOI: 10.1002/aur.1270 PMID: 23413037

Milosavljevic, B., Leno, V. C., Simonoff, E., Baird, G., Pickles, A., Jones, C. R. G., Erskine, C., Charman, T., & Happé, F. (2015). Alexithymia in Adolescents with Autism Spectrum Disorder: Its Relationship to Internalising Difficulties, Sensory Modulation and Social Cognition. *Journal of Autism and Developmental Disorders*, *46*(4), 1354–1367. DOI: 10.1007/s10803-015-2670-8 PMID: 26659552

Milton, D. E. M. (2012). On the ontological status of autism: The 'double empathy problem.'. *Disability & Society*, *27*(6), 883–887. DOI: 10.1080/09687599.2012.710008

Milton, D., Gurbuz, E., & López, B. (2022). The 'double empathy problem': *Ten years on. Autism : The International Journal of Research and Practice*, *26*(8), 1901–1903. DOI: 10.1177/13623613221129123 PMID: 36263746

Mingins, J. E., Tarver, J., Waite, J., Jones, C., & Surtees, A. (2020). Anxiety and intellectual functioning in autistic children: A systematic review and meta-analysis. *Autism : The International Journal of Research and Practice*, *25*(1), 18–32. DOI: 10.1177/1362361320953253 PMID: 33198481

Ministry of Education. (2020). National [Government of India.]. *Educational Policy*, •••, 2020.

Minshew, N. J., & Goldstein, G. (2001). The pattern of intact and impaired memory functions in autism. *Journal of Child Psychology and Psychiatry, and Allied Disciplines*, *42*(8), 1095–1101. DOI: 10.1111/1469-7610.00808 PMID: 11806691

Misra, D. P., & Agarwal, V. (2018). Systematic Reviews: Challenges for Their Justification, Related Comprehensive Searches, and Implications. *Journal of Korean Medical Science*, *33*(12), e92. Advance online publication. DOI: 10.3346/jkms.2018.33.e92 PMID: 29542301

Mithyantha, R., Kneen, R., McCann, E., & Gladstone, M. (2017). Current evidence-based recommendations on investigating children with global developmental delay. *Archives of Disease in Childhood*, *102*(11), 1071–1076. DOI: 10.1136/archdischild-2016-311271 PMID: 29054862

Miyake, A., Friedman, N. P., Emerson, M. J., Witzki, A. H., Howerter, A., & Wager, T. D. (2000). The unity and diversity of executive functions and their contributions to complex "frontal lobe" tasks: A latent variable analysis. *Cognitive Psychology*, *41*(1), 49–100. DOI: 10.1006/cogp.1999.0734 PMID: 10945922

Mokhtari, S., & Parchini, P. (2024). The application of drawing tasks in studying cognitive functions in Autism Spectrum Disorder: A systematic review. *Review Journal of Autism and Developmental Disorders*, *11*(2), 180–193.

Mokrova, I., O'Brien, M., Calkins, S., & Keane, S. (2010). Parental ADHD symptomology and ineffective parenting: The connecting link of home chaos. *Parenting, Science and Practice, 10*(2), 119–135. DOI: 10.1080/15295190903212844 PMID: 20454604

Montaser, J., Umeano, L., Pujari, H. P., Nasiri, S. M. Z., Parisapogu, A., Shah, A., & Khan, S. (2023). Correlations Between the Development of Social Anxiety and Individuals With Autism Spectrum Disorder: A Systematic Review. *Cureus, 15*(9), e44841. DOI: 10.7759/cureus.44841 PMID: 37809175

Moore, D. S.. (2017). *The developing genome*. Oxford University Press.

Morelli, G. (2014). The evolution of attachment theory and cultures of human attachment in infancy and early childhood.

Morie, K. P., Jackson, S. L. J., Zhai, Z. W., Potenza, M. N., & Dritschel, B. (2019). Mood Disorders in High-Functioning Autism: The Importance of Alexithymia and Emotional Regulation. *Journal of Autism and Developmental Disorders, 49*(7), 2935–2945. DOI: 10.1007/s10803-019-04020-1 PMID: 31028592

Morris, A. S., Hays-Grudo, J., Kerr, K. L., & Beasley, L. O. (2021). The heart of the matter: Developing the whole child through community resources and caregiver relationships. *Development and Psychopathology, 33*(2), 533–544. DOI: 10.1017/S0954579420001595 PMID: 33955346

Morris-Rosendahl, D. J., & Crocq, M.-A. (2022). Neurodevelopmental disorders—The history and future of a diagnostic concept. *Dialogues in Clinical Neuroscience, 22*(1), 65–72. DOI: 10.31887/DCNS.2020.22.1/macrocq PMID: 32699506

Mualem, R., Morales-Quezada, L., Farraj, R. H., Shance, S., Bernshtein, D. H., Cohen, S., Mualem, L., Salem, N., Yehuda, R. R., Zbedat, Y., Waksman, I., & Biswas, S. (2024). Econeurobiology and brain development in children: Key factors affecting development, behavioral outcomes, and school interventions. *Frontiers in Public Health, 12*, 1376075. DOI: 10.3389/fpubh.2024.1376075 PMID: 39391155

Mul, C., Stagg, S. D., Herbelin, B., & Aspell, J. E. (2018). The Feeling of Me Feeling for You: Interoception, Alexithymia and Empathy in Autism. *Journal of Autism and Developmental Disorders, 48*(9), 2953–2967. DOI: 10.1007/s10803-018-3564-3 PMID: 29644587

Murphy, C. M., Deeley, Q., Daly, E., Ecker, C., O'Brien, F. M., Hallahan, B., Loth, E., Toal, F., Reed, S., Hales, S., Robertson, D. M., Craig, M. C., Mullins, D., Barker, G. J., Lavender, T., Johnston, P., Murphy, K. C., & Murphy, D. (2011). Anatomy and aging of the amygdala and hippocampus in autism spectrum disorder: An in vivo magnetic resonance imaging study of asperger syndrome. *Autism Research : Official Journal of the International Society for Autism Research*, *5*(1), 3–12. DOI: 10.1002/aur.227 PMID: 21948742

Murphy, K. R., & Barkley, R. A. (1996). Attention deficit hyperactivity disorder in adults: Comorbidities and adaptive impairments. *Comprehensive Psychiatry*, *37*(6), 393–401. DOI: 10.1016/S0010-440X(96)90022-X PMID: 8932963

National Institute of Mental Health and Neurosciences. (2019). *NIMHANS index for specific learning disabilities*. NIMHANS.

National Research Council. (2001). *Educating children with autism*. National Academy Press.

Nejati, V., & Derakhshan, Z. (2024). Attention Training Improves Executive Functions and Ameliorates Behavioral Symptoms in Children with Attention-Deficit Hyperactivity Disorder: Implication of Tele-Cognitive-Rehabilitation in the Era of Coronavirus Disease. *Games for Health Journal*, *13*(1), 40–49. Advance online publication. DOI: 10.1089/g4h.2023.0002 PMID: 38300525

Nelson, C. A., de Haan, M., & Thomas, K. M. (2006). *Neuroscience of cognitive development*. Wiley.

Nelson, C. A., Thomas, K. M., & de Haan, M. (2006). Neural Basis of cognitive development. In Kuuhn, D., & Siegler, R. (Eds.), Handbook of child psychology: Vol. 2. *Cognition, perception, and language* (6th ed., pp. 3–57). Wiley.

Niarchou, M., Lazary, J., Zhou, R., & Reichenberg, A. (2023). Common genetic risk factors in ASD and ADHD co-occurring families. *Psychiatry Research*, *327*, 115384. Advance online publication. DOI: 10.1016/j.psychres.2023.115384

Nigg, J. T. (2016). Annual Research Review: On the relations among self-regulation, self-control, executive functioning, effortful control, cognitive control, impulsivity, risk-taking, and inhibition for developmental psychopathology. *Journal of Child Psychology and Psychiatry, and Allied Disciplines*, *58*(4), 361–383. DOI: 10.1111/jcpp.12675 PMID: 28035675

Nigg, J. T., Stavro, G., Ettenhofer, M., Hambrick, D. Z., Miller, T., & Henderson, J. M. (2005). Executive functions and ADHD in adults: Evidence for selective effects on ADHD symptom domains. *Journal of Abnormal Psychology*, *114*(4), 706–717. DOI: 10.1037/0021-843X.114.3.706 PMID: 16351391

Ni, H., Lin, H., Tseng, W. I., & Gau, S. S. (2020). Association of self-regulation with white matter correlates in boys with and without autism spectrum disorder. *Scientific Reports*, *10*(1), 13811. Advance online publication. DOI: 10.1038/s41598-020-70836-y PMID: 32796900

Noble, K. G., Houston, S. M., Brito, N. H., Bartsch, H., Kan, E., Kuperman, J. M., Akshoomoff, N., Amaral, D. G., Bloss, C. S., Libiger, O., Schork, N. J., Murray, S. S., Casey, B. J., Chang, L., Ernst, T. M., Frazier, J. A., Gruen, J. R., Kennedy, D. N., Van Zijl, P., & Sowell, E. R. (2015). Family income, parental education and brain structure in children and adolescents. *Nature Neuroscience*, *18*(5), 773–778. DOI: 10.1038/nn.3983 PMID: 25821911

Nobre, A. C., & Gresch, D. (2025). How the brain shifts between external and internal attention. *Neuron*, *113*(15), 2382–2398. DOI: 10.1016/j.neuron.2025.06.013 PMID: 40675155

Norbury, C. F., & Sparks, A. (2013). Difference or disorder? Cultural issues in understanding neurodevelopmental disorders. *Developmental Psychology*, *49*(1), 45–58. DOI: 10.1037/a0027446 PMID: 22390668

Nordin, V., Palmgren, M., Lindbladh, A., Bölte, S., & Jonsson, U. (2024). School absenteeism in autistic children and adolescents: A scoping review. *Autism : The International Journal of Research and Practice*, *28*(7), 1622–1637. DOI: 10.1177/13623613231217409 PMID: 38159071

Nowell, S. W., Watson, L. R., Boyd, B., & Klinger, L. G. (2019). Efficacy study of a social communication and self-regulation intervention for school-age children with autism spectrum disorder: A randomized controlled trial. *Language, Speech, and Hearing Services in Schools*, *50*(3), 416–433. DOI: 10.1044/2019_LSHSS-18-0093 PMID: 31287766

Oakley, B., Jones, E. J. H., Crawley, D., Charman, T., Buitelaar, J. K., Tillmann, J., Murphy, D., & Loth, E. (2020). Alexithymia in autism: Cross-sectional and longitudinal associations with social-communication difficulties, anxiety and depression symptoms. *Psychological Medicine*, *52*(8), 1458–1470. DOI: 10.1017/S0033291720003244 PMID: 33028432

Olusanya, B. O., Davis, A. C., Wertlieb, D., Boo, N. Y., Nair, M. K. C., Halpern, R., & Kofumn, G.Global Research on Developmental Disabilities Collaborators. (2018). Developmental disabilities among children younger than five years in low- and middle-income countries. *The Lancet. Global Health*, *6*(10), e1100–e1121. DOI: 10.1016/S2214-109X(18)30309-7 PMID: 30172774

Otterman, D. L., Koopman-Verhoeff, M. E., White, T. J., Tiemeier, H., Bolhuis, K., & Jansen, P. W. (2019). Executive functioning and neurodevelopmental disorders in early childhood: A prospective population-based study. *Child and Adolescent Psychiatry and Mental Health*, *13*(1), 38. DOI: 10.1186/s13034-019-0299-7 PMID: 31649749

Otto, H. (2014). Don't show your emotions! Emotion regulation and attachment in the Cameroonian Nso. *Different faces of attachment*, 215-229.

Oviogun, P. V., & Veerdee, P. S. (2020). Definition of language and linguistics: Basic competence. *Macrolinguistics and Microlinguistics*, *1*(1), 1–12. DOI: 10.21744/mami.v1n1.1

Owen, A., Curran, M., Cook, S. W., Cole, R. S., & McGregor, K. K. (2023). Teaching little kids big sentences: A randomized controlled trial showing that children with DLD respond to complex syntax intervention embedded within the context of preschool/kindergarten science instruction. *International Journal of Language & Communication Disorders*, *58*(5), 1551–1569. DOI: 10.1111/1460-6984.12882 PMID: 37129110

Ozonoff, S., & Jensen, J. (1999). Brief report: Specific executive function profiles in three neuro-de velopmental disorders. *Journal of Autism and Developmental Disorders*, *29*(2), 171–177. DOI: 10.1023/A:1023052913110 PMID: 10382139

Ozsivadjian, A., Hollocks, M. J., Magiati, I., Happé, F., Baird, G., & Absoud, M. (2020). Is cognitive inflexibility a missing link? The role of cognitive inflexibility, alexithymia and intolerance of uncertainty in externalising and internalising behaviours in young people with autism spectrum disorder. *Journal of Child Psychology and Psychiatry, and Allied Disciplines*, *62*(6), 715–724. DOI: 10.1111/jcpp.13295 PMID: 32827150

Paananen, M., Husberg, H., Katajamäki, H., & Aro, T. (2022). School-based group intervention in attention and executive functions: Intervention response and moderators. *Frontiers in Psychology*, *13*, 975856. Advance online publication. DOI: 10.3389/fpsyg.2022.975856 PMID: 36186366

Paas, F., Renkl, A., & Sweller, J. (2003). Cognitive load theory and instructional design: Recent developments. *Educational Psychologist*, *38*(1), 1–4. DOI: 10.1207/S15326985EP3801_1

Palumbo, M. L., Mody, M., Klykylo, W. M., Ballard, K. J., McDougle, C. J., & Guenther, F. H. (2024). Neurodevelopmental disorders: Speech and language disorders. In Tasman, A., Riba, M. B., Alarcón, R. D., Alfonso, C. A., Kanba, S., Lecic-Tosevski, D., Ndetei, D. M., Ng, C. H., & Schulze, T. G. (Eds.), *Tasman's Psychiatry* (pp. 1533–1559). Springer Nature Switzerland AG., DOI: 10.1007/978-3-030-51366-5_86

Papalia, D. E., & Martorell, G. (2021). *Experience human development* (15th ed.). McGraw-Hill.

Pardo-Salamanca, A., Paoletti, D., Pastor-Cerezuela, G., De Stasio, S., & Berenguer, C. (2024). Executive Functioning Profiles in Neurodevelopmental Disorders: Parent–Child Outcomes. *Children (Basel, Switzerland)*, *11*(8), 909. DOI: 10.3390/children11080909 PMID: 39201844

Parke, R. D., & Bornstein, M. H. (2002). Handbook of parenting: Vol. 3: Being and becoming a parent.

Park, J. L., Hudec, K. L., & Johnston, C. (2017). Parental ADHD symptoms and parenting behaviors: A meta-analytic review. *Clinical Psychology Review*, *56*, 25–39. DOI: 10.1016/j.cpr.2017.05.003 PMID: 28601690

Park, J. L., & Johnston, C. (2019). Parental ADHD symptoms and parenting behaviors. *The ADHD Report*, *27*(3), 1–7. DOI: 10.1521/adhd.2019.27.3.1

Park, K., Kihl, T., Park, S., Kim, M., & Chang, J. (2018). Fairy tale directed game-based training system for children with ADHD using BCI and motion sensing technologies. *Behaviour & Information Technology*, *38*(6), 564–577. DOI: 10.1080/0144929X.2018.1544276

Parlatini, V., Bellato, A., Gabellone, A., Margari, L., Marzulli, L., Matera, E., Petruzzelli, M. G., Solmi, M., Correll, C. U., & Cortese, S. (2024). A state-of-the-art overview of candidate diagnostic biomarkers for Attention-deficit/hyperactivity disorder (ADHD). *Expert Review of Molecular Diagnostics*, *24*(4), 259–271. DOI: 10.1080/14737159.2024.2333277 PMID: 38506617

Pasini, A., Paloscia, C., Alessandrelli, R., Porfirio, M. C., & Curatolo, P. (2007). Attention and executive functions profile in drug naive ADHD subtypes. *Brain & Development*, *29*(7), 400–408. DOI: 10.1016/j.braindev.2006.11.010 PMID: 17207595

Pastorino, G. M. G., Operto, F. F., Padovano, C., Vivenzio, V., Scuoppo, C., Pastorino, N., Roccella, M., Vetri, L., Carotenuto, M., & Coppola, G. (2021). Social Cognition in Neurodevelopmental Disorders and Epilepsy. [Secondary Pediatric Neurology]. *Frontiers in Neurology*, *12*, 658823. Advance online publication. DOI: 10.3389/fneur.2021.658823 PMID: 33935956

Patel, V., Belkin, G. S., Chockalingam, A., Cooper, J., Saxena, S., & Unützer, J. (2011). Grand challenges: Integrating mental health services into priority health care platforms. *PLoS Medicine*, *8*(5), e1001448. DOI: 10.1371/journal.pmed.1001448 PMID: 23737736

Patel, V., Saxena, S., Lund, C., Thornicroft, G., Baingana, F., Bolton, P., Chisholm, D., Collins, P. Y., Cooper, J. L., Eaton, J., Herrman, H., & Lomola, S.. (2018). The Lancet Commission on global mental health and sustainable development. *Lancet*, *392*(10157), 1553–1598. DOI: 10.1016/S0140-6736(18)31612-X PMID: 30314863

Patil, O., & Kaple, M. (2023). Sensory Processing Differences in Individuals With Autism Spectrum Disorder: A Narrative Review of Underlying Mechanisms and Sensory-Based Interventions. *Cureus*, *15*(10), e48020. DOI: 10.7759/cureus.48020 PMID: 38034138

Paul, M. L., Sheth, P., Davis, R., Chrusciel, T., & Messias, E. (2025). Incidence of attention-deficit/hyperactivity disorder between 2016 and 2023: A retrospective cohort. *Psychiatric Research and Clinical Practice*, *7*(1), 18–24. Advance online publication. DOI: 10.1176/appi.prcp.20240121 PMID: 40171065

Pellicano, E., Lawson, W., Hall, G., Mahony, J., Lilley, R., Heyworth, M., Clapham, H., & Yudell, M. (2022). "I Knew She'd Get It, and Get Me": Participants' Perspectives of a Participatory Autism Research Project. *Autism in Adulthood: Challenges and Management*, *4*(2), 120–129. DOI: 10.1089/aut.2021.0039 PMID: 36605972

Peng, P., & Kievit, R. A. (2019). The development of academic achievement and cognitive abilities: A bidirectional perspective. *Child Development Perspectives*, *14*(1), 15–20. DOI: 10.1111/cdep.12352 PMID: 35909387

Pereira, T., Ramalho, A. M., & Lousada, M. (2025). Parents' and Early Childhood Educators' Perceptions after the Implementation of the Pragmatic Intervention Programme (PICP). *Autism & Developmental Language Impairments*, *10*, 23969415251330465. Advance online publication. DOI: 10.1177/23969415251330465 PMID: 40370932

Pérez-Vigil, A., Ilzarbe, D., Garcia-Delgar, B., Morer, A., Pomares, M., Puig, O., Lera-Miguel, S., Rosa, M., Romero, M., Escalona, R. C., & Lázaro, L. (2024). Theory of mind in neurodevelopmental disorders: Beyond autistic spectrum disorder. *Neurología : Publicación Oficial de la Sociedad Española de Neurología, 39*(2), 117–126. DOI: 10.1016/j.nrleng.2024.01.005 PMID: 38272257

Peristeri, E., Frantzidis, C. A., & Andreou, M. (2024). Editorial: Neural mechanisms of language and cognitive performance in individuals with neurodevelopmental disorders. *Frontiers in Psychology, 15*, 1414354. Advance online publication. DOI: 10.3389/fpsyg.2024.1414354 PMID: 38741752

Peterson, R. L., & Pennington, B. F. (2015). Developmental dyslexia. *Lancet, 379*(9830), 1997–2007. DOI: 10.1016/S0140-6736(12)60198-6 PMID: 22513218

Peters-Scheffer, N., Didden, R., Sigafoos, J., Green, V. A., & Korzilius, H. (2013). Behavioral flexibility in children with autism spectrum disorder and intellectual disability. *Research in Autism Spectrum Disorders, 7*(6), 699–709. DOI: 10.1016/j.rasd.2013.02.016

Peverill, S., Smith, I. M., Duku, E., Szatmari, P., Mirenda, P., Vaillancourt, T., Volden, J., Zwaigenbaum, L., Bennett, T., Elsabbagh, M., Georgiades, S., & Ungar, W. J. (2019). Developmental trajectories of feeding problems in children with autism spectrum disorder. *Journal of Pediatric Psychology, 44*(8), 988–998. DOI: 10.1093/jpepsy/jsz033 PMID: 31089730

Phelan, H. L., Filliter, J. H., & Johnson, S. A. (2011). Brief report: Memory performance on the California Verbal Learning Test – Children's Version in autism spectrum disorder. *Journal of Autism and Developmental Disorders, 41*(4), 518–523. DOI: 10.1007/s10803-010-1069-9 PMID: 20652387

Piaget, J. (1952). *The origins of intelligence in children*. International Universities Press. DOI: 10.1037/11494-000

Pinderhughes, E. E., Dodge, K. A., Bates, J. E., Pettit, G. S., & Zelli, A. (2000). Discipline responses: Influences of parents' socioeconomic status, ethnicity, beliefs about parenting, stress, and cognitiveemotional processes. *Journal of Family Psychology : JFP : Journal of the Division of Family Psychology of the American Psychological Association (Division 43), 14*(3), 380–400. DOI: 10.1037/0893-3200.14.3.380 PMID: 11025931

Pini, S., Nardi, B., Carpita, B., Amatori, G., Cremone, I. M., & Dell'Osso, L. (2025). Relevance of separation anxiety in the autism spectrum and related disorders. *Journal of Psychopathology, 31*. Advance online publication. DOI: 10.36148/2284-0249-N615

Plomin, R., DeFries, J. C., Knopik, V. S., & Neiderhiser, J. M. (2016). Top 10 replicated findings from behavioral genetics. *Perspectives on Psychological Science : A Journal of the Association for Psychological Science, 11*(1), 3–23. DOI: 10.1177/1745691615617439 PMID: 26817721

Pohl, A. L., Crockford, S. K., Blakemore, M., Allison, C., & Baron-Cohen, S. (2020). A comparative study of autistic and non-autistic women's experience of motherhood. *Molecular Autism, 11*(1), 1–12. DOI: 10.1186/s13229-019-0304-2 PMID: 31911826

Posner, M. I., & Rothbart, M. K. (2007). Research on attention networks as a model for the integration of psychological science. *Annual Review of Psychology, 58*(1), 1–23. DOI: 10.1146/annurev.psych.58.110405.085516 PMID: 17029565

Potard, C., Auger, A. C., Lenoir-Perrotel, S., & Jarry, C. (2022). Examining frustration intolerance beliefs among adults with dyslexia or developmental coordination disorder. *Research in Developmental Disabilities, 123*, 104184. DOI: 10.1016/j.ridd.2022.104184 PMID: 35121415

Pouretemad, H. R., Sadeghi, S., Badv, R. S., & Brand, S. (2022). Differentiating Post–Digital Nannying Autism Syndrome from Autism Spectrum Disorders in Young Children: A Comparative Cross-Sectional Study. *Journal of Clinical Medicine, 11*(22), 6786. DOI: 10.3390/jcm11226786 PMID: 36431264

Powell, K., O'Brien, S. E., Chawarska, K., & Klin, A. (2022). Elevated symptoms of executive dysfunction predict lower adaptive functioning in 3-year-olds with ASD. *Autism Research : Official Journal of the International Society for Autism Research, 15*(7), 1336–1347. DOI: 10.1002/aur.2715 PMID: 35388596

Power, T. J., Soffer, S. L., Fives, C. J., & Nissley-Tsiopinis, J. (2013). Family-school intervention for children with ADHD. *School Psychology Review, 42*(3), 251–271.

Praslova, L. N. (2024). *The canary code: A guide to neurodiversity, dignity, and intersectional belonging at work*. Berrett-Koehler Publishers.

Provenzi, L., Bussu, G., & Riva, V. (2023). Editorial: Risk and protective factors, family environment and (a)typical neurodevelopmental outcomes. *Frontiers in Psychology, 14*, 1221338. DOI: 10.3389/fpsyg.2023.1221338 PMID: 37408973

Psychogiou, L., Daley, D. M., Thompson, M. J., & Sonuga-Barke, E. J. S. (2008). Do maternal attention-deficit/hyperactivity disorder symptoms exacerbate or ameliorate the negative effect of child attention-deficit/hyperactivity disorder symptoms on parenting? *Development and Psychopathology, 20*(1), 121–137. DOI: 10.1017/S0954579408000060 PMID: 18211731

Punshon, C., Skirrow, P., & Murphy, G. (2009). The not guilty verdict' Psychological reactions to a diagnosis of Asperger syndrome in adulthood. *Autism : The International Journal of Research and Practice*, *13*(3), 265–283. DOI: 10.1177/1362361309103795 PMID: 19369388

Ramji, R., Rämgård, M., & Kottorp, A. (2023). Psychometric properties of the WHOQOL-BREF in citizens from a disadvantaged neighborhood in Southern Sweden. *Frontiers in Psychology*, *14*, 1118575. DOI: 10.3389/fpsyg.2023.1118575 PMID: 37113124

Ramsay, J. R., & Rostain, A. (2008). *Cognitive-behavioral therapy for adult ADHD: An integrative psychosocial and medical approach.* Routledge/Taylor & Francis Group. New York, NY: Routledge.

Rasinski, T. V. (2012). Why reading fluency should be hot. *The Reading Teacher*, *65*(8), 516–522. DOI: 10.1002/TRTR.01077

Raud, L., Westerhausen, R., Dooley, N., & Huster, R. J. (2020). Differences in unity: The go/no-go and stop signal tasks rely on different mechanisms. *NeuroImage*, *210*, 116582. DOI: 10.1016/j.neuroimage.2020.116582 PMID: 31987997

Raymaker, D. M., Teo, A. R., Steckler, N. A., Lentz, B., Scharer, M., Santos, A. D., Kapp, S. K., Hunter, M., Joyce, A., & Nicolaidis, C. (2020). "Having all of your internal resources exhausted beyond measure and being left with no clean-up crew": Defining autistic burnout. *Autism in Adulthood: Challenges and Management*, *2*(2), 1–12. DOI: 10.1089/aut.2019.0079 PMID: 32851204

Rehman, A., Heldal, I., Costescu, C., David, C., & Lin, J. C.-W. (2025). *An Adaptive Scoring Framework for Attention Assessment in NDD Children via Serious Games.* IEEE Access. https://arxiv.org/pdf/2509.08353

Reid, R., Mason, L., & Asaro-Saddler, K. (2013). Self-regulation strategies for students with autism spectrum disorder. In *Interventions for autism spectrum disorders: Translating science into practice* (pp. 257–281). Springer New York., DOI: 10.1007/978-1-4614-5301-7_13

Renno, P., & Wood, J. (2013). Discriminant and convergent validity of the anxiety construct in children with autism spectrum disorders. *Journal of Autism and Developmental Disorders*, *43*(9), 2135–2146. DOI: 10.1007/s10803-013-1767-1 PMID: 23354538

Retalis, S., Korpa, T., Skaloumpakas, C., Boloudakis, M., Kourakli, M., Altanis, I., & Pervanidou, P. (2014). Empowering children with ADHD learning disabilities with the kinems kinect learning games. In *8th European Conference on Games Based Learning* (pp. 469–477).

Richey, J. A., Damiano, C. R., Sabatino, A., Rittenberg, A., Petty, C., Bizzell, J., Voyvodic, J., Heller, A., Coffman, M. C., Smoski, M., Davidson, R. J., & Dichter, G. S. (2015). Neural mechanisms of emotion regulation in autism spectrum disorder. *Journal of Autism and Developmental Disorders*, *45*(11), 3409–3423. DOI: 10.1007/s10803-015-2359-z PMID: 25618212

Richter, L. M., Daelmans, B., Lombardi, J., Heymann, J., Boo, F. L., Behrman, J. R., Lu, C., Lucas, J. E., Perez-Escamilla, R., Dua, T., Bhutta, Z. A., Stenberg, K., Gertler, P., & Darmstadt, G. L.Paper Steering Committee. (2019). Investing in the foundation of sustainable development: Pathways to scale up for early childhood development. *Lancet*, *389*(10064), 103–118. DOI: 10.1016/S0140-6736(16)31698-1 PMID: 27717610

Ridderinkhof, A., de Bruin, E. I., van den Driesschen, S., & Bögels, S. M. (2020). Attention in Children With Autism Spectrum Disorder and the Effects of a Mindfulness-Based Program. *Journal of Attention Disorders*, *24*(5), 681–692. DOI: 10.1177/1087054718797428 PMID: 30222027

Roberts, M., Ashinoff, B. K., Castellanos, F. X., & Carrasco, M. (2018). When attention is intact in adults with ADHD. *Psychonomic Bulletin & Review*, *25*(4), 1423–1434. DOI: 10.3758/s13423-017-1407-4 PMID: 29181782

Rodgers, J., Wigham, S., McConachie, H., Freeston, M., Honey, E., & Parr, J. (2016). Development of the anxiety scale for children with autism spectrum disorder (asc-asd). *Autism Research : Official Journal of the International Society for Autism Research*, *9*(11), 1205–1215. DOI: 10.1002/aur.1603 PMID: 26887910

Rodríguez-Prieto, P., Giral-Oliveros, N. A., Simpson, I. C., & Ibáñez-Alfonso, J. A. (2024). Cognitive stimulation in socioeconomically disadvantaged children with neurodevelopmental disorders: A case series. [Secondary Pediatric Psychology]. *Frontiers in Psychology*, *15*, 1365697. Advance online publication. DOI: 10.3389/fpsyg.2024.1365697 PMID: 39045438

Rogers, C., Lepherd, L., Ganguly, R., & Jacob-Rogers, S. (2017). Perinatal issues for women with high functioning autism spectrum disorder. *Women and Birth : Journal of the Australian College of Midwives*, *30*(2), e89–e95. DOI: 10.1016/j.wombi.2016.09.009 PMID: 27751685

Rogers, S. J., & Dawson, G. (2010). *Early Start Denver Model for young children with autism*. Guilford Press.

Rogers, S. J., Estes, A., Lord, C., Vismara, L., Winter, J., Fitzpatrick, A., Guo, Y., & Dawson, G. (2012). Early Start Denver Model intervention for young children with autism. *Journal of the American Academy of Child and Adolescent Psychiatry, 51*(1), 105–115.

Roording-Ragetlie, S., Pieters, S., Wennekers, E., Klip, H., Buitelaar, J. K., & Slaats-Willemse, D. (2023). Working memory training in children with neurodevelopmental disorders and intellectual disabilities, the role of coaching: A double-blind randomised controlled trial. *Journal of Intellectual Disability Research : JIDR, 67*(9), 842–859. DOI: 10.1111/jir.13047 PMID: 37313626

Root, J. R., Jimenez, B., & Saunders, A. (2021). Leveraging the UDL framework to plan grade-aligned mathematics in inclusive settings. *In Practice, 1*(1), 13–2. PMID: 33039648

Ros-DeMarize, R., Garcia, A., & Graziano, P. A. (2022). The impact of parental ADHD symptoms on Parenting practices and stress after behavioral intervention: Comparisons across co-occurring presentations. *Journal of Child and Family Studies, 31*(7), 1869–1879. DOI: 10.1007/s10826-021-02217-6

Rose, D. H., & Meyer, A. (2002). *Teaching every student in the digital age*. ASCD.

Rosenthal, R., & Jacobson, L. (1968). *Pygmalion in the classroom*. Holt, Rinehart & Winston. DOI: 10.1007/BF02322211

Rosqvist, H. B., & Lövgren, V. (2013). Doing adulthood through parenthood: Notions of parenthood among people with cognitive disabilities. *Alter (Paris), 7*(1), 56–68. DOI: 10.1016/j.alter.2012.11.002

Rostami, M., & Saadati, N. (2018). Role of maternal parenting styles in predicting oppositional defiant, behavior, conduct, mood, and separation anxiety disorders among students. *Journal of Research and Health, 8*(5), 418–424. DOI: 10.29252/jrh.8.5.418

Rothbart, M. K., Sheese, B. E., Rosario Rueda, M., & Posner, M. I. (2011). Developing Mechanisms of Self-Regulation in Early Life! *Emotion Review, 3*(2), 207–213. DOI: 10.1177/1754073910387943 PMID: 21892360

Rubia, K. (2018). Cognitive neuroscience of attention deficit hyperactivity disorder (ADHD) and its clinical translation. *Frontiers in Human Neuroscience, 12*, 100. DOI: 10.3389/fnhum.2018.00100 PMID: 29651240

Rubia, K., Westwood, S., Aggensteiner, P. M., & Brandeis, D. (2021). Neurotherapeutics for Attention Deficit/Hyperactivity Disorder (ADHD): A Review. *Cells, 10*(8), 2156. DOI: 10.3390/cells10082156 PMID: 34440925

Rueda, M. R., Posner, M. I., & Rothbart, M. K. (2005). The development of executive attention: Contributions to the emergence of self-regulation. *Developmental Neuropsychology, 28*(2), 573–594. DOI: 10.1207/s15326942dn2802_2 PMID: 16144428

Russell, A. E. (2022). Neurodevelopmental Disorders and Attendance at School. In Moore, D. A., Finning, K., & Ford, T. (Eds.), *Mental Health and Attendance at School* (pp. 78–105). Cambridge University Press., https://www.cambridge.org/core/books/abs/mental-health-and-attendance-at-school/neurodevelopmental-disorders-and-attendance-at-school/DC186CBEF0D46CD6D3D92129DF78EEC6 DOI: 10.1017/9781911623151.006

Russell, J. (1997). How executive disorders can bring about an inadequate "theory of mind.". In Russell, J. (Ed.), *Autism as an executive disorder* (pp. 256–304). Oxford University Press.

Rutter, M. (1989). Pathways from childhood to adult life. *Journal of Child Psychology and Psychiatry, and Allied Disciplines, 30*(1), 23–51. DOI: 10.1111/j.1469-7610.1989.tb00768.x PMID: 2647779

Rutter, M. (2006). Genes and behavior. *Nature, 443*(7114), 924–925. PMID: 17066023

Rutter, M. (2011). Research Review: Child psychiatric diagnosis and classification: concepts, findings, challenges and potential. *Journal of Child Psychology and Psychiatry, and Allied Disciplines, 52*(6), 647–660. DOI: 10.1111/j.1469-7610.2011.02367.x PMID: 21434914

Rutter, M. (2012). Resilience as a dynamic concept. *Development and Psychopathology, 24*(2), 335–344. DOI: 10.1017/S0954579412000028 PMID: 22559117

Rylaarsdam, L., & Guemez-Gamboa, A. (2019). Genetic causes and modifiers of autism spectrum disorder. *Frontiers in Cellular Neuroscience, 13*, 385. DOI: 10.3389/fncel.2019.00385 PMID: 31481879

Sacrey, L. R., Zwaigenbaum, L., Bryson, S., Brian, J., Smith, I. M., Raza, S., Roberts, W., Szatmari, P., Vaillancourt, T., Roncadin, C., & Garon, N. (2018). Developmental trajectories of adaptive behavior in autism spectrum disorder: A high-risk sibling cohort. *Journal of Child Psychology and Psychiatry, and Allied Disciplines, 60*(6), 697–706. DOI: 10.1111/jcpp.12985 PMID: 30295313

Sadozai, A. K., Sun, C., Demetriou, E. A., Lampit, A., Munro, M., Perry, N., Boulton, K. A., & Guastella, A. J. (2024). Executive function in children with neurodevelopmental conditions: A systematic review and meta-analysis. *Nature Human Behaviour*, *8*(12), 2357–2366. DOI: 10.1038/s41562-024-02000-9 PMID: 39424962

Sáez-Suanes, G. P. (2024). Mood Alternations on the Autistic Spectrum. *The Palgrave Encyclopedia of Disability*, 1-13. https://doi.org/DOI: 10.1007/978-3-031-40858-8_5-1

Safren, S. A., Perlman, C. A., Sprich, S., & Otto, M. W. (2005). *Mastering your adult ADHD: A cognitive-behavioral treatment program*. Oxford University Press.

Sahuquillo-Leal, R., Perea, M., Moreno-Giménez, A., Salmerón, L., Andreu, J., Pons, D., Vento, M., & García-Blanco, A. (2025). Emotional face processing in autism spectrum condition: A study of attentional orienting and inhibitory control. *Journal of Autism and Developmental Disorders*, *55*(2), 440–448. DOI: 10.1007/s10803-023-06200-6 PMID: 38238508

Sameroff, A. J. (2000). Developmental systems and psychopathology. *Development and Psychopathology*, *12*(3), 297–312. DOI: 10.1017/S0954579400003035 PMID: 11014740

Sameroff, A. J. (2010). A unified theory of development. *Child Development*, *81*(1), 6–22. DOI: 10.1111/j.1467-8624.2009.01378.x PMID: 20331651

Sami, R., & Tarek, G. (2025). Multimodal approaches in language therapy for children with developmental language delay: Enhancing engagement and outcomes using Let's Learn Program. *The Egyptian Journal of Otolaryngology*, *41*(1), 64. DOI: 10.1186/s43163-025-00804-8

Samson, A. C., Hardan, A. Y., Podell, R. W., Phillips, J. M., & Gross, J. J. (2014). Emotion Regulation in Children and Adolescents With Autism Spectrum Disorder. *Autism Research : Official Journal of the International Society for Autism Research*, *8*(1), 9–18. DOI: 10.1002/aur.1387 PMID: 24863869

Sandin, S., Lichtenstein, P., Kuja-Halkola, R., Hultman, C., Larsson, H., & Reichenberg, A. (2017). The heritability of autism spectrum disorder. *Journal of the American Medical Association*, *318*(12), 1182. DOI: 10.1001/jama.2017.12141 PMID: 28973605

Saragih, B. D., & Fuadah, F. (2024). The Influence of Parenting Styles on the Early Childhood Development at TKK Kasih Mulia Cimahi. Int. J. Pharm. *Bio-Medical Sci*, *4*(10), 861–864. DOI: 10.47191/ijpbms/v4-i10-12

Sarmukadam, K., Bitsika, V., & Sharpley, C. F. (2023). Frontoparietal connectivity, sensory features, and anxiety in children and adolescents with autism spectrum disorder. *Advances in Neurodevelopmental Disorders*, *7*(1), 14–26. DOI: 10.1007/s41252-022-00271-9

Sassone-Corsi, P., & Christen, Y. (2016). *Research and perspectives in endocrine interactions: A time for metabolism and hormones*. https://library.oapen.org/bitstream/handle/20.500.12657/27865/1/1002139.pdf

Satterstrom, F. K., Kosmicki, J. A., Wang, J., Breen, M. S., De Rubeis, S., An, J.-Y., Peng, M., Collins, R., Grove, J., Klei, L., Stevens, C., Reichert, J., Mulhern, M. S., Artomov, M., Gerges, S., Sheppard, B., Xu, X., Bhaduri, A., Norman, U., & Buxbaum, J. D. (2020). Large-scale exome sequencing study implicates both developmental and functional changes in the neurobiology of autism. *Cell*, *180*(3), 568–584.e23. DOI: 10.1016/j.cell.2019.12.036 PMID: 31981491

Sayers, N., Sayers, E., & O'Brien, S. (2011). Stereotyped behaviour in children with autism and intellectual disability: An examination of the executive dysfunction hypothesis. *Journal of Intellectual Disability Research : JIDR*, *55*(7), 701–710. DOI: 10.1111/j.1365-2788.2010.01370.x PMID: 21199048

Scatliffe, N., Casavant, S. G., Vittner, D., & Cong, X. (2019). Oxytocin and early parent-infant interactions: A systematic review. *International Journal of Nursing Sciences*, *6*(4), 445–453. DOI: 10.1016/j.ijnss.2019.09.009 PMID: 31728399

Schaie, K. W. (1996). *Intellectual development in adulthood*. Cambridge University Press.

Schalock, R. L.. (2021). *Intellectual disability: Definition, diagnosis, classification, and systems of supports* (12th ed.). AAIDD.

Schiele, T., Mues, A., Wirth, A., Christner, N., Paulus, M., Birtwistle, E., & Niklas, F. (2024). Bridging the gap: A longitudinal study on the relation between preschool children's moral self-concept, normative stances, and sharing behavior. *Social and Emotional Learning: Research, Practice, and Policy*, *3*, 100027. DOI: 10.1016/j.sel.2024.100027

Schilling, R. F., Schinke, S. P., Blythe, B. J., & Barth, R. P. (1982). Child maltreatment and mentally retarded parents: Is there a relationship? *Mental Retardation*, *20*(5), 201. PMID: 6757649

Schiltz, H. K., & Magnus, B. E. (2021). Differential Item Functioning Based on Autism Features, IQ, and Age on the Screen for Child Anxiety Related Disorders (SCARED) Among Youth on the Autism Spectrum. *Autism Research : Official Journal of the International Society for Autism Research*, *14*(6), 1220–1236. DOI: 10.1002/aur.2481 PMID: 33543824

Schmitt, L. M., Herrington, T. M., & Mosconi, M. W. (2018). Cognitive mechanisms of inhibitory control deficits in autism spectrum disorder. *Journal of Child Psychology and Psychiatry, and Allied Disciplines*, *59*(5), 586–595. DOI: 10.1111/jcpp.12837 PMID: 29052841

Schoeman, R., Enright, J., James, A., Vermeulen, C., & De Beer, N. (2018). Removing mental health barriers to education: A community project. *South African Journal of Psychiatry*, *24*. Advance online publication. DOI: 10.4102/sajpsychiatry.v24i0.1293

Schuck, R. K., & Fung, L. K. (2024). A dual design thinking – universal design approach to catalyze neurodiversity advocacy through collaboration among highschoolers. *Frontiers in Psychiatry*, *14*, 1250895. DOI: 10.3389/fpsyt.2023.1250895 PMID: 38268559

Schulze, M., Coghill, D., Lux, S., Philipsen, A., & Silk, T. (2024). Assessing brain iron and its relationship to cognition and comorbidity in children with Attention-Deficit/Hyperactivity Disorder with quantitative susceptibility mapping. *Biological Psychiatry. Cognitive Neuroscience and Neuroimaging*. Advance online publication. DOI: 10.1016/j.bpsc.2024.08.015 PMID: 39218036

Schweitzer, J. B., Faber, T. L., Grafton, S. T., Tune, L. E., Hoffman, J. M., & Kilts, C. D. (2000). Alterations in the functional anatomy of working memory in adult attention deficit hyperactivity disorder. *The American Journal of Psychiatry*, *157*(2), 278–280. DOI: 10.1176/appi.ajp.157.2.278 PMID: 10671402

Seeley, W. W. (2019). The salience network: A neural system for perceiving and responding to homeostatic demands. *The Journal of Neuroscience : The Official Journal of the Society for Neuroscience*, *39*(50), 9878–9882. DOI: 10.1523/JNEUROSCI.1138-17.2019 PMID: 31676604

Segura, P., Pagani, M., Bishop, S. L., Thomson, P., Colcombe, S., Xu, T., Factor, Z. Z., Hector, E. C., Kim, S. H., Lombardo, M. V., Gozzi, A., Castellanos, X. F., Lord, C., Milham, M. P., & Di Martino, A. (2024). Connectome-based symptom mapping andin silicorelated gene expression in children with autism and/or attention-deficit/hyperactivity disorder. medRxiv *(Cold Spring Harbor Laboratory)*. https://doi.org/ DOI: 10.1101/2024.12.09.24318621

Segura, P.. (2025). Connectome-based symptom mapping and in silico related gene expression in neurodevelopmental conditions. *Molecular Psychiatry*. Advance online publication. DOI: 10.1038/s41380-025-03205-8 PMID: 41131279

Sethi, C., Harrop, C., Zhang, W., Pritchett, J., Whitten, A., & Boyd, B. A. (2018). Parent and professional perspectives on behavioral inflexibility in autism spectrum disorders: A qualitative study. *Autism : The International Journal of Research and Practice*, *23*(5), 1236–1248. DOI: 10.1177/1362361318810217 PMID: 30394796

Shaffer, R. C., Schmitt, L., Reisinger, D. L., Coffman, M. C., Horn, P. S., Goodwin, M. S., Mazefsky, C. A., Randall, S., & Erickson, C. A. (2022). Regulating Together: Emotion Dysregulation Group Treatment for ASD Youth and Their Caregivers. *Journal of Autism and Developmental Disorders*, *53*(5), 1942–1962. DOI: 10.1007/s10803-022-05461-x PMID: 35141815

Shahaeian, A., Haynes, M., & Frick, P. J. (2023). The role of language in the association between theory of mind and executive functioning in early childhood: New longitudinal evidence. *Early Childhood Research Quarterly*, *62*, 251–258. DOI: 10.1016/j.ecresq.2022.09.003

Shapiro, E. G., Hughes, S. J., August, G. J., & Bloomquist, M. L. (1993). Processing of emotional information in children with attention-deficit hyperactivity disorder. *Developmental Neuropsychology*, *9*(3–4), 207–224. DOI: 10.1080/87565649309540553

Shaw, P.. (2018). *Opportunities for neurodevelopmental plasticity from infancy through early adulthood*. Society for Research in Child Development., DOI: 10.1111/cdev.13073

Shaw, R., Grayson, A., & Lewis, V. (2005). Inhibition, ADHD, and Computer Games: The Inhibitory Performance of Children with ADHD on Computerized Tasks and Games. *Journal of Attention Disorders*, *8*(4), 160–168. DOI: 10.1177/1087054705278771 PMID: 16110046

Shear, K., Jin, R., Ruscio, A. M., Walters, E. E., & Kessler, R. C. (2006). Prevalence and correlates of estimated dsm-iv child and adult separation anxiety disorder in the national comorbidity survey replication. *The American Journal of Psychiatry*, *163*(6), 1074–1083. DOI: 10.1176/ajp.2006.163.6.1074 PMID: 16741209

Shimizu, V. T., Bueno, O. F. A., & Miranda, M. C. (2014). Sensory processing abilities of children with ADHD. *Brazilian Journal of Physical Therapy*, *18*(4), 343–352. DOI: 10.1590/bjpt-rbf.2014.0043 PMID: 25076000

Shokrkon, A., & Nicoladis, E. (2022). The directionality of the relationship between executive functions and language skills: A literature review. *Frontiers in Psychology*, *13*, 848696. DOI: 10.3389/fpsyg.2022.848696 PMID: 35928417

Sholihah, R. A. (2022). Language and Brain: Neurological Aspects in Language Acquisition. *MUHARRIK: Jurnal Dakwah Dan Sosial*, *5*(1), 220–230. Advance online publication. DOI: 10.37680/muharrik.v5i1.1069

Shonkoff, J. P., Garner, A. S., Siegel, B. S., Dobbins, M. I., Earls, M. F., Garner, A. S., McGuinn, L., Pascoe, J., & Wood, D. L. (2012). The lifelong effects of early childhood adversity and toxic stress. *Pediatrics*, *129*(1), e232–e246. DOI: 10.1542/peds.2011-2663 PMID: 22201156

Shonkoff, J. P., & Phillips, D. A. (2000). *From neurons to neighborhoods*. National Academy Press.

Shuai, L., Wang, Y., Li, W., Wilson, A., Wang, S., Chen, R., & Zhang, J. (2020). Executive Function Training for Preschool Children With ADHD: A Randomized Controlled Trial. *Journal of Attention Disorders*, *25*(14), 2037–2047. Advance online publication. DOI: 10.1177/1087054720956723 PMID: 32964771

Sibley, M. H., Arnold, L. E., Swanson, J. M., Hechtman, L. T., Kennedy, T. M., & Owens, E.MTA Cooperative Group. (2022). Defining ADHD symptom persistence in adulthood. *Journal of Child Psychology and Psychiatry, and Allied Disciplines*, *63*(2), 123–135. DOI: 10.1111/jcpp.13449 PMID: 27642116

Sibley, M. H., Ross, J. M., Gnagy, E. M., Dixon, L. J., Conn, B., & Pelham, W. E.Jr. (2013). An intensive summer treatment program for ADHD reduces parent–adolescent conflict. *Journal of Psychopathology and Behavioral Assessment*, *35*(1), 10–19. DOI: 10.1007/s10862-012-9314-5

Siegler, R. S. (2016). *Cognitive development* (4th ed.). Pearson.

Silverman, C. (2015). Steve Silberman, NeuroTribes: The Legacy of Autism and the Future of Neurodiversity. *Anthropological Quarterly*, *88*(4), 1111–1122. DOI: 10.1353/anq.2015.0057

Singer, J. (2016). *Neurodiversity: The birth of an idea.* [Kindle edition].

Singer, J. (1999). Why can't you be normal for once in your life? In Corker, M., & French, S. (Eds.), *Disability discourse* (pp. 59–67). Open University Press.

Singer, J. (2017). *NeuroDiversity: The birth of an idea*. Judy Singer.

Singh, J., Arun, P., & Bajaj, M. K. (2021). Theory of Mind and Executive Functions in Children With Attention Deficit Hyperactivity Disorder and Specific Learning Disorder. *Indian Journal of Psychological Medicine*, *43*(5), 392–398. Advance online publication. DOI: 10.1177/0253717621999807 PMID: 34584303

Siugzdaite, R., Bathelt, J., Holmes, J., & Astle, D. E. (2020). Transdiagnostic brain mapping in developmental disorders. *Current Biology : CB*, *30*(7), 1245–1257. DOI: 10.1016/j.cub.2020.01.078 PMID: 32109389

Slattery, E. J., Ryan, P., Fortune, D. G., & McAvinue, L. P. (2023). Evaluation of a School-Based Attention Training Program for Improving Sustained Attention. *Mind, Brain and Education : The Official Journal of the International Mind, Brain, and Education Society*, *18*(1), 103–124. DOI: 10.1111/mbe.12396

Smith, A. (2009). The empathy imbalance hypothesis of autism: A theoretical approach to cognitive and emotional empathy in autistic development. *The Psychological Record*, *59*(3), 489–510. DOI: 10.1007/BF03395675

Smith, E., Koerting, J., Latter, S., Knowles, M. M., McCann, D. C., Thompson, M., & Sonuga-Barke, E. J. (2015). Overcoming barriers to effective early parenting interventions for attention-deficit hyperactivity disorder (ADHD): Parent and practitioner views. *Child: Care, Health and Development*, *41*(1), 93–102. DOI: 10.1111/cch.12146 PMID: 24814640

Smith, J. N., Raiker, J. S., Fosco, W. D., Jusko, M. L., Campez, M., Little, K., Mattfeld, A., Espinal, K., Sanchez, G., Merrill, B., Musser, E. D., Gnagy, E., Greiner, A., Coles, E., & Pelham, W. E.Jr. (2020). Executive Functioning and Activity in Children: A Multimethod Examination of Working Memory, Inhibition, and Hyperactivity. *Journal of Abnormal Child Psychology*, *48*(9), 1143–1153. DOI: 10.1007/s10802-020-00665-0 PMID: 32557161

Smith, K. E., & Pollak, S. D. (2020). Early life stress and development: Potential mechanisms for adverse outcomes. *Journal of Neurodevelopmental Disorders*, *12*(1), 34. DOI: 10.1186/s11689-020-09337-y PMID: 33327939

Smolak, E., McGregor, K. K., Arbisi-Kelm, T., & Eden, N. (2020). Sustained Attention in Developmental Language Disorder and Its Relation to Working Memory and Language. *Journal of Speech, Language, and Hearing Research: JSLHR*, *63*(12), 4096–4108. DOI: 10.1044/2020_JSLHR-20-00265 PMID: 33166200

Snowling, M. J., & Hulme, C. (2012). Annual research review: The nature and classification of reading disorders—a commentary on proposals for DSM-5. *Journal of Child Psychology and Psychiatry, and Allied Disciplines*, *53*(5), 593–607. DOI: 10.1111/j.1469-7610.2011.02495.x PMID: 22141434

Söldner, L., & Paulus, M. (2024). I help, therefore, I am?–A registered report on longitudinal inter-relations of the three-dimensional moral self-concept and prosocial behaviours in preschool children. *The British Journal of Developmental Psychology, 42*(2), 257–284. DOI: 10.1111/bjdp.12481 PMID: 38483075

Soler-Gutiérrez, A.-M., Sánchez-Carmona, A. J., Albert, J., Hinojosa, J. A., Cortese, S., Bellato, A., & Mayas, J. (2025). Emotion processing difficulties in ADHD: A Bayesian meta-analysis study. *European Child & Adolescent Psychiatry, 34*(8), 2369–2390. Advance online publication. DOI: 10.1007/s00787-025-02647-3 PMID: 39853403

Soliman, D., Frydenberg, E., Liang, R., & Deans, J. (2020). Enhancing empathy in preschoolers: A comparison of social and emotional learning approaches! *Educational and Developmental Psychologist, 38*(1), 64–76. DOI: 10.1080/20590776.2020.1839883

Solomon, M., Ozonoff, S., Ursu, S., Ravizza, S., Cummings, N., Ly, S., & Carter, C. (2009). The neural substrates of cognitive control deficits in autism spectrum disorders. *Neuropsychologia, 47*(12), 2515–2526. DOI: 10.1016/j.neuropsychologia.2009.04.019 PMID: 19410583

Song, X., Hou, Y., Shi, W., Wang, Y., Fan, F., & Hong, L. (2025). Exploring the impact of different types of exercise on working memory in children with ADHD: A network meta-analysis. *Frontiers in Psychology, 16*, 1522944. DOI: 10.3389/fpsyg.2025.1522944 PMID: 39931282

Sonuga-Barke, E. J., Daley, D., & Thompson, M. (2002). Does maternal ADHD reduce the effectiveness of parent training for preschool children's ADHD? *Journal of the American Academy of Child and Adolescent Psychiatry, 41*(6), 696–702. DOI: 10.1097/00004583-200206000-00009 PMID: 12049444

Sörnyei, D., Vass, Á., Németh, D., & Farkas, K. (2023). Autistic and schizotypal traits exhibit similarities in their impact on mentalization and adult attachment impairments. https://doi.org/DOI: 10.31234/osf.io/8ga3f

South, M., Chamberlain, P. D., Wigham, S., Newton, T., Le Couteur, A., McConachie, H., Gray, L., Freeston, M., Parr, J., Kirwan, C. B., & Rodgers, J. (2014). Enhanced decision making and risk avoidance in high-functioning autism spectrum disorder. *Neuropsychology, 28*(2), 222–228. DOI: 10.1037/neu0000016 PMID: 24219603

South, M., & Rodgers, J. (2017). Sensory, Emotional and Cognitive Contributions to Anxiety in Autism Spectrum Disorders. *Frontiers in Human Neuroscience, 11*, 20. DOI: 10.3389/fnhum.2017.00020 PMID: 28174531

Southon, C. (2022). The relationship between executive function, neurodevelopmental disorder traits, and academic achievement in university students. *Frontiers in Psychology*, *13*, 958013. Advance online publication. DOI: 10.3389/fpsyg.2022.958013 PMID: 36118426

Sowden, S., Koehne, S., Catmur, C., Dziobek, I., & Bird, G. (2015). Intact automatic imitation and typical spatial compatibility in autism spectrum disorder: Challenging the broken mirror theory. *Autism Research : Official Journal of the International Society for Autism Research*, *9*(2), 292–300. DOI: 10.1002/aur.1511 PMID: 26112060

Spreng, R. N., Stevens, W. D., Chamberlain, J., Gilmore, A. W., & Schacter, D. L. (2010). Default network activity, coupled with the frontoparietal control network, supports goal-directed cognition. *NeuroImage*, *53*(1), 303–317. DOI: 10.1016/j.neuroimage.2010.06.016 PMID: 20600998

Sridhar, S., Khamaj, A., & Asthana, M. K. (2023). Cognitive neuroscience perspective on memory: Overview and summary. *Frontiers in Human Neuroscience*, *17*, 1217093. Advance online publication. DOI: 10.3389/fnhum.2023.1217093 PMID: 37565054

Sroufe, L. A. (1997). Psychopathology as an outcome of development. *Development and Psychopathology*, *9*(2), 251–268. DOI: 10.1017/S0954579497002046 PMID: 9201444

Sroufe, L. A., Egeland, B., Carlson, E., & Collins, W. A. (2005). *The development of the person*. Guilford Press.

Steed, E. A., & Kranski, T. A. (2020). Participant characteristics in research on interventions for young children with challenging behavior: A systematic review. *Topics in Early Childhood Special Education*, *40*(2), 110–123. DOI: 10.1177/0271121419832969

Sterrett, K., Shire, S., & Kasari, C. (2017). Peer relationships among children with ASD: Interventions targeting social acceptance, friendships, and peer networks. *International Review of Research in Developmental Disabilities*, *52*, 37–74. DOI: 10.1016/bs.irrdd.2017.07.006

Stiles, J. (2000). Neural plasticity and cognitive development. *Developmental Neuropsychology*, *18*(2), 237–272. DOI: 10.1207/S15326942DN1802_5 PMID: 11280966

Stobernack, T., de Vries, S. P. W., Rodrigues Pereira, R., Pelsser, L. M., Ter Braak, C. J. F., Aarts, E., van Baarlen, P., Kleerebezem, M., Frankena, K., & Hontelez, S. (2019). Biomarker Research in ADHD: The Impact of Nutrition (BRAIN) - study protocol of an open-label trial to investigate the mechanisms underlying the effects of a few-foods diet on ADHD symptoms in children. *BMJ Open*, *9*(11), e029422. DOI: 10.1136/bmjopen-2019-029422 PMID: 31694844

Sudre, G., Frederick, J., Sharp, W., Ishii-Takahashi, A., Mangalmurti, A., Choudhury, S., & Shaw, P. (2020). Mapping associations between polygenic risks for childhood neuropsychiatric disorders, symptoms of attention deficit hyperactivity disorder, cognition, and the brain. *Molecular Psychiatry*, *25*(10), 2482–2492. DOI: 10.1038/s41380-019-0350-3 PMID: 30700802

Šulc, L., Wu, F., Lashari, A., Remnélius, K. L., Pyko, A., Nevriana, A., Lissåker, C., Sjöström, M., Wiebert, P., Bölte, S., Gustavsson, P., Albin, M., & Selander, J. (2025). The impact of maternal occupational exposure on ADHD and autism diagnoses in children. *Occupational and Environmental Medicine*, *A31*, 2–A32. DOI: 10.1136/oemed-2025-EPICOHabstracts.77

Supekar, K., Iyer, T., & Menon, V. (2017). The influence of sex and age on prevalence rates of comorbid conditions in autism. *Autism Research : Official Journal of the International Society for Autism Research*, *10*(5), 778–789. DOI: 10.1002/aur.1741 PMID: 28188687

Super, C. M., & Harkness, S. (1986). The developmental niche. *International Journal of Behavioral Development*, *9*(4), 545–569. DOI: 10.1177/016502548600900409

Susman, E. J., & Dorn, L. D. (2009). Puberty: Its role in development. In Lerner, R. M., & Steinberg, L. (Eds.),; 3rd ed.). Handbook of adolescent psychology. Wiley. DOI: 10.1002/9780470479193.adlpsy001006

Syriopoulou-Delli, C. K., & Filiou, A. (2022). A systematic review of dysfunctional thoughts, feelings and phobias of children and adolescents with autism. Solutions and therapeutic methods. *International Journal of Developmental Disabilities*, *69*(5), 756–776. PMID: 36210890

Szatmari, P., Georgiades, S., Duku, E., Bennett, T. A., Bryson, S., Fombonne, E., Mirenda, P., Roberts, W., Smith, I. M., Vaillancourt, T., Volden, J., Waddell, C., Zwaigenbaum, L., Elsabbagh, M., & Thompson, A. (2015). Developmental trajectories of symptom severity and adaptive functioning in an inception cohort of preschool children with autism spectrum disorder. *JAMA Psychiatry*, *72*(3), 276. DOI: 10.1001/jamapsychiatry.2014.2463 PMID: 25629657

Tager-Flusberg, H. (2001). Neuropsychological components of language acquisition in autism. *The Journal of Developmental and Learning Disorders*, *5*, 57–80.

Takahashi, N., Ono, T., Omori, Y., Iizumi, M., Kato, H., Kasuno, S., Persing, B., & Tsuchiya, K. J. (2024). Assessment of executive functions using a 3D-video game in children and adolescents with ADHD. *Frontiers in Psychiatry*, *15*, 1407703. DOI: 10.3389/fpsyt.2024.1407703 PMID: 39238936

Talcer, M. C., Duffy, O., & Pedlow, K. (2021). A qualitative exploration into the sensory experiences of autistic mothers. *Journal of Autism and Developmental Disorders*. Advance online publication. DOI: 10.1007/s10803-021-05188-1 PMID: 34251566

Tallal, P. (1985). Auditory temporal perception, phonics and reading disabilities in children. *Brain and Language*, *9*(2), 182–198. DOI: 10.1016/0093-934X(80)90139-X PMID: 7363063

Tasiou, K., & Nikolaou, E. N. (2025). Well-Being Among Parents Raising a Child Diagnosed With Attention Deficit Hyperactivity Disorder (ADHD) and Intervention Programs: A Literature Review. In *Exploring Cognitive and Psychosocial Dynamics Across Childhood and Adolescence*, (pp. 229-248). IGI Global.

Tasiou, K., & Nikolaou, E. N. (2023). Psychological resilience of families of children with attention deficit hyperactivity disorder. In *New trends and approaches in child and adult psychopathology and mental health* (pp. 99–121). Gutenberg.

Teicher, M. H., Andersen, S. L., Polcari, A., Anderson, C. M., & Navalta, C. P. (2002). Developmental neurobiology of childhood stress and trauma. *The Psychiatric Clinics of North America*, *25*(2), 397–viii. DOI: 10.1016/S0193-953X(01)00003-X PMID: 12136507

Tercan, H., & Bayhan, P. (2025). The interplay of family dynamics, lifestyle, and ADHD: A case–control study on sociodemographic risk factors. *Brain and Behavior*, *15*(9), e70830. Advance online publication. DOI: 10.1002/brb3.70830 PMID: 40916512

Thapar, A., Cooper, M., & Rutter, M. (2021). Neurodevelopmental disorders. *The Lancet Psychiatry, 8*(4), 339–346. *(Note: This reference is an alternative entry or updated correspondence to the 2017 iteration included in the original text).*

Thapar, A., & Cooper, M. (2016, March 19). Attention deficit hyperactivity disorder. *Lancet*, *387*(10024), 1240–1250. DOI: 10.1016/S0140-6736(15)00238-X PMID: 26386541

Thapar, A., Cooper, M., & Rutter, M. (2016). Neurodevelopmental disorders. *The Lancet. Psychiatry*, *4*(4), 339–346. DOI: 10.1016/S2215-0366(16)30376-5 PMID: 27979720

Thatcher, R. W., Walker, R. A., & Giudice, S. (1987). Human, cerebral, hemispheris develop at different rates and ages. *Science*, *236*(4805), 1110–1113. DOI: 10.1126/science.3576224 PMID: 3576224

Thelen, E., & Smith, L. B. (1994). *A dynamic systems approach to the development of cognition and action*. MIT Press. DOI: 10.7551/mitpress/2524.001.0001

Theodoratou, M., Katsarou, D. V., Megari, K., Papadopoulou, S. L., Efthymiou, E., Sofologi, M., Kougioumtzis, G. A., Yotsidi, V., Koundourou, C., Toki, E. I., Argyrides, M., & Mantsos, E. (2025). Innovative Neuropsychological Interventions for ADHD and Asperger's Syndrome and Clinical Implications for Practitioners: Integrating Traditional Approaches With Emerging Technologies (Chapter 19, pages 391-410). *Clinical Applications of Pediatric Neuropsychology from Infancy to Adolescence*. Pennsylvania / USA: IGI Global.

Theodoratou, M., Kougioumtzis, G. A., Yotsidi, V., Andriopoulou, P., Megari, K., Koundourou, C., Siouti, Z., & Argyrides, M. (2025). Clinical Neuropsychological Profile and Interventions for Co-Occurrence of ADHD and ASD. In Sofologi, M., Katsarou, D., & Efthymiou, E. (Eds.), *Exploring Cognitive and Psychosocial Dynamics Across Childhood and Adolescence* (pp. 211–228). IGI Global., DOI: 10.4018/979-8-3693-4022-6.ch011

Theule, J., Wiener, J., Rogers, M. A., & Marton, I. (2011). Predicting parenting stress in families of children with ADHD: Parent and contextual factors. *Journal of Child and Family Studies*, *20*(5), 640–647. DOI: 10.1007/s10826-010-9439-7

Thijssen, S., Riem, M. M. E., Vijayakumar, N., Cima, M. J., & Whittle, S. (2023). Editorial: Nurturing the brain: Associations between family environment and child brain development. *Frontiers in Neuroscience*, *17*, 1119838. Advance online publication. DOI: 10.3389/fnins.2023.1119838 PMID: 36798461

Thom-Jones, S., Brownlow, C., & Abel, S. (2026). Experiences of autistic parents, from conception to raising adult children: A systematic review of the literature. *Autism in Adulthood: Challenges and Management*, *8*(3), 284–304. DOI: 10.1089/aut.2024.0181

Thompson, M. J. J., Laver-Bradbury, C., Ayres, M., Le Poidevin, E., Mead, S., Dodds, C., & Weeks, A. (2009). A small-scale randomized controlled trial of the revised new forest parenting programme for preschoolers with attention deficit hyperactivity disorder. *European Child & Adolescent Psychiatry*, *18*(10), 605–616. DOI: 10.1007/s00787-009-0020-0 PMID: 19404717

Tick, B., Bolton, P., Happé, F., Rutter, M., & Rijsdijk, F. (2016). Heritability of autism spectrum disorders: A meta-analysis of twin studies. *Journal of Child Psychology and Psychiatry, and Allied Disciplines*, *57*(5), 585–595. DOI: 10.1111/jcpp.12499 PMID: 26709141

Timimi, S., & Taylor, E. (2004). ADHD is best understood as a cultural construct. *The British Journal of Psychiatry : The Journal of Mental Science*, *184*(1), 8–9. DOI: 10.1192/bjp.184.1.8 PMID: 14702221

Toppelberg, C. O., & Collins, B. A. (2010). Language, culture, and adaptation in immigrant children. *Child and Adolescent Psychiatric Clinics of North America*, *19*(4), 697–717. DOI: 10.1016/j.chc.2010.07.003 PMID: 21056342

Torralva, T., Gleichgerrcht, E., Lischinsky, A., Roca, M., & Manes, F. (2013). "Ecological" and highly demanding executive tasks detect real-life deficits in high-functioning adult ADHD patients. *Journal of Attention Disorders*, *17*(1), 11–19. DOI: 10.1177/1087054710389988 PMID: 22826512

Tottenham, N., & Galván, A. (2016). Stress and the adolescent brain: Amygdala-prefrontal cortex circuitry and ventral striatum as developmental targets. *Neuroscience and Biobehavioral Reviews*, *70*, 217–227. Advance online publication. DOI: 10.1016/j.neubiorev.2016.07.030 PMID: 27473936

Trane, F. E., & Willcutt, E. G. (2022). Attention-Deficit/Hyperactivity Disorder and Academic Functioning: Reading, Writing, and Math Abilities in a Community Sample of Youth with and without ADHD. *Research on Child and Adolescent Psychopathology*, *51*(4), 583–596. DOI: 10.1007/s10802-022-01004-1 PMID: 36480079

Trent, J. W., Jr. (1994). *Inventing the feeble mind: A history of mental retardation in the United States*. University of California Press. tankona.free.fr/trent1994.pdf

Trinczer, I. L., & Shalev, L. (2024). Computerised Attention Functions Training Versus Computerised Executive Functions Training for Children with Attention Deficit/Hyperactivity Disorder: A Randomised Controlled Trial. *Journal of Clinical Medicine*, *13*(23), 7239. DOI: 10.3390/jcm13237239 PMID: 39685698

Tsang, T. W., Kohn, M., Efron, D., Clarke, S. D., Clark, C. R., Lamb, C., & Williams, L. M. (2012). Anxiety in young people with adhd. *Journal of Attention Disorders, 19*(1), 18–26. DOI: 10.1177/1087054712446830 PMID: 22713359

Tseng, M. H., Henderson, A., Chow, S. M., & Yao, G. (2004). Relationship between motor proficiency, attention, impulse, and activity in children with ADHD. *Developmental Medicine and Child Neurology, 46*(6), 381–388. Advance online publication. DOI: 10.1017/S0012162204000623 PMID: 15174529

Tung, I., Brammer, W. A., Li, J. J., & Lee, S. S. (2015). Parenting behaviour mediates the intergenerational association of parent and child offspring ADHD symptoms. *Journal of Clinical Child and Adolescent Psychology : The Official Journal for the Society of Clinical Child and Adolescent Psychology, American Psychological Association, Division 53, 44*(5), 787–799. DOI: 10.1080/15374416.2014.913250 PMID: 24926775

Turnbull, A., Turnbull, R., Wehmeyer, M., & Shogren, K. (2015). *Exceptional lives* (8th ed.). Pearson.

Tye, C., Battaglia, M., Bertoletti, E., Ashwood, K. L., Azadi, B., Asherson, P., Bolton, P., & McLoughlin, G. (2014). Altered neurophysiological responses to emotional faces discriminate children with ASD, ADHD and ASD+ADHD. *Biological Psychology, 103*, 125–134. DOI: 10.1016/j.biopsycho.2014.08.013 PMID: 25179537

Tymchuk, A. J. (1992). Predicting adequacy of parenting by people with mental retardation. *Child Abuse & Neglect, 16*(2), 165–178. DOI: 10.1016/0145-2134(92)90025-M PMID: 1559166

Tymchuk, A. J., & Feldman, M. A. (1991). Parents with mental retardation and their children: Review of research relevant to professional practice. *Canadian Psychology = Psychologie Canadienne, 32*(3), 486–496. DOI: 10.1037/h0079023

Tyrka, A. R., Burgers, D. E., Philip, N. S., Price, L. H., & Carpenter, L. L. (2013). The neurobiological correlates of childhood adversity and implications for treatment. *Acta Psychiatrica Scandinavica, 128*(6), 434–447. DOI: 10.1111/acps.12143 PMID: 23662634

Uddin, L. Q., Supekar, K., Lynch, C. J., Khouzam, A., Phillips, J. M., Feinstein, C., Ryali, S., & Menon, V. (2013). Salience network–based classification and prediction of symptom severity in children with autism. *JAMA Psychiatry, 70*(8), 869. DOI: 10.1001/jamapsychiatry.2013.104 PMID: 23803651

Uher, R. (2022). Gene–environment interactions in severe mental illness. *World Psychiatry; Official Journal of the World Psychiatric Association (WPA), 21*(1), 72–73.

Ullman, M. T., Earle, F. S., Walenski, M., & Janacsek, K. (2020). The neurocognition of developmental disorders of language. *Annual Review of Psychology*, *71*(1), 389–417. DOI: 10.1146/annurev-psych-122216-011555 PMID: 31337273

Ung, D., Arnold, E. B., Nadai, A. S. D., Lewin, A. B., Phares, V., Murphy, T. K., & Storch, E. A. (2013). Inter-rater Reliability of the Anxiety Disorders Interview Schedule for DSM-IV in High-Functioning Youth with Autism Spectrum Disorder. *Journal of Developmental and Physical Disabilities*, *26*(1), 53–65. DOI: 10.1007/s10882-013-9343-3 PMID: 24683302

Unger, O., & Howes, C. (1988). Mother-Child Interactions and Symbolic Play between Toddlers and Their Adolescent or Mentally Retarded Mothers. *The Occupational Therapy Journal of Research*, *8*(4), 237–249. DOI: 10.1177/153944928800800405

UNICEF. (2019). *Children with disabilities: Ensuring inclusion and equity*. UNICEF.

United Nations Educational, Scientific and Cultural Organization. (2024). *Q&A: How inclusion in education has evolved*. UNESCO. https://www.unesco.org/en/articles/qa-what-you-need-know-about-inclusion-education

Unsworth, N. (2016). Working memory capacity and recall from long-term memory: Examining the influences of encoding strategies, study time allocation, search efficiency, and monitoring abilities. *Journal of Experimental Psychology. Learning, Memory, and Cognition*, *42*(1), 50–61. DOI: 10.1037/xlm0000148 PMID: 26076331

Ursache, A., & Noble, K. G. (2016). Socioeconomic status, white matter and executive function in children. *Developmental Science*, *19*(5), 672–685. DOI: 10.1111/desc.12334 PMID: 27781144

Üstün, N. S. G., Gümüş, Ş. N., & Soylu, N. (2023). Oxytocin Levels in Children with Separation Anxiety and Their Mothers before and after Treatment. *Clinical Psychopharmacology and Neuroscience : The Official Scientific Journal of the Korean College of Neuropsychopharmacology*, *21*(3), 499–515. DOI: 10.9758/cpn.22.1008 PMID: 37424418

van den Hoofdakker, B. J., Nauta, M. H., Veen-Mulders, L., van der Sytema, S., Emmelkamp, P. M. G., Minderaa, R. B., & Hoekstra, P. J. (2009). Behavioral parent training as an adjunct to routine care in children with attention-deficit/hyperactivity disorder: Moderators of treatment response. [PubMed: 19633060]. *Journal of Pediatric Psychology*, *35*(3), 317–326. DOI: 10.1093/jpepsy/jsp060 PMID: 19633060

Van Der Maas, H. L. J., Dolan, C. V., Grasman, R. P. P. P., Wicherts, J. M., Huizenga, H. M., & Raijmakers, M. E. J. (2006). A dynamical model of general intelligence: The positive manifold of intelligence by mutualism. *Psychological Review, 113*(4), 842–861. DOI: 10.1037/0033-295X.113.4.842 PMID: 17014305

van der Wel, P., & van Steenbergen, H. (2018). Pupil dilation as an index of effort in cognitive control tasks: A review. *Psychonomic Bulletin & Review, 25*(6), 2005–2015. DOI: 10.3758/s13423-018-1432-y PMID: 29435963

van Son, D., de Rover, M., De Blasio, F. M., van der Does, W., Barry, R. J., & Putman, P. (2019). Electroencephalography theta/beta ratio covaries with mind wandering and functional connectivity in the executive control network. *Annals of the New York Academy of Sciences, 1452*(1), 52–64. DOI: 10.1111/nyas.14180 PMID: 31310007

van Steensel, F. J., Bögels, S. M., & Perrin, S. (2011). Anxiety disorders in children and adolescents with autistic spectrum disorders: A meta-analysis. *Clinical Child and Family Psychology Review, 14*(3), 302–317. DOI: 10.1007/s10567-011-0097-0 PMID: 21735077

van Stralen, J. (2016). Emotional dysregulation in children with attention-deficit/hyperactivity disorder. *Attention Deficit and Hyperactivity Disorders, 8*(4), 175–187. DOI: 10.1007/s12402-016-0199-0 PMID: 27299358

Vandewouw, M. M., Safar, K., Mossad, S. I., Lu, J., Lerch, J. P., Anagnostou, E., & Taylor, M. J. (2021). Do shapes have feelings? Social attribution in children with autism spectrum disorder and attention-deficit/hyperactivity disorder. *Translational Psychiatry, 11*(1), 493. DOI: 10.1038/s41398-021-01625-y PMID: 34564704

VanTieghem, M. R., & Tottenham, N. (2017). Neurobiological programming of early life stress: functional development of amygdala-prefrontal circuitry and vulnerability for stress-related psychopathology. Behavioral neurobiology of PTSD, 117-136.

Veenman, B., Luman, M., & Oosterlaan, J. (2017). Further Insight into the Effectiveness of a Behavioral Teacher Program Targeting ADHD Symptoms Using Actigraphy, Classroom Observations and Peer Ratings. *Frontiers in Psychology, 8*, 1157. DOI: 10.3389/fpsyg.2017.01157 PMID: 28744244

Veenstra-VanderWeele, J. (2018). Recognizing the problem of suicidality in autism spectrum disorder. *Journal of the American Academy of Child and Adolescent Psychiatry, 57*(5), 302–303. DOI: 10.1016/j.jaac.2018.03.003 PMID: 29706156

Vermeij, B., Wiefferink, C. H., Knoors, H., & Scholte, R. H. J. (2023). Effects in language development of young children with language delay during early intervention. *Journal of Communication Disorders*, *103*, 106326. DOI: 10.1016/j.jcomdis.2023.106326 PMID: 37086608

Vertel, A. (2023) Mary Ainsworth's attachment theory and its significance for understanding a child's early social-emotional development! *Humanities science current issues,* 1, 304-310. DOI https://doi.org/DOI: 10.24919/2308-4863/70-1-46

Vincenzo, C. D. (2026). Pediatric obsessive–compulsive disorder as a developmental disorder of cognitive–emotional control: A transdiagnostic and family-integrated perspective. *Frontiers in Psychiatry*, *16*, 1750938. Advance online publication. DOI: 10.3389/fpsyt.2025.1750938 PMID: 41625616

Vogan, V. M., Leung, R. C., Safar, K., Martinussen, R., Smith, M. L., & Taylor, M. J. (2018). Longitudinal Examination of Everyday Executive Functioning in Children With ASD: Relations With Social, Emotional, and Behavioral Functioning Over Time. *Frontiers in Psychology*, *9*, 1774. Advance online publication. DOI: 10.3389/fpsyg.2018.01774 PMID: 30364134

Volkan-Yazici, M., Elbasan, B., & Yazici, G. (2018). Motor Performance and Activities of Daily Living in Children with Neurodevelopmental Disorders. *Iranian Journal of Pediatrics*, *28*(6), e65396. DOI: 10.5812/ijp.65396

Volkmar, F., & McPartland, J. C. (2014). From Kanner to DSM-5. *Annual Review of Clinical Psychology, 10* , 193–212.

Vyas, A., Mitra, R., Shankaranarayana Rao, B. S., & Chattarji, S. (2002). Chronic stress induces contrasting patterns of dendritic remodeling in hippocampal and amygdaloid neurons. *The Journal of Neuroscience : The Official Journal of the Society for Neuroscience*, *22*(15), 6810–6818. DOI: 10.1523/JNEUROSCI.22-15-06810.2002 PMID: 12151561

Vygotsky, L. S. (1978). *Mind in society*. Harvard University Press.

Vygotsky, L. S. (1987). *Thinking and speech.* Plenum Press.

Wade, M., Prime, H., Jenkins, J. M., Yeates, K. O., Williams, T., & Lee, K. (2018). On the relation between theory of mind and executive functioning: A developmental cognitive neuroscience perspective. *Psychonomic Bulletin & Review*, *25*(6), 2119–2140. DOI: 10.3758/s13423-018-1459-0 PMID: 29619648

Wagner, S., & Harony-Nicolas, H. (2017). Oxytocin and animal models for autism spectrum disorder. In *Behavioral pharmacology of neuropeptides* (pp. 213–237). Oxytocin., DOI: 10.1007/7854_2017_15

Waisman, T. C., Williams, Z. J., Cage, E., Santhanam, S. P., Magiati, I., Dwyer, P., Stockwell, K. M., Kofner, B., Brown, H., Davidson, D., Herrell, J., Shore, S. M., Caudel, D., Gurbuz, E., & Gillespie-Lynch, K. (2022). Learning from the experts: Evaluating a participatory autism and universal design training for university educators. *Autism : The International Journal of Research and Practice*, *27*(2), 356–370. DOI: 10.1177/13623613221097207 PMID: 35652315

Walker, N. (2021). *Neuroqueer heresies: Notes on the neurodiversity paradigm, autistic empowerment, and postnormal possibilities*. Autonomous Press. Weird Books for Weird People.

Wang, L., Wang, B., Wu, C., Wang, J., & Sun, M. (2023). Autism spectrum disorder: Neurodevelopmental risk factors, biological mechanism, and precision therapy. *International Journal of Molecular Sciences*, *24*(3), 1819. DOI: 10.3390/ijms24031819 PMID: 36768153

Wang, Q., Chang, J., & Chawarska, K. (2020). Atypical Value-Driven Selective Attention in Young Children With Autism Spectrum Disorder. *JAMA Network Open*, *3*(5), e204928. DOI: 10.1001/jamanetworkopen.2020.4928 PMID: 32374399

Wang, Y. (2023). Influence of Early Family Nurturing Environment on Children's Psychological and Emotional Social Development. *Iranian Journal of Public Health*, *52*(10), 2138–2147. DOI: 10.18502/ijph.v52i10.13852 PMID: 37899924

Wang, Y., Zhang, Y. B., Liu, L. L., Cui, J. F., Wang, J., Shum, D. H. K., & Chan, R. C. K. (2017). A meta-analysis of working memory impairments in autism spectrum disorders. *Neuropsychology Review*, *27*(1), 46–61. DOI: 10.1007/s11065-016-9336-y PMID: 28102493

Wan, M. W., Meera, S. S., & Swanson, M. R. (2025). Emerging neurodivergence in infancy and toddlerhood. *Infant Behavior & Development*, *80*, 102133. DOI: 10.1016/j.infbeh.2025.102133 PMID: 40903314

Wanni Arachchige Dona, S., Badloe, N., Sciberras, E., Gold, L., Coghill, D., & Le, H. N. D. (2023). The Impact of Childhood Attention-Deficit/Hyperactivity Disorder (ADHD) on Children's Health-Related Quality of Life: A Systematic Review and Meta-Analysis. *Journal of Attention Disorders*, *27*(6), 598–611. DOI: 10.1177/10870547231155438 PMID: 36800919

Watkins, L., Kuhn, M., Ledbetter-Cho, K., Gevarter, C., & O'Reilly, M. (2015). Evidence-based social communication interventions for children with autism spectrum disorder. *Indian Journal of Pediatrics*, *84*(1), 68–75. DOI: 10.1007/s12098-015-1938-5 PMID: 26581197

Weiss, M., Hechtman, L., & Weiss, G. (2000). ADHD in parents. *Journal of the American Academy of Child and Adolescent Psychiatry*, *39*(8), 1059–1061. DOI: 10.1097/00004583-200008000-00023 PMID: 10939236

Weisz, J. R., Kuppens, S., Ng, M. Y., Eckshtain, D., Ugueto, A. M., Vaughn-Coaxum, R., Jensen-Doss, A., Marchette, L. K., Fordwood, S. R., & Cortés, R. C. (2017). Psychotherapy for children and adolescents. *Annual Review of Clinical Psychology*, *13*, 337–363. PMID: 27442352

Westwood, S. J., Parlatini, V., Rubia, K., Cortese, S., Sonuga-Barke, E. J. S., Banaschewski, T., Baeyens, D., Bölte, S., Brandeis, D., Buitelaar, J., Carucci, S., Coghill, D., Daley, D., Döpfner, M., Ferrin, M., Galera, C., Hollis, C., Holtmann, M., Purper-Ouakil, D., & Zuddas, A. (2023). Computerized cognitive training in attention-deficit/hyperactivity disorder (ADHD): A meta-analysis of randomized controlled trials with blinded and objective outcomes. *Molecular Psychiatry*, *28*(4), 1402–1414. DOI: 10.1038/s41380-023-02000-7 PMID: 36977764

White, S. W., Mazefsky, C. A., Dichter, G. S., Chiu, P. H., Richey, J. A., & Ollendick, T. H. (2014). Social-cognitive, physiological, and neural mechanisms underlying emotion regulation impairments: Understanding anxiety in autism spectrum disorder. *International Journal of Developmental Neuroscience : The Official Journal of the International Society for Developmental Neuroscience*, *39*(1), 22–36. DOI: 10.1016/j.ijdevneu.2014.05.012 PMID: 24951837

Wijnhoven, L. A. M. W., Creemers, D. H. M., Vermulst, A. A., & Granic, I. (2018). Prevalence and Risk Factors of Anxiety in a Clinical Dutch Sample of Children with an Autism Spectrum Disorder. *Frontiers in Psychiatry*, *9*, 50. Advance online publication. DOI: 10.3389/fpsyt.2018.00050 PMID: 29551982

Williams, D. L., Goldstein, G., Kojkowski, N., & Minshew, N. J. (2008). Do individuals with high functioning autism have the IQ profile associated with nonverbal learning disability. *Research in Autism Spectrum Disorders*, *2*(2), 353–361. DOI: 10.1016/j.rasd.2007.08.005 PMID: 18516234

Williams, D. L., Hultman, C. I., Haxby, J. V., & Minshew, N. J. (2012). Brief report: Verbal mediation and planning ability in adolescents with autism spectrum disorder. *Journal of Autism and Developmental Disorders*, *42*(7), 1530–1534.

Williams, D. L., Minshew, N. J., & Goldstein, G. (2006). Visual short-term memory in autism. *Neuropsychology*, *20*(4), 458–461.

Williamson, D., & Johnston, C. (2019). Maternal ADHD symptoms and parenting stress: The roles of parenting self-efficacy beliefs and neuroticism. *Journal of Attention Disorders*, *23*(5), 493–505. DOI: 10.1177/1087054717693373 PMID: 28201945

Williams, Z. J., Suzman, E., & Woynaroski, T. G. (2021). Prevalence of decreased sound tolerance (hyperacusis) in individuals with autism spectrum disorder: A meta-analysis. *Ear and Hearing*, *42*(5), 1137–1150. DOI: 10.1097/AUD.0000000000001005 PMID: 33577214

Willsey, A. J., & State, M. W. (2015). Autism spectrum disorders: From genes to neurobiology. *Current Opinion in Neurobiology*, *30*, 92–99. DOI: 10.1016/j.conb.2014.10.015 PMID: 25464374

Wiltgen, B., Sanders, M., Anagnostaras, S., Sage, J., & Fanselow, M. (2006). Context fear learning in the absence of the hippocampus. *The Journal of Neuroscience : The Official Journal of the Society for Neuroscience*, *26*(20), 5484–5491. DOI: 10.1523/JNEUROSCI.2685-05.2006 PMID: 16707800

Woodbury-Smith, M., & Scherer, S. W. (2018). Progress in the genetics of autism spectrum disorder. *Developmental Medicine and Child Neurology*, *60*(5), 445–451. DOI: 10.1111/dmcn.13717 PMID: 29574884

Woods, K. E., Mazursky-Horowitz, H., Thomas, S. R., Dougherty, L. R., & Chronis-Tuscano, A. (2019). The unique effects of maternal ADHD symptoms and emotion dysregulation on parenting behavior. *Journal of Attention Disorders*. Advance online publication. DOI: 10.1177/1087054719829820 PMID: 30762448

World Health Organization. (1992). *The ICD-10 Classification of Mental and Behavioural Disorders: Clinical Descriptions and Diagnostic Guidelines*. https://cdn.who.int/media/docs/default-source/classification/other-classifications/9241544228_eng.pdf

World Health Organization. (2013). *Mental health action plan 2013–2020*. WHO.

World Health Organization. (2019). *Clinical descriptions and diagnostic requirements for ICD-11 mental, behavioural and neurodevelopmental disorders*. https://faculty.ksu.edu.sa/sites/default/files/icd-_11_2018.pdf

World Health Organization. (2019). *International classification of diseases for mortality and morbidity statistics* (11th rev.). WHO.

World Health Organization. (2023). *Autism spectrum disorders*. WHO.

World Health Organization. (2023). *Global report on children with developmental disabilities: From the margins to the mainstream*. World Health Organization. https://iris.who.int/server/api/core/bitstreams/b699c175-08a7-4670-b757-8f6a143de6fe/content

World Health Organization. (2023). *Nurturing care for early childhood development*. WHO.

Wright, C., Shin, J. H., Rajpurohit, A., Deep-Soboslay, A., Collado-Torres, L., Brandon, N. J., Hyde, T. M., Kleinman, J. E., Jaffe, A. E., Cross, A. J., & Weinberger, D. R. (2017). Altered expression of histamine signaling genes in autism spectrum disorder. *Translational Psychiatry*, *7*(5), e1126. Advance online publication. DOI: 10.1038/tp.2017.87 PMID: 28485729

Wu, M., Joubran, E., Kumar, D., Assadi, N. D., & Nguyen, H. M. (2023). Variations in anxiety and related psychiatric comorbidity levels among youths with individual diagnoses of autism spectrum disorder or attention deficit hyperactivity disorder and those with both diagnoses. *Cureus*. Advance online publication. DOI: 10.7759/cureus.41759 PMID: 37575727

Wu, Z., Wang, P., Liu, L., Liu, J., Cao, X., Sun, L., Cao, Q., Yang, L., Wang, Y., & Yang, B. (2022). ADHD-inattentive versus ADHD-Combined subtypes: A severity continuum or two distinct entities? A comprehensive analysis of clinical, cognitive and neuroimaging data. *Journal of Psychiatric Research*, *149*, 28–36. DOI: 10.1016/j.jpsychires.2022.02.012 PMID: 35219873

Wymbs, B. T., Dawson, A. E., Egan, T. E., Sacchetti, G. M., Tams, S. T., & Wymbs, F. A. (2017). ADHD and depression symptoms in parent couples predict response to child ADHD and ODD behavior. *Journal of Abnormal Child Psychology*, *45*(3), 471–484. DOI: 10.1007/s10802-016-0220-2 PMID: 27796690

Xiang, X., Cho, J., Sun, Y., & Wang, X. (2022). Childhood adversity and cognitive impairment in later life. *Frontiers in Psychology*, *13*, 935254. DOI: 10.3389/fpsyg.2022.935254 PMID: 36051218

Xi, D. (2025). The Impact of Family Environment on Children's Education: An Analytical Study. *Lecture Notes in Education Psychology and Public Media*, *86*(1), 12–15. DOI: 10.54254/2753-7048/2025.21814

Xie, Q., Pan, N., Ou, X., Shen, S., Jing, J., Weng, X., Shi, L., Lin, L., Yang, J., Li, X., Zhang, K., Chen, F., Wang, Y., Wu, J., & Wang, X. (2025). Chronic Physical Pain in Children With and Without Autism Spectrum Disorder in the United States: Findings from the 2016 – 2021 National Survey of Children's Health. *Journal of Autism and Developmental Disorders*. Advance online publication. DOI: 10.1007/s10803-025-06846-4 PMID: 40301196

Xu, J., Dam, N. T. V., Feng, C., Luo, Y., Ai, H., Gu, R., & Xu, P. (2019). Anxious brain networks: A coordinate-based activation likelihood estimation meta-analysis of resting-state functional connectivity studies in anxiety. *Neuroscience and Biobehavioral Reviews*, *96*, 21–30. DOI: 10.1016/j.neubiorev.2018.11.005 PMID: 30452934

Xu, Y., Meng, Y., Dong, X., Wang, S., & Yu, L. (2024). Relationship between family socioeconomic status and toddlers' social-emotional development: the mediation effects of home rearing environment. *Research Square*. https://doi.org/DOI: 10.21203/rs.3.rs-4725276/v1

Yang, S., Dong, X., Guo, X., Han, Y., Song, H., Gao, L., Dai, W., Su, Y., & Zhang, X. (2017). Serum oxytocin levels and an oxytocin receptor gene polymorphism (rs2254298) indicate social deficits in children and adolescents with autism spectrum disorders. *Frontiers in Neuroscience*, *11*, 221. Advance online publication. DOI: 10.3389/fnins.2017.00221 PMID: 28484366

Yan, H. (2025). Neuroimaging Biomarkers for ADHD and ASD: Recent advances, transdiagnostic overlaps, and implications for precision Psychiatry. *Lecture Notes in Education Psychology and Public Media*, *111*(1), 31–44. DOI: 10.54254/2753-7048/2025.ND26282

Yarger, H. A., Nordahl, C. W., & Redcay, E. (2022). Examining Associations Between Amygdala Volumes and Anxiety Symptoms in Autism Spectrum Disorder. *Biological Psychiatry. Cognitive Neuroscience and Neuroimaging*, *7*(9), 916–924. DOI: 10.1016/j.bpsc.2021.10.010 PMID: 34688922

Yaşgüçlükal, M. A., Elmalı, A. D., & Korkmaz, B. (2024). Social Cognition and Theory of Mind. *Neuropsychiatric Investigation*, *62*(3), 100–108. DOI: 10.5152/NeuropsychiatricInvest.2024.24016

Yen, C., Valentine, E. P., & Chiang, M. C. (2024). The Use of Transcranial Magnetic Stimulation in Attention Optimization Research: A Review from Basic Theory to Findings in Attention-Deficit/Hyperactivity Disorder and Depression. *Life (Basel, Switzerland)*, *14*(3), 329. DOI: 10.3390/life14030329 PMID: 38541654

Yoon, S., Choi, J., Lee, W., & Do, J. (2020). Genetic and epigenetic etiology underlying autism spectrum disorder. *Journal of Clinical Medicine*, *9*(4), 966. Advance online publication. DOI: 10.3390/jcm9040966 PMID: 32244359

Yuan, S., Wu, H., Wu, Y., Xu, H., Yu, J., Zhong, Y., Zhang, N., Li, J., Xu, Q., & Wang, C. (2022). Neural effects of cognitive behavioral therapy in psychiatric disorders: A systematic review and activation likelihood estimation meta-analysis. *Frontiers in Psychology*, *13*, 853804. Advance online publication. DOI: 10.3389/fpsyg.2022.853804 PMID: 35592157

Yu, Y., & Bailey, A. L. (2025). Self-concept in first grade and academic performance trajectories: Roles of gender and dual-language immersion versus English-medium Program Enrollment. *International Multilingual Research Journal*, *19*(4), 1–20. DOI: 10.1080/19313152.2024.2387990

Zaidman-Zait, A., & Shilo, I. (2018). Parental ADHD symptoms and inhibitory control in relation to parenting among mothers of children with and without ADHD. *Journal of Attention Disorders*, *39*. Advance online publication. DOI: 10.1177/1087054718808063 PMID: 30442044

Zantinge, G., van Rijn, S., Stockmann, L., & Swaab, H. (2017). Physiological arousal and emotion regulation strategies in young children with autism spectrum disorders. *Journal of Autism and Developmental Disorders*, *47*(9), 2648–2657. DOI: 10.1007/s10803-017-3181-6 PMID: 28593596

Zelazo, P. D., & Lyons, K. E. (2012). The potential benefits of mindfulness training in early childhood. *Child Development Perspectives*, *6*(2), 154–160. DOI: 10.1111/j.1750-8606.2012.00241.x

Zelazo, P. D., Müller, U., Frye, D., Marcovitch, S., Argitis, G., Boseovski, J., Chiang, J. K., Hongwanishkul, D., Schuster, B. V., & Sutherland, A. (2003). The development of executive function in early childhood. *Monographs of the Society for Research in Child Development*, *68*(3), vii–137. DOI: 10.1111/j.0037-976X.2003.00269.x PMID: 14723273

Zhang, Q., He, Q., & Hou, Y. (2025). A resting-state functional magnetic resonance imaging meta-analysis of differences in brain activity between children and adolescents with attention-deficit/hyperactivity disorder using activation likelihood estimation. *European Child & Adolescent Psychiatry*. Advance online publication. DOI: 10.1007/s00787-025-02906-3 PMID: 41222592

Zhao, L., Agazzi, H., Du, Y., Meng, H., Maku, R., Li, K., Aspinall, P., Garvan, C. W., & Fang, S. (2024). A Digital Cognitive-Physical Intervention for Attention-Deficit/Hyperactivity Disorder: Randomized Controlled Trial. *Journal of Medical Internet Research*, *26*, e55569. DOI: 10.2196/55569 PMID: 38728075

Zhong, R., Li, M., Chen, Q., Li, J., Li, G., & Lin, W. (2019). The P300 Event-Related Potential Component and Cognitive Impairment in Epilepsy: A Systematic Review and Meta-analysis. *Frontiers in Neurology*, *10*, 943. DOI: 10.3389/fneur.2019.00943 PMID: 31543861

Zhou, X., Jia, F., Bambling, M., Edirippulige, S., Whiteford, H., & Lin, J. (2026). Associations between multiple neurodevelopmental disorders and mental health in children. *Journal of Affective Disorders*, *393*, 120397. DOI: 10.1016/j.jad.2025.120397 PMID: 41072876

Zoppé, H., Trocmet, L., Rambault, A., Abtroun, Y., Defresne, D., Ansoborlo, M., Hazard, M., & Bonnet-Brilhault, F. (2025). Early detection of neurodevelopmental disorders in children with delayed milestones: Navigating between overlapping trajectories and the limits of a single-diagnosis categorical approach (A Preliminary Study for the CONDOR Cohort). *Asian Journal of Psychiatry*, *109*, 104561. DOI: 10.1016/j.ajp.2025.104561 PMID: 40466582

Zwaigenbaum, L., Bauman, M. L., Stone, W. L., Yirmiya, N., Estes, A., Hansen, R. L., McPartland, J. C., Natowicz, M. R., Choueiri, R., Fein, D., Kasari, C., Pierce, K., Buie, T., Carter, A., Davis, P. A., Granpeesheh, D., Mailloux, Z., Newschaffer, C., Robins, D., Roley, S. S., … Wetherby, A. (2015). Early Identification of Autism Spectrum Disorder: Recommendations for Practice and Research. *Pediatrics, 136 Suppl 1*(Suppl 1), S10–S40. DOI: 10.1542/peds.2014-3667C

Zwaigenbaum, L., Bauman, M. L., Choueiri, R., Kasari, C., Carter, A., Granpeesheh, D., Mailloux, Z., Smith-Roley, S., Wagner, S., Fein, D., Pierce, K., Buie, T., Davis, P. A., Newschaffer, C., Robins, D., Wetherby, A., Stone, W. L., Yirmiya, N., Estes, A., & Natowicz, M. R. (2021). Early intervention for children with autism spectrum disorder under 3 years of age. *Pediatrics*, *136*(Suppl. 1), S60–S81. DOI: 10.1542/peds.2014-3667E PMID: 26430170

About the Contributors

Kalliopi Megari is a Postdoctoral researcher of Aristotle University of Thessaloniki, Greece, Academic Director of MSc in Clinical Psychology and Clinical supervisor at City College, University of York, Europe Campus. She is Adjunct lecturer at University of Western Macedonia in Florina, Greece. Dr. Megari is a psychologist with a history of working in the hospital & health care industry, skilled in Clinical Neuropsychology, Clinical Research, Medical Education, Psychological Assessment and Learning Disabilities. She works both in clinical and in research practice and she provides strong professional healthcare services, graduated from Aristotle University of Thessaloniki, and attended further education from Department of Educational and Social Policy, University of Macedonia, in people with special needs and disabilities. She holds undergraduate degrees in Nursing and Psychology, as well as a Master' s and a PhD in Neuropsychology from Aristotle University of Thessaloniki. She has some years of occupational and research experience working with patients who have neurological, psychiatric, and cognitive disorders, as well as chronic disease patients suffering from cancer and cardiovascular diseases. She is the head of the Centre of creative activities of children and adults with disabilities and she also works as a counseling psychologist in Prison, Diavata Thessaloniki, at the school of second chance. She was the Global Engagement Representative of SLC International Neuropsychological Society from 2018-2021 and she was a research fellow in the Department of Cardiovascular Surgery in AHEPA Hospital. Currently she is a Global Membership Committee member of International Neuropsychological Society and leader of Rehabilitation of COVID-19 patients working group of NeuroCOVID International Neuropsychology Taskforce SIG. In addition, she is the General Secretary of the board of directors of Hellenic Neuropsychological Society and Ethics Committee president of Hellenic Neuropsychological Society. Since 2021, she is a member of PIAC Community Outreach Subcommittee of AMERICAN PSYCHOLOGICAL ASSOCIATION Membership and a member of Engagement Committee of American Group Psychotherapy Association (AGPA).

Her work has earned her many prestigious international awards and was an Ambassador of National Academy of Neuropsychology (NAN), USA Leadership and Ambassador Development Program (2022-23). Currently she is the leader of Pediatric Neuropsychology Topical Group of FESN - Federation of the European Societies of Neuropsychology and serves as an auditor of the board of Directors. She has given lectures at Aristotle University of Thessaloniki, University of Warsaw, Maria Curie-Sklodowska University in Lublin – UMCS, and Norwegian University of Science and Technology in Oslo. She is committed to leadership skills and issues on equity, diversity, and inclusion as her clinical and research work states.

***

Jessica Arun Robert is a 2nd year student at PES University where she is pursuing her Bachelors of Science in Psychology. Her interested fields of research include Forensic, Criminal and Clinical Psychology.

Bhumika B. N. is a psychologist and educator holding a Master's degree in Psychology. She currently serves as an Assistant Professor of Psychology at PES University, RR Nagar, Bengaluru. In addition to her academic role, she has professional experience as a counselor, pediatric neuropsychologist, and corporate trainer. She has guided and co-authored several research papers and book chapters, reflecting her engagement with scholarly work and applied psychology. She holds certifications in Reiki (Degree I) and Hypnotherapy (Level I), which complement her integrative approach to psychological well-being. As an educator, she emphasizes a student-centric and experiential learning environment, enabling learners to meaningfully connect psychological theory with real-world applications.

Sara Begum is Professor and Ex – Dean, Faculty of Education, Jamia Millia Islamia, New Delhi, and a senior academic with more than three decades of experience in teacher education, special and inclusive education, and disability studies. She has supervised 25 doctoral and numerous postgraduate research scholars. She has played a significant role in curriculum development, policy advisory bodies and national academic committees. Prof. Begum has authored and edited multiple books, serves as Editor – in – Chief of the Jamia Journal of Education, and has led several funded research projects in inclusive education, assistive technology and disability rights. Her academic leadership and scholarship have made substantial contributions to advancing inclusive and rights-based education in India.

Efthymia Efthymiou, Associate Professor at Zayed University (UAE), studies inclusive teaching, classroom discourse, and learning environments that enable every student with disabilities to belong and participate. She brings this lens to medical education, promoting disability-competent, technology-enhanced training. She also works with UAE federal schools to turn research on inclusion and digital access into classroom practice.

Shreya Ghosh is an Assistant Professor at PES University, Bangalore, and a research scholar with a strong passion for inquiry and innovation. Her interests lie in neuroscience, psychology, human relations, and sustainable development. She explores how psychological principles and neuroscientific insights support emotional regulation, cognitive balance, sustainable practices, and elder well-being, while integrating perspectives from wisdom traditions.

Veera Gupta is an eminent Indian educationist, researcher and teacher educator with extensive experience in educational policy, teacher education, inclusive education and vocational education. She currently serves as Professor and Head, Department of Educational Policy at National Institute of Educational Planning and Administration. Earlier, she was Professor at Jamia Millia Islamia, where she also served as Director of the Malaviya Mission Teacher Training Centre (MMTTC). Prof. Gupta has contributed significantly to educational research, policy formulation, curriculum development and teacher training in collaboration with organizations such as UNICEF, UGC, NCTE and the Ministry of Education. Her areas of expertise include inclusive education, guidance and counselling, educational leadership, school assessment and skill development. She has published widely in national and international journals and has guided several research scholars in the field of education.

Mohd. Faijullah Khan is an Associate Professor of Special Education (Learning Disabilities) at the Institute of Advanced Studies in Education (IASE), Jamia Millia Islamia, New Delhi. He holds a Ph.D. in Education from Jamia Millia Islamia, with research focusing on stress, quality of life and coping strategies of parents of children with special needs. With academic training in Special Education and Applied Psychology, he has extensive experience in teacher education, research and disability studies. Dr. Khan has guided several Ph.D. scholars and postgraduate dissertations in the field of special and inclusive education. He has published widely in national and international journals and authored books on learning disabilities, disability laws and intervention strategies. Actively involved in policy, training and advocacy, he has contributed to government bodies and professional organizations related to disability and education. His work reflects a strong commitment to inclusive education and the empowerment of persons with disabilities.

Georgios A. Kougioumtzis is an Associate Professor of Counseling, ICT, and Teaching Methodology, in the Department of Turkish and Modern Asian Studies, at National and Kapodistrian University of Athens, Greece; a Visiting Professor in the School of Psychology, at Neapolis University Pafos, Cyprus, in the field of Counseling / Educational Psychology, and Specific Learning Difficulties, and a Visiting Academic in the School of Social Sciences, at Hellenic Open University, Patras, Greece, in the field of Psychology / Counseling. He holds a Ph.D. in Pedagogics, Teaching Methodology, and Counseling / Teacher Mentoring, from the Department of Philosophy, Pedagogy, and Psychology - National and Kapodistrian University of Athens. He has published 12 books by IGI Global Scientific Publishing (USA) and Grigori Publications (Greece) in the fields of Educational Psychology, Counseling Psychology, Specific Learning Difficulties, and Teaching Methodology and ICT, and over than two hundred (200) papers. He is married and the father of three daughters.

Phillip Marais has trained as a psychologist and holds a master's degree in Cognitive and Research Psychology, as well as a master's degree in Education. His interests focus on the neurocognitive mechanisms which underpin memory, learning, and executive functioning in neurodiverse populations - and how these profiles may differ when examined dimensionally. Phillip currently works within inclusive education, with a strong focus on positive behaviour management, and learning mechanisms in neurodiverse populations.

Eleni Nikolaou is an Associate Professor at the department of Sciences of Preschool Education and Educational Design, University of the Aegean. She has been teaching at the University of the Aegean, since 2006. In addition to her teaching duties at the undergraduate level, she also teaches in the Postgraduate Programs of "Environmental Education", as well as in the "Models of Educational Planning and Development" of T.E.P.A.E.S of the University of the Aegean. She has worked for almost fifteen consecutive years in a counseling and mental health service for children, adolescents and their families in Rhodes, Greece. During her career she has given a lot of lectures in schools regarding mental health issues and she has been participated in professional development training courses for teachers. She holds a Ph.D. from the Department of Preschool Education and Educational Design, University of the Aegean (2005). She completed her postgraduate studies at City University, London (M.Sc. in Counseling Psychology, 1999). She holds a Bachelor's Degree in Psychology from the University of Crete (1996). Her articles have been published in reputable scientific peer reviewed journals and Conferences, either in national or international level. She participates as a reviewer in Greek as well as in International Journals. She has also co-edited several collective volumes in Greek and international level. Her research interests include school counselling, psychological resilience, psychological wellbeing, mental health promotion, bullying and issues of developmental psychopathology.

Maria Sofologi is an Adjunct Ass. Professor at the Department of Early Childhood and Education at the University of Ioannina in Greece. She delivers the courses "Cognitive Psychology", and "Developmental Psychology". She is also a postdoctoral researcher at the University of Ioannina in Greece. She holds a Ph.D. in Cognitive Psychology from the Aristotle University of Thessaloniki. She also holds a Master of Science degree in Cognitive Psychology from the Aristotle University of Thessaloniki. During her master's degree years she trained and practiced different assessment cognitive tools to evaluate all cognitive functions like memory, attention, language, executive functions both in adults and children. She is the key speaker in many European and Hellenic conferences concerning cognitive psychology, educational psychology, special education in children and adults, as well. Her academic work includes a series of many scientific publications, books, and book chapters concerning Cognitive Psychology, Special Education, Educational Psychology, and Cognitive impairments in children and adults as well.

Anuj Srivastava is a researcher in special and inclusive education whose work examines neurodevelopmental disabilities across childhood and adolescence with particular focus on mental health, psychosocial interventions and prosocial development. He is currently pursuing his Ph.D. in Education at Jamia Millia Islamia, New Delhi. His research work is indexed in Scopus, Web of Science (ESCI) and Google Scholar, with publications appearing in Springer Nature journals and other peer – reviewed international outlets. Mr. Srivastava brings more than a decade of experience in teaching and training master – level professionals in special education and rehabilitation sciences. He has supervised multiple postgraduate dissertations in special education and has completed government funded research projects related to disability and inclusion. He has contributed Scopus – indexed book chapters and serves as a peer reviewer for Scopus Q2 & Q4 – indexed journal, reflecting active engagement in international scholarly publishing. He holds multiple degrees such as M.Ed. Special Education (Intellectual Disability), B.Ed. Special Education (Intellectual Disability & Learning Disability), M.Sc. Psychology and M.A. Geography. He has research interests on Inclusive education, Special Education, Intellectual and Developmental Disabilities, Neurodevelopmental Disorders, Skill Development, psychosocial at risk and resilience, Psychosocial Training, family – centered and school – based interventions, assistive and digital technologies, Mental Illness, Early Childhood Care and Development, Persons with Disabilities, Children with Disabilities, Rehabilitation and rights – based practice for individuals with Neurodevelopmental disabilities.

Kyriaki Tasiou is a teacher and works for the last 17 years at a primary school as a special education teacher. She holds a Master's degree on the topic: "Gender and New Educational and Working Environments in the Information Society" of the T.E.P.A.E.S.-University of the Aegean and Master's degree with the title: "Sciences of Education: Special Education and Education of Persons with Problems of Oral and Written Communication" of the Inter-University MSc of the EAP with the University of Thessaly. She has been trained in Greek Sign Language. She is a PhD candidate at the T.E.P.A.E.S of the University of the Aegean.

Maria Theodoratou-Bekou holds a Ph.D. in Psychology from the National and Kapodistrian University of Athens, complemented by a Maitrise and D.E.S.S. in Clinical Psychology and Psychopathology from the University of Provence (Aix Centre), France. With over 30 years of academic experience, she has held prominent teaching and research positions at the Hellenic Open University, Neapolis University of Cyprus, the University of Patras, and the Technological Educational Institute of Western Greece. Her distinguished careerintegrates rigorous academic research in social and clinical psychology Dr. Theodoratou-Bekou's professional expertise is characterized by a specialized focus on group-based psychosocial interventions, particularly within educational and health settings. Her work emphasizes: Student Group Interventions: Designing and implementing therapeutic and supportive protocols tailored to the unique psychosocial needs of student population. Her extensive body of research, published in numerous peer-reviewed scientific journals, continues to contribute significantly to the fields of social and clinical psychology.

Kiara Tiwari is currently studying a Bachelor of Science at PES University, majoring in Psychology. She is interested in research, mainly aiming to focus towards the fields of Neuropsychology, and Neurodivergence.

Index

A

B

C

D

E

www.ingramcontent.com/pod-product-compliance
Lightning Source LLC
LaVergne TN
LVHW062330300926
849161LV00007B/1642
9798337370729